Evidence:
Cases and Argument

Peter Murphy MA, LLB
and
John Beaumont LLM

Financial
Training

First published in Great Britain 1982 by Financial Training Publications Limited,
Avenue House, 131 Holland Park Avenue, London W11 4UT.

© Financial Training Publications Limited 1982

ISBN: 0 906322 10 3

Photoset by Top Type Phototypesetting Co. Ltd., London, W1
Printed in Great Britain by Biddles Ltd, Guildford, Surrey

Contents

A: The admissibility of evidence   1.1 Facts which may be proved: introductory notes   1.2 Authorities: res gestae   1.3 Authorities: facts relevant to facts in issue   1.4 Authorities: standards of comparison   1.5 Judicial discretion: introductory notes   1.6 Authorities: judicial discretion   1.7 Evidence illegally or unfairly obtained: introductory notes   1.8 Authorities: evidence illegally and unfairly obtained   1.9 The 'best evidence' rule   B: Proof without evidence   1.10 Introductory notes   1.11 Authorities: formal admissions   1.12 Authorities: judicial notice   1.13 Authorities: presumption of legitimacy   1.14 Authorities: presumption of marriage   1.15 Authorities: presumption of death   1.16 Authorities: presumption of regularity   1.17 Authorities: conflicting presumptions

A: The Queen v Coke and Littleton   2.1 Brief for the prosecution   2.2 Brief for the defence   B: Blackstone v Coke   2.3 Brief for the plaintiff   2.4 Brief for the defendant

A: The burden and standard of proof in civil cases   3.1 Introductory notes   3.2 Commentary   3.3 Argument   B: The burden and standard of proof in criminal cases   3.4 Introductory notes   3.5 Commentary   3.6 Argument   C: The burden and standard of proof on secondary issues   3.7 Introductory notes   3.8 Commentary   3.9 Argument   3.10 Commentary   3.11 Argument   3.12 Questions for Counsel

10 Public Policy and Privilege

A: Public policy 10.1 Introductory notes 10.2 Commentary 10.3 Argument 10.4 Commentary 10.5 Argument B: Private evidential privileges 10.6 Self-incrimination: introductory notes 10.7 Commentary 10.8 Argument 10.9 Legal professional privilege: introductory notes 10.10 Commentary 10.11 Argument 10.12 Commentary 10.13 Argument 10.14 Commentary 10.15 Argument 10.16 Matrimonial communications: introductory notes 10.17 Commentary 10.18 Argument 10.19 Questions for Counsel

11 Competence and Compellability: Oaths and Affirmations

A: Competence and Compellability 11.1 Introductory notes 11.2 Commentary 11.3 Argument 11.4 Commentary 11.5 Argument 11.6 Spouses: Introductory notes 11.7 Commentary 11.8 Argument 11.9 Children: Introductory notes 11.10 Commentary 11.11 Course of evidence and argument B: Oaths and Affirmations 11.12 Introductory notes 11.13 Commentary 11.14 Argument 11.15 Questions for Counsel

12 Evidence in Chief

A: Introduction 12.1 B: Refreshing the memory 12.2 Introductory notes 12.3 Commentary 12.4 Course of evidence 12.5 Commentary 12.6 Argument 12.7 Commentary 12.8 Course of evidence 12.9 Commentary 12.10 Argument 12.11 Commentary 12.12 Argument C: Previous consistent statements 12.13 Introductory notes 12.14 Commentary 12.15 Argument 12.16 Commentary 12.17 Argument 12.18 Commentary 12.19 Course of evidence D: Unfavourable and hostile witnesses 12.20 Introductory notes 12.21 Commentary 12.22 Argument 12.23 Questions for Counsel

13 Cross-examination and Beyond

A: Cross-examination generally 13.1 Introductory notes 13.2 Commentary 13.3 Argument 13.4 Commentary 13.5 Argument B: Previous inconsistent statements 13.6 Introductory notes 13.7 Commentary 13.8 Course of evidence 13.9 Commentary 13.10 Argument C: Finality of answers on collateral issues 13.11 Introductory notes 13.12 Commentary 13.13 Argument 13.14 Commentary 13.15 Argument 13.16 Commentary 13.17 Argument D: Cross-examination on documents 13.18 Introductory notes 13.19 Commentary 13.20 Course of evidence 13.21 Commentary 13.22 Course of evidence E: Beyond cross-examination 13.23 Introductory notes 13.24 Commentary 13.25 Argument 13.26 Commentary 13.27 Argument 13.28 Questions for Counsel

14   Corroboration   422

14.1 Introductory notes 14.2 Commentary 14.3 Argument 14.4
Commentary 14.5 Argument 14.6 Commentary 14.7 Argument 14.8
Commentary 14.9 Argument 14.10 Questions for Counsel.

15   Documentary and Real Evidence   449

A: Documentary evidence 15.1 Proof of contents: introductory notes 15.2
Commentary 15.3 Argument 15.4 Proof of due execution: introductory
notes 15.5 Commentary 15.6 Argument B: Real evidence 15.7
Introductory notes 15.8 Commentary 15.9 Argument 15.10 Questions for
Counsel

Preface

When the preface was written to *A Practical Approach to Evidence,* the rape or non-rape of Margaret Blackstone was less than a year old. Its second anniversary has now passed and the sequel of a civil suit against the luckless Coke has been added to the teaching armament of this companion volume. Every practising lawyer is aware that legal authorities bear a marked resemblance to statistics. Both can be employed within limits to demonstrate a wide variety of propositions. In the field of evidence, where problems rarely have the courtesy to arise one at a time, cases seem to vie with each other to comprehend and analyse as many problems as they can.

Accordingly, it seemed right when contemplating a source book for use along side *A Practical Approach to Evidence,* to seek to put the authorities into some sort of meaningful context. Our efforts to achieve this goal have been centred on demonstrating the role which the authorites might play in evidential arguments arising from *R v Coke and Littleton* and *Blackstone v Coke.* The argument to which the authorities seem germane are put into the mouths of counsel representing the various parties and of the judges before whom the arguments are made. The arguments arise sometimes at pre-trial stages, sometimes during trial, and sometimes on appeal. The choice of forum in this respect is fortuitous, and has been made so as to present what seemed to the authors to be the most realistic and attractive setting for the presentation of the arguments. In the same chapter, the reader will find arguments presented at one or more of these stages. Each episode should be treated separately and should not be seen as bearing any chronological relationship to the episode which precedes it or the episode which follows it.

So far as we are aware, the form of this book represents a novel departure from traditional case books and source books. This book is designed to be read on its own but may be used in conjunction with *A Practical Approach to Evidence,* which itself represented some measure of departure from the traditional textbook format. The exchanges between judge and counsel should not, of course, be regarded as a model of what would occur in court. The lengthy arguments presented by counsel in this book would drive even the most patient tribunal to distraction, and the degree of departure from the precise issue before the court attributed both to judge and counsel would play a major part in bringing the administration of justice to a standstill. But the dialogue is intended to illustrate, albeit in expanded form, the thought patterns which lie behind a well-reasoned argument and perhaps more importantly to illustrate the vital process of applying law to the facts of a case, without which the most brilliant piece of legal research will be utterly lacking in persuasive value. At the same time, if the length and scope of the arguments themselves go beyond the realities of practice, care has been taken to reproduce accuracy in the procedural settings and in the style of the dialogue. Like the facts of a case, these matters are inseparable from the law of evidence and are useful subjects to study for any intending advocate.

Regrettably, space and coherence alike dictate that there must be some selectivity in the authorities cited. We have discarded with reluctance many useful cases, some of which are referred to in the text, in order to give due prominence to what seem to us to be the most useful in practical terms.

It is hoped that this book, like *A Practical Approach to Evidence,* will commend itself alike to students for the Bar and Solicitors Final Examinations and those concerned with degree courses. We recommend that as far as possible, each section be studied as a whole so that the various authorities set out are seen in the sequence of the argument which accompanies them. The practice of including questions for counsel at the conclusion of each chapter seems to have been well received in *A Practical Approach to Evidence* and is continued here.

An attempt has been made to reflect the law as at 31 December 1981.

We wish to extend our grateful thanks to our publishers, particularly Heather Saward, whose energy and resourcefulness in the face of the pressure of time seems to be matched only by their detailed concern for the quality of that which they produce. Our thanks are also due to Heather D. Pow, who typed much of the manuscript, to Betty Downing, the law librarian at Leeds Polytechnic, and to Joe Palmer who prepared the indexes.

Finally, a tribute is due to our wives, Hilary Pearson, MA (Oxon) LLB (Lond), Barrister-at-Law and Judith Beaumont, without whose love and patience this book would not have been written.

Leeds   John Beaumont
San Francisco   Peter Murphy
February 1982

Table of Cases

Table of Statutes

Table of Orders, Rules and Regulations

Acknowledgements

The authors and publishers wish to thank the following for permission to reprint extracts from the sources indicated: Incorporated Council of Law Reporting for England and Wales: *Law Reports* and *Weekly Law Reports*. Butterworth & Co (Publishers) Ltd: *The All England Law Report*. Law Book Company Ltd: *Commonwealth Law Report*. Sweet & Maxwell Ltd: *The Criminal Appeal Reports*.

1 Evidence: The Science of Proof

A: THE ADMISSIBILITY OF EVIDENCE

1.1 Facts which may be proved: introductory notes

1.1.1 The purpose of evidence is to demonstrate to the court the truth or probability of those facts upon which a party's case or defence depends in law. Accordingly, evidence must be confined to the proof of those facts, and will not be permitted in relation to supernumerary or unrelated facts, which have no relevance to proof, but may be prejudicial to the party against whom those facts are offered. The facts that a party is permitted to prove with a view to establishing his claim or defence are:

(a) facts in issue in the case;
(b) facts constituting part of, or accompanying and explaining facts in issue, described as part of the *res gestae;*
(c) facts relevant to facts in issue; and
(d) where appropriate, standards of comparison.

1.1.2 Facts in issue. These are the facts which a party must prove in order to succeed in his claim or defence, or in a criminal case to obtain a conviction or to establish a defence where the onus of proof is with the defendant. What these facts are depends in each case on the substantive law applicable to the claim, charge or defence. They may be derived from the pleadings, indictment or charge as the case may be. Such facts are properly described as 'primary' facts in issue. To take the example of a typical action for negligence, the primary facts in issue will be those which, if proved, will establish that the defendant owed a duty of care to the plaintiff, that the defendant was in breach of that duty of care and that such breach caused to the plaintiff loss and damage for which he is entitled in law to recover; together with any further facts dictated by the nature of the defence, if it goes beyond a mere denial of those pleaded by the plaintiff, for example such facts as may establish contributory negligence or *volenti non fit injuria*. There also exists a category of 'secondary' facts in issue which are facts affecting either the credibility of a witness or the admissibility of evidence. Therefore, evidence may be called, for example, tending to show that a witness for the other side is biased or partial; or that a confession is admissible inasmuch as it was made voluntarily.

1.1.3 Facts forming part of the res gestae. A fact stated in isolation from its antecedents in time, place or surrounding circumstances may be difficult or even impossible to comprehend. Other facts or circumstances may be so closely connected with the fact in issue as to be part and parcel of the same transaction. Examples may be the tone of voice in which words were spoken, the manner in which a blow was struck or the appearance of the victim afterwards. Such other facts are said to be part of the *res gestae* and may be proved by evidence. The purpose of this rule is to render comprehensible and useful facts in issue in the case, and it is not confined by any strict rules as to length of time or distance. Facts forming part of the *res gestae* are usually, though not always, hearsay and admissible only by virtue of an exception to the rule against hearsay. This exception is considered in 6.6.2, 6.7 and 6.8 post.

1.1.4   Facts relevant to facts in issue.   A fact is relevant if its proof tends to make some other fact more or less probable. For example, on a charge of murder by stabbing it would be relevant that the defendant was seen carrying a bloodstained knife from the scene. Similarly, on a charge of theft the fact that the property was found in the possession of the defendant shortly after it was missed, and he was unwilling or unable to give an adequate explanation of how he came by it, would be relevant. It is a general rule of the law of evidence that no evidence is admissible unless it is relevant to the facts in issue. The converse proposition, however, is not true. Much relevant evidence is inadmissible by virtue of the rules of evidence. The test of relevance is, therefore, basic to the admissibility of any piece of evidence, and irrelevant or insufficiently relevant evidence will be excluded. In certain cases, evidence may be admitted as conditionally relevant where its relevance is to be demonstrated by facts which have not yet been proved but will be proved at a later stage. Certain facts have multiple relevance, in that they tend to prove or disprove more than one fact in issue in the case. Other facts are relevant to one issue only, and the jury must be directed to consider them only in relation to the fact in issue to which they are relevant.

1.1.5   In appropriate cases, where it is necessary to judge the conduct of a person against an objective standard, evidence may be given to prove what such objective standard is or was at the material time. A common example is negligence. The standard of a reasonable man may call for evidence of how a reasonable person would have behaved in the circumstances in which the accused found himself. Where the standard of comparison is one outside the every day experience of the court, for example the standard of behaviour of a professional man, the objective standard should be proved by expert evidence. The evidence must show what the generally accepted conduct would be, and not merely what a witness himself would have done. (*A Practical Approach to Evidence*, pp 3–13).

1.2   Authorities: res gestae

O'Leary v R (1946) 73 CLR 252 (High Court of Australia)

A number of men employed at a timber camp went on a drunken orgy lasting several hours, after which one of their number was found dying, having been savagely beaten about the head. The defendant was found guilty of his murder. At the trial evidence was admitted that the defendant at various times during the orgy had violently assaulted other employees. Some of these assaults were unprovoked and all consisted of brutal blows at the head. The defendant had also aimed a blow at the deceased.

DIXON J said: 'In my opinion the evidence objected to was admissible, because, from the time on Saturday 6th July when the prisoner and the party with him came under the influence of drink right up to the conclusion of the scene in the early hours of the following Sunday morning in the presence of the deceased's body lying in front of the huts, a connected series of event occurred which should be considered as one transaction. The part which the prisoner took in the drunken orgy which, as the facts suggest, culminated in the fatal attack upon the deceased man would appear to me to be relevant to the question whether the prisoner was the assailant and, if so, whether he was at the time capable of forming, and did form, the intention which would make his crime murder.

The evidence disclosed that, under the influence of the beer and wine he had drunk and continued to drink, he engaged in repeated acts of violence which might be regarded as amounting to a connected course of conduct. Without evidence of what, during that time, was done by those men who took any significant part in the matter and especially evidence of the behaviour of the prisoner, the transaction of which the alleged murder formed an integral part could not be truly understood and, isolated from it, could only be presented as an unreal and not very intelligible event. The prisoner's generally violent and hostile conduct might will serve to explain his mind and attitude and, therefore, to implicate him in the resulting homicide.'

See also: *R v Nye and Loan* (1977) 66 Cr App R 252; *Ratten v R* 1972 AC 378; *R v Conde* (1868) 10 Cox CC 547, 6.8 post.

1.3 Authorities: Facts relevant to facts in issue

Stephen's Digest of the Law of Evidence, 12th ed, art 1

The word 'relevant' means that any two facts to which it is applied are so related to each other that according to the common course of events one either taken by itself or in connection with other facts proves or renders probable the past, present, or future existence or non-existence of the other.

DPP v Kilbourne [1973] AC 729 (HL) (For facts see 6.8 post)

LORD SIMON OF GLAISDALE said: [The terms 'relevance' and 'admissibility']...are frequently, and in many circumstances legitimately, used interchangeably; but I think it makes for clarity if they are kept separate, since some relevant evidence is inadmissible and some admissible evidence is irrelevant (in the senses that I shall shortly submit). Evidence is relevant if it is logically probative or disprobative of some matter which requires proof. I do not pause to analyse what is involved in "logical probativeness," except to note that the term does not of itself express the element of experience which is so significant of its operation in law, and possibly elsewhere. It is sufficient to say, even at the risk of etymological tautology, that relevant (i.e. logically probative or disprobative) evidence is evidence which makes the matter which requires proof more or less probable...Evidence is admissible if it may be lawfully adduced at a trial. "Weight" of evidence is the degree of probability (both intrinsically and inferentially) which is attached to it by the tribunal of fact once it is established to be relevant and admissible in law.'

Holcombe v Hewson (1810) 2 Camp 391 (KB)

The plaintiff, a brewer, brought an action against a publican for breach of covenant to buy beer from the brewer. In reply to a defence that the beer previously supplied to him was bad, the plaintiff proposed to call several other publicans to say that they were supplied with good beer by him.

LORD ELLENBOROUGH said: 'This is *res inter alios acta*. We cannot here enquire into the quality of different beer furnished to different persons. The plaintiff might deal well with one, and not with the others. Let him call some of those who frequented the defendant's house, and there drank the beer which he sent in; or let him give any other evidence of the quality of this beer; but I cannot admit witnesses to his general character and habits as a brewer.'

Joy v *Phillips, Mills & Co. Ltd.* [1916] 1 KB 849 (CA)

A claim was made for workmen's compensation in respect of the death of a stable boy caused by a kick from a horse. There was no direct evidence as to how the accident happened. The deceased was found near the horse, clutching a halter which at that time he had no reason to use. Evidence was admitted that some time previously the boy had hit the horses with a halter and teased them.

PHILLIMORE LJ said: 'In my judgment the evidence which was put before him was entirely admissible. Wherever an inquiry has to be made into the cause of the death of a person, and, there being no direct evidence, recourse must be had to circumstantial evidence, any evidence as to the habits and ordinary doings of the deceased which may contribute to the circumstances by throwing light upon the probable cause of death is admissible, even in the case of a prosecution for murder. Especially in these cases under the Workmen's Compensation Act the books are full of cases where evidence as to the habits or practice of the deceased or even in his class has been admitted both in favour of the applicant and against him or her, both to contribute towards the conclusion that the accident to the deceased arose out of and in the course of the employment, and to contribute towards the opposite result.'

LORD COZENS-HARDY MR said: 'If the question was whether a man was drowned in a stream in one circumstance or another, could you not ask whether the man was in the habit of going to his work by the side of the stream and then crossing over a bridge? It seems to me that you could. Otherwise you would be shutting your eyes altogether to facts necessary for drawing the proper inferences. So it is here.'
(SARGANT J agreed).

Woolf v *Woolf* [1931] P 134 (CA)

On an undefended petition by a wife for divorce by reason of the adultery of her husband, the evidence was that the husband passed two nights in a bedroom at an hotel with a woman.

LORD HANWORTH MR said: 'In *Loveden* v *Loveden* 2 Hagg Con 1, Sir William Scott said that it was not necessary to prove the direct fact of adultery, for "if it were otherwise, there is not one case in a hundred in which that proof would be attainable: it is very rarely indeed that the parties are surprised in the direct fact of adultery. In every case almost the fact is inferred from circumstances that lead to it by fair inference as a necessary conclusion; and unless this were the case, and unless this were so held, no protection whatever could be given to marital rights." That passage has been quoted with approval in the Court of Appeal by Lopes LJ in *Allen* v *Allen* [1894] P 248, 252, where he says: "To lay down any general rule, to attempt to define what circumstances would be sufficient and what insufficient upon which to infer the fact of adultery, is impossible. Each case must depend on its own particular circumstances."

It seems to me that, human nature being what it is, adultery must be inferred here. The husband was twenty-five, and no more, and he had been married, and there is no reason to assume that his sexual appetite was less than that of a normal healthy man. I think that to say that an adulterous inclination should be proved is to lay an unjustifiable burden on the petitioner. The case is one of an innocent woman proving opportunity for adultery, and the fact that the parties spent two nights in the same bedroom. In my opinion in this case the Court ought to be satisfied that adultery has been proved.
(LAWRENCE and ROMER LJJ agreed.)

1.4 Authorities: standards of comparison

Chapman v *Walton* (1833) 10 Bing 57 (CP)

The plaintiff alleged that the defendant, a broker, had been negligent in failing to take steps to have varied the terms upon which goods at sea were insured, after receiving a letter concerning their destination. The letter was unclear on the question of the destination and the point at issue was whether the defendant might call other brokers to state what they would have done in similar circumstances.

TINDAL CJ said: 'It is objected on the part of the Plaintiffs, that to allow this question to be put to the witnesses is, in effect and substance, to allow them to be asked what is the meaning of the letter; that it is to ask them, whether the letter told the Defendant that the vessel was going to the Canaries; whereas the letter ought to be allowed to speak for itself; or if there were any doubt upon the meaning, it ought to be determined by the Court and jury, and not by the evidence of insurance brokers or any other witnesses.

It may be admitted, that if such were the real nature of the question, the evidence offered would have been inadmissible. But we think, upon reference to the issue between the parties, it was different. The action is brought for the want of reasonable and proper care, skill, and judgment shewn by the Defendant under certain circumstances in the exercise of his employment as a policy broker. The point, therefore, to be determined is, not whether the Defendant arrived at a correct conclusion upon reading the letter, but whether, upon the occasion in question, he did or did not exercise a reasonable and proper care, skill and judgment. This is a question of fact, the decision of which appears to us to rest upon this further enquiry, viz whether other persons exercising the same profession or calling, and being men of experience and skill therein, would or would not have come to the same conclusion as the Defendant. For the Defendant did not contract that he would bring to the performance of his duty, on this occasion, an extraordinary degree of skill, but only a reasonable and ordinary proportion of it; and it appears to us, that it is not only an unobjectionable mode, but the most satisfactory mode of determining this question, to shew by evidence whether a majority of skilful and experienced brokers would have come to the same conclusion as the Defendant. If nine brokers of experience out of ten would have done the same as the Defendant under the same circumstances, or even if as many out of a given number would have been of his opinion as against it, he who only stipulates to bring a reasonable degree of skill to the performance of his duty, would be entitled to a verdict in his favour. And there is no hardship upon the Plaintiffs by this course of proceeding, for they might have called members of the same profession or trade to give opposite evidence, if the facts would have warranted it; and the jury would then have decided upon such conflicting testimony, according to the relative skill or experience of the witnesses on either side, or according to the strength of the reasons which were advanced by the witnesses in support of their respective opinions. If this is the point to be decided, as we all think it is, neither the Judge nor the jury can, upon reading the letter, arrive at any conclusion upon the question. If the letter, indeed, had contained an express or explicit order to obtain leave to touch at the Canaries, there would have been no question at all: evidence as to the conduct of other men, on reading such a letter, would never have been received, because perfectly useless if received. But it is not a simple abstract question, as is supposed by the Plaintiffs, what the words of the letter mean: it is what others conversant with the business of a policy broker would have understood it to mean, and how they would have acted upon it under the same circumstances. The time of year at which the voyage is performed; the nature of the cargo on board; the objects of the voyage, as disclosed in the letter; above all, the circumstance that the original voyage described in the policy itself comprehended Teneriffe, the greatest and most important of the Canary Islands, would all operate in the minds of experienced men in determining whether it was intended the alteration should include a liberty to touch and stay at the Canaries in general. And this conclusion, it appears to us, neither Judge nor jury could arrive at from the simple perusal of the letter, unassisted by evidence; because they would not have the experience upon which a judgment could be formed.'

Noble and another v *Kennoway* (1780) 2 Doug KB 510

The question at issue was whether underwriters were entitled to repudiate liability on the insurance of a ship's cargo on the ground that there had been unreasonable delay in landing it in Labrador. Evidence was adduced of a practice of delaying the landing of cargo while ships were used for fishing in the Newfoundland trade in order to show that a similar practice prevailed in the Labrador trade.

BULLER J said: 'I think the evidence objected to was properly admitted. If it can be shown, that the time would have been reasonable in one place, that is a degree of evidence to prove that it was so in another. The effect of such evidence may be taken off, by a proof of a difference of circumstances. It is very true, that the custom of one manor is no evidence of another; that has been determined in many cases; but the point here is very different; it is a question concerning the nature of a particular branch of trade.'
(LORD MANSFIELD and WILLES and ASHHURST JJ agreed.)

Fleet v Murton (1871) LR 7 QB 126

The defendants, fruit brokers in London, being employed by the plaintiffs, merchants in London, to sell for them, gave them the following contract note addressed to the plaintiffs: 'We have this day sold for your account to our principal' so many tons of raisins. (Signed) 'M & W, brokers.' The defendants' principal having accepted part of the raisins, and not having accepted the rest, the plaintiffs brought an action on the contract against the defendants, and sought to make the defendants personally liable by giving evidence that, in the London fruit trade, if the brokers did not give the names of their principals in the contract, they were held personally liable, although they contracted as brokers for a principal. Evidence was also given of a similar custom in the London colonial market.

COCKBURN CJ, after holding that the evidence of the custom in the same trade was admissible as not inconsistent with the written contract, continued: 'This case seems to me to go further than the case of *Noble* v *Kennoway* 2 Doug 510...At the same time it is impossible to shut one's eyes to the fact that the moral effect of the evidence would operate on a reasonable mind with very considerable force. If there exists a custom to the effect that the agent makes himself liable under given circumstances, in a large and extensive trade like the colonial trade, it makes it more probable that in the fruit trade in the Mediterranean or elsewhere a similar custom would obtain. I am not quite so clear on the point, but still I do not think that the argument addressed to us goes as far as to shew that this evidence was not admissible.'

MELLOR J said: 'But with reference to the last point as to the admissibility of the evidence of the custom in the colonial trade, which is a new point as far as I am aware, I think this case goes further than any case has actually gone; yet I cannot help thinking that the evidence was relevant to this case and admissible, on the ground that, shewing, as it did, what was the custom in other trades, though not so analogous, no doubt, to the trade in question, as was the trade in *Noble* v *Kennoway* 2 Doug 510, it tended to shew the probability, that in the fruit trade as well as in the colonial trade the broker did under given circumstances undertake a similar responsibility.'
(BLACKBURN J agreed).

1.5 Judicial discretion: introductory notes

1.5.1 By judicial discretion is meant the power, if any, of a judge to admit evidence which is strictly inadmissible in law, or to exclude evidence which is strictly admissible in law. Such power, where it exists, is exercised in the interest of securing a fair trial for all parties, and with a view to avoiding prejudice threatened to one or more parties by some piece of evidence. In general, the common law has proceeded upon strictly legal questions of admissibility and inadmissibility, and has avoided any wide recognition of discretionary powers to admit or exclude.

1.5.2 At common law there is no discretion to admit inadmissible evidence either in civil or criminal cases. This rule is of general application and is to be distinguished from certain statutory powers to override formal defects in evidence as presented to the court, or to admit evidence notwithstanding failure to observe some applicable procedural requirement, such as those laid down for the admission of hearsay evidence by the Civil Evidence Act 1968 and RSC, Order 38.

1.5.3 It is uncertain whether any discretion exists in civil cases to exclude admissible evidence. Where a judge sits alone as a tribunal both of law and fact, as in most civil matters, the question is not crucial as the judge may simply accord little or no weight to such evidence as he would tend to exclude in the exercise of his discretion. However, the existence of discretion to exclude evidence seems to have been assumed by the Civil Evidence Act 1968, s.18(5), and the Civil Evidence Act 1972, s.5(3), which purport to preserve such a discretion. There appears also to be some discretion to restrain the disclosure of confidential communications (see 10.14) but it may be that this so-called 'discretion' must ultimately give way to the insistence of the party seeking to compel disclosure.

1.5.4 In criminal cases, there is a general judicial discretion to exclude evidence, even though admissible in law, which is so prejudicial as to make it virtually impossible for the jury to take a dispassionate view of the crucial facts of a case. This discretion is available simply in the interests of securing a fair trial. The test is usually said to be whether any probative value possessed by the evidence is substantially outweighed by the possible prejudicial effect thereof. There is only one such discretion, in the terms stated above, albeit that such discretion may operate in a number of different situations and upon quite diverse items of evidence. Common examples of the exercise of the discretion are:

1.5.4.1 Where evidence is admissible technically under the 'similar fact' principle (see Chapter 5), but is seriously prejudicial because of its disclosure of a specific and damaging aspect of the defendant's character.

1.5.4.2 Where the prosecution propose to adduce evidence permitted by the Theft Act 1968, s.27(3), and, in the opinion of the judge, the prejudicial value of such evidence is serious in terms of the exposure of the defendant's previous bad character.

1.5.4.3 Where the defendant has become liable to be cross-examined as to his character by virtue of the Criminal Evidence Act 1898, s.1(e) or 1(f), the judge may exclude such cross-examination altogether or confine it to those aspects of the defendant's character which appear likely to assist the jury as to his credibility.

1.5.4.4 Where a confession has been obtained in breach of the judge's rules, the judge may exclude such a confession if, by reason of the breach and the other circumstances of the case, its admission would be unfair to the defendant. (*A Practical Approach to Evidence*, pp 15–22).

1.6 Authorities: judicial discretion

1.6.1 Inclusionary

Myers v *DPP* [1965] AC 1001 (HL) (For facts, see 6.3 post)

LORD REID said: 'It is true that a judge has a discretion to exclude legally admissible evidence if justice so requires, but it is a very different thing to say that he has a discretion to admit legally inadmissible evidence.'

1.6.2. Exclusionary: civil cases

Civil Evidence Act 1968, s.18(5)

18.(5) Nothing in this Act shall prejudice:
(a) any power of a court, in any legal proceedings, to exclude evidence (whether by preventing questions from being put or otherwise) at its discretion...

1.6.3 Exclusionary: criminal cases

R v *List* [1966] 1 WLR 9 (York Assizes)

The defendant was charged with receiving stolen goods. The prosecution, in reliance on the Larceny Act 1916, s.43(1), sought to adduce evidence that the defendant had, within the five years preceding the date of the offence charged, been convicted of offences involving fraud or dishonesty.

ROSKILL J said: 'A trial judge always has an overriding duty in every case to secure a fair trial, and if in any particular case he comes to the conclusion that, even though certain evidence is strictly admissible, yet its prejudicial effect once admitted is such as to make it virtually impossible for a dispassionate view of the crucial facts of the case to be thereafter taken by the jury, then the trial judge, in my judgment, should exclude that evidence.' (His Lordship ruled that the evidence could not be adduced.)

R v *Sang* [1980] AC 402 (HL) (For facts, see 1.8 post)

LORD DIPLOCK said: 'Recognition that there may be circumstances in which in a jury trial the judge has a discretion to prevent particular kinds of evidence that is admissible from being adduced before the jury, has grown up piecemeal. It appears first in cases arising under proviso (f) of Section 1 of the Criminal Evidence Act 1898, which sets out the circumstances in which an accused may be cross-examined as to his previous convictions or bad character. The relevant cases starting in 1913 with *R* v *Watson* (1913) 109 LT 335 are conveniently cited in the speech of Lord Hodson in *R* v *Selvey* [1970] AC 304, a case in which this House accepted that in such cases the trial judge had a discretion to prevent such cross-examination, notwithstanding that it was strictly admissible under the statute, if he was of opinion that its prejudicial effect upon the jury was likely to outweigh its probative value.
Next the existence of a judicial discretion to exclude evidence of "similar facts," even where it was technically admissible, was recognised by Lord du Parcq, delivering the opinion of the Privy Council in *Noor Mohamed* v *The King* [1949] AC 182, 192. He put the grounds which justified its exercise rather more narrowly than they had been put in the "previous conviction" cases to which I have been referring; but in *Harris* v *Director of Public Prosecutions* [1952] AC 694, Viscount Simon, with whose speech the other members of this House agreed, said that the discretion to exclude "similar facts" evidence should be exercised where the "probable effect" (sc prejudicial to the accused) "would be out of proportion to its true evidential value."
That phrase was borrowed from the speech of Lord Moulton in *R* v *Christie* [1914] AC 545. That was neither a "previous conviction" nor a "similar facts" case, but was one involving evidence of an accusation made in the presence of the accused by the child victim of an alleged indecent assault and the accused's failure to answer it, from which the prosecution sought to infer an admission by the accused that it was true. Lord Moulton's statement was not confined to evidence of inferential confessions but was general in its scope and has frequently been cited as applicable in cases of cross-examination as to bad character or previous convictions under the Criminal Evidence Act 1898 and in "similar facts" cases. So I would hold that there has now developed a general rule of practice whereby in a trial by jury the judge has a discretion to exclude evidence which, though technically admissible, would probably have a prejudicial influence on the minds of the jury, which would be out of proportion to its true evidential value.'

VISCOUNT DILHORNE said: 'That a judge has such a discretion in some circumstances is now established beyond all doubt. He can refuse to allow the cross-examination of an accused as to character when the provision of the Criminal Evidence Act 1898 would permit it and he can refuse to allow the prosecution to call evidence tending to prove the commission of offences other than those charged. In my opinion these are not the only cases in which he has that discretion. He can in my opinion disallow the use in any trial of admissible relevant evidence if in his opinion its use would be accompanied by effects prejudicial to the accused which would outweigh its probative value.

In *R v Selvey* [1970] AC 304, a decision of this House which somehow escaped the attention of the Court of Appeal and of counsel, the Crown contended that a judge had no discretion to refuse to permit cross-examination as to character when the Criminal Evidence Act 1898 sanctioned it. Dealing with this contention, I said after reviewing a number of cases, at p 341:

> In the light of what was said in all these cases by judges of great eminence, one is tempted to say, as Lord Hewart said in *R v Dunkley* [1927] 1 KB 323 that it is far too late in the day even to consider the argument that a judge has no such discretion. Let it suffice for me to say that in my opinion the existence of such a discretion is now clearly established.

Lord Hodson in the same case at p 364 said that there were two answers to the argument that a judge had no such discretion:

> First, there is a long line of authority to support the opinion that there is such a discretion to be exercised under this subsection. In the second place, what is I think more significant, there is abundant authority that in criminal cases there is discretion to exclude evidence, admissible in law, of which the prejudicial effect against the accused outweighs its probative value in the opinion of the trial judge.

And Lord Pearce at p 360 said the discretion came

> from the inherent power of the courts to secure a fair trial for the accused or, to use the words of Viscount Simon [in *Harris v Director of Public Prosecutions* [1952] AC 694, 707] ' the duty of a judge when trying a charge of crime to set the essentials of justice above the technical rule if the strict application of the latter would operate unfairly against the accused.'

In the "similar fact" cases of which *Noor Mohamed v The King* [1949] AC 182 and *Harris v Director of Public Prosecutions* [1952] AC 694 are examples, a similar conclusion was reached. That the use of evidence of which the probative value is outweighed by its prejudicial effect should not occur appears first to have been clearly stated in *R v Christie* [1914] AC 545 in the speeches of Lord Moulton and Lord Reading. That was a case in which the admissibility of a statement made in the presence of the accused had to be considered and the fact that their statements were made in that case is a strong indication that the exercise of this power by a judge is not limited to "character" and "similar fact" cases.

I referred in *R v Selvey* [1970] AC 304 to the overriding duty of the judge to ensure that a trial is fair. His discretion to control the use of relevant admissible evidence is exercised in the discharge of this duty. It is the use of the evidence, not, save in relation to confessions and admissions by the accused, the manner in which it has been obtained with which he is concerned.'

LORD SALMON said: 'I consider that it is a clear principle of the law that a trial judge has the power and the duty to ensure that the accused has a fair trial. Accordingly, amongst other things, he has a discretion to exclude legally admissible evidence if justice so requires: see Lord Reid's speech in *Myers v Director of Public Prosecutions* [1965] AC 1001, 1024. It follows that:

1. An accused cannot be convicted unless the prosecution proves his guilt beyond a reasonable doubt. To allow an accused to be convicted when there is no evidence before the court capable of proving his guilt beyond a reasonable doubt would obviously be unfair.

2. A confession by an accused which has been obtained by threats or promises is inadmissible as evidence against him, because to admit it would be unfair.

3. The judge has a discretion to exclude evidence procured, after the commission of the alleged offence, which although technically admissible appears to the judge to be unfair. The classical example of such a case is where the prejudicial effect of such evidence would be out of proportion to its evidential value. *Harris* v *Director of Public Prosecutions* [1952] AC 694, 707; *Kuruma* v *The Queen* [1955] AC 197; *R* v *Selvey* [1970] AC 304.

4. Very recently, at "a trial within a trial" an accused gave evidence (accepted as true by the judge) that a confession upon which the Crown wished to rely was forced out of him; but nevertheless the accused admitted in cross-examination that the confession was true. The Privy Council ruled that when the trial was resumed the Crown could not offer evidence or cross-examine the accused about anything he had said at the "trial within a trial." To allow the Crown to do so would have been unfair: see *Wong Kam-ming* v *The Queen* [1980] AC 247.

I recognise that there may have been no categories of cases, other than those to which I have referred, in which technically admissible evidence proffered by the Crown has been rejected by the court on the ground that it would make the trial unfair. I cannot, however, accept that a judge's undoubted duty to ensure that the accused has a fair trial is confined to such cases. In my opinion the category of such cases is not and never can be closed except by statute.

LORD FRASER OF TULLYBELTON said: 'The starting point is, in my opinion, that by the law of England all evidence which is relevant is also admissible: see *Kuruma* v *The Queen* [1955] AC 197, 203, Lord Goddard. Nevertheless evidence that is admissible in law may, in certain cases, be excluded by the judge in the exercise of a discretion which he undoubtedly possesses. One such case is where evidence of "similar facts" would be admissible, for example to prove guilty intent or to exclude a defence of accident, but where the judge considers that its effect in prejudicing the jury against the accused would exceed its value in tending to prove his guilt. The judge in these circumstances has a discretion to exclude the evidence not only if its probative weight is "trifling" — see *Noor Mohamed* v *The King* [1949] AC 182, 192 — but whenever its prejudicial effect would be "out of proportion to its true evidential value" — see *Harris* v *Director of Public Prosecutions* [1952] AC 694, 707, Viscount Simon quoting Lord Moulton in *R* v *Christie* [1914] AC 545. I read the latter expression as meaning that the discretion can be exercised where the prejudicial value of the evidence would greatly exceed its probative value. Another such case is that a judge has a discretion to exclude evidence of the previous record or character of the accused and to refuse to allow him to be cross-examined as to his character notwithstanding that such evidence or cross-examination may be legally admissible under section 1(f)(ii) of the Criminal Evidence Act 1898. In *R* v *Selvey* [1970] AC 304, 341, Viscount Dilhorne said that the existence of such a discretion was "now clearly established."

These cases are in my opinion examples of the exercise of a single discretion founded upon the duty of the judge to ensure that every accused person has a fair trial. That is the basis upon which it was put by Lord Goddard in *Kuruma* v *The Queen* [1955] AC 197 where he said, at p 204:

> No doubt in a criminal case the judge always has a discretion to disallow evidence if the strict rules of admissibility would operate unfairly against an accused.

If there were not some underlying discretionary power it would be difficult to explain how the judges were able, when the Criminal Evidence Act 1898 came into force, to exclude legally admissible evidence of the type to which I have referred. The statute does not in terms confer a discretion...

The result will be to leave judges with a discretion to be exercised in accordance with their individual views of what is unfair or oppressive or morally reprehensible. These adjectives do undoubtedly describe standards which are largely subjective and which are therefore liable to variation. But I do not think there is any cause for anxiety in that. Judges of all courts are accustomed to deciding what is reasonable and to applying other standards containing a large subjective element. In exercising the discretion with which this appeal is concerned, judges will have the benefit of the decision of this House fixing certain limits beyond which they should not go and they will also have valuable guidance of a more general nature in the opinion of Lord Widgery CJ in *Jeffrey* v *Black* [1978] QB 490. I do not think it would be practicable to attempt to lay down any more precise rules because the purpose of the discretion is that it should be sufficiently wide and flexible to be capable of being exercised in a variety of circumstances that may occur from time to time but which cannot be foreseen.

LORD SCARMAN said: 'In my judgment, certain broad conclusions emerge from a study of the case law. They are:

(1) that there is one general discretion, not several specific or limited discretions;

(2) that the discretion now extends further than was contemplated by Lord Halsbury and Lord Moulton in *Christie's* case, or even by Lord Simon in *Harris* v *Director of Public Prosecutions* [1952] AC 694: it is now the law that "a judge has a discretion to exclude legally admissible evidence if justice so requires" (Lord Reid in *Myers* v *Director of Public Prosecutions* [1965] AC 1001, 1024);

(3) that the formula of prejudicial effect outweighing probative value, which has been developed in the "similar fact" cases, is not a complete statement of the range or the principle of the discretion;

(4) that the discretion is, however, limited to what my noble and learned friend, Viscount Dilhorne, calls the "unfair use" of evidence at trial: it does not confer any judicial power of veto upon the right of the prosecution to prosecute or to present in support of the prosecution's case admissible evidence, however obtained.

These broad conclusions leave unresolved the critical question as to the limits of the discretion and the principle upon which it is founded. It may be, as Lord MacDermott CJ said in *R* v *Murphy* [1965] NI 138, 149, that unfairness, which will be found to be its modern justification, cannot be closely defined. One must, however, emerge from the last refuge of legal thought — that each case depends on its facts — and attempt some analysis of principle.

It is tempting to accept that there are several discretions specific to certain situations. Certainly the law has developed by reference to specific situations in which admissible evidence has been either excluded or said to be liable, at the judge's discretion, to be excluded.

A discretion has been recognised to exclude "similar fact" evidence where its prejudicial effect would outweigh its probative value: *Noor Mohamed* v *The King* [1949] AC 182. A discretion to refuse to permit a cross-examination of the accused to his record, though permissible under the Criminal Evidence Act 1898, was recognised by this House in *R* v *Selvey* [1970] AC 304. Other relevant evidence may also be excluded. Examples are: a voluntary confession obtained in breach of the Judges' Rules; evidence obtained where the defendant has been misled into providing it (*R* v *Payne* [1963] 1 WLR 637); evidence obtained illegally after the commission of the offence (*Kuruma* v *The Queen* [1955] AC 197). The instances of actual exclusion are rare: but too many distinguished judges have said that the discretion exists for there to be any doubt that it does.

Notwithstanding its development case by case, I have no doubt that the discretion is now a general one in the sense that it is to be exercised whenever a judge considers it necessary in order to ensure the accused a fair trial. *R* v *Selvey* [1970] AC 304 can be seen to be of critical importance. Viscount Dilhorne, though he was directing his attention to the specific situation in that case (cross-examination of the accused to his record) referred to cases concerned with other situations, e.g. *R* v *Christie* [1914] AC 545, *Noor Mohamed* v *The King* [1949] AC 182, *Harris* v *Director of Public Prosecutions* [1952] AC 694 and *Kuruma* v *The Queen* [1955] AC 197, and concluded by saying, at pp 341–342:

> It [i.e. its exercise] must depend on the circumstances of each case and *the overriding duty of the judge to ensure that a trial is fair* (my emphasis).

Lord Hodson, Lord Guest and Lord Pearce, with whom Lord Wilberforce agreed, were clearly of the opinion that the discretion was a general one. Lord Hodson said at p 349: "Discretion ought not to be confined save by the limits of fairness." Lord Guest said at p 352, that the discretion "springs from the inherent power of the judge to control the trial before him and to see that justice is done in fairness to the accused": and Lord Pearce echoed his words at p 360F.

The review of the authorities by this House in *Selvey's* case reveals how comparatively recent a judicial development this discretion is. Its history is associated with the recognition of the admissibility of "similar fact" evidence. As this rule of evidence became established, judges were alert to prevent its abuse where probative value was slight and prejudicial effect upon a jury likely to be great. But other more basic matters contributed to the development: in particular, the common law principle against self-incrimination, and the side-effects of the Criminal Law Evidence Act 1898 which by conferring upon the accused the right to give evidence on his own behalf exposed him to the perils of cross-examination. Against this comparatively modern background the judges have had to discharge their duty of ensuring the accused a fair trial. Long before 1898, however, the courts were faced with the problem of reconciling fairness at trial with the admissibility of evidence obtained as a consequence of an inadmissible confession. The problem was resolved in *R* v *Warickshall* (1783) 1 Leach 263 by the court declaring, at p 300:

> Facts thus obtained, however, must be fully and satisfactorily proved, without calling in the aid of any part of the confession from which they may have been derived;...

The discovery of the stolen goods in that case, or (as in *R* v *Berriman* (1854) 6 Cox 388) the finding of the remains of the corpse, is the best possible evidence of the truth of the confession (compare and contrast the Canadian approach in the Supreme Court decision *R* v *Wray* (1970) 11 DLR (3d) 673): but in English law the confession is inadmissible, not because it is unreliable (its reliability is established by what has been found), but because to admit it would be unfair. Similar considerations influenced the judges after 1898 in protecting an accused from a permissible cross-examination to his record or in excluding admissible "similar fact" evidence. At first, the judge would be expected to use his influence (*R* v *Christie* [1914] AC 545) to dissuade the prosecution from doing what the statute or the common law allowed: but by the time *Kuruma* v *The Queen* [1955] AC 197 was decided influence had become power. Lord Goddard CJ was able to say, in that case, at p 204:

> No doubt in a criminal case the judge always has a discretion to disallow evidence if the strict rules of admissibility would operate unfairly against an accused.

R v *Christie* [1914] AC 545 is, therefore, only a staging-post in the development of the law. The modern discretion is a general one to be exercised where fairness to the accused requires its exercise.'

1.7 Evidence illegally or unfairly obtained: introductory notes

1.7.1 Evidence is not inadmissible merely because it has been obtained unfairly or even illegally by the party seeking to tender it. The test is whether the evidence is relevant, and whether it is otherwise admissible by virtue of the law of evidence in general. This rule extends to evidence obtained by means of entrapment or through the agency of an agent provocateur.

1.7.2 Further, there is no discretion to exclude evidence merely because it has been obtained illegally or unfairly. However, as noted in 1.5 ante, the judge does have a general discretion to exclude evidence where probative value is outweighed substantially by its possible prejudicial effect. This is not however because of the method by which the evidence is obtained, but because of the effect of the evidence once admitted.

1.7.3 The above rules do not effect the specific laws of evidence governing the admissibility of confessions and other incriminating evidence obtained by search or inquiry from the defendant. The admissibility of confessions may depend upon the manner in which they are obtained, and the detailed rules on this subject are dealt with in Chapter 7. To this extent, confessions and other incriminating material obtained by search must now be regarded as an exception to the general rule of English law that evidence is not rendered inadmissible merely because of the manner in which it is obtained. (*A Practical Approach to Evidence*, pp 22–7.)

1.8 Authorities: evidence illegally and unfairly obtained

R v Leatham (1861) 8 Cox 498 (QB)

The question arose as to whether a letter referred to by the defendant in an inquiry by Commissioners under the Corrupt Practices Act was admissible in evidence against him even though the Act provided that testimony before the Commissioners should not be admissible.

CROMPTON J said: 'Suppose by threats and promises a confession of murder obtained, which would not be admissible, but you also obtain a clue to a place where a written confession may be found, or where the body of a person murdered is secreted; could not that latter evidence be made use of because the first clue to it came from the murderer? It matters not how you get it; if you steal it even, it would be admissible in evidence.'

Kuruma, son of Kaniu v R [1955] AC 197 (PC)

The appellant was convicted of the unlawful possession of ammunition during a period of emergency in Kenya. The ammunition was found during an illegal search.

LORD GODDARD, delivering the judgment of their Lordships' said: 'In their Lordships' opinion the test to be applied in considering whether evidence is admissible is whether it is relevant to the matters in issue. If it is, it is admissible and the court is not concerned with how the evidence was obtained. While this proposition may not have been stated in so many words in any English case there are decisions which support it, and in their Lordships' opinion it is plainly right in principle. In *R v Leatham* (1861) 8 Cox CC 498 an information for penalties under the Corrupt Practices Act, objection was taken to the production of a letter written by the defendant because its existence only became known by answers he had given to the commissioners who held the inquiry under the Act, which provided that answers before that tribunal should not be admissible in evidence against him. The Court of Queen's Bench held that though his answers could not be used against the defendant, yet if a clue was thereby given to other evidence, in that case the letter, which would prove the case it was admissible. Crompton J said Ibid 501: "It matters not how you get it; if you steal it even, it would be admissible." *Lloyd v Mostyn* (1842) 10 M&W 478 was an action on a bond. The person in whose possession it was objected to produce it on the ground of privilege. The plaintiff's attorney, however, had got a copy of it and notice to produce the original being proved the court admitted the copy as secondary evidence. To the same effect was *Calcraft v Guest* [1898] 1 QB 759. There can be no difference in principle for this purpose between a civil and a criminal case. No doubt in a criminal case the judge always has a discretion to disallow evidence if the strict rules of admissibility would operate unfairly against an accused. This was emphasised in the case before this Board of *Noor Mohamed v The King* [1949] AC 182 at 191–2, and in the recent case in the House of Lords, *Harris v Director of Public Prosecutions* [1952] AC 694. If, for instance, some admission of some piece of evidence, e.g. a document, had been obtained from a defendant by a trick, no doubt the judge might properly rule it out.
Appeal dismissed.

Jeffrey v Black [1978] QB 490 (DC)

The defendant was arrested by two police officers of the drug squad for stealing a sandwich from a public house. The officers then quite improperly searched his home and found cannabis and cannabis resin. He was charged with possession of those drugs. The justices ruled that evidence obtained during the search was inadmissible and dismissed the informations. The prosecutor appealed.

LORD WIDGERY CJ said: 'It is firmly established according to English law that the mere fact that evidence is obtained in an irregular fashion does not of itself prevent that evidence from being relevant and acceptable to a court. The authority for that is *Kuruma* v *The Queen* [1955] AC 197...There one has that pronouncement from the Privy Council, and I have not the least doubt that we must firmly accept the proposition that an irregularity in obtaining evidence does not render the evidence inadmissible. Whether or not the evidence is admissible depends on whether or not it is relevant to the issues in respect of which it is called.

At this point it would seem that the prosecutor ought to succeed in his appeal because at this point what he appears to have shown is that the justices were wrong in failing to recognise the law as stated in *Kuruma* v *The Queen* [1955] AC 197. But that is not in fact the end of the matter because the justices sitting in this case, like any other tribunal dealing with criminal matters in England and sitting under the English law, have a general discretion to decline to allow any evidence to be called by the prosecution if they think that it would be unfair or oppressive to allow that to be done. In getting an assessment of what this discretion means, justices ought, I think, to stress to themselves that the discretion is not a discretion which arises only in drug cases. It is not a discretion which arises only in cases where police can enter premises. It is a discretion which every judge has all the time in respect of all the evidence which is tendered by the prosecution. It would probably give justices some idea of the extent to which this discretion is used if one asks them whether they are appreciative of the fact that they have the discretion anyway, and it may well be that a number of experienced justices would be quite ignorant of the possession of this discretion. That gives them, I hope, some idea of how relatively rarely it is exercised in our courts. But if the case is exceptional, if the case is such that not only have the police officers entered without authority, but they have been guilty of trickery or they have misled someone, or they have been oppressive or they have been unfair, or in other respects they have behaved in a manner which is morally reprehensible, then it is open to the justices to apply their discretion and decline to allow the particular evidence to be let in as part of the trial. I cannot stress the point too strongly that this is a very exceptional situation, and the simple, unvarnished fact that evidence was obtained by police officers who had gone in without bothering to get a search warrant is not enough to justify the justices in exercising their discretion to keep the evidence out.

(FORBES and CROOM-JOHNSON JJ agreed.)
Appeal allowed.

R v *Sang* [1980] AC 402 (HL)

Two defendants were indicted on counts of conspiracy to utter forged banknotes and unlawful possession of forged banknotes. They pleaded not guilty and counsel invited the trial judge to allow a trial within a trial to determine whether the activities referred to in the indictment came about as a result of incitement by an agent provocateur. Counsel hoped that, having established the facts, he would persuade the judge to exercise his discretion to exclude any prosecution evidence of the commission of offences so incited. The judge, doubting the existence of any such discretion, invited counsel to argue the point on the assumption that the necessary facts had been established. After argument, the judge ruled that he had no such discretion. Thereupon the defendants changed their pleas, and each pleaded guilty to one count and was sentenced. The Court of Appeal upheld the judge's ruling. One defendant appealed to the House of Lords.

LORD DIPLOCK said: 'What has been regarded as the fountain head of all subsequent dicta on this topic is the statement by Lord Goddard delivering advice of the Privy Council in *Kuruma* v *The Queen* [1955] AC 197. That was a case in which the evidence of unlawful possession of ammunition by the accused was obtained as a result of an illegal search of his person. The Board held that this evidence was admissible and had rightly been admitted; but Lord Goddard although he had earlier said at p 203 that if evidence is admissible "the court is not concerned with how the evidence was obtained," nevertheless went on to say, at p 204:

> No doubt in a criminal case the judge always has a discretion to disallow evidence if the strict rules of admissibility would operate unfairly against an accused. This was

emphasised in the case before this Board of *Noor Mohamed* v *The King* [1949] AC 182, and in the recent case in the House of Lords, *Harris* v *Director of Public Prosecutions* [1952] AC 694. *If, for instance, some admission of some piece of evidence, e.g. a document, had been obtained from a defendant by a trick, no doubt the judge might properly rule it out.*

Up to the sentence that I have italicised there is nothing in this passage to suggest that when Lord Goddard spoke of admissible evidence operating "unfairly" against the accused he intended to refer to any wider aspect of unfairness than the probable prejudicial effect of the evidence upon the minds of the jury outweighing its true evidential value; though he no doubt also had in mind the discretion that had long been exercised in England under the Judges' Rules to refuse to admit confessions by the accused made after the crime even though strictly they may be admissible. The instance given in the passage I have italicised appears to me to deal with a case which falls within the latter category since the document "obtained from a defendant by a trick" is clearly analogous to a confession which the defendant has been unfairly induced to make, and had, indeed, been so treated in *R* v *Barker* [1941] 2 KB 381 where an incriminating document obtained from the defendant by a promise of favours was held to be inadmissible.

It is interesting in this connection to observe that the only case that has been brought to your Lordships' attention in which an appellate court has actually excluded evidence on the ground that it had been unfairly obtained (*R* v *Payne* [1963] 1 WLR 637) would appear to fall into this category. The defendant, charged with drunken driving, had been induced to submit himself to examination by a doctor to see if he was suffering from any illness or disability, upon the understanding that the doctor would not examine him for the purpose of seeing whether he were fit to drive. The doctor in fact gave evidence of the defendant's unfitness to drive based upon his symptoms and behaviour in the course of that examination. The Court of Criminal Appeal quashed his conviction on the ground that the trial judge ought to have exercised his discretion to exclude the doctor's evidence. This again, as it seems to me, is analogous to unfairly inducing a defendant to confess to an offence, and the short judgment of the Court of Criminal Appeal is clearly based upon the maxim *nemo debet prodere se ipsum*.

In no other case to which your Lordships' attention has been drawn has either the Court of Criminal Appeal or the Court of Appeal allowed an appeal upon the ground that either magistrates in summary proceedings or the judge in a trial upon indictment ought to have exercised a discretion to exclude admissible evidence upon the ground that it had been obtained unfairly or by trickery or in some other way that is morally reprehensible; though they cover a wide gamut of apparent improprieties from illegal searches, as in *Kuruma* v *The Queen* itself and in *Jeffrey* v *Black* [1978] QB 490 (which must be the high water mark of this kind of illegality) to the clearest case of evidence obtained by the use of agents provocateur. Of the latter an outstanding example is to be found in *Browning* v *J W H Watson (Rochester) Ltd.* [1953] 1 WLR 1172 where Lord Goddard CJ remitted the case to the magistrates with a direction that the offence had been proved, but pointedly reminded them that it was open to them to give the defendant an absolute discharge and to award no costs to the prosecution.

Nevertheless it has to be recognised that there is an unbroken series of dicta in judgments of appellate courts to the effect that there is a judicial discretion to exclude admissible evidence which has been 'obtained' unfairly or by trickery or oppressively, although except in *R* v *Payne* [1963] 1 WLR 637, there never has been a case in which those courts have come across conduct so unfair, so tricky or so oppressive as to justify them in holding that the discretion ought to have been exercised in favour of exclusion. In every one of the cases to which your Lordships have been referred where such dicta appear, the source from which the evidence sought to be excluded had been obtained has been the defendant himself or (in some of the search cases) premises occupied by him; and the dicta can be traced to a common ancestor in Lord Goddard's statement in *Kuruma* v *The Queen* [1955] AC 197 which I have already cited. That statement was not, in my view, ever intended to acknowledge the existence of any wider discretion than to exclude (1) admissible evidence which would probably have a prejudicial influence upon the minds of the jury that would be out of proportion to its true evidential value; and (2) evidence tantamount to a self-incriminatory admission which was obtained from the defendant, after the offence had been committed, by means which would justify a judge in excluding an actual confession which had the like self-incriminating effect. As a matter of language, although not as a matter of application, the subsequent dicta go much further than this; but in so far as they do so they have never yet been considered by this House.

My Lords, I propose to exclude, as the certified question does, detailed consideration of the role of the trial judge in relation to confessions and evidence obtained from the defendant after commission of the offence that is tantamount to a confession. It has a long history dating back to the days before the existence of a disciplined police force, when a prisoner on a charge of felony could not be represented by counsel and was not entitled to give evidence in his own defence either to deny that he had made the confession, which was generally oral, or to deny that its contents were true. The underlying rationale of this branch of the criminal law, though it may originally have been based upon ensuring the reliability of confessions is, in my view, now to be found in the maxim *nemo debet prodere se ipsum,* no one can be required to be his own betrayer or in its popular English mistranslation 'the right to silence.' That is why there is no discretion to exclude evidence discovered as the result of an illegal search but there is discretion to exclude evidence which the accused has been induced to produce voluntarily if the method of inducement was unfair.

Outside this limited field in which for historical reasons the function of the trial judge extended to imposing sanctions for improper conduct on the part of the prosecution before the commencement of the proceedings in inducing the accused by threats, favour or trickery to provide evidence against himself, your Lordships should, I think, make it clear that the function of the judge at a criminal trial as respects the admission of evidence is to ensure that the accused has a fair trial according to law. It is no part of a judge's function to exercise disciplinary powers over the police or prosecution as respects the way in which evidence to be used at the trial is obtained by them. If it was obtained illegally there will be a remedy in civil law; if it was obtained legally but in breach of the rules of conduct for the police, this is a matter for the appropriate disciplinary authority to deal with. What the judge at the trial is concerned with is not how the evidence sought to be adduced by the prosecution has been obtained, but with how it is used by the prosecution at the trial.

A fair trial according to law involves, in the case of a trial upon indictment, that it should take place before a judge and a jury; that the case against the accused should be proved to the satisfaction of the jury beyond all reasonable doubt upon evidence that is admissible in law; and, as a corollary to this, that there should be excluded from the jury information about the accused which is likely to have an influence on their minds prejudicial to the accused which is out of proportion to the true probative value of admissible evidence conveying that information. If these conditions are fulfilled and the jury receive correct instructions from the judge as to the law applicable to the case, the requirement that the accused should have a fair trial according to law is, in my view, satisfied; for the fairness of a trial according to law is not all one-sided; it requires that those who are undoubtedly guilty should be convicted as well as that those about whose guilt there is any reasonable doubt should be acquitted. However much the judge may dislike the way in which a particular piece of evidence was obtained before proceedings were commenced, if it is admissible evidence probative of the accused's guilt it is no part of his judicial function to exclude it for this reason. If your Lordships so hold you will be reverting to the law as it was laid down by Lord Moulton in *R v Christie* [1914] AC 545, Lord du Parcq in *Noor Mohamed v The King* [1949] AC 182 and Viscount Simon in *Harris v Director of Public Prosecutions* [1952] AC 694 before the growth of what I believe to have been a misunderstanding of Lord Goddard's dictum in *Kuruma v The Queen* [1955] AC 197.

LORD SCARMAN said: 'The accused is to be tried according to law. The law, not the judge's discretion, determines what is admissible evidence. The law, not the judge, determines what defences are available to the accused. It is the law that, subject to certain recognised exceptions, evidence which is relevant is admissible. It is the law that there is no defence of entrapment. The judge may not use his discretion to prevent a prosecution being brought merely because he disapproves of the way in which legally admissible evidence has been obtained. The judge may not by the exercise of his discretion to exclude admissible evidence secure to the accused the benefit of a defence unknown to the law. Judges are not responsible for the bringing or abandonment of prosecutions: nor have they the right to adjudicate in a way which indirectly usurps the functions of the legislature or jury. For legislation would be needed to introduce a defence of entrapment: and, if it were to be introduced, it would be for the jury to decide whether in the particular case effect should be given to it.

I can now answer the questions posed at the beginning of this opinion. The role of the judge is confined to the forensic process. He controls neither the police nor the prosecuting authority. He neither initiates nor stifles a prosecution. Save in the very rare situation, which is not this case, of an abuse of the process of the court (against which every court is in duty bound to protect itself), the judge is concerned only with the conduct of the trial. The Judges' Rules, for example, are not a judicial control of police interrogation, but notice that, if certain steps are not taken, certain evidence, otherwise admissible, may be excluded at the trial. The judge's control of the criminal process begins and ends with trial, though his influence may extend beyond its beginning and conclusion. It follows that the prosecution has rights, which the judge may not override. The right to prosecute and the right to lead admissible evidence in support of its case are not subject to judicial control. Of course when the prosecutor reaches court, he becomes subject to the directions as to the conduct of the trial by the judge, whose duty it then is to see that the accused has a fair trial according to law.

What does "fair" mean in this context? It relates to the process of trial. No man is to be compelled to incriminate himself; *nemo tenetur se ipsum prodere*. No man is to be convicted save upon the probative effect of legally admissible evidence. No admission or confession is to be received in evidence unless voluntary. If legally admissible evidence be tendered which endangers these principles (as, for example, in *R* v *Payne* [1963] 1 WLR 637), the judge may exercise his discretion to exclude it, thus ensuring that the accused has the benefit of principles which exist in the law to secure him a fair trial; but he has no power to exclude admissible evidence of the commission of a crime, unless in his judgment these principles are endangered...

The question remains whether evidence obtained from an accused by deception, or a trick, may be excluded at the discretion of the trial judge. Lord Goddard CJ thought it could be: *Kuruma* v *The Queen* [1955] AC 197, 204, Lord Parker CJ and Lord Widgery CJ thought so too: see *Callis* v *Gunn* [1964] 1 QB 495, 502 and *Jeffrey* v *Black* [1978] QB 490. The dicta of three successive Lord Chief Justices are not to be lightly rejected. It is unnecessary for the purposes of this appeal, to express a conclusion upon them. But, always provided that these dicta are treated as relating exclusively to the obtaining of evidence from the accused, I would not necessarily dissent from them. If an accused is misled or tricked into providing evidence (whether it be an admission or the provision of fingerprints or medical evidence or some other evidence), the rule against self-incrimination — *nemo tenetur se ipsum prodere* — is likely to be infringed. Each case must, of course, depend on its circumstances. All I would say is that the principle of fairness, though concerned exclusively with the use of evidence at trial, is not susceptible to categorisation or classification and is wide enough in some circumstances to embrace the way in which, after the crime, evidence has been obtained from the accused.'

(VISCOUNT DILHORNE and LORD SALMON and FRASER agreed.)

Appeal dismissed.

1.9 The 'best evidence' rule

1.9.1   The best evidence rule states that only the best available evidence of a fact will be admitted. If it appears that better evidence might have been obtained, for example the production of an actual object as contrasted with an oral description of it given by a witness, evidence which is not the best will be rejected. The rule originated in the 18th century and is generally considered to be obsolete. It is generally thought to survive only in the rule that where it is sought to rely upon the contents of a document as evidence, the original document must generally be produced in preference to a copy or oral evidence of the contents. The rule is, however, occasionally revived for the purpose of excluding evidence.

1.9.2   Irrespective of the impact of the rule upon admissibility, the best available evidence is always likely to carry more weight that any other evidence of a fact, and it is a legitimate matter for comment that available better evidence has been neglected in favour of less satisfactory or less reliable evidence. (*A Practical Approach to Evidence*, pp 27–8).

B: PROOF WITHOUT EVIDENCE

1.10 Introductory notes

1.10.1 The court will accept as proved, without the need for evidence, any fact which is formally admitted for the purpose of proceedings, or of which the court is entitled to take judicial notice. The court will find proved a fact presumed in favour of a party, in the absence of evidence to the contrary.

1.10.2 Formal admissions In civil cases, any fact in issue may be admitted on the pleadings, in response to a notice to admit or to interrogatories or at any stage by agreement between the parties before or at trial. The fact admitted is conclusively taken to be true for the purpose of the proceedings only. For the purpose of the proceedings, a party may rely on a fact admitted for any purpose including the signing of judgment provided that no further facts are needed to prove the case, and provided also that no inferences must be drawn from admitted facts in order to lend effect to them. In criminal cases, the admission of facts for the purpose of proceedings is governed by statute and is subject to procedural safeguards. Principal among these safeguards is that an admission may, with leave of the court, be withdrawn for the purpose of the proceedings in which it is made, or any subsequent criminal proceedings relating to the same matter.

1.10.3 Judicial notice The court will take judicial notice of certain facts and thereby acknowledge the truth of those facts without the necessity for proof by evidence. Such facts are those which are notorious or which are readily demonstrable by reference to proper sources. Such proper sources include works of reference, and even the taking of evidence by the judge. A judge may not act on his personal knowledge of the particular facts of the case before him. But he may, properly and within reasonable limits, apply such general knowledge as he may have of the subject matter of the case to the process of understanding and evaluating the evidence. In the case of magistrates and jurors, it is proper for those persons to use general or local knowledge in considering a case. Judicial notice is taken of the existence and contents of public statutes and of the Law of England, of the procedure and privileges of both Houses of Parliament and of the jurisdiction and rules of each Division of the High Court. Similarly, judicial notice will be taken of well-established customs, such as those of the City of London, of professional practice, of political matters and affairs of state and of readily demonstrable public facts, for example facts of historical or geographical notoriety or the meaning of words in common usage.

1.10.4 Presumptions A presumption is a device for fixing the burden of proof in relation to certain facts, notwithstanding the incidence of the burden of proof in relation to the case generally. Where a presumption operates in favour of a party who seeks to prove a fact, the court may find proved and act on that fact without evidence unless the opponent rebuts the presumption by adducing evidence satisfactory to the court, and thereby restores the burden of proof applicable to the case generally. A presumption requires the party in whose favour it operates to prove certain 'primary facts', on proof of which the 'presumed fact' is taken by the court to be true in the absence of satisfactory evidence to the contrary. An example of this is that where a party proves that H and W have been through a ceremony of marriage, it is presumed that H and W were validly married. The important examples of presumptions follow.

1.10.4.1 Presumption of legitimacy. On proof of the primary facts that a child was born to a wife, that it was born during lawful wedlock or within the normal period of gestation thereafter, and that the husband was alive at the date of conception, it will be presumed that the child is the legitimate child of husband and wife and that access took place between them resulting in the conception. The mere fact of voluntary separation during the marriage, or the institution of divorce proceedings, will not affect the operation of the presumption. However, if the separation is by virtue of an order of the court, there is a contrary presumption that the order of the court was obeyed, and consequently where the child is born more than nine months after such an order it will be presumed to be illegitimate. By statute, any presumption as to legitimacy or illegitimacy may be rebutted in civil proceedings on the balance of probabilities. It is likely that the same test would now apply in criminal proceedings governed by the common law. The parties to a marriage are now competent witnesses as to the occurrence or non-occurrence of sexual intercourse, and save in criminal proceedings, are compellable to give evidence on that subject.

1.10.4.2 Presumption of marriage. On proof of either of the alternative primary facts that H and W went through a ceremony of marriage, or that H and W have cohabited together and been regarded as man and wife, it will be presumed that H and W are validly married. The presumption extends to include any necessary presumption of formal capacity to marry. Strong evidence is needed to rebut the presumption, but rebutting evidence may be found in evidence of incapacity to marry or of the existence of a valid prior marriage.

1.10.4.3 Presumption of death. On proof of the primary facts that there is no acceptable evidence that the subject has been alive at some time during a continuous period of seven years or more, that there are persons likely to have heard from him were he alive who have not heard of him during that period, and that all due inquiries have been made with a view to locating the subject without success, it will be presumed that the subject died at some time during the period of seven years. What amounts to the absence of acceptable evidence that the subject is alive and what amounts to the making of reasonable inquiries are questions of fact in every case. The presumption is only that the subject died at some time during the period. His death on any particular day will not be presumed and must be proved by evidence if relevant. However, the presumption will, under modern law, extend to dates during the period of seven years before the date of trial. The period of seven years is strictly insisted upon. There is no presumption that the subject died from any particular cause, died childless or died celibate. In dealing with this presumption, it should be remembered that it is always open to the court to infer death (or continued life) from the evidence as a question of fact.

1.10.4.4 Presumption of regularity. This expression really embodies three separate presumptions, as follows:

(a) On proof of the primary fact that some official or public act has been performed or that a person acted in an official public capacity, it is presumed that the act done complied with any necessary formalities or that the person so acting was properly appointed for the purpose as the case may be.

(b) On proof of the primary fact that a mechanical instrument is usually in order and working correctly, it will be presumed that it was so working and in order when used on a relevant occasion.

(c) On proof that necessary business transactions have been carried out that required to be effected in a certain order, it will be presumed that they were effected in that order.

1.10.4.5 Where there are two or more conflicting presumptions applying to the same facts, they cancel each other out and the burden of proof operates as though neither presumption applied. (*A Practical Approach to Evidence*, pp 28–41.)

1.11 Authorities: formal admissions

Rules of the Supreme Court, Order 18

13(1) Subject to paragraph (4), any allegation of fact made by a party in his pleading is deemed to be admitted by the opposite party unless it is traversed by that party in his pleading or a joinder of issue under Rule 14 operates as a denial of it.

(2) A traverse may be made either by a denial or by a statement of non-admission and either expressly or by necessary implication.

(3) Subject to paragraph (4), every allegation of fact made in a statement of claim or counterclaim which the party on whom it is served does not intend to admit must be specifically traversed by him in his defence or defence to counterclaim, as the case may be; and a general denial of such allegations, or a general statement of non-admission of them, is not a sufficient traverse of them.

(4) Any allegation that a party has suffered damage and any allegation as to the amount of damages is deemed to be traversed unless specifically admitted.

14(1) If there is no reply to a defence, there is an implied joinder of issue on that defence.

(2) Subject to paragraph (3)

(a) there is at the close of pleadings an implied joinder of issue on the pleading last served, and

(b) a party may in his pleading expressly join issue on the next preceding pleading.

(3) There can be no joinder of issue, implied or express, on a statement of claim or counterclaim.

(4) A joinder of issue operates as a denial of every material allegation of fact made in the pleading on which there is an implied or express joinder of issue unless, in the case of an express joinder of issue, any such allegation is excepted from the joinder and is stated to be admitted, in which case the express joinder of issue operates as a denial of every other such allegation.

Rules of the Supreme Court, Order 27

27(1) Without prejudice to Order 18, rule 13, a party to a cause or matter may give notice, by his pleading or otherwise in writing, that he admits the truth of the whole or any part of the case of any other party.

Criminal Justice Act 1967, s.10

10(1) Subject to the provisions of this section, any fact of which oral evidence may be given in any criminal proceedings may be admitted for the purpose of those proceedings by or on behalf of the prosecutor or defendant, and the admission by any party of any such fact under this section shall as against that party be conclusive evidence in those proceedings of the fact admitted.

(2) An admission under this section —

(a) may be made before or at the proceedings;

(b) if made otherwise than in court, shall be in writing;

(c) if made in writing by an individual, shall purport to be signed by the person making it...

(d) if made on behalf of a defendant who is an individual, shall be made by his counsel or solicitor;

(e) if made at any stage before the trial by a defendant who is an individual must be approved by his counsel or solicitor (whether at the time it was made or subsequently) before or at the proceedings in question.

(3) An admission under this section for the purpose of proceedings relating to any matter shall be treated as an admission for the purpose of any subsequent criminal proceedings relating to that matter (including any appeal or retrial).

(4) An admission under this section may with the leave of the court be withdrawn in the proceedings for the purpose of which it is made or any subsequent criminal proceedings relating to the same matter.

1.12 Authorities: judicial notice

Oxford Poor Rate Case (1857) 8 E&B 184 (Exch Ch)

The University claimed exemption from liability to poor rate in respect of certain buildings and land.

COLERIDGE J said: 'The University of Oxford, without attempting an exact or complete definition of it, may at least be said to be a national institution created for a great national purpose, the advancement, namely, of religion and learning through the nation. We are bound judicially so to regard it; for the Legislature in public Acts of Parliament, so deals with its title and property, its discipline and government, as to declare that it holds the one and must be compelled, if necessary, to regulate the other, not merely with a view to any private interests of the corporation or corporators, but so as best to advance the interests of the public in the two respects we have named, of learning and religion.'

Burns v *Edman* [1970] 2 QB 541

The plaintiff's husband was killed in a motor accident involving the defendant. Home Office records disclosed that he had received two prison sentences, one for robbery and another for being an accessory to a felony, and there was nothing to show that during his lifetime he had any honest employment and he possessed no capital assets. The plaintiff, who was aware that such money as her husband gave her came from the proceeds of crime, brought an action against the defendant under the Law Reform (Miscellaneous Provisions) Act 1934 on behalf of the deceased's estate.

CRIGHTON J said: 'Counsel for the plaintiff argued that the maximum figure for loss of expectation of life these days is £500, and there is no reason why the deceased, as a strong and healthy man of 32 should not receive that figure or his estate receive that figure. On the other hand, counsel for the defendant argued that damages for loss of expectation of life — and he is quite right about this in the light of the authorities — is really damages for loss of a happy life or the element of happiness, in so far as it outweighs the element of unhappiness in life. Now this man, as I find, was a criminal and I think I am entitled to take judicial notice of the fact that the life of a criminal is an unhappy one, and I think that that fact sounds, in the assessment of damages, under the Law Reform Act for loss of expectation of life. Accordingly, I would award the plaintiff under that head, as administratrix of the estate of the deceased, the sum of £250 reduced by a quarter in respect of the deceased's contributory negligence.'

Judgment for £187 10s.

McQuaker v *Goddard* [1940] 1 KB 687 (CA)

The defendant was the proprietor of a zoo. The plaintiff, a visitor to the zoo, was bitten by a camel while feeding it. In an action for damages for personal injuries, one issue was whether a camel was a wild or domestic animal. The judge consulted books about camels and heard conflicting expert evidence about their behaviour. Having done so he took judicial notice of the fact that a camel was a domestic animal.

CLAUSON LJ said: 'I should like, however, to add a word as to the part taken in the matter by the evidence given as to the facts of nature in regard to camels. That evidence is not, it must be understood, in the ordinary sense evidence bearing upon an issue of fact. In my view the exact position is this. The judge takes judicial notice of the ordinary course of nature, and in this particular case of the ordinary course of nature in regard to the position of camels among other animals. The reason why the evidence was given was for the assistance of the judge in forming his view as to what the ordinary course of nature in this regard in fact is, a matter of which he is supposed to have complete knowledge. The point is best explained by reading a few lines from that great work, the late Mr Justice Stephen's, "Digest of the Law of Evidence." In the 12th edition, Article 62 is as follows: "No evidence of any fact of which the Court will take judicial notice need be given by the party alleging its existence; but the judge, upon being called upon to take judicial notice thereof, may, if he is unacquainted with such fact, refer to any person or to any document or book of reference for his satisfaction in relation thereto, or may refuse to take judicial notice thereof unless and until the party calling upon him to take such notice produces any such document or book of reference." From that statement it appears that the document or book of reference only enshrines the knowledge of those who are acquainted with the particular branch of natural phenomena; and in the present case, owing to some extent to the fact that there appears to be a serious flaw in a statement in a well known book of reference on the matter here in question, the learned judge permitted, and properly permitted, oral evidence to be given before him by persons who had, or professed to have, special knowledge with regard to this particular branch of natural history. When that evidence was given and weighed up with the statements in the books of reference which were referred to, the facts became perfectly plain; and the learned judge was able without any difficulty whatever to give a correct statement of the natural phenomena material to the matter in question, of which he was bound to take judicial notice.'
(SCOTT and MACKINNON LJJ agreed.)

Duff Development Co. Ltd. v *Government of Kelantan* [1924] AC 797 (HL)

An arbitration award was made in favour of the company against the Government of Kelantan. The government applied for an order setting aside the award. In reply to an inquiry from the Master, the Secretary of State for the Colonies wrote an official letter stating that Kelantan was an independent state and its Sultan the sovereign ruler thereof.

VISCOUNT CAVE said: 'It has for some time been the practice of our Courts, when such a question is raised, to take judicial notice of the sovereignty of a State, and for that purpose (in any case of uncertainty) to seek information from a Secretary of State; and when information is so obtained the Court does not permit it to be questioned by the parties.'

VISCOUNT FINLAY said: 'It is settled law that it is for the Court to take judicial cognisance of the status of any foreign Government. If there can be any doubt on the matter the practice is for the Court to receive information from the appropriate department of His Majesty's Government, and the information so received is conclusive. The judgment of Farwell J in *Foster* v *Glove Venture Syndicate* [1900] 1 Ch 811 seems to me to be a perfectly accurate statement of the law and practice on this point. There are a great many matters of which the Court is bound to take judicial cognisance, and among them are all questions as to the status and boundaries of foreign powers. In all matters of which the Court takes judicial cognisance the Court may have recourse to any proper source of information. It has long been settled that on any question of the status of any foreign power the proper course is that the Court should apply to His Majesty's Government, and that in any such matter it is bound to act on the information given to them through the proper department. Such information is not in the nature of evidence; it is a statement by the Sovereign of this country through one of his Ministers upon a matter which is peculiarly within his cognisance.'

LORD SUMNER said: 'Without contesting in the least either the inconvenience or the impropriety of any conflict between the High Court and the Secretary of State upon the grave question of the sovereignty of the Sultan of Kelantan, I venture to think that the mere obligation of deference to any statement made in His Majesty's name hardly constitutes the whole legal basis for the rule laid down in the *Johore Case* [1894] 1 QB 149.

The status of foreign communities and the identity of the high personages who are the chiefs of foreign states, are matters of which the Courts of this country take judicial notice. Instead of requiring proof to be furnished on these subjects by the litigants, they act on their own knowledge or, if necessary, obtain the requisite information for themselves. I take it that in so doing the Courts are bound, as they would be on any other issue of fact raised before them, to act on the best evidence and, if the question is whether some new State or some older State, whose sovereignty is not notorious, is a sovereign State or not, the best evidence is a statement, which the Crown condescends to permit the appropriate Secretary of State to give on its behalf. It is the prerogative of the Crown to recognise or to withhold recognition from States or chiefs of States, and to determine from time to time the status with which foreign powers are to be deemed to be invested. This being so, a foreign ruler, whom the Crown recognises as a sovereign, is such a sovereign for the purposes of an English Court of law, and the best evidence of such recognition is the statement duly made with regard to it in His Majesty's name. Accordingly where such a statement is forthcoming no other evidence is admissible or needed. I think this is the real judicial explanation why it was held that the Sultan of Johore was a foreign sovereign. In considering the answer given by the Secretary of State, it was not the business of the Court to inquire whether the Colonial Office rightly concluded that the Sultan was entitled to be recognised as a sovereign by international law. All it had to do was to examine the communication in order so see if the meaning of it really was that the Sultan had been and was recognised as a sovereign.

(LORDS DUNEDIN and CARSON delivered concurring opinions on this point.)

Reynolds v *Llanelly Associated Tinplate Co. Limited* [1948] 1 All ER 140 (CA)

The appellant was awarded workmen's compensation for an injury to an eye. The county court judge based his decision on some local knowledge which he had relating to the employment prospects of a workman of such skill and age.

LORD GREENE MR said: 'The practice of county court judges of supplementing evidence by having recourse to their own local knowledge and experience has been criticised, praised as most beneficial, objected to, and encouraged in different decisions. I think it is impossible to suggest at this time of day that the county court judge is not entitled, within limits to which I shall refer in a moment, to take into account his own knowledge of general conditions in the neighbourhood.

I do not desire to express any opinion, and it is not necessary to do so, whether or not the rather stringent limits suggested for the operation of that rule by Romer, LJ, ought to be observed. I need not quote them, but he does criticise and suggest limits for its operation in *Owens* v *Llay Main Collieries, Ltd.* 25 BWCC 593. I am content myself to refer to this statement by Lord Buckmaster in *Keane* v *Mount Vernon Colliery Co., Ltd.* 26 BWCC 252:

> In order to get rid of the question that the arbitrator has raised as to the admissibility of... knowledge [of local conditions of the varying wages of miners employed in the district] I may say that I think that, properly applied, and within reasonable limits, he was entitled to use it. To hold otherwise would involve that a number of witnesses would have to be called in order to bring under judicial notice by local proof facts within the common knowledge of everyone in the district. I see no objection to his having made his judicial experience in this respect available.

It is worth noticing that the type of case to which Lord Buckmaster is referring is that where the judge uses his knowledge of matters which are within the common knowledge of everyone in the district, and he limits his right to call his own knowledge into play by the words "properly applied and within reasonable limits." The question, therefore, I apprehend for this court, whenever a judge is said improperly to have used his local knowledge, is whether he has used that knowledge properly and within reasonable limits. That leaves the function of this court rather vague. It would mean that in every individual case where the point is raised we should have to decide whether or not we thought that the judge had acted in relation to the facts of the case in a reasonable manner. When one looks at the type of case where this practice has been adopted and approved one finds that they are cases of a quite general nature. Take the case last referred to, *Keane* v *Mount Vernon Colliery Co. Ltd.* The question there was what was necessary to give the family of a deceased man sufficient provision for the ordinary necessaries of life. In arriving at his finding, the judge said he had taken into consideration the evidence and also his own judicial knowledge of local conditions and the average wage of miners employed in the district. That type of knowledge is of quite a general character and is not liable to be varied by specific individual characteristics of the individual case...One more example was a judgment of Scrutton, LJ, in *Mothersdale* v *Cleveland Bridge & Engineering Co.* which is quoted in *Owens* v *Llay Main Collieries, Ltd.* 25 BWCC 587. Scrutton, LJ said (23 BWCC 51):

> If the learned county court judge had properly directed himself, and was referred to *Tannock* v *Brownieside Coal Co.*, and had read it, and using his local knowledge, and his knowledge as a man, as he is entitled to do, of the condition of things in Durham, he has found that the failure to obtain employment is largely due to the state of the labour market in Durham, and not wholly or mainly due to the consequences of the injury, I cannot possibly say that he is wrong in coming to that view when it is a matter of fact for him whether in the evidence, plus his local knowledge, there is evidence on which he could find that it was the state of the labour market in Durham which causes the man to be unemployed.

There the question was whether the workman's failure to obtain employment was a consequence of the injury and the judge, knowing the conditions of employment in Durham, found that it was not.

That is the sort of general knowledge which is quite unobjectionable if the judge makes use of it, but, in my opinion, in the present case it is not general knowledge, which has been drawn on. It must be some particular knowledge that the judge drew on relating to the possibility of a man of this high degree of skill at his age obtaining a job at as high a rate of wages as 10 guineas a week. There are factors in the case of such an individual of a particular nature, and the judge ought not to have drawn on knowledge which could only be helpful if it was of a highly specialised nature. The knowledge required to answer the question here was not, in my opinion, the sort of knowledge to which Lord Buckmaster was referring when he spoke of knowledge which everybody in the district would have. Even treating those words as of rather too limiting a character, this seems to me to be quite a different class of case from that where what was implied was some general knowledge relating to employment in general and the cases of men in all categories of that sort. This is a very special and individual case, and, in my view, the county court judge ought not to have answered the crucial question on his own knowledge of the locality.'
(COHEN and ASQUITH LJJ agreed.)
Appeal dismissed.

Ingram v *Percival* [1969] 1 QB 548

The defendant was charged with unlawfully using a net secured by anchors of weights in tidal waters for taking salmon and migratory trout. The justices made use of their knowledge of local conditions to decide on the extent of tidal waters, and convicted the defendant, who appealed.

LORD PARKER CJ said: '...on the view I take of this case, the result depends upon whether the justices were entitled to make use of the knowledge which they said that they had.

In my judgment they were fully entitled to do so. It has always been recognised that justices may and should — after all they are local justices — take into consideration matters which they know of their own local knowledge, and particularly matters in regard to the locality, whether it be on land, as it seems to me, or in water.'
(WALLER and FISHER JJ agreed.)
Appeal dismissed.

Wetherall v *Harrison* [1976] QB 773 (DC)

The defendant was charged with failure to provide a specimen for a laboratory test without reasonable excuse contrary to s.9(3) of the Road Traffic Act 1972. The defendant had reacted abnormally and struggled when a doctor attempted to take a specimen of blood. The doctor gave evidence that the defendant's behaviour had not been genuine and he was simulating a fit. The defendant gave evidence that he had been apprehensive in the past when required to have an injection and had felt unwell. After the justices retired, a doctor among them gave his opinion that the defendant's behaviour might be genuine and the justices also related their experience and viewpoint of war-time inoculations. They decided that the defendant's behaviour was due to a hysterical reaction resulting from a fear of the needle, that he had not refused to give a specimen of blood without reasonable excuse and dismissed the charge. The prosecutor appealed.

LORD WIDGERY CJ said: 'Mr Barker, in putting the matter before us, is really inviting us to say, for the advantage of justices hereafter, what should happen when a justice has specialised knowledge of this kind; should he use it or should he not.

In argument we were referred to three authorities. The only one I need refer to, and the most recent, is *Reynolds* v *Llanelly Associated Tinplate Co. Ltd.* [1948] 1 All ER 140. That was concerned with arbitrators and judges and the extent to which they could have regard to their own personal knowledge. I do not think that the position of a justice of the peace is the same, in this regard, as the position of a trained judge. If you have a judge sitting alone, trying a civil case, it is perfectly feasible and sensible that he should be instructed and trained to exclude certain factors from his consideration of the problem. Justices are not so trained. They are much more like jurymen in this respect. I think it would be wrong to start with the proposition that justices' use of their own local or personal knowledge is governed by exactly the same rule as is laid down in the case of trained judges. I do not believe that a serious restriction on a justice's use of his own knowledge or the knowledge of his colleagues can really be enforced. Laymen (by which I mean non-lawyers) sitting as justices considering a case which has just been heard before them lack the ability to put out of their minds certain features of the case. In particular, if the justice is a specialist, be he a doctor, or an engineer or an accountant, or what you will, it is not possible for him to approach the decision in the case as though he had not got that training, and indeed I think it would be a very bad thing it he had to. In a sense, the bench of justices are like a jury, they are a cross-section of people, and one of the advantages which they have is that they bring a lot of varied experience into the court room and use it.

So I start with the proposition that it is not improper for a justice who has special knowledge of the circumstances forming the background to a particular case to draw on that special knowledge in interpretation of the evidence which he has heard. I stress that last sentence, because it would be quite wrong if the justice went on, as it were, to give evidence to himself in contradiction of that which has been heard in court. He is not there to give evidence to himself, still more is he not there to give evidence to other justices; but that he can employ his basic knowledge in considering, weighing up and assessing the evidence given before the court is I think beyond doubt.

Furthermore, I do not see why he should not, certainly if requested to by his fellow justices, tell his fellow justices the way in which his specialised knowledge has caused him to look at the evidence. In no bench of justices should there be a leader, so aggressive that he tries to assume responsibility for the decision and excludes the others, whether he is proceeding on the basis of a specialised subject or not, and that certainly goes for justices with a specialised knowledge, because it would be quite wrong for the doctor in the present case to have gone into the justices' retiring room and immediately proceeded to persuade all the justices because of his specialised knowledge. He ought really to have waited until asked to make a contribution on his specialist subject. Whether he is asked or not, he should not press his views unduly on the rest of the bench. He should tell them in a temperate and orderly way what he thinks about the case, if they want to know, and then leave them to form their own conclusion if they wish so to do. Here again it is most important that the justice with specialised knowledge should not proceed to give evidence himself to his fellow justices contradictory to that which they have heard in the court. He can explain the evidence they have heard: he can give his own view as to how the case should go and how it should be decided; but he should not be giving evidence himself behind closed doors which is not available to the parties.

Applying those principles to the instant case, there was certainly no reason why Dr Robertson should not, when forming his own conclusion about this case, have referred to his own knowledge, and his own knowledge and experience was that this kind of fit was genuine, and knowing that it would be right that in reviewing and considering the evidence in this case he should have that knowledge in the background and use it if he thought fit. Since his fellow justices obviously knew he was a doctor and I think asked him for the benefit of his views, I see no reason at all why he should not tell them what his views were. That does not seem to me to be contrary to any principle to be applied here, and I do not believe in this case either that the doctor went beyond the scope of the authority which I am trying to apply.' (O'CONNOR and LAWSON JJ agreed.)
Appeal dismissed.

1.13 Authorities: presumption of legitimacy

Knowles v *Knowles* [1962] P 161

On May 22, 1957, the husband was granted a decree nisi of divorce on the ground of the wife's desertion. On July 5, 1957, that decree was made absolute. On April 19, 1958, the wife gave birth to a child. Thereafter, the wife applied in the suit for an order against her husband for maintenance of the child. The husband resisted the application. An issue was tried to determine the child's paternity, and its date of conception.

WRANGHAM J said: 'There is undoubtedly a presumption (strong, but capable of being rebutted by satisfactory evidence) that a child born in wedlock to a married woman is the child of her husband. That presumption applies not only to a child born during wedlock but also to a child clearly conceived during wedlock. That appears from such cases as *In re Heath* [1945] Ch 417 and *In re Overbury* [1955] Ch 122, where what was being considered was the paternity of a child which must, according to the laws of nature, have been conceived during wedlock but which had been born after the death of the husband. The presumption that a child conceived during wedlock is a legitimate child of the husband applies just as much whether the husband and wife are living together in the ordinary way or whether they are separated by agreement, or by a deed, or simply separated, even if the wife has obtained from the magistrates an order for maintenance, unless that order contains a non-cohabitation clause. That appears from *Bowen* v *Norman* [1938] 1 KB 689 and *Ettenfield* v *Ettenfield* [1940] P 96. The presumption ceases to operate if the parties are separated under an order of the court such as, for example, a decree of judicial separation, which does away with the duty of the spouses to live together. It seems to me that the basis of the presumption is that the law contemplates spouses as fulfilling their marital duties to each other unless there has been an actual order of the court dispensing with the performance of such duties. So long as the law contemplates the spouses as performing their marital duties to each other, so long will it contemplate that a married woman, if she bears a child, will be bearing it as a result of intercourse with her husband only.

Now, it does not seem to me that the presentation of a petition for divorce can possibly be equivalent to a decree of judicial separation or a non-cohabitation order by magistrates so as to dispense with the mutual marital duties of the spouses. Indeed, it appears to follow from such cases as *W* v *W* (No 2) [1954] P 486 and *Cohen* v *Cohen* [1940] AC 631 that even after a decree nisi has been pronounced the parties still owe to each other the marital duties which were imposed upon them by marriage. It has been repeatedly said that a decree nisi does not dissolve a marriage, and if, as appears from the cases that I have cited, a spouse who has deserted the other spouse remains under a duty to resume married life with that spouse even after a decree nisi has been pronounced, whether it be for nullity or divorce, it seems to me to be clear that the law contemplates marital duties as still in existence, and, therefore, will treat the parties, from one point of view, as fulfilling them. If this reasoning be correct, it seems that the presumption that a child conceived during wedlock is legitimate continues to operate after the presentation of a petition for divorce or nullity, or even the pronounciation of a decree nisi either for nullity or for divorce.

The authority which seems at first sight to be contrary to that reasoning is *Maturin* v *Attorney-General* [1938] 2 All ER 214. That was a case in which no formal judgment was given, but there is reported a discussion between Hodson J and Mr Valentine Holmes, who was appearing for the Attorney-General, from which it appears that Hodson J, in deciding whether or not a child which had been conceived during the marriage was or was not a child of the husband, paid some attention to the fact that it was conceived after a petition for divorce had been presented. There is no indication that Hodson J was intending to lay down the law in considered terms, but he did say that Ibid 216: "The original petition in the *Stone* case, unreported, was presented on March 14, 1929. I suppose that that is some indication that they were not living together after that?" To which the answer from Mr Valentine Holmes was "Yes." I cannot think that by that question Hodson J meant to indicate a view that the presumption of legitimacy of a child conceived during wedlock finished as soon as a petition for divorce was presented. I think that all he meant was that the presumption would operate less strongly where the child was conceived after the presentation of a petition for divorce, or, to put it another way, would be more easily rebutted by evidence. That seems to me, if I may say so, with great respect to Hodson J, to be the plainest common sense. This would apply equally in a case where it appeared that the parties were separated, for example, under a deed. It is plain that the presumption continues to operate when the parties are separated under a deed, but in common sense it must be more easily rebuttable. It seems to me, equally, that it continues to operate after the presentation of a petition or after the pronounciation of a decree nisi, although in each case, no doubt, more easily rebutted by other evidence than it would be in the case of a husband and wife who were living together in the same house in the normal way. I therefore come to the conclusion that there was in the circumstances of this case a presumption that the child born to the wife was a legitimate child.

Now that involves, of course, not merely a presumption as to the paternity, as to the person with whom the wife had intercourse, it involves also a presumption as to the date of conception; but I think that if one has a presumption as to legitimacy it operates as to both, where both go to show legitimacy. In this case, for the child to be legitimate it has not merely to be conceived as the result of intercourse between husband and wife, but to have been conceived before the decree absolute. If there be a presumption of legitimacy at all it seems to me to be a presumption as to both matters which in this case constitute legitimacy; that is to say, a presumption that the child was conceived before the decree absolute, and equally a presumption that it was child of the husband. Of course, the presumptions as to both those facts are rebuttable by evidence.

So far as the date of conception is concerned, as I have indicated, the evidence appears to me to be extremely nicely balanced. Taking into account the presumption, I find that the date of conception was between June 9 and June 23, 1957.

Now comes the question of the evidence upon the question of paternity. I have already held that there is a presumption that the husband is the father; but it by no means follows that I shall find he is the father, because that presumption is rebuttable by evidence and, in the circumstances of a case like this, rebuttable by much less strong evidence that would be required in many other cases.

I therefore turn back to the facts in this matter. [His Lordship referred to the evidence and continued:] I accept the evidence that the husband and wife had intercourse at any rate during July, 1957. Mr Garland submitted to me that if I find that the husband and wife were upon such terms that they were prepared to have intercourse with each other, or, to put it another way, that the husband was having access to his wife, access in the sense of sexual intercourse in July, 1957, that finding affords a basis for the presumption that the sexual intercourse had occurred not merely after, but also before, the decree absolute, so that the child born to the wife was a legitimate child. I think Mr Garland's contention is correct, and, having regard to the presumption, I find that intercourse did take place between these parties in June, 1957, and that this child was conceived as a result of that intercourse so that the husband is the father of the child.'

Hetherington v *Hetherington* (1887) 12 PD 112

This was an application to discharge a matrimonial order made by the justices, on the ground that since the date of the order the wife had been guilty of adultery, and had given birth to a child, born more than nine months after the separation, of which the husband was not the father.

Sir James Hannen, President, said: 'There is no doubt that from the time such an order is made — which is equivalent to a judicial separation and the ancient divorce à mensâ et thoro — the parties are authorised to live apart, and from that moment all the presumption which exists in the case of married persons as to access and the legitimacy of children is reserved. If a child is born mo e than nine months after the separation, it is presumed to be illegitimate, unless it be shewn as a matter of evidence that the husband and wife have come together again.'

Matrimonial Causes Act 1965, s.43

43 (1) [The evidence of a husband or wife shall be admissible in any proceedings to prove that marital intercourse did or did not take place between them during any period;[1]] [But a husband or wife shall not be compellable in any proceedings to give evidence of the matters aforesaid.[2]]

Civil Evidence Act 1968, s.16(4)

16(4) In section 43(1) of the Matrimonial Causes Act 1965 (under which the evidence of a husband or wife is admissible in any proceedings to prove that marital intercourse did or did not take place between them during any period but a husband or wife is not compellable in any proceedings to give evidence of the matters aforesaid), the words from 'but a husband or wife' to the end of the subsection shall cease to have effect except in relation to criminal proceedings.

Matrimonial Causes Act 1973 s.48(1)

48(1) The evidence of a husband or wife shall be admissible in any proceedings to prove that marital intercourse did or did not take place between them during any period.

Family Law Reform Act 1969, s.26

26. Any presumption of law as to the legitimacy or illegitimacy of any person may in any civil proceedings be rebutted by evidence which shows that it is more probable than not that that person is illegitimate or legitimate, as the case may be, and it shall not be necessary to prove that fact beyond reasonable doubt in order to rebut the presumption.

1.14 Authorities: presumption of marriage

Piers and another v *Piers* (1849) 2 HL Cas 331

The question arose as to the validity of a marriage. The two persons in question had shown

---

[1]Words repealed by the Matrimonial Causes Act 1973, s.54(1), Sched 3, but reproduced for the purpose of construing the remaining provisions of this Act.
[2]Words repealed except in relation to criminal proceedings by the Civil Evidence Act 1968, s.16(4).

an intention to marry, and a marriage had been, in form, celebrated between them, by a regularly ordained clergyman, in a private house, as if by special licence, and the parties, by their acts at the time, shewed that they believed such marriage to be a real and valid marriage.

THE LORD CHANCELLOR said: 'My Lords, I have not found that the rule of law is anywhere laid down more to my satisfaction than it is by Lord Lyndhurst in the case of *Morris* v *Davies*, as determined in this House (5 Clark and Fin 163). It is not precisely the same presumption as exists in the present case; but the principle is strictly applicable to the presumption which we are considering. He says (see p 265), "The presumption of law is not lightly to be repelled. It is not to be broken in upon or shaken by a mere balance of probability. The evidence for the purpose of repelling it must be strong, distinct, satisfactory and conclusive." No doubt, every case must vary as to how far the evidence may be considered as "satisfactory and conclusive;" but he lays down this rule that the presumption must prevail unless it is most satisfactorily repelled by the evidence in the cause appearing conclusive to those who have to decide upon that question.'

LORD CAMPBELL said: 'My Lords, it seems to me that this case depends entirely upon the effect to be given to the presumption of law in favour of the marriage. It is allowed that there is a presumption in its favour, and, until the contrary is proved, we are bound to draw the inference that everything existed which was necessary to constitute a valid marriage, and among other things, that there was a special license from the Bishop of Sodor and Man. But it is likewise admitted on the other hand, that this is not a *praesumptio juris,* that it may be rebutted, and that it can only stand subject to the contrary being proved. The whole question therefore depends upon what sort of evidence is required to prove the negative, and to give effect to it...

My Lords, my opinion is, that a presumption of this sort, in favour of a marriage, can only be negatived by disproving every reasonable possibility. I do not mean to say that you must shew the impossibility of any supposition which can be suggested to support the validity of the marriage; but you must shew that this is most highly improbable, and that it is not reasonably possible.'

(LORD BROUGHAM delivered a concurring judgment.)

Re Taplin, Watson v *Tate* [1937] 3 All ER 105 (Ch D)

A declaration was sought that certain children were the lawful children of TB and his wife, EB. TB lived in Rockhampton from 1860-1870 with a certain lady; they held themselves out to be husband and wife, and they and their children were received in local society, which would not have been the case had there been any suggestion of irregularity. TB at his death was one of the most prominent solicitors in Rockhampton. The birth certificates of the children recorded the marriage of the parents as having taken place at Ballan, Victoria, on January 10,1860, but no such marriage was registered there, although registration had there been compulsory for some years. In 1873, TB's father, who lived in England, executed a deed covenanting to make certain payments to the children or their mother and this deed contained these words: 'the following reputed children of his deceased son,' TB, 'which children are now in England with their mother EM, otherwise EB.'

SIMONDS J said: 'The evidence before me is not cogent; but it is adequate to satisfy me that the man and woman lived together at Rockhampton for ten years as man and wife in the sight of that small community. They were there received into society, which was not a society of loose and uncertain morals, but with proper views as to marital relations, and were at all times regarded as man and wife. This being so, the presumption of our law is that they were man and wife. This presumption is not to be disturbed except by evidence of the most cogent kind. Here it is sought to displace the presumption in two ways. First of all, because the parties pinned themselves to a marriage at a certain date and place, and the records contain no entry of such a marriage. Whatever the compulsory nature of the administration, this cannot, in my view, displace the presumption of marriage. The absence of a record is always a possibility. The presumption rests mainly upon the notorious fact of their living together, which has been fully proved.

The other ground upon which the presumption is sought to be displaced is that, in 1873, the deed of trust was executed; but I cannot draw from that deed any inference contrary to the presumption that I would otherwise draw. I cannot guess the motive which induced the grandparent to put into that deed those words of stigma on his son, and I find no sufficient reason in the deed for saying that the children were illegitimate.

In the circumstances, I declare that the children are the lawful children of Thomas Bellas and Emily his wife.'

Mahadervan v *Mahadervan* [1964] P 233

The parties were married in 1951 in Ceylon. A local statute required compliance with certain preliminaries, that the marriage should be solemnised by a registrar in his office or other authorised place, and that, in the course of the ceremony, the registrar should address the parties as to the nature of the union. The certificate of marriage purported to show that the marriage had been solemnised by the registrar at his office. The parties cohabited as husband and wife until early in 1952, after which the husband came to England, from whence, until march 1954, he wrote a number of letters to the wife acknowledging her as such. In August 1958, the husband went through a ceremony of marriage with an English woman with whom he, thereafter, lived in England as husband and wife. In September 1960, the first purported wife came to England and subsequently issued a complaint on the ground of the husband's adultery. At the hearing before the justices her evidence as to the marriage, which was accepted, was that the ceremony had taken place at the house of her parents; she made no reference to the registrar's address to the parties. The justices rejected the husband's contention that the marriage was invalid for failure to comply with the local formalities and made an order in favour of the wife. The husband appealed.

SIR JOCELYN SIMON said: 'He draws attention to the following facts. First of all, duress being no longer in issue, these parties intended to get married. Secondly, they went through a ceremony of marriage. Thirdly, the certificate is correct on the face of it and presupposes proper steps having been taken to lead up to it. Fourthly, the parties cohabited as if husband and wife and purporting to be such. And, fifthly, the husband wrote letters acknowledging the wife as his wife. Two rules of law expressed in latin maxims therefore come into play: *omnia praesumuntur rite esse acta* as regard the acts of the officials and *omnia praesumuntur pro matrimonio*. Where there is a ceremony followed by cohabitation as husband and wife, a strong presumption arises that the parties are lawfully married. The leading case as to this is *Piers* v *Piers* (1849) 2 HL Cas 331. The validity of the marriage in question depended on the issue of a special licence; but there was no trace of its issue and the bishop of the diocese had no recollection of issuing it. Nevertheless the House of Lords affirmed the marriage. Lord Cottenham cited with approval the words of Lord Lyndhurst in *Morris* v *Davies* (1837) 5 Cl&Fin 163. "The presumption of law is not lightly to be repelled. It is not to be broken in upon or shaken by a mere balance of probability. The evidence for the purpose of repelling it must be strong, distinct, satisfactory and conclusive." Lord Campbell said "you must show a high degree of probability that there was not a licence...a presumption of this sort, in favour of a marriage, can only be negatived by disproving every reasonable possibility." The principle has been applied and those passages have been repeatedly cited in cases of the highest authority. A particularly striking and relevant example is *Sastry Velaider Aronegary* v *Sembecutty Vaigalie* (1881) 6 App Cas 364. It related to a marriage between Tamils in Ceylon, and it was admitted that not all the necessary ceremonies had been performed owing to disturbances which took place when the marriage was going on. But the Privy Council held the parties to be married, Sir Barnes Peacock saying Ibid 371: "It does not, therefore, appear to their Lordships that the law of Ceylon is different from that which prevails in this country; namely, that where a man and woman are proved to have lived together as man and wife, the law will presume, unless the contrary be clearly proved, that they were living together in consequence of a valid marriage, and not in a state of concubinage."

Counsel for the husband argues, however, that today the proper standard of proof is the mere balance of probability, relying on *In re Peete, Peete* v *Crompton* [1952] 2 TLR 383. To my mind it is unnecessary to examine this authority further, because it was expressly limited to the question of capacity to marry and did not go to the formalities of the marriage; and the

two cases where it had been cited with approval, *In re Watkins, Watkins* v *Watkins* [1953] 1
WLR 1332 and *Chard* v *Chard (orse. Northcott),* [1956] p 259 also related to capacity to
marry. The general principles stated in *Piers* v *Piers* 2 HL Cas 331 relied upon by counsel for
the wife stand untouched by any later authority so far as the ceremonies of marriage are
concerned, although some question had been raised as to the actual terms in which the
standard of proof was phrased. Lord Brougham in *Piers* v *Piers* itself had demurred to the
use of the word "conclusive" in the judgment of Lord Cottenham CL: he preferred[17] "clear,
distinct and satisfactory evidence." Sir Barnes Peacock in *Sastry Vclaider Aronegary* v
Sembecutty Vaigalie used the words "the clearest and most satisfactory evidence." Harman
LJ in a recent case, *In re Taylor, decd,* [1961] 1 WLR 9 has also criticised the word
"conclusive." Certainly today "conclusive" does suggest an irrebutable presumption, and, as
Harman LJ pointed out, it is clear that the presumption can be rebutted, though the evidence
in rebuttal must be firm and clear. In *Hill* v *Hill* [1959] 1 WLR 172 the judgment of the Privy
Council delivered by Lord Somervell cited *Piers* v *Piers* and went on: "It is clear that a
balance of probabilities is insufficient to rebut the presumption. Various epithets have been
used, but their Lordships accepted the word in the passage cited by the judge." That was a
passage from Halsbury's *Laws of England* (2nd ed, vol 16, p 599) "The evidence must be
decisive." I would need," he continued, "very strong evidence to justify a conclusion that
Winter did not conduct the service in accordance with the form in his book...there is no
sufficiently satisfactory or decisive evidence to establish the invalidity of this ceremony." If it
is not presumptuous to say so, it seems to me that "decisive" might be said to beg the
question: what is the weight of evidence which is required to decide the issue? In my view,
where a ceremony of marriage is proved followed by cohabitation as husband and wife, a
presumption is raised which cannot be rebutted by evidence which merely goes to show on a
balance of probabilities that there was no valid marriage: it must be evidence which satisfies
beyond reasonable doubt that there was no valid marriage. In other words, the presumption
in favour of marriage in such circumstances is of the same weight as the presumption of
innocence in criminal and matrimonial causes. A jury would have to be directed that to
displace the presumption, the husband must prove his case in such a way that they can feel
sure that there was no marriage.

As for the argument of counsel for the husband that there is no presumption in favour of a
marriage where it is a foreign one and its establishment would invalidate a subsequent English
one, no ground of principle and no authority could be cited to support it. To accept it would
give expression to a legal chauvinism that has no place in any rational system of private
international law. Our courts in my view apply exactly the same weight of presumption in
favour of a foreign marriage as of an English one, and the nationality of any later marriage
brought into question is quite immaterial.
(BAKER J agreed.)
Appeal dismissed.

1.15   Authorities: presumption of death

Chard v *Chard* [1956] P 259

A wife who was party to a marriage in 1909 was last heard of in 1917 as a normally healthy
woman who would, in 1933, have attained the age of 44. She had reasons for not wishing to
be heard of by the husband and his family and it was not possible to trace anyone who, since
1917, would naturally have heard of her. No trace of the registration of her death could be
found. The husband having remarried in 1933, he and the 1933 wife sought decrees of nullity
based on the bigamous character of the 1933 marriage. The husband had spent almost all of
the period between 1917 and 1933 in prison, and there was no reason to suppose that he was
likely to have heard of his first wife between those dates.

SACHS J said: 'My view is thus that in matters where no statute lays down an applicable
rule, the issue of whether a person is, or is not to be presumed dead, is generally speaking one
of fact and not subject to a presumption of law.

To that there is an exception which can be assumed without affecting the present case. By
virtue of a long sequence of judicial statements, which either assert or assume such a rule, it

appears accepted that there is a convenient presumption of law applicable to certain cases of seven years' absence where no statute applies. That presumption in its modern shape takes effect (without examining its terms too exactly) substantially as follows. Where as regards "AB" there is no acceptable affirmative evidence that he was alive at some time during a continuous period of seven years or more, then if it can be proved first, that there are persons who would be likely to have heard of him over that period, secondly that those persons have not heard of him, and thirdly that all due inquiries have been made appropriate to the circumstances, "AB" will be presumed to have died at some time within that period. (Such a presumption would, of course be one of law, and could not be one of fact, because there can hardly be a logical inference from any particular set of facts that a man had not died within 2,555 days but had died within 2,560.)'

(SACHS J granted a decree nisi of nullity granted to both the petitioner and the respondent, holding that there was no evidence of the first wife's death.)

Re Phene's Trusts (1870) 5 Ch App 139

A testator died on the 5th of January 1861, having bequeathed his residurary estate equally between his nephews and nieces. One of his nephews, Nicholas Phene Mill, was born in 1829, had gone to America in 1853, had frequently written home till August 1858, when he wrote from on board an American ship of war, but from that time no letter had been received from him, and nothing was afterwards heard about him, except that he was entered in the books of the American Navy as having deserted on the 16th June 1860, while on leave. His personal representative petitioned for a share of the testator's estate, and an order was made to this effect.

GIFFARD LJ said: 'It is a general, well-founded rule that a person seeking to recover property must establish his title by affirmative proof. This was one of the grounds of decision in *Doe* v *Nepean* 5 B & Ad 86, and to assert as an exception to the rule that the onus of proving death at any particular period, either within the seven years or otherwise, should be with the party alleging death at such particular period, and not with the person to whose title that fact is essential, is not consistent with the judgment of the present Lord Chancellor, when Vice-Chancellor, in *In re Green's Settlement* Law Rep 1 Eq 288, or with the *dictum* of Lord Justice Rolt when he said, in *In re Benham's Trusts,* that the question was one, not of presumption, but of proof; or with the real substance of the actual decisions, or the sound parts of the reasoning, in *Doe* v *Nepean,* or with the judgments in *R* v *Inhabitants of Harborne* 2 A & E 540, and *R* v *Lumley* Law Rep ICC 196, or with the principles to be deduced from the judgment in *Underwood* v *Wing* 8 HLC 183. The true proposition is, that those who found a right upon a person having survived a particular period must establish that fact affirmatively by evidence; the evidence will necessarily differ in different cases, but sufficient evidence there must be, or the person asserting title will fail.

This case happens to be one of an alleged member of a class of legatees. Survivorship of a testator is requisite to clothe a person with the character of a member of that class. This is a tacit condition annexed by law to the gift, and it follows that the representatives of a person alleged to be a member of the class must prove as against the other members of the class who prove their survivorship, that he survived the testator, otherwise he was not a legatee at all. For these reasons, and upon a review of the authorities, and the judgments on which they rest, I am of opinion that there is no presumption of law as to the particular period at which *Nicholas Phene Mill* died, that it is a matter of fact to be proved by evidence, and that the onus of proof rests on his representative.'

Order discharged.

Chipchase v Chipchase [1939] P 391

A wife, having according to her evidence neither seen nor heard of her husband since 1916, married again in 1928 on the assumption that he was dead. In 1939 she summoned her second husband on the grounds of alleged adultery, desertion and wilful neglect to maintain. The magistrates dismissed the summons, because as there was no evidence that the first husband was dead, the wife had failed to prove that her second marriage was valid. The wife appealed.

SIR BOYD MERRIMAN said: 'The magistrates have given their decision that they gave expressly on the ground that, there being no evidence that Leetch was dead, they were of opinion for that reason that the first marriage was still subsisting. It seems to me impossible to say that there was no evidence that Leetch was dead having regard to the presumption which arises in circumstances of this kind. That presumption — I am taking the statement of it from the judgment of Giffard LJ in *Phene's Trusts* (1869) LR 5 Ch 139 — is that the law presumes a person who has not been heard of for over seven years to be dead, but in the absence of special circumstances draws no presumption from that fact as to the particular period at which he died. I need not read for present purposes the rest of the statement of the legal doctrine. Once it is shown that the wife has not heard of her husband for seven years, that presumption arises. Of course, it is not an irrebuttable presumption and it may take very little evidence to rebut it, having regard to the particular circumstances of a particular case, but, if that proposition is established affirmatively to the satisfaction of the magistrates, then it is impossible to say there is no evidence of a husband having been dead.

It is in that connection, in my opinion, that the question of the nature of any such inquiries that the wife has made arises. There is nothing in this statement of the presumption which I have quoted about reasonable belief, or inquiries, or probability of life, or any of those things to which Mr Horner has referred us. But, of course, if a person was given ground for supposing that the other party to the marriage was alive and deliberately turned a blind eye and refused to make obvious inquiries, it might very well be that the Court would not accept as proved that the party had not been heard of for seven years. It seems to me that it is in discussing this question that the reasonableness of inquiries that have been made in regard to the circumstances of the case, whatever they may be, should be ascertained. It is in this connection that that matter is important, but once it has been established to the satisfaction of the tribunal that the party has not been heard of for seven years, then the presumption arises, although, of course, it is a presumption which can be rebutted.

In this particular case the question is whether the wife was entitled to rely on that presumption. At the time when she went through the ceremony of marriage in 1928 not merely seven but twelve years had elapsed, but it goes without saying that the magistrates have got to judge of that question as it appears to them in 1939. The wife, on the one hand, is entitled to pray in aid the lapse of yet another ten years, during which, she says, she has not heard of her husband. The husband, on the other hand, might be shown by some evidence, the nature of which we are unaware, but which it is suggested is in existence, actually to have been alive in 1928. In taking into account the further lapse of ten years since the ceremony of marriage in 1928 it will, no doubt, be open to the magistrates to discount that further lapse of time in connection with the non-appearance of the husband, by reason of the fact that the marriage itself did not take place in the name of Leetch but took place in the wife's maiden name. Putting it another way, there was nothing in the nature of the second marriage itself to attract the attention of the first husband if, in fact, he was alive. Those are all circumstances which the magistrates will be able to take into account.

At the end of it all, the question remains: Is it established that the husband had not been heard of for twelve years or so before the second ceremony of marriage and is there anything in the evidence to rebut the presumption that he was dead? I do not feel that that approach to the matter has been considered by the magistrates at all.'
(HENN COLLINS J agreed.)
Case remitted to magistrates.

Law of Property Act 1925, s.184

184. In all cases where, after the commencement of this Act, two or more persons have died in circumstances rendering it uncertain which of them survived the other or others, such deaths shall (subject to any order of the court), for all purposes affecting the title to property, be presumed to have occurred in order of seniority, and accordingly the younger shall be deemed to have survived the elder.

Matrimonial Causes Act 1973, s.19

19(1) Any married person who alleges that reasonable grounds exist for supposing that the other party to the marriage is dead may... present a petition to the court to have it presumed that the other party is dead and to have the marriage dissolved, and the court may, if satisfied that such reasonable grounds exist, grant a decree of presumption of death and dissolution of the marriage.

(3) In any proceedings under this section the fact that for a period of seven years or more the other party to the marriage has been continually absent from the petitioner and the petitioner has no reason to believe that the other party has been living within that time shall be evidence that the other party is dead until the contrary is proved.

Offences against the Person Act 1861, s.57

57. Whosoever, being married, shall marry any other person during the life of the former husband or wife, whether the second marriage shall have taken place in England or Ireland or elsewhere, shall be guilty of [an offence], and being convicted thereof shall be liable to [imprisonment] for any term not exceeding seven years...: Provided, that nothing in this section contained shall extend to any second marriage contracted elsewhere than in England and Ireland by any other than a subject of Her Majesty, or to any person marrying a second time whose husband or wife shall have been continually absent from such person for the space of seven years then last past, and shall not have been known by such person to be living within that time, or shall extend to any person who , at the time of such second marriage, shall have been divorced from the bond of the first marriage, or to any person whose former marriage shall have been declared void by the sentence of any court of competent jurisdiction.

1.16   Authorities: presumption of regularity

R v *Roberts* (1878) 14 Cox CC 101 (CCCR)

An indictment for perjury alleged the offence to have been committed before JU, then being and sitting as the duly qualified and appointed deputy judge of the County Court of W. Proof was given that the perjury took place in the presence of JU at the County Court, and a certified minute of the proceedings of the court was put in evidence.

LORD COLERIDGE CJ said: 'I am of opinion that the conviction should be affirmed. One of the best recognised principles of law, *Omnia praesumuntur esse rite et solemniter acta donec probetur in contrarium* is applicable to public officers acting in discharge of public duties. The mere acting in a public capacity is sufficient prima facie proof of their proper appointment; but it is only a prima facie presumption, and it is capable of being rebutted, and in the case of *R* v *Verelst* 3 Camp 433 that presumption was rebutted in fact, and the person who there had acted as surrogate for twenty years, was proved to have been improperly appointed. The case of *R* v *Verelst* is exceedingly like this; there the fact of Dr Parson having acted as surrogate was held by Lord Ellenborough, CJ, to be sufficient prima facie evidence that he was duly appointed, and had competent authority to administer an oath, and for that proposition *R* v *Verelst* was referred to as good law by Lord Campbell, CJ, in *Wolton* v *Gavin* 16 QB 48. But it was further shown in *R* v *Verelst* that Dr Parson had never been regularly appointed as surrogate, and Lord Ellenborough then held that the evidence that Dr Parson was not duly appointed a surrogate could not be shut out, however long he might have acted in that capacity, and that the presumption arising from his acting only stood until the contrary was proved. That is an instructive case, as showing the true rule as to the prima facie presumption in such cases. It is laid down in all the text books as a recognised principle that a person acting in the capacity of a public officer is prima facie to be taken to be so, and that principle was adopted by Patteson, J, in *Doe dem Bowley* v *Barnes* 8 QB 1043. In that case there was demise by the churchwardens and overseers of some parish property, and the fact that they acted as churchwardens and overseers at the time of the demise was held to be sufficient prima facie proof for the purpose of an action of ejectment without proving their appointment. His Lordship then referred to the decision of Tindal, CJ, to the same effect in *R* v *Newton* (Car & Kir 469), and to *R* v *Jones* (2 Camp 131). This objection, if it were good, would extend very widely, for, suppose perjury committed on the first time of acting in his office before a judge or a recorder, or a County Court judge, or any person who fills a responsible public position, would it lie on the prosecution to show the appointment of such an officer in the strictest possible way? Mr Jelf has not satisfied me that it would, and no member of the court has any doubt that there is no ground for such a contention. Conviction affirmed.

Berryman v ***Wise*** (1791) 4 TR 366 (KB)

This was an action of slander by an attorney for words spoken of him in the way of his profession.

BULLER J said that in the case of all peace-officers, justices of the peace, constables etc, it was sufficient to prove that they acted in those characters without producing their appointments, and that even in the case of murder.

R v ***Cresswell*** (1876) 1 QBD 446 (CCCR)

On an indictment for bigamy it was proved that the first marriage was solemnised, not in the parish church of the parish, but in a chamber in a building a few yards from the church, while the church was under repair. It was further proved that divine service had several times been performed in the building in question.

LORD COLERIDGE CJ said: 'This conviction must be affirmed. The case states that divine service had been several times celebrated in the place where the marriage in question was solemnised. This is sufficient, in accordance with the maxim *omnia praesumuntur rite esse acta,* to give rise to the presumption that the building was licensed. The presumption is the stronger because the clergyman who celebrated the marriage might, by 6 & 7 Wm 4, c.85, s.3, have been indicted for felony if he knowingly did so in an unlicensed place.'
(MELLOR, LUSH and GROVE JJ, and AMPHLETT B, concurred.)
Conviction affirmed.

Tingle Jacobs and Co. v ***Kennedy*** [1964] 1 WLR 638(n)

This concerned an action for negligence arising out of a collision at a crossroads controlled by traffic lights. The county court judge held that the lights were not working properly, although there was evidence of regular inspection of them and there had been no complaints or reported trouble.

LORD DENNING MR stated the facts and continued: 'It seems to me in the face of that evidence it would not be right to suggest the lights were not working properly. Furthermore, when you have a device of this kind set up for public use in active operation, I should have thought the presumption should be that it is in proper working order unless there is evidence to the contrary; and there was none here. Therefore, I cannot go with the suggestion of the judge that the lights were not working properly. I think the case should be decided on the basis that they were working properly.'
(PEARSON and SALMON LJJ agreed.)
Order for new trial.

1.17 Authorities: conflicting presumptions

R v ***Willshire*** (1881) 6 QBD 366 (CCCR)

In 1864 the defendant married A. In 1868 he was charged with bigamy in marrying B in 1868, his wife A being then alive, and was convicted. In 1879 he married C, and in 1880, C being then alive, the defendant was convicted of bigamy, it being held by the judge that the burden of proof was on the defendant and that there was no evidence that A was alive when the defendant married C, or that the marriage with C was invalid by reason of A being then alive.

LORD COLERIDGE CJ said: 'It is said, and I think rightly, that there is a presumption in favour of the validity of this latter marriage, but the prisoner shewed that there was a valid marriage in 1864, and that the woman he then married was alive in 1868. He thus set up the existence of a life in 1868, which, in the absence of any evidence to the contrary will be presumed to have continued to 1879. It is urged, in effect, that the presumption in favour of innocence, a presumption which goes to establish the validity of the marriage of 1879, rebuts the presumption in favour of the duration of life. It is sufficient to raise a question of fact for the jury to determine. It was for the jury to decide whether the man told and acted a falsehood for the purpose of marrying in 1879, or whether his real wife was then dead. The Common Serjeant did not leave the question to the jury, but on these conflicting presumptions held, that the burden of proof was on the prisoner, who was bound to adduce other or further evidence of the existence of his wife in 1879; thus withdrawing from the jury the determination of the fact from these conflicting presumptions. I am clearly of opinion that in this the learned common serjeant went beyond the rules of law. The prisoner was only bound to set up the life; it was for the prosecution to prove his guilt.

(LINDLEY, HAWKINS, LOPES and BOWEN JJ agreed.)

Conviction quashed.

2   The Papers

A: THE QUEEN v COKE AND LITTLETON

2.1   Brief for the prosecution

2.1.1   Instructions to Counsel.   Counsel is instructed in the prosecution of these two defendants, who are due to stand trial at the Oxbridge Crown Court upon the indictment sent with these papers. Counsel also has the statements of witnesses tendered in the committal proceedings on behalf of the prosecution, and a letter from solicitors representing the defendant Littleton, giving notice of alibi as required by s. 11 of the Criminal Justice Act 1967.

There are a number of matters of evidence which Counsel will no doubt wish to consider. Both complainants are under the age of eighteen. The elder sister, Margaret, has been in trouble for shoplifting. On the other hand, the defendant Coke has a previous conviction for rape, said to have been committed under very similar circumstances. In the case of Littleton, the evidence of identification will be of crucial importance, especially in view of his defence of alibi.

The fact of sexual intercourse between Coke and Margaret Blackstone seems to be undisputed, but is in any event supported by the forensic evidence suggesting that the girl had had recent sexual intercourse. There is also the fact which appears to be strongly disputed, that the same defendant was probably the author of the questioned written exhibit, which may assist in the question of his state of mind at the relevant time. Counsel will no doubt wish to consider the state of the expert evidence.

Certain issues arise from the evidence of the police officers, in respect of the search of Coke's flat, apparently without a search warrant, and from the circumstances in which Coke subsequently made his incriminating statement under caution. Counsel's attention is also drawn to the admission of guilt said to be contained in the tape-recorded conversation at the police station between Littleton and his wife. Questions arise concerning the use of the tape and the possibility of privilege in relation to the conversation.

Counsel is instructed to consider and advise on these and any other points of evidence which may arise.

Indictment

IN THE CROWN COURT AT OXBRIDGE

THE QUEEN v HENRY EDWARD COKE and
                    MARTIN STEPHEN LITTLETON

Charged as follows:

COUNT 1

Statement of Offence

Rape contrary to section 1(1) of the Sexual Offences Act 1956.

Particulars of Offence

Henry Edward Coke on the 8th day of July 1979 raped Margaret Ann Blackstone.

COUNT 2

Statement of Offence

Indecent Assault contrary to section 14(1) of the Sexual Offences Act 1956.

Particulars of Offence

Martin Stephen Littleton on the 8th day of July 1979 indecently assaulted Angela Hazel Blackstone.

W. RUSSELL COX
Officer of the Court

Depositions

STATEMENT OF WITNESS
(Criminal Justice Act 1967, s.2, s.9; Magistrates' Courts Rules 1968, r.58)[1]
Statement of: Margaret Ann Blackstone
Age of Witness: 17 (born 3 May 1962)
Occupation of Witness Schoolgirl
Address of Witness 4 The Hyde, Oxbridge.

This statement, consisting of 2 pages, each signed by me, is true to the best of my knowledge and belief, and I make it knowing that if it is tendered in evidence, I shall be liable to prosecution if I have wilfully stated in it anything which I know to be false or do not believe to be true.

Dated the 12th day of July 1979.

Signed: M.A. Blackstone
Witnessed: Dennis Bracton D/S
Helen Blackstone (mother)

I am a schoolgirl aged seventeen and live with my parents and my sister Angela at the above address. I have known Henry Coke for quite a long time, because he goes to a youth club which my friends and I go to at weekends. I think he lives in Plowden Drive in Oxbridge. From time to time he has approached me at the club and asked me to go to bed with him, but I have always refused.

On Sunday, 8 July, I was walking after lunch in the park with Angela, when I saw Henry Coke coming towards us with another man who looked rather older, whom I did not know. We all started talking, and Henry said he had a new album by a band we liked and invited us to his flat to listen to it. I did not really want to go, but Angela was very excited about the idea and so we did. When we got there, Henry put the record on and made us all some coffee. I was sitting on the divan and Henry came and sat next to me. Angela was sitting on the window-ledge next to a large armchair where the other man was sitting.

After a while, Henry started making suggestions to me that we should have sexual intercourse. I told him to stop and that I did not want him even saying such things while my sister was around. At first he seemed to accept this, but then he got very persistent and started trying to hold my hand and put his arm round my shoulder. I pushed him away. All of a sudden, he pushed me backwards very hard, so that I fell on my back on the divan. I was so taken by surprise that I did not get up straight away, and then Henry put his hand up my skirt and pulled my pants down to my ankles. I was very frightened and just lay there. It was only when I saw that he was unzipping his trousers that I started to scream and fight. I was expecting the other man to stop him, but he did nothing. Henry was far too strong for me and he had sexual intercourse with me. I understand what this means, and that is what happened. I did not consent to it, and did nothing to lead Henry to think that I might consent.

---

[1]Now Magistrates' Courts Act 1980, s.102; Criminal Justice Act 1967, s.9; Magistrates' Courts Rules 1981, r.70.

When it was over, I got up quickly. I was terribly distressed. To my horror, I saw that Angela was sitting on the other man's lap and that he had his hand up her skirt. I shouted at her to come with me, and we both ran out of the flat and home. Neither of them made any effort to stop us.

When we got home, I could not bring myself to say anything to my mother, and ran straight upstairs, but Angela said something, and shortly afterwards, my mother came up and asked me what had happened. I didn't want to say anything, but after some time my mother more or less dragged the truth out of me, and then called the police. I then went to bed until a bit later, when a lady doctor came and examined me.

I didn't see what was happening to Angela while Henry was having intercourse with me. It was only afterwards that I noticed that she was sitting with the other man. I think I would recognise the other man if I saw him again.

Signed: M. A. Blackstone   **Witnessed:** Dennis Bracton D/S
                                                   Helen Blackstone (mother)

STATEMENT OF WITNESS

(Criminal Justice Act 1967, s.2, s.9; Magistrates' Courts Rules 1968, r.58)

Statement of: Angela Hazel Blackstone

Age of Witness 13 (born 4 June 1966)

Occupation of Witness Schoolgirl

Address of Witness 4 The Hyde, Oxbridge.

This statement, consisting of 1 page, signed by me, is true to the best of my knowledge and belief, and I make it knowing that if it is tendered in evidence, I shall be liable to prosecution if I have wilfully stated in it anything which I know to be false or do not believe to be true.

Dated the 12th day of July 1979.

Signed: Angela H. Blackstone

Witnessed: Dennis Bracton D/S

Helen Blackstone (mother)

I am a schoolgirl aged thirteen and I live with my parents and my sister Margaret at 4 The Hyde, Oxbridge. On Sunday after lunch, Margaret and I went for a walk in the park. We quite often do that. While we were walking, we met two men who I didn't know. One was a bit older than Margaret, and the other was even older, about the same as my uncle Paul, who is about thirty, I think. The older man didn't say much, but the younger one said he had the Least's new album and said we could listen to it. So we went home with him, and the older man came as well.

When we got there, I sat on the window ledge drinking some coffee and listening to the record, which was great. The younger man was sitting next to Margaret on the sofa. They were talking and messing about. Then they seemed to be having an argument and I saw Margaret fall backwards and the man fall on top of her. Margaret was shouting to the man to stop. I didn't understand what was going on, and I was frightened. The older man who was sitting in an armchair by the window told me not to worry, they were only playing. He lifted me off the window-ledge and sat me on his lap. He didn't want me to watch Margaret, and asked me if I liked boys. I wanted to listen to the music, which was very good. Then he put his hand up my skirt and asked me if I liked it. I said I didn't, but he still kept on, and he was rubbing his leg against me.

After one or two minutes, Margaret got up off the sofa. She was crying a lot and shouted to me to come home with her, which I did. Margaret was crying all the way home but she wouldn't tell me what was the matter, and she went straight to her room when we got home. I thought I had better tell mummy in case anything was the matter with Margaret, so I told her everything that had happened.

Later on Sunday afternoon, a policeman came round with a lady police officer and I told them what had happened. Then we went out in the police car, and drove round the streets near the park. While we were doing this, I saw the older man walking along. I am sure it was the same man. We got out and went up with the police to the man, and I pointed at him and said it was the same man who had been sitting in the armchair. Then mummy took me back home while the police spoke to the man. Later on, a lady doctor came and examined me.

Signed: Angela H. Blackstone   **Witnessed:** Dennis Bracton D/S

Helen Blackstone (mother)

STATEMENT OF WITNESS
(Criminal Justice Act 1967, s.2, s.9; Magistrates' Courts Rules 1968, r.58)
Statement of: Helen Blackstone
Age of Witness Over 21
Occupation of Witness Housewife
Address of Witness 4 The Hyde, Oxbridge.

This statement, consisting of 1 page, signed by me, is true to the best of my knowledge and belief, and I make it knowing that if it is tendered in evidence, I shall be liable to prosecution if I have wilfully stated in it anything which I know to be false or do not believe to be true.

Dated the 12th day of July 1979.

Signed: Helen Blackstone
Witnessed: Dennis Bracton D/S

I live with my husband and two children, Margaret Ann (aged seventeen, born on 3 May 1962) and Angela Hazel (aged thirteen, born on 4 June 1966) at the above address. I now produce copies of the certificates of birth of both my children, marked 'HB1' and 'HB2' respectively.

On Sunday, 8 July, the children went for a walk together after lunch round the park, as they quite often do. They left the house at about 2 o'clock. They are usually back by 3 o'clock to half past, and on this occasion, I noticed that it was a little after 4 o'clock. I heard Margaret running upstairs, and Angela went into the kitchen very quietly, which is unusual. I went into the kitchen and asked Angela if everything was all right. She told me that she and Margaret had been with two men at a flat, and that one of the men had done something to Margaret which upset her. They seemed to be fighting. Angela also said that the other man had sat her on his lap and put his hand up her skirt and kept rubbing his leg against her. She said she didn't like it.

I was very alarmed by all this, and I went up to Margaret's bedroom, where I found her on the bed sobbing violently. She did not want to talk about it, but being sure by now that something terrible had just happened, I shouted at her and slapped her. She then told me that she had been raped by Henry Coke at his flat. I at once went and called the police, and when they came some time later, they talked to both children. They said that Margaret should go to bed until a doctor came to look at her. Angela and I were asked to go out in the police car with them to have a look round.

As we were driving in Plowden Drive, which is not far from the park, Angela suddenly pointed to a man walking towards the police car, and said that it was the man who had touched her while they were sitting in the chair. The car stopped, and the officers and I and Angela approached the man. Angela pointed to the man and said: 'That's him.' The man said he didn't know what she was talking about, or words to that effect, and the officers told me to take Angela home, which I did.

Shortly after we got back home, a doctor arrived from the police and examined both children in my presence.

Signed: Helen Blackstone   **Witnessed:** Dennis Bracton D/S

STATEMENT OF WITNESS

(Criminal Justice Act 1967, s.2, s.9; Magistrates' Courts Rules 1968, r.58)

Statement of: Dr Susan Geraldine Vesey
Age of Witness Over 21
Occupation of Witness Medical Practitioner
Address of Witness 27 Random Cuttings, Oxbridge.

This statement consisting of 1 page, signed by me, is true to the best of my knowledge and belief, and I make it knowing that if it is tendered in evidence, I shall be liable to prosecution if I have wilfully stated in it anything which I know to be false or do not believe to be true.

Dated the 16th day of July 1979.

Signed: Susan Vesey
Witnessed: Dennis Bracton D/S

I am a medical practitioner in general practice at the above address. I also act as one of the surgeons to the Oxbridge Constabulary. On Sunday 8 July 1979, I was on call as duty police surgeon when as a result of a call from D/I Glanvil, I went to 4 The Hyde, Oxbridge, where I examined Margaret Ann Blackstone (D.O.B. 3 May 1962) and Angela Hazel Blackstone (D.O.B. 4 June 1966) who were identified to me by their mother, Mrs Helen Blackstone.

RESULTS OF EXAMINATION

Margaret Ann Blackstone

This girl was evidently distressed and crying at the time of my visit, though not hysterical. She was generally in excellent health. Examination of the genital area showed signs of recent sexual intercourse. There were traces of what appeared to be semen, and some reddening of the vaginal region. There was no bruising of or damage to the genitals. I took a vaginal swab which I placed in a sealed polythene bag and labelled 'SGV1'. I later handed this to D/S Bracton.

Angela Hazel Blackstone

This girl was composed and able to tell me what had happened to her. She was in excellent general health and examination revealed nothing of relevance to the inquiry.

Signed: Susan Vesey   **Witnessed:** Dennis Bracton D/S

STATEMENT OF WITNESS
(Criminal Justice Act 1967, s.2, s.9; Magistrates' Courts Rules 1968, r.58)
Statement of: Geoffrey Glanvil
Age of Witness Over 21
Occupation of Witness Detective Inspector
Address of Witness Oxbridge Police Station.

This statement, consisting of 2 pages, each signed by me, is true to the best of my knowledge and belief, and I make it knowing that if it is tendered in evidence, I shall be liable to prosecution if I have wilfully stated in it anything which I know to be false or do not believe to be true.
Dated the 16th day of July 1979.

Signed: Geoffrey Glanvil D/I
Witnessed: Dennis Bracton D/S

On Sunday 8 July 1979, at about 4.15 p.m., I was on duty in plain clothes when as a result of information received, I went in an unmarked police car with D/S Bracton and WPC Raymond to 4 The Hyde, Oxbridge. I there saw a Mrs Helen Blackstone and her two daughters, Miss Margaret Ann Blackstone aged seventeen and Miss Angela Hazel Blackstone aged thirteen. As a result of what they told me, I advised Margaret Blackstone to go to bed at once and I called for the duty police surgeon to attend. WPC Raymond remained with Margaret at my request.

Together with D/S Bracton, Mrs Blackstone and Angela I then drove the police car slowly through a number of streets around the public park near The Hyde. As we were driving along Plowden Drive, I noticed a man walking towards us, tall, slightly built, about thirty to thirty-five, dark hair, wearing a light shirt and blue jeans. Angela pointed out this man at once as the man who had assaulted her. I stopped the car, and with the other occupants got out and approached the man. Angela looked at him, pointed at him and said: 'That's him.' The man replied: 'What on earth is she talking about?' I then asked Mrs Blackstone to take Angela home.

I said to the man: 'What is your name?' He said: Martin Littleton. Why?' I said: 'We are police officers. It is alleged that earlier this afternoon you assaulted that girl indecently.' He said: 'Rubbish. I've never seen her before in my life.' I said: 'Have you been at Henry Coke's flat today? Littleton said: 'I know Henry Coke, but I haven't been there today. I've been at home on my own. In fact, I've only just got up. This must be some sort of mistake.' I said: 'Where do you live?' Littleton said: 'Eldon Villas, number 17.' I then arrested Littleton for indecent assault and cautioned him, and he replied: 'You've got the wrong man, I tell you.' We then conveyed him to Oxbridge police station where he was detained.

At about 5.30 p.m. the same afternoon with D/S Bracton, I went to a first floor flat at 52 Plowden Drive, where the door was opened by a youth of about eighteen years of age, medium build, fair hair and casually dressed. I said:

'Henry Edward Coke?' He said: 'Yes.' I said: 'We are police officers. You are under arrest for raping Margaret Blackstone earlier this afternoon,' and cautioned Coke, who replied: 'Yes, all right, I was expecting you.' While D/S Bracton sat with Coke, I then searched the flat. In a drawer of the bedside cabinet I found several sheets of notepaper upon which were written in ink references to Margaret Blackstone. I took possession of these sheets, which I now produce marked 'GG1'. We then conveyed Coke to Oxbridge Police Station, where he too was detained.

Later, at 7 p.m. the same day, with D/S Bracton, I interviewed Littleton at the police station in the CID office. I reminded him of the caution, and said: 'Now, what about it, Mr Littleton?' Littleton said: 'I'm not answering any questions. I want to see my solicitor.' I said: 'You can see a solicitor at a time convenient to me. I am investigating a serious offence.' Littleton said: 'Nothing to say.' I said: 'Very well, you will be detained over night and I will see you in the morning,' Littleton said: 'No. Please give me bail. My wife will be so worried.' I said: 'Bail is not on at the moment, but I will make sure your wife knows where you are.'

At 7.20 p.m. the same day, with D/S Bracton, I interviewed Henry Coke in the CID office. I said: 'You are still under caution. Do you want to tell me about it?' Coke said: 'Yes, I may as well. With form for the same thing, I reckon I'm going down for a while. Will you write a statement for me?' I said: 'Certainly.' I then wrote at Coke's dictation a statement under caution, between 7.30 and 8 p.m. without any break. I now produce this statement marked 'GG2'. After completing this statement, I said to Coke: 'You have not mentioned the sheets of paper referring to Margaret which I found in your room.' Coke said: 'No. Actually, those are not mine. Lots of my mates fancy Margaret.' I said: 'How do they come to be in your room on this particular day when you rape her?' Coke said: 'They may have been there for months.' I said: 'Will you supply me with specimens of your handwriting so that I can have a scientific comparison made?' He said: 'Yes, all right.' Coke then wrote at my dictation on a piece of paper which I now produce marked 'GG3'. I then handed exhibits 'GG1' and 'GG3' to D/S Bracton for transmission to the forensic science laboratory.

At about 8.45 p.m. the same day, Mrs Davina Littleton arrived at the police station, and was allowed to see her husband in a cell. I positioned myself nearby, so that I could hear clearly what was said, and recorded the conversation using a pocket cassette recorder. After some general conversation, Mrs Littleton asked: 'Martin, tell me the truth. Is there any truth in what the police say?' Littleton replied: 'Yes, I'm afraid so. I don't know what came over me. I just felt her up. I couldn't help myself. I can't explain it.' I now produce the cassette as exhibit 'GG4'.

The next morning at about 9 a.m. I formally charged Coke with rape and Littleton with indecent assault. They were cautioned and neither made any reply.

Signed: Geoffrey Glanvil D/I   **Witnessed:** Dennis Bracton D/S

STATEMENT UNDER CAUTION

Oxbridge Police Station
Date: 8 July 1979
Time: 7.30 p.m.

Statement of: Henry Edward Coke
Address: 52 Plowden Drive, Oxbridge
Age: 18
Occupation: Apprentice Tailor.

 I, Henry Edward Coke, **wish to make a statement. I want someone to write down what I say. I have been told that I need not say anthing unless I wish to do so and that whatever I say may be given in evidence.**

Signed: H.E. Coke
Witnessed: Geoffrey Glanvil D/I

It's difficult to know where to start really. I've known Margaret for years from the club and seeing her around. I've always fancied her. She's really lovely. I saw her down the club last night wearing one of those see-through blouses. I went home and thought about it a lot, and decided to do something about it. My mate Martin Littleton came round this morning and he had a couple of drinks with me at lunchtime. I told him that Margaret and her sister always went for a stroll in the park after lunch and I was telling him how much I fancied Margaret. We agreed we would meet them if we could and find some reason to take them back to my place. I was really only going to chat Margaret up a bit. Martin said he would look after the little girl for me. So we went up the park, and it went all right. They said they would come back with us to listen to a new record which is very popular down the club at the moment. I put the record on and started chatting Margaret up, while Martin talked to the little girl. Margaret didn't want to know. She was giving me no joy at all. I suddenly came over all funny. I felt I had to have her at all costs. It wasn't difficult. She was

sitting next to me on my divan bed. I pushed her backwards on to the bed. She looked rather surprised more than anything else. She had taken her shoes off and wasn't wearing tights, so I had her pants off quite easily. It was only then she started struggling. It was no trouble. I had if off with her. Then she started crying, which was a bit silly, because she would have enjoyed it if she'd thought about it. She called over to her sister and dragged her off. She was carrying her shoes. I don't think she remembered her pants. I threw them out afterwards.

After she went I was worried. Obviously, I knew you would probably come for me, but actually, I was more worried about Martin. It was only when I had finished with Margaret that I saw what he was up to with the little girl. He was touching her up and fondling her. I know I was a bit forceful with Margaret, but at least she is old enough. Doing that to a kiddy is really sick. No way was I involved with that. I want to make that clear. That is down to Martin on his own. Once I discovered what was going on, I gave Martin a mouthful. We had quite an argument and I threw him out. I don't know what happened to him after that.

I would like to say I'm sorry for what happened. I really like Margaret and I didn't want to hurt her. It's all very silly. Why can't girls say yes sometimes and just enjoy it?

Signed: H.E. Coke
Witnessed: Geoffrey Glanvil D/I

I have read the above statement and I have been told that I can correct, alter or add anything I wish. This statement is true. I have made it of my own free will.

Signed: H.E. Coke
Witnessed: Geoffrey Glanvil D/I

Statement taken by me Geoffrey Glanvil **between** 7.30 p.m. and 8 p.m. **No breaks for refreshments.**

Signed: Geoffrey Glanvil D/I

STATEMENT OF WITNESS
(Criminal Justice Act 1967, s.2, s.9; Magistrates' Courts Rules 1968, r.58)
Statement of: Dennis Bracton
Age of Witness: Over 21
Occupation of Witness Detective Sergeant
Address of Witness Oxbridge Police Station
This statement, consisting of 2 pages, each signed by me, is true to the best of my knowledge and belief, and I make it knowing that if it is tendered in evidence, I shall be liable to prosecution if I have wilfully stated in it anything which I know to be false or do not believe to be true.
Dated the 16th day of July 1979.

Signed: Dennis Bracton D/S
Witnessed: Geoffrey Glanvil D/I

On Sunday 8 July 1979 at about 4.15 p.m. I was on duty in plain clothes when as a result of information received, I went in an unmarked police car with D/I Glanvil and WPC Raymond to 4 The Hyde, Oxbridge. I there saw a Mrs Helen Blackstone and her two daughters, Miss Margaret Blackstone aged seventeen and Miss Angela Blackstone aged thirteen. As a result of what they said, D/I Glanvil advised Margaret Blackstone to go to bed and await the arrival of a doctor. D/I Glanvil then called for the duty police surgeon, Dr Vesey, to attend. WPC Raymond remained at the house with Margaret.

Together with D/I Glanvil, Mrs Blackstone and Angela, I then drove in the police car slowly around various streets near the park just by The Hyde. As we were driving along Plowden Drive, I saw Angela point to a man walking towards us, tall, slightly built, about thirty to thirty-five, dark hair, wearing a light shirt and blue jeans. D/I Glanvil stopped the car, and we all got out and approached the man. Angela looked at him, pointed to him and said: 'That's him.' The man replied: 'What on earth is she talking about?' D/I Glanvil then asked Mrs Blackstone to take Angela home.

D/I Glanvil said to the man: 'What is your name?' He said: 'Martin Littleton. Why?' D/I Glanvil said: 'We are police officers. It is alleged that earlier this afternoon you assaulted that girl indecently.' He said: 'Rubbish. I've never seen her before in my life.' D/I Glanvil said: 'Have you been at Henry Coke's flat today? Littleton said: 'I know Henry Coke, but I haven't been there today. I've been at home on my own. In fact, I've only just got up. This must be some sort of mistake.' D/I Glanvil said: 'Where do you live?' Littleton said: 'Eldon Villas, Number 17.' D/I Glanvil then arrested Littleton for indecent asault and cautioned him, and Littleton replied: 'You've got the wrong man, I tell you.' We then conveyed Littleton to Oxbridge police station where he was detained.

At about 5.30 p.m. the same day, with D/I Glanvil, I went to a first-floor flat at 52 Plowden Drive, where the door was opened by a youth of about eighteen years, medium build, fair hair and casually dressed. D/I Glanvil said: 'Henry Edward Coke?' He said: 'Yes'. D/I Glanvil said: 'We are police officers. You are under arrest for raping Margaret Blackstone earlier this afternoon' and cautioned Coke, who said: 'Yes, all right, I was expecting you.' I then sat with Coke while D/I Glanvil searched the flat. In a drawer in a bedside cabinet I saw D/I Glanvil find a number a number of sheets of notepaper, of which he took possession. Coke was then detained at Oxbridge police station.

Later the same day at 7 p.m. with D/I Glanvil I interviewed Littleton in the CID office at Oxbridge police station. D/I Glanvil reminded Littleton of the caution and said: 'Now, what about it, Mr Littleton?' Littleton said: 'I'm not answering any questions. I want to see my solicitor.' D/I Glanvil said: 'You can see a solicitor at a time convenient to me. I am investigating a serious offence.' Littleton said: 'Nothing to say.' D/I Glanvil said: 'Very well, you will be detained overnight and I will see you in the morning.' Littleton said: 'No. Please give me bail. My wife will be so worried.' D/I Glanvil said: 'Bail is not on at the moment, but I will make sure your wife knows where you are.'

At 7.30 p.m. the same day, with D/I Glanvil I interviewed Henry Coke in the CID office. D/I Glanvil said: 'You are still under caution. Do you want to tell me about it?' Coke said: 'Yes, I may as well. With form for the same thing, I reckon I'm going down for a while. Will you write a statement for me?' D/I Glanvil said: 'Certainly.' D/I Glanvil then took a statement under caution from Coke, and while this was being done, I left the room to attend to other matters.

The next morning at about 9 a.m. I was present when D/I Glanvil formally charged Coke and Littleton with rape and indecent assault respectively. They were cautioned and made no reply.

During the evening of 8 July, I had taken possession from D/I Glanvil of exhibits GG1 and GG3. After the defendants had been charged, I took these exhibits from the police station to the surgery of Dr Susan Vesey at 27 Random Cuttings, Oxbridge. I there collected from the doctor a swab contained in a polythene bag marked 'SGV1'. I then conveyed these exhibits personally to the appropriate departments of the Oxbridge forensic science laboratory.

Signed: Dennis Bracton D/S   **Witnessed:** Geoffrey Glanvil D/I

STATEMENT OF WITNESS
(Criminal Justice Act 1967, s.2, s.9; Magistrates' Courts Rules 1968, r.58)
Statement of: Lorraine Raymond
Age of Witness   Over 21
Occupation of Witness   Police Constable 24
Address of Witness   Oxbridge Police Station.

This statement, consisting of 1 page, signed by me, is true to the best of my knowledge and belief, and I make it knowing that if it is tendered in evidence, I shall be liable to prosecution if I have wilfully stated in it anything which I know to be false or do not believe to be true.
Dated   the 16th day of July 1979.

Signed: Lorraine Raymond WPC 24
Witnessed: Dennis Bracton D/S

On Sunday 8 July 1979, at about 4.15 p.m. I was on duty in uniform at Oxbridge Police Station, when as a result of information received, I went with D/I Glanvil and D/S Bracton, to 4 The Hyde, Oxbridge, where I saw a Mrs Helen Blackstone and her two daughters, Miss Margaret Blackstone aged seventeen and Miss Angela Blackstone aged thirteen. As a result of what they said, D/I Glanvil advised Margaret Blackstone to go to bed and await the arrival of the police surgeon. At D/I Glanvil's request, I remained in the bedroom with Margaret while the other officers went out in the police car with Mrs Blackstone and Angela.

While we were together, Margaret was initially upset but recovered her composure rapidly. I asked her various questions, in reply to which she gave me an account of her having been raped by a young man known to her called Henry Coke.

At about 4.50 p.m. just after Mrs Blackstone and Angela had returned to the house, the duty police surgeon, Dr Susan Vesey, arrived and I then left and returned to the police station.

Signed: Lorraine Raymond WPC 24 **Witnessed:** Dennis Bracton D/S

STATEMENT OF WITNESS
(Criminal Justice Act 1967, s.2, s.9; Magistrates' Courts Rules 1968, r.58)
Statement of: Philip Hale BSc
Age of Witness Over 21
Occupation of Witness Higher Scientific Officer
Address of Witness Forensic Science Laboratory, Portland Road, Oxbridge.

This statement, consisting of 1 page, signed by me, is true to the best of my knowledge and belief, and I make it knowing that if it is tendered in evidence, I shall be liable to prosecution if I have wilfully stated in it anything which I know to be false or do not believe to be true.
Dated the 20th day of July 1979.

Signed: Philip Hale
Witnessed: Dennis Bracton D/S

I have specialised for the last seven years in the scientific examination of documents and comparison of handwriting. On Monday, 9 July 1979, I received from D/S Bracton exhibits GG1 and GG3 which were identified by means of labels.

Exhibit GG1

This was a bundle of four sheets of lined white notepaper containing various short passages in cursive handwriting in blue ball-point ink. The passages contained references in sexual context to someone called Margaret Blackstone. I took this to be questioned writing.

Exhibit GG3

This was a single sheet of plain notepaper containing the following words in cursive handwriting in blue ball-point ink: 'Margaret. Margaret Blackstone. I want you. I need you. I must have you. I think about Margaret all the time.'
I took this to be the known handwriting of Henry Edward Coke.
I examined and compared these exhibits.

Results of examination

I found a high probability that the writer of exhibit GG3 also wrote the text of exhibit GG1. I cannot wholly exclude the possibility that the writer of GG1 was a different person from the writer of GG3 but in my opinion this is unlikely.
After examination, I returned the exhibits to Oxbridge police station where I handed then to D/S Bracton.
I have prepared a chart of comparison of the two exhibits which I can use to illustrate my conclusions if necessary.

Signed: Philip Hale   **Witnessed:** Dennis Bracton D/S

STATEMENT OF WITNESS
(Criminal Justice Act 1967, s.2, s.9; Magistrates' Courts Rules 1968, r.58)
Statement of: Ernest Espinasse MSc, PhD
Age of Witness Over 21
Occupation of Witness   Higher Scientific Officer
Address of Witness Forensic Science Laboratory, Portland Road, Oxbridge.
   This statement, consisting of 1 page, signed by me, is true to the best of my knowledge and belief, and I make it knowing that if it is tendered in evidence, I shall be liable to prosecution if I have wilfully stated in it anything which I know to be false or do not believe to be true.
Dated the 16th day of July 1979.

Signed: Ernest Espinasse
Witnessed: Dennis Bracton D/S

On Monday 9 July 1979, I received from D/S Bracton a polythene bag bearing an identifying label marked 'SGV1' and containing a sterilised cotton swab.

   I specialise in the detection and identification of traces of blood, semen and other biological matter and in the scientific examination of specimens and exhibits within these fields. I examined exhibit SGV1.

Results of examination

This exhibit yielded positive and readily detectable evidence of human spermatozoa, seminal acid phosphatase and seminal blood-group antigens. From the presence of these factors and the high level at which they were detected, I am able to say that the subject of the swab had had sexual intercourse within a recent time of the taking of the swab. I can say that such intercourse definitely occurred within forty-eight hours of the taking of the swab, and in all probability, within a very much shorter time. I can illustrate and support my conclusions if necessary.

   After examination, I resealed the exhibit in sterile material and placed it in a safe place in the laboratory.

Signed: Ernest Espinasse   **Witnessed:** Dennis Bracton D/S

Previous convictions of defendants and witness

CONVICTIONS RECORDED AGAINST: Henry Edward Coke
CONVICTED IN NAME OF: (As above)
C.R.O. No: HEC 3421   D.O.B.: 4/3/61

DATE	COURT	OFFENCE	SENTENCE
16/4/76	Oxbridge Crown	Rape (M/O Induced girl to visit him to listen to records and raped her)	Borstal training (released on 14/10/77)

CONVICTIONS RECORDED AGAINST: Martin Stephen Littleton
CONVICTED IN NAME OF:
C.R.O. No: D.O.B.: 11/2/46

DATE	COURT	OFFENCE	SENTENCE
		NONE RECORDED	

CONVICTIONS RECORDED AGAINST: Margaret Ann Blackstone
CONVICTED IN NAME OF: (As above)
C.R.O. No: D.O.B.: 3/5/62

DATE	COURT	OFFENCE	SENTENCE
27/11/78	Oxbridge Juvenile	Theft (shoplifting)	Conditional discharge 2 years

Notice of alibi

THOMAS, WATSON & CO.

Solicitors and   19 College Row   A. Hughes-Thompson
Commissioners for   Oxbridge   R. Sims LLB
Oaths   Oxshire XX5 3BR
                                Tel: Oxbridge 7541

Our Ref: RS/MSL
Your Ref:

The Prosecuting Solicitor
Oxbridge Constabulary
Police Headquarters
Oxbridge

23 July 1979

Dear Sir

The Queen v *Coke and Littleton*

We act in the above matter for the defendant Martin Stephen Litttleton, who is charged with indecent assault.

We are instructed by our client to supply you now, at the first practicable opportunity, with details of our client's alibi, which will be his defence at trial.

On 8 July 1979, a Sunday, our client was asleep in bed until about 2 o'clock that afternoon, having retired to bed after a heavy day's work on the Saturday, shortly before midnight. He got up between 2.30 and 3 p.m., had something to eat, and feeling slightly unwell, went out for a walk at about 4.15 p.m. or a little after. This was the first time our client had left his house at 17 Eldon Villas, Oxbridge, on that day. It was in the course of that walk that he was stopped by police and arrested.

There are no witnesses in support of the alibi. Our client was alone at home at all material times.

Yours faithfully

Thomas, Watson & Co

2.2 Brief for the defence

2.2.1 Instructions to Counsel on behalf of the defendant Coke   Counsel is instructed on behalf of the defendant Coke, who is charged with rape, as appears from the indictment and statements of the prosecution witnesses sent herewith. The defendant wishes to plead not guilty to this charge, and Counsel will see from his proof of evidence which follows, that he does not deny having sexual intercourse with Margaret Blackstone on the relevant occasion, but says that such intercourse took place with her consent. Counsel will please consider the implications of this defence, and of the fact that according to Coke, the girl is somewhat promiscuous, in the light of the defendant's previous conviction for rape.

The defendant Littleton is of course separately represented, because of the clear conflict of interest between the two, and it is not known what he may say about Coke. It is believed that he may be putting forward a defence of alibi, which would result in a direct conflict of evidence between the defendants. Littleton is apparently a man of previous good character.

Counsel will see that Coke has some serious challenges to the police evidence, both with regard to the search of his flat and his arrest, and his subsequent treatment at the police station. It may be that these matters will affect the admissibility of Coke's alleged oral and written admissions to the police, which on the face of it are very damaging to his case. There is also concern about the written notes found by the police. Coke is adamant that he did not write these, and Counsel will no doubt wish to consider carefully the evidence of the handwriting expert.

Counsel will please consider these matters and the evidence in general.

2.2.2   Proof of evidence of Coke

HENRY EDWARD COKE of 52 Plowden Drive, Oxbridge, will state as follows. I have been charged with raping a girl called Margaret Blackstone at my flat on 8 July 1979. To this charge I wish to plead not guilty. I admit that I had sexual intercourse with her, but it was with her consent. What happened was as follows.

I have known Margaret for quite a long time, because we both go to the same youth club at weekends. Margaret is a really good-looking girl, and all my mates fancy her as well. I have never made any secret of the fact that I do. I have tried chatting her up at the club on various occasions, and although she was usually with someone else, she gave me the impression that I would be all right if I played my cards right. I decided to try my luck. By this, I mean that I was going to try to have sexual intercourse with her, but not by force or against her will. I saw Margaret the night before the alleged rape, Saturday the 7th at the club, and I made up by mind to meet her 'accidentally' the next afternoon when she was walking with her sister in the park, as she usually does.

In fact, the next morning, my mate Martin Littleton came round. He is a fair bit older than my crowd, and is married, but he helps out at the pub I use as my local and we get on very well. I told him about what I had in mind while we were having a drink at lunchtime. Martin agreed to talk to the little girl while I made my number with Margaret, if we could persuade them to come back to my place with us. We went round the park, and there they were, so we asked them back to listen to a new album from the Least, which all the kids like at the moment, and they came.' Margaret

seemed quite happy about it. She came and sat next to me on the divan bed and we
drank coffee while we listened to the album. She took her shoes off. We were getting
on really well. Martin was laughing and talking to the little girl the other side of the
room near the window.

Margaret and I then lay down on the sofa, and she made it clear that she wanted to
have sexual intercourse with me. She took off her pants, and we had intercourse. This
was entirely with her consent. The story she has told to her mother and the police is
quite untrue. I think she has made this up because she is embarrassed about doing it
with her sister there, and because obviously she was going to be asked how her
younger sister came to be interfered with while Margaret was with her. Also, Margaret
was not a virgin at the time. Several of my mates have had it off with her. She will do
it with anyone. Apparently she threatened to complain that my mate Kevin had raped
her last year, when he hadn't at all. She was convicted of shoplifting last year, and it
seems she is rather dishonest.

I want to make it clear that I had nothing to do with Martin interfering with the
little girl. All I saw was that he was touching her up, when Margaret and I had
finished. Margaret must have seen that as well, because she dragged the little girl off
pretty quickly. She didn't even wait to put on her shoes, which she carried, and she left
her pants behind. I threw them away later on. I was disgusted with Martin. We had a
big row, and I threw him out.

I thought then that the police would be round, but there was nothing I could do. Mr
Glanvil and Mr Bracton came round at about 5.30 that afternoon. They did not say
anything to me, as they say. They rushed in without a word, and started searching the
room. I knew who they were. I did say: 'I was expecting you,' which was true, but this
was while they were searching the room. I also asked them if they had a search
warrant, and was told to shut up. Glanvil found some pieces of paper with a few
bawdy remarks about Margaret on them. I think they had been there for ages. My
mates used to come round and we would talk about girls and so on, and I think one of
them must have written it for a laugh. I certainly did not. I did give the police
specimens of my handwriting later, and I am surprised at the conclusions reached by
the expert. I definitely did not write those remarks, and I note that he cannot say for
certain that I did.

After they had finished the search, Glanvil just said: 'Right, come on.' They took me
to the police station. I was not told I was being arrested, and I was not cautioned.
Later that day, the officers came to see me in an office and questioned me. It is true
that I signed a statement under caution, but this was only because the officers shouted
at me and threatened me that if I did not admit raping Margaret, they would do me
for interfering with the little girl as well, and Glanvil said they would 'lock me up and
throw away the key' for that. I believed this, because I was really horrified by the idea
of touching up children, and I could see that they could make it look bad for me. So I
made up the statement and dictated it to them. Some of it was of course true, but not
the bit about how the intercourse came about. I did not say before making the
statement: 'Yes, I may as well. With form for the same thing, I reckon I'm going down
for a while.' I just agreed at the end of a session of threats to make one.

It is true that, unfortunately, I have been convicted of rape before. This was in April
1976. I was sent to Borstal, and was there until October 1977. On this occasion, I was
guilty and pleaded guilty. I did intend to persuade the girl to make love but I went too
far. However, I learned my lesson from this, and I would not have done this again. I

have never been in trouble apart from this, and am now apprentice to a tailor. I started this after a course we had in Borstal, and I want to get on with it and lead a useful life.

2.2.3 Instructions to Counsel on behalf of the defendant Littleton

Counsel is instructed on behalf of the defendant Littleton, a man of good character who has been charged with indecently assaulting a girl of thirteen, as appears from the indictment and statements of the witnesses for the prosecution. Littleton wishes to plead not guilty to this charge, and sets out his defence in the proof of evidence which follows. A proof of evidence from Mrs Littleton is also available, which supports what the defendant has to say in certain important respects.

Counsel will appreciate that in view of the defence of alibi, the issue of identification is crucial to the case. The admissibility and quality of the evidence for the prosecution must be questionable in this respect. Unfortunately, no witness is available to support the alibi itself. It will be particularly important to ensure that the jury hear the whole of the tape of the conversation between the defendant and his wife if it is used in evidence at all, but Counsel will no doubt be anxious to exclude it if this can be done.

Unfortunately, it is believed that the defendant Coke will say that Littleton was at his flat on the day in question and may say that Littleton did in some way assault the girl. In this connection, it is worth observing that Coke has a previous conviction for rape, and it may be that he is protecting the man who was actually there.

Counsel will please consider the matters of evidence which arise in this case.

2.2.4 Proof of evidence of Littleton

MARTIN STEPHEN LITTLETON of 17 Eldon Villas, Oxbridge, will state as follows:

I have been charged with indecently assaulting a girl of thirteen called Angela Blackstone. I wish to plead not guilty. I am a man of thirty-three years of age, married and I am of good character.

I have a number of part-time occupations, one of which is helping out at a public house called the Turk's Head in Oxbridge. I have come across a youth called Henry Coke there, and I have been to his place in Plowden Drive once or twice. On Sunday, 8 July 1979, the day of the alleged assault, I got up late, about 2.30 or 3 o'clock, as far as I can remember. My wife had been at her sister's over the previous night. I had a bite to eat. Then, because I felt a bit headachy, I went out for a walk in the direction of the park.

I started walking down Plowden Drive in the course of my walk, as this road is on the way from my house to the park. I noticed that there was a car coming towards me rather slowly, but I thought nothing of it until it stopped, and a small girl whom I have never seen before in my life got out with a woman and two men, and came up to me. The girl said something like: 'That's him' and pointed at me. I had no idea what was going on. The police officers then told me what was alleged, and they have correctly recorded my answers, which were to the effect that there had been a mistake over the identity of the attacker. I am sure the girl is genuinely convinced that I assaulted her, but I was not at Coke's flat that day and have no idea what happened. The police did not believe me, and I was arrested and taken to the police station.

Later on, the officers wanted to ask me some more questions, but I refused to answer until I had seen my solicitor, and I was not allowed to see him. Because of this, I was kept in overnight, which really upset me. My wife was due back that afternoon and would have been worried. In fact, the police contacted her, and she arrived at the station to see me later that evening. It now appears that the police recorded what we said to each other during the few minutes we were allowed in my cell. It is true that we had the conversation to which D/I Glanvil refers in his statement, but as should appear from the cassette, my wife's question was asked under the great stress which she felt at what had happened. I very foolishly lost my temper and answered in an ironical vein, intending to convey nothing more than anger that she should even have asked the question. I had in fact told her the truth already, exactly as it appears in this statement, and I hope this is also recorded on the cassette. I was not making any sort of admission that I had committed the offence.

I see that Henry Coke has told the police that I was at his flat and somehow helped him in his plan to rape Margaret Blackstone, and then myself molested her sister. This is quite untrue. I cannot think why he should have said this, as I have never offended him as far as I know, except that he is obviously trying to shield whoever was there, to cover up his own guilt. Coke has been in trouble of this sort before. He has been to Borstal for some offence involving a different girl, although I do not know the details of this.

2.2.5 Proof of evidence of Mrs Littleton

DAVINA MARY LITTLETON of 17 Eldon Villas, Oxbridge, will state as follows: I am the wife of Martin Stephen Littleton and live with him at the above address.

On Saturday, 7 July 1979, I went for the day to my sister who lives at Winchelham, because it was her little boy's birthday. Martin was working all day on that Saturday, so he remained at home, and I arranged to stay the night and return the next day.

On the Sunday, 8 July, I arrived home at about 6 o'clock in the evening to find the house empty. This was rather unusual, as Martin usually stays in if he is not working. By 8 o'clock, I was getting worried. Just about then, I had a telephone call from the Oxbridge police saying that Martin had been arrested. They wouldn't tell me why over the phone. I was frantic. I got to the police station as quickly as I could and I saw Inspector Glanvil, who told me what they said had happened. I told him it was absurd, and said I wanted to see my husband. After some discussion, I was granted permission to do this, and after some delay, I was shown into a cell, where he was.

It appears that our conversation was recorded by the police, and I have done my best to recall it. Unfortunately, I was in such a state that only two things stand out clearly. Firstly, Martin told me that there must have been a mistake because he had been at home when the offence was supposed to have been committed. Then, a bit later, I very foolishly begged him to tell me whether there was any truth in what was said about him. I only did this because of the state I was in. It caused Martin to lose his temper, and he did reply in the words recorded by the police. However, it was quite clear that he was speaking in a bitter, sarcastic tone, and he did not mean that he was really guilty. If he had meant that, I think I would have had complete hysteria on the spot, and it would have shown in the recording. I would have been very angry and distressed.

From my knowledge of Martin, which goes back about nine years, six of them as his wife, the suggestion that he would interfere with children sexually is ludicrous. I have often seen him with children of friends and relatives, and his attitude towards them has always been quite normal. He is very popular with everyone who knows him, and has a good reputation for honesty and helpfulness.

B: *BLACKSTONE* v *COKE*

2.3 Brief for the Plaintiff

2.3.1 Instructions to Counsel. Counsel is instructed on behalf of the plaintiff in this action, which arises from the rape of the plaintiff by the defendant in July 1979. Counsel will observe that the plaintiff is assisted by the defendant's conviction of this offence in the Crown Court on 10 January 1980. The defendant asserts that he was wrongly convicted, and counsel will no doubt consider how the matter should be presented, in the light of s.11 of the Civil Evidence Act 1968. The defendant has never, so far as is known to your instructing solicitors, attempted to deny his paternity of the child until these proceedings, but it is thought that he may try to impute this to one Henneky, who is in the United States at the present time. No notice has been given on behalf of the defendant of an intention to adduce his hearsay evidence, but counsel will find interesting the letter from Henneky's American lawyer.

The plaintiff has available expert evidence from Dr Gray dealing with the plaintiff's psychological sufferings, and from Dr Vesey who saw her just after the rape and subsequently dealing with the reasons why the pregnancy was not terminated. Both will be available as witnesses. On instructing solicitors' advice, the plaintiff has declined to submit herself or the child to blood tests. Frankly, we regard the evidence as very strong, and were not prepared to risk exacerbating her suffering. The other side may seek to make some capital.

The defendant's solicitors have issued a subpoena duces tecum against the Director of the Oxbridge City Children's Department apparently in the belief that Miss Blackstone made some damaging admission to him about paternity when consulting the Department on the subject of long term fostering. The Director has refused to answer enquiries from either side, claiming that public policy prevents this, and it seems that the issue may have to be determined by the Court. Miss Blackstone states that she said nothing inconsistent with her case. For our part, we have issued a subpoena to a Fr Wigmore, a Roman Catholic priest consulted by Mr Coke. It is thought that the defendant may well have said something incriminating to Fr Wigmore, who, subject to counsel's advice, seems to us to be compellable to repeat it to the court. This information was gleaned from a letter which the defendant's solicitors inadvertently enclosed with a letter to instructing solicitors, and a copy of which counsel will find herewith. The original was returned to Mansfield & Co. in accordance with counsel's advice, but it is hoped that the copy may be useful in evidence.

Counsel will please consider the evidence and advise generally, and appear for the plaintiff.

Pleadings

IN THE HIGH COURT OF JUSTICE   1980 B No: 123
QUEEN'S BENCH DIVISION
OXBRIDGE DISTRICT REGISTRY
Writ issued the 19th day of May 1980
BETWEEN:

MARGARET ANN BLACKSTONE   PLAINTIFF
and
HENRY EDWARD COKE   DEFENDANT

STATEMENT OF CLAIM

1.   On the 8th day of July 1979 the Defendant lured the Plaintiff to his flat at
52 Plowden Drive in the City and County of Oxbridge under pretence of a
social occasion for listening to music and drinking coffee and there assaulted
and beat the Plaintiff by having sexual intercourse with her by force and
without her consent.
2.   Further and alternatively the Defendant falsely and against her will
imprisoned the Plaintiff in his said flat by force despite the Plaintiff's repeated
requests that she be allowed to leave.
3.   Pursuant to the provisions of section 11 of the Civil Evidence Act 1968 the
Plaintiff will rely upon the conviction of the Defendant on indictment on the
10th day of January 1980 at the Oxbridge Crown Court before the Honourable
Mr Justice Holt and a jury of having raped the Plaintiff on the 8th day of July
1979. Such conviction is relevant in this suit to the Plaintiff's allegations herein
that the Defendant had sexual intercourse with the Plaintiff on the said date,
that he did so without the Plaintiff's consent and that the Defendant is the
father of the Plaintiff's child referred to in the particulars under paragraph 4
hereof.
4.   By reason of the Defendant's assault and battery and/or false imprisonment
of the Plaintiff as aforesaid the Plaintiff has suffered personal injury, loss and
damage.

PARTICULARS OF PERSONAL INJURY

(i)   Severe pain and irritation of the genital region;

(ii)   Unwanted pregnancy resulting in the confinement of the Plaintiff and the birth to her on the 22nd day of April 1980 of a male child, Kenneth Arthur Blackstone;

(iii)   Post-natal complications and depression;

(iv)   Continuing depression, emotional distress, fear of social ostracism, anxiety over normal social contact with others and lack of self confidence, all requiring psychiatric treatment.

PARTICULARS OF LOSS AND DAMAGE

Expenses of confinement and birth:	£500.00
Psychiatrist's fees:	£70.00
	£570.00

AND THE PLAINTIFF CLAIMS: (i) The said sum of £570.00

(ii) Damages.

ALEXANDER NOY

Served this 19th day of May 1980 by Eldon & Co., 12, The Low, Oxbridge, Solicitors for the Plaintiff.

IN THE HIGH COURT OF JUSTICE   1980 B No: 123
QUEEN'S BENCH DIVISION
OXBRIDGE DISTRICT REGISTRY
BETWEEN:

MARGARET ANN BLACKSTONE   PLAINTIFF
— and —
HENRY EDWARD COKE   DEFENDANT

DEFENCE

1.   With reference to paragraph 1 of the Statement of Claim the Defendant
admits only that on the 8th day of July 1979 at his said flat he had sexual
intercourse with the Plaintiff. The Plaintiff consented to such intercourse. The
Defendant denies that he used any force or assaulted or beat the Plaintiff as
alleged or at all. Save as expressly admitted above the Defendant denies each
and every allegation contained in the said paragraph 1.

2.   With reference to paragraph 2 of the Statement of Claim the Defendant
denies that he falsely imprisoned the Plaintiff as alleged or at all. At all material
times the Plaintiff was a willing visitor to the Defendant's flat and was free to
leave as she wished.

3.   With reference to paragraph 3 of the Statement of Claim the Defendant
admits that he was in fact convicted of rape as alleged but denies that he was
guilty of the said or any offence. The Defendant will seek to show that he was
wrongly convicted and will invite this Honourable Court so to find.

4.   The Defendant admits that the Plaintiff gave birth to a child on the date
alleged but denies that he is the father of the said child.

5.   The Defendant makes no admissions with regard to the alleged or any
personal injury, loss or damage. If (which is not admitted) the Plaintiff suffered
any personal injury, loss or damage the Defendant denies that such injury, loss
or damage was caused or contributed to by his said sexual intercourse with the
Plaintiff or that he is in any manner responsible therefor.

6.   Further and alternatively such injury, loss or damage as the Plaintiff may
prove flowing from her said pregnancy, confinement or giving birth (which is
not admitted) was caused by or contributed to by the Plaintiff's refusal or
failure to undergo an abortion at the proper time after conception.

7.   In the premises the Defendant denies that the Plaintiff is entitled to the
relief claimed or any relief.

HORACE ATKYN

Served this 13th day of June 1980 by Mansfield & Co, Oldschool Buildings,
Oxbridge, Solicitors for the Defendant.

Correspondence

Solicitors	ELDON & Co	12, The Low,
Commissioners for Oaths		Oxbridge XX5 2BR
		Tel: Oxbridge 62847

Geoffrey J. Eldon LL.B
Paul Birch
Stephen M. Paynter B.A.
Mary L. Driver LL.B
Kenneth Stacey
Geraldine C. Eldon M.A.

Messrs. Mansfield & Co.,
Oldschool Bldgs.,
Oxbridge.

Our ref: GJE/MAB
Your ref: SPM/HEC

5 February 1980

Dear Sirs,

Re:

Miss Margaret Blackstone

We act for Miss Blackstone in matters arising from the rape committed on her by your client Mr Henry Coke on the 8 July, 1979, an offence of which he was convicted by a jury at the Oxbridge Crown Court on the 10 January of this year. As a result of this act, our client is now pregnant with Mr Coke's child, and is expected to give birth in April.

We are advised by Counsel that our client is entitled to substantial damages against Mr Coke in respect of the birth, and her severe psychological injury and distress. Your client may consider himself fortunate that our client wishes no more to do with him and is prepared to maintain the child herself with the help of her family. Unless we hear from you within 14 days of this letter with your proposals for settlement of our client's claim, we shall have no alternative but to instruct Counsel to settle proceedings in the High Court.

Yours Faithfully,

Eldon & Co.

MANSFIELD & Co.

Stanley P. Mansfield
Philip Garrity LL.B

Solicitors and Commissioners for Oaths   Heather L. Morris

Peter G. Bullimore

Oldschool Buildings,
Oxbridge
Tel: 0411

Messrs. Eldon & Co.,
12, The Low,
Oxbridge.

Our ref: SPM/HEC
Your ref: GJE/MAB

8 February 1980

Dear Sirs,

Re:

Miss Blackstone and Mr Coke

We are in receipt of your letter of the 5th, inst. and confirm that we act for Mr Coke in this matter. If your client does not require maintenance for the child, we are unable to see what damages your client may be entitled to. Our client instructs us that Miss Blackstone was offered the opportunity of an abortion, but declined it. In those circumstances, her damages are no more than nominal. Mr Coke is prepared to pay her the sum of £500 to avoid this unnecessary litigation, provided that it is understood that this is to end the matter once and for all.

Yours Faithfully,

Mansfield & Co.

ELDON & Co.

Solicitors
Commissioners for Oaths

12, The Low,
Oxbridge XX5 2BR
Tel: Oxbridge 6284

Geoffrey J. Eldon LL.B
Paul Birch
Stephen M. Paynter B.A.
Mary L. Driver LL.B
Kenneth Stacey
Geraldine C. Eldon M.A.

Mansfield & Co.,
Oldschool Bldgs.,
Oxbridge.

Our ref: GJE/MAB
Your ref: SPM/HEC

14 February 1980

Dear Sirs,

Re:

Miss Margaret Blackstone

We are in receipt of your letter of the 8 February, which both we and our client consider to be outrageous. In our view, an unwelcomed pregnancy induced by forcible sexual intercourse, and the inevitable mental and emotional complications which this must entail in one so young can hardly be written off as 'nominal'. Your client's offer is rejected.

In view of your client's attitude, we see no purpose in discussing this matter with you any further, and we are sending our papers to Counsel.

Yours Faithfully,

Eldon & Co.

MANSFIELD & Co.

	Stanley P. Mansfield
	Philip Garrity LL.B
Solicitors and Commissioners for Oaths	Heather L. Morris
	Peter G. Bullimore

Oldschool Buildings,
Oxbridge
Tel: 0411

Messrs. Eldon & Co.,
12, The Low,
Oxbridge.

Our ref: SPM/HEC
Your ref: GJE/MAB

20 February 1980

Dear Sirs,

    Re:

Miss Blackstone and Mr Coke

Thank you for your letter of the 14th inst. We regret that this matter cannot be concluded without resort to the courts. We have instructions to accept service. We shall of course have to apply for Legal Aid on our client's behalf, and you may in due course like to let us know what kind of 'substantial damages' you feel our client, who is an apprentice tailor approaching his 19th birlthday, should be in a position to pay.

We wish to advise you that our client continues to maintain his innocence, and will if necessary seek to prove that the verdict of the jury was wrong. He instructs us that both Miss Blackstone and himself know who the father of her child is, and we hope to have evidence available to confirm what he tells us. You may take this letter as notice to your client to submit herself and the child, when it is born, to a suitable blood test.

If in these circumstances, you wish to proceed, so be it.

Yours Faithfully,

Mansfield & Co.

ELDON & Co.

Solicitors
Commissioners for Oaths

12, The Low,
Oxbridge XX5 2BR.
Tel: Oxbridge 6284.

Geoffrey J. Eldon LL.B
Paul Birch
Stephen M. Paynter B.A.
Mary L. Driver LL.B
Kenneth Stacey
Geraldine C. Eldon M.A.

Messrs. Mansfield & Co.
Oldschool Bldgs.,
Oxbridge.

Our ref: GJE/MAB
Your ref: SPM/HEC

3 March 1980

Dear Sirs,

Re:

Miss Blackstone and Mr Coke

Thank you for your letter of the 20 February. We too regret that proceedings should be necessary, but your client's attitude leaves us no alternative. It seems to us extraordinary that a man convicted of the offence of rape after a full trial should respond in this way.

We are instructed to reply particularly to your observations as to the paternity of the child with which Miss Blackstone. Firstly, while there may be no reason why Miss Blackstone should not have undergone an abortion, we find it incredible that your client should have the temerity, having impregnated ours by force, to dictate to Miss Blackstone what she should or should not do in this regard. If our client had wished to terminate the pregnancy, she was perfectly free to do so, but it was and is for her to decide on these matters and not for your client. Nor is our client prepared to submit herself or her child to any blood test. Our client has indeed no doubt as to the identity of the father, and we have advised her that in view of the available evidence, no further proof is called for.

We take this opportunity of enclosing a letter which, no doubt by inadvertence, you enclosed with your letter to us of the 20 February. On the advice of Counsel, we apprehend that you are entitled to have the original back, but we wish to make it clear that we have copied it for our own use and will in due course tender it as evidence, unless the original is produced or admitted.

Yours Faithfully,

Eldon & Co.

MANSFIELD & Co.

Stanley P. Mansfield
Philip Garrity LL.B
Solicitors and Commissioners for Oaths   Heather L. Morris
Peter G. Bullimore

Oldschool Buildings,
Oxbridge
Tel: 0411

H.E. Coke Esq.,
52, Plowden Drive,
Oxbridge.

STRICTLY PERSONAL AND CONFIDENTIAL

Our ref: SPM/HEC
Your ref: GJE/MAB

20 February, 1980

Dear Sirs,

Re:

Yourself and Miss Blackstone

As we discussed yesterday, I have written to the other side in fairly strong terms. As I explained when you telephoned this morning, the court will look at the matter from a strictly legal point of view, although you may see it in other terms too. Certainly, I would not object to your seeking personal advice from Fr. Wigmore about your moral position, but I shall continue, as your solicitor, to uphold your legal rights, subject of course to your instructions.

I have noted what you said about the possibility that Margaret may have given a quite different account of the paternity to the Local Authority Children's Department, and of course I shall look into it.

With my best wishes,

Yours Sincerely,

Stanley P. Mansfield

WARREN B. WITKIN
Attorney at Law

3251 Wontshire Blvd.,
Suite 3400,
Los Angeles, Ca. 90064
Tel: (213) 500 5000

Ms. Margaret A. Blackstone
4, The Hyde,
Oxbridge, England.

8 November 1979

Re: Mr Anthony F. Henneky

Dear Ms. Blackstone:

Mr Anthony F. Henneky has asked me to reply to your recent letter, which hinted obliquely that he might be the father of a child with which you are pregnant at this point in time.

My client tells me that nothing could be further from the truth, and that you are both aware that the father is a Mr Henry E. Coke. Mr Henneky and I hope that this will be the end of the matter, and that you will not repeat such allegations.

If this was not the intent of your letter, please forgive the presumption of this letter.

Very Truly Yours,

Warren B. Witkin
Attorney for Anthony F. Henneky.

2.4 Brief for the Defendant

2.4.1 Instructions to Counsel. Counsel will be familiar with this case, having appeared for Mr Coke at his criminal trial, and having settled the pleadings and advised throughout. There is little to add to what counsel already knows. The plaintiff's solicitors have not disclosed any expert medical evidence apart from Dr Gray, and have never responded to our request for blood tests.

Mr Henneky refuses to return from the United States to give evidence, and it seems that we shall have to rely on his written statement under the Civil Evidence Act 1968. Unfortunately, the plaintiff's solicitors have issued a subpoena against Fr Wigmore, of whom they learnt when regrettably, your instructing solicitors sent astray a letter to Mr Coke. It is hoped that counsel will be able to rely on some privilege for his confidence in Fr Wigmore, who is minded to refuse to answer any questions on the subject and will no doubt be held in contempt unless some privilege can be found.

The Director of the Children's Department continues to object to revealing any communications passing between his department and the plaintiff, and counsel is asked to ask the judge to rule on this matter, as it may be of some significance to the defence.

As counsel requested, a transcript of the evidence given at the criminal trial has been agreed with the other side and will be available at court for the judge's use.

Counsel will please advise as may be necessary and appear for Mr Coke.

2.4.2 Proof of evidence of: Anthony Filbert Henneky

1245, Robert E. Lee Boulevard, Gilroy, California USA
5 June 1980.
I am now 32 years of age and reside at the above address. Between 1976 and 1979 I was a student at Oxbridge College of Technology, studying Botany and the technical and economic aspects of market gardening. I came to college rather late in life compared to most of the students, because I worked in market gardening for some years after leaving school. A paper I wrote on the California garlic industry while at college attracted the attention of Mr Jefferson T. Budweiser III, the President of Budweiser Garlic, of Gilroy, California. Mr Budweiser wrote to me and offered me an executive position with his company in Gilroy, which is the major garlic production center in the world. I accepted, and having obtained permission to reside and work in the United State, I moved here in September 1979.

During my stay in Oxbridge, I met a girl called Margaret Blackstone. I think this would be early in 1977. I can only describe Margaret as somewhat promiscuous. She was attracted to me as a rather older person than her other friends. We started to have sexual intercourse on a regular basis. On legal advice, I am not prepared to state when this intercourse began. We had sexual intercourse during 1979, and quite frequently during May and June 1979, when my course was ending and I was preparing to move to the States. I recall specifically the weekend when Margaret states that she was raped by Henry Coke. To my certain recollection, Margaret and I had sexual intercourse on the Friday and Saturday nights in the back of my car after attending the youth club. We might well have seen each other on the Sunday night as well, had it not been for what happened with Coke. After this, we had sexual intercourse once or twice two or three weeks after the Coke incident, and that was the end of our relationship.

After I arrived in the United States, I received a letter from Margaret, to the effect that she was pregnant. She asked me to destroy the letter after reading it which unfortunately I did. I cannot now remember the date on which I received the letter, but it must have been sometime in October 1979. Although the letter did not say so expressly, I formed the impression that Margaret was hinting that the child was mine. This is possible, as we were rather lax over contraception, and often took risks. I took legal advice, and did not reply. I was told by someone I know in England that Henry Coke had been charged with raping Margaret, and it was suggested to me that I might return to give evidence for him. I know nothing of what happened between Coke and Margaret, except that I had the impression that she wasn't interested in him, but I must say that it would not surprise me to hear that she consented to have sex with him, or anyone, for that matter. In any event, I was not then and am not now prepared to return to England to give evidence, as my attorney has advised me not to do so. If this statement is of any use, I am happy for Coke to make use of it, but I am not prepared to leave the United States or to give evidence.

3 The Burden and Standard of Proof

A: THE BURDEN AND STANDARD OF PROOF IN CIVIL CASES

3.1 Introductory notes

3.1.1 The term 'burden of proof' refers to the obligation of a party to satisfy the tribunal of fact of the truth or probability of each fact necessary to establish the elements of his claim or defence (where the defence goes beyond a mere denial of the plaintiff's claim). The burden may be discharged by the adduction of evidence, or by the assertion of presumptions in a party's favour, by reliance on formal admissions or by the taking of judicial notice by the judge of certain facts, or by any combination of these.

3.1.2 However, the term 'burden of proof' has two meanings, and is habitually employed in both senses.
    3.1.2.1 The 'legal' or ' persuasive' burden describes the obligation to prove each essential element of a claim or affirmative defence. Hence, failure to discharge this burden, when the whole of the evidence is assessed by the tribunal of fact, will be fatal to that claim or defence.
    3.1.2.2 The 'evidential' burden refers to the burden of adducing sufficient evidence or other proof of a given fact to justify a favourable finding on that fact. Failure to discharge this burden gives rise to the risk of an adverse finding on that fact (unless the contrary evidence is insufficient or is rejected) and hence ultimately to the risk of failure on some essential issue to which the fact relates. If sufficiently serious, this may entail failure in the claim or defence as a whole. But mere failure to discharge an evidential burden is not in itself fatal to the claim or defence, and the tribunal of fact must still weigh the whole of the evidence given on both sides, before deciding the case in the light of the legal burden.
    At the outset of the case, the legal and evidential burdens generally coincide, but while the legal burden remains on the same party throughout, the evidential burden may shift once evidence has been given which is sufficient to establish a *prima facie* case in support of a particular fact. The opponent may then have to adduce evidence to the contrary, or risk an adverse finding on that fact.

3.1.3 In civil cases, the legal burden of proving any issue lies on the party to the success of whose claim or defence proof of that issue is essential in law. The question of what facts fall to be proved by which party is one of substantive law, and is usually apparent from the pleadings. The answer is always to be found in the rules of substantive law governing the cause of action or defence in issue. In cases where the law is unclear, or it is uncertain what substantive rules should be applied, the court will decide as a matter of law where the burden lies, and will generally treat the question as one of broad convenience and justice, by requiring proof of the party to whom the least embarrassment or difficulty will be occasioned by bearing the burden. This will usually suggest that the party asserting the affirmative rather than the negative of a proposition bear the burden of proof in that instance. The court will look beyond the language of the pleading in ascertaining which party asserts an affirmative proposition, and will have regard to the substance of the proposition.

3.1.4   The term 'standard of proof' describes the extent or degree to which a party bearing a burden of proof must discharge that burden, in order that the tribunal of fact may render him a favourable finding. It is therefore a measurement of the quality and cogency of evidence tendered for the purpose of discharging the burden of proof, a statement of the degree of conviction that must be produced in the mind of the tribunal of fact, before the law will allow that tribunal to find in favour of the party bearing the burden of proof.

3.1.5   In all civil cases, the standard of proof is that on the balance of probabilities. The tribunal of fact need only be persuaded that the asserter's case is more probable than not. If the tribunal of fact is wholly undecided, and therefore finds the sides of the scale evenly balanced, the party bearing the burden of proof has failed. But if that party has tipped the scales even very slightly in his favour, the standard is met.

3.1.6   Even where a party to a civil case alleges facts which, if proved, would amount to conduct by his opponent of a criminal or quasi-criminal nature, the standard remains that of the balance of probabilities, and does not escalate to the criminal standard of proof (see 3.4 post). Nevertheless, any court will require cogent evidence before finding that a grave allegation has been proved on the balance of probabilities, and the graver the allegation the more cogent the evidence required.

3.1.7   The above observations apply to matrimonial causes. Although the authorities conflict, it is now generally accepted that the normal civil standard applies to matrimonial causes. The concept of the matrimonial offence with its quasi-criminal stigma has now gone, and with it the need for any higher standard of proof. Marital breakdown is now regarded as a misfortune befalling both parties, and the sole ground for divorce is the irretrievable breakdown of the marriage. (*A Practical Approach to Evidence,* pp 66–9, 73–4, 79–82.)

3.2 Commentary

Blackstone v *Coke* at trial.   Hardwicke J. invites Mr Noy for the plaintiff and Mr Atkyn for the defendant to address him in argument, after the close of the evidence, on the burden and standard of proof applicable to various issues in the case.

3.3 Argument

Hardwicke J: Mr Atkyn, I would be grateful if you would help me on one or two matters regarding the burden and standard of proof. Do you accept that you bear the burden of proving what I might call the affirmative parts of your defence, namely that the plaintiff consented to have sexual intercourse with your client on the assault and battery cause of action, and that the plaintiff was free to leave, on the false imprisonment allegation?

Mr Atkyn: No, my Lord. In my submission, although those matters seem to be affirmative allegations in the defence, they really do no more than deny part of the plaintiff's case, which the plaintiff must establish in order to succeed.

Hardwicke J: I had in mind the observations of the House of Lords in *Joseph Constantine Steamship Line* v *Imperial Smelting Corporation,* which is reported at [1942] AC 154. It seemed to me that the House of Lords was saying in that case that a party should be required to prove the affirmative allegations which he makes.

Mr Atkyn: My Lord, that is a sound rule where it is unclear who is asserting the issue, or where the rules of law are unclear. But ordinarily, one has to look to the law underlying the cause of action. Here, the plaintiff has undertaken to prove that the defendant assaulted and beat her. That is an affirmative allegation, even though in this case, the assault consists of sexual intercourse without her consent. If one looks at *Constantine* v *Imperial Smelting,* it becomes clear. A difficult point arose with regard to the doctrine of frustration of contract.

Joseph Constantine Steamship Line v *Imperial Smelting Corporation* [1942] AC 154 (HL)

The charterers of a ship claimed damages from the owners for failure to load. The defendants pleaded that the contract had been frustrated by the destruction of the ship owing to an explosion, the cause of which was unclear. Such frustration would have concluded the case in favour of the defendants in the absence of any fault on their part. Atkinson J held that the onus of proving that the frustration was induced by the defendant's default lay upon the charterers. The Court of Appeal reversed this decision and the defendants appealed to the House of Lords.

VISCOUNT SIMON LC said: 'The question here is where the onus of proof lies; i.e. whether, when a supervening event has been proved which would, apart from the defendant's 'default' put an end to the contract, and when at the end of the case no inference of "default" exists and the evidence is equally consistent with either view, the defence fails because the defendant has not established affirmatively that the supervening event was not due to his default.

I may observe, in the first place, that, if this were correct, there must be many cases in which, although in truth frustration is complete and unavoidable, the defendant will be held liable because of his inability to prove a negative — in some cases, indeed, a whole series of negatives. Suppose that a vessel while on the high seas disappears completely during a storm. Can it be that the defence of frustration of the adventure depends on the owner's ability to prove that all his servants on board were navigating the ship with adequate skill and that there was no "default" which brought about the catastrophe? Suppose that a vessel in convoy is torpedoed by the enemy and sinks immediately with all hands. Does the application of the doctrine require that the owners should affirmatively prove that those on board were keeping a good look-out, were obscuring lights, were steering as directed, and so forth? There is no reported case which requires us so to hold. The doctrine on which the defence of frustration depends is nowhere so stated as to place this onus of proof on the party relying on it.

In this connection it is well to emphasize that when "frustration" in the legal sense occurs, it does not merely provide one party with a defence in an action brought by the other. It kills the contract itself and discharges both parties automatically. The plaintiff sues for breach at a past date and the defendant pleads that at that date no contract existed. In this situation the plaintiff could only succeed if it were shown that the determination of the contract were due to the defendant's "default," and it would be a strange result if the party alleging this were not the party required to prove it.'

LORD WRIGHT said: 'The appeal can, I think, be decided according to the generally accepted view that frustration involves as one of its elements absence of fault, by applying the ordinary rules as to onus of proof. If frustration is viewed (as I think it can be) as analogous to an exception, since it is generally relied on as a defence to a claim for failure to perform a contract, the same rule will properly be applied to it as to the ordinary type of exceptions. The defence may be rebutted by proof of fault, but the onus of proving fault will rest on the plaintiff. This is merely to apply the familiar rule which is applied, for instance, where a carrier by sea relies on the exception of perils of the seas. If the goods owner then desires to rebut that prima facie defence on the ground of negligence or other fault on the part of the shipowner, it rests on the goods owner to establish the negligence or fault.'
(LORDS RUSSELL of KILLOWEN, MAUGHAM AND PORTER delivered concurring judgments)
Appeal allowed.

In those circumstances, as can be seen, their Lordships thought it right that the affirmative proposition, that there had been fault, should be affirmatively proved.

My Lord, in relation to the problem of fundamental breach, the Court of Appeal applied much the same principal in:

Levison and another v Patent Steam Carpet Cleaning Co. Ltd. [1978] QB 69 (CA)

The defendants were guilty of the unexplained loss of a Chinese carpet which had been delivered to them for cleaning and which belonged to the plaintiffs. A clause in the contract signed by the plaintiffs would have exempted the defendants from liability for negligence, but not for any fundamental breach. The plaintiffs sued the cleaners for the loss of the carpet. The county court judge gave judgment against the cleaners who appealed.

LORD DENNING MR said: 'This brings me to the crux of the case. On whom is the burden of proof? Take the present case. Assuming that clause 2 (a) or clause 5, or either of them, limits or exempts the cleaners from liability for negligence: but not for a fundamental breach. On whom is the burden to prove that there was fundamental breach?

Upon principle, I should have thought that the burden was on the cleaners to prove that they were not guilty of a fundamental breach. After all, Mrs Levison does not know what happened to it. The cleaners are the ones who know, or should know, what happened to the carpet, and the burden should be on them to say what it was. It was so held by McNair J. in *Woolmer* v *Delmer Price Ltd.* [1955] 1 QB 291; and by me in *J. Spurling Ltd.* v *Bradshaw* [1956] 1 WLR 461, 466, and by the East African Court of Appeal in *United Manufacturers Ltd.* v *WAFCO Ltd.* [1974] EA 233. A contrary view was expressed by this court in *Hunt & Winterbotham (West of England) Ltd.* v *B.R.S. (Parcels) Ltd.* [1962] 1 QB 617, 635. And there is a long line of shipping cases in which it has been held that, if a shipowner makes a prima facie case that the cause of the loss was one of the excepted perils, the burden is on the shipper to prove that it was not covered by the exceptions: see *The Glendarroch* [1894] P 226 and *Munro, Brice & Co.* v *War Risks Association Ltd.* [1918] 2KB 78. To which there may be added *Joseph Constantine Steamship Line Ltd.* v *Imperial Smelting Corporation Ltd.* [1942] AC 154 on frustration.

It is, therefore, a moot point for decision. On it I am clearly of the opinion that, in a contract of bailment, when a bailee seeks to escape liability on the ground that he was not negligent or that he was excused by an exception or limitation clause, then he must show what happened to the goods. He must prove all the circumstances known to him in which the loss or damage occurred. If it appears that the goods were lost or damaged without any negligence on his part, then, of course, he is not liable. If it appears that they were lost or damaged by a slight breach — not going to the root of the contract — he may be protected by the exemption or limitation clause. But, if he leaves the cause of loss or damage undiscovered and unexplained — then I think he is liable: because it is then quite likely that the goods were stolen by one of his servants; or delivered by a servant to the wrong address; or damaged by reckless or wilful misconduct; all of which the offending servant will conceal and not make known to his employer. Such conduct would be a fundamental breach against which the exemption or limitation clause will not protect him.

The cleaning company in this case did not show what happened to the carpet. They did not prove how it was lost. They gave all sorts of excuses for non-delivery and eventually said it had been stolen. Then I would ask: By whom was it stolen? Was it by one of their own servants? Or with his connivance? Alternatively, was it delivered by one of their servants to the wrong address? In the absence of any explanation, I would infer that it was one of these causes. In none of them would the cleaning company be protected by the exemption or limitation clause.
(ORR LJ AND SIR DAVIS CAIRNS agreed)
Appeal dismissed.

My Lord, there is no such difficulty here, the law is clear enough.

Hardwicke J: So you say that even in the case of false imprisonment, the plaintiff must prove each element of the case set out in the Statement of Claim. You are merely denying the allegation made against you.

Mr Atkyn: Yes, My Lord. It is not as though I am going beyond a mere denial and setting up some separate and positive defence such as one sees in negligence cases with defences of contributory negligence or Act of God.

Hardwicke J: Mr Noy, what do you say?

Mr Noy: My Lord, I agree with what my learned friend says, and I hope to persuade Your Lordship that the burden has been discharged. Of course, Your Lordship was with me at an earlier stage when Your Lordship rejected my learned friend's submission of no case to answer.

Hardwicke J: Yes, but that meant no more than that you had established a *prima facie* case. It was then up to Mr Atkyn to decide whether to adduce evidence. Now that he has done so, I must consider the evidence as a whole. You had discharged the evidential burden, but I must now consider the legal burden which we have been discussing. You have pleaded a cause of action which involves your proving affirmatively that your client was assaulted and beaten, and was falsely imprisoned. In my judgment, that involves your showing that she did not consent, and was not actually free to leave by reasonable means, because on the facts of this case, those facts are essential to your claim.

Mr Noy: Yes, My Lord[1].

Hardwicke J: The next matter relates to the standard of proof in this case. Ordinarily of course, the standard would be the balance of probabilities. That is the well known test which was described as follows:

Miller v Minister of Pensions [1947] A All ER 372 (DC)

DENNING J said: 'The degree of cogency...required to discharge a burden in a civil case...is well settled. It must carry a reasonable degree of probability, but not so high as is required in a criminal case. If the evidence is such that the tribunal can say, "We think it more probable than not," the burden is discharged, but, if the probabilities are equal, it is not.'

Hardwicke J: But here, I have two problems. The first is that I am faced with an allegation that the defendant committed a serious criminal offence, an allegation which he denies, despite having been convicted. The second is that I am being asked, in effect, to decide the paternity of the plaintiff's child, which seems to me to raise issues which may require a higher standard than merely saying, 'I find it more

---

[1]For argument on the burden of proof of the correctness of Coke's criminal conviction, see 9.12 post.

probable than not'.

Mr Noy: My Lord, I would argue that the balance of probabilities is appropriate, despite the matters to which Your Lordship has referred. On the first problem of criminal conduct, a number of cases have held that even in this context, the civil standard continues to apply. For example, the Court of Appeal applied the civil standard to the following case, where the allegations were of fraudulent misrepresentation:

Hornal v **Neuberger Products Ltd.** [1957] 1 QB 247 (CA)

The plaintiff claimed damages for breach of warranty and fraud on the ground that the defendant had falsely stated that a machine sold by him to the plaintiff had been reconditioned. The defendants denied this. The judge held that he was satisfied on the balance of probability that the statement was made, but not beyond reasonable doubt.

DENNING LJ said: 'I must say that, if I was sitting as a judge alone, and I was satisfied that the statement was made, that would be enough for me, whether the claim was put in warranty or on fraud. I think it would bring the law into contempt if a judge were to say that on the issue of warranty he finds the statement was made, and that on the issue of fraud he finds it was not made.

HODSON LJ said: 'The comparative dearth of express authority on this topic is not surprising. No responsible counsel undertakes to prove a serious accusation without admitting that cogent evidence is required, and judges approach serious accusations in the same way without necessarily considering in every case whether or not there is a criminal issue involved. For example, in the ordinary case arising from a collision between two motor-cars involving charges of negligence, I have never heard of a judge applying the criminal standard of proof, on the ground that his judgment might involve the finding of one of the parties guilty of a criminal offence...

Notwithstanding the existence of some cases where the point appears to have been argued and decided in a contrary sense, I think the true view, and that most strongly supported by authority, is that which the judge took, namely, that in a civil case the balance of probability standard is correct.'

MORRIS LJ said: 'It is, I think, clear from the authorities that a difference of approach in civil cases has been recognised. Many judicial utterances show this. The phrase "balance of probabilities" is often employed as a convenient phrase to express the basis upon which civil issues are decided. It may well be that no clear-cut logical reconciliation can be formulated in regard to the authorities on these topics. But perhaps they illustrate that "the life of the law is not logic but experience". In some criminal cases liberty may be involved; in some it may not. In some civil cases the issues may involve questions of reputation which can transcend in importance even questions of personal liberty. Good name in man or woman is "the immediate jewel of their souls".

But in truth no real mischief results from an acceptance of the fact that there is some difference of approach in civil actions. Particularly is this so if the words which are used to define that approach are the servants but not the masters of meaning. Though no court and no jury would give less careful attention to issues lacking gravity than to those marked by it, the very elements of gravity become a part of the whole range of circumstances which have to be weighed in the scale when deciding as to the balance of probabilities. This view was denoted by Denning LJ when in his judgment in *Bater* v *Bater* [1951] P 35, 36, 37 he spoke of a "degree of probability which is commensurate with the occasion" and of "a degree of probability which is proportionate to the subject-matter".

In English law the citizen is regarded as being a free man of good repute. Issues may be raised in a civil action which affect character and reputation, and these will not be forgotten by judges and juries when considering the probabilities in regard to whatever misconduct is alleged. There will be reluctance to rob any man of his good name: there will also be reluctance to make any man pay what is not due or to make any man liable who is not or not liable who is. A court will not be deterred from a conclusion because of regret at its consequences: a court must arrive at such conclusion as is directed by the weight and preponderance of the evidence.'

Hardwicke J: But am I not to have any regard to the gravity of the offence which the plaintiff says the defendant committed?

Mr Noy: Certainly, Your Lordship would require cogent evidence before finding proved any serious allegation, and I shall hope to persuade Your Lordship of the cogency of the evidence in this case. But the question is not one of sliding scales, the standard varying with the gravity of the offence. May I refer Your Lordship to the following judgment:

Re Dellow's Will Trusts [1964] 1 WLR 451 (Ch D)

A husband and wife made mutual wills, the husband leaving all his estate to his wife, provided that she survived him, with other bequests if she did not, and the wife providing in similar terms for the husband with gifts over. On January 1, 1958, both spouses were found dead in their homes from coal gas poisoning. The trustees of the wills issued a summons asking, inter alia, whether the husband or the wife had died first or whether, if the evidence was not conclusive, the presumption in section 184 of the Law of Property Act 1925, was applicable and the husband, being the elder, should be presumed to have died first. If the latter proposition was correct, the summons asked for an inquiry as to whether the wife feloniously killed the husband. Thereupon the question arose as to the standard of proof required in civil matters to establish felonious killing...

UNGOED-THOMAS J stated the facts and continued: 'It seems to me that in civil cases it is not so much that a different standard of proof is required in different circumstances varying according to the gravity of the issue, but, as Morris LJ says in *Hornal v Neuberger Products Ltd.* [1957] 1 QB 247, 266 the gravity of the issue becomes part of the circumstances which the court has to take into consideration in deciding whether or not the burden of proof has been discharged. The more serious the allegation the more cogent is the evidence required to overcome the unlikelihood of what is alleged and thus to prove it. This is perhaps a somewhat academic distinction and the practical result is stated by Denning LJ: "The more serious the allegation the higher the degree of probability that is required: but it need not, in a civil case, reach the very high standard required by the criminal law". In this case the issue is whether or not the wife feloniously killed the husband. There can hardly be a graver issue than that, and its gravity weighs very heavily against establishing that such a killing took place, even for the purposes of deciding a civil issue.'
Order accordingly.

Hardwicke J: So I should assess the weight of the evidence in deciding whether I am satisfied that the scales have been tipped in your client's favour, but I need only be satisfied on the balance of probabilities, is that right?

Mr Noy: Yes, My Lord.

Hardwicke J: Very well. Mr Atkyn?

Mr Atkyn: My Lord, I agree with what my learned friend has said.

Hardwicke J: Mr Atkyn, I would like your help on the second question. Your case is that despite the act of sexual intercourse between Mr Coke and Miss Blackstone, Mr Coke is not the father of the child born to Miss Blackstone. Your evidence is that Mr Henneky is the father.

Mr Atkyn: Yes, my Lord.

Hardwicke J: Well, that seems to me to be a matter involving a quasi-matrimonial allegation, and one which may bear some stigma so far as Mr Henneky is concerned.

Of course, if Miss Blackstone is right, the same may apply to your client. How should I view the standard of proof on that point?

Mr Atkyn: My Lord in my submission, there is no reason to depart from the usual civil standard. Of course, Miss Blackstone's child is illegitimate, whichever view Your Lordship takes. But it may be helpful to look at what Parliament requires for proof of the issue of legitimacy or illegitimacy:

Family Law Reform Act 1969, s.26

> 26. Any presumption of law as to the legitimacy or illegitimacy of any person may in any civil proceedings be rebutted by evidence which shows that it is more probable than not that that person is illegitimate or legitimate, as the case may be, and it shall not be necessary to prove that fact beyond reasonable doubt in order to rebut the presumption.

Hardwicke J: Yes, I take your point that the issue in this case is hardly any more serious than those covered by that section. But am I not right in thinking that some authorities would have imposed a higher standard in matrimonial cases than in civil cases generally?

Mr Atkyn: My Lord, there are certainly some older cases which suggest that. For example, *Ginesi* v *Ginesi* [1948] P 179 related to a petition on the ground of adultery. The same standard had been applied to a case of cruelty in *Bater* v *Bater* [1951] P 35. But those were both well before the Divorce Reform Act 1969, and the subsequent view taken in such cases as *Wachtel* v *Wachtel* [1973] Fam 72 that the concept of the matrimonial offence had disappeared. Indeed, even earlier, the House of Lords had inclined to the normal civil standard when Lord Denning, in a passage from his speech in *Blyth* v *Blyth* [1966] AC 643 with which Lord Pearce concurred, espoused that view, at least in relation to the issue of condonation. The Court of Appeal has advocated the same standard as follows:

Bastable* v *Bastable and Sanders [1968] 1 WLR 1684 (CA)

> The husband petitioned for divorce on the ground of desertion and also adultery with S. The evidence of adultery was purely circumstantial. The judge granted the husband a decree on both grounds. The wife did not dispute the desertion, but she and S appealed against the finding of adultery.

> WILLMER LJ said: 'I confess that I have found the question raised by this appeal an exceedingly difficult one. It seems to me that much must depend upon what is the appropriate standard of proof to be expected in relation to a charge such as that made here. If I may say so with all possible respect, sitting in this court I do not find it altogether easy to follow the directions contained in various statements made by members of the House of Lords. There have been two cases in relatively recent years in which various members of the House of Lords expressed views with regard to the standard of proof required in matrimonial cases. One was *Preston-Jones* v *Preston-Jones* [1951] AC 391 and the other was *Blyth* v *Blyth* [1966] AC 643 in both of which various members of the House made statements which we can treat only with the utmost respect in relation to the standard of proof required. But it is fair to say that in both cases what they said was not strictly necessary for the decision of the matter in hand, but must be regarded as obiter. In *Preston-Jones* v *Preston-Jones* the question being debated was whether adultery was to be inferred from an unusual period of gestation, and their lordships were concerned with an argument that in such circumstances nothing short of proof with scientific certainty would satisfy the burden upon a petitioner. The House of Lords rejected that submission. But Lord MacDermott [1951] AC 417, in a passage in his speech which has often been cited, expressed the view that nothing short of

proof beyond a reasonable doubt would be sufficient to satisfy the burden of proof on a petitioner. With that expression of view Lord Simonds agreed, and so did Lord Morton of Henryton.

In *Blyth* v *Blyth* the question under consideration was not the standard of proof required in relation to a matrimonial offence, but what was the standard of proof in relation to condonation. Again the members of the House discussed in their speeches what they conceived to be the appropriate standard of proof in support of an allegation of a matrimonial offence. The dissenting minority, consisting of Lord Morris of Borth-y-Gest and Lord Morton of Henryton, adhered to the view which had been expressed in *Preston-Jones*, to which I have already referred. On the other hand, Lord Denning though that a considerably lower standard of proof could be adopted. He pointed out [1966] AC 667 et seq, that what had been said in *Preston-Jones* was obiter, and he for his part preferred the view which had been expressed in an Australian case of *Wright* v *Wright*, [1948] 77 CLR 191, as against that which had been decided by the Court of Appeal in this country in *Ginesi* v *Ginesi*, Lord Pearce took the same view as Lord Denning had taken. So far, therefore, the House of Lords in *Blyth* v *Blyth* was divided, two against two, on the question what is the appropriate standard of proof to be exacted in support of a charge of a matrimonial offence. The fifth member of the House, Lord Pearson, adopted what I can only describe as an intermediate position. Having quoted at some length from what Lord MacDermott said in *Preston-Jones* v *Preston-Jones*, Lord Pearson commented:

> "This language is consistent with the view that the word 'satisfied' does not, as a matter of interpretation, mean 'satisfied beyond reasonable doubt,' and that the requirement of proof beyond reasonable doubt may be limited to the grounds for dissolution and may not extend to the matters referred to in subparagraphs *(b)* and *(c)*."

which relate to matters of connivance, condonation, and so forth. In other words, as I read what Lord Pearson was saying, he would have been disposed to apply the standard of "satisfaction beyond reasonable doubt" where proof of a matrimonial offence is being considered, but would not apply that standard in relation to such matters as condonation, which was the subject-matter of the appeal to the House of Lords in that case. It will be seen, therefore, that for us who sit in this court it is not altogether easy to determine exactly what standard of proof should be applied in relation to proof of a matrimonial offence such as adultery.

When *Blyth* v *Blyth and Pugh* [1965] P 411 was before this court I ventured to say that I agreed with the view expressed by Denning LJ in *Bater* v *Bater* [1951] P 35 and adopted by this court in *Hornal* v *Neuberger Products Ltd.* [1957] 1 QB 247. In that oft-quoted passage Denning LJ said [1951] P 37: "The difference of opinion which has been evoked about the standard of proof in recent cases may well turn out to be more a matter of words than anything else. It is, of course, true that by our law a higher standard of proof is required in criminal cases than in civil cases. But this is subject to the qualification that there is no absolute standard in either case. In criminal cases the charge must be proved beyond reasonable doubt, but there may be degrees of proof within that standard. As Best CJ and many other great judges have said: 'in proportion as the crime is enormous, so ought the proof to be clear.' So also in civil cases, the case may be proved by a preponderance of probability, but there may be degrees of probability within that standard. The degree depends on the subject-matter. A civil court, when considering a charge of fraud, will naturally require for itself a higher degree of probability than that which it would require when asking if negligence is established. It does not adopt so high a degree as a criminal court, even when it is considering a charge of a criminal nature; but still it does require a degree of probability which is commensurate with the occasion. Likewise, a divorce court should require a degree of probability which is proportionate to the subject-matter."

Until the matter has been further considered by the House of Lords, and further guidance has been received, I propose to direct myself in accordance with that statement of principle.

In the present case, what is charged is "an offence." True, it is not a criminal offence; it is a matrimonial offence. It is for the husband petitioner to satisfy the court that the offence has been committed. Whatever the popular view may be, it remains true to say that in the eyes of the law the commission of adultery is a serious matrimonial offence. It follows, in my view, that a high standard of proof is required in order to satisfy the court that the offence has been committed.

EDMUND DAVIES LJ said: 'When one is thus contrasting the standard of proof in criminal charges on the one hand with that applicable to civil cases on the other, the distinction is certainly capable of being expressed in terms which a juryman can be expected to understand. But how he is to be instructed in the proper approach to his duty when he is trying civil cases of a matrimonial character is not very clear to me. "In proportion as the offence is grave, so ought the proof to be clear," observed Lord Denning in *Blyth* v *Blyth* [1966] AC 643, but with the utmost deference I take leave to doubt that such a distinction could effectively be made by a jury, or indeed by many judges and lawyers. I should have thought, with respect, that an offence is either proved or it is not proved, in accordance with the standard (civil or criminal) appropriate to the case under consideration.

Be that as it may, *Blyth's* case dealt solely with a matter of condonation, and in relation to that it decisively and authoritatively laid down that the petitioner need show, only on a balance of probability, that he did not connive or condone, as the case may be. Lord Denning's observations in relation to the standard of proof appropriate to the establishment of a matrimonial offence, on the other hand, must ex necessitatis be regarded as obiter. (WINN LJ agreed with WILLMER LJ)
Appeal allowed.

My Lord, it would seem inappropriate in a case of this kind to apply a higher standard now.

Hardwicke J: Yes, thank you.

B: THE BURDEN AND STANDARD OF PROOF IN CRIMINAL CASES

3.4 Introductory notes

3.4.1 In criminal cases, the legal burden of proving the guilt of the defendant rests upon the prosecution. This means that the prosecution must prove each element of the offence charged. The defendant need not prove his innocence, and indeed bears no legal burden of proving any issue in his defence. The essential elements of an offence are a matter of substantive criminal law, and will be reflected in the indictment or summons.

3.4.2 The above rule, although of general application, is subject to the following exceptions:

3.4.2.1 In certain cases, by statute, the legal burden of proving some particular issue is made to rest upon the defendant, for example proof of diminished responsibility under the Homicide Act 1957, s.2(2). In all respects other than that provided for by the statute in question, the burden lies upon the prosecution to prove the guilt of the defendant.

3.4.2.2 Where a statutory offence proscribes certain conduct subject to a proviso, exception, exemption, excuse or qualification, permitting such conduct by persons belonging to a class holding certain qualifications or licences, the burden of proving membership of the excepted class lies upon the defendant. In all other respects, the prosecution bear the burden of proving his guilt.

3.4.2.3 Where the defendant seeks a verdict of not guilty by reason of insanity, the burden of proving such insanity lies on him. The burden of proving guilt in other respects lies on the prosecution. The prosecution also bear the burden of proving insanity where they set out to do so in order to refute a defence of diminished responsibility tendered by the defence, a course open to the prosecution under the Criminal Procedure (Insanity) Act 1964, s.6.

3.4.3 The evidential burden of proof coincides with the legal burden at the outset of a criminal case, but as to any fact of which the prosecution adduce *prima facie* evidence, the defence may run the risk of failure if they call no evidence to the contrary. This in no way alters the incidence of the legal burden of proof.

3.4.4 Where the defence raise an issue which goes beyond a mere denial of the prosecution case, and approximates to an affirmative defence in a civil case, the legal burden is not borne by the defendant on such an issue (as would be the case in a civil suit) but the defendant must raise the issue by evidence, before it may be considered. This is generally thought of as an evidential burden. If such an issue is raised, the prosecution bear the legal burden of rebutting it because of their overall burden of proving guilt. Exampes of such issues are non-insane automatism, provocation, self-defence and duress.

3.4.5 The standard of proof required of the prosecution on the issue of guilt is a high one. It is normally formulated for the jury as proof 'beyond reasonable doubt' or 'satisfied so that you are sure of guilt'. But any form of words which adequately conveys the high degree required will suffice, and the judge may explain the standard in any appropriate words which he feels are likely to be understood by the jury he is directing. Words which fail to convey a sufficiently high standard will amount to a serious misdirection. The direction on the burden and standard of proof must come early in the summing-up and occupy a prominent part in it.

3.4.6 In the exceptional cases where the defence bear the legal burden of proof on an issue (*3.4.2.* ante) the standard required of them is only the civil standard, i.e. proof on the balance of probabilities. (*A Practical Approach to Evidence*, pp. 69-75, 76-78.)

3.5 Commentary

R v *Coke and Littleton* on appeal against conviction to the Court of Appeal, Criminal Division (Leach, East and Cox L JJ). Mr Atkyn for Coke and Mr Bacon for Littleton complain of the following passages in the summing-up of Holt J to the jury at the trial:

'Now, members of the jury, I have explained to you the meaning in law of these two charges, rape and indecent assault. You now know that each charge consists of a number of elements, and I will now tell you who must prove what elements and to what standard of proof. Let me deal first with the charge of rape against Coke. Once the prosecution prove the fact that sexual intercouse took place between Coke and Miss Blackstone on the relevant date, you are then faced with the problem of consent. The prosecution have had no trouble proving that sexual intercouse took place, because Coke does not dispute it. So there you have no difficulty. The difficulty focuses on consent. Coke says she consented. Miss Blackstone says she did not consent. How do you decide? Well, members of the jury, you may think it would be a matter of some difficulty for the prosecution to prove a negative. If Coke says she did consent, let him prove the affirmative to you. Consider whether he has succeeded in proving that consent to you on the whole of the evidence.'

'Littleton, members of the jury, has told you that he was not at Coke's flat at the time of the alleged assault on Angela Blackstone. He has raised what is sometimes termed an alibi. Of course, he is therefore doing more than just say, 'I didn't do it'; he is saying 'I wasn't there'. Now if he had confined himself to denying the assault ('I was there, but I didn't touch her') well, that would be one thing — you would have to ask yourselves, 'Have the prosecution proved their case?'. But where the defendant asserts a positive defence which goes beyond a mere denial, that is quite another thing, and it is then up to him to prove that fact before you need consider it.'

'But members of the jury, in both cases, you must bear in mind that these are criminal charges. The law says that you must not convict either man, unless you are fairly sure it is right to do so on the whole of the evidence. You must be satisfied, in other words be pretty certain of their guilt. Otherwise you should acquit.'

3.6 Argument

Mr Atkyn (having read the above passages to the court):   My Lords, the first point I make is with regard to the burden of proof on the charge of rape. The learned judge directed the jury, in effect, that the burden of disproving an essential element of the charge, namely lack of consent, lay upon the defendant.

Leach LJ: Of course, on the evidence adduced by the prosecution, your client lured this young girl to his flat and on his own admission had sexual intercourse with her. What were the jury to make of that?

Mr Atkyn: My Lord, the jury were entitled to draw inferences from the evidence, but they should have been directed that it was for the prosecution to prove every element of the offence of rape. Lack of consent is an essential element of that offence, even though it is expressed as a negative proposition. The situation is exactly that of the following leading case:

Woolmington v *DPP* [1935] AC 462 (HL)

The defendant was charged with the murder of his wife from whom he was separated. He gave evidence to the effect that whilst endeavouring to induce her to return to live with him by threatening to shoot himself, he had shot her and killed her accidentally. The jury were directed that, once it was proved that the defendant shot his wife, it was for him to prove the absence of malice, although malice was an essential element of the charge of murder. The defendant was convicted of murder and appealed unsuccessfully to the Court of Criminal Appeal. He further appealed to the House of Lords.

VISCOUNT SANKEY LC said: 'If at any period of a trial it was permissible for the judge to rule that the prosecution had established its case and that the onus was shifted on the prisoner to prove that he was not guilty and that unless he discharged that onus the prosecution was entitled to succeed, it would be enabling the judge in such a case to say that the jury must in law find the prisoner guilty and so make the judge decide the case and not the jury, which is not the common law. It would be an entirely different case from those exceptional instances of special verdicts where a judge asks the jury to find certain facts and directs them that on such facts the prosecution is entitled to succeed. Indeed, a consideration

of such special verdicts shows that it is not till the end of the evidence that a verdict can properly be found and that at the end of the evidence it is not for the prisoner to establish his innocence, but for the prosecution to establish his guilt. Just as there is evidence on behalf of the prosecution so there may be evidence on behalf of the prisoner which may cause a doubt as to his guilt. In either case, he is entitled to the benefit of the doubt. But while the prosecution must prove the guilt of the prisoner, there is no such burden laid on the prisoner to prove his innocence and it is sufficient for him to raise a doubt as to his guilt; he is not bound to satisfy the jury of his innocence...Throughout the web of the English Criminal Law one golden thread is always to be seen, that it is the duty of the prosecution to prove the prisoner's guilt subject to what I have already said as to the defence of insanity and subject also to any statutory exception. If, at the end of and on the whole of the case, there is a reasonable doubt, created by the evidence given by either the prosecution or the prisoner, as to whether the prisoner killed the deceased with a malicious intention, the prosecution has not made out the case and the prisoner is entitled to an acquittal. No matter what the charge or where the trial, the principle that the prosecution must prove the guilt of the prisoner is part of the common law of England and no attempt to whittle it down can be entertained. When dealing with a murder case the Crown must prove (*a*) death as the result of a voluntary act of the accused and (*b*) malice of the accused. It may prove malice either expressly or by implication. For malice may be implied where death occurs as the result of a voluntary act of the accused which is (i) intentional and (ii) unprovoked. When evidence of death and malice has been given (this is a question for the jury) the accused is entitled to show, by evidence or by examination of the circumstances adduced by the Crown that the act on his part which caused death was either unintentional or provoked. If the jury are either satisfied with his explanation or, upon a review of all the evidence, are left in reasonable doubt whether, even if his explanation be not accepted, the act was unintentional or provoked, the prisoner is entitled to be acquitted. It is not the law of England to say, as was said in the summing-up in the present case: "if the Crown satisfy you that this woman died at the prisoner's hands then he has to show that there are circumstances to be found in the evidence which has been given from the witness-box in this case which alleviate the crime so that it is only manslaughter or which excuse the homicide altogether by showing it was a pure accident.'
(LORDS ATKIN, HEWART, TOMLIN and WRIGHT concurred)
Appeal allowed.

East LJ: You would not say that there is no case in which a defendant may be called upon to prove some part of his defence?

Mr Atkyn: No, My Lord. There are of course some instances in which Parliament expressly lays that burden upon a defendant. For example, diminished responsibility is provided for as follows:

Homicide Act 1957, s.2(2)

2(2) On a charge of murder, it shall be for the defence to prove that the person charged is by virtue of this section not liable to be convicted of murder.

Cox LJ: Then of course, there is the class of cases where the offence consists of conduct which may be indulged in by certain persons, if not by the public at large.

Mr Atkyn: My Lord, yes. Of course, in the cases tried before magistrates' courts, the position there is governed as follows:

Magistrates' Courts Act 1980 s.101

101. Where the defendant to an information or complaint relies for his defence on any exception, exemption, proviso, excuse or qualification, whether or not it accompanies the description of the offence or matter of complaint in the enactment creating the offence or on which the complaint is founded, the burden of proving the exception, exemption, proviso,

excuse or qualification shall be on him; and this notwithstanding that the information or complaint contains an allegation negativing the exception, exemption, proviso, excuse or qualification.

My Lords, in due course, the position was accorded recognition at common law for cases on indictment by the decision of this court as follows:

R v *Edwards* [1975] QB 27 (CA)

The defendant was convicted of selling intoxicating liquor without a justices' licence contrary to section 160 (1) (*a*) of the Licensing Act 1964. He was unrepresented at the trial and did not give evidence, but made an unsworn statement denying the occupation of the premises. He appealed against conviction on the ground that, since the prosecution had access to the register of licences under section 34(2) of the Act, the prosecution should have called evidence to prove that there was no justices' licence in force.

LAWTON LJ, reading the judgment of the court, related the facts and the terms of s.81 of the Magistrates' Courts Act 1952 [the precursor of s.101 of the 1980 Act], and continued: 'Mr Leonard, on behalf of the prosecution, submitted that section 81 is a statutory statement of a common law rule applicable in all criminal courts. If it were not, the law would be in an unsatisfactory state, because the burden of proof in summary trials would be different from that in trials on indictment.

Mr Underhill, for the defendant, submitted, however, that at common law the burden of proving an exception, exemption, proviso, excuse or qualification only shifts when the facts constituting it are peculiarly within the accused's own knowledge and that they were not in this case because section 30 (1) of the Licensing Act 1964 requires the clerk to the licensing justices for a licensing district to keep a register of licences, containing particulars of all justices' licences granted in the district, the premises for which they were granted, the names of the owners of those premises, and the names of the holders of the licences. It follows, submitted Mr Underhill, that the Brixton police had available to them in their own area a public source of knowledge which they could go to at any reasonable time: see section 34 (2). If the rule about shifting the onus of proof only applies when the facts initiating the operation of the exception are peculiarly in the accused's own knowledge, there is much to be said for Mr Underhill's submission.

Mr Underhill accepted that there are three exceptions to the fundamental rule of our criminal law that the prosecution must prove every element of the alleged offence. The first relates to insanity and the second to those cases in which a statute expressly imposes a burden of proof upon an accused. The third exception has been under consideration in this appeal and questions have arisen as to its nature and the circumstances in which it applies.

The phrase which Mr Underhill used in making his submission, namely, "facts peculiarly within the accused's own knowledge" has been used many times in textbooks and judgments: for example, *per* Lord Goddard CJ in *John* v *Humphreys* [1955] 1 WLR 325, 327; *Phipson on Evidence*, 11th ed (1970), p 108 and *Cross, Evidence*, 3rd ed (1967), p 81. It has been taken from the judgment of Bayley J in *R* v *Turner* (1816) 5 M & S 206, 211. If the rule only applies when the facts constituting exculpation are peculiarly within the defendant's own knowledge, we would have expected to have found reported cases giving some help as to how the courts were to decide this. If a query arises, should the judge or the jury decide who had what knowledge? Should evidence be called on this issue? If not, why not? In the century and a half since 1816 the defendant is unlikely to have been the first defendant wishing to query the extent of the prosecution's knowledge. Counsel brought no such cases to our attention and we have found none for ourselves.

Since 1816 there are number of cases in the reports illustrating the shifting of the onus of proof on to the defendant to prove either that he held a licence to do an act which was otherwise prohibited by a statute or that he was exempted in some way. Thus in *R* v *Scott* [1921] 86 JP 69 the question arose whether the prosecution should have proved, which they did not, that the defendant, who was charged with an offence under the Dangerous Drugs Act 1920, was not authorised to supply specified drugs. That Act provided that no person should supply any of the specified drugs unless he was licensed by the Secretary of State to do so. Swift J held that if the defendant was licensed, it was a fact which was peculiarly within his own knowledge and there was no hardship on him in being put to the proof. We can see no difference between that case (which was approved by the Court of Criminal Appeal in *R* v *Oliver* [1944] KB 68 and cited by Lord Pearson with approval in *Nimmo* v *Alexander Cowan & Sons Ltd.* [1968] AC 107) and this. There would have been no difficulty whatsoever in calling someone on the Secretary of State's staff to say that the defendant had not been licensed to supply the drugs.

The statutory prohibition of acts otherwise than under licence granted by a government department was a commonplace of life during the war years 1939 to 1945 and for some time afterwards. The problem as to who was to prove lack of a licence was considered fully in *R* v *Oliver* [1944] KB 68, 69–70. The appellant had been convicted on an indictment charging him with supplying sugar otherwise than under the terms of a licence, permit or other authority granted by the Ministry of Food, contrary to regulation 55 of the Defence (General) Regulations 1939 and article 2 of the Sugar Control Order 1940. The prosecution did not prove that he had not been granted a licence and he appealed on that ground. Mr Slade, for the appellant, submitted that the rule shifting the onus to the defendant to prove he came within an exception did not apply "as the information could easily have been obtained by the prosecution from official sources": see p 69. The Solicitor-General, who appeared for the prosecution, put his case in these terms, at p 70:

If a statute lays down that an act is prohibited except in the case of persons who are excepted, the onus is on the defendant to prove that he is within the excepted class.

The Court of Criminal Appeal accepted this submission; and in his judgment Viscount Caldecote CJ dealt with two points which Mr Slade had put forward in support of his main submission. Both had been canvassed in the 18th century and had echoed through the courts in the 19th; first, that although there was no need for the prosecution to prove that a proviso in a statute did not apply, this was not so with an exception; and secondly, the prosecution should have given prima facie evidence of the non-existence of a licence. As we have sought to show in this judgment, the old distinction between provisos and exceptions had been moribund, if not dead, for well over a century, although some life had been injected into it by Lord Alverstone CJ in *R* v *James* [1902] 1 KB 540, 545. As to this, Viscount Caldecote CJ said in *R* v *Oliver* [1944] KB 68, 73:

With the greatest respect to the judgment of Lord Alverstone in *R* v *James,* it seems to us to be very difficult to make the result depend on the question whether the negative is of a proviso or of an exception. We think it makes no difference at all that the order was drafted as it now appears instead of being in a form which absolutely prohibits the supply of sugar except as thereinafter provided, with a later clause providing that if a person is supplied under a licence he should be excused."

As to the second point Viscount Caldecote CJ said plainly that the prosecution were under no necessity of giving prima facie evidence of the non-existence of a licence. As this point had been raised we infer that the court did not consider that the availability of evidence to the prosecution was a relevant factor in shifting the burden of proof.

R v *Oliver* was cited to the House of Lords in *Nimmo* v *Alexander Cowan & Sons Ltd.* [1968] AC 107, which was concerned with the onus of pleading and proving in cases under section 29 (1) of the Factories Act 1961 that it was not reasonably practicable to make and keep working places safe. Where the onus lay would, of course, be the same in both civil and criminal cases brough under that Act, although the standard of proof would be higher in criminal cases that in civil. None of their Lordships criticised *R* v *Oliver;* Lord Pearson clearly approved it. Not everyone has done so; for an example, see *Glanville Williams, Criminal Law,* 2nd ed [1961], pp 901–904. In *R* v *Putland and Sorrell* [1946] 1 All ER 85 some judicial doubt was expressed as to how far *R* v *Oliver* went. The appellants were charged with having conspired to acquire, and having acquired, rationed goods, namely, silk stockings, without surrendering the appropriate number of coupons, in contravention of the Consumer Rationing Order 1944. No evidence was called by the prosecution to prove that coupons had not been surrendered. *R* v *Oliver* was cited, but Humphreys J, who delivered the judgment of the court, distinguished that case by stating that there was a very broad distinction between a statutory prohibition against doing an act, in which case it was for the defendant to prove that he might do it lawfully, and a statutory prohibition against doing an act otherwise than in a particular way, as for example by surrendering coupons, in which case it was for the prosecution to give prima facie evidence that the specified lawful way had not been followed. We have been unable to appreciate the difference between the two types of case. The court had clearly been impressed, as had Lord Kenyon CJ, 150 years before in *R* v *Stone*, 1 East 639, by the argument that the shifting of the onus of proof could be oppressive; but under the Defence (General) Regulations the only difference between a wholesaler of sugar called upon to justify his trade in that commodity and a man wearing a new shirt (one of the examples given by Humphreys J) called upon to prove that he had acquired it lawfully might be that one could do so more easily than the other. We find this difference not substantial enough to justify distinguishing *R* v *Oliver*.

In *John* v *Humphreys* [1955] 1 WLR 325 the Divisional Court had to consider the problem of the onus of proof in a case of a defendant who had been charged with driving a motor vehicle on a road without being the holder of a licence. He did not appear at the hearing before the justices and no evidence was called other than to prove that he had driven a motor vehicle along a road. The justices were of the opinion that mere proof of driving (that not being in itself an unlawful act) was not enough to support the charge and that before the burden of proving that he was the holder of a licence passed to the defendant the prosecution should have established a prima facie case. They dismissed the information. The prosecutor appealed. Before the justices he had argued that the burden of proving the holding of a licence lay on the defendant since it was a fact peculiarly within his knowledge; as indeed it was. It would have been impracticable for the prosecution to have proved that no licensing authority had issued a licence. It follows that this case is of little help on the question whether *R* v *Turner*, 5 M & S 206 applies when the prosecution can prove a defendant's lack of qualification or lawful excuse. The court decided that there was no need for the prosecution to establish a prima facie case. Ormerod J expressed some hesitation on his point but concluded that the court was bound by the decision in *R* v *Oliver*.

In our judgment this line of authority establishes that over the centuries the common law, as a result of experience and the need to ensure that justice is done both to the community and to defendants, has evolved an exception to the fundamental rule of our criminal law that the prosecution must prove every element of the offence charged. This exception, like so much else in the common law, was hammered out on the anvil of pleading. It is limited to offences arising under enactments which prohibit the doing of an act save in specified circumstances or by persons of specified classes or with specified qualifications or with the licence or permission of specified authorities. Whenever the prosecution seeks to rely on this exception, the court must construe the enactment under which the charge is laid. If the true construction is that the enactment prohibits the doing of acts, subject to provisos, exemptions and the like, then the prosecution can rely upon the exception.

In our judgment its application does not depend upon either the fact, or the presumption, that the defendant has peculiar knowledge enabling him to prove the positive of any negative averment. As Wigmore pointed out in his great *Treatise on Evidence* [1905], vol 4 p 3525, this concept of peculiar knowledge furnishes no working rule. If it did, defendants would have to prove lack of intent. What does provide a working rule is what the common law evolved from a rule of pleading. We have striven to identify it in this judgment. Like nearly all rules it could be applied oppressively; but the courts have ample powers to curb and discourage oppressive prosecutors and do not hesitate to use them.

Two consequences follow from the view we have taken as to the evolution and nature of this exception. First, as it comes into operation upon an enactment being construed in a particular way, there is no need for the prosecution to prove a prima facie case of lack of excuse, qualification or the like; and secondly, what shifts is the onus: it is for the defendant to prove that he was entitled to do the prohibited act. What rests on him is the legal or, as it is sometimes called, the persuasive burden of proof. It is not the evidential burden.

When the exception as we have adjudged it to be is applied to this case it was for the defendant to prove that he was the holder of a justices' licence, not the prosecution. Appeal dismissed.

And, My Lords, to complete the picture, one has to take account of the defence of insanity, as follows:

Daniel M'Naghten's Case (1843) 10 Cl & F 200

The defendant, intending to murder Sir Robert Peel, killed the statesman's secretary by mistake. He was acquitted of murder on the ground of insanity. The verdict was made the subject of debate in the House of Lords and it was determined to take the opinion of all the judges on the law governing such cases. The judges attended and five questions were put to them:

TINDAL CJ said: 'Your Lordships are pleased to inquire of us, secondly:

What are the proper questions to be submitted to the jury when a person alleged to be afflicted with insane delusion respecting one or more particular subjects or persons is charged with the commission of a crime (murder, for example), and insanity is set up as a defence?

And, thirdly:

In what terms ought the question to be left to the jury as to the prisoner's state of mind at the time when the act was committed?

As these two questions appear to us to be more conveniently answered together we have to submit our opinion to be that the jurors ought to be told in all cases that every man is to be presumed to be sane and to possess a sufficient degree of reason to be responsible for his crimes until the contrary be proved to their satisfaction, and that to establish a defence on the ground of insanity it must be clearly proved that, at the time of committing of the act the party accused was labouring under such a defect of reason, from disease of the mind, as not to know the nature and quality of the act he was doing, or, if he did know it, that he did not know he was doing what was wrong.'

Leach LJ: Mr Atkyn, none of those exceptional cases appear to apply to this case.
Mr Atkyn: My Lord, that is right. And in those circumstances, I respectfully submit that the learned judge misdirected the jury with regard to the burden of proof. It was for the prosecution to prove that there was no consent. The rule in *Woolmington* v *DPP* applies, as it does in most criminal cases, to its full extent.
Leach LJ: Mr Bacon, you also have a point on the burden of proof? What concerns me in Littleton's case is whether the learned judge may not have been correct in directing the jury that Littleton bore some burden of adducing evidence to raise the issue of his alibi, without of course in any way affecting the prosecution's overall burden.
Mr Bacon: My Lord, I respectfully adopt what Mr Atkyn has said about the burden of proving guilt. In my submission, an alibi does not go beyond a denial of the case for the prosecution, and is not a positive defence raising new issues. Only where the defence goes beyond a mere denial, must they adduce evidence to lay a foundation for the new matter.
East LJ: What amounts to 'going beyond a denial' for this purpose?
Mr Bacon: My Lord, anything which amounts to a positive assertion by the defence of matters not raised as part of the prosecution case. As an example, where the defendant raises self-defence he must do so by some evidence which serves to lay the issue before the jury. May I refer Your Lordships to the following two cases in which self-defence and automatism were raised.

R v Lobell [1957] QB 547 (CCA)

The appellant was convicted of wounding with intent to do grievous bodily harm. At the trial the sole defence was that in inflicting the wound the appellant was acting in self-defence. The trial judge directed the jury that it was for the defence to establish that plea to the jury's satisfaction.

LORD GODDARD CJ, reading the judgment of the court, said: It must, however, be understood that maintaining the rule that the onus always remains on the prosecution does not mean that the Crown must give evidence-in-chief to rebut a suggestion of self-defence before that issue is raised, or indeed need give any evidence on the subject at all. If an issue relating to self-defence is to be left to the jury there must be some evidence from which a jury would be entitled to find that issue in favour of the accused, and ordinarily no doubt such evidence would be given by the defence. But there is a difference between leading evidence which would enable a jury to find an issue in favour of a defendant and in putting the onus upon him. the truth is that the jury must come to a verdict on the whole of the evidence that has been laid before them. If on a consideration of all the evidence the jury are left in doubt whether the killing or wounding may not have been in self-defence the proper verdict would be not guilty. A convenient way of directing the jury is to tell them that the burden of establishing guilt is on the prosecution, but that they must also consider the evidence for the defence which may have one of three results: it may convince them of the innocence of the accused, or it may cause them to doubt, in which case the defendant is entitled to an acquittal, or it may and sometimes does strengthen the case for the prosecution. It is perhaps a fine distinction to say that before a jury can find a particular issue in favour of an accused person he must give some evidence on which it can be found but none the less the onus remains on the prosecution; what it really amounts to is that if in the result the jury are left in doubt where the truth lies the verdict should be not guilty, and this is as true of an issue as to self-defence as it is to one of provocation, though of course the latter plea goes only to a mitigation of the offence.
Appeal allowed.

Hill v Baxter [1958] 1 QB 277 (DC)

The defendant drove a van across a road junction at a fast speed, ignoring a 'Halt' sign. At his trial for dangerous driving, he gave evidence that he had become unconscious as a result of a sudden illness. No evidence of this was produced. The magistrates acquitted him and the prosecutor appealed to the Divisional Court.

LORD GODDARD CJ said: 'The justices' finding that the respondent was not capable of forming any intention as to the manner of driving is really immaterial. What they evidently mean is that the respondent was in a state of automation. But he was driving and, as the case finds, exercising some skill, and undoubtedly the onus of proving that he was in a state of automation must be on him. This is not only akin to a defence of insanity, but it is a rule of the law of evidence that the onus of proving a fact which must be exclusively within the knowledge of a party lies on him who asserts it. This, no doubt, is subject to the qualification that where an onus is on the defendant in a criminal case the burden is not as high as it is on a prosecutor.'

DEVLIN J said: 'I am satisfied that even in a case in which liability depended upon full proof of mens rea, it would not be open to the defence to rely upon automatism without providing some evidence of it. If it amounted to insanity in the legal sense, it is well established that the burden of proof would start with and remain throughout upon the defence. But there is also recognised in the criminal law a lighter burden which the accused discharges by producing some evidence, but which does not relieve the prosecution from having to prove in the end all the facts necessary to establish guilt. This principle has manifested itself in different forms; most of them relate to the accused's state of mind and put it upon him to give some evidence about it. Thus the fact that an accused is found in possession of property recently stolen does not of itself prove that he knew of the stealing.

Nevertheless, it is not open to the accused at the end of the prosecution's case to submit that he has no case to answer; he must offer some explanation to account for his possession though he does not have to prove that the explanation is true: *R v Aves* [1950] 2 All ER 330. In a charge of murder it is for the prosecution to prove that the killing was intentional and unprovoked, and that burden is never shifted: *Woolmington v Director of Public Prosecutions* [1935] AC 462. But though the prosecution must in the end prove lack of provocation, the obligation arises only if there is some evidence of provocation fit to go to the jury: *Holmes v Director of Public Prosecution* [1946] AC 588. The same rule applies in the case of self-defence: *Reg. v Lobell* [1957] 1 QB 547. In any crime involving mens rea the prosecution must prove guilty intent, but if the defence suggests drunkenness as negativing intent, they must offer evidence of it, if, indeed, they do not have to prove it: *Director of Public Prosecutions v Beards* [1920] AC 479, 507. It would be quite unreasonable to allow the defence to submit at the end of the prosecution's case that the Crown had not proved affirmatively and beyond a reasonable doubt that the accused was at the time of the crime sober, or not sleepwalking or not in a trance or black out. I am satisfied that such matters ought not to be considered at all until the defence has produced at least prima facie evidence. I should wish to reserve for future consideration when necessary the question of where the burden ultimately lies.

As automatism is akin to insanity in law there would be great practical advantage if the burden of proof was the same in both cases. But so far insanity is the only matter of defence in which under the common law the burden of proof has been held to be completely shifted.

In my judgment there is not to be found in the case stated evidence of automatism of a character which would be fit to leave to a jury.

(PEARSON J agreed with DEVLIN J)

Appeal allowed.

Cox LJ: The same would be true, would it not, of provocation or duress?

Mr Bacon: Yes, My Lord. In the present case, however, no such question arises. The defendant's presence at the scene is clearly a necessary part of the prosecution case, and he has done no more than deny it. In any event, My Lords, the learned judge misdirected the jury, in that his words can only have been taken as referring to the legal burden of proof. The authorities agree that the defence need do no more than lay a foundation of evidence, which can mean no more than an evidential burden. The point was made in the House of Lords as follows:

Bratty v Attorney-General for Northern Ireland [1963] AC 386 (HL)

The appellant was convicted of the murder by strangulation of an 18-year-old girl. Two of his defences were insanity and automatism. He appealed to the Court of Criminal Appeal in Northern Ireland and the House of Lords against the trial judge's refusal to put the defence of automatism to the jury. Their Lordships dismissed the appeal, but during the course of their speeches uttered certain dicta on the question of the burden of proof in such cases.

LORD MORRIS OF BORTH-Y-GEST said: 'The "golden" rule of the English criminal law that it is the duty of the prosecution to prove an accused person's guilt (subject to any statutory exception and subject to the special position which arises where it is given in evidence that an accused person is insane), does not involve that the prosecution must speculate as to and specifically anticipate every conceivable explanation that an accused person might offer. The evidence of the commission of certain acts may suffice to prove that they were intentional. In a charge of murder, malice may by implication be proved where death occurs as the result of a voluntary act of the accused which is (i) intentional and (ii) unprovoked. When evidence of death and malice has been given an accused person may, however, either by adducing evidence or by examining the circumstances adduced by the Crown, show that his actions were either unintentional or provoked. In such a situation the continuing and constant obligation of the prosecution to satisfy the jury beyond any reasonable doubt is in no way abated (see *Woolmington* v *DPP* [1935] AC 462). In the conceivably possible case that I have postulated (of a violent act committed by a sleep-walker) it would not necessarily be the duty of the prosecution in leading their evidence as to the commission of the act specifically to direct such evidence to negativing the possibility of the act having been committed while sleep-walking. If, however, during the trial the suggested explanation of the act was advanced and if such explanation was so supported that it had sufficient substance to merit consideration by the jury, then the onus which is upon the prosecution would not be discharged unless the jury, having considered the explanation, were sure that guilt in regard to the particular crime charged was established so that they were left in no reasonable doubt. The position would be analogous to that which arises where a defence of self-defence is raised. Though the onus is upon the prosecution to negative that defence, the obligation to do so only arises effectively when there is a suggestion of such defence (see *R* v *Lobell* [1957] 1 QB 547).

Before an explanation of any conduct is worthy of consideration such explanation must be warranted by the established facts or be supported by some evidence that has been given by some witness. Though questions as to whether evidence should or should not be accepted or as to the weight to be attached to it are for the determination of the jury, it is a province of the judge to rule whether a theory or a submission has the support of evidence so that it can properly be passed to the jury for their consideration. As human behaviour may manifest itself in infinite varieties of circumstances it is perilous to generalise, but it is not every facile mouthing of some easy phrase of excuse that can amount to an explanation. It is for a judge to decide whether there is evidence fit to be left to a jury which could be the basis for some suggested verdict.'

The present case is on all fours with *R* v *Johnson*.

R v *Johnson* [1961] 1 WLR 1478 (CCA)

The appellant was convicted of robbery with violence. At his trial he denied taking part in the robbery and put forward an alibi, calling witnesses to support it. The trial judge, in summing up, indicated that the appellant had assumed the burden of proof when he put forward his defence of alibi.

ASHWORTH J, delivering the judgment of the court, stated the facts and continued: 'The main ground of appeal is based on an alleged misdirection by the judge in regard to the answer which the appellant put forward in the shape of the alibi. As Mr Skellhorn submits, an alibi is commonly called a defence, but it is to be distinguished from some of the statutory defences, such as the defence of diminished responsibility under the Homicide Act, 1957, where Parliament has specifically provided for a defence, and has further indicated that the burden of establishing such a defence rests on the accused. It may be that the true view of an alibi is the same as that of self-defence or provocation. It is the answer which a defendant puts forward, and the burden of proof, in the sense of establishing the guilt of the defendant, rests throughout on the prosecution. If a man puts forward an answer in the shape of an alibi or in the shape of self-defence, he does not in law thereby assume any burden of proving that answer. So much, in the opinion of the court, is plain on the authorities.'
Appeal allowed.

My Lord, there was no such exceptional case here as to lay any legal burden on the defendent, and the direction should have been clear on that point.

Leach LJ: Yes, very well. Now, I believe both of you wish to present arguments on the question of the learned judge's treatment of the standard of proof. Mr Atkyn?

Mr Atkyn: My Lords, yes. In my submission, the words used by the learned judge did not adequately convey the high standard of proof required of the prosecution in a criminal case. Indeed, My Lords, the words employed in the summing up have been expressly disapproved in this court and the Court of Criminal Appeal before it. In the following case, where the Court of Appeal examined the matter in some depth, the word 'satisfied' was held to be insufficient.

R v Hepworth and Fearnley [1955] 2 QB 600 (CCA)

LORD GODDARD CJ, delivering the judgment of the court said: 'The appellants were convicted before the recorder of Bradford of the offence of receiving wool, an offence which is by no means uncommon in Yorkshire. I have no doubt that for the most part, at any rate, juries drawn from the citizens of Bradford know perfectly well what their duty is in trying offences of that description. They have to find and feel sure that the goods have been stolen, that they have got into the possession of the accused persons and that the accused knew that they were stolen.

Another thing that is said in the present case is that recorder only used the word "satisfied." It may be, especially considering the number of cases recently in which this question has arisen, that I misled courts because I said in R v Summers (1952) 36 Cr App R 14, 15 — and I still adhere to it — that I thought that it was very unfortunate to talk to juries about "reasonable doubt" because the explanations given as to what is and what is not a reasonable doubt are so very often extraordinarily difficult to follow and it is very difficult to tell a jury what is a reasonable doubt. To tell a jury that it must not be a fanciful doubt is something that is without any real guidance. To tell them that a reasonable doubt is such a doubt as to cause them to hesitate in their own affairs never seems to me to convey any particular standard; one member of the jury might say he would hesitate over something and another member might say he would hesitate over something and another member might say that that would not cause him to hesitate at all. I therefore suggested that it would be better to use some other expression, by which I meant to convey to the jury that they should only convict if they felt sure of the guilt of the accused. It may be that in some cases the word "satisfied" is enough. Then, it is said that the jury in a civil case has to be satisfied and, therefore, one is only laying down the same standard of proof as in a civil case. I confess that I have had some difficulty in understanding how there is or there can be two standards; therefore, one would be on safe ground if one said in a criminal case to a jury: "You must be satisfied beyond reasonable doubt" and one could also say: "You, the jury, must be completely satisfied," or better still: "You must feel sure of the prisoner's guilt." But I desire to repeat what I said in R v Kritz [1950] 1 KB 82, 89. It is not the particular formula that matters: it is the effect of the summing up. If the jury are made to understand that they have to be satisfied and must not return a verdict against a defendant unless they feel sure, and that the onus is all the time on the prosecution and not on the defence," that is enough. I should be very sorry if it were thought that these cases should depend on the use of a particular formula or particular word or words. The point is that they jury should be directed first, that the onus is always on the prosecution; secondly, that before they convict they must feel sure of the accused's guilt. If that is done, that will be enough.'
Appeal allowed.

The same criticism of 'reasonably sure' was made in R v Head and Warrener (1961) 45 Cr App R 225 (CCA).

East LJ: Are you submitting that the judge must employ a certain formula in order to direct the jury on this point, and if so, what is it?

Mr Atkyn: My Lord, the judge need not employ a formula, but his words must convey the high degree of proof required. I have cited to Your Lordships the view expressed by Lord Goddard CJ in R v Hepworth and Fearnley that 'satisfied beyond reasonable doubt' or 'sure of guilt' would be enough. Both are very much stronger than the words used by the learned judge in this case.

Cox LJ: Those phrases could aptly be termed 'formulae'.

Mr Atkyn: My Lord, they could. But other phrases having the same effect have been upheld, and appellate courts have stressed the effect of the words taken in the context of the summing up as a whole, rather than insisting on some invariable form of words. Indeed, the Judicial Committee of the Privy Council indicated in the next case that the precise words should vary from jury to jury, according to the judge's view of their individual characteristics.

Walters v *R* [1969] 2 AC 26 (PC)

The petitioner was charged with murder. In the course of his summing up the trial judge sought to explain the phrase 'a reasonable doubt' as follows: 'Sometimes it is put this way, that a reasonable doubt is that quality and mind of doubt which, when you are dealing with matters of importance in your own affairs, you allow to influence you one way or the other.' The Court of Appeal of Jamaica confirmed the conviction and refused the petitioner leave to appeal against his conviction for murder. The petitioner applied to the Privy Council for special leave to appeal.

LORD DIPLOCK delivering the judgment of the court, said: 'By the time he sums up the judge at the trial has had an opportunity of observing the jurors. In their Lordships' view it is best left to his discretion to choose the most appropriate set of words in which to make *that* jury understand that they must not return a verdict against a defendant unless they are sure of his guilt; and if the judge feels that any of them, through unfamiliarity with court procedure, are in danger of thinking that they are engaged in some task more esoteric than applying to the evidence adduced at the trial the common sense with which they approach matters of importance to them in their ordinary lives, then the use of such analogies as that used by Small J in the present case, whether in the words in which he expressed it or in those used in any of the other cases to which reference has been made, may be helpful and is in their Lordships' view unexceptionable. Their Lordships would deprecate any attempt to lay down some precise formula or to draw fine distinctions between one set of words and another. It is the effect of the summing up as a whole that matters.'
Petition dismissed.

And in *Ferguson* v *R* the Privy Council upheld a combination of Lord Goddard's phrases.

Ferguson v *R* [1979] 1 WLR 94 (PC)

The defendant was charged with murder. The trial judge directed: '...it is required to satisfy you beyond reasonable doubt that from the evidence before you...the defendant is guilty of murder...If you entertain the kind of doubt, which might affect the mind of a person in the conduct of important affairs, then you entertain a reasonable doubt...' The defendant was convicted of murder and appealed on the ground, inter alia, that the judge misdirected the jury as to the intent necessary to establish the crime of murder.

LORD SCARMAN, delivering the judgment of their Lordships, said: It is submitted that the judge encouraged "too subjective" an approach by telling the jury that the doubt must be such as "might affect the mind of a person in the conduct of important affairs."
    Their Lordships were told and accepted that in certain Commonwealth jurisdictions some judges avoid this forumulation. It is criticised as being unhelpful and possibly dangerous, in that questions arising in the conduct of important affairs often have little resemblance to the issues in a criminal trial and individual jurors may well decide such questions by applying standards lower than satisfaction beyond reasonable doubt and analogous, if to anything, to the civil standard of the balance of probabilities. In *Walters* v *The Queen* [1969] 2 AC 26 their Lordships had to consider a direction almost identical in part with that in this case. Delivering the judgment in that case (which was not an appeal, but an application for special leave to appeal) Lord Diplock pointed out that a distinction between "objective" and "subjective" tests is not apt in this context. The Board expressed the view in that case that the formula used in summing up does not matter so long as it is made clear to the jury, whatever words are used, that they must not return a verdict against a defendant unless they are sure of

his guilt. Their Lordships' Board agree with these comments with one reservation. Though the law requires no particular formula, judges are wise, as a general rule, to adopt one.

The time-honoured formula is that the jury must be satisfied beyond reasonable doubt. As Dixon CJ said in *Dawson v The Queen* (1961) 106 CLR 1, 18, attempts to substitute other expressions have never prospered. It is generally sufficient and safe to direct a jury that they must be satisfied beyond reasonable doubt so that they feel sure of the defendant's guilt. Nevertheless, other words will suffice, so long as the message is clear.

Appeal dismissed.

Leach LJ: Of course, Lord Goddard CJ had himself some doubt on the phrase 'beyond reasonable doubt' in *R* v *Summers.*

R v *Summers* (1952) 36 Cr App R 14 (CCA)

LORD GODDARD CJ referred to the facts and the use of the phrase 'reasonable doubt' in the summing-up, and continued: 'I have never yet heard a court give a satisfactory definition of what is a reasonable doubt, and it would be very much better if summings-up did not use that expression, for it seems to me that, whenever a court attempts to explain what is meant by a reasonable doubt, it gives a definition or tries to explain the term in a way which is often likely to cause more confusion than clarity. It is far better, instead of using the words "reasonable doubt" and then trying to explain what is a reasonable doubt, to direct a jury: "You must not convict unless you are satisfied by the evidence that the offence has been committed." The jury should be told that it not for the prisoner to prove his innocence, but for the prosecution to prove his guilt. If a jury is told that it is their duty to regard the evidence and see that it satisfies them so that they can feel sure when they return a verdict of Guilty, that is much better than using the expression "reasonable doubt" and I hope in future that that will be done. I never use the expression when summing-up. I always tell a jury that, before they convict, they must feel sure and must be satisfied that the prosecution have established the guilt of the prisoner.'

Mr Atkyn: Yes, my Lord. It seems that what Lord Goddard may have had in mind was the difficulty of understanding that sometimes arises, and the feasibility of amplifying the direction, should the jury require further guidance. But Lord Goddard did approve the phrase in *R* v *Hepworth and Fearnley,* and amplifying directions can be found that satisfy the need to stress the high standard. I would refer to:

R v *Ching* (1976) 63 Cr App R 7 (CA)

The defendant was charged with theft from a supermarket. After retiring, the jury returned to the court and the foreman asked the judge to give further directions about the standard of proof. The judge gave a further direction in these terms: 'It is the duty of the prosecution to prove the charge on the whole of the evidence beyond a reasonable doubt. A reasonable doubt, it has been said, is a doubt to which you can give a reason as opposed to a mere fanciful sort of speculation such as "Well, nothing in this world is certain, nothing in this world can be proved." It is sometimes said the sort of matter which might influence you if you were to consider some business matter. A matter, for example, of a mortgage concerning your house, something of that nature.' The jury convicted the defendant who appealed.

LAWTON LJ, giving the judgment of the court, said: 'Mr. Latham accepted that when this Court comes to consider the effect of the final direction which the judge gave to the jury, it must be looked at against the whole background of the case, and in particular against the whole of the summing-up. That has been said time and time again in this Court. If any authority is required for the proposition it is to be found in *Hepworth and Fernley*...

The next ground of complaint was that by using the mortgage of a house analogy, the learned judge was doing something which had been condemned a number of times in this Court. Counsel called our attention to two recent decisions. One was *Gray* (1973) 58 Cr App

R 177. In that case the phrase which was disapproved of was "doubt which might affect you in the conduct of your everyday affairs." The other, even more recently, is the decision of this Court, on January 13, 1976, in *Knott*. In that case the phrase "the sort of doubt that can influence you as prudent men and women in the conduct of your everyday affairs." In the past this Court has criticised trial judges for using that kind of analogy. The use of any analogy is to be avoided whenever possible.

The final criticism was that when giving the direction of which complaint is made, the judge did not emphasise once again that the jury had to be sure. But we have no doubt that by the time the jury retired for the last time, they must have appreciated that they had to be sure before they could return a verdict of guilty.

Nevertheless, in most cases — but not in this one — judges would be well advised not to attempt any gloss upon what is meant by "sure" or what is meant by "reasonable doubt." In the last two decades there have been numerous cases before this Court, some of which have been successful, some of which have not, which have come here because judges have thought it helpful to a jury to comment of what the standard of proof is. Experience in this Court has shown that such comments usually create difficulties. They are more likely to confuse than help. But the exceptional case does sometimes arise. This is the sort of case in which, as I have already pointed out, the jury possibly wanted help as to what was meant by "doubt," The judge thought they want help and he tried to give them some. He was right to try and that is all he was doing. He seems to have steered clear of the formulas which have been condemned in this Court such as "such doubt as arises in your everyday affairs or your everyday life"; or using another example which has been before the Court, "the kind of doubts which you may have when trying to make up your minds what kind of motor car to buy."

Mr. Latham said that the judge did not stress that the relevant doubts were those which have to be overcome in *important* business affairs. What he did was to pick an example, which for sensible people would be an important matter. We can see nothing wrong in his so doing.'

Appeal dismissed.

My Lords, that decision may be contrasted with that in *R* v *Gray* (1973) 58 Cr App R 177 (CA), where the amplifying direction fell short of what is required.

East LJ: You say that the learned judge's words here, even taken together, fell short of the force needed to convey the high standard, even looked at as a whole.

Mr Atkyn: Yes, My Lord. Not only were the words themselves inadequate, but they did not occupy the pivotal position in the summing up that would stamp them on the mind of the jury as being of central importance to their task in relation to the evidence. This was held to be important by this court in *R* v *Ching*. Hence, the summing up on a vital issue was insufficient, read as a whole.

Mr Bacon: My Lords, I have nothing to add to what my learned friend has said, except perhaps that only in the exceptional cases where the defence bear some legal burden of proof (see 3.4.2 ante) may the sort of standard suggested by the learned judge be appropriate. The learned judge may by his words have effectively conveyed the civil standard of the balance of probabilities, which might properly be applied to a defence burden. I refer to:

R v *Carr-Briant* [1943] KB 607 (CCA)

The defendant who was charged with corruption contrary to the Prevention of Corruption Act 1906, was a director of a firm which entered into a contract for work to be done with the War Department. Payments in respect of work done under the contracts were made on the certificate of an engineer named Baldock, an employee of the War Department, that it had been satisfactorily performed. The appellant gave or lent to Baldock £60 so that Baldock might pay for a car which he had agreed to buy. The trial judge directed the jury that the defendant had not only to discharge the burden of proof and show that he gave the money without a corrupt motive, but had also to do so beyond all reasonable doubt. The defendant was convicted and appealed.

HUMPHREYS J, reading the judgment of the court, said: 'We see no reason why the rebuttable presumption created by the section should not be construed in the same manner as similar words in other statutes or similar presumptions at common law; for instance, the presumption of sanity in the case of an accused person who is setting up the defence of insanity. We agree with and adopt for the purpose of this judgment the language of Lord Hailsham LC, in delivering the judgment of the Privy Council in *Sodeman* v *Regem* [1936] WN 190, 191 where he said: "The suggestion made by the petitioner was that the jury may have been misled by the judge's language into the impression that the burden of proof resting upon the accused to prove the insanity was as heavy as the burden of proof resting upon the prosecution to prove the facts which they had to establish. In fact there was no doubt that the burden of proof for the defence was not so onerous... It was certainly plain that the burden in cases in which an accused had to prove insanity might fairly be stated as not being higher than the burden which rested upon a plaintiff or defendant in civil proceedings. That that was the law was not challenged."
    In our judgment, in any case where, either by statute or at common law, some matter is presumed against an accused person "unless the contrary is proved," the jury should be directed that it is for them to decide whether the contrary is proved, that the burden of proof required is less than that required at the hands of the prosecution in proving the case beyond a reasonable doubt, and that the burden may be discharged by evidence satisfying the jury of the probability of that which the accused is called upon to establish.
Appeal allowed.

That standard is wholly inappropriate in this case.
    Leach LJ: Yes, thank you.

C: THE BURDEN AND STANDARD OF PROOF ON SECONDARY ISSUES

3.7 Introductory notes

3.7.1 Secondary facts, as that expression is used in the present context, are facts which fall to be proved in order to demonstrate the admissibility or inadmissibility of evidence. Two quite distinct situations exist, which call for the application of different rules as to the burden and standard of proof of secondary facts.
    3.7.1.1 In cases where the judge has to rule on the admissibility of evidence as a matter of law, and must first investigate secondary facts in order to satisfy himself that certain conditions are shown to exist, the party asserting that the challenged evidence is admissible as part of his case bears the burden of proof of those secondary facts which are necessary to establish the admissibility of that evidence.
    3.7.1.2 In cases where a party is entitled to put evidence before the tribunal of fact, subject only to scrutiny by the judge of the credentials of the evidence to determine whether it is, on the face of it, that which it purports to be, is original and untampered with, the party relying on the evidence bears the burden of satisfying the judge of those matters.

3.7.2 In cases where the admissibility of the evidence falls to be decided as a question of law, the standard of proof to be employed is the same as on the main issue (i.e. as the primary facts of the case). Where the judge need only scrutinise the evidence in the preliminary way described in *3.7.1.2,* the party tendering the evidence need do no more than demonstrate the apparent originality and authenticity of the evidence on the balance of probabilities in any given case. (*A Practical Approach to Evidence,* pp 75–6, 78–9.)

3.8 Commentary

R v *Coke and Littleton* at trial: Mr Bunbury for the prosecution has invited the judge to hear evidence in the absence of the jury with a view to establishing the voluntariness and consequently the admissibility of the oral and written confessions allegedly made to the police by Coke. Mr Atkyn has called evidence tending to show that the statements were involuntary and therefore inadmissible. (For the authorities and argument on the actual issues of voluntariness and discretion relating to the Coke confessions, see 7.4 et seq.)

3.9 Argument

Holt J: Gentlemen, before you come to address me on the substance of the evidence I have heard, what do you say about the burden and standard of proof on the issue of voluntariness? How should I apply my mind to that issue?

Mr Bunbury: My Lord, I am glad to say that my learned friend and I take the same position as to the law. The authorities are clear that the prosecution bear the burden of proving the voluntariness of confessions, voluntariness being a necessary condition of their admissibility in law. Moreover, My Lord, the prosecution must discharge that burden to the criminal standard of proof, that is to say beyond reasonable doubt. My Lord, this is true generally of those cases in which the prosecution seek to prove facts that render some piece of hearsay evidence admissible. Of course, in practice, confessions are the most common example. My Lord, the matter was put clearly in one or two older cases, for example:

R v *Thompson* [1893] 2 QB 12 (CCR)

The defendant was convicted of embezzling the money of a company. The main issue at the trial was the question of the admissibility of a purported confessions.

CAVE J said: 'To be admissible, a confession must be free and voluntary. If it proceeds from remorse and a desire to make reparation for the crime, it is admissible. If it flows from hope or fear, excited by a person in authority, it is inadmissible. On this point the authorities are unanimous...The material question consequently is whether the confession has been obtained by the influence of hope or fear; and the evidence to this point being in its nature preliminary, is addressed to the judge, who will require the prosecutor to show *affirmatively,* to his satisfaction, that the statement was *not* made under the influence of an improper inducement, and who *in the event of any doubt subsisting on this head,* will reject the confession.''...

If these principles and the reasons for them are, as it seems impossible to doubt, well founded, they afford to magistrates a simple test by which the admissibility of a confession may be decided. They have to ask, Is it proved affirmatively that the confession was free and voluntary — that is, was it preceded by any inducement to make a statement held out by a person in authority? If so, and the inducement has not clearly been removed before the statement was made, evidence of the statement is inadmissible.'

(LORD COLERIDGE CJ, HAWKINS, DAY and WILLS JJ concurred)

Conviction quashed.

The same principle has been re-affirmed in recent times by the House of Lords in:

DPP v *Ping Lin* [1976] AC 574 (HL)

LORD HAILSHAM LC said: 'To be admissible, confessions, however convincing, must be voluntary in the sense that the prosecution must prove, and prove beyond reasonable doubt, in the classical words of Lord Sumner in *Ibrahim* v *The King* [1914] AC 599, 609: "that it has not been obtained from him either by fear of prejudice or hope of advantage exercised (sic) or held out by a person in authority."... But, on the sujbect of confessions, English law is not wholly rational. It is subject to the general rule, described by Lord Sumner as a "rule of policy" to which I have already referred, viz that, before a confession is to be admitted in evidence, it must be proved by the prosecution beyond reasonable doubt, "as a fundamental condition of its admissibility" that it is "voluntary in the sense that it has not been obtained by fear or prejudice or hope of advantage excited or held out by a person in authority." '

Holt J: Very well, thank you.

3.10 Commentary

R v *Coke and Littleton* at trial: Mr Bunbury for the prosecution tenders evidence of the obtaining and contents of the cassette recording, exhibit GG4. After ruling that the cassette and its contents are admissible, and that there is no reason of discretion for excluding them,[1] Holt J raises the issue of preliminary scrutiny.

3.11 Argument

Holt J: Mr Bunbury, am I correct in thinking that I should enquire into the tape-recording before allowing it to go to the jury? Of course, I have heard Detective Inspector Glanvil's evidence of how it came to be made.

Mr Bunbury: Yes, My Lord. And Your Lordship has heard that there is no dispute that the conversation was accurately recorded by the detective inspector.

Holt J: Yes, but that is not enough, is it? Because as I understand it, something may turn on the tone of voice of the speakers, and the physical impression and context of the conversation, is that right, Mr Atkyn?

Mr Atkyn: Yes, My Lord. It may be very important to the defence. In my submission, Your Lordship must be satisfied as to the condition of the recording as an original and as having remained untampered with from the date when it was made until now.

Holt J: Is that a question of admissibility, so that Mr Bunbury must persuade me beyond reasonable doubt?

Mr Atkyn: No, My Lord. This is one of those rare instances in which Your Lordship must to some extent weigh the evidence in order to be satisfied that the recording is original and untampered with. My Lord, this does in one sense trespass on the function of the jury, but there is good authority for examining such real evidence in this way, even where its contents are admissible from the standpoint of the law of evidence, as Your Lordship has held them to be. If Your Lordship looks at the case of *R* v *Maqsud Ali; R* v *Ashiq Hussain* [1966] 1 QB 688, at the end of the of the judgment of the Court of Criminal Appeal, there appears this *per curiam* observation:

In the normal case of a trial within a trial the issue clearly raised is whether evidence such

---

[1]As to the admissibility of tape-recordings generally, see 15.9 post.

as statements are voluntary or if voluntary whether they were obtained in conformity with the Judge's Rules. Here the judge was pressed to undertake an inquiry into the weight of the evidence and although reluctant at first, he ultimately agreed to do so. In the view of this court the cases must be rare where the judge is justified in undertaking his own investigation into the weight of the evidence which, subject to proper directions from the judge, is really the province of the jury, but the court sees that there can be cases — but they must be rare —where the issue of admissibility and weight can overlay each other. We think this was one of those rare cases in which the judge was justified in doing what he did.'

Holt J: Yes. Neither that case nor a rather later decision in *R* v *Stevenson* [1971] 1 WLR 1 (CA) helps as to the standard of proof.

Mr Bunbury No, My Lord, but perhaps I might refer Your Lordships to the judgment of Shaw J in *R* v *Robson; R* v *Harris* [1972] 1 WLR 651. There, it was held that the standard of weighing what will ultimately be a question of weight for the jury is no more than that required to show a *prima facie* case of originality and authenticity, which cannot mean more than the balance of probabilities and may be somewhat less.

R v *Robson; R* v *Harris* [1972] 1 WLR 651 (Central Criminal Court)

At the defendants' trial the prosecution intended to rely on certain tape-recordings of conversations; they were put forward as original recordings. The defendants objected to the admissibility of the recordings.

SHAW J said: 'I may say in passing that in a recent criminal trial, *R* v *Stevenson* [1971] 1 WLR 1, where a similar question arose it was contended that the standard of proof of originality was that which applied to any issue which had to be resolved by the jury in such a trial, namely, proof beyond reasonable doubt. This is, of course, right if and when the issue does come before the jury as a matter they have to decide as going to weight and cogency. In the first stage, when the question is solely that of admissibility — i.e. whether the evidence is competent to be considered by the jury at all — the judge, it seems to me, would be usurping their function if he purported to deal with not merely the primary issue of admissibility but what is the ultimate issue of cogency. My own view is that in considering that limited question the judge is required to do no more than to satisfy himself that a prima facie case of originality has been made out by evidence which defines and describes the provenance and history of the recordings up to the moment of production in court. If that evidence appears to remain intact after cross-examination it is not incumbent on him to hear and weigh other evidence which might controvert the prima facie case. To embark on such an inquiry seems to me to trespass on the ultimate function of the jury.

It is true that in determining whether an alleged confession is admissible or not the judge has the duty of deciding a contentious issue and he has to apply the same criteria as a jury would have to do: but this is an anomalous case deriving from its own special history and from considerations peculiar to confessions. It is perhaps worth noticing that, if in regard to an alleged confession the issue is not whether it was made voluntarily but whether it was made at all, that question is solely for the jury's determination; the trial judge has no part to play except to sum the matter up to them.

Although in the present case the objection was taken on the question of originality of the tape recordings, the real gravamen of the objection was an attack on their authenticity. This larger issue is manifestly one for the jury in the same way as is the credibility of any witness although, of course, the jury's consideration must be confined to evidence which is in the first place admissible. However, for the purposes of this case I accepted the proposition that I ought to conduct a comprehensive inquiry into not only the history of the tapes but also their nature and condition and that for this purpose I should hear evidence on both sides and decide the question on the balance of probabilities in the light of all the material before me. At the conclusion of that evidence there was a strong prima facice case for the originality of the recordings. As I have already ventured to suggest, that was, as I see it, the apt and proper stage at which to rule on the fundamental question of admissibility. If I had then been called upon to make a decision on the evidence adduced by the Crown I would have had no hesitation in overruling the objections, whether as a matter of strict law or as a matter of discretion.

In *R* v *Stevenson* [1971] 1 WLR 1, to which I have already referred, Kilner Brown J felt himself obliged to hear evidence from both sides in order to decide whether evidence in the form of tape recordings should be excluded on the ground that they were copies. He too had misgivings as to where the line should be drawn between matters going to admissibility and matters which really went to weight and cogency. He said, at p 3: "Consequently in this case an extremely lengthy and detailed examination of the evidence has taken place upon the voire dire. This examination has been conducted with very great care. It has been highly technical and very scientific at times and extremely burdensome for everybody engaged in this case. I interpolate to say that I have been greatly assisted by the way in which this examination has taken place, greatly assisted by those who had the technical duty of producing it, to those who have given evidence and to counsel who have probed that evidence before me. Nevertheless, as a general rule it seems to me to be highly undesirable, and indeed wrong, for such an investigation to take place before the judge. If it is regarded as a general practice it would lead to the ludicrous situation that in every case where an accused person said that the prosecution evidence is fabricated the judge would be called upon to usurp the functions of the jury." Kilner Brown J went on to say: "Notwithstanding the wide area over which this inquiry has ranged I intend to limit my approach to one single issue which in my view is legitimately within the province of admissibility. It may be alternatively, if I am wrong in that, a question of discretion. I decide this matter on the narrow but vital question as to whether or not the so-called original tapes are established as original."

I would venture to qualify what the judge was there saying by inserting the words "prima facie," so that it would state that the judge is called upon to decide the narrow but vital issue whether or not the so-called original takes are shown prima facie to be original.
Ruling accordingly.

(Holt J then considered the evidence, and ruled that the cassette, together with a transcript of its contents might be placed before the jury.)

3.12 Questions for Counsel

3.12.1 Blackstone v *Coke:* Can any argument be made against the position taken by Hardwicke J (3.3) that it was for the plaintiff to show (i) that she did not consent to the sexual intercourse, and (ii) that she was not in fact free to leave Coke's flat?

3.12.2 Blackstone v *Coke:* Assume for this question only that at the criminal trial Coke had been acquitted of the charge of rape. If in the present action, both Margaret Blackstone and Coke give evidence along the lines of their respective statements set out in chapter 2, how would you argue for the plaintiff the question of the plaintiff's burden and standard of proof to the judge?

3.12.3 R v *Coke and Littleton:* Construct a passage for Holt J to include in his summing up that would adequately deal with the burden and standard of proof relating to the issue of guilt of (a) Coke and (b) Littleton on the offences charged.

3.12.4 R v *Coke and Littleton:* What arguments would you put before Holt J for the prosecution on the question of the burden and standard of proof in relation to evidence called for the purpose (a) of showing the admissibility of the Littleton cassette over an objection of matrimonial communication privilege (see 10.16) and (b) of showing that the Coke handwriting samples might be put in evidence, together with the evidence of Mr Hale of expert comparison (see 153 et seq).

4 Evidence of Character

4.1 Introductory notes

4.1.1 The word 'character' has at least three possible meanings. First, it may refer to a person's general reputation in the community. Second, it may refer to his disposition to behave in a certain way. Third, it may refer to specific acts in his personal history, such as previous criminal convictions. Character may have a creditable or a discreditable connotation, and is known as 'good' or 'bad' character accordingly.

4.1.2 In some cases, the character of a person may be a fact in issue or a relevant fact. Such cases include actions for defamation which concern the plaintiff's reputation directly. Certain criminal offences require proof of a limited element of character by providing that a person may only be convicted if he is of known bad character, or if he has previously been convicted of certain crimes, or been sentenced in certain ways. In these cases, the necessary element of character is just one fact which must be proved to establish the case.

4.1.3 In most cases, however, character is not a fact in issue and will be evidentially irrelevant to the facts in issue. For this reason, where character is not a fact in issue, evidence of character is usually inadmissible on the issues in the case. This does not exclude such evidence for all purposes. With the exception of a defendant giving evidence in a criminal case, (4.4 post) witnesses may be discredited by attacks on their character to the extent permitted by the rules governing collateral issues, but such evidence will go only to the credit of the witness, and can affect only indirectly the issue in the case.

4.1.4 In a civil case where character is not itself in issue, such evidence is inadmissible to prove or disprove the facts in issue, whether it is evidence of good or bad character.

4.1.5 In criminal cases in which character is not in issue, the prosecution may not tender evidence of the defendant's bad character for the purpose of proving his guilt by suggesting the likelihood of guilt in the light of his record. If evidence is directly relevant to the proof of guilt, however, it is not inadmissible merely because it happens also to disclose something discreditable to the defendant. Similar fact evidence (Chapter 5) is the major, though not the only example of relevant evidence which reveals some element of character. What is forbidden is 'giving a dog a bad name and hanging him'.

4.1.6 In all criminal cases, the defendant may at his option assert his own good character by way of defence, by cross-examination of prosecution witnesses and by giving and calling evidence of character himself. If he does so, his whole character is opened to scrutiny and, subject to the court's discretion, he may be cross-examined and his evidence may be rebutted or discredited. The evidence of good character is treated, illogically but out of latitude to the defendant, as going to the issue of his guilt or innocence, even though it does no more than assert the unlikelihood of guilt by an appeal to the defendant's past record. It is probable that, with the exception of specific creditable acts on other occasions which are excluded, the defendant may assert his good character in every respect and is not limited to evidence of his reputation in the community. (*A Practical Approach to Evidence*, pp 85–92.)

4.2 Commentary

R v *Coke and Littleton* on appeal against conviction. Mr Bacon on behalf of Littleton complains that at the trial, Holt J limited his cross-examination of the prosecution witnesses to the question of his reputation in Oxbridge and did not permit evidence of his lack of previous convictions. Moreover, the learned judge did not permit Mrs Littleton to give evidence of Littleton's general disposition and behaviour with children on other occasions. Mr Bacon further complains of a passage in the summing up. Littleton elected not to give evidence, but to make an unsworn statement from the dock (see 12.4 et seq). The passage complained of was as follows:

Members of the jury, you may be wondering what to make of the evidence that Mr Littleton is a man who enjoys a good reputation in Oxbridge. It is rather unfortunate that you heard that evidence, because I must now direct you to disregard it. The only relevance which that evidence could have had, would have been to enhance Littleton's credibility, had he elected to give evidence. You might have been more inclined to accept his evidence knowing him to be a man of good reputation than might otherwise have been the case. But he has not given evidence, and you are not judging him as a witness. No question of his credit as a witness arises, and so there is no issue to which the evidence of his reputation can be relevant.

4.3 Argument

Mr Bacon: My Lords, in my submission the learned judge was wrong in not allowing me to cross-examine Detective Inspector Glanvil about the appellant Littleton's good character in terms of the absence of a criminal record.
Leach LJ: That does seem rather curious, Mr Bacon. It would appear that the learned judge took the view that evidence of good character must be confined to matters concerning general reputation.
Mr Bacon: Yes, My Lords. That view was at one time prevalent at common law, as Your Lordships know from the decision in:

R v *Rowton* (1865) Le & Ca 520 (CCR)

The defendant was charged with indecent assault on a boy and called several witnesses to his character. The prosecution called a witness to give evidence in rebuttal, and the witness was asked about the defendant's general character for decency and morality of conduct. He replied: 'I know nothing of the neighbourhood's opinion, because I was only a boy at school when I knew him; but my own opinion, and the opinion of my brothers who were also pupils of his, is that his character is that of a man capable of the grossest indecency and the most flagrant immorality'.

COCKBURN CJ said: 'There are two questions to be decided. The first is whether, when evidence of good character has been given in favour of a prisoner, evidence of his general bad character can be called in reply. I am clearly of opinion that it can be. It is true that I do not remember any case in my own experience where such evidence has been given; but that is easily explainable by the fact that evidence of good character is not given when it is known that it can be rebutted; and it frequently happens that the prosecuting counsel, from a spirit of fairness, gives notice to the other side, when he is in a position to contradict such evidence. But, when we come to consider whether the evidence is admissible, it is only possible to come to one conclusion. It is said that evidence of good character raises only a collateral issue; but I think that, if the prisoner thinks proper to raise that issue as one of the elements for the consideration of the jury, nothing could be more unjust than that he should have the advantage of a character which, in point of fact, may be the very reverse of that which he really deserves.

Assuming, then, that evidence was receivable to rebut the evidence of good character, the second question is, was the answer which was given in this case, in reply to a perfectly legitimate question, such an answer as could properly be left to the jury? Now, in determining this point, it is necessary to consider what is the meaning of evidence of character. Does it mean evidence of general reputation or evidence of disposition? I am of opinion that it means evidence of general reputation. What you want to get at is the tendency and disposition of the man's mind towards committing or abstaining from committing the class of crime with which he stands charged; but no one has ever heard the question — what is the tendency and disposition of the prisoner's mind? — put directly. The only way of getting at it is by giving evidence of his general character founded on his general reputation in the neighbourhood in which he lives. That, in my opinion, is the sense in which the word "character" is to be taken, when evidence of character is spoken of. The fact that a man has an unblemished reputation leads to the presumption that he is incapable of committing the crime for which he is being tried. We are not now considering whether it is desirable that the law of England should be altered — whether it is expedient to import the practice of other countries and go into the prisoner's antecedents for the purpose of shewing that he is likely to commit the crime with which he is charged, or, stopping short of that, whether it would be wise to allow the prisoner to go into facts for the purpose of shewing that he is incapable of committing the crime charged against him. It is quite clear that, as the law now stands, the prisoner cannot give evidence of particular facts, although one fact would weigh more than the opinion of all his friends and neighbours. So too, evidence of antecedent bad conduct would form equally good ground for inferring the prisoner's guilt, yet it is quite clear evidence of that kind is inadmissible. The allowing evidence of good character has arisen from the fairness of our laws and is an anomalous exception to the general rule. It is quite true that evidence of character is most cogent, when it is preceded by a statement shewing that the witness has had opportunities of acquiring information upon the subject beyond what the man's neighbours in general would have; and in practice the admission of such statements is often carried beyond the letter of the law in favour of the prisoner. It is, moreover, most essential that a witness who comes forward to give a man a good character should himself have a good opinion of him; for other wise he would only be deceiving the jury; and so the strict rule is often exceeded. But, when we consider what, in the strict interpretation of the law, is the limit of such evidence, in my judgment it must be restricted to the man's general reputation, and must not extend to the individual opinion of the witness. Some time back, I put this question —Suppose a witness is called who says that he knows nothing of the general character of the accused, but that he had had abundant opportunities of forming an individual opinion as to his honesty or the particular moral quality that may be in question in the particular case. Surely, if such evidence were objected to, it would be inadmissible.

If that be the true doctine as to the admissibility of evidence to character in favour of the prisoner, the next question is, within what limits must the rebutting evidence be confined? I think that that evidence must be of the same character and confined within the same limits —that, as the prisoner can only give evidence of general good character, so the evidence called to rebut it must be evidence of the same general description, shewing that the evidence which has been given in favour of the prisoner is not true, but that the man's general reputation is bad.

ERLE CJ (dissenting) said: 'Now, what is the principle on which evidence of character is admitted? It seems to me that such evidence is admissible for the purpose of shewing the disposition of the party accused, and basing thereon a presumption that he did not commit the crime imputed to him. Disposition cannot be ascertained directly; it is only to be ascertained by the opinion formed concerning the man, which must be founded either on personal experience, or on the expression of opinion by others, whose opinion again ought to be founded on their personal experience. The question between us is, whether the Court is at liberty to receive a statement of the disposition of a prisoner, founded on the personal experience of the witness, who attends to give evidence and state that estimate which long personal knowledge of and acquaintance with the prisoner has enabled him to form? I think that each source of evidence is admissible. You may give in evidence the general rumour prevalent in the prisoner's neighbourhood, and, according to my experience, you may have also the personal judgment of those who are capable of forming a more real, substantial, guiding opinion than that which is to be gathered from general rumour. I never saw a witness examined to character without an inquiry being made into his personal means of knowledge of that character. The evidence goes to the jury depending entirely upon the personal experience of the witness who has offered his testimony. Suppose a witness to character were to say, "This man has been in my employ for twenty years. I have had experience of his conduct; but I have never heard a human being express an opinion of him in my life. For my own part, I have always regarded him with the highest esteem and respect, and have had an abundant experience that he is one of the worthiest men in the world." The principle the Lord Chief Justice has laid down would exclude this evidence; and that is the point where I differ from him. To my mind personal experience gives cogency to the evidence; whereas such a statement as, "I have heard some persons speak well of him," or "I have heard general report in favour of the prisoner," has a very slight effect in comparison. Again, to the proposition that general character is alone admissible the answer is that it is impossible to get at it. There is no such thing as general character; it is the general inference supposed to arise from hearing a number of separate and disinterested statements in favour of the prisoner. But I think that the notion that general character is alone admissible is not accurate. It would be wholly inadmissible to ask a witness what individual he has ever heard give his opinion of a particular fact connected with the man. I attach considerable weight to this distinction, because, in my opinion, the best character is that which is the least talked of'.
(The other learned judges concurred in the judgment delivered by COCKBURN CJ: WILLES J also dissented.)

East LJ: Has that case ever been overruled?

Mr Bacon: My Lords, it has never been expressly overruled, and indeed was approved recently by the Court of Appeal in *R* v *Redgrave* [1981] Crim LR 556, but the majority of modern decisions has proceeded on the assumption that it is no longer good law in so far as it restricts the adduction of evidence of character. In *R* v *Dunkley* Lord Hewart CJ showed that an entirely different view of the word 'character' has been taken consistently by the courts since the coming into effect of the Criminal Evidence Act 1898. Of course, the decision in *R* v *Rowton* was well before the Act and was decided when the law was very different. And My Lords, since the decision of the House of Lords in *Jones* v *DPP,* the better view is that character is to be considered on a basis wider than mere reputation.

R v *Dunkley* [1927] 1 KB 323 (CCA)

The appellant was convicted of stealing and receiving certain property. A witness for the prosecution gave evidence that the appellant brought the articles to her and asked her to dispose of them. In cross-examination it was suggested to the witness that her story was a pure invention fabricated out of a feeling of revenge against the appellant. The trial judge allowed the prosecution to cross-examine the appellant as to his previous convictions on the ground that he had cast imputations upon the character of a witness for the prosecution within s.1 (f) (ii) of the Criminal Evidence Act 1898 (see 4.8 post).

LORD HEWART CJ, delivering the judgment of the court, referred to s.1(f) of the Criminal Evidence Act and continued: 'It is apparent that within the space of a very few lines the word "character" is used in this part of the section no fewer than four times. It is also apparent that the imputations which are spoken of in the closing words of the passage I have read are described, not as imputations on the prosecutor or the witnesses for the prosecution, but as imputations on the character of the prosecutor or the witnesses for the prosecution. In those circumstances it is not difficult to suppose that a formidable argument might have been raised on the phrasing of this statute, that the character which is spoken of is the character which is so well known in the vocabulary of the criminal law — namely, the general reputation of the person referred to; in other words, that "character" in that context and in every part of it, in the last part no less than in the first, in the third part no less than in the second, bears the meaning which the term "character" was held to bear, for example, in the case of *R* v *Rowton* (1865) Le & Ca 520, where the question was considered by the Court of Crown Cases Reserved,.... Nevertheless, when one looks at the long line of cases beginning very shortly after the passing of the Criminal Evidence Act, 1898, it does not appear that that argument has ever been so much as formulated. It was formulated yesterday. One can only say that it is now much too late in the day even to consider that argument, because that argument could not now prevail without the revision, and indeed to a great extent the overthrow, of a very long series of decisions.'
Appeal dismissed.

Jones v *DPP* [1962] AC 635 (HL) (For the facts see 4.6 post)

LORD DEVLIN said: 'It is not difficult to see what has happened. The dam that was patiently constructed over the centuries by the judges of England to hold back the natural flow of evidence on character, that is, evidence about those acts and omissions of a man which show truly what he is, has broken down and some parts of it at any rate are beyond repair. Every practitioner knows that questions are asked and answered every day in the courts that conflict with the rule; see Taylor on Evidence, 12th ed. Vol. I, section 350. The courts have recognised this but at the same time they have given to the Act of 1898 the effect which I firmly believe it was intended to have but which it may be can be justified as a matter of language only if it is construed in the light of a rule of evidence that is now no longer in force. They have been able to do this because they have declared the law as they understand it to be without attempting to reconcile their decisions exactly with the language used.
Your Lordships are now told that you should return to the words of the Act and give them their literal meaning whatever the consequences may be. For my part I find it impossible to think about construing the words of the Act literally until I have made up my mind whether "character" means or includes the moral disposition of the man or only his reputation. That is crucial; any other approach is piecemeal. Unfortunately, your Lordships have not been asked to consider *R* v *Dunkley* [1927] 1 KB 323 which, subject to your Lordships' view of it, governs the law on this point. It appears to me to be inevitable that sooner or later your Lordships will have to consider whether *R* v *Dunkley* was rightly decided. If it was, is, then, proviso (*f*) to be construed as "a universal and absolute prohibition" against asking the accused any question in cross-examination that tends to show that he is of a bad moral disposition? I do not believe that anyone would be prepared to answer that question with an unqualified affirmative; for so answered it would make effective cross-examination of an accused person practically impossible. Sooner or later, then, the courts will have to determine what diminishment there is to be of the universality and absoluteness of the rule; and, if relevance to an issue be not the test, what sort of aspersions may be cast upon the accused in cross-examination and what may not....

If *R* v *Dunkley* is to be upheld, it can in my opinion be upheld only on the reasoning on which the judgment is itself based, namely, that it is too late to argue — at any rate in relation to the Act of 1898 — that "character" should bear the meaning of reputation only. Indeed, I cannot see any other ground on which the decision could be defended. To take only one point, is it possible to argue that when Parliament in proviso (*f*) (ii) referred to the accused as giving "evidence of his good character," it contemplated that he might give evidence to show that he was a man of good moral disposition when 30 years before the court which was then of final appeal had in one of the most fully considered judgments in its history decided that that was precisely what he could not do? If the Court of Criminal Appeal in *R* v *Dunkley* had thought that there was any argument on the construction of the Act which would have fortified their decision, no doubt they would have incorporated it in their judgment; but they relied solely on authority, consisting of decisions given since the passing of the Act, which they said ought not to be disturbed.'...

My Lords, this, I think, is the result that has so far been achieved by the decisions that have been given on the effect of section 1 of the Act of 1898; and I should hesitate long before I started to examine and analyse afresh the construction and working of that section. One way or another, and it may be without a sufficiently strict attention to the text of the section, the decisions of the Court of Criminal Appeal in the past have as a whole produced a sensible result.

LORD DENNING said: 'I find myself in complete agreement with the speech which my noble and learned friend, Lord Devlin, has prepared, with only this addition, that I think it far too late now to argue that "character" in section 1(f) means only reputation.'

Cox LJ: Assuming that your argument is right, what evidence do you say you were entitled to adduce?

Mr Bacon: My Lords, it is common practice to lead that a defendant is a man of previous good character in the police sense, in that he has not previously been convicted of any criminal offence. In the present case, my learned friend for the Crown has indicated to me that that evidence would not have been disputed.

Mr Bunbury: My Lords, that is correct. No convictions are recorded against Mr Littleton.

Mr Bacon: And My Lords, in addition there would be no reason why evidence should not have been given of Mr Littleton's disposition generally, and in particular with regard to children.

Leach LJ: You would not contend that you could lead evidence that did no more than show that on other occasions he had been in the company of children and had done nothing wrong?

Mr Bacon: My Lord, I accept that. Evidence of specific creditable acts would have no relevance, but I would be entitled to ask questions as to his general disposition...

East LJ: ...if he had given evidence...

Mr Bacon: ...if he had given evidence, it would have been more satisfactory, My Lord, but in my submission even Mrs Littleton could have dealt with it as a character witness. She would, of course, have been liable to be cross-examined.

Leach LJ: Mr Bacon, assuming that we are with you on that point, what complaint do you make about the passage in the summing up of the learned judge which you read to us earlier?

Mr Bacon: My Lords, that relates to the evidential value of Littleton's good character and the use which the jury were entitled to make of it. The learned judge directed the jury to ignore that evidence simply because the defendant did not give evidence.

Cox LJ: As I understand it, that is the view taken by this court in *R* v *Falconer-*

Atlee (1973) 58 Cr App R 348.

Mr Bacon: My Lords, that is perfectly true. There are two views about evidence of good character given by the defence. On one view, the evidence can go only to credit and so is irrelevant if the defendant chooses not to give evidence. But on another view, the evidence may be relevant on the main issue, and that view was endorsed by this court in *R* v *Bryant; R* v *Oxley.* The facts of that case were very close to those of the present case. The court held that the evidence was capable of going beyond a mere matter of credit and might actually be relevant as making it appear to the jury less likely that the defendant was guilty.

R v *Bryant; R* v *Oxley* [1979] QB 108 (CA)

The defendants were jointly charged with robbery. One defendant applied for leave to appeal against his conviction on the ground that the trial judge had misdirected the jury in stating that evidence given of his good character went to credibility and, in the circumstances, had little relevance to the issue whether he had committed the offence.

WATKINS J, giving the judgment of the court, said: 'If...as seems to be so, the judge was intending to convey to the jury the impression that a good character is relevant only when a defendant gives evidence and, therefore, is a matter only to be taken into consideration when the credibility of what he and other witnesses have said is being assessed, he was being too restrictive about its possible uses. The possession of a good character is a matter which does go primarily to the issue of credibility. This has been made clear in a number of recent cases. But juries should be directed that it is capable of bearing a more general significance which is best illustrated by what was said by Williams J in *R* v *Stannard* (1837) 7 C & P 673, 675: "I have no doubt, if we are put to decide the unwelcome question, that evidence to character must be considered as evidence in the cause. It is evidence, as my brother Patteson has said, to be submitted to the jury, to induce them to say whether they think it likely that a person with such a character would have committed the offence."...

We have no doubt that the omission to direct the jury in this way in the present case could not possibly have had the effect of rendering the jury's verdict unsafe or unsatisfactory. Application refused.

B: THE DEFENDANT IN CRIMINAL CASES: THE CRIMINAL EVIDENCE ACT 1898

4.4 Introductory notes

4.4.1 The Criminal Evidence Act 1898 for the first time made the defendant in criminal cases competent, though not compellable, as a witness for the defence. If he elects to give evidence, the defendant is invested with a statutory 'shield' under s.1(f) of the Act, which provides him with an immunity, not enjoyed by witnesses generally, against being cross-examined about his (bad) character. The shield may be lost in certain cases prescribed by the Act, namely where:

    (a) the evidence of character is relevant to guilt as charged, or

    (b) he has sought to establish his good character, or the nature or conduct of the defence is such as to involve imputations on the character of the prosecutor or the witnesses for the prosecution, or

    (c) he has given evidence against any person charged in the same proceedings.

4.4.2 In the first of the cases set out above, the cross-examination, where permitted, will go to the guilt of the defendant, whereas in the circumstances of the second and third sub-paragraphs, the same evidence will go only to the credit of the defendant as a witness. The Act provides only for cross-examination and does not affect the common law rules which govern the circumstances in which evidence may be called in rebuttal.

4.4.3   Even where the shield is lost, the trial judge may in his discretion forbid or limit cross-examination about character where the prosecution seek to avail themselves of the statutory rights to cross-examine. However, where a co-defendant is entitled to cross-examine, the judge has no discretion to restrain that course.

4.4.4   Cross-examination as to character and evidence of character may also be permitted when tendered by one defendant against another, where such evidence is relevant to the case of the tendering defendant, just as evidence relevant to guilt may be tendered by the prosecution even though it may reveal some aspect of the defendant's character (4.1.5).

4.4.5   Where an inadvertent reference to character is made during a trial, the judge may discharge the jury and order a re-trial, and should do so unless the error is insignificant in the context of the trial as a whole and an appropriate warning to the jury can be relied upon to remedy the situation.

4.4.6   Even where it is proper to refer to character, all concerned should bear in mind the provisions of the Rehabilitation of Offenders Act 1974, and the Children and Young Persons Act 1963, s.16(2), which restrict the use of certain previous convictions and findings of guilt. (*A Practical Approach to Evidence,* pp 92–107).

4.5   Commentary

R v *Coke and Littleton* at trial.   Mr Atkyn's cross-examination of Margaret has been confined to the question of consent on the occasion complained of, and in his evidence in chief, Coke avoids all attacks on her character and all reference to his own character. Mr Bunbury, in the absence of the jury, applies to Holt J for leave to cross-examine Coke about his previous conviction for rape. Mr Atkyn objects.

4.6   Argument

Mr Atkyn: My Lord, I object most strongly to this proposed line of questioning on the ground that it is prohibited by section 1 of the Criminal Evidence Act 1898. My Lord, that section, which for the first time made the defendant a competent witness for the defence, laid down that the defendant was not to be treated as other witnesses by being exposed to cross-examination about his character. My Lord, the section was made quite specific as to the circumstances in which such cross-examination by the prosecution may be permissible, and none of the cases in which this can occur is applicable to the present case.

---

[1]This is of course an improbable way for Coke to give evidence and perhaps an unlikely one for Mr Atkyn to cross-examine, but it does isolate s.1(f)(i).

Criminal Evidence Act 1898 s.1(e) and (f)

(e) A person charged and being a witness in pursuance of this Act may be asked any question in cross-examination notwithstanding that it would tend to criminate him as to the offence charged:

(f) A person charged and called as a witness in pursuance of this Act shall not be asked, and if asked shall not be required to answer, any question tending to show that he has committed or been convicted of or been charged with any offence other than that wherewith he is then charged, or is of bad character, unless—

(i) the proof that he has committed or been convicted of such other offence is admissible evidence to show that he is guilty of the offence wherewith he is then charged; or

(ii) he has personally or by his advocate asked questions of the witnesses for the prosecution with a view to establish his own good character, or has given evidence of his good character, or the nature or conduct of the defence is such as to involve imputations on the character of the prosecutor or the witnesses for the prosecution; or

(iii) he has given evidence against any other person charged in the same proceedings.

My Lord, the defendant Coke has not in his evidence made any reference to his good character or any imputation on any witness for the prosecution. And in so far as he may have given evidence unfavourable to the case for the defendant Littleton, that is a matter which is for my learned friend Mr Bacon to deal with.

Holt J: You are thinking primarily of section 1(f) rather than section 1(e), because it is 1(f) which prohibits the exploration of character.

Mr Atkyn: Yes, My Lord.

Holt J: Well, let us look at what the subsection does purport to prohibit. First of all, it says that the defendant 'shall not be required to answer'. I rather think from what Lord Reid said in *Jones* v *DPP* that this means that it is cross-examination which is prohibited. He said: 'It was suggested that this applies to examination in chief as well as to cross-examination. I do not think so. The words "shall not be required to answer" are quite inappropriate for examination in chief. The proviso is obviously intended to protect the accused. It does not prevent him from volunteering evidence, and does not in my view prevent his counsel from asking questions leading to disclosure of a previous conviction or bad character if such disclosure is thought to assist in his defence.' The section does not stop the defendant from putting in his character in chief.

Then the section prohibits 'any question tending to show'.

Mr Atkyn: Yes, My Lord. That would appear to mean simply tending to reveal to the jury something which was previously unknown to them. I would again refer Your Lordship to *Jones* v *DPP*, where this was held to be the case.

Jones v *DPP* [1962] AC 635 (HL)

The appellant was charged with the murder of a girl guide. Before the trial the defendant set up a false alibi. At the trial he testified instead that he was with a prostitute on the night in question and deposed to his wife's angry reaction to his late return. He accounted for the change in his alibi by saying in his evidence in chief that he 'had been in trouble with the police before' and therefore had been reluctant to give an alibi which could not be corroborated. This testimony was strikingly similar to that given by him at an earlier trial during which he was convicted of raping a girl guide. He was cross-examined with regard to these similarities on the footing that it was an extraordinary coincidence that he should have an identical alibi for the two occasions on which he had been in trouble. The appellant was convicted of murder and appealed on the ground that the cross-examination was inadmissible because the questions were excluded by s.1(f) of the Criminal Evidence Act 1898, as 'tending to show' that he had committed or been convicted of or had been charged with an offence other than that with which he was then charged, or was of bad character.

VISCOUNT SIMONDS said: 'As to the meaning of the words "tend to show" I see no difficulty. It is not the intention of the question that matters but the effect of the question and, presumably, the possible answer. Nor is the word "show" in its context ambiguous. Primarily it may mean a visual demonstration, but in relation to the giving of oral evidence it can only mean "make known." The issue, then, is whether the challenged questions made known anything to the jury which they did not know before. Learned counsel for the defence had, for reasons which were, no doubt, adequate and probably imperative, made it known to the jury that the appellant had previously been in trouble with the police. In doing so he took a calculated risk. I think that it would be too strict a view to hold that the challenged questions tended to make known to the jury that the appellant had committed or been convicted of or charged with any other offence than that of the murder for which he was standing his trial. They had been told that he had been in trouble with the police: what the trouble was they were not told. He was asked whether on some occasion he had answered certain questions in a certain way. He was not asked what the occasion was. Vagueness was matched with vagueness. The jury could not be expected to know what your Lordships now are told, that his trouble with the police referred to one incident and his answers to questions to another. This was the view taken by the experienced judges of the Court of Criminal Appeal, and I agree with them.'

LORD REID said: 'The questions prohibited are those which "tend to show" certain things. Does this mean tend to prove or tend to suggest? Here I cannot accept the argument of the Attorney-General. What matters is the effect of the questions on the jury. A veiled suggestion of a previous offence may be just as damaging as a definite statement. In my judgment, "tends to show" means tends to suggest to the jury. But the crucial point in the present case is whether the questions are to be considered in isolation or whether they are to be considered in the light of all that had gone before them at the trial. If the questions or line of questioning has to be considered in isolation I think that the questions with which this appeal is concerned would tend to show at least that the accused had previously been charged with an offence. The jury would be likely to jump to that conclusion, if this was the first they had heard of this matter. But I do not think that the questions ought to be considered in isolation. If the test is the effect the questions would be likely to have on the minds of the jury that necessarily implies that one must have regard to what the jury had already heard. If the jury already knew that the accused had been charged with an offence, a question inferring that he had been charged would add nothing and it would be absurd to prohibit it. If the obvious purpose of the proviso is to protect the accused from possible prejudice, as I think it is, then "show" must mean "reveal," because it is only a revelation of something new which could cause such prejudice.'
(LORD MORRIS of BORTH-Y-GEST delivered a judgment agreeing with VISCOUNT SIMONDS and LORD REID).

LORD DENNING (dissenting): My Lords, much of the discussion before your Lordships was directed to the effect of section 1(f) of the Criminal Evidence Act, 1898: and, if that were the sole paragraph for consideration, I should have thought that counsel for the Crown ought not to have asked the question he did. My reasons are these:
   First: The questions tended to show that Jones had previously been charged in a court of law with another offence. True it is that they did not point definitely to that conclusion, but they conveyed that impression, and that is enough. Counsel may not have intended it, but that does not matter. What matters is the impression the questions would have on the jury. The Attorney-General said that, if the questions left the matter evenly balanced, so that there was some other conclusion that could equally well be drawn, as, for instance, that Jones had not been "charged" in a court of law but had only been interrogated in a police station, there was no bar to the questions being asked I cannot agree. If the questions asked by the Crown

are capable of conveying two impressions — one objectionable and the other not — then they "tend to show" each of them: and the questions must be excluded, lest the jury adopt the worse of the two impressions. I do not think that it is open to the prosecution to throw out prejudicial hints and insinuations — from which a jury might infer that the man had been charged before — and then escape censure under the cloak of ambiguity.

Second: I think that the questions tended to show that Jones had been "in trouble" before. It is one thing to confess to having been in trouble before. It is quite another to have it emphasised against you with devastating detail. Before these questions were asked by the Crown, all that the jury knew was that at some unspecified time in the near or distant past, this man had been in trouble with the police. After the questions were asked, the jury knew, in addition, that he had been very recently in trouble for an offence on a Friday night which was of so sensational a character that it featured in a newspaper on the following Sunday —in these respects closely similar to the present offence — and that he had been charged in a court of law with that very offence. It seems to me that questions which tend to reveal an offence, thus particularised, are directly within the prohibition in section 1(f) and are not rendered admissible by his own vague disclosure of some other offence. I do not believe that the mere fact that he said.he had been in trouble before with the police — referring as he did to an entirely different matter many years past — let in this very damaging cross-examination as to recent events.

(LORD DEVLIN also dissented on this point, but both he and LORD DENNING agreed with the majority that the line of cross-examination was proper; see *A Practical Approach to Evidence* p 94, n 28.)

Holt J: Then it goes on, 'committed or been convicted of or been charged with'. Obviously, the subsection is not confined to actual convictions, but is intended to deal with other discreditable conduct. It may not matter here, but what is the meaning of 'charged with'?

Mr Atkyn: My Lord, it would seem to mean a formal charge, not just that the defendant was suspected of some offence. I would refer Your Lordship to:

Stirland v DPP [1944] AC 315 (HL)

The appellant, on trial for forgery, put his character in issue and asserted in examination in chief that he had never been 'charged' with any offence. He was asked in cross-examination questions suggesting that on a previous occasion he had been 'questioned about a suggested forgery' by his former employers.

VISCOUNT SIMON LC said: It is necessary, however, to guard against a possible confusion in the use of the word "charged." In para. (f) of s.1 of the Act of 1898 the word appears five times and it is plain that its meaning in the section is "accused before a court" and not merely "suspected or accused without prosecution." When the appellant denied that he had ever been "charged," he may fairly be understood to use the word in the sense it bears in the statute and to mean that he had never previously been brought before a criminal court. Questions whether his former employer had suspected him of forgery were not, therefore, any challenge to the veracity of what he had said. Neither were they relevant as going to disprove good character. The most virtuous may be suspected, and an unproved accusation proves nothing against the accused, but the questions, while irrelevant both to the charge which was being tried and to the issue of good character, were calculated to injure the appellants in the eyes of the jury by suggesting that he had been in trouble before, and were, therefore, not fair to him. They should not have been put, and, if put, should have been disallowed.

(LORDS RUSSELL OF KILLOWEN, THANKERTON, WRIGHT and PORTER agreed).

My Lord, the prohibition extends to 'any offence', so tnat even subsequent offences are protected. I refer for example to a case in which, had the defendant's shield remained intact, the cross-examination would have been improper, namely:

R v *Coltress* (1978) 68 Cr App R 193 (CA)

The defendant was charged with the theft of a bottle of whisky from a store. At his trial his defence involved imputations on the character of witnesses for the prosecution. At the time of his arrest, the defendant had been a man of good character, but ten months later, before his trial, he had been convicted of the theft of a credit card and of obtaining credit by the use of that card. The judge, in his discretion, permitted the prosecution to cross-examine the defendant as to those convictions under s.1(f)(ii) of the Criminal Evidence Act 1898. The defendant was convicted and appealed.

ORR LJ, giving the judgment of the court, said: 'The next ground of appeal was that the judge wrongly exercised his discretion in allowing cross-examination of the defendant as to the convictions in question, which took place 10 months after his arrest for the offence on which he was being tried, and it was argued that at the time of the offence the accused was a man of good character and would have remained so had the trial taken place before the subsequent convictions of which evidence was admitted. For this reason it was said, it was a wrong exercise of discretion to admit the convictions in evidence.'
We have no doubt that the judge had in mind the fact that these were subsequent convictions in coming to the conclusion whether they should be admitted in evidence, and we find no substance in this ground of appeal.
Appeal dismissed.

Holt J: And the prohibition is evidently wider than just previous convictions because the subsection adds specifically, 'or is of bad character'. What may that involve?

Mr Atkyn: My Lord, it is now capable of extending to general disposition and conduct and of course to previous convictions as well, whereas at common law before the Act, it was thought that evidence of character was confined to evidence of reputation.
(Mr Atkyn referred to *R* v *Dunkley* [1927] 1 KB 323 and the matters dealt with in 4.3 ante, and continued:)
My Lord, in my submission, the course proposed by my learned friend offends against the subsection on any view.

Holt J: Mr Bunbury, how do you put your argument?

Mr Bunbury: My Lord, my learned friend's objection relates only to the possibility of cross-examination where the defendant himself does something to expose himself to it, where he loses his shield, so to speak. But the section also provides two instances where the prosecution are entitled to cross-examine as a matter of law, irrespective of the nature or conduct of the defence.

Holt J: You are presumably referring to sections 1(e) and 1(f)(i) whereas Mr Atkyn may have had in mind sections 1(f)(ii) and 1(f)(iii).

Mr Bunbury: Yes, My Lord. Section 1(e) relates to questions tending to show that the defendant is guilty of the offence charged in the indictment, that is to say questions directly related to the offence charged.

Holt J: Mr Atkyn, you would not object to that kind of questioning, would you? If a defendant elects to give evidence, the prosecution must be entitled to seek to convict him.

Mr Atkyn: My Lord, I respectfully agree, but section 1(e) makes no reference to cross-examination as to character, or to offences other than that charged.

Mr Bunbury: My Lord, I base my argument on the second of the two subsections to which Your Lordship referred, section 1(f)(i). That part of the section is within the prohibition of section 1(f), but specifically permits cross-examination as to character where the evidence of character is admissible to prove guilt as charged. It is a case where exceptionally, cross-examination of a defendant about his character, including other offences, is permitted for the purpose of introducing admissible evidence on the issue of his guilt.

Holt J: I do not find it at all easy to imagine in what cases it can be admissible evidence of an offence to show that a man has been convicted on another occasion, or is of bad character.

Mr Bunbury: My Lord, the cases are not numerous. The first category is where a previous conviction is actually made part of the offence charged by statute. One example is the offence under the Firearms Act 1968.

Firearms Act 1968, s.21

(21)(1) A person who has been sentenced to imprisonment for a term of three years or more, shall not at any time have a firearm or ammunition in his possession.
(4) It is an offence for a person to contravene any of the foregoing provisions of this section.

Holt J: Well, that is a case where the statute makes that particular aspect of character a fact in issue, rather like the example of driving while disqualified. But while you could establish that fact as part of your case, his character generally would be protected by section 1(f). Much the same would apply where the statute said that some part of his character was to be relevant to an aspect of the case, for instance under the Theft Act 1968.

Theft Act 1968, s.27

27(3) Where a person is being proceeded against for handling stolen goods (but not for any offence other than handling stolen goods), then at any stage of the proceedings, if evidence has been given of his having or arranging to have in his possession the goods the subject of the charge, or of his undertaking or assisting in, or arranging to undertake or assist in, their retention, removal, disposal or realisation, the following evidence shall be admissible for the purpose of proving that he knew or believed the goods to be stolen goods:—
(a) evidence that he has had in his possession, or has undertaken or assisted in the retention, removal, disposal or realisation of, stolen goods from any theft taking place not earlier than twelve months before the offence charged; and
(b) ...evidence that he has within the five years preceding the date of the offence charged been convicted of theft or of handling stolen goods.

Again, what the Act is doing there is not to expose his character as a whole, but to say that that peculiarly relevant and specific part of it shall have a limited evidential value as to his state of mind, and no more. That is not really of much help in the present case.

Mr Bunbury: No, My Lord. May I come to the second category which may assist. There are cases where obviously relevant evidence happens also to involve some exposure of character. In such a case, as Lord Herschell LC said in *Makin and Makin v Attorney-General for New South Wales* [1894] AC 57 at 65: '...the mere fact that the evidence adduced tends to show the commission of other crimes does not render it inadmissible if it be relevant to an issue before the jury, and it may be so relevant if it bears upon the question whether the acts alleged to consistute the crime charged in the indictment were designed or accidental, or to rebut a defence which would otherwise be open to the accused.'

I would refer Your Lordship to:

R v *Chitson* [1909] 2 KB 945 (CCA)

The defendant was convicted of having unlawful sexual intercourse with a girl aged fourteen. The girl gave evidence that on the day after the alleged offence the defendant had told her that he had previously done the same thing to another girl, who was alleged by the prosecution to have been under sixteen at the time. The defendant gave evidence, and was asked in cross-examination (and the questions were allowed by the judge) whether he had made the statement.

A T LAWRENCE J, delivering the judgment of the court, stated the facts and continued: 'Although the latter questions did no doubt tend to prove that he was of bad character, still they also in our opinion tended to show that he was guilty of the offence with which he was charged, for if he had made that statement to the prosecutrix at the time alleged by her, that fact would strongly corroborate her evidence that the prisoner was the person who had had connection with her. We are therefore of the opinion that the learned judge rightly admitted the questions, not in order to prove a habit or system, as was the case in *Makin* v *Attorney-General for New South Wales* [1894] AC 57 and *R* v *Bond* [1906] 2 KB 389, but because the evidence was material as tending to show that the statement was one likely to have been made to the prosecutrix by the prisoner, and was not invented by her or learnt from someone else, and it was therefore material to the issue as to whether the prisoner did commit the offence for which he was then being tried.

Appeal dismissed.

Similarly, My Lord, in *R* v *Kurasch:*

R v *Kurasch* [1915] 2 KB 749 (CCA)

The appellant and four other men were convicted of conspiring by means of false pretences to defraud the prosecutor, the false pretences alleged being the holding of a mock auction. The appellants denied the false pretences and also alleged that they were all merely the servants of a woman who was the proprietress of the auction business. The appellant gave evidence and was asked in cross-examination whether it was not the fact that he and the proprietress of the business were at the date of the offence living together as man and wife. The appellant answered that he was.

LORD READING CJ, delivering the judgment of the court, stated the facts and continued: 'In *R* v *Rodley* [1913] 3 KB 472, the following passage from the judgment of Channell J in *R* v *Fisher* [1910] 1 KB 152 was quoted by Bankes J in delivering the judgment of the Court: "The principle is clear, however, and if the principle is attended to I think it will usually be found that the difficulty of applying it to a particular case will disappear. The principle is that the prosecution are not allowed to prove that a prisoner has committed the offence with which he is charged by giving evidence that he is a person of bad character and one who is in the habit of committing crimes, for that is equivalent to asking the jury to say that because the prisoner has committed other offences he must therefore be guilty of the particular offence for which he is being tried. But if the evidence of other offences does go to prove that he did commit the offence charged, it is admissible because it is relevant to the issue, and it is admissible not because, but notwithstanding that, it proves that the prisoner has committed another offence"... We do not desire in the least to depart from the principles of law as there laid down. The only difficulty that arises is in applying those principles to the facts of this case, but we have come to the conclusion that it is impossible to say that a question as to the real relations which existed between the appellant and Mrs Dyas was not material to the issue. It would materially assist the prosecution to establish their case if they could show that the appellant was not a mere servant of Mrs Dyas, but that he occupied a more important

position, and that, according to the evidence of the police officer, he had said he had employed one of the men engaged in the auction. In these circumstances it cannot, in our opinion, be said that a question as to the relations between the appellant and Mrs Dyas was not relevant to the issue. The case seems to us to come very close to the decision in *R v Chitson* [1909] 2 KB 945, and to come within the principle laid down in the other cases to which attention has been drawn.'
Appeal dismissed.

My Lord, in my submission, the reason why the cross-examination was proper in those cases was not that it referred to character, but that it was relevant to the issue before the jury on the facts of those cases and so was permissible despite the reference to the defendant's character.

Holt J: The relevance there seems to have stemmed from things that the defendant himself had said, though presumably this need not be so.

Mr Bunbury: My Lord, yes. One sees from this that I ought to be permitted to cross-examine about Coke's previous conviction here, because he has given evidence that Miss Blackstone consented to sexual intercourse and that he had no reason to think otherwise. I say that his state of mind as a man previously convicted of rape in similar circumstances is relevant to that issue before the jury. Indeed, the jury may be misled by being denied this cross-examination in view of Coke's own assertions regarding his state of mind.

Holt J: You say 'in similar circumstances'. Do I take it that you propose to cross-examine not just on the existence of the previous conviction, but as to the detail of the offence?

Mr Bunbury: Yes, My Lord. This is not a case where the court is concerned merely with the defendant's credit as a witness, as would be the case under s.1(f)(ii) or (iii). Here, the very detail provides the relevance to guilt as charged. My Lord, it is true that in *R v France and France* this court held that in a case where the defendants denied their very presence at the scene, cross-examination as to the detail of a previous offence could not be justified.

R v France and France, unreported, 11 September 1978 (CA)

SWANWICK J, delivering the judgment of the court, said: 'These two appellants were unanimously convicted by the jury of theft. They had been jointly indicted with a man called Melvyn Fearn who had on a previous occasion pleaded guilty to theft and who, in fact, gave evidence for the Crown.

Very briefly, the facts of the charge against them were that whilst Mary France and Fearn took some steps to distract the assistant in a jewellery shop, Terence France stole two gold bracelets to a value of £300 from the window display and later transferred them to a green bag in the possession of Fearn outside the shop. The Appellants, on the other hand, claimed that Fearn was the person who had committed the crime and they had had nothing to do with it whatsoever and that they had never been in the jewellery shop at all....

The whole of the prosecution case was said to be a conspiracy by the police who had been watching Fearn, knew of the Appellants' records and wanted to involve them and had embroidered their evidence in order to do so. This attack having been made on the police meant that inevitably the characters of both accused were going to be put in issue. Mr Bullimore, who appeared for them both, very understandably and properly grasped the nettle and asked Terence France in chief about his record. He then admitted that he had an extensive criminal record...

What was put by the defence before the jury in the cross-examination of the police and in the examination-in-chief of Terence France was that he had an extensive criminal record for dishonesty, including convictions for embezzlement, larceny, theft, burglary and false accounting and had served terms of imprisonment. When it came to his cross-examination, counsel for the prosecution reminded him that he had already told the jury that on numerous occasions in the past he had been dishonest and elicited from him that in 1975, he had received twelve months' imprisonment, that in 1973 he had been to prison for theft, which involved going into shops, distracting people and stealing items, and that in March, 1975, he had gone into a jeweller's shop and stolen a ring. At that stage, and not until that stage, the defence raised an objection in the presence of the jury that the prosecution were well entitled to ask the defendant what previous convictions he had got, in so far as that went to credibility. They submitted that the detail of the offences that had been elicited in cross-examination had gone far beyond that issue and was highly prejudicial and quite unfair. Mr Bullimore has told us that in making that submission he did not intend nor did he apply for discharge of the jury but he hoped that if the submission was successful, the jury might forget the details and indeed he was prepared to take the risk of them doing so if nothing further was said about the matter. However, the learned Judge then ruled that if the evidence was that the defendant was sent to prison for twelve months for stealing, if that was rightly in evidence before the jury, and indeed it was conceded that it was, then, in his words: "It cannot be inappropriate for the jury to have before them evidence of the kind of stealing."

When it came to the evidence of Mary France, she supported her husband's account, including the allegation of conspiracy by the police, and therefore exposed herself to cross-examination of her record. The prosecution applied to the learned Judge, in the absence of the jury, to cross-examine her on her record, she not having given evidence of it in chief. The defence conceded that they would be entitled to do so but again resisted the prosecution asking her more than the mere fact of conviction. However, the learned Judge, following his previous ruling, again ruled that the prosecution were entitled to put the details, whereupon they elicited from her that on the 19th March, 1975, she was convicted of a joint offence with her husband of stealing a ring from a jeweller's shop. We will come later to the summing up.

Complaint is now made that the learned Judge should not have allowed those details to be put in cross-examination of these Appellants. In the grounds of appeal, it was firstly suggested that it was inadmissible because it was not relevant to any issue, it not being suggested — and Mr Worsley confirms this — that this would be admissible as similar fact evidence. One reason was that the Crown had not elected to call such evidence in chief as would have been proper, normal, fair and desirable if they had intended to call such evidence. Secondly, the Crown were not and are not in a position to suggest that the evidence went far enough to be similar fact evidence. Thirdly, the issue was not one appropriate to similar fact evidence because the issue was not one of intent or anything of that sort; it was a straightforward issue as to what had happened....

We do not think that it is desirable to lay down hard and fast rules as to what questions precisely can be asked in each case where an accused person has, by his cross-examination of Crown witnesses or otherwise, put his character in issue. Suffice it to say that in this case, taking an overall view of the matter, we regard these questions, directed as they were specifically to previous convictions which bore some similarity to the charges before the court, was ill-directed in that respect and should have been excluded by the learned Judge — quite apart from the question of admissibility — as being prejudicial rather than probative. It must have been highly prejudicial and we feel that the extent to which the cross-examination went was beyond the bounds of legitimate cross-examination as to credibility, the bounds of which we are not prepared to define more precisely than to say obviously it may be relevant on an issue of credibility to test or bring out the sort of scale of the previous offences or something of that sort. However, we do not propose to lay down hard and fast rules or indeed guidelines for that evidence. We consider this individual case and we consider in this case those questions were wrongly allowed and we think they must have prejudiced the jury. Appeal allowed.

This decision was distinguished by a subsequent court in *R v Duncalf* where the question for the jury was not whether the defendant was present, but his intent, as is the case here.

R v Duncalf [1979] 1 WLR 918 (CA)

The defendants were convicted of conspiracy to steal from shops and stores.

ROSKILL L J, reading the judgment of the court, dealt with other grounds of appeal and continued: 'The other matter argued before us was that the appellants who had attacked the police and thus caused their own characters to be placed before the jury had been improperly cross-examined, not merely as to facts which led to those convictions. Those underlying facts in truth showed that the appellants had previously been convicted of doing very much the same thing on a previous occasion. This cross-examination though not objected to at the trial, was said to be contrary to the decision of this court in *R v France* [1979] Crim LR 48.

A very similar argument was recently advanced before this court as presently constituted in *R v Dudley* (unreported), April 2, 1979, and rejected. The offending evidence in *R v France* was not relevant to any question of intent — indeed the judgment of this court given by Swanwick J shows that if that evidence had been directed to the intent, the position would have been different. The appellants in *R v France* had denied being present at all at the scene of the alleged theft. In the present case the appellants' presence was admitted and the sole issue was one of their intent. We do not see why this evidence was not admissible on this issue within proviso (f)(i) to section 1 of the Criminal Evidence Act 1898, subject, of course, in such a case to the judge's right to exclude such evidence if invited so to do on the ground that it is prejudicial rather than probative: see also the speech of Viscount Sankey L C, in *Maxwell v Director of Public Prosecutions* [1935] AC 309, 319, 320. We respectfully agree with what this court said in *R v France* [1979] Crim LR 48, namely, that hard and fast rules cannot be laid down as to what questions may or may not be asked in circumstances such as these.'

Holt J: Mr Atkyn, what do you say?

Mr Atkyn: My Lord, if this evidence was relevant in this way, it was open to my learned friend to apply to have it admitted as similar fact evidence (see Chapter 5). In *R v France and France* it was for exactly that reason — that the prosecution had not sought to admit the previous conviction as similar fact evidence — that the court held the cross-examination could go only to credit, so that the fact of the previous conviction might be used to attack the defendant's credit, but the detail was beyond what was permissible, and was, of course prejudicial.

(Holt J then considered these arguments and a further argument by Mr Atkyn that grounds existed for excluding the cross-examination in the exercise of his discretion (as to discretion see 1.5 ante), and allowed the cross-examination both as to the fact of the previous conviction, and the manner in which it was committed, as being relevant to the issue of Coke's state of mind and therefore admissible evidence to prove the offence charged under s.1(f)(i).)

4.7 Commentary

R v Coke and Littleton at trial. Mr Atkyn for Coke has cross-examined Margaret Blackstone with a view to showing that she consented to have sexual intercourse with Coke. With the leave of Holt J[1], he has further cross-examined her about her previous sexual experience, suggesting specifically that she is promiscuous, and that she falsely accused Kevin of raping her last year. Mr Atkyn asks her about her previous conviction for theft, and suggests that she is dishonest generally and in relation to this case. Mr Atkyn, suggesting that the confession is inadmissible, has also cross-examined D/I Glanvil and D/S Bracton to the effect that they threatened Coke at the police station to induce him to make a confession of guilt, made up an alleged verbal admission attributed to Coke and were guilty of a number of breaches of the Judges' Rules, notably by failing to caution him. Mr Atkyn's purpose was to seek to

---

[1]For the necessity for leave before cross-examination of the complainant about her previous sexual experience, see 13.3.

demonstrate that Coke's alleged confessions were not voluntary and should not be admitted into evidence, or should be treated as having little weight if placed before the jury. Coke has given evidence in chief, stating that he is honest and hardworking, and that Margaret consented to have sexual intercourse with him. Mr Bunbury for the prosecution asks Holt J to send the jury out and applies for leave to cross-examine Coke about his character.

4.8 Argument

Mr Bunbury: My Lord, in my submission, I am entitled to cross-examine the defendant Coke as to his previous conviction for rape, under the provisions of s.1(f)(ii) of the Criminal Evidence Act 1898. I rest my submission on both grounds postulated by the subsection. Coke has both given evidence of his good character, and, by counsel, made the clearest possible imputations on the character of three prosecution witnesses, namely Miss Blackstone, D/I Glanvil and D/S Bracton.

Holt J: You say that the jury should be told about his past record because it goes to credit.

Mr Bunbury: Yes, My Lord. The jury are entitled to be shown the full picture, and to know the full background about a defendant who seeks to create a favourable impression in terms of character. They are also entitled to know from what kind of man the imputations on character emanate. It may be that they will take a very different view, knowing that the author of these attacks is a man with a previous conviction for rape. My Lord, I do not seek to put the detail of the conviction before the jury. (See *R* v *France and France; R* v *Duncalf,* 4.6 ante.)

Holt J: His evidence of good character, according to my note, was limited to saying that he is honest and hardworking. What is the relevance of proving a previous conviction for rape, if what you want to do is discredit his assertion of honesty?

Mr Bunbury: With respect, My Lord, character is indivisible. Where a defendant asserts his good character in whatever terms, he leads the jury to suppose him to be a person less likely to have committed the offence charged than they might think if they knew the truth. I would refer Your Lordship to:

R v *Winfield* [1939] 4 All ER 164 (CCA)

The defendant, who was charged with indecent assault on a woman, called a witness and asked her questions to establish his good character with regard to sexual morality. The witness and/or the defendant (there being a conflict between the two reports of the case, in [1939] 4 All ER 164 and in 27 Cr App R 139) were cross-examined on the defendant's previous convictions of offences involving dishonesty. On appeal against conviction, it was contended that the evidence as to his general character was improperly admitted.

HUMPHREYS J, delivering the judgment of the court said: 'The deputy chairman knew, though probably the prisoner did not, that there is no such thing known to our procedure as putting half your character in issue and leaving out the other half. A man is not entitled to say, "Well, I may have a bad character as a dishonest rogue, but at all events nobody has ever said that I have acted indecently towards women." That cannot be done. If a man who is accused chooses to put his character in issue, he must take the consequences. It is quite clear that this man did. He asked questions about his character quite apart from the facts of this case. The result was that he was properly cross-examined as to character.'
(The appeal was, however, allowed and conviction quashed on the ground of want of corroboration.)

And there is a dictum of Lord Simon LC in which your Lordship will find the same point:

Stirland v *DPP* [1944] AC 315 (HL) (For the facts, see 4.6 ante)

LORD SIMON said: 'An accused who "puts his character in issue" must be regarded as putting the whole of his past record in issue. He cannot assert his good conduct in certain respects without exposing himself to enquiry about the rest of his record so far as this tends to disprove a claim for good character.'

Subject to Your Lordship's discretion, I should be entitled to draw the jury's attention to the previous conviction, not of course as being evidence of guilt, but to attack the defendant Coke in terms of his credit as a witness.

My Lord, the position is even clearer where a defendant makes imputations on the character of the prosecution witnesses, because there the jury are weighing his credibility against that of the witness attacked, and that process might be vitally affected by the consideration whether the defendant is a man of good character or not.

Holt J: Mr Atkyn, it seems to me, subject to what you say, that your client has lost his shield under s.1(f)(ii) as a matter of law.

Mr Atkyn: My Lord, so far as Coke's alleged assertion of good character is concerned, Your Lordship must consider the issue of relevance. What he said was that he was honest and hardworking. He made no assertions about his character in any other respect. There is a question of relevance in allowing the jury to hear about this conviction, which does not assist them by refuting anything said by the defendant in evidence. I would refer Your Lordship to:

Maxwell v *DPP* [1935] AC 309 (HL)

The appellant was charged with manslaughter. It was alleged that he had performed an illegal abortion which had resulted in death. He gave evidence of his general good character, and was then cross-examined to show that on a previous occasion he had been charged with, but acquitted of, the same offence in similar circumstances. The appellant was convicted, and appealed unsuccessfully to the Court of Criminal Appeal. He further appealed to the House of Lords.

VISCOUNT SANKEY LC said: 'When it is sought to justify a question it must not only be brought within the terms of the permission, but also must be capable of justification according to the general rules of evidence and in particular must satisfy the test of relevance. Exception (i) deals with the former of the two main classes of evidence referred to above, that is, evidence falling within the rule that where issues of intention or design are involved in the charge or defence, the prisoner may be asked questions relevant to these matters, even though he has himself raised no question of his good character. Exceptions (ii) and (iii) come into play where the prisoner by himself or his witnesses has put his character in issue, or has attacked the character of others. Dealing with exceptions (i) and (ii), it is clear that the test of relevance is wider in (ii) than in (i); in the latter, proof that the prisoner has committed or been convicted of some other offence, can only be admitted if it goes to show that he was guilty of the offence charged. In the former (exception ii), the questions permissible must be relevant to the issue of his own good character and if not so relevant cannot be admissible. But it seems clear that the mere fact of a charge cannot in general be evidence of bad character or be regarded otherwise than as a misfortune. It seemed to be contended on behalf of the respondent that a charge was per se such evidence that the man charged, even though acquitted, must thereafter remain under a cloud, however innocent. I find it impossible to accept any such view. The mere fact that a man has been charged with an offence is no proof that he committed the offence. Such a fact is, therefore, irrelevant; it neither goes to show that the prisoner did the acts for which he is actually being tried nor does it go to his credibility as a witness. Such questions must, therefore, be excluded on the principle which is fundamental in the law of evidence as conceived in this country, especially in criminal cases, because, if allowed, they are likely to lead the minds of the jury astray into false issues; not merely do they tend to introduce suspicion as if it were evidence, but they tend to distract the jury from the true issue — namely, whether the prisoner in fact committed the offence on which he is actually standing his trial. It is of the utmost importance for a fair trial that the evidence should be prima facie limited to matters relating to the transaction which forms the subject of the indictment and that any departure from these matters should be strictly confined.

It does not result from this conclusion that the word "charged" in proviso (f) is otiose: it is clearly not so as regards the prohibition; and when the exceptions come into play there may still be cases in which a prisoner may be asked about a charge as a step in cross-examination leading to a question whether he was convicted on the charge, or in order to elicit some evidence as to statements made or evidence given by the prisoner in the course of the trial on a charge which failed, which tend to throw doubt on the evidence which he is actually giving, though cases of this last class must be rare and the cross-examination permissible only with great safeguards.

Again, a man charged with an offence against the person may perhaps be asked whether he had uttered threats against the person attacked because he was angry with him for bringing a charge which turned out to be unfounded. Other probabilities may be imagined. Thus, if a prisoner has been acquitted on the plea of autrefois convict such an acquittal might be relevant to his credit, though it would seem that what was in truth relevant to his credit was the previous conviction and not the fact that he was erroneously again charged with the same offence; again, it may be, though it is perhaps a remote supposition, that an acquittal of a prisoner charged with rape on the plea of consent may possibly be relevant to a prisoner's credit.

But these instances all involve the crucial test of relevance. And in general no question whether a prisoner has been convicted or charged or acquitted should be asked or, if asked, allowed by the judge, who has a discretion under proviso (f), unless it helps to elucidate the particular issue which the jury is investigating, or goes to credibility, that is, tends to show that he is not to be believed on his oath; indeed the question whether a man has been convicted, charged or acquitted ought not to be admitted, even if it goes to credibility, if there is any risk of the jury being misled into thinking that it goes not to credibility but to the probability of his having committed the offence of which he is charged. I think that it is impossible in the present case to say that the fact that the prisoner had been acquitted on a previous charge of murder or manslaughter, was relevant, or that it tended in the present case to destroy his credibility as a witness.

(LORDS ATKIN, BLANESBURGH, THANKERTON and WRIGHT agreed)
Appeal allowed.

This may be contrasted with the decision in:

R v *Waldman* (1934) 24 Cr App R 204 (CCA)

The appellant, who was charged with receiving stolen property, put his character in issue and was asked in cross-examination about a previous conviction and a previous acquittal for the same offence.

AVORY J, giving the judgment of the court, said: 'Now upon the first point — whether or not the question was admissible — it is to be observed that there is a not unimportant distinction between this case and the case of *Maxwell* v *DPP*, which was the subject of the judgment in the House of Lords. In the present case the appellant put his character in issue, and not only himself put it in issue, but called a witness to testify as to his good character. That witness was asked whether in fact the appellant had been convicted of the offence of receiving stolen goods in 1920, and the appellant himself had to admit that he had been convicted in 1920 of receiving. Both the appellant and this witness were also asked about a

charge made two years later against the appellant for a similar offence of receiving stolen property, on which occasion he had been acquitted. In *Maxwell* v *DPP* there was no suggestion that the appellant had ever been convicted at all, and whether the House of Lords would have decided the question in the same way as they did if they had had to deal with a case where a man had been previously acquitted may be open to doubt. It is not necessary for this Court to consider what the decision of the House of Lords would have been in such a case. It is not necessary either to consider or to express an opinion on the point which Mr Christmas Humphreys has taken, that, in a case where the charge is one of receiving, the admissibility of a question as to a previous acquittal may be relevant. We do not express any opinion on the point, although it may be one worthy of consideration. The charge of receiving stands on an exceptional footing in that it is one of the few charges in which the prosecution, for the purpose of proving the guilty knowledge of the accused, are allowed to give evidence of a previous conviction within the last five years and of other stolen property being found within twelve months on the premises of the accused. No doubt also there is much to be said for making a distinction between a charge of receiving stolen goods and a charge such as that with which the House of Lords dealt in Maxwell.'
The court nevertheless dismissed the appeal applying the proviso to s.4 of the Criminal Appeal Act 1907.

Holt J: But Mr Atkyn, as Mr Bunbury told me, and I am inclined to accept, character is indivisible. The defendant Coke has sought, in my view, to lead the jury to accept him as a man of good character and so one less likely to have committed this offence. This is not a case concerned with a previous acquittal. I think it would be entirely wrong to leave them with that impression uncontradicted. Be that as it may, it seems clear that the imputations made by Coke through you in cross-examination are enough to deprive him of his shield.

Mr Atkyn: My Lord, may I make two observations about that, relating to what are said to be imputations on the character of these witnesses. The first is that at least so far as Margaret Blackstone is concerned, the suggestions made to her do no more than deny, admittedly in emphatic terms, the substance of the case against my client. It is clear law that a defendant is entitled to defend himself, if necessary in strong terms, by denying the charge without losing his shield. Were this not the case, the whole purpose of the protection given to him under s.1 of the 1898 Act would be defeated. I refer Your Lordship to:

R v *Rouse* [1904] 1 KB 184 (CCR)

LORD ALVERSTONE CJ said: 'Having regard to the statement that has been made to us by the counsel for the prosecution, I wish to make it perfectly clear that our decision proceeds upon the particular facts as stated in the case, and that we are not laying down any general rule. The real question which we decide is whether the answer which the defendant gave to the question put to him was sufficient to justify cross-examination as to his antecedents. The indictment was for conspiring to induce the prosecutor by false pretences to sell a mare to the defendant Rouse, and the prosecutor in the course of his evidence said that on a previous occasion Rouse had offered to buy the mare from him for 19*l*. Rouse was called as a witness for the defence, and was asked this question in cross-examination: "Did you ask the prosecutor to sell you the mare in April for 19*l*, or has he invented all that?" If the expression "all that" referred to matters outside those with which the prosecution was dealing, different considerations might arise, for the answer, "No, it is a lie, and he is a liar," might then perhaps be construed as an attack upon the prosecutor's general character as regards truthfulness. But under the circumstances of the case, I think that the prosecution is in a dilemma; either the answer amounted to no more than a plea of not guilty put in forcible language such as would not be unnatural in a person in the defendant's rank in life, or it had nothing to do with the conduct of the defence. In my opinion, the answer given by the

defendant was not sufficient to bring the case within s.1, sub-s (f)(ii), of the Criminal Evidence Act, 1898; the defence itself, by the plea of not guilty, involves the allegation that the charge is not true, and this answer of the defendant was no more than a denial, emphatic in its terms, to the same effect.'
(WRIGHT, KENNEDY, DARLING and PHILLIMORE JJ agreed)
Convictions quashed.

Mr Bunbury: My Lord, I accept that a defendant may deny the charge without losing his shield. The question is whether he may go beyond a denial without losing it.
Mr Atkyn: He has gone so far as to allege consent, which is the equivalent of a denial in a rape case. I would refer Your Lordships to:

R v Turner [1944] KB 463 (CCA)

At the trial of the appellant on a charge of rape his counsel in cross-examination of the prosecutrix suggested to her that she not merely consented to intercourse, but also offered to commit an act of gross indecency on him, and the appellant in his examination in chief gave evidence to the same effect.

HUMPHREYS J, reading the judgment of the court, stated the facts and continued: 'It must be conceded that to allege to a woman that she permitted a man other than her husband to have intercourse with her would be regarded by most persons as an imputation on her character. In the same way, in former times, one of the deadliest insults which could be offered to a gentleman was to call him a liar, and such conduct has often led to a duel, with fatal results, but if an accused person refers to a witness for the prosecution as a liar it does not follow that he is making an imputation on his character so as to render himself liable to cross-examination to character: see *R v Rouse.* We think that wider considerations are involved in the solution of this problem. On a charge of rape the Crown has to prove two things:— (1) intercourse, and (2) the non-consent of the woman. For centuries the law has jealously guarded the right of an accused person to put forward at his trial any defence open to him on the indictment without running the risk of his character, if a bad one, being disclosed to the jury. It would be strange, indeed, if the Act of Parliament which allowed him, in most cases for the first time, to give evidence on oath had virtually deprived him of that right in the case of one serious felony, by enacting that he could only do so at the risk of having his character exposed. What is commonly referred to as the defence of consent in rape is, in truth, nothing more than a denial by the accused that the prosecution has established one of the two essential ingredients of the charge.'
Conviction quashed.

Holt J: Mr Atkyn, I accept of course that he may deny consent, but he has gone rather beyond that. You cited *R v Rouse* to me, but what about:

R v Rappolt (1911) 6 Cr App R 156 (CCA)

The accused was convicted of causing grievous bodily harm to one Stevens. He applied for leave to appeal.

RIDLEY J, giving the judgment of the court, said: 'There was a general attack on the character of Stevens (a witness for the prosecution) when the applicant stated on oath that Stevens was "a horrible liar.".... That is an attack on the general character of the prosecutor, and goes far beyond anything that this court has allowed to pass without rendering the accused liable to cross-examination.
Application refused.

In the present case, she was accused of promiscuity and of another false accusation of rape against someone else. I leave aside her conviction for theft which she admitted, but the allegations to which I have referred seem to me to go well beyond a mere denial. I bear in mind also that he has accused two police officers of fabrication of evidence, and intimidation for the purpose of inducing a confession. How much further does he have to go before he makes an imputation on character?

Mr Atkyn: I accept that allegations of fabrication would amount to an imputation on character, My Lord. This much would seem to be clear from:

R v Clark [1955] 2 QB 469 (CCA)

The appellant was charged with burglary and larceny. At the trial it was suggested by the defence that a purported confession signed by the defendant had been manufactured by a police officer and was untrue. Cross-examination as to the defendant's previous convictions was allowed on the ground that the nature and conduct of the defence was such as to involve imputations on the character of the witnesses for the prosecution. The appellant was convicted and appealed on the ground that in the circumstances the cross-examination as to his character had been improperly allowed.

LORD GODDARD CJ, delivering the judgment of the court, said: 'I think that this matter, so far as this court is concerned, can really be said to be concluded by two cases, both of them fairly early in the history of the court, which so far as I know have never been reversed. One is *R v Wright* (1910) 5 Cr App R 131, when the court consisted of Darling, Phillimore and Bucknill JJ. In that case the prisoner, who had made a complete confession, said that the confession had been got out of him by bribery, by being given tobacco and being allowed to smoke. Darling J, giving the judgment of the court, said (p 133): "If the appellant puts it that he was improperly induced to make and sign the statement that was produced, it is difficult to imagine anything more like an imputation on a witness for the prosecution. It is imputed to the witness that, having a man in his custody, he bribed him, and so by that means got him to make the confession. It is contended by Mr Churchill that this case comes within *Preston* [1909] 1 KB 568 in which Channell J delivered judgment. But on what ground did Channell J really put the decision?...he says: "The present case obviously is very near the line," and...he says: "The statement in the present case was "a mere unconsidered remark made by the prisoner without giving any serious attention to it," etc. The imputation in the case now before us was that the police inspector was not a fit person to remain in the force; had he done what was imputed to him there is no doubt he could have been dismissed from the force; it is the gravest possible imputation, and cannot be excused by the contention that it was the only way open to the appellant of meeting the case against him." I observe that the judge said that it was difficult to imagine anything more like an imputation on the witness for the prosecution. This case is even worse, because in *R v Wright* it was merely suggested that to get the confession out of the prisoner the police officers bribed him with tobacco, while in the present case it is said that they concocted the confession, and that the confession was never that of the appellant, but was dictated by the police officer.

The other case to which I would refer is *R v Jones* (1923) 17 Cr App R 117, where the matter was very much the same as it is here. In the course of the argument Shearman J said: "Here appellant said that the police deliberately held him up on remand after remand, and as they could not get evidence they concocted it" — that is what is said here, that as the police had not evidence they concocted it — and Lord Hewart CJ said: "It is one thing to deny a statement; it is another thing to say that the statement has been deliberately and elaborately manufactured."

Those two cases seem to be entirely in point. This was an attack by the appellant, not on the evidence of the police inspector, but on his conduct outside that evidence. It is one thing to say: "That is not my statement"; it is another thing to say, as prisoners very often do: "Well yes, but he misunderstood me; he has got down something I did not say; I missed it when it was being read over, but what I said was something else," and very often a specious and plausible paraphrase of something which would make the sense of the statement different is given; or sometimes the prisoner says: "The officer left out something." In all such cases there is really no difficulty, and it should be remembered that it is always in the discretion of the judge to rule out a cross-examination and to tell counsel for the prosecution that he is not going to allow a cross-examination as to previous convictions. I do not want to make any joke about the matter or to put it otherwise than perfectly seriously, but one knows well that police officers are regarded as fair game for cross-examination and to make charges against, and I do not believe that any judge would allow a roving cross-examination into the prisoner's past merely because he said, "The police constable is a liar," or "The police constable is not telling the truth"; for all he is doing is pleading not guilty with emphasis, or, as Darling J said in *R* v *Rouse* [1904] 1 KB 184, that is "merely an emphatic mode of denial." It is quite another thing to make the suggestion against police officers that they have been conspiring together to defeat the ends of justice.

For these reasons the court is of opinion that the cross-examination was properly admitted in the present case.

Appeal dismissed.

I did, however, seek to suggest that the officers may have been mistaken in certain respects.

Holt J: I have to look to the reality of the situation, Mr Atkyn, not just to the form of the questions. The Court of Appeal emphasised that point in:

R v **Tanner** (1977) 66 Cr App R 56 (CA)

The appellant was indicted on two counts of theft. Police officers testified that when the appellant was being questioned about the thefts he had made admissions. At the trial the appellant denied this. Counsel did not cross-examine the officers on the basis that they were lying, but simply that they were wrong in saying that the admissions were made. However, during his cross-examination, in answer to a question by the trial judge, the appellant said that the police evidence on that matter was a complete invention. The trial judge in his discretion then granted the prosecution's application to cross-examine the appellant about his previous convictions. The appellant was convicted and appealed on the ground that the judge had exercised his discretion wrongly, it being contended that a simple denial by a defendant of evidence given by a prosecution witness, even if he said that that witness was lying, did not involve an imputation on the character of the witness within the proviso to s.1(f) of the Criminal Evidence Act 1898.

BROWNE LJ, reading the judgment of the court, said: 'In our judgment, the nature and conduct of the defence in the present case did involve imputations on the character of the police officers. This was not a case of a denial of a single answer, nor was there any suggestion or possibility of mistake or misunderstanding. The appellant was denying not only his admission, but in the case of each interview a series of subsequent important answers attributed to him by the police.

In spite of Mr de Lotbiniere's skilful handling of the cross-examination of the police officers, and of the defendants evidence in chief, it necessarily followed, in the circumstances of this case, that the appellant was saying impliedly that the police officers had made up a substantial and vital part of their evidence and that Detective Constable Tuck and Dectective Constable Mytton had conspired together to do so. He also said expressly that one of the police officers said that if he admitted the offence he would get bail. The judge's intervention was, in our judgment, merely bringing into the open what was already necessarily implicit. Appeal dismissed.

Mr Atkyn: My Lord, yes. Perhaps I might mention my second point which relates partly to the question of law of admissibility, whether the shield has been lost, and partly to Your Lordship's discretion. It is that the matters which were put were an integral part of the defence, and indeed, it would have been impossible to conduct the defence on the basis of my instructions without putting those matters.

Holt J: Yes. I should like to hear Mr Bunbury on that point.

Mr Bunbury: In my submission, My Lord, however much imputations on character may be essential to the proper presentation of the defence, as a matter of law the shield is lost. The point was specifically made by the House of Lords in *Selvey* v *DPP*, although I accept that their Lordships did recognise the existence of a discretion to prevent any unfairness which may, in the judge's opinion, arise from the application of the subsection.

Selvey v *DPP* [1970] AC 304 (HL)

The appellant was charged with buggery. There was medical evidence that the complainant had been sexually interfered with by someone on the day in question, and also indecent photographs were found in the appellant's room. The defence was that the complainant had told him that he had already "been on the bed" with a man for £1 and that he would do the same for him for £1. The appellant denied knowledge of the photographs and suggested that they had been planted on him by the complainant in annoyance at the rejection of the offer. The trial judge allowed the appellant to be cross-examined on his previous convictions for homosexual offences. The appellant was convicted and appealed on the ground, *inter alia,* that as the nature of his defence necessarily involved the imputation against the complainant, the judge in accordance with 'the general rule' should have exercised his discretion under s.1(f)(ii) of the Criminal Evidence Act 1898, in his favour by excluding his previous record.

LORD PEARCE said: 'My Lords, ever since the Criminal Evidence Act 1898, came into force there has been difficulty and argument about the application of the words in section 1(f)(ii) "the nature or conduct of the defence is such as to involve imputations on the character of the prosecutor or the witnesses for the prosecution."

Two main views have been put forward. One view adopts the literal meaning of the words. The prosecutor is cross-examined to show that he has fabricated the charge for improper reasons. That involves imputations on his character. Therefore, it lets in the previous convictions of the accused. The practical justification, for this view is the "tit for tat" argument. If the accused is seeking to cast discredit on the prosecution, then the prosecution should be allowed to do likewise. If the accused is seeking to persuade the jury that the prosecutor behaved like a knave, then the jury should know the character of the man who makes these accusations, so that it may judge fairly between them instead of being in the dark as to one of them.

The other view would limit the literal meaning of the words. For it cannot, it is said, have been intended by Parliament to make a man liable to have his previous convictions revealed whenever the essence of his defence necessitates imputations on the character of the prosecutor. This revelation is always damaging and often fatal to a defence. The high-water mark of this argument is the ordinary case of rape. In this the vital issue (as a rule) is whether the woman consented. Consent (as a rule) involves imputations on her character. Therefore, in the ordinary case of rape, the accused cannot defend himself without letting in his previous convictions. The same argument extends in varying lesser degrees to many cases.

The argument in favour of a construction more liberal to the accused is supported in two ways.

First, it is said that character is used in the sense in which it was used in *R* v *Rowton,* 10 Cox CC 25, where the full court ruled that evidence of good character must be limited solely to general reputation and not to a man's actual disposition;
[his Lordship reviewed the authorities bearing on this point (see 4.3 ante) and continued]

Late as it may be, it might be justifiable to consider whether "character" means in the context solely general reputation, if a reassessment could lead to any clarification of the problem. But in my opinion it leads nowhere. For I cannot accept the proposition that to accuse a person of a particular knavery does not involve imputations on his general reputation. The words "involve" and "imputations" are wide. It would be playing with words to say that the allegation of really discreditable matters does not involve imputations on his general reputation, if only as showing how erroneous that reputation must be. The argument is, however, a valuable reminder that the Act is intending serious and not trivial imputations.

The second part of the argument in favour of a construction more liberal to the accused is concerned with the words "the conduct or nature of the defence." One should, it can be argued, read conduct or nature as something superimposed on the essence of the defence itself.

In *O'Hara* v *HM Advocate* 1948 SC(J) 90, 98, the learned Lord Justice-Clerk (Lord Thomson), after a careful review of the English cases, construed "conduct" as meaning the actual handling of the case by the accused or his advocate. He found difficulty with "nature" but said: "But the more general considerations which I have mentioned persuade me to the view that 'nature' is to be read, not as meaning something which is inherent in the defence, but as referable to the mechanism of the defence; nature being the strategy of the defence and conduct the tactics." This argument has obvious force, particularly in a case of rape, where the allegation of consent is in truth no more than a mere traverse of the essential ingredient which the Crown have to prove, namely, want of consent. But the argument does not, and I think cannot, fairly stop short of contending that *all* matters which are relevant to the crime, that is, of which rebutting evidence could be proved, are excluded from the words "conduct or nature of the defence."

To take the present case as an example, the evidence having established physical signs on the victim of the alleged offence, his admission that he had previously committed it with somebody else was relevant. So, too, was his admission that he had been paid £1 for it, since, when the conversation was relevant, it could not be right to bowdlerise it. And, therefore, it is said, the putting of the allegation in cross-examination and the evidence given by the accused was an essentially relevant part of the defence and therefore was not within the words "the nature or conduct of the defence." If Mr Jeremy Hutchison's forceful argument on the proper construction of the subsection is right, the story told by the accused did not let in the convictions.

So large a gloss upon the words is not easy to justify, even if one were convinced that it necessarily produced a fair and proper result which Parliament intended. But there are two sides to the matter. So liberal a shield for an accused is in many cases unfair to a prosecution. Provided it is all linked up to the defence put forward by an accused there would be no limit to the amount of mud which could be thrown against an unshielded prosecutor while the accused could still crouch behind his own shield.

VISCOUNT DILHORNE said: 'The cases to which I have referred, some of which it is not possible to reconcile, in my opinion finally establish the following propositions:

(1)   The words of the statute must be given their ordinary natural meaning (*Hudson* [1912] 2 KB 464; *Jenkins,* 31 Cr App R 1; *Cook* [1959] 2 QB 340).

(2)   The section permits cross-examination of the accused as to character both when imputations on the character of the prosecutor and his witness are cast to show their unreliability as witnesses independently of the evidence given by them and also when the casting of such imputations is necessary to enable the accused to establish his defence (*Hudson; Jenkins; Cook*).

(3)   In rape cases the accused can allege consent without placing himself in peril of such cross-examination (*Sheean,* 21 Cox CC 561; *Turner* [1944] KB 463). This may be because such cases are sui generis (*per* Devlin J in *R* v *Cook* [1959] 2 QB 340, 347), or on the ground that the issue is one raised by the prosecution.

(4)   If what is said amounts in reality to no more than a denial of the charge, expressed, it may be, in emphatic language, it should not be regarded as coming within the section (*Rouse* [1904] 1 KB 184; *R* v *Crout* (1909) 3 Cr App R 64; *R* v *Jones,* 17 Cr App R 117; *Clark* [1955] 2 QB 469).

Applying these propositions to this case, it is in my opinion clear beyond all doubt that the cross-examination of the accused was permissible under the statute.

I now turn to the question whether a judge has discretion to refuse to permit such cross-examination of the accused even when it is permissible under the section.... In *Maxwell* [1935] AC 309 and in *Stirland* [1944] AC 315 it was said in this House that a judge has that discretion. In *Jenkins,* 31 Cr App R 1, 15, Singleton J said: "If and when such a situation arises" (the question whether the accused should be cross-examined as to character) "it is open to counsel to apply to the presiding judge that he may be allowed to take the course indicated... Such an application will not always be granted, for the judge has a discretion in the matter. He may feel that even though the position is established in law, still the putting of such questions as to the character of the accused person may be fraught with results which immeasurably outweigh the result of questions put by the defence and which make a fair trial of the accused person almost impossible. On the other hand, in the ordinary and normal case he may feel that if the credit of the prosecutor or his witnesses has been attacked, it is only fair that the jury should have before them material on which they can form their judgment whether the accused person is any more worthy to be believed than those he has attacked. It is obviously unfair that the jury should be left in the dark about an accused person's character if the conduct of his defence has attacked the character of the prosecutor or the witnesses for the prosecution within the meaning of the section. The essential thing is a fair trial and that the legislature sought to ensure by section 1, subsection (f)."

Similar views were expressed in *Noor Mohamed* v *The King* [1949] AC 182 by Lord du Parcq, in *Harris* v *DPP* [1952] AC 694, in *Cook* [1959] 2 QB 340, in *Jones* v *Director of Public Prosecutions* [1962] AC 635, and in other cases.

In the light of what was said in all these cases by judges of great eminence, one is tempted to say, as Lord Hewart said in *Dunkley* [1927] 1 KB 323 that it is far too late in the day even to consider the argument that a judge has no such discretion. Let it suffice for me to say that in my opinion the existence of such a discretion is now clearly established.

Mr Caulfield posed the question, on what principles should such a discretion be exercised....

I do not think it possible to improve upon the guidance given by Singleton J in the passage quoted above from *Jenkins*, 31 Cr App R 1, 15, by Lord du Parcq in *Noor Mohamed* [1949] 182 or by Devlin J, in *Cook* [1959] 2 QB 340 as to the matters which should be borne in mind in relation to the exercise of the discretion. It is now so well established that on a charge of rape the allegation that the woman consented, although involving an imputation on her character, should not expose an accused to cross-examination as to character, that it is possible to say, if the refusal to allow it is a matter of discretion, that there is a general rule that the discretion should be so exercised. Apart from this, there is not, I think, any general rule as to the exercise of discretion. It must depend on the circumstances of each case and the overriding duty of the judge to ensure that a trial is fair.

It is desirable that a warning should be given when it becomes apparent that the defence is taking a course which may expose the accused to such cross-examination. That was not given in this case but the failure to give such a warning would not, in my opinion, justify in this case the allowing of the appeal.

(LORDS HODSON and GUEST delivered concurring judgments and Lord Wilberforce agreed.)

Appeal dismissed.

Further, the Court of Appeal in *R* v *Bishop* held that the same rule of law applied where the cross-examination was directed not to the credit of the witness against whom the imputation was made, but at contesting an element of the offence, in that case that the defendant was a trespasser.

R v *Bishop* [1975] QB 274 (CA)

On a charge of burglary, the defendant sought to explain his presence in a room where his fingerprints were found by alleging that he had had a homosexual relationship with the occupier, who was a witness for the prosecution. The prosecution were allowed to cross-examine the defendant about his previous convictions for offences of dishonesty and he was convicted.

STEPHENSON LJ, reading the judgment of the court, related the facts and continued: 'Mr Bate submitted that in these progressive (or permissive) days it was no longer an imputation on a man's character to say of him that he was a homosexual or that he practised homosexuality. Since 1967, when section 1 of the Sexual Offences Act 1967 became law, it was no longer an offence to commit a homosexual act with another man of full age in private. No reasonable person would now think the worse of a man who committed such acts; he might not wish to associate with him but he would not condemn him. We think that this argument goes too far and that the gap between what is declared by Parliament to be illegal and punishable and what the common man or woman still regards as immoral or wrong is not wide enought to support it. Most men would be anxious to keep from a jury in any case the knowledge that they practised such acts and many would be debarred from going to the police to charge another with any offence if they thought that he might defend himself by making such an allegation, whether baseless or not. If this is still true, we are not behind the times in holding that Mr Price's character was clearly impugned by the allegation of homosexual conduct made against him by the defendant.

Then it is contended that even if the allegation reflects upon his character, it does not reflect upon his integrity, his honesty or his reliability so that he is thereby rendered less likely to be a truthful witness, or if in fact it has that effect it was not made with that intention.

Mr Bate says that the defendant's allegation against Mr Price was made not for the purpose of discrediting his testimony but for the purpose of explaining his presence in Mr Price's room.

We do not consider that this argument can succeed against the plain words of section 1(f)(ii) given their natural and ordinary meaning. If we give them that meaning, as we are now required to do by the House of Lords in *Selvey's* case (see for instance what Viscount Dilhorne said [1970] AC 304, 339), they cannot be restricted in the way suggested by the words of the judgment which we have just quoted. Though we agree that the general nature of the Act and the general principle underlying it are as there stated we do not accept the submission that an imputation of homosexual immorality against a witness may not reflect upon his reliability — generally or in the witness box; nor do we accept the submission that a defendant can attack the character of a witness without risk of the jury's learning that his own character is bad by disclaiming any intention to discredit the witness's testimony. Such a construction of the section would enable many guilty men to resort to variations of "the Portsmouth defence" with success by unfairly keeping the jury in ignorance of their true character and would fly in the face of the decision in *Selvey's* case to strip the plain words of section 1(f)(ii) of the gloss put upon them in earlier cases....

...Once it is conceded, as Mr Bate rightly conceded, that an imputation on character covers charges of faults or vices, whether reputed or real, which are not criminal offences it is difficult to restrict the statutory exception of s.1(f)(ii) in any such way as has been suggested on behalf of the defendant.

Appeal dismissed.

Holt J: Yes. I think it is really a question of discretion in the present case. I see that in *Selvey's* case, Stable J in his discretion limited the cross-examination to sexual matters, no doubt because he took the view that the jury would be sufficiently assisted, and that anything else would be unduly prejudicial to the defendant.

(Holt J held that Coke had lost his shield both by reason of giving evidence of his good character and of making imputations on the characters of the prosecution witnesses, under s.1(f)(ii). He further held that no reason of discretion existed to disallow the cross-examination, and that accordingly, Mr Bunbury's application should succeed.)

4.9 Commentary

R v *Coke and Littleton* on appeal against conviction. In the course of evidence in chief, Coke stated that Littleton was at his flat at the time of the alleged assault on Angela Blackstone. Mr Bacon for Littleton suggested to Coke that this is untrue. Mr Bacon then applied for and was granted leave to cross-examine Coke about his character, on the ground that Coke had 'given evidence against' Littleton, and within the meaning of s.1(f)(iii). On appeal against conviction, Coke contends that this decision was wrong. He also complains that Holt J misdirected the jury in summing up, in the following passage, which Mr Atkyn reads to the Court of Appeal:

Members of the jury, when you come to consider the evidence of Coke's previous conviction for rape, bear in mind how it was you heard of it. It was not from the prosecution, but from Littleton. His motive in introducing it, quite properly, was to invite you to assess the evidence of the man who says to you in evidence, 'Littleton was at my flat' — a fact which Littleton denies and has denied from the first. You will have to consider whether that conviction weakens your faith in Coke's evidence so that you are not sure whether to accept it to the point where you would rely on it to convict. That is the use which Littleton invites you to make of it. But now that you know about it, you cannot close your eyes to it, can you? You may think that it must also have some impact on the Crown's case against Coke himself. Do you think, having heard that evidence, that it makes it at least somewhat more likely that Coke is guilty? Can you now view his allegation that Miss Blackstone consented in quite the same light?

4.10   Argument

Mr Atkyn: First of all, My Lords, the learned judge was wrong in allowing this line of cross-examination, for two reasons. May I begin with the question whether Coke and Littleton were 'charged in the same proceedings' as required by s.1(f)(iii). In my submission, they were not, because although they were before the same jury, they were charged with different offences.

Leach LJ: I think that argument may be too late, Mr Atkyn. Before the amendment introduced by the Criminal Evidence Act 1979 when the Act said, 'charged with the same offence', authority would have constrained us to agree. But the amendment was designed to overcome this technicality.

East LJ: They were before the same jury. What else can the expression 'the same proceedings' mean?

Mr Atkyn: My Lords, I take Your Lordships' point. I will come, if I may, to my second point, which is that the learned judge erred in holding that Coke had 'given evidence against' Littleton within the meaning of the subsection.

Leach LJ: I think you are on stronger ground there, Mr Atkyn. What do you say that expression means?

Mr Atkyn: My Lords, in my submission the wording covers any evidence which would warrant the conviction of the other person charged in the same proceedings.

Cox LJ: But not necessarily given with the intent that the co-defendant be convicted?

Mr Atkyn: No, My Lord. Usually, the overriding motive of the co-defendant will be to exculpate himself rather than convict the co-accused, although not infrequently those two motives would run parallel to each other.

Leach LJ: I think I am right in saying that assuming that the appellant Coke did give evidence against his co-accused within the meaning of s.1(f)(iii), the judge had no discretion to restrain Counsel for the co-accused from cross-examining as to character.

Mr Atkyn: Your Lordship is quite correct. This case differs from that where the prosecution apply to cross-examine under s.1(f)(i) or (ii). My Lords, no doubt the trial judge has to permit full rein to both defendants to allow a proper presentation of their respective defences, and is concerned to apply the rules of evidence between them, whereas as between the Crown and a defendant, additional factors of fair play must be taken into account. My Lords, all these points were reviewed by the House of Lords in:

Murdoch v *Taylor* [1965] AC 574 (HL)

Murdoch, who had a criminal record, was jointly tried with Lynch, who was previously of good character. Each was charged with receiving stolen cameras. Lynch gave evidence implicating Murdoch and Murdoch gave evidence alleging that Lynch alone was in control and possession of a box containing the stolen cameras. The judge held that Lynch's counsel was entitled to take advantage of section 1(f)(iii) and cross-examine as to his previous convictions. Murdoch was convicted and appealed.

LORD MORRIS OF BORTH-Y-GEST said: 'It is to be remembered that section 1(f) of the Act refers only to a person who is charged with an offence and who is called (upon his own application) as a witness for the defence. One situation in which such a person loses the protection given to him is where he has given evidence against any other person charged with the same offence.

If an accused person becomes a witness his sworn testimony, if admissible, becomes a part of the evidence in the case. What he says in cross-examination is just as much a part of that evidence as is what he says in examination in chief. The word "against" is one that is well understood. It is a clear and robust word. It has more decisiveness than is possessed by such phrases as "tending to show" or "such as to involve." It is a word that needs neither explanation nor translation. It calls for no synonym.

The Act does not call for any investigation as to the motives or wishes which may have prompted the giving of evidence against another person charged with the same offence. It is the nature of the evidence that must be considered. Its character does not change according as to whether it is the product of pained reluctance or of malevolent eagerness. If, while ignoring anything trivial or casual, the positive evidence given by the witness would rationally have to be included in any survey or summary of the evidence in the case which, if accepted, would warrant the conviction of the "other person charged with the "same offence," then the witness would have given evidence against such other person. Such other person would then have that additional testimony against him. From his point of view that testimony would be just as damaging whether given with regret or whether given with relish. Such other person might then wish, in order to defend himself, to show that credence ought not to be attached to the evidence which had been given against him. In such circumstances the Act removes one barrier which would otherwise be in his way.

It may be noted that if A and B are jointly charged with the same offence and if A chooses to give evidence which is purely in defence of himself and is not evidence against B he may be asked questions in cross-examination by B notwithstanding that such questions would tend to criminate him (A) as to the offence charged. In similar circumstances B would be likewise placed. But questions of the kind denoted by section 1(f) could not be put. No doubt during any such cross-examination a judge would be alert to protect a witness from being cajoled into saying more than it was ever his plan or wish or intention to say.

If an accused person, when giving evidence for the defence, has given evidence against any other person charged with the same offence, the question arises whether the latter needs the permission of the court before putting to the witness any question of the kind denoted in section 1(f). In my judgment he must have liberty to defend himself by such legitimate means as he thinks it wise to employ. This does not, however, mean that the judge has no function to discharge. In the first place it will be for him to rule as a matter of law whether a witness has or has not given evidence against any other person charged with the same offence. In the present case I consider that it could fairly and properly be said that the appellant had given evidence against Lynch. In the second place, it is always for a judge to rule in regard to the relevance of any evidence and therefore in regard to the propriety of any question which it is desired to ask. Section 1(f) of the Act provides that except in particular circumstances certain questions may not be asked. The section does not state that in the particular circumstances certain questions may be asked. The test of relevance must always be satisfied.'

[His Lordship referred with approval to the speech of VISCOUNT SANKEY LC in *Maxwell v DPP* and continued:]

The result, in my judgment, is that where it is claimed that an accused person has given evidence against another person charged with the same offence and it is desired to put questions of the kind denoted in section I(f), intimation of this desire should (in such way as may be appropriate) be given to the court and to counsel concerned. The temporary withdrawal of the jury might become desirable. It will then be for the judge to rule in regard to the matters to which I have referred. If he rules as a matter of law that the proposed questions may be put, then he is not called upon either to give or to withhold any permission to put them.

The present case is concerned only with the situation where it is a co-accused person who desires to put questions to another co-accused who has given evidence against him. Different considerations apply where it is the desire of the prosecution to put questions of the kind denoted in section I(f)....

LORD DONOVAN said: 'What kind of evidence is contemplated by proviso (f)(iii), that is, what is "evidence against" a co-accused is perhaps the most difficult part of the case. At one end of the scale is evidence which does no more than contradict something which a co-accused has said without further advancing the prosecution's case in any significant degree. I agree with the view expressed by Winn J in giving judgment in *Stannard* that this is not the kind of evidence contemplated by proviso (f)(iii). At the other end of the scale is evidence which, if the jury believes it, would establish the co-accused's guilt, for example, in a case of theft: "I saw him steal the purse" or in a case of assault, "I saw him strike the blow." It is this kind of evidence which alone, so the appellant contends, will satisfy the words "has given evidence against." Again, I reget I cannot share that view. There may well be evidence which regarded in isolation would be quite innocuous from the co-accused's point of view and, so regarded, could not be regarded as evidence "against" him. For example, what would be proved if one co-accused said of his co-accused: "He told me he knew of an easy job and persuaded me to help him"? If such evidence is kept unrelated to anything else it proves nothing criminal. But juries hear the whole of the evidence and they will consider particular parts of it, not in isolation but in conjunction with all the other evidence, and part of that other evidence may establish that "job" meant a housebreaking job. Then the item of evidence I have taken as an example obviously becomes evidence "against" the accused. If, therefore, the effect of the evidence upon the minds of the jury is to be taken as the test, it cannot be right to regard it in isolation in order to decide whether it is evidence against the co-accused. If Parliament had meant by proviso (f)(iii) to refer to evidence which was by itself conclusive against the co-accused it would have been easy to say so.

The test prescribed by the Court of Criminal Appeal in *Stannard* was whether the evidence in question tended to support the prosecution's case in a material respect or to undermine the defence. I have no substantial quarrel with this definition. I would, however, observe that some danger may lurk in the use of the expression "tended to." There will probably be occasions when it could be said that evidence given by one accused "tended to" support the prosecution's case simply because it differed from the evidence of his co-accused; and the addition of the words "in a material respect" might not wholly remove the danger. The difficulty is not really one of conception but of expression. I myself would omit the words "tended to" and simply say that "evidence against" means evidence which supports the prosecution's case in a material respect or which undermines the defence of the co-accused.

The evidence in the present case was clearly against Lynch in that sense. It was evidence which, if the jury accepted it, put Lynch in sole control and possession of property which according to the rest of the evidence had been stolen the day before, and which Lynch had tried to sell for a price which was a fraction of its real value. Murdoch's evidence thus supported the case of the prosecution in a material respect and none the less so because Coles had already given evidence to a somewhat similar effect.

On the question of discretion, I agree with the Court of Criminal Appeal that a trial judge has no discretion whether to allow an accused person to be cross-examined as to his past criminal offences once he has given evidence against his co-accused. Proviso (f)(iii) in terms confers no such discretion and, in my opinion, none can be implied. It is true that in relation to proviso (f)(ii) such a discretion does exist; that is to say, in the cases where the accused has attempted to establish his own good character or where the nature and conduct of the defence is such as to involve imputations on the character of the prosecutor or of a witness for the prosecution.

But in these cases it will normally, if not invariably, be the prosecution which will want to bring out the accused's bad character — not some co-accused; and in such cases it seems to me quite proper that the court should retain some control of the matter. For its duty is to secure a fair trial and the prejudicial value of evidence establishing the accused's bad character may at times wholly outweigh the value of such evidence as tending to show that he was guilty of the crime alleged.

(LORD EVERSHED agreed with LORD DONOVAN: LORD PEARCE dissented on the question of discretion. LORD REID agreed.)

Appeal dismissed.

Leach LJ: Of course, in reading any case decided before the Criminal Evidence Act 1979 came into force, one has to remember the different wording of the subsection under the original statute, and bear it in mind. But I do not think it alters the points made by the House of Lords in that case. How do you put your case, Mr Atkyn?

Mr Atkyn: My Lords, I say that the present case is similar to that of:

R v Bruce and others [1975] 1 WLR 1252 (CA)

Eight youths surrounded a passenger on a train and took money from him, realising that he had been frightened. They were charged with robbery. One defendant, McGuiness, supported the prosecution case that there was a plan to rob, but said that he had played no part in carrying it out. The defendent Bruce denied in evidence that there was a plan to rob. Counsel for McGuiness was allowed to cross-examine Bruce about his previous convictions on the basis that Bruce had given "evidence against" McGuiness. The defendants were acquitted of robbery but convicted of theft.

STEPHENSON LJ, reading the judgment of the court, said: 'Did Bruce give that evidence against McGuinness? Yes, in the sense that he contradicted McGuinness and said that that part of his defence which agreed with the prosecution that there was a plan to rob a Pakistani was untrue; no, in the sense that he supported McGuinness' defence that he did not rob Mr Lecerf and that he provided McGuinness with a different, and possibly a better, defence to the charge than he himself had put forward.

We cannot help thinking that reading the words of sub-paragraph (iii) in their context in their ordinary meaning a lawyer and a layman would alike regard Bruce's evidence denying that there was a plan to rob as given more in McGuinness' favour than against him. On balance it exculpated him of robbery and did not incriminate him. We think it right to give the words their ordinary meaning, if we can, without adding any gloss to them: cf *R v Selvey* [1970] AC 304, especially, *per* Viscount Dilhorne at p 339. But the cases cited to us at first sight show that a gloss has been put upon these words which this court is bound to put upon them. In *Murdoch v Taylor* [1965] AC 574 the House of Lords — or certainly a majority of their Lordships — approved with a minor modification the construction put upon the words in *R v Stannard* [1965] 2 QB 1 and held that "evidence against" means evidence which supports the prosecution's case in a material respect or which undermines the defence of the co-accused; see *per* Lord Donovan, at p 592. But neither in that case nor in *Stannard's* case, nor in *R v Davis (Alan)* [1975] 1 WLR 345, where this court recently applied that interpretation or test to a conflict between the only two persons charged with the same offence which went to the very root of the case, were there under consideration any facts like those of this unusual conflict. Usually evidence which undermines the defence of another defendant supports the prosecution's case against him. Here the evidence did more to undermine the prosecution's case than to undermine the co-accused's defence.

Appeals dismissed.

My Lords, I accept that the two cases are not exactly alike, because Coke's evidence certainly did not mean that Littleton was more likely to be acquitted. But Coke was doing no more than giving evidence of a fact almost coincidental to his defence.

East LJ: I would not agree with that, Mr Atkyn. As I understand it, the undisputed evidence was that Littleton played some part in Coke's plan to entertain the girls at his flat. He also sought to dissociate himself from what Littleton was allegedly doing while he was there. The motive with which Coke gave that evidence is immaterial, as we have seen. I must say I take the view that Coke's evidence in fact supported a material part of the prosecution's case against Littleton.

(Leach and Cox LJ indicated their agreement with this view, and Mr Atkyn was invited to deal with the summing up).

Mr Atkyn: My Lords, the learned judge clearly invited the jury to treat the evidence of Coke's character as relevant to his guilt as charged. Had the cross-examination been permitted by the prosecution under s.1(f)(i) as admissible evidence to prove the charge, then such a direction would have been proper. But in my submission, where the shield is lost by reason of s.1(f)(ii) or (iii) the evidence goes only to the defendant's credit as a witness. My Lord, I refer to:

R v Preston [1909] 1 KB 568 (CCA)

CHANNEL J stated the rationale of the second half of s.1(f)(ii) as follows: 'It appears to us to mean this: that if the defence is so conducted, or the nature of the defence is such, as to involve the proposition that the jury ought not to believe the prosecutor or one of the witnesses for the prosecution upon the ground that his conduct — not his evidence in the case, but his conduct outside the evidence given by him — makes him an unreliable witness, then the jury ought also to know the character of the prisoner who either gives that evidence or makes that charge, and it then becomes admissible to cross-examine the prisoner as to his antecedents and character with the view of showing that he has such a bad character that the jury ought not to rely upon his evidence.'

East LJ: Yes, and of course as Lord Morris pointed out in his speech in *Murdoch* v *Taylor* to which you referred us earlier, the judge has the task of assessing whether the evidence is relevant to the credit of the witness, and there is certainly no indication that it can be used for any other purpose.

Mr Atkyn: I would also refer Your Lordships to *R* v *France and France*, (see 4.6 ante).

My Lords, in my submission, the direction given by the learned judge wrongly invited the jury to go beyond the proper use of the evidence for purposes of credit and gave them the impression that the previous conviction was somehow probative of guilt. This was a serious misdirection.

Cox LJ: Mr Atkyn, we have been assuming thus far that the right of Littleton to cross-examine Coke about credit could have been justified only under s.1(f)(iii). But am I not correct in thinking that the judge might have justified the same course under s.1(f)(ii), assuming that he took the view that Coke had put in his character or made imputations against the prosecution witnesses?

Mr Atkyn: My Lords, that possibility was canvassed in:

R v Lovett [1973] 1 WLR 241 (CA)

The defendant was charged, *inter alia*, with the theft of a television set and one Gregory was charged with dishonestly assisting with the disposal of the set. At their joint trial, the defendant gave evidence against Gregory and also made imputations against the character of a prosecution witness. Counsel for Gregory without giving any prior intimation to the court, cross-examined the defendant on his criminal record, thereby forestalling an application by the prosecution, under section 1(f)(ii) of the Criminal Evidence Act 1898, for leave to cross-examine the defendant on his criminal record. The defendant was convicted and Gregory was acquitted.

EDMUND DAVIES LJ, delivering the judgment of the court, having stated that cross-examination under section 1(f)(iii) as it was then worded was improper because the two defendants were not charged with "the same offence", said: '...Widgery LJ said in *R v Russell (George)* [1971] 1 QB 151, 154:

> Lord Donovan [in *Murdoch v Taylor* [1965] AC 574, at 592] clearly contemplated the possibility that a co-accused might take advantage of proviso (ii) and also that the prosecution might take advantage of proviso (iii). But the case is not authority on any of these points...

In *R v Russell (George)* one co-accused had not only given evidence against another co-accused charged, as the court held, with the same (albeit not joint) offence, but he had also made imputations against a witness for the prosecution, and counsel for the attacked co-accused had at the trial unsuccessfully sought to cross-examine his attacker as to his past record under both (ii) and (iii) of proviso (f). But holding that the latter clearly applied, the court found it unnecessary to decide whether the former could also have been invoked.
We know of only one reported case where it appears that the prosecution was permitted to cross-examine one of the two co-accused under proviso (iii). This is *R v Seigley* (1911) 6 Cr App R 106. The case is in some ways an odd one, but Hamilton J said at p 107 that the course adopted was "clearly permissible under section 1(f)(iii) of the Criminal Evidence Act 1898." On the other hand, we have no knowledge of any case where a co-accused who has not been attacked in circumstances coming within proviso (iii) has proceeded to cross-examine his co-accused pursuant to proviso (ii) on the ground that the latter has made imputations against a Crown witness.
In principle, ought he to be allowed to do so? We think that under the existing law circumstances could well arise when he should, and those of the present case afford one example. Gregory could not legitimately cross-examine the defendant on his previous record, despite his extremely damaging evidence, solely because they were not, as we have held, "charged with the same offence." But the resulting prejudice against Gregory was none the less real on that account.'
In *R v Roberts* (1936) 25 Cr App R 158, 161, Talbot J said:

> One can easily conceive an argument for...allowing a further exception to the exemption of prisoners from this particular line of cross-examination, but one must interpret the Act as it is.

And a "liberal" interpretation could lead to injustice. For example, A and B are jointly charged with the same offence; A (who has a criminal record) gives no evidence against B, but he does make imputations against a Crown witness. On the other hand, B (with a clean record) has it in mind to throw all the blame on A and, for this purpose, it would obviously be helpful to him if he could discredit A by cross-examining him on his bad record. In such circumstances, the Crown themselves may or may not have it in mind to cross-examine A on these lines, but in either case they unquestionably must first seek and obtain the court's permission. Then ought B, against whom A has alleged nothing, to be in a position to cross-examine Á *as of right* on these matters? We think that justice demands a negative answer to that question....
Having reflected upon the matter, the conclusion we have accordingly come to in relation to the present case is this: Although a final decision upon the point is not now called for, we incline to the view that the circumstances were such as to empower the court to rule that cross-examination of the defendant on his past history by Gregory was permissible under

proviso (ii). But we are firmly of the view that Gregory was not entitled as of right to do this, and that all would depend upon whether the court in the exercise of its discretion granted him leave to follow that course.
Appeal dismissed.

My Lords, in that case, it was postulated that the prosecution might similarly make use of s.1(f)(iii) in an appropriate case, subject in that case to the judge's discretion. But in my submission, the point cannot be taken as settled. If Your Lordships were minded to consider that possibility here, I would say, with respect, that I should have been entitled to a determination at first instance of whether s.1(f)(ii) applied.

4.11 Commentary

R v *Coke and Littleton* at trial. In cross-examination of the witnesses for the prosecution, Mr Atkyn for Coke has made the suggestions to Margaret Blackstone, D/I Glanvil and D/S Bracton described in commentary 4.7. Mr Bacon for Littleton has cross-examinated D/I Glanvil to seek to show his good reputation in the community of Oxbridge. Subsequently, both Coke and Littleton decline to give evidence. Mr Bunbury applies to call evidence in rebuttal, consisting in Coke's case of evidence of his previous conviction for rape, and in Littleton's case of evidence unfavourable to his reputation.

4.12 Argument

Holt J: So far as the defendant Littleton is concerned, of course you would be entitled to lead evidence in rebuttal of the impression he sought to create by cross-examination. I think that follows from *R* v *Rowton* (4.3 ante) and has always been accepted where an accused by whatever means asserts his good character. But in Coke's case, what you have are imputations. Your only remedy is the statutory one of cross-examination given by s.1(f)(ii) of the Criminal Evidence Act 1898. Cross-examination is possible only where a defendant gives evidence. Indeed, just such a situation arose in:

R v *Butterwasser* [1948] 1 KB 4 (CCA)

The defendant was convicted of wounding with intent to do grievous bodily harm. At the trial the evidence for the prosecution was given by the prosecutor and his wife. The defendant's counsel in cross-examination attacked the character of the prosecutor and his wife, putting to them a number of previous convictions including convictions of offences of violence, which they admitted, and thereby suggesting that it was really the prosecutor who attacked the defendant. The defendant was not called to give evidence and he neither called witnesses to his character nor cross-examined the witnesses for the prosecution on this subject. Thereupon, with the leave of the court, a police officer was called for the prosecution and read out a record of the defendant's previous convictions.

LORD GODDARD CJ, giving the judgment of the court said: 'It is elementary law that even since it became the practice, as it has been for the last one hundred and fifty or two hundred years, of allowing a prisoner to call evidence of good character, or where he has put questions to witnesses for the Crown and obtained or attempted to obtain admissions from them that he is a man of good character, in other words, where the prisoner himself puts his character in issue, evidence in rebuttal can be given by the prosecution to show that he is in fact a man of bad character.... There is no case to be found in the books — and it is certainly

contrary to what all the present members of the court have understood during the whole of the time they have been in the profession — that where the prisoner does not put his own character in issue, but has merely attacked the witnesses for the prosecution, evidence can be called for the prosecution to prove that the prisoner is a man of bad character. It is, of course, permissible, where a prisoner takes advantage of the Act of 1898, which made prisoners competent witnesses on their trial in all cases, and goes into the witness box and attacks the witnesses for the prosecution, to cross-examine him with regard to convictions and matters of character; and no doubt if a conviction is put to him and he denies it, the provisions of Denman's Act would apply and the conviction could be proved against him. But it is admitted that there is no authority, and I do not see on what principle it could be said, that if a man does not go into the box and put his own character is issue, he can have evidence given against him of previous bad character when all that he has done is to attack the witnesses for the prosecution. The reason is that by attacking the witnesses for the prosecution and suggesting they are unreliable, he is not putting his character in issue; he is putting their character in issue. And the reason why, if he gives evidence, he can be cross-examined if he has attacked the witnesses for the prosecution is that the statute says he can. It seems to the court, therefore, that it is impossible to say that because the prisoner in this case attacked the witnesses for the prosecution but did not himself give evidence, evidence of his bad character was admissible. In those circumstances, the learned recorder should have declined to allow the evidence to be given, and therefore inadmissible evidence on a most vital point was admitted in this case.
Appeal allowed.

You will have to rely on the jury's good sense to assess the weight to be attached to the imputations in these circumstances. I cannot allow rebuttal in such a case.

4.13 Questions for Counsel

4.13.1 R v *Coke and Littleton:* In the argument 4.3, what questions regarding Littleton's character should Mr Bacon have been permitted to ask of the prosecution witnesses, and Mrs Littleton?

4.13.2 R v *Coke and Littleton:* In the light of his ruling at the end of argument 4.6, how should Holt J direct the jury on the evidence of Coke's previous conviction?

4.13.3 R v *Coke and Littleton:* Same question in the light of the conclusion at the end of argument 4.8.

4.13.4 R v *Coke and Littleton:* Argument 4.10 — do you agree with the Court of Appeal that Coke had 'given evidence against (another person) charged in the same proceedings'? Do you agree with Mr Atkyn's criticism of the summing up? How might Holt J have improved it?

5   *Similar Fact Evidence*

5.1   Introductory notes

5.1.1   In a criminal case, the prosecution may not introduce evidence of the defendant's bad character in order to prove his guilt as charged (4.1). However, where the prosecution can point to something in the defendant's past character or disposition which offers probative value in relation to the offence charged, such evidence is not inadmissible merely because it happens to reveal to the jury some aspect of the defendant's bad character.

5.1.2   Accordingly, evidence of 'similar facts' will be admissible on the issue of guilt provided that such evidence goes beyond mere evidence of character or disposition, and offers positive proof which would tend to lead the tribunal of fact to say 'these offences are the work of the same man'.

5.1.3   In order to demonstrate the required degree of probative value, the similar facts must demonstrate a 'striking similarity' to the facts of the offence charged. This similarity must relate to the offence itself, as opposed to the peripheral surrounding circumstances of the offence, and must bear a striking similarity in significant rather than commonplace features of the crime.

5.1.4   Although it was for some time thought that sexual offences, and particularly offences of a homosexual nature those relating to children, fell within a special category, it is now recognised that the above tests apply to all criminal offences. Accordingly, the mere repetition of sexual offences does not in itself give rise to a sufficient striking similarity, unless the offences are of such an unusual nature as to fall within the rule by their mere repetition. Moreover, it should only be in exceptional circumstances that evidence of a defendant's sexual propensity without more (e.g. whether or not he is a homosexual) or evidence of the defendant's possession of sexual materials, should be regarded as admissible evidence of the commission of the particular offence.

5.1.5   It was at one time thought that similar fact evidence might only be admitted in order to rebut some specific defence such as accident, coincidence or innocent association, the defendant thus denying any systematic course of conduct. However, it is now established that if similar fact evidence is admissible, it is admissible at the outset as part of the prosecution case and should be proved as such. Of course, it remains true that the rebuttal of such defences is one of the most important uses of similar fact evidence. But there is no objection to the admission of such evidence even where the defence is one of a complete denial.

5.1.6 Similar fact evidence in criminal cases generally consists of evidence of previous convictions. However, there is no ojection to evidence of previous offences of which the defendant has not been convicted, provided that the jury understand that they must act on such matters only if they are sure they are proved. In a case where the indictment charges a number of different offences of an ostensibly similar kind, the jury may be directed that each may be regarded as similar fact evidence in relation to the other, provided the above tests are satisfied. If they are not satisfied, it may be necessary to sever the indictment and order separate trials.

5.1.7 In an appropriate case, similar fact evidence may be tendered for the defence and in such a case, exactly the same rules of admissibility apply.

5.1.8 In all cases where similar fact evidence is involved, the trial judge has a discretion to exclude such evidence even where it may technically be admissible, on the ground that its probative value would be outweighed by the prejudice that may result to the defendant by the admission of the evidence. This is a balancing test, in which the judge must weigh what assistance the jury will derive from the evidence in relation to the offence charged, and the potential of the similar fact evidence to damn the defendant in the eyes of the jury and perhaps make a fair trial impossible.

5.1.9 In civil cases, as in criminal cases, the judge will determine the issue of admissibility and the question of the exercise of his discretion at the same time, and will probably decide both having regard to how much value he considers the evidence is likely to have if admitted. In civil cases, similar fact evidence will consist of other tortious or otherwise wrongful acts committed or alleged to have been committed by the defendant. (*A Practical Approach to Evidence,* pp 108–22.)

5.2 Commentary

R v Coke and Littleton at trial. Mr Bunbury for the prosecution, in the absence of the jury, invites Holt J to rule on the admissibility as similar fact evidence of Coke's previous conviction for rape, which he proposes to prove by adducing a certificate of conviction and by calling the victim of that offence to give evidence as to the *modus operandi*. Although questions of the admissibility of evidence are generally dealt with as and when they arise in the natural course of the trial, Mr Bunbury explains to Holt J that it would be difficult for him fully to open the case unless the matter were considered as a preliminary point. Mr Atkyn on behalf of Coke has no objection to this course, but disputes the admissibility of the evidence, contending both that it is inadmissible in law and that Holt J should in any event exercise his discretion to exclude it.

5.3 Argument

Holt J: Mr Bunbury, am I not right in thinking that English criminal law has always forbidden the prosecution to prove the defendant's guilt by reference to his previous bad character? That is like giving a dog a bad name and hanging it.

Mr Bunbury: My Lord, that is true. However, I have two arguments to advance before Your Lordship. The first is that on the facts of the present case, there is such a striking similarity between the evidence in this case and the way in which Coke was proved to have committed his previous rape, that the previous offence has a substantial probative value in the present case. The second is that in an offence of this nature, the repetition of offences bearing such a close resemblance to each other is itself enough to enable the jury to find evidence of some intent or system.

Holt J: Well, let us deal with your first argument first.

Mr Bunbury: Certainly, My Lord. May I begin with the classic statement by Lord Herschell LC in:

Makin and Makin v Attorney-General for New South Wales [1894] AC 57 (PC)

The defendants were charged with the murder of a baby, whose body was found in the back yard of a house occupied by them. The defendants had 'adopted' it from its mother in return for a sum of money, stating that they wished to bring it up because they had lost their own child. The facts were consistent with an allegation that the defendants had killed the child for the maintenance, but equally were consistent with death by natural causes followed by an irregular burial. There was, however, evidence that the bodies of other babies, similarly adopted by the defendants, were found buried in the yards of houses occupied by the defendants. This evidence was held to be admissible, and the defendants were convicted. They appealed to the Supreme Court of New South Wales and from there to the Privy Council.

LORD HERSCHELL LC, delivering the judgment of their Lordships, said: 'In their Lordships' opinion the principles which must govern the decision of the case are clear, though the application of them is by no means free from difficulty. It is undoubtedly not competent for the prosecution to adduce evidence tending to show that the accused has been guilty of criminal acts other than those covered by the indictment, for the purpose of leading to the conclusion that the accused is a person likely from his criminal conduct or character to have committed the offence for which he is being tried. On the other hand, the mere fact that the evidence adduced tends to shew the commission of other crimes does not render it inadmissible if it be relevant to an issue before the jury, and it may be so relevant if it bears upon the question whether the acts alleged to constitute the crime charged in the indictment were designed or accidental, or to rebut a defence which would otherwise be open to the accused.

   Under these circumstances their Lordships cannot see that it was irrelevant to the issue to be tried by the jury that several other infants had been received from their mothers on like representations, and upon payment of a sum inadequate for the support of the child for more than a very limited period, or that the bodies of infants had been found buried in a similar manner in the gardens of several houses occupied by the prisoners.'

Appeal dismissed.

My Lord, Lord Herschell obviously had two considerations in mind. The first was to exclude mere evidence of character which would do no more than assert the defendant's general criminal disposition. But the second was to admit evidence relevant to the issue of guilt, even though it might tend to expose some element of the defendant's character.

Another example was:

R v George Joseph Smith (1915) 11 Cr App R 229 (CCA)

The appellant was convicted of the murder of Bessie Munday, a woman with whom he had gone through a ceremony of marriage. Evidence of the deaths of two other women with whom the appellant had gone through a ceremony of marriage was admitted. In each case, the deceased woman was found drowned in her bath; in each case, the door of the bathroom would not lock; in each case, the appellant had informed a doctor that the woman suffered from epileptic fits; and, in each case, the woman's life was insured for the benefit of the appellant.

LORD READING CJ, delivering the judgment of the court, said: 'Whether the evidence was admissible or not depends on principles of law which have been considered by this Court many times, and which depend in the main on the statement of the law by Lord Herschell in *Makin* v *Attorney-General for New South Wales.*
[His Lordship set out the statement of Lord Herschell and continued:]
    Now in this case the prosecution tendered the evidence, and it was admitted by the judge on the ground that it tended to shew that the act charged had been committed, that is, had been designed. A question has been raised on which we have heard valuable agruments, but it is a matter which we need not, and do not intend to decide in this case. It is undesirable that we should decide the point unless it has been fully argued. It is sufficient to say that it is not disputed, and could not be disputed, that if as a matter of law there was *prima facie* evidence that the appellant committed the act charged, evidence of similar acts became admissible, and the other point does not arise for the reason that we have come to the conclusion that there was undoubtedly, as a matter of law, *prima facie* evidence that the appellant committed the act charged apart altogether from the other cases. Viewing the case put forward with regard to Bessie Munday only, we are of opinion that there was a case which the judge was bound in strict law to put to the jury. The case was reinforced by the evidence admitted with reference to the other two cases for the purpose of shewing the design of the appellant. We think that that evidence was properly admitted, and the judge was very careful to point out to the jury the use they could properly make of the evidence. He directed them more than once that they must not allow their minds to be confused and think that they were deciding whether the murders of Burnham and Lofty had been committed; they were trying the appellant for the murder of Munday. We are of opinion therefore that the first point fails.
    The second point taken is that even assuming that evidence of the death of the other two women was admissible, the prosecution ought only to have been allowed to prove that the women were found dead in their baths. For the reasons already given in dealing with the first point, it is apparent that to cut short the evidence there would have been of no assistance to the case. In our opinion it was open to the prosecution to give, and the judge was right in admitting, evidence of the facts surrounding the deaths of the two women.'
Appeal dismissed.

My Lord, in both those cases the degree of similarity was so great that it effectively excluded any consideration of coincidence, accident or innocent association which might have been raised by the defence. In this case, the prosecution alleges that Coke has employed the same method on both occasions, that is to say by inviting a young girl to his flat under the pretence of listening to music, and using that occasion to commit the offence. If the jury considered the present case in isolation, any defence that the sexual intercourse was consensual and that the defendant used no deception will appear very different to the jury than it would were they to be informed of what the defendant had done on another occasion less than two years before.
    Holt J: Yes, I see the force of that. Mr Atkyn, what do you say?
    Mr Atkyn: My Lord, I accept the principle for which my learned friend contends but I say that this case does not fall within it. Secondly, My Lord, I would invite Your Lordships to exclude the evidence in the exercise of Your Lordship's discretion even if it should be technically admissible. On the question of admissibility, I say that this case bears less resemblance to *Smith* and *Makin* than it does to the following case:

Noor Mohamed v R [1949] AC 182 (PC)

The appellant, a goldsmith, was convicted of murdering by potassium cyanide poisoning a woman, Ayesha, who was living with him as his wife. At his trial, evidence, led for the purpose of meeting a possible defence of accident or suicide, was admitted that some two years earlier his wife, Gooriah, had died of potassium cyanide poisoning in similar circumstances although her death had not been the subject of any criminal charge.

LORD DU PARCQ, delivering the judgment of their Lordships, said: 'Their Lordships have considered with care the question whether the evidence now in question can be said to be relevant to any issue in the case. They have asked themselves, adopting the language of Lord Sumner in *Thompson's* case [1918] AC 221, 236, "What exactly does this purport to prove?" At the trial the learned counsel for the Crown, when submitting that the evidence should be admitted, referred to the possible defences of accident and suicide. In his address to the jury he said, according to the note, that the evidence was led "to meet the defence of suicide," and pointed out that the circumstances surrounding the deaths of the two women "followed a similar pattern." At their Lordships' bar it was submitted that this similarity of circumstances would lead to the inference that the appellant administered poison to Ayesha with felonious intent.

There can be little doubt that the manner of Ayesha's death, even without the evidence as to the death of Gooriah, would arouse suspicion against the appellant in the mind of a reasonable man. The facts proved as to the death of Gooriah would certainly tend to deepen that suspicion, and might well tilt the balance against the accused in the estimation of a jury. It by no means follows that this evidence ought to be admitted. If an examination of it shows that it is impressive just because it appears to demonstrate, in the words of Lord Herschell in *Makin's* case [1894] AC 57 "that the accused is a person likely from his criminal conduct or character to have committed the offence for which he is being tried," and if it is otherwise of no real substance, then it was certainly wrongly admitted. After fully considering all the facts which, if accepted, it revealed, their Lordships are not satisfied that its admission can be justified on any of the grounds which have been suggested or on any other ground. Assuming that it is consistent with the evidence relating to the death of Ayesha that she took her own life, or that she took poison accidentally (one of which assumptions must be made for the purpose of the Crown's argument at the trial) there is nothing in the circumstances of Gooriah's death to negative these possible views. Even if the appellant deliberately caused Gooriah to take poison (an assumption not lightly to be made, since he was never charged with having murdered her) it does not follow that Ayesha may not have committed suicide. As to the argument from similarity of circumstances, it seems on analysis to amount to no more than this, that if the appellant murdered one woman because he was jealous of her, it is probable that he murdered another for the same reason. If the appellant were proved to have administered poison to Ayesha in circumstances consistent with accident, then proof that he had previously administered poison to Gooriah in similar circumstances might well have been admissible. There was, however, no direct evidence in either case that the appellant had administered the poison. It is true that in the case of Gooriah there was evidence from which it might be inferred that he persuaded her to take the poison by a trick, but this evidence cannot properly be used to found an inference that a similar trick was used to deceive Ayesha, and so to fill a gap in the available evidence. The evidence which was properly adduced as to Ayesha shows her to have been acquainted, as were, it may be supposed, most of the inhabitants of the village in which the appellant lived, with the fact that suspicion rested on him in respect of Gooriah's death, and the theory that Ayesha was deceived into taking poison by a similar ruse to that which is supposed to have succeeded with Gooriah seems to their Lordships to rest on an improbable surmise. The effect of the admission of the impugned evidence may well have been that the jury came to the conclusion that the appellant was guilty of the murder of Gooriah, with which he had never been charged, and having thus, adjudged him a murderer, were satisfied with something short of conclusive proof that he had murdered Ayesha. In these circumstances the verdict cannot stand, notwithstanding the care with which the learned judge summed up the case, and the fairness with which the trial was conducted in all other respects.'
Appeal allowed.

The case illustrates the danger of admitting evidence where the similarity between the offence charged and the previous matter is no more than superficial.

Holt J: On what basis ought I to assess whether the similarity is sufficient?

Mr Atkyn: My Lord, in two ways. The first is that the similarity must be one relating to the offence itself. Evidence which does no more than suggest similar behaviour in other or peripheral respects should not be admitted. I would refer Your Lordship to:

R v *Rodley* [1913] 3 KB 468 (CCA)

The appellant was convicted of breaking into a dwelling-house with intent to rape. The prosecution evidence was that after entering the house he had seized the complainant, but ran away on being surprised by her father. The defence at the trial was that the appellant went to the house for the purpose of courting the complainant with her consent, and that he did not break into the house and did not intend or attempt to ravish her. The prosecution tendered evidence that one hour later on the same day the appellant went to the house of another woman, about three miles away, gained access to her bedroom down the chimney, and with her consent had intercourse with her.

BANKES J, reading the judgment of the court, said 'In *R v Fisher* [1910] 1 KB 149, 152 Channell J puts the point thus. He says: "The principle is clear, however, and if the principle is attended to I think it will usually be found that the difficulty of applying it to a particular case will disappear. The principle is that the prosecution are not allowed to prove that a prisoner has committed the offence with which he is charged by giving evidence that he is a person of bad character and one who is in the habit of committing crimes, for that is equivalent of asking the jury to say that because the prisoner has committed other offences he must therefore be guilty of the particular offence for which he is being tried. But if the evidence of other offences does go to prove that he did commit the offence charged, it is admissible because it is relevant to the issue, and it is admissible not because, but notwithstanding that, it proves that the prisoner has committed another offence." As here pointed out by Channell J, the governing rule must always be that any evidence to be admissible must be relevant to the issue.... This Court is of opinion that the evidence is not admissible. At the point in the trial at which the evidence was tendered the defences really in issue were: (1) That the appellant never broke into the house at all; (2) that the appellant did not break into the house with any intention of committing a rape; (3) that the prosecutrix's story as to what occurred in the house was not true.

The evidence which was objected to was not, in the opinion of this Court, relevant to any of those issues, and was not therefore admissible to rebut any of the above defences. If the jury believed the evidence of the prosecutrix, the only issue was as to whether, in the opinion of the jury, the acts of the appellant amounted to an attempt to rape, and whether from his acts the jury would infer that the appellant broke into the house with the intention of committing a rape. In the opinion of this Court upon neither of those issues was the evidence objected to relevant. The conclusion therefore arrived at by this Court is that the evidence objected to was not admissible on any ground and ought to have been rejected.'
Conviction quashed.

I would rely also on the decision in:

R v *Tricoglus* (1976) 65 Cr App R 16 (CA)

The defendant was convicted of raping A. A gave evidence that she had accepted a lift from a bearded man driving a Mini. He had driven her to a cul-de-sac and there raped her. The manner of the rape was peculiar, the rapist having odd sexual tastes. Evidence was admitted from G that, a few days before the rape of A, she (G) had been raped in the same cul-de-sac as A by a bearded man from whom she had accepted a lift. The method of raping her was virtually the same as in A's case and her ravisher had the same peculiar sexual tastes. G identified the defendant's car when shown it, after some uncertainty about its make. Evidence was also admitted from M and C that in the same vicinity they had been offered, but had refused, lifts from a bearded man driving a Mini. C took the number of the car, which corresponded, except for one figure, with that of the defendant's car, a Mini.

LAWTON LJ, giving the judgment of the court, said: 'In our judgment the evidence of Mrs G as to the manner in which she was raped did bear a uniquely and strikingly similar resemblance to the manner in which Ann was raped. Therefore, prima facie, as a matter of law Mrs G's evidence as to how she was raped was admissible. That was the view which Nield J took and, in our judgment, rightly took. On the other hand the evidence of Mrs M and Miss C as to the unpleasant experience that they had had of being accosted by a man who, to use a colloquial expression, was "kerb crawling" really has no bearing at all upon the manner in which Ann was raped. In our judgment it merely went to show, if it did tie up in any way with the appellant (as it probably did on the evidence of Miss C and on an admission which the appellant made in the witness box when he was giving evidence) that he has unpleasant social habits. Beyond that it does not go. Therefore it ought not, in our judgment, to have been admitted.

Mr Chadwin, on behalf of the Crown, sought to satisfy the Court that it had got probative value outside similar fact evidence by saying that it showed that the appellant was a man who possessed a Mini similar to that in which Ann had been raped. In our judgment that is far too tenuous a link to justify the admission of this evidence.

Evidence of this kind must have had a considerable prejudicial effect because in a case where the issue was, "was this the man who had raped Ann?" the prosecution, by calling the evidence of Mrs M and Miss C, was calling evidence of a type which was bound to lead the jury to think that this appellant had a propensity towards approaching women who were strangers to him and trying to get them into his motorcar for the purpose of sexual intercourse. As has been pointed out many times in this Court and in the House of Lords, it is not permissible to call evidence to show that a man has a propensity towards a particular type of crime. The evidence of Mrs G, as I have already indicated, was in a different category altogether.'

Appeal allowed.

Holt J: Yes, but is not this case one where we are concerned with the evidence of the equivalent of G? There is no doubt that your client was in fact convicted of the rape on the previous occasion. Of course, I should have to be satisfied that it was not just another act of rape, but one which did bear a striking similarity in the manner of its commission.

Mr Atkyn: My Lord, yes. In any event the second matter which Your Lordship should take into account is whether any such similarity related to a significant feature of the offence, and not just to a matter which is so commonplace that it could apply to almost any case of rape.

Holt J: Yes. As I understand Mr Bunbury's argument, he would say that these offences are of such a nature that the very fact that there are two of them is enough to give rise to striking similarity. Is that right, Mr Bunbury?

Mr Bunbury: Yes, My Lord. I rely principally on the decision of the House of Lords in:

Thompson v *R* [1918] AC 221 (HL)

The appellant was convicted of committing acts of gross indecency with boys on 16 March. At his trial his defence was that he was not the man and he adduced evidence to establish an alibi. It was proved that the man who committed the offence made an appointment to meet the boys on 19 March at the time and place where the offence was committed and that the appellant met the boys at the appointed time and place and gave them money. The prosecution tendered evidence that on this occasion, when he was arrested, the appellant was carrying powder puffs and that he had indecent photographs of boys in his rooms.

LORD SUMNER said: '...There must be something to connect the circumstance tendered in evidence, not only with the accused, but with his participation in the crime. It is this something which he expressed in the judgment under appeal in the words "ordinary men do not keep indecent photographs of naked boys in their possession. Men who commit the offences charged do...The man who did the acts on March 16 was a man who would be likely to have such photographs in his possession. The man arrested on the 19th in fact had such photographs in his possession at his rooms." Illustrations, it is true, were employed during the argument, both at your Lordships' Bar and in the Court below, and I think in one passage in the judgment, which went considerably beyond the limits of admissibility, but as applied to the facts of the case I think the meaning of the above passage may be restated more fully as follows: The actual criminal made an appointment to meet the same boys at the same time and place three days later and presumably for the same purpose. This tends to show that his act was not an isolated act, but was an incident in the habitual gratification of a particular propensity. The appellant, as his possession of the photographs tend to show, is a person with the same propensity. Indeed, he went to the place of the appointment with some of the outfit, and he had the rest of it at home. The evidence tends to attach to the accused a peculiarity which, though not purely physical, I think may be recognised as properly bearing that name. Experience tends to show that these offences against nature connote an inversion of normal characteristics which, while demanding punishment as offending against social morality, also partake of the nature of an abnormal physical property. A thief, a cheat, a coiner, or a house-breaker is only a particular specimen of the genus rogue, and, though no doubt each tends to keep to his own line of business, they all alike possess the by no means extraordinary mental characteristic that they propose somehow to get their livings dishonestly. So common a characteristic is not a recognisable mark of the individual. Persons, however, who commit the offences now under consideration seek the habitual gratification of a particular perverted lust, which not only takes them out of the class of ordinary men gone wrong, but stamps them with the hall-mark of a specialised and extraordinary class as much as if they carried on their bodies some physical peculiarity. So expanded and understood, I accept the passage which I have quoted above, and think that the photographs, found as they were and after a short interval of time, tend to show that the accused had this recognisable propensity, which it was shown was also the propensity of the criminal of March 16. It was accordingly admissible evidence of his identity with that criminal. Its weight was for the jury. No doubt it required considerable discretion in introducing it at all and a careful direction from the learned judge, but it is admitted that this was given in unexceptionable terms.'

LORD FINLEY LC said: 'What was done on the 16th shows that the person who did it was a person with abnormal propensities of this kind. The possession of the articles tends to show that the person who came on the 19th, the prisoner, had abnormal propensities of the same kind. The criminal of the 16th and the prisoner had this feature in common, and it appears to me that the evidence which is objected to afforded some evidence tending to show the probability of the truth of the boys' story as to identity.'
(LORDS DUNEDIN and PARKER of WADDINGTON concurred. LORDS ATKINSON and PARMOOR also delivered judgments dismissing the appeal.)
Appeal dismissed.

My Lord, the same point was made in:

R v Sims [1946] KB 531 (CCA)

The defendant was charged with sodomy with three men and gross indecency with a fourth. All the offences were alleged to have taken place on different occasions. At the trial the defendant made an application that the charges be tried separately in respect of each separate man. The application was refused and the defendant was convicted subsequently of sodomy on each of the three charges, but acquitted on the indecency charge.

LORD GODDARD CJ, reading the written judgment of the court, which he stated had been largely prepared by DENNING J, said: 'In all these cases the evidence of other acts may tend to show the accused to be of a bad disposition, but it also shows something more. The other acts have specific features connecting him with the crime charged and are on that account admissible in evidence.... The specific feature in such cases lies in the abnormal and perverted propensity which stamps the individual as clearly as if marked by a physical deformity. We think that in all the cases where the evidence has been admitted there have been special features connecting the evidence with the crime charged as distinct from evidence that he is of a bad disposition.... Applying these principles, we are of opinion that on the trial of one of the counts in this case, the evidence on the others would be admissible. The evidence of each man was that the accused invited him into the house and there committed the crime charged. The acts they describe bear a striking similarity. That is a special feature sufficient in itself to justify the admissibility of the evidence; but we think it should be put on a broader basis. Sodomy is a crime in a special category...'

[His Lordship referred with approval to Lord Sumner's speech in *Thompson* v *R* and continued:]

'On this account, in regard to this crime we think that the repetition of the acts is itself a specific feature connecting the accused with the crime and that evidence of this kind is admissible to show the nature of the act done by the accused. The probative force of all the acts together is much greater than one alone; for, whereas the jury might think one man might be telling an untruth, three or four are hardly likely to tell the same untruth unless they were conspiring together. If there is nothing to suggest a conspiracy their evidence would seem to be overwhelming. Whilst it would no doubt be in the interests of the prisoner that each case should be considered separately without the evidence on the others, we think that the interests of justice require that on each case the evidence on the others should be considered, and that, even apart from the defence raised by him, the evidence would be admissible.

In this case the matter can be put in another and very simple way. The visits of the men to the prisoner's house were either for a guilty or an innocent purpose: that they all speak to the commission of the same class of acts upon them tends to show that in each case the visits were for the former and not the latter purpose. The same considerations would apply to a case where a man is charged with a series of indecent offences against children, whether boys or girls: that they all complain of the same sort of conduct shows that the interest the prisoner was taking in them was not of a paternal or friendly nature but for the purpose of satisfying lust.

If we are right in thinking that the evidence was admissible, it is plain that the accused would not be prejudiced or embarrassed by reason of all the counts being tried together, and there was no reason for the judge to direct the jury that, in considering whether a particular charge was proved, they were to shut out other charges from their minds.'

Appeal dismissed.

Mr Atkyn: My Lord, if I may interrupt my learned friend, those cases must be read in the light of more recent authority. In my submission, sexual offences are no longer in any special category as was supposed in those earlier cases, but are subject to the test applicable to criminal cases generally. May I refer Your Lordship to the decision of the House of Lords in *DPP* v *Boardman* which is now the leading authority:

DPP v *Boardman* [1975] AC 421 (HL)

The appellant, the headmaster of a boarding school, was convicted of attempted buggery with S, one of his pupils, and of inciting H, another pupil, to commit buggery with him. The defence was that S and H were lying and that the alleged incidents never took place. The trial judge ruled that the evidence of H was admissible on the count concerning S and *vice versa*. This was because, in each case, the homosexual conduct alleged by both boys against the appellant was of an unusual kind, in that it involved a request by a middle aged man to an adolescent to play the active role in buggery. There were, however, other similarities in the evidence of S and H. Both said that they were woken up by the appellant at about midnight whilst asleep in the dormitory; both said that he used similar words to induce their participation. The jury convicted the appellant, and his appeal against conviction on the ground, *inter alia*, that the judge's ruling had been wrong was dismissed by the Court of Appeal. A further appeal was made to the House of Lords.

LORD WILBERFORCE said: 'We can dispose at once of the suggestion that there is a special rule or principle applicable to sexual, or to homosexual offences. This suggestion had support at one time — eminent support from Lord Sumner in *Thompson* v *R* [1918] AC 221 — but is now certainly obsolete: see *per* Lord Reid (at p 751) and the other learned lords in *R* v *Kilbourne* [1973] AC 729. Evidence that an offence of a sexual character was committed by A against B cannot be supported by evidence that an offence of a sexual character was committed by A against C, or against C, D and E.

The question certified suggests that the contrary may be true if the offences take a "particular form." I do not know what this means: all sexual activity has some form or other and the varieties are not unlimited: how particular must it be for a special rule to apply? The general salutary rule of exclusion must not be eroded through so vague an epithet. The danger of it being so is indeed well shown in the present case for the judge excluded the (similar fact) evidence of one boy because it showed "normal" homosexual acts while admitting the (similar fact) evidence of another boy because the homosexual acts assumed a different, and, in his view, "abnormal," pattern. Distinctions such as this, rightly called fine distinctions by the judge, lend an unattractive unreality to the law.

If the evidence was to be received, then, it must be on some general principle not confined to sexual offences.'

LORD MORRIS OF BORTH-Y-GEST said: 'If the question is raised whether there is a special rule in cases where there is a charge involving an allegation of homosexual conduct the answer must be that there is no such special rule. But in such cases there may be, depending upon the particular facts, room for the application of the principle to which I have been referring. The word "thereby" in the certified point of law seems to raise a question whether there is a rule which gives automatic admissibility to evidence where proclivities take a particular form. There is no such specific rule which would automatically give admissibility. But there may be cases where a judge, having both limbs of Lord Herschell LC's famous proposition (*Makin* v *Attorney-General for New South Wales* [1894] AC 57, 65) in mind, considers that the interests of justice (of which the interests of fairness form so fundamental a component) make it proper that he should permit a jury when considering the evidence on a charge concerning one fact or set of facts also to consider the evidence concerning another fact or set of facts if between the two there is such a close or striking similarity or such an underlying unity that probative force could fairly be yielded.'

Holt J: Yes, Mr Bunbury, what do you say about that case?

Mr Bunbury: My Lord, I accept that *DPP* v *Boardman* represents the law at present. But there is still authority in the Court of Appeal which indicates that sexual offences may still form something of a separate class. I refer Your Lordship to:

R v *Johannsen* (1977) 65 Cr App R 101 (CA)

The defendant was charged with homosexual offences with five schoolboys aged fourteen and fifteen. Two counts in respect of each boy charged (i) buggery, and (ii) gross indecency. The defendant had been committed for trial without oral examination of the prosecution witnesses, the five boys, but on their depositions. After arraignment, defending counsel moved to sever the indictment so that there would be separate trials on each of the coupled counts on the ground that there were no striking similarities between each of the coupled counts so as to make the evidence on one admissible on the others. The trial judge ruled against that submission upholding the prosecution submission that the evidence on the depositions revealed striking similarities between the coupled counts. Save in the case of one boy, each of the other four gave evidence about one or more incidents. The defendant was convicted on all counts, and appealed.

LAWTON LJ, reading the judgment of the court, said: 'We do not find it necessary to set

out in much detail the sordid evidence given in this case.... The prosecution's case was that between May and December 1975 he made a practice of accosting boys in amusement arcades and similar places, offering them money or a meal or treating them to a game, taking them to his accommodation or on the beach and there committing the offences charged. His particular homosexual propensities were to handle the boys' penises and getting them to do the same with his, fellatio and buggery.... We have no hesitation in deciding that there were striking similarities about what happened to each of the boys — the accostings in the same kind of places, the enticements, the visits to his accommodation, his homosexual propensities and his ways of gratifying them.
Appeal dismissed.

Holt J: If I may say so with respect, that seems to me to be difficult to reconcile with the approach of the House of Lords in *DPP* v *Boardman*.
Mr Atkyn: Perhaps I might point out, My Lord, a case in which the Court of Appeal arrived at a quite different decision on facts which were virtually indistinguishable from those in *R* v *Johannsen*. I refer to:

R v Novac (1976) 65 Cr App R 107 (CA)

An application to sever an indictment containing various counts against the appellant alleging buggery and gross indecency with boys said to have been accosted by the appellant in amusement arcades was rejected. The appellant was said to have offered them money or a meal and then taken them to his home or the beach to commit the offences.

BRIDGE LJ, reading the judgment of the court, said: 'We cannot think that two or more alleged offences of buggery or attempted buggery committed in bed at the residence of the alleged offender with boys to whom he had offered shelter can be said to have been committed in a uniquely or strikingly similar manner. If a man is going to commit buggery with a boy he picks up, it must surely be a commonplace feature of such an encounter that he will take the boy home with him and commit the offence in bed. The fact that the boys may in each case have been picked up by Raywood in the first instance at amusement arcades may be a feature more nearly approximating to a "unique or striking similarity" within the ambit of Lord Salmon's principle. It is not, however, a similarity in the commission of the crime. It is a similarity in the surrounding circumstances and is not, in our judgment sufficiently proximate to the commission of the crime itself to lead to the conclusion that the repetition of this feature would make the boys' stories inexplicable on the basis of coincidence.'
Appeal allowed.

In my submission, the test of admissibility is one of relevance as was laid down by Their Lordships in:

DPP v Boardman [1975] AC 421 (HL) (Facts set out above).

LORD WILBERFORCE said: 'There are obvious difficulties in the way of formulating any such rule in such a manner as, on the one hand, to enable clear guidance to be given to juries, and, on the other hand, to avoid undue rigidity.
    The prevailing formulation is to be found in the judgment of the Court of Criminal Appeal in *R* v *Sims* [1946] KB 531 where it was said, at pp 539–540: "The evidence of each man was that the accused invited him into the house and there committed the acts charged. The acts they describe bear a striking similarity. That is a special feature sufficient in itself to justify the admissibility of the evidence;... The probative force of all the acts together is much greater than one alone; for, whereas the jury might think that one man might be telling an untruth, three or four are hardly likely to tell the same untruth unless they were conspiring together. If there is nothing to suggest a conspiracy their evidence would seem to be overwhelming."
Sims has not received universal approbation or uniform commentary, but I think that it must

be taken that this passage has received at least the general approval of this House in *R* v *Kilbourne* [1973] AC 529. For my part, since the statement is evidently related to the facts of that particular case, I should deprecate its literal use in other cases. It is certainly neither clear nor comprehensive. A suitable adaptation, and, if necessary, expansion, should be allowed to judges in order to suit the facts involved. The basic principle must be that the admission of similar fact evidence (of the kind now in question) is exceptional and requires a strong degree of probative force. This probative force is derived, if at all, from the circumstance that the facts testified to by the several witnesses bear to each other such a striking similarity that they must, when judged by experience and common sense, either all be true, or have arisen from a cause common to the witnesses or from pure coincidence. The jury may, therefore, properly be asked to judge whether the right conclusion is that all are true, so that each story is supported by the other(s).

I use the words "a cause common to the witnesses" to include not only (as in *R* v *Sims* [1946] KB 531) the possibility that the witnesses may have invented a story in concert but also the possibility that a similar story may have arisen by a process of infection from media or publicity or simply from fashion. In the sexual field, and in others, this may be a real possibility: something much more than mere similarity and absence of proved conspiracy is needed if this evidence is to be allowed. This is well illustrated by *R* v *Kilbourne* [1973] AC 529 where the judge excluded "intra group" evidence because of the possibility, *as it appeared to him,* of collaboration between boys who knew each other well. This is, in my respectful opinion, the right course rather than to admit the evidence unless a case of collaboration or concoction is made out.

If this test is to be applied fairly, much depends in the first place upon the experience and common sense of the judge. As was said by Lord Simon of Glaisdale in *R* v *Kilbourne,* at p 756, in judging whether one fact is probative of another, experience plays as large a place as logic. And in matters of experience it is for the judge to keep close to current mores. What is striking in one age is normal in another: the perversions of yesterday may be the routine or the fashion of tomorrow. The ultimate test has to be applied by the jury using similar qualities of experience and common sense after a fair presentation of the dangers either way of admission or of rejection. Finally, whether the judge has properly used and stated the ingredients of experience and common sense may be reviewed by the Court of Appeal.

The present case is, to my mind, right on the border-line. There were only two relevant witnesses, S and H. The striking similarity as presented to the jury was and was only the active character of the sexual performance to which the accused was said to have invited the complainants. In relation to the incident which was the subject of the second charge, the language used by the boy was not specific: the "similarity" was derived from an earlier incident in connection with which the boy used a verb connoting an active role. I agree with, I think, all your Lordships in thinking that all of this, relating not very specifically to the one striking element, common to two boys only, is, if sufficient, only just sufficient. Perhaps other similarities could have been found in the accused's approaches to the boys (I do not myself find them particularly striking), but the judge did not rest upon them to direct the jury as to their "similarity." I do not think that these ought now to be relied upon. The dilution of the "striking" fact by more prosaic details might have weakened the impact upon the jury rather than strengthened it. The judge dealt properly and fairly with the possibility of a conspiracy between the boys.

These matters lie largely within the field of the judge's discretion, and of the jury's task; the Court of Appeal has reviewed the whole matter in a careful judgment. I do not think that there is anything which justifies the interference of this House. But I confess to some fear that the case, if regarded as an example, may be setting the standard of "striking similarity" too low.

LORD HAILSHAM OF ST MARYLEBONE said: 'Another contention put forward by appellant's counsel was that the decision in *R* v *Sims* [1946] KB 531 was wrong, and that any cases founded on *Sims* fell with it. It is true, as I have said, that the passage relating to evidence which is logically probative, at p 537, must now be read in the light of Lord du Parcq's criticisms in *Noor Mohamed* v *The King* [1949] AC 182, 194. It is also true that in *R* v *Kilbourne* [1973] AC 729 both Lord Reid and I expressed the view that the opinion expressed in *R* v *Sims* [1946] KB 531, 540, which seems to put sodomy as a "crime in a special category" goes a great deal too far, and that Lord Sumner's statement in *Thompson* v *The King* [1918] AC 221, 222 ought not to be read in this sense. Lord Reid said, at p 751:

> Then there are indications of a special rule for homosexual crimes. If there ever was a time for that, that time is past, and on the view which I take of the law, any such special rule is quite unnecessary.

Both Lord Morris of Borth-y-Gest and I said the same by implication. But, subject to these two points, and the specific point decided in *Kilbourne*, *Sims* has never been successfully challenged and was expressly approved in general terms in *Kilbourne* by myself, Lord Reid and Lord Morris of Borth-y-Gest, and by implication by Viscount Simon in *Harris* v *Director of Public Prosecutions* [1952] AC 694, 708, and followed in *R* v *Campbell* [1956] 2 QB 432.

The truth is that, apart from these qualifications, *Sims* was never in need of support, for in the sense explained in Professor Cross's book on *Evidence*, 3rd ed, p 319, it was only a particular example of a general principle which stems from *Makin* v *Attorney-General for New South Wales* [1894] AC 57, especially at p 65, and goes down through a long list of cases, English and Scottish, including *Moorov* v *HM Advocate*, 1930 JC 68 and *Ogg* v *HM Advocate*, 1938 JC 152 to the present time. This rule is contained in the classic statement of Lord Herschell LC in *Makin*, at p 65, cited above, which I quote here once again solely for convenience:

> It is undoubtedly not competent for the prosecution to adduce evidence tending to show that the accused has been guilty of criminal acts other than those covered by the indictment, for the purpose of leading to the conclusion that the accused is a person likely from his criminal conduct or character to have committed the offence for which he is being tried. On the other hand, the mere fact that the evidence adduced tends to show the commission of other crimes does not render it inadmissible if it be relevant to an issue before the jury, and it may be so relevant if it bears upon the question whether the acts alleged to constitute the crime charged in the indictment were designed or accidental, or to rebut a defence which would otherwise be open to the accused.

This statement may be divided into its component parts. The first sentence lays down a general rule of exclusion. "Similar fact" evidence, or evidence of bad character is not admissible for the purpose of leading to the conclusion that a person, from his criminal conduct or character, is likely to have committed the offence for which he is being held.

Two theories have been advanced as to the basis of this, and both have respectable judicial support. One is that such evidence is simply irrelevant. No number of similar offences can connect a particular person with a particular crime, however much they may lead the police, or anyone else investigating the offence, to concentrate their inquiries upon him as their prime suspect. According to this theory, similar fact evidence excluded under Lord Herschell LC's first sentence has no probative value and is to be rejected on that ground. The second theory is that the prejudice created by the admission of such evidence outweighs any probative value it may have. An example of this view is to be found in the speech of Lord Simon of Glaisdale in *R* v *Kilbourne* [1973] AC 729 where he said, at p 757:

> The reason why the type of evidence referred to by Lord Herschell LC in the first sentence of the passage is inadmissible is, not because it is irrelevant, but because its logically probative significance is considered to be grossly outweighed by its prejudice to the accused, so that a fair trial is endangered if it is admitted;...

With respect, both theories are correct. When there is nothing to connect the accused with a particular crime except bad character or similar crimes committed in the past, the probative value of the evidence is nil and the evidence is rejected on that ground. When there is some evidence connecting the accused with the crime, in the eyes of most people, guilt of similar offences in the past might well be considered to have probative value (cf the statutory exceptions to this effect in the old law of receiving and under the Theft Act 1968). Nonetheless, in the absence of a statutory provision to the contrary, the evidence is to be excluded under the first rule in *Makin* [1894] AC 57, 65 because its prejudicial effect may be more powerful than its probative effect, and thus endanger a fair trial because it tends to undermine the integrity of the presumption of innocence and the burden of proof. In other words, it is a rule of English law which has its roots in policy, and by which, in Lord du Parcq's phrase in *Noor Mohamed* v *The King* [1949] AC 182, 194, logicians would not be bound.

But there is a third case, to which the second rule in *Makin* [1894] AC 57, 65 applies. The mere fact that the evidence adduced tends to show the commission of other crimes does not by itself render it inadmissible *if it is relevant to an issue before the jury and it may be so relevant if it bears upon the question whether the acts alleged to constitute the crime charged in the indictment were designed or accidental, or to rebut a defence which would otherwise be open to the accused.*

Contrary to what was suggested in argument for the appellant, this rule is not an exception grafted on to the first. It is an independent proposition introduced by the words: "On the other hand" and the two propositions together cover the entire field. If one applies, the other does not.

Thus in *R* v *Ball* [1911] AC 47, evidence of inclination and affection of a sexual kind was admitted to show inclination in a case of brother and sister incest; in *Thompson* v *The King* [1918] AC 221, evidence of a particular tendency was admitted to show that the accused was present at a particular time and place of meeting as the result of previous assignation, and was not purely fortinuitous as claimed by the accused; in *R* v *Smith* (1915) *The Trial of George Joseph Smith*, edited by Eric R Watson, *Notable British Trials Series* (1922) (the "brides in the bath" case) evidence of similar circumstances was admitted to exclude coincidence where there was no other evidence either of the fact of killing or the intent; similar considerations seem to have prevailed in *R* v *Straffen* [1952] 2 QB 911. The permutations are almost indefinite. In *Moorov* v *HM Advocate*, 1930 JC 68 coincidence of story as distinct from coincidence in the facts was held to be admissible and corroborative, and this, after some fairly agonised appraisals, was what was thought in *R* v *Kilbourne* [1973] AC 729. The fact is that, although the categories are useful classes of example, they are not closed (see *per* Viscount Simon in *Harris* v *Director of Public Prosecutions* [1952] AC 694, 705), and they cannot in fact be closed by categorisation. The rules of logic and common sense are not susceptible of exact codification when applied to the actual facts of life in its infinite variety.

What is important is not to open the door so widely that the second proposition merges in the first: see, for example, what was said in *R* v *Flack* [1969] 1 WLR 937, *R* v *Chandor* [1959] 1 QB 545 and *Ogg* v *HM Advocate* 1938 JC 152. Contrary to what was said in *R* v *Flack* and *R* v *Chandor* I do not see the logical distinction between innocent association cases and cases of complete denial, since the permutations are too various to admit of universally appropriate labels. The truth is that a mere succession of facts is not normally enough (see *Moorov* v *HM Advocate*, 1930 JC 68 on "a course of criminal conduct"), whether the cases are many or limited to two as in *HM Advocate* v *AE*, 1937 JC 96. There must be something more than mere repetition. What there must be is variously described as "underlying unity" (*Moorov* v *HM Advocate*), "system" (see *per* Lord Reid in *R* v *Kilbourne*), "nexus," "unity of intent, project, campaign or adventure" (*Moorov* v *HM Advocate*), "part of the same criminal conduct," "striking resemblance" (*R* v *Sims* [1946] KB 531). These are all highly analogical not to say metaphorical expressions and should not be applied pedantically. It is true that the doctrine "must be applied with great caution" (see *Ogg* v *HM Advocate*, 1938 JC 152, *per* the Lord Justice-Clerk (Lord Aitchison), at p 158), but:

> The test in each case, and in considering each particular charge, is, was the evidence with regard to other charges relevant to that charge? (*per* Lord Wark, at p 160).

The test is (*per* Lord Simon of Glaisdale in *R* v *Kilbourne* [1973] AC 729, 759) whether there is "...such an underlying unity between the offences as to make coincidence an affront to common sense" or, to quote Hallett J in *R* v *Robinson*, 37 Cr App R 95, 106–107, in the passage cited by Professor Cross, *Evidence*, 3rd ed, p 316:

> If a jury are precluded by some rule of law from taking the view that something is a coincidence which is against all the probabilities if the accused person is innocent, then it

would seem to be a doctrine of law which prevents a jury from using what looks like ordinary common sense.

This definition would seem easy enough were it not for the fact that the judge must, as a matter of law, withhold from the jury evidence which is outside the definition. The jury can treat the matter as one of degree and weight, which it is. The judge is constrained to assert a line of principle before he allows it to go to the jury. I do not know that the matter can be better stated that it was by Lord Herschell LC in *Makin* v *Attorney-General for New South Wales* [1894] AC 57, 65, remembering the note of caution sounded in *Ogg* v *HM Advocate,* 1938 JC 152 and perhaps finding useful as guides, but not as shackles, the kind of factor enumerated there, as, for example, the number of instances involved, any interrelation between them, the intervals or similarities of time, circumstances and the details and character of the evidence. Reference may also be made to the passage in Lord du Parcq's judgment in *Noor Mohamed* v *The King* [1949] AC 182, 192 noticed with approval by Viscount Simon in *Harris* v *Director of Public Prosecutions* [1952] AC 694, 707. It is perhaps helpful to remind oneself that what is *not* to be admitted is a chain of reasoning and not necessarily a state of facts. If the inadmissible chain of reasoning is the *only* purpose for which the evidence is adduced as a matter of law, the evidence itself is not admissible. If there is some other relevant, probative purpose than for the forbidden type of reasoning, the evidence is admitted, but should be made subject to a warning from the judge that the jury must eschew the forbidden reasoning. The judge also has a discretion, not as a matter of law but as a matter of good practice, to exclude evidence whose prejudicial effect, though the evidence be technically admissible on the decided cases, may be so great in the particular circumstances as to outweigh its probative value to the extent that a verdict of guilty might be considered unsafe or unsatisfactory if ensuing (cf *per* Lord Simon in *Harris* v *Director of Public Prosecutions* [1952] AC 694, 707). In all these cases it is for the judge to ensure as a matter of law in the first place, and as a matter of discretion where the matter is free, that a properly instructed jury, applying their minds to the facts, can come to the conclusion that they are satisfied so that they are sure that to treat the matter as pure coincidence by reason of the "nexus," "pattern," "system," "striking resemblances" or whatever phrase is used is "an affront to common sense" [*R* v *Kilbourne* [1973] AC 729, *per* Lord Simon of Glaisdale, at p 759]. In this the ordinary rules of logic and common sense prevail, whether the case is one of burglary and the burglar has left some "signature" as the mark of his presence, or false pretences and the pretences alleged have too many common characteristics to have happened coincidentally, or whether the dispute is one of identity and the accused in a series of offences has some notable physical features or behaviourial or psychological characteristics or, as in some cases, is in possession of incriminating articles, like a jemmy, a set of skeleton keys or, in abortion cases, the apparatus of the abortionist. Attempts to codify the rules of common sense are to be resisted. The first rule in *Makin* [1894] AC 57, 65 is designed to exclude a particular kind of inference being drawn which might upset the presumption of innocence by introducing more heat than light. When that is the only purpose for which the evidence is being tendered, it should be excluded altogether, as in *R* v *Horwood* [1970] 1 QB 133. Where the purpose is an inference of another kind, subject to the judge's overriding discretion to exclude, the evidence is admissible, if in fact the evidence be logically probative. Even then it is for the jury to assess its weight, which may be greater or less according as to how far it accords with other evidence, and according as to how far that other evidence may be conclusive.

There are two further points of a general character that I would add. The "striking resemblances" or "unusual features," or whatever phrase is considered appropriate, to ignore which would affront common sense, may either be in the objective facts, as for instance in *R* v *Smith, Notable British Trials Series,* or *R* v *Straffen* [1952] 2 QB 911, or may constitute a striking similarity in the accounts by witnesses of disputed transactions. For instance, whilst it would certainly not be enough to identify the culprit in a series of burglaries that he climbed in through a ground floor window, the fact that he left the same humorous limerick on the walls of the sitting room, or an esoteric sysmbol written in lipstick on the mirror, might well be enough. In a sex case, to adopt an example given in argument in the Court of Appeal, whilst a repeated homosexual act by itself might be quite insufficient to admit the evidence as confirmatory of identity or design, the fact that it was alleged to have been performed wearing the ceremonial head-dress of a Red Indian chief or other eccentric garb might well in appropriate circumstances suffice.'

LORD SALMON said: 'My Lords, evidence against an accused which tends only to show that he is a man of character with a disposition to commit crimes, even the crime with which he is charged, is inadmissible and deemed to be irrelevant in English law. I do not pause to discuss the philosophic basis for this fundamental rule. It is certainly not founded on logic, but on policy. To admit such evidence would be unjust and would offend our concept of a fair trial to which we hold that everyone is entitled. Nevertheless, if there is some other evidence which may show that an accused is guilty of the crime with which he is charged, such evidence is admissible against him, notwithstanding that it may also reveal his bad character and disposition to commit crime.

I have no wish to add to the anthology of guidance concerning the special circumstances in which evidence is relevant and admissible against an accused, notwithstanding that it may disclose that he is a man of bad character with a disposition to commit the kind of crime with which he is charged. The principles upon which such evidence should be admitted or excluded are stated with crystal clarity in the celebrated passage from the judgment delivered by Lord Herschell LC in *Makin* v *Attorney-General for New South Wales* [1894] AC 57, 65. I doubt whether the learned analyses and explanations of that passage to which it has been subjected so often in the last 80 years add very much to it.

It is plain from what has fallen from your Lordships (with which I respectfully agree) that the principles stated by Lord Herschell are of universal application and that homosexual offences are not exempt from them as at one time seems to have been supposed: see *Thompson* v *The King* [1918] AC 221, *per* Lord Sumner, at p 232, and *R* v *Sims* [1946] KB 531, 537.

The doctrine that evidence which is admissible and relevant to prove guilt might at the same time be incapable of constituting corroboration was finally laid to rest in *R* v *Kilbourne* [1973] AC 729. It was a strange doctrine resting on the fallacy that evidence which might itself require corroboration was therefore incapable of corroborating any other evidence. If corroborating evidence is suspect that no doubt goes to its weight but not to its admissibility. After all, corroboration is only evidence tending to implicate an accused in the commission of the offence with which he is charged.

[It] confirms in some material particular not only the evidence that the crime has been committed, but also that the prisoner committed it": *R* v *Baskerville* [1916] 2 KB 658, 667, *per* Lord Reading CJ.

My Lords, whether or not evidence is relevant and admissible against an accused is solely a question of law. The test must be: is the evidence capable of tending to persuade a reasonable jury of the accused's guilt on some ground other than his bad character and disposition to commit the sort of crime with which he is charged? In the case of an alleged homosexual offence, just as in the case of an alleged burglary, evidence which proves merely that the accused has committed crimes in the past and is therefore disposed to commit the crime charged is clearly inadmissible. It has, however, never been doubted that if the crime charged is committed in a uniquely or strikingly similar manner to other crimes committed by the accused the manner in which the other crimes were committed may be evidence upon which a jury could reasonably conclude that the accused was guilty of the crime charged. The similarity would have to be so unique or striking that common sense makes it inexplicable on the basis of coincidence. I would stress that the question as to whether the evidence is capable of being so regarded by a reasonable jury is a question of law. There is no easy way out by leaving it to the jury to see how they decide it. If a trial judge wrongly lets in the evidence and the jury convict, then, subject to the proviso [to section 2 (1) of the Criminal Appeal Act 1968], the conviction must be quashed. If, for example, A is charged with burglary at the house of B and it is shown that the burglar, whoever he was, entered B's house by a ground floor window, evidence against A that he had committed a long series of burglaries, in every case entering by a ground floor window, would be clearly inadmissible. This would show nothing from which a reasonable jury could infer anything except bad character and a disposition to burgle. The factor of unique or striking similarity would be missing. There

must be thousands of professional burglars who habitually enter through ground floor windows and the fact that B's house was entered in this way might well be a coincidence. Certainly it could not reasonably be regarded as evidence that A was the burglar. On the other hand, if, for example, A had a long series of convictions for burglary and in every case he had left a distinctive written mark or device behind him and he was then charged with burglary in circumstances in which an exactly similar mark or device was found at the site of the burglary which he was alleged to have committed, the similarity between the burglary charged and those of which he had previously been convicted would be so uniquely or strikingly similar that evidence of the manner in which he had committed the previous burglaries would, in law, clearly be admissible against him. I postulate these facts merely as an illustration. There is a possibility but only, I think, a theoretical possibility that they might arise. In such a case, A would no doubt say, quite rightly, that, with his record it is inconceivable that he would have left the mark or device behind him had he been the burglar: he might just as well have published a written confession: the mark or device must have been made at the time of or just after the burglary by someone trying to implicate him. This, however, would be a question for the jury to decide.'
(LORDS MORRIS OF BORTH-Y-GEST and CROSS OF CHELSEA delivered concurring judgments.)
Appeal dismissed.

I would also refer Your Lordships to a decision which emphasises that each case must be looked at on its own facts. I refer to:

R v *Scarrott* [1978] QB 1016 (CA)

The defendant was tried on an indictment, containing 13 counts, charging him with buggery, attempted buggery, assault with intent to commit buggery and indecent assault involving eight young boys over a period of 4½ years. Before arraignment, counsel for the defendant applied to sever the indictment and asked for separate trials in respect of each boy, as a multiple indictment would be prejudicial to the defendant. The application was refused. During the course of the trial the judge ruled that the evidence given by each boy relating to the count or counts concerning him had a striking similarity to the evidence given by the other boys, and was admissible on the other counts. The defendant was convicted on one count of buggery, one count of attempted buggery and eight counts of indecent assault on seven boys.

SCARMAN LJ, giving the judgment of the court, said: 'To be admissible, the evidence by its striking similarity has to reveal an underlying link between the matters with which it deals and the allegations against the defendant upon the count under consideration. Subject to one comment, which really goes only to choice of language, we would respectfully accept the way in which the general principle was put by Lord Salmon in *R v Boardman* [1975] AC 421, 462. Lord Salmon puts the general principle as follows:

...whether or not evidence is relevant and admissible against an accused is solely a question of law. The test must be: is the evidence capable of tending to persuade a reasonable jury of the accused's guilt on some ground other than his bad character and disposition to commit the sort of crime with which he is charged? In the case of an alleged homosexual offence, just as in the case of an alleged burglary, evidence which proves merely that the accused has committed crimes in the past and is therefore disposed to commit the crime charged is clearly inadmissible. It has, however, never been doubted that if the crime charged is committed in a uniquely or strikingly similar manner to other crimes committed by the accused the manner in which the other crimes were committed may be evidence upon which a jury could reasonably conclude that the accused was guilty of the crime charged. The similarity would have to be so unique or striking that common sense makes it inexplicable on the basis of coincidence. I would stress that the question as to whether the evidence is capable of being so regarded by a reasonable jury is a question of law. There is no easy way out by leaving it to the jury to see how they decide it....

I now come to the one comment which this court would make on the statement of general principle made by Lord Salmon. Hallowed though by now the phrase "strikingly similar" is (it was used by Lord Goddard CJ in *R v Sims* [1946] KB 531 and has now received the accolade of use in the House of Lords in *Boardman*) it is no more than a label. Like all labels it can mislead; it is a possible passport to error. It is, we repeat, only a label and it is not to be confused with the substance of law which it labels....

Positive probative value is what the law requires, if similar fact evidence is to be admissible. Such probative value is not provided by the mere repetition of similar facts; there has to be some feature or features in the evidence sought to be adduced which provides a link — an underlying link as it has been called in some of the cases. The existence of such a link is not to be inferred from mere similarity of facts which are themselves so commonplace that they can provide no sure ground for saying that they point to the commission by the accused of the offence under consideration.

Lord Cross of Chelsea put the matter, as we think, in its correct perspective at the end of the day when, in the course of his speech in *R v Boardman* [1975] AC 421, 459, he said:

> The likelihood of such a coincidence obviously becomes less and less the more people there are who make the similar allegations and the more striking are the similarities in the various stories. In the end, as I have said, it is a question of degree....

...In our view, we are here in that area of judgment upon particular facts from which the criminal law can never depart. Plainly some matters, some circumstances may be so distant in time or place from the commission of an offence as not to be properly considered when deciding whether the subject matter of similar fact evidence displays striking similarities with the offence charged. On the other hand, equally plainly, one cannot isolate, as a sort of laboratory specimen, the bare bones of a criminal offence from its surrounding circumstances and say that it is only within the confines of that specimen, microscopically considered, that admissibility is to be determined. Indeed, in one of the most famous cases of all dealing with similar fact evidence, the brides in the bath case, *R v Smith* (1915) 11 Cr App R 229, the court had regard to the facts that the accused man married the women, and that he insured their lives. Some surrounding circumstances have to be considered in order to understand either the offence charged or the nature of the similar fact evidence which it is sought to adduce and in each case it must be a matter of judgment where the line is drawn. One cannot draw an inflexible line as a rule of law....

...We think, however, that in this very difficult class of case where trial judges do face a very complex problem in both the conduct of the trial and in summing up, we should attempt to give some practical guidance to judges at certain stages of the trial. What we now say is not to be considered as any advance or development of the law; it is merely an attempt upon the basis of *R v Kilbourne* [1973] AC 729 and *R v Boardman* [1975] AC 421 to give some guidance which may be helpful to judges who have this very difficult task to discharge.

The help that we can give deals really with a number of phases of the trial process. The first phase is before arraignment when a defendant submits that the indictment should be severed. Of course the question as to whether a judge should allow an indictment to contain a number of counts initially has to be dealt with under the discretion given to a judge by the Indictment Rules 1971, and in particular rule 9, which only repeats the law as it has been ever since 1915:

> Charges for any offences may be joined in the same indictment if those charges are founded on the same facts, or form or are a part of a series of offences of the same or a similar character.

It is not very difficult for a judge to reach a conclusion under that rule, but, having come to the conclusion, as Judge Vowden plainly did in this case, that the offences were of a similar character and a series, he then has to consider how to deal with the application to sever. It appears to us that when such an application at this stage is made a judge must, as Lawton LJ said in *R v Johannsen* (unreported), May 17, 1977, act not on some judicial speculation as to what may happen in the trial but on such factual material as is then available to him, i.e. the depositions or the statements, according to the nature of the committal proceedings. He must ask himself at that stage, whether in his judgment it would be open to a jury, properly directed and warned, to treat the evidence available upon a study of the depositions or statements as strikingly similar to the evidence to be adduced in respect of the various counts and he must, we think, be able even at that stage to take the matter a little further; he must be able to say that if this evidence is believed, it could be accepted as admissible similar fact evidence or, as in the circumstances of this class of case, as evidence capable of corroborating the direct evidence. Of course he will also at this stage, as at all stages of a criminal trial when a ruling is required of him, consider whether the evidence appears to be, upon the information then available, independent or untainted evidence and whether there is a real chance that there is falsity or conspiracy to give false evidence and he must also consider at this, as at every stage when a ruling is sought, the balance, upon the information then available to him, between the possible prejudicial effect of the evidence and its probative value. If the judge takes all those well known matters into account, and reaches his decision upon the basis of the factual information which is available to him, it does not seem to us possible to fault the exercise of his discretion whichever way it goes. It is important to appreciate that at this stage, the pre-arraignment stage, the ultimate decision of the judge is an exercise of judicial discretion. So long as he does not err in law, takes into account all relevant matters and excludes consideration of irrelevant matters, his discretion will stand. Of course at this stage the judge is taking no final decision as to the admissibility of evidence. If he decides to allow the multi-count indictment to proceed, it will still be for his ruling as to whether the evidence, for instance, on counts 1 to 7 will be admitted as similar fact evidence to assist in the proof of the offence charged in count 8 and so on throughout the indictment. It does not follow that because a multi-count indictment has been allowed to proceed that therefore the evidence given will be evidence on all the counts contained in the indictment. Similarly, if he decides at that stage to sever and if the trial proceeds upon the basis of only, let us say, one count, it will still be open to the prosecution, at the appropriate moment, to adduce evidence relating to the other (and now put aside) counts as similar fact evidence of that count and it will then be for the judge to rule, in accordance with the laws of evidence, whether the evidence is admissible or not.

The next phase of the trial process, on which we think, in the light of the authorities, we can give some practical guidance, is when the judge's ruling is sought as to the admissibility of the similar fact evidence. His task, though a difficult exercise of judgment, can be stated in simple terms. He first has to reach a view upon what he then knows of the facts of the case and of the nature of the evidence to be adduced as to whether the evidence possesses the features of striking similarity or probative value which have been canvassed earlier in this judgment. If he reaches the view that it does, he then has to consider whether the evidence is such that it ought to be put to the jury. He may be impressed with the very real possibility that the evidence is tainted by conspiracy or ganging up, the group objection, or he may, because of the group objection or for some other reason, take the view that, though strikingly similar and therefore, prima facie, admissible, the evidence is so prejudicial that its prejudicial effect outweighs its probative value. If he admits the evidence, he will in his summing up have to make sure that the jury is left with the task of deciding whether to accept the evidence and whether to treat the evidence as in fact corroboration or not.'
Appeal dismissed.

Holt J: Yes, I think I must look at this case on its own facts. I would not accept that there is any general principle that sexual offences are admissible purely because of mere repetition. Mr Bunbury, it may be helpful if I look at one or two examples of non-sexual cases on the general application of the principle.

Mr Bunbury: Certainly, My Lord. A good example is: *R* v *Rance; R* v *Herron* where the court approved the admission of similar fact evidence on a charge alleging a corrupt payment of money.

R v Rance; R v Herron (1975) 62 Cr App R 118 (CA)

Rance, the managing director of a building company, was convicted of corruptly procuring a payment of money to Herron, a local councillor (who was convicted of corruptly receiving the money). The payment was made on a certificate signed by Rance describing Herron as a 'subcontractor' which he was not. Rance said that he must have been deceived into signing the certificate. Evidence was received of similar payments to other councillors supported by other false certificates. The defendants applied for leave to appeal against conviction.

LORD WIDGERY CJ, delivering the judgment of the court, said: 'The question whether evidence of those two other cases should be admitted had to depend on the recent conclusions of the House of Lords in the case of *DPP* v *Boardman* (1974) 60 Cr App R 165; [1975] AC 421. There are two very helpful passages which indicate a crisp, modern test to decide the vexed and oft-argued question of how far evidence of similar criminal transactions can be admitted.
I take first a passage from Lord Cross's speech at pp 185, 457. He says:

> As Viscount Simon said in *Harris* v *DPP* (1952) 36 Cr App R 39, 51; [1952] AC 694, 705, it is not possible to compile an exhaustive list of the sort of cases in which "similar fact" evidence — to use a compendious phrase — is admissible. The question must always be whether the similar fact evidence taken together with the other evidence would do no more than raise or strengthen a suspicion that the accused committed the offence with which he is charged or would point so strongly to his guilt that only an ultra-cautious jury, if they accepted it as true, would acquit in face of it. In the end — although the admissibility of such evidence is a question of law, not of discretion — the question as I see it must be one of degree.

Then later Lord Salmon, dealing with the same point, uses these words at pp 188 and 462 of the respective reports. He said:

> My Lords, whether or not evidence is relevant and admissible against an accused is solely a question of law. The test must be: is the evidence capable of tending to persuade a reasonable jury of the accused's guilt on some ground other than his bad character and disposition to commit the sort of crime with which he is charged? In the case of an alleged homosexual offence, just as in the case of an alleged burglary, evidence which proves merely that the accused has committed crimes in the past and is therefore disposed to commit the crime charged is clearly inadmissible. It has, however, never been doubted that if the crime charged is committed in a uniquely or strikingly similar manner to other crimes committed by the accused, the manner in which the other crimes were committed may be evidence upon which a jury could reasonably conclude that the accused was guilty of the crime charged.

It seems to us that one must be careful not to attach too much importance to Lord Salmon's vivid phrase "uniquely or strikingly similar." The gist of what is being said both by Lord Cross and by Lord Salmon is that evidence is admissible as similar fact evidence if, but only if, it goes beyond showing a tendency to commit crimes of this kind and is positively probative in regard to the crime now charged. That, we think, is the test which we have to apply on the question of the correctness or otherwise of the admission of the similar fact evidence in this case.
We think quite clearly that the evidence of the other transactions — Bowes and McKenna — did, if accepted by the jury, go beyond merely showing that Rance was a person who was not above passing a bribe. The essence of each of these three cases is that a bribe was paid out to a councillor in respect of a contract in which Rance's company was interested, and in every case (each of the three — the instant one and the other two) there is the bogus document of some kind with Rance's signature on it which is the basis upon which the bribe was to be covered up. We have no doubt in saying that in those circumstances the similar fact evidence of Bowes's case and McKenna's case did go beyond merely showing a tendency on the part of Rance to commit the offence. Therefore it passed the test in *DPP* v *Boardman* (supra) and so far was correctly admitted.'
Applications refused.

And in the second example, My Lord, the court upheld the admission of similar fact evidence of arson, namely:

R v *Mansfield* [1977] 1 WLR 1102 (CA)

The appellant was charged, *inter alia,* with three counts of arson. The fires were started within a period of three weeks, the first in an hotel where the appellant lived, the second and third in an hotel where he worked as a kitchen porter. In each case, the method of starting the fire was distinctive; in each the appellant had an opportunity to start the fire; in each case, he was seen nearby acting suspiciously, and lied to the police when questioned; and in the case of the third fire, a waste-paper bin from the appellant's room was found near the site of the fire. At the trial the appellant submitted that there should be separate trials in respect of each fire because the alleged similarities between them were not sufficiently striking to justify admission of the evidence relating to all of them in respect of each one of them. The judge refused to sever the indictment and the appellant was convicted on all three counts.

LAWTON LJ, delivering the judgment of the court, related the facts and continued: 'The Crown's case was that those various factors showed a degree of similarity between the fires which could reasonably lead to a court inferring that the same man had started each of them. Counsel for the appellant's answer to that submission was that there was nothing striking about those similarities; there was nothing about them which would lead any reasonable person to consider that they had been started by the same man. Counsel for the appellant invited our attention in detail to the speeches of their Lordships in *Boardman* v *Director of Public Prosecutions* [1975] AC 421. In those speeches picturesque examples were given by Lord Hailsham of St Marylebone of the kind of similarities which could result in evidence being admitted of a number of cases other than the one actually charged. Lord Salmon [1975] AC 421, in the course of his speech, used the memorable phrase: "uniquely or strikingly similar". Lord Cross [1975] AC 421 used the vivid expression: "other than an ultra-cautious jury".

   As a result of the use of the illustrations which Lord Hailsham gave and the striking phrases which Lord Salmon and Lord Cross used, counsel for the appellant submitted that the points of similarity relied on by the Crown lacked the qualities which those examples and those phrases indicated were essential.

   The court queried this in the course of argument because similarity may depend on pieces of evidence which have no striking or unusual qualities about them at all; nevertheless they would be similarities for the purposes of the rule of evidence. In the course of his final submissions counsel for the appellant invited our attention to the decision of this court in *R* v *Rance* (1975) 62 Cr App Rep 118. He did so in order to establish that this court had accepted and acted on the speech of Lord Cross as set out in *Boardman* v *Director of Public Prosecutions* [1975] AC 421. No doubt through inadvertence he did not go on to invite our attention to a passage in which Lord Widgery CJ said (1975) 62 Cr App Rep 118 at 121:

   It seems to us that one must be careful not to attach too much importance to Lord Salmon's vivid phrase "uniquely or strikingly similar" [1975] AC 421 at 462. The gist of what is being said both by Lord Cross and by Lord Salmon is that evidence is admissible as similar fact evidence if, but only if, it goes beyond showing a tendency to commit crimes of this kind and is positively probative in regard to the crime now charged. That, we think is the test which we have to apply on the question of the correctness or otherwise of the admission of the similar fact evidence in this case.

   That is the test we have applied. I suggested to both counsel in the course of argument that another way of putting the test is for the court to ask itself whether the evidence can be explained away as coincidence, and only if it cannot does the question of admitting it as a method of proof come to be considered at all. Both counsel said they accepted that way of stating the test. Counsel for the appellant asked us to add, if we thought that was the right test, the phrase: "The judge must approach the problem with caution." It is manifest that the trial judge in this case did approach the problem with caution.'
Appeal dismissed.

Holt J: Those cases make it very clear. What I now have to do is consider the detail of the previous offence. But, before I do so, you are going to submit, Mr Atkyn, are you not, that I should exercise some discretion to exclude the evidence, even if I find it to be technically admissible?

Mr Atkyn: Yes, My Lord. There is abundant authority that Your Lordship has a discretion. It is the general discretion to ensure a fair trial, and it is a matter for Your Lordship to weigh the probative value of the similar fact evidence against the possible prejudice to the defendant. Of course, in this case, the prejudice may be very great indeed because of the proximity in time and the nature of the offences. Your Lordship has already been referred to the facts of *Noor Mohamed* v *R* [1949] AC 182. May I refer Your Lordship to the words of Lord du Parcq at page 192:

> ...in all such cases the judge ought to consider whether the evidence which it is proposed to adduce is sufficiently substantial, having regard to the purpose to which it is professedly directed, to make it desirable in the interest of justice that it should be admitted. If, so far as that purpose is concerned, it can in the circumstances of the case have only trifling weight, the judge will be right to exclude it. To say this is not to confuse weight with admissibility. The distinction is plain, but cases must occur in which it would be unjust to admit evidence of a character gravely prejudicial to the accused even though there may be some tenuous ground for holding it technically admissible. The decision must then be left to the discretion and the sense of fairness of the judge.

Holt J: Yes, thank you. Mr Bunbury, I am rather wondering whether I should wait to see in what way the defence develops, before admitting the evidence, if I admit it at all. It occurs to me that the evidence may assist the jury if the defence is to be that the defendant believed Miss Blackstone consented, because in the light of his previous experience they may think he would have been more careful on the question of consent. But can I admit it as part of your case and allow you to open it to the jury at this stage, before I know what the defence is

Mr Bunbury: My Lord, in my submission Your Lordship should allow the evidence from the outset. It is true that in older cases such as *Thompson* v *R* [1918] AC 221, which has been referred to already the Court took the view that the purpose of similar fact evidence was to rebut certain specific defences. This is no longer the position. In *Thompson* v *R,* Lord Sumner said at 232:

> The mere theory that a plea of not guilty puts everything material in issue is not enough for this purpose. The prosecution cannot credit the accused with fancy defences in order to rebut them at the outset with some damning piece of prejudice.

But the law has now changed. May I refer Your Lordship again to the words of Lord Goddard CJ in *R* v *Sims* [1946] 1 KB 531 at 539:

> It has often been said that the admissibility of evidence of this kind depends on the nature of the defence raised by the accused: see, for instance, the observations of Lord Sumner in *Thompson* v *Rex* [1918] AC 232, and of this court in *Rex* v *Lewis Cole* (1941) Cr App R 43. We think that that view is the result of a different approach to the subject. If one starts with the assumption that all evidence tending to show a disposition towards a particular crime must be excluded unless justified, then the justification of evidence of this kind is that it tends to rebut a defence otherwise open to the accused; but if one starts with the general proposition that all evidence that is logically probative is admissible unless excluded, then

evidence of this kind does not have to seek a justification but is admissible irrespective of the
issues raised by the defence, and this we think is the correct view.

The position was confirmed by the House of Lords in:

Harris v DPP [1952] AC 694 (HL)

A series of eight larcenies having common characteristics occurred in May, June and July
1951, in an office in an enclosed and extensive market at times when most of the gates were
shut and in periods during part of which the defendant, a police officer, was on solitary duty
there. The precise time of only one larceny, the last which occurred in July, was known and
then the defendant was found to be in the immediate vicinity of the office. He was charged on
indictment with all the larcenies and, having been tried on all eight counts simultaneously, he
was acquitted on the first seven and convicted on the eighth, that relating to the larceny in
July.

VISCOUNT SIMON LC said: 'In my opinion, the principle laid down by Lord Herschell
LC in *Makin's* case [1894] AC 57 remains the proper principle to apply and I see no reason
for modifying it. *Makin's* case [1894] AC 57 was a decision of the Judicial Committee of the
Privy Council, but it was unanimously approved by the House of Lords in *R v Ball* [1911]
AC 47, 71, and has been constantly relied on ever since. It is, I think, an error to attempt to
draw up a closed list of the sort of cases in which the principle operates: such a list only
provides instances of its general application, whereas what really matters is the principle itself
and its proper application to the particular circumstances of the charge that is being tried. It
is the application that may sometimes be difficult, and the particular case now before the
House illustrates that difficulty.... When Lord Herschell speaks of evidence of other
occasions in which the accused was concerned as being admissible to "rebut" a defence which
would otherwise be open to the accused, he is not using the vocabulary of civil pleadings and
requiring a specific line of defence to be set up before evidence is tendered which would
overthrow it. If it were so, instances would arise where magistrates might be urged not to
commit for trial, or it might be ruled at the trial, at the end of the prosecution's case, that
enough had not been established to displace the presumption of innocence, when all the time
evidence properly available to support the prosecution was being withheld. "In criminal cases,
and especially in those where the justices have summary jurisdiction, the admissibility of
evidence has to be determined in reference to all the issues which have to be established by the
prosecution, and frequently without any indication of the particular defence that is going to
be set up": *per* Avory J in giving the judgment of the Divisional Court in *Perkins v Jeffery*
[1915] 2 KB 702, 707.'
    Lord du Parcq pointed out in *Noor Mohamed v The King* [1949] AC 182, 191 in
commenting on what Lord Sumner had said in *Thompson v The King* [1918] AC 221, 232:
'An accused person need set up no defence other than a general denial of the crime alleged.
The plea of not guilty may be equivalent to saying 'let the prosecution prove its case, if it can,'
and having said so much the accused may take refuge in silence. In such a case it may appear
(for instance) that the facts and circumstances of the particular offence charged are consistent
with innocent intention, whereas further evidence, which incidentally shows that the accused
has committed one or more other offences, may tend to prove that they are consistent only
with a guilty intent. The prosecution could not be said, in their Lordships' opinion, to be
'crediting the accused with a fancy defence' if they sought to adduce such evidence."
    The substance of the matter appears to me to be that the prosecution may adduce all
proper evidence which tends to prove the charge. I do not understand Lord Herschell's words
to mean that the prosecution must withhold such evidence until after the accused has set up a
specific defence which calls for rebuttal. Where, for instance, mens rea is an essential element
in guilt, and the facts of the occurrence which is the subject of the charge, standing by
themselves, would be consistent with mere accident, there would be nothing wrong in the
prosecution seeking to establish the true situation by offering, as part of its case in the first
instance, evidence of similar action by the accused at another time which would go to show
that he intended to do what he did on the occasion charged and was thus acting criminally. *R*

v *Mortimer* 25 Cr App R 150 is a good example of this. What Lord Sumner meant when he denied the right of the prosecution to "credit the accused with fancy defences" (in *Thompson* v *The King* [1918] AC 221, 232) was that evidence of similar facts involving the accused ought not to be dragged in to his prejudice without reasonable cause.'

(His Lordship held that as regards the larceny of July, the evidence of the previous larcenies, which occurred when he was not proved to have been near the office, should have been excluded from the consideration of the jury and, the judge having omitted to direct them to that effect, the conviction should be quashed. LORDS PORTER, TUCKER, and MORTON OF HENRYTON agreed. LORD OAKSEY agreed with the principles stated by the LORD CHANCELLOR as to the admissibility of evidence, but disagreed with the application of those principles to the facts of the case.)

Appeal allowed.

In my submission, My Lord, I should be entitled to open the similar fact evidence to the jury and to call the evidence relating to the previous offence as part of my case.

(Holt J then considered the detailed nature of the similar fact evidence, held it to be admissible in law, and further held that there was no reason to exercise his discretion in favour of exclusion. The learned judge gave leave to Mr Bunbury to open the evidence to the jury and to call it as part of his case.)

5.4 Commentary

R v *Coke* and *Littleton* at trial. Mr Bunbury for the prosecution proposes to call evidence of the finding in Coke's flat by D/I Glanvil of the written material referring to Margaret Blackstone. Mr Atkyn objects.

5.5 Argument

Mr Atkyn: My Lord, I object to this evidence, because quite irrespective of the scientific comparison of handwriting and the fact that my client denies having written the note, it is in any event no more than prejudice and has no probative value. Coke does not dispute and has never disputed that he wished to have sexual relations with Miss Blackstone and indeed has always maintained that he did so with her consent.

Holt J: Yes. Mr Bunbury, what do you say?

Mr Bunbury: My Lord, I say that the evidence is probative. At an earlier stage of the trial Your Lordship was referred to the case of *Thompson* v *R* [1918] AC 221. In that case, the House of Lords upheld the admission of evidence of the finding of photographs of naked boys and other items in a sexual context, in the defendant's room. Their Lordships did so on the basis that such evidence was directly relevant to the acts charged, in that they indicated the defendant's intent or state of mind. I accept that there must be a showing of relevance, but, My Lord, I say that the explicit reference to Margaret Blackstone in this context is enough. It shows what was in the defendant's mind with regard to her, although it is of course for the jury to evaluate it. Courts in more modern times have followed the same principle, for example in:

R v **Reading** [1966] 1 WLR 836 (CCA)

The defendant was convicted of robbery and taking a motor vehicle, arising out of the hijacking of a lorry. Evidence was given of possession by him of goods hijacked from another lorry, a walkie-talkie radio set, earphones and police-type uniform. This evidence was given to rebut a defence of alibi and mistaken identity.

EDMUND DAVIES J, giving the judgment of the court, said: 'What is submitted by Mr Simpson, and submitted with great clarity, is this: Those articles should not have been admitted in evidence at all, for there is no evidence here that any of them were used in relation to either the November 11 or November 30 robberies, and, relying upon principally *R v Taylor* (1923) 17 Cr App Rep 109, in those circumstances the jury should not have been permitted to hear about any of those articles. Reference has also been made to the House of Lords decision in *R v Thompson* [1918] AC 221. This submission, if it is a good one, affects others besides Reading. It is therefore of considerable importance and we have reflected upon it with the care which it demands. The conclusion we have come to is that the submission is invalid. In *Taylor's* case the accused man with another was seen to emerge from a shop doorway. The defence was "We were in the doorway for a lark and accidentally broke the door." The defence therefore was "We never committed a crime at all." Evidence was admitted that some days later a jemmy was found in Taylor's possession. The evidence was that no jemmy had been used to break the door open. The conviction of Taylor on those facts was quashed by this court on the grounds that, in view of the absence of any evidence of a jemmy having been used to perpetrate a crime, testimony that a jemmy was later found upon him could have this, and only this, significance, to show that he was a man of criminal disposition and therefore likely not to have been in that doorway for an innocent purpose. There are other decisions to the same effect, *R v Manning* (1923) 17 Cr App Rep 85, being of that ilk, but that case is wholly removed from the present case. The issue upon which what was found on December 8 was admissible evidence was that of identification. These men were all denying that they were present either on November 11 or 30. It was, in our judgment, admissible evidence on that issue to show what the scene was as the police found it on December 8. There are a number of reported decisions where, despite the fact that material found on an accused person was not used in the perpetration of the crime, possession is nevertheless provable in evidence on the issue of identification. Indeed *Thompson's* case, relied upon so strongly by Mr Simpson, illustrates that type of case to perfection. In *Thompson* the powder puffs and the indecent photographs found on the accused man had in no way been utilised by him at the time of committing offences on little boys on October 16. Nevertheless they were admitted in order to link him up with the offences committed on that date.'
Appeal dismissed.

Holt J: Yes, very well.
(Holt J then heard from Mr Atkyn regarding the probative value of the evidence and held it to be admissible).

5.6   Commentary

R v Coke and *Littleton* on appeal against conviction: Mr Atkyn for Coke appeals on the ground that Holt J refused to admit the evidence of Coke's friend Kevin to the effect that on a previous occasion, Margaret Blackstone threatened without justification to accuse him of rape. Mr Atkyn points out to the Court of Appeal that it was specifically suggested to Margaret in cross-examination that the accusation was deliberately false and that she had consented to have sexual intercourse with Coke.

5.7   Argument

Leach LJ: But, Mr Atkyn, what do you say the relevance of this evidence would have been to the case?
Mr Atkyn: My Lord, it would have shown that Miss Blackstone had lied on the same subject on another occasion, which might lead the jury to take a very different

view of her evidence than would be the case if they knew only of this occasion. There is authority that similar fact evidence may be admitted for the defence. I refer Your Lordships to *R* v *Neale* where, although the evidence was rejected on the facts, the principle of admissibility was accepted:

R v Neale (1977) 65 Cr App R 304 (CA)

The defendant was charged, together with one Burr, with arson and manslaughter. A fire had occurred at a youth hostel where both lived, which had been started deliberately and had caused loss of life. The defendant said that at the time of the fire he had been asleep in bed at the hostel. Counsel for the defendant sought a ruling from the trial judge which would enable him either by cross-examination from prosecution witnesses or if necessary by adducing evidence in the course of the development of the defence case, to elicit that Burr had admitted on five different occasions he had started fires by himself. The trial judge came to the conclusion that that evidence was not relevant — it was evidence of propensity or disposition only and contained nothing which bore upon the defence which was that the defendant was elsewhere and therefore did not do it. The defendant was subsequently convicted. He applied for leave to appeal.

SCARMAN LJ, giving the judgment of the court, stated the facts and continued: 'The question is whether that evidence if extracted or adduced would be admissible evidence in the trial of the applicant Neale. It was a co-accused who was seeking to adduce this evidence, and therefore it is clear upon the authorities that if this evidence were relevant either to the case against him or to his defence, he would be able, as of right, to extract it or adduce it, notwithstanding its prejudicial effect upon Burr. The discretionary control the judge has in a joint trial or indeed in any trial, that is to say the discretion to refuse to allow the Crown to adduce, or elicit, evidence which though probative is so prejudicial that it should not be accepted, does not exist or arise when application is being made by a co-defendant. Mr Hillman, for the applicant, was therefore right in our judgment to make the point that the only issue, and it is a very short issue, is whether or not this evidence was relevant.

The learned judge reached the same analysis of the situation as that which I have just given, and he came to the conclusion that the evidence was not relevant. The view that he took was that this was evidence of propensity or disposition only, and contained nothing which bore upon the defence which was that the applicant was elsewhere and did not therefore do it. We have come to the conclusion that the learned judge was right and that it really is, in the circumstances of this case, a *non sequitur* to deduce from the existence of a propensity in Burr to raise fires that Neale was not there or participating when this fire, which did the damage and caused the death, was raised. Mr Hillman really revealed or exposed the logical fallacy in his argument, when in the course of a succinct and extremely well developed submission he submitted that evidence to Burr's propensity to commit wanton and unaided arson was needed in order to support the defence that the applicant Neale was not there at the time the fire was raised.

In our judgment this is a *non sequitur*. We have been referred helpfully to two authorities, both of which reinforce the approach to this problem which we have developed. The earlier, and indeed the famous, case of *Miller* (1952) 36 Cr App R 169; [1952] 2 All ER 667, was a decision by Devlin J dealing with a case where the facts were very different from those with which we have been confronted. Devlin J said at p 171 and p 668 respectively: "The fundamental principle, equally applicable to any question that is asked by the defence as to any question that is asked by the prosecution, is that it is not normally relevant to inquire into a prisoner's previous character, and, particularly, to ask questions which tend to show that he has previously committed some criminal offence. It is not relevant because the fact that he has committed an offence on one occasion does not in any way show that he is likely to commit an offence on any subsequent occasion. Accordingly, such questions are, in general, inadmissible, not primarily for the reason that they are prejudicial, but because they are irrelevant."

Then he goes on to the difference in application of the principle when it is the prosecution which is seeking to lead the evidence as distinct from the case in which, as here, a co-defendant is seeking to lead the evidence. There is a clear general principle, that, in general, evidence of propensity to commit a crime is not evidence that the man with that propensity committed the crime on the particular occasion, but of course in the present case the logical gap is greater. Here the relevance of the evidence has to be borne in mind by reference to the defence, which was, "I was not there."

Mr Hillman also referred us to a recent decision of this court, again on different facts and really dealing with a different question. The cited case is the decision in *Rance* and *Herron* (1976) 62 Cr App R 118. I quote one sentence from the headnote because it again shows an emphasis on the general principle to which Devlin J was referring in *Miller's* case *(supra)*. *Rance (supra)* was concerned with the problem of similar fact evidence, and the headnote reads as follows: "Evidence is admissible as 'similar fact' evidence if, but only if, it goes beyond showing a tendency on the part of the defendant to commit crimes of the kind charged and is positively probative in regard to the crime charged." Again a little later there is an emphasis on the necessity for some positive probative link between the evidence sought to be adduced and the issue to which it is said to be relevant.'

Application refused.

East LJ: I think your difficulty is that even if you are right in saying there was a sufficient degree of similarity, the evidence would have gone only to the collateral issue of Margaret Blackstone's credit, and it is a clear rule of law that you cannot contradict answers as to credit given during cross-examination (see 13.0).

Leach LJ: I agree.

5.8 Commentary

Blackstone v *Coke* at trial. Mr Noy for the plaintiff invites Hardwicke J to consider evidence of Coke's previous offence of rape. After referring His Lordship to the general principles worked out in the criminal cases, as set out above, Mr Noy switches his argument to civil matters.

5.9 Argument

Hardwicke J: Mr Noy, I have in mind:

Managers of Metropolitan Asylum District v Hill and others (1882) 47 LT 29

LORD WATSON said: '...there appears to me to be an appreciable distinction between evidence having a direct relation to the principal question in dispute and evidence relating to collateral facts, which will, if established, tend to elucidate that question. It is the right of the party tendering it to have evidence of the former kind admitted, irrespective of its amount or weight, these remaining for consideration when his case is closed; but I am not prepared to hold that he has the same absolute right when he tenders evidence of facts collateral to the main issue. In order to entitle him to give such evidence, he must, in the first instance, satisfy the court that the collateral fact which he proposes to prove will, when established, be capable of affording a reasonable presumption or inference as to the matter in dispute; and I am disposed to hold that he is also bound to satisfy the court that the evidence which he is prepared to adduce will be reasonably conclusive, and will not raise a difficult and doubtful controversy of precisely the same kind as that which the jury have to determine. It appears to me that it might lead to unfortunate results if the court had not the power to reject evidence of collateral fact which does not satisfy both of the conditions which I have endeavoured to indicate.'

I am not sure whether I should entertain such evidence in the ordinary civil case.
Mr Noy: My Lord, there is more recent authority that Your Lordship can feel free

to entertain such evidence, especially in the absence of a jury. May I refer Your Lordship to the decision of the Court of Appeal in:

Mood Music Publishing Company Limited v De Wolfe Limited [1976] Ch 119 (CA)

The plaintiffs were the owners of the copyright in a musical work called '*Sogno Nostalgico*'. They alleged that the defendants had infringed such copyright by supplying for broadcasting a work entitled 'Girl in the Dark'. It was not disputed that the works were similar, but the defendants argued that the similarity was coincidental, and denied copying even though '*Sogno Nostalgico*' was composed prior to 'Girl in the Dark'. The plaintiffs were permitted to adduce evidence to show that on other occasions the defendants had reproduced works subject to copyright.
The defendants appealed.

LORD DENNING MR stated the facts and continued: 'The admissibility of evidence as to "similar facts" has been much considered in the criminal law. Some of them have reached the highest tribunal, the latest of them being *R* v *Boardman* [1975] AC 421. The criminal courts have been very careful not to admit such evidence unless its probative value is so strong that it should be received in the interests of justice: and its admission will not operate unfairly to the accused. In civil cases the courts have followed a similar line but have not been so chary of admitting it. In civil cases the courts will admit evidence of similar facts if it is logically probative, that is, if it is logically relevant in determining the matter which is in issue: provided that it is not oppressive or unfair to the other side: and also that the other side has fair notice of it and is able to deal with it. Instances are *Brown* v *Eastern & Midlands Railway Co.* (1889) 22 QBD 391; *Moore* v *Ransome's Dock Committee* (1898) 14 TLR 539 and *Hales* v *Kerr* [1908] 2 KB 601.
   The matter in issue in the present case is whether the resemblances which "Girl in the Dark" bear to "*Sogno Nostalgico*" are mere coincidences or are due to copying. Upon that issue it is very relevant to know that there are these other cases of musical works which are undoubtedly the subject of copyright, but that the defendants have nevertheless produced musical works bearing close resemblance to them. Whereas it might be due to mere coincidence in one case, it is very unlikely that they would be coincidences in four cases. It is rather like *Rex* v *Sims* [1946] KB 531, 540, where it was said: "The probative force of all the acts together is much greater than one alone." So the probative force of four resemblances together is much better than one alone.... It seems to me the judge was right.'
(ORR LJ and BROWNE LJ agreed.)
Appeal dismissed.

My Lord, in this case, the defendants certainly cannot contend that they had no notice and in the circumstances, it is difficult to see how they could be prejudiced.

(Hardwicke J then considered an argument from Mr Atkyn that the evidence was merely prejudicial, and ruled that he would admit it but would bear in mind throughout the risk of prejudice and scrutinise its weight very carefully.)

5.10 Questions for Counsel

5.10.1   R v *Coke* and *Littleton:* Construct a passage to be included in the summing up of Holt J directing the jury as to the nature and use of the evidence of Coke's previous conviction.

5.10.2   R v *Coke* and *Littleton:* Are there any further points which you might have made to the Court of Appeal with regard to the exclusion of Kevin's evidence? Would these arguments be likely to succeed?

6   The Rule Against Hearsay: I

A: SCOPE AND APPLICATION OF THE RULE

6.1   Introductory notes

6.1.1   Evidence is inadmissible if it consists of any statement made by a person other than while giving evidence in the instant proceedings and it is tendered for the purpose of proving the truth of any fact contained in such statement. Evidence which is inadmissible for this reason is referred to as 'hearsay', and may be contrasted with 'direct' evidence which consists of evidence by a witness as to what he himself perceived or did.

The rule against hearsay is justified by three considerations, namely:

(a)   that hearsay carries the inherent danger of unreliability through repetition of the facts stated in one or more successive communications;

(b)   the fear of manufactured or exaggerated evidence; and most importantly

(c)   that hearsay cannot be usefully challenged in cross-examination, except on the inadequate basis of the veracity or reliability of the source of the communication and therefore the court cannot see and hear the evidence directly tested.

6.1.2   Although the rule against hearsay at common law was and is very wide, the fact that hearsay evidence was often the most reliable evidence, or the only evidence available led to the growth of a number of exceptions. The common law exceptions to the rule are dealt with in section B of this chapter. There are also in modern law very important statutory exceptions which are considered in Chapter 8. In civil cases, the Civil Evidence Acts 1968 and 1972 operate to permit the admission of most hearsay evidence in civil cases, subject to procedural safeguards and close scrutiny of the weight of the evidence admitted. In criminal cases, however, which continue to be governed by common law principles, the common law rule against hearsay still applies subject to the common law exceptions.

6.1.3   The rule against hearsay applies to all adversarial proceedings. It does not apply to the narrow category of non-adversarial proceedings, in which the court's purpose is not to determine a dispute between the parties, but to investigate questions on an inquisitorial basis. Where the rule applies, it applies to evidence tendered by any party, including evidence tendered by the defendant in a criminal case.

6.1.4   The only certain way of distinguishing statements which are admissible as **direct** evidence from statements which are inadmissible as hearsay is to test the evidence by reference to two questions:

6.1.4.1 What is the source of the statement? A hearsay statement will always be one made by a person other than while giving evidence in the proceedings at hand (including statements made by a witness on a previous occasion). The statement may be made by a variety of ways; orally, in writing, by gesture or by an action intended to have communicative effect. Opinions differ as to whether conduct not intended to communicate a fact, but which nonetheless has that effect, should be excluded as hearsay.

6.1.4.2 For what purpose is the evidence tendered? Out of court statements are not necessarily hearsay. They may be direct evidence, where it is sought to prove simply that the statement was made, or simply that the statement was made in a certain form. Such a case would be where a plaintiff seeks to prove the actual making of a statement alleged to be defamatory, or a prosecutor to prove the uttering of certain words alleged to be obscene. The reason why such statements are direct evidence is that the actual making or the actual form of the statement is in issue and not the truth of any fact stated by the maker of the statement. Conversely, if the statement is tendered with a view to showing that some relevant fact stated in it is true, then the statement is for that purpose inadmissible hearsay. Some statements, while admissible as direct evidence, also have an objectionable hearsay character. In such cases, the statements may be admitted, but the jury must be carefully directed that the only use they may make of the statement is as direct evidence and not as evidence of the truth of any fact stated therein. (*A Practical Approach to Evidence*, pp 123–39.)

6.2 Commentary

R v *Coke* and *Littleton* at trial. As part of the prosecution case, Mr Bunbury proposes to adduce evidence of medical and psychiatric records kept at a hospital administered by the National Health Service relating to diagnosis of and treatment given to Margaret Blackstone shortly following the alleged rape. The records are voluminous and were compiled by a number of different doctors and nurses, some of whom are unavailable to give evidence. Mr Atkyn for Coke objects to the admissibility of the evidence, firstly on the ground that it is irrelevant to any issue in the case (see also 1.1.4 and 1.3 ante). Having heard argument on this matter, Holt J considers Mr Atkyn's second argument.

6.3 Argument

Mr Atkyn: My Lord, I have another substantial objection to the admissibility of this evidence, namely that it offends against the rule against hearsay. The evidence is not admissible under any exception to the rule[1].

Holt J: This evidence appears to me to be perfectly reliable, having been compiled by professional men and women in the exercise of their duty.

Mr Atkyn: My Lord, in my submission, hearsay evidence is frequently apparently reliable, but because of the difficulties of ensuring reliability and of challenging it in

---

[1]If the hospital had been privately owned, it might be claimed that the records were those of a trade or business, and thus admissible under Criminal Evidence Act 1965, s.1: see 8.3 post.

cross-examination it is excluded at common law.

Holt J: What do you say makes this evidence hearsay?

Mr Atkyn: My Lord, there are two factors. The first is that the reports consist of statements made by a number of different people other than while giving evidence in this case. The second is that the prosecution's obvious intention in adducing this evidence is to seek to prove the truth of the facts stated in that evidence. If I may deal with the first of those points, the rule applies to all statements made other than while giving evidence in these proceedings, even including those made on oath on other occasions.

Holt J: These of course are statements made in writing.

Mr Atkyn: My Lord, yes. In my submission, that makes no difference to the rule. Written statements are of course a common source of hearsay and are subject to the same rules as statements made in any other form. May I refer Your Lordship to the speeches of the House of Lords in:

Myers v *DPP* [1965] AC 1001 (HL)

The appellant was convicted of offences of dishonesty in relation to motor vehicles. His practice was to buy up wrecked cars with their log-books, to disguise stolen cars so that they corresponded as nearly as possible with the wrecks and their log-books, and to sell the stolen cars as if they were the wrecks, repaired by him. In order to prove their case, the prosecution adduced evidence from a witness in charge of records which were kept on microfilm, containing details of every car made at the works of a certain manufacturer. The microfilm was prepared from records compiled by workmen on cards, which were destroyed after being filmed, and which recorded the cylinder-block number of each car. Since the cylinder-block number was stamped indelibly on the engine of each vehicle, the evidence was of some value to the prosecution in proving the true identity of the cars in question. The trial judge admitted this evidence and the Court of Criminal Appeal upheld this.

LORD REID said: 'I find no sign of a more liberal approach in any of the speeches in these two cases. And since the latter was decided in 1886, there appears to be no case in which any new exception or any considerable extension of an existing exception has been approved.

I have never taken a narrow view of the functions of this House as an appellate tribunal. The common law must be developed to meet changing economic conditions and habits of thought, and I would not be deterred by expressions of opinion in this House in old cases. But there are limits to what we can or should do. If we are to extend the law it must be by the development and application of fundamental principles. We cannot introduce arbitrary conditions or limitations: that must be left to legislation. And if we do in effect change the law, we ought in my opinion only to do that in cases where our decision will produce some finality or certainty. If we disregard technicalities in this case and seek to apply principle and common sense, there are a number of other parts of the existing law of hearsay susceptible of similar treatment, and we shall probably have a series of appeals in cases where the existing technical limitations produce an unjust result. If we are to give a wide interpretation to our judicial functions questions of policy cannot be wholly excluded, and it seems to me to be against public policy to produce uncertainty. The only satisfactory solution is by legislation following on a wide survey of the whole field, and I think that such a survey is overdue. A policy of make do and mend is no longer adequate. The most powerful argument of those who support the strict doctine of precedent is that if it is relaxed judges will be tempted to encroach on the proper field of the legislature, and this case to my mind offers a strong temptation to do that which ought to be resisted. I must now explain why I think that to hold this evidence competent would be to change the law.

It was not disputed before your Lordships that to admit these records is to admit hearsay. They only tend to prove that a particular car bore a particular number when it was assembled if the jury were entitled to infer that the entries were accurate, at least in the main; and the entries on the cards were assertions by the unidentifiable men who made them that they had entered numbers which they had seen on the cars. Counsel for the respondent were unable to argue that these records fell within any of the established exceptions or to adduce any reported case or any textbook as direct authority for their admission.

LORD MORRIS of BORTH-Y-GEST said: 'It was submitted that documents of a private character should be admissible if some independent evidence establishes that the maker of them cannot be identified or called and if it is proved that they were made contemporaneously and in the course of duty and if it is proved that the documents are of such a nature that they are probably accurate. A new rule on some such lines may prove to be desirable: it has not been shown that any such rule now exists or that the scope of judicial discretion makes its introduction permissible.

There is no doubt that in earlier centuries hearsay evidence was extensively received, but as long ago as the early part of the eighteenth century it became established that in general it could not be given. Over 80 years ago the speeches in your Lordships' House in *Sturla* v *Freccia* showed that the law is that as a general rule hearsay evidence is not admissible, and that authority must be found to justify its reception within some established and existing exception to the rule. Just as no authority could in that case be cited to warrant the reception of the evidence so also none has been cited in the present case.

LORD HODSON said: 'There is not, in my opinion, any justification for endeavouring to extend the rule as declared in the case of *Sturla* v *Freccia* so as to say that not only public records but private records which are not open to inspection are nevertheless admissible in evidence. Hedge the extension about with safeguards as you will, this surely would be judicial legislation with a vengeance in an attempt to introduce reform of the law of evidence which if needed can properly be dealt with only by the legislature.
(LORDS PEARCE and DONOVAN dissented.)
[The court applied the proviso to s.4(1) of the Criminal Appeal Act 1907.][1]
Appeal dismissed.

Holt J: I suppose the form of the statement is less important that the fact that it was made out of court.

Mr Atkyn: My Lord, yes. Statements can be made in various ways. In some cases for example, some conduct such as a sign or gesture may be enough, as was the case in:

Chandrasekera v *R* [1937] AC 220 (PC)

A woman whose throat had been cut was unable to speak owing to the nature of the wound. She was fully conscious, however, and able to understand what was said to her, to make signs and to nod her head slightly. After making certain signs which, it was alleged, possibly indicated the appellant, she was asked the direct question whether it was the appellant who had cut her throat, and in answer she nodded her head. She died shortly afterwards.

LORD ROCHE, delivering the judgment of their Lordships, said: 'The case under consideration closely resembles the case of a person who is dumb and is able to converse by means of a finger alphabet. Upon proper evidence proving the words used in a conversation so held their Lordships think that a statement so made would be a verbal statement within the meaning of the section. So here, their Lordships think that there was proper and sufficient evidence of a verbal statement by the deceased to the effect that it was the accused who cut her neck. As to the remainder of the evidence as to signs made by the deceased, it was necessarily given in order that it might be understood in what circumstances and context the vital question came to be asked and to be answered.
Appeal dismissed.

---

[1]The actual decision on the admissibility of the records would now be reversed by virtue of the Criminal Evidence Act 1965 (see 8.3 post), but the principle of the decision survives.

I must concede that there are some cases involving conduct which are less simple. These are cases where, unlike *Chandrasekera,* the conduct is not intended to communicate a fact but nonetheless tends to do so. In my submission, the better view is still that such conduct is objectionable as hearsay. This point of view was taken by Baron Parke in:

Wright v Doe d.Tatham (1837) 7 A&E 313 (Exch)

The issue was whether a testator, John Marsden, had sufficient mental capacity to make a valid will. As evidence of his competency letters were produced in evidence, written at various periods and in which the writers addressed him in terms which implied that they thought him capable of acting in a rational manner. It was argued that the letters were not hearsay because they were tendered, not to prove the truth of anything said in them, but to show the state of mind of their writers and how they conducted themselves towards Marsden.

PARKE B, said: 'I am of opinion that, according to the established principles of the law of evidence, the letters are all inadmissible....One great principle in this law is, that all facts which are relevant to the issue may be proved; another is, that all such facts as have not been admitted by the party against whom they are offered, or some one under whom he claims, ought to be proved under the sanction of an oath (or its equivalent introduced by statute, a solemn affirmation), either on the trial of the issue or some other issue involving the same question between the same parties or those to whom they are privy. To this rule certain exceptions have been recognised; some from very early times, on the grounds of necessity or convenience; such as the proof of the quality and intention of acts by declarations accompanying them; of pedigrees, and of public rights by the statement of deceased persons presumably well acquainted with the subject, as inhabitants of the district in the one case, or relations within certain limits in the other. Such also is the proof of possession by entries of deceased stewards or receivers charging themselves, or of facts of a public nature by public documents; within none of which exceptions is it contended that the present case can be classed.

That the three letters were each of them written by the persons whose names they bear, and sent, at some time before they were found, to the testator's house, no doubt are facts, and those facts are proved on oath; and the letters are without doubt admissible on an issue in which the fact of sending such letters by those persons, and within that limit of time, is relevant to the matter in dispute; as, for instance, on a feigned issue to try the question whether such letters were sent to the testator's house, or on any issue in which it is the material question whether such letters or any of them had been sent. Verbal declarations of the same parties are also facts, and in like manner admissible under the same circumstances; and so would letters of declarations to third persons upon the like supposition.

But the question is, whether the contents of these letters are evidence of the fact to be proved upon this issue, — that is, the actual existence of the qualities which the testator is, in those letters, by implication, stated to possess: and those letters may be considered in this respect to be on the same footing as if they had contained a direct and positive statement that he was competent. For this purpose they are mere hearsay evidence, statements of the writers, not on oath, of the truth of the matter in question, with this addition, that they have acted upon the statements on the faith of their being true, by their sending the letters to the testator. That the so acting cannot give a sufficient sanction for the truth of the statement is perfectly plain; for it is clear that, if the same statements had been made by parol or in writing to a third person, that would have been insufficient; and this is conceded by learned counsel for the plaintiff in error.

Many other instances of a similar nature, by way of illustration, were suggested by the learned counsel for the defendant in error, which, on the most cursory consideration, any one would at once declare to be inadmissible in evidence. Others were supposed on the part of the plaintiff in error, which, at first sight, have the appearance of being mere facts, and therefore admissible, though on further consideration they are open to precisely the same objection. Of the first description are the supposed cases of a letter by a third person to any one demanding a debt, which may be said to be a treatment of him as a debtor, being offered as proof that the debt was really due; a note, congratulating him on his high state of bodily vigour, being proposed as evidence of his being in good health; both of which are manifestly at first sight objectionable. To the latter class belong the supposed conduct of the family or relations of a testator, taking the same precautions in his absence as if he were a lunatic; his election, in his absence, to some high and responsible office; the conduct of a physician who permitted a will to be executed by a sick testator; the conduct of a deceased captain on a question of seawothiness, who, after examining every part of the vessel, embarked in it with his family; all these, when deliberately considered, are, with reference to the matter in issue in each case, mere instances of hearsay evidence, mere statements, not on oath, but implied in or vouched by the actual conduct of persons by whose acts the litigant parties are not to be bound.'

Holt J: I imagine the same principle could apply to words which are not intended to communicate facts but nonetheless have that effect?

Mr Atkyn: My Lord, certainly.

Holt J: Mr Bunbury, the statements contained in these records were clearly made by persons other than while giving evidence in this case. Is it right that by seeking to introduce them into evidence, you wish to prove the truth of the various facts contained in them?

Mr Bunbury: My Lord, I must accept that there is great force in what my learned friend says, but in my submission, these records could be admissible as direct evidence, because they tend to show by reason of Margaret's very presence in hospital what her condition was at that time. In my submission, the case is analogous to that of:

R v Rice and Others [1963] 1 QB 857 (CCA)

Rice, Moore and Hoather were tried with other men on two counts of conspiracy. Part of the prosecution case against Rice was that he had taken a flight to Manchester on or about a certain date, in the company of Hoather. This was denied. The prosecution produced an airline ticket to Manchester in respect of a date at about the relevant time, affording two seats in the names of Rice and Moore. The prosecution suggested that Hoather flew in place of Moore. The ticket was put to Rice in cross-examination, and, he having denied all knowledge of it, it was exhibited and shown to the jury. All the defendants were convicted. On appeal it was argued that the ticket was hearsay and had been wrongly admitted.

WINN J, delivering the judgment of the court, said: 'The court thinks that it would have been more accurate had the recorder said that the production of the tickets from the place where used tickets would properly be kept was a fact from which the jury might infer that probably two people had flown on the particular flight and that it might or might not seem to them by applying their common knowledge of such matters that the passengers bore the surnames which were written on the ticket.

It is plain that the latter inference was not one to be readily accepted in a case where it was not suggested that Moore, whose name was on the ticket, had actually flown; indeed it is obvious that pro tanto the potential inference was excluded. Nevertheless it remained open for partial acceptance in respect of Rice...

So far as Rice was concerned the ticket was treated differently and assumed importance from the direction given that the jury might, if they saw fit, regard it as a corroboration of Hoather's evidence that Rice flew with him to Manchester and that Rice booked the ticket...The court finds no misdirection in that passage...

The court doubts whether the air ticket could constitute admissible evidence that the booking was effected either by Rice or even by any man of that name but it does not think that for relevant purposes the distinction between the booking of the ticket and the use of it was material with regard either to the case against Rice or to his defence.'

Appeal dismissed.

Holt J: With all respect to the Court of Appeal, I cannot say that I find that decision an easy one to follow.

Mr Bunbury: My Lord, it is not easy to isolate the use made of the air ticket as direct evidence from its hearsay character. Perhaps a clearer example would be:

Ratten v *R* [1972] AC 378 (PC)

The appellant was convicted of the murder of his wife by shooting her. His defence was that the gun had gone off accidentally whilst he was cleaning it. To rebut that defence evidence was called from a telephone operator who stated that shortly before the time of the shooting she had received a call from the address where the deceased lived with her husband. The witness said that the call was from a female who, in a voice sobbing and becoming hysterical, said, 'Get me the police, please? but then hung up. The appellant objected to the evidence on the ground that it was hearsay.

LORD WILBERFORCE, delivering the judgment of their Lordships, said: 'In their Lordships' opinion the evidence was not hearsay evidence and was admissible as evidence of fact relevant to an issue.

The mere fact that evidence of a witness includes evidence as to words spoken by another person who is not called, is no objection to its admissibility. Words spoken are facts just as much as any other action by a human being. If the speaking of the words is a relevant fact, a witness may give evidence that they were spoken. A question of hearsay only arises when the words spoken are relied on "testimonially," i.e. as establishing some fact narrated by the words....

The evidence relating to the act of telephoning by the deceased was, in their Lordship's view, factual and relevant. It can be analysed into the following elements.

(1) At about 1.15 p.m. the number Echuca 1494 rang. I plugged into that number.
(2) I opened the speak key and said "Number please."
(3) A female voice answered.
(4) The voice was hysterical and sobbed.
(5) The voice said "Get me the police please."

The factual items numbers (1)–(3) were relevant in order to show that, contrary to the evidence of the appellant, a call was made, only some 3–5 minutes before the fatal shooting, by a woman. It not being suggested that there was anybody in the house other than the appellant, his wife and small children, this woman, the caller, could only have been the deceased. Items (4) and (5) were relevant as possibly showing (if the jury thought fit to draw the inference) that the deceased woman was at this time in a state of emotion or fear (cf *Averson* v *Lord Kinnaird* (1805) 6 East 188, 193, *per* Lord Ellenborough CJ). They were relevant and necessary evidence in order to explain and complete the fact of the call being made. A telephone call is a composite act, made up of manual operations together with the utterance of words (cf *McGregor* v *Stokes* [1952] VLR 347 and remarks of Salmond J therein quoted). To confine the evidence to the first would be to deprive the act of most of its significance. The act had content when it was known that the call was made in a state of emotion. The knowledge that the caller desired the police to be called helped to indicate the nature of the emotion — anxiety or fear at an existing or impending emergency. It was a matter for the jury to decide what light (if any) this evidence, in the absence of any explanation from the appellant, who was in the house, threw upon what situation was occurring, or developing at the time.

If then, this evidence had been presented in this way, as evidence purely of relevant facts, its admissibility could hardly have been plausibly challenged.

Appeal dismissed.

Holt J: I do not think that the mere fact of Miss Blackstone's being in hospital is what is intended here. If I were to admit this evidence, its only true significance would lie in the jury's acceptance of the truth of what is contained in the reports. In my view it is hearsay and should be excluded.

6.4 Commentary

R v Coke and *Littleton* on appeal against conviction. During his evidence in chief, Coke sought to give evidence that prior to 8 July 1979, he had been told by friends at the youth club that Margaret Blackstone was promiscuous and that she had expressed interest in having sexual relations with Coke. This evidence having been objected to by Mr Bunbury on behalf of the prosecution, Holt J ruled it to be inadmissible. Mr Atkyn now appeals on Coke's behalf, on the ground that the evidence was wrongly excluded.

6.5 Argument

Leach LJ: Why do you say that this evidence should have been admitted? The appellant Coke seems to have been trying to tell the jury what he had been told by others, apparently with a view to proving that what those others had said was true. But there are many cases which say that such evidence is inadmissible. One well-known example is that of:

Jones v Metcalfe [1967] 1 WLR 1286 (DC)

A collision took place between two cars, caused by the action of a lorry. An eye witness reported the registration number of the lorry to the police. The appellant was charged with driving without due care and attention. The eye witness gave evidence that he had reported the number to the police, but was unable to quote the number to the court. The other evidence was that of a police officer who said that as a result of information, he interviewed the appellant, put to him what was alleged to have taken place, stated that his information was that the motor lorry concerned was EWH 820 and that the appellant admitted that he was the driver of a lorry bearing that number at the time and date in question, but denied that any accident occurred due to his driving. The appellant was convicted.

DIPLOCK LJ, said: 'Like Lord Parker CJ I have every sympathy with the justices because the inference of fact that the appellant was the driver of the lorry at the time of the accident is irresistible as a matter of common sense. But this is a branch of the law which has little to do with common sense. The inference that the appellant was the driver of the lorry was really an inference of what the independent witness had said to the police when he gave them the number of the lorry, and since what he had said to the police would have been inadmissible as hearsay, to infer what he said to the police is inadmissible also. What makes it even more absurd is, as Lord Parker pointed out, that if when the independent witness gave the number of the lorry to the police officer, the latter had written it down in his presence, then the police officer's note could have been shown to the independent witness and he could have used it, not to tell the justices what he told the police officer, but to refresh his memory.'
(WIDGERY J agreed and LORD PARKER CJ delivered a judgment to the same effect.) Appeal allowed.

Mr Atkyn: My Lord, of course I accept the principle of those cases.
East LJ: You do not say that the defence are entitled to adduce hearsay evidence where the prosecution would not be entitled to do so?
Mr Atkyn: My Lord, no. The cases are quite clear on that point. I would refer to:

Sparks v R [1964] AC 964 (PC)

The appellant, a white man, was convicted of indecently assaulting a girl of three. At the trial, the girl did not give evidence and the judge ruled that the evidence of the girl's mother that the girl had told her that the attacker was coloured was not admissible.

LORD MORRIS of BORTH-Y-GEST, delivering the judgment of their Lordships, said: 'The mother would clearly be giving hearsay evidence if she were permitted to state what her girl had said to her. It becomes necessary, therefore, to examine the contentions which have been advanced in support of the admissibility of the evidence. It was said that "it was manifestly unjust for the jury to be left throughout the whole trial with the impression that the child could not give any clue to the identity of her assailant." The cause of justice is, however, best served by adherence to rules which have long been recognised and settled. If the girl had made a remark to her mother (not in the presence of the appellant) to the effect that it was the appellant who had assaulted her and if the girl was not to be a witness at the trial, evidence as to what she had said would be the merest hearsay. In such circumstances it would be the defence who would wish to challenge a contention, if advanced, that it would be "manifestly unjust" for the jury not to know that the girl had given a clue to the identity of her assailant. If it is said that hearsay evidence should freely be admitted and that there should be concentration in any particular case upon deciding as to its value or weight it is sufficient to say that our law has not been evolved upon such lines but is firmly based upon the view that it is wiser and better that hearsay should be excluded save in certain well defined and rather exceptional circumstances.
The Appeal was allowed on other grounds.

Much the same principle was laid down in *R* v *Turner and Others* (1975) 61 Cr App R 67.

Cox LJ: Then how do you put your argument?

Mr Atkyn: My Lord, while it is true that the appellant Coke wished to say what others had told him, he wished to do so not in order to prove the truth of what was said but to prove the appellant's state of mind. It was the appellant's case that on 8 July 1979, he believed that Margaret Blackstone consented to have intercourse with him. The information he received from the others was directed to proving his state of mind, and not the truth of anything that was said.

Leach LJ: That may be so, but merely because the defendant's state of mind is involved does not make hearsay admissible. For example, a defendant may make a confession based solely on what he has been told by others. That confession is just as valueless as the hearsay on which it is based, despite the fact that confessions are generally admissible evidence to prove the defendant's guilt. I have in mind the case of:

Surujpaul v *R* [1958] 1 WLR 1050 (PC)

The appellant was charged with murder as an accessory before the fact. He made an admission that the murder in question had in fact been commited.

LORD TUCKER, delivering the judgment of their Lordships, said: 'This necessitates a close examination of the statement, but it may here be observed that although such statement may afford very strong corroboration of Dhajoo's evidence with regard to the part taken by the appellant in the plot and as to his counselling or inciting the others to commit robbery or murder, it is difficult to see how it can afford any evidence as to the actual commission of the crime at which by their verdict the jury have found he was not proved to have been present and assisting. A voluntary statement made by an accused person is admissible as a "confession." He can confess as to his own acts, knowledge or intentions, but he cannot "confess" as to the acts of other persons which he has not seen and of which he can only have knowledge by hearsay. A failure by the prosecution to prove an essential element in the offence cannot be cured by an "admission" of this nature.'
Appeal allowed.

East LJ: I seem to recall similarly the case of *Comptroller of Customs* v *Western Lectric Co. Limited* (1966) AC 367.

Mr Atkyn: My Lords, of course I accept the principle of those cases. But had the confessions been admitted, they would have been admitted as evidence of the truth of the facts stated in them. This is the purpose for which confessions are used. In the present case, it was the appellant's state of mind as such that was relevant. The case is akin to that of:

Subramaniam v Public Prosecutor [1956] 1 WLR 965 (PC)

The appellant was charged with unlawful possession of ammunition. It would have been a defence that the appellant had a lawful excuse for his possession, and he sought to give evidence that he had been captured by terrorists and was acting under duress. The trial judge ruled that he could not state in evidence what the terrorists had said to him. The appellant was convicted and appealed.

MR L M D DE SILVA, delivering the judgment of their Lordships, said: 'Evidence of a statement made to a witness by a person who is not himself called as a witness may or may not be hearsay. It is hearsay and inadmissible when the object of the evidence is to establish the truth of what is contained in the statement. It is not hearsay and is admissible when it is proposed to establish by the evidence, not the truth of the statement, but the fact that it was made. The fact that the statement was made, quite apart from its truth, is frequently relevant in considering the mental state and conduct thereafter of the witness or of some other person in whose presence the statement was made. In the case before their Lordships statements could have been made to the appellant by the terrorists, which, whether true or not, if they had been believed by the appellant, might reasonably have induced in him an apprehension of instant death if he failed to conform to their wishes.'
Appeal allowed.

That of course was a case where the defendant's state of mind was relevant to the defence of duress. However, the defendant's state of mind may be relevant to other defences. A very different case where the defendant's belief was relevant to his defence was:

R v Willis [1960] 1 WLR 55 (CCA)

The appellant, a director of a scrap metal business, was charged jointly with his foreman with the larceny of a drum of metal cable. The cable had been taken from the owners and delivered two days later to one of the firm's customers. The appellant's defence was that he was unaware of the taking and delivery of the cable, and that he was first made suspicious by a phone conversation with the customer's representative a few hours after its delivery. The prosecution case was largely founded on the appellant's failure candidly to inform the police of these suspicions. The appellant sought to explain this failure by giving evidence of the content of a conversation with the foreman shortly before the appellant's interview with the police. The evidence was rejected as inadmissible, and the appellant was convicted.

LORD PARKER CJ, giving the judgment of the court, said: 'This court is of opinion that that ruling was wrong. It is quite clear that evidence of what has been said by a person who is not called as a witness may be perfectly good evidence of the state of mind in which the defendant was.
(His Lordship referred to the statement of the law in *Subramaniam* v *Public Prosecutor, ante,* and continued:)
In the opinion of this court, that statement of the law is applicable to the present case. It is true that the Board were there considering the state of mind and conduct of the defendant at the time of the commission of the offence, but provided the evidence as to his state of mind

and conduct is relevant, it matters not whether it was in regard to the conduct at the time of the commission of the offence or, as here, at a subsequent time, to explain his answer to the police and his conduct when charged. Accordingly, that evidence in the present case was wrongly excluded.

(The court nevertheless dismissed the appeal, applying the proviso to the Criminal Appeal Act 1907, s.4(1).)

In this case, My Lords, the defendant's state of mind was something that was central to his defence and something of which he was permitted to give evidence. The information he had received from others was relevant to that state of mind and evidence of it should have been admitted. It was direct evidence and not hearsay.

B: MINOR COMMON LAW EXCEPTIONS

6.6 Introductory notes

6.6.1 Before the more recent statutory reforms, the common law had recognised that in certain exceptional cases, hearsay evidence should be admitted as an exception to the general rule. These were cases where, in the absence of such hearsay, no evidence would be available, or the available evidence would be hopelessly unsatisfactory or unintelligible. In civil cases, these exceptions have been incorporated into the Civil Evidence Act 1968, but in criminal cases they remain governed by the common law. Each of the three major common law exceptions about to be discussed has some built-in safeguard designed to ensure the reliability of the evidence admitted, and each can be justified on the basis that it makes it possible to prove facts which otherwise might be incapable of proof. There were at common law one or two other specific exceptions. These were of importance chiefly in civil cases and are now included in the Civil Evidence Act 1968.

6.6.2 The res gestae principle. This exception enables hearsay statements to be given when they are contemporaneous with and an integral part of some act or conduct relevant to the case. The requirement of contemporaneity of the statement with the conduct was designed to ensure that the statement was reliable and not concocted for the advantage of the speaker. The absence of concoction is the deciding factor in modern cases. The rule applies typically to statements of intention by the persons who perform relevant acts, and to spontaneous excited statements by participants in or observers of relevant events. The rule also applies to contemporaneous declarations of the physical and mental state of the speaker. Evidence admitted under this exception is said to be admitted under the *res gestae* principle.

6.6.3 Declarations by persons since deceased. The death of relevant witnesses presents a final and unique problem of unavailable evidence. The common law responded by allowing the admission of declarations by persons since deceased, in cases where such statements appeared presumptively reliable, for example, when made they were against the interest of the maker, or made in the course of some duty, or made during a settled and hopeless expectation of death. Declarations by persons since deceased were also admitted to prove matters of public concern, such as custom, prescriptive rights, public and general rights and the like, and in this case their admission was justified by the fact that the proof of such matters habitually requires evidence of declarations made in times past, and that failing their admission evidence would usually be unavailable.

6.6.4 Facts contained in public documents. At common law, statements made in public documents are admissible as *prima facie* evidence of the facts contained in them. A certified copy of the document is generally sufficient proof of its contents. Unlike private documents, which were and are subject to the general rule against hearsay, public documents were regarded as reliable because they were compiled by public servants acting under a duty, and for the express purpose of future reference. At the same time, in order to ensure reliability, the common law imposes conditions that:

(a)   the contents sought to be proved must relate to matters of public interest,
(b)   the document must be open to public inspection,
(c)   the entry in question must have been promptly made, and
(d)   the entry must have been made by a person having a duty to inquire into and satisfy himself of the truth of the facts recorded.

Though the last of these conditions has been modified to take account of contemporary practice in keeping records, these conditions remain essentially in force. (*A Practical Approach to Evidence,* pp 140–152.)

6.7   Commentary

R v *Coke* and *Littleton* at trial.   During the course of her evidence in chief, Margaret Blackstone indicates for the first time that she recalls having had a conversation with Angela on the way home from Coke's flat after the alleged rape. Before any further questions are put, the jury retire and in their absence, Margaret gives evidence that she said to Angela: 'Henry Coke raped me. I am in terrible pain.' Margaret estimates that this conversation took place within three or four minutes of leaving Coke's flat. Mr Atkyn on behalf of Coke objects to this evidence.

6.8   Argument

Holt J: I really cannot see how this evidence can be admissible.
Mr Bunbury: My Lord, in my submission it could be admitted under the *res gastae* principle.
Holt J: As I understand it, that principle applies to statements which are admitted as accompanying and explaining relevant acts. Surely the statement must bear some relationship of that kind to the act sought to be explained. There is no act on Margaret Blackstone's part which needs explanation or to which this statement can be relevant. Is not this clear from:

R v **Bliss** (1837) 7 A&E 550 (QB)

At a trial for obstructing a public highway, the issue was whether a particular road, admitted to exist, was public or private, evidence was offered that a person, since deceased, had planted a 'willow on a spot adjoining the road, on ground of which he was a tenant, saying, at the same time, that he planted it to show where the boundary of the road was when he was a boy.

LORD DENMAN CJ said: 'It is not every declaration accompanying an act that is receivable in evidence: if it were so, persons would be enabled to dispose of the rights of others in the most unjust manner. The facts that Ramplin planted a willow on the spot, and that persons kept within the line pointed out by it, would have been evidence; but a declaration to shew that the party planted it with a particular motive is not so.... Then it was said that the declaration might be proved as accompanying an act; but whether it accompanied the act, as explanatory of it, is equivocal; and, at any rate, the declaration signified nothing in this case, the question being not of boundary, but as to the character of the road, whether public or private. The mere fact of the tree being placed there could not, I think, be relevant, unless as introductory to other matters.'

Mr Bunbury: My Lord, with respect, the *res gestae* principle is not restricted to such cases. The rule extends also to spontaneous statements by participants in or observers of events. This is an ancient rule going back to *Thompson* v *Trevanion* (1693) Skin 402.

Holt J: I observe that in such cases, the statement must be proved to be spontaneous. I have in mind the decision in *R* v *Bedingfield* where a very high standard of spontaneity was called for.

R v *Bedingfield* (1879) 14 Cox CC 341 (Norwich Winter Assizes)

The defendant was charged with murder. The victim came out of a room where she had been alone with the defendant, her throat cut through, and said, 'See what Harry has done'. She died a few minutes later. The prosecution proposed to call a witness to state what the victim had said. The defence objected.

COCKBURN CJ said he had carefully considered the question and was clear that it could not be admitted, and therefore ought not to be stated, as it might have a fatal effect. 'I regret,' he said, 'that according to the law of England, any statement made by the deceased should not be admissible. Then could it be admissible having been made in the absence of the prisoner, as part of the *res gestae,* but it is not so admissible, for it was not part of anything done, or something said while something was being done, but something said after something done. It was not as if, while being in the room, and while the act was being done, she had said something which was heard.

Counsel for the prosecution consequently did not state what the deceased said, but said they should tender it in evidence, and accordingly, when the witness was called — one of the assistants who heard the statement — she was first asked as to the circumstances, and stated that "the deceased came out of the house bleeding very much at the throat, and seeming very much frightened," and then said something, and died in ten minutes.

It was then proposed to prove what she said, but Cockburn CJ said it was not admissible. Anything, he said, uttered by the deceased at the time the act was being done would be admissible, as, for instance, if she had been heard to say something, as "Don't, Harry!" But here it was something stated by her after it was all over, whatever it was, and after the act was completed.

Verdict, guilty.

Mr Atkyn: My Lord, I accept that that would exclude the present evidence. But the test in *R* v *Bedingfield* has been somewhat modified by the decision of the Privy Council in:

Ratten v *R* [1972] AC 378 (PC) For the facts, see 6.3 ante.

LORD WILBERFORCE said: 'The Crown defended the admissibility of words as part of the "res gestae" a contention which led to the citation of numerous authorities.

The expression "res gestae", like many Latin phrases, is often used to cover situations insufficiently analysed in clear English terms. In the context of the law of evidence it may be used in at least three different ways:

1. When a situation of fact (e.g. a killing) is being considered, the question may arise when does the situation begin and when does it end. It may be arbitrary and artificial to confine the evidence to the firing of the gun or the insertion of the knife, without knowing in a broader sense, what was happening. Thus in *O'Leary* v *The King* (1946) 73 CLR 566 evidence was admitted of assaults, prior to a killing, committed by the accused during what was said to be a continuous orgy. As Dixon J said at p 577: "Without evidence of what, during that time, was done by those men who took any significant part in the matter and especially evidence of the behaviour of the prisoner, the transaction of which the alleged murder formed an integral part could not be truly understood and, isolated from it, could only be presented as an unreal and not very intelligible event."

2. The evidence may be concerned with spoken words as such (apart from the truth of what they convey). The words are then themselves the res gestae or part of the res gestae, i.e. are the relevant facts or part of them.

3. A hearsay statement is made either by the victim of an attack or by a bystander — indicating directly or indirectly the identity of the attacker. The admissibility of the statement is then said to depend on whether it was made as part of the res gestae. A classical instance of this is the much debated case of *R* v *Bedingfield* (1879) 14 Cox CC 341, and there are other instances of its application in reported cases. These tend to apply different standards, and some of them carry less than conviction. The reason, why this is so, is that concentration tends to be focused upon the opaque or at least imprecise Latin phrase rather than upon the basic reason for excluding the type of evidence which this group of cases is concerned with. There is no doubt what this reason is: it is twofold. The first is that there may be uncertainty as to the exact words used because of their transmission through the evidence of another person than the speaker. The second is because of the risk of concoction of false evidence by persons who have been victims of assault or accident. The first matter goes to weight. The person testifying to the words used is liable to cross-examination: the accused person (as he could not at the time when earlier reported cases were decided) can give his own account if different. There is no such difference in kind or substance between evidence of what was said and evidence of what was done (for example between evidence of what the victim said as to an attack and evidence that he (or she) was seen in a terrified state or was heard to shriek) as to require a total rejection of one and admission of the other.

The possibility of concoction, or fabrication, where it exists, is on the other hand an entirely valid reason for exclusion, and is probably the real test which judges in fact apply. In their Lordships' opinion this should be recognised and applied directly as the relevant test: the test should be not the uncertain one whether the making of the statement was in some sense part of the event or transaction. This may often be difficult to establish: such external matters as the time which elapses between the events and the speaking of the words (or vice versa) and differences in location being relevant factors but not, taken by themselves, decisive criteria. As regards statements made after the event it must be for the judge, by preliminary ruling, to satisfy himself that the statement was so clearly made in circumstances of spontaneity or involvement in the event that the possibility of concoction can be disregarded. Conversely, if he considers that the statement was made by way of narrative of a detached prior event so that the speaker was so disengaged from it as to be able to construct or adapt his account, he should exclude it. And the same must in principle be true of statements made before the event. The test should be not the uncertain one, whether the making of the statement should be regarded as part of the event or transaction. This may often be difficult to show. But if the drama, leading up to the climax, has commenced and assumed such intensity and pressure that the utterance can safely be regarded as a true reflection of what was unrolling or actually happening, it ought to be received. The expression "res gestae" may conveniently sum up these criteria, but the reality of them must always be kept in mind: it is this that lies behind the best reasoned of the judges' rulings.

Holt J: Even on this new test, I would have to be satisfied that there was no reasonable possibility of concoction, and here I am dealing with a period of three or four minutes.

Mr Bunbury: My Lord, that is true. On the other hand, it would be a period of some excitement during which Margaret would be hardly likely to invent a story. The case may be compared to that of *R* v *Nye* and *Loan* where some considerable period of time was involved but the evidence was still admitted.

R v *Nye and Loan* (1977) 66 Cr App R 252 (CA)

The driver of a vehicle involved in a road traffic accident was assaulted by a passenger in another vehicle. He then sat in his car, recovering from the effect of the assault, and some minutes later, when the police arrived, identified his assailant to them.

LAWTON LJ, delivering the judgment of the court, said: 'We have to apply the opinion of Lord Wilberforce [in *Ratten* v *R,* (ante)]. Was there spontaneity in this identification? It is difficult to imagine a more spontaneous identification. Mr Lucas had been savagely attacked. He called for the help of the police and when police officers arrived, one of them asked what had happened. Mr Lucas pointed out Loan to him and alleged that Loan was the man who had hit him. He did this in the presence of the crowd which had collected.

Was there an opportunity for concoction? The interval of time was very short indeed. During part of that interval Mr Lucas was sitting down in his car trying to overcome the effects of the blows which had been struck. Commonsense and experience of life tells us that in that interval he would not be thinking of concocting a case against anybody. He would have been trying to clear his head. So we can put out of mind altogether, in our judgment, any possibility of concoction.

There is however the possibility of error, as Mr Thom has pointed out to us and that, if we may put a gloss upon what Lord Wilberforce said, is an additional factor to be taken into consideration. Perhaps Lord Wilberforce envisaged error in the word "concocted." Was there in this case any real possibility of error?

Mr Lucas appreciated that there were two men in the car. There is no doubt at all about that. He appreciated that the man who had assaulted him, not once but twice, had come from the passenger side of the car. Anyone who has been assaulted usually has good reason for remembering what his assailant's face looks like. Mr Lucas also appreciated that the driver at some stage had intervened to stop further assaults. He appreciated too that the man who had come to his car window and had threatened him with further violence if he did not move his car quickly, was not the man who had assaulted him but was the driver. Although the matter was never gone into at the trial, the statement which was made by Mr Lucas to the police and which formed part of the depositions, indicated that there were some differences in clothing between the two men. There is no doubt that Mr Lucas did make one mistake about the appearance of the two men. They are both young men, but one is considerably taller than the other. Mr Lucas got their height the wrong way round. He said that the driver was taller than the man who had assaulted him, whereas Loan is taller than the driver. That point was much canvassed at the trial. The jury were reminded of it by the learned judge in his summing-up.

Was the evidence of identification admissible at all? In our judgment, having regard to the tests which are set out in *Ratten* v *R (supra),* we consider that it was. There was no opportunity here for concoction and there was no chance of an error being made.

The fact that the evidence is admissible is of course not conclusive of the matter, if the Court looking at the case as a whole comes to the conclusion that its weight was unsatisfactory.'
Appeals dismissed.

Holt J: Yes, I see.

Mr Bunbury: In my submission, the evidence would equally be admissible as a contemporaneous declaration of the physical state of the speaker. The case of *R* v *Conde* shows that such statements may be admitted under the *res gestae* principle.

R v *Conde* (1867) 10 Cox CC 547 (Central Criminal Court)

The defendants were charged with the murder of their child by depriving it of food. A prosecution witness said, '...the deceased child came into my room...He looked very thin and emaciated...He spoke to me.' Counsel for the defendants objected to the reception of any statement made by the child in the absence of the defendants.

CHANNELL B said he was clearly of opinion that the evidence was admissible, upon the ground that it was not so much a statement as an act. A complaint of hunger was an act; although the particulars of the statement might not be receivable, the fact of the complaint was clearly so.
(Mary Conde found guilty of manslaughter, John George Conde not guilty.)

Mr Atkyn: My Lord, in my submission, all that would be admissible under that principle would be Margaret's complaint of being in pain. The cause of that pain would not be admissible.
(After hearing argument from Mr Atkyn, Holt J held that there was a risk of concoction and excluded the evidence.)

6.9 Commentary

R v *Coke* and *Littleton* on appeal against conviction. After a period of nine months from the date of Coke's alleged rape, but before Coke has been brought to trial, Margaret enters hospital to give birth to her child. During labour, she unexpectedly suffers a cardiac arrest and despite efforts to revive her, dies giving birth to a living child. In a brief period of consciousness, just before her death, Margaret said to a doctor standing by: 'Don't let them blame Henry Coke. The father is Anthony Henneky.' At the trial, Coke sought to call the doctor who heard the statement to give evidence of it, but the evidence was rejected by Holt J as inadmissible hearsay. Coke appeals on the ground that the evidence was wrongly excluded.

6.10 Argument

Leach LJ: Mr Atkyn, I do recall cases where the declaration of a deceased person was admitted where it was shown that the statement was made pursuant to some duty. But I cannot see that such a principle fits the present case.
Mr Atkyn: My Lord, I respectfully agree. In any event, in that kind of case, the duty must surely be in the nature of a legal or professional one. It must also be reasonably contemporaneous. An illustration would be:

R v *Buckley* (1873) 13 Cox CC 293 (Chester Spring Assizes)

The defendant was charged with the murder of a police constable. The prosecution sought to introduce into evidence a statement made by the deceased shortly before his death to his superior officer that he was about to go to keep observation on the defendant.

LUSH. J thought that the statement made by the deceased man was quite admissible, but went to the other court to consult with Mellor J on the point. After an absence of some minutes the learned judge returned, and said that his learned friend had no doubt at all of its admissibility, and the statement was therefore received in evidence.

East LJ: I wonder if counsel took the point that what Mellor J had said was hearsay! [Laughter] I also understand that the dying declarations of a deceased person were sometimes admissible in certain cases quite apart from any element of duty.

Mr Atkyn: Your Lordship is quite right. Such a declaration would be admissible where the maker was at the time under a settled, hopeless expectation of death, with no hope of recovery. The leading case is that of:

R v Woodcock (1789) 1 Leach 500 (Old Bailey)

The defendant was charged with the murder of his wife. She made a statement implicating him at a time when her death was inevitable because of the serious wounds which she had received. The deceased retained her senses until death, but never expressed any realisation of dying.

EYRE CB, said: 'Now the general principle on which this species of evidence is admitted is, that they are declarations made in extremity, when the party is at the point of death, and when every hope of this world is gone: when every motive to falsehood is silenced, and the mind is induced by the most powerful considerations to speak the truth; a situation so solemn, and so awful, is considered by the law as creating an obligation equal to that which is imposed by a positive oath administered in a Court of Justice. But a difficulty also arises with respect to these declarations; for it has not appeared, and it seems impossible to find out, whether the deceased herself apprehended that she was in such a state of mortality as would inevitably oblige her soon to answer before her Maker for the truth or falsehood of her assertions. The several witnesses could give no satisfactory information as to the sentiments of her mind upon this subject.... Upon the whole of this difficulty, however, my judgment is, that inasmuch as she was mortally wounded, and was in a condition which rendered almost immediate death inevitable; as she was thought by every person about her to be dying, though it was difficult to get from her particular explanations as to what she thought of herself and her situation; her declarations, made under these circumstances, ought to be considered by a Jury as being made under the impression of her approaching dissolution; for, resigned as she appeared to be, she must have felt the hand of death, and must have considered herself as a dying woman.

(The defendant was convicted.)

In my submission, the declaration of Miss Blackstone would fit within that description. And it is admissible under the rule, even though its contents may be favourable to the defendant, as in the case of:

R v Scaife (1836) 2 Lew CC 150 (York Summer Assizes)

COLERIDGE J held that dying declaractions may be given in evidence in favour of the accused as well as against him; and the following declaration was accordingly received: 'He would not have struck me but that I provoked him to it.'

Mr Bunbury: My Lords, if I may intervene. It is clear law that dying declarations are admissible only in homicide cases and for the purpose of proving the cause and circumstances of the death. I would refer to *R* v *Newton and Carpenter* which is a decision which has never been doubted.

R v Newton and Carpenter (1859) 1 F&F 641 (York Summer Assizes)

A woman was raped and the next day, in distress of mind, cut her throat. As she was likely to die a magistrate was sent for and, in the presence of the defendants, her deposition was taken. At the trial of the defendants for the rape the deposition was tendered in evidence by the prosecution.

HILL J said: 'It is not admissible as a dying declaration, as it does not relate to the offence which caused her death.'

East LJ: The learned judge would also have had to satisfy himself that the statement was a complete one and not incoherent or unreliable. I seem to remember such objection being taken in the case of:

Waugh v R [1950] AC 203 (PC)

The appellant was convicted of murder. At his trial a dying declaration was admitted where the deceased said, referring to the appellant, 'The man has an old grudge for me simply because...', and died before he could complete the sentence.

LORD OAKSEY, delivering the judgment of their Lordships, said: 'Their Lordships are of opinion that the dying declaration was inadmissible because on its face it was incomplete and no one can tell what the deceased was about to add; that it was in any event a serious error to admit it in part; and that it was a further and even more serious error not to point out to the jury that it had not been subject to cross-examination.'
Appeal allowed.

Leach LJ: In any event, I think Mr Bunbury's objection is fatal.

Mr Atkyn: In those circumstances, My Lords, I submit that the declaration is nonetheless admissible as a declaration against interest. Where a person makes a declaration which, when made, is contrary to that person's material interests, such declaration may be admitted after the person's death. Margaret Blackstone's purpose in making the declaration does not limit its use as evidence for other purposes subsequently. I would refer Your Lordships to:

Higham v Ridgway (1808) 10 East 109 (KB)

The question at issue was the date of birth of a child. In order to prove this, it was sought to adduce a statement made by a deceased male midwife that he had delivered a woman of a child on a certain day and referring to the payment of his fees.

LORD ELLENBOROUGH CJ said: 'The discharge in the book, in his own hand-writing repels the claim which he would otherwise have had against the father from the rest of the evidence as it now appears. Therefore the entry made by the party was to his own immediate prejudice, when he had not only no interest to make it, if it were not true, but he had an interest the other way, not to discharge a claim which it appears from other evidence that he had... Here the entries were made by a person who, so far from having any interest to make them, had an interest the other way; and such entries against the interest of the party making them are clearly evidence of the fact stated, on the authority of the case of *Warren* v *Greenville* 2 Stra 1129, and of all those cases where the books of receivers have been admitted.'

BAYLEY J: 'This was no officious entry made by one who had no concern in the transaction: he had no interest in making it: and as he thereby discharged an individual against whom he would otherwise have had a claim, I think the entry was evidence by all the authorities... But the principle to be drawn from all the cases, beginning with *Warren* v *Greenville* down to *Roe* v *Rawlings* 7 East 279, is that if a person have peculiar means of knowing a fact, and make a declaration of that fact, which is against his interest, it is clearly evidence after his death, if he could have been examined to it in his lifetime. And that principle has been constantly acted upon in the case of receivers' accounts.'

Cox LJ: For what reason do you say that this statement was against Miss Blackstone's interest?

Mr Atkyn: My Lord, because it tended to disprove a serious allegation that she had made which, if proved, might have led to an award of damages.

East LJ: I am not sure that that follows, because she made an allegation against a different putative father. But leaving that aside, what are the limits of the rule?

Mr Atkyn: My Lords, it would seem that even a declaration which does no more than create some moral obligation on the part of the speaker may be enough. I would refer to:

Coward v Motor Insurers' Bureau [1963] 1 QB 259 (CA)

A was a pillion passenger on B's motor-cycle when they were involved in an accident in which, by B's negligence, both were killed. A's widow obtained judgment for damages against B's representatives, which was unsatisfied because his insurance policy did not cover pillion passengers. Mrs A therefore sued the Motor Insurers' Bureau under their agreement with the Ministry, alleging that the risk to A was a liability required to be covered by a policy or security within that agreement, as B was carrying A for hire or reward. Evidence was tendered of payments by A to B and of statements by A to the effect that he paid a weekly sum to B for driving him to work. The judge refused to admit the evidence about the statements because they did not amount to a recognition of a contractual obligation, and dismissed the action. Mrs A appealed.

UPJOHN LJ, delivering the judgment of the court, said: 'The first question, therefore, that we have to determine is whether the judge is correct in his conclusion that a statement against pecuniary interest is only admissible if it is an acknowledgment or recognition of a legal obligation, but not if it recognises only a moral obligation.

We cannot agree that the law is as stated by the judge and that evidence is only admissible where the declaration recognises a contractual obligation. No authority supports that proposition and the books of Professor Cross and Dr Nokes on evidence, to which we have been referred, do not, in our view, support a contrary view.

The rule is, we think, clearly settled. We take it from one of the earliest and leading cases in the House of Lords, the *Sussex Peerage* case (1841) 11 Cl&F 85, HL, where Lord Campbell LC said: " But as to the point of interest, I have always understood the rule to be, that the declaration, to be admissible, must have been one which was contrary to the interests of the party making it, in a pecuniary point of view." This does not suggest the test of a legal or contractual obligation; the test is whether it is against the pecuniary interest of the declarant, that is, that it must appear to be against his interest. Whether in the end there is a contractual obligation can surely only be established when the whole of the relevant admissible evidence has been considered.'

Appeal dismissed on other grounds.

There is certainly authority that it is against the interest of the declarant to risk a finding of adultery against him, as is shown by *B v Attorney General* [1965] P 278.

Cox LJ: I think that mere exposure to a possible criminal penalty would not be enough, in light of the *Sussex Peerage Case* which is unfortunate from your client's point of view since Miss Blackstone might possibly have put herself in that position.

Sussex Peerage Case (1844) 11 Cl&F 85 (HL)

The claimant to a peerage had to prove his legitimacy. In order to do so he adduced evidence of the statement of a deceased clergyman to his son, to the effect that the clergyman had celebrated a marriage between the deceased peer and his alleged wife. It was argued that this was admissible as a declaration against interest, since in the particular circumstances in which the marriage was celebrated, the clergyman was liable to criminal punishment under the Royal Marriages Act 1772.

LORD BROUGHAM said: 'The case of *Higham v Ridgway* [10 East 109] declares the law on the point at issue. The more we look at that case, the more clearly must we come to two conclusions. In the first place we must see that the evidence there was admitted, not because the subject-matter of the declaration was within the peculiar knowledge of the party making the declaration, but that it was a declaration made against an interest of a very specific nature, *viz.*, a pecuniary interest. I may further say, that one of the learned judges who is now present to assist your Lordships, I mean Mr Justice Williams, was a counsel in that very case, and argued it with Mr Serjeant Manley in 1808, against the admission of the evidence; and he remembers perfectly well that the evidence was received on the express and specific ground that it was an entry against the pecuniary interest of the party. Another conclusion to which we must come is that, considering the nature and tendencies of such evidence unless properly restricted, we ought to be careful and cautious of extending the rule as laid down in the case of *Higham* v *Ridgway*, beyond the limits settled by that case. To say, if a man should confess a felony for which he would be liable to prosecution, that therefore, the instant the grave closes over him, all that was said by him is to be taken as evidence in every action and prosecution against another person, is one of the most monstrous and untenable propositions that can be advanced. Lord Kenyon never could have entertained the opinion or held the doctrine imputed to him in the case of *Standen* v *Standen* (1 Peake's NP.45). The law in *Higham* v *Ridgway* has been carried far enough, although not too far. The rule, as understood now, is that the only declarations of deceased persons receivable in evidence, are those made against the proprietary or pecuniary interests of the party making them, when the subject-matter of such declarations is within the peculiar knowledge of the party so making them.'

LORD CAMPBELL said: 'By the law of England the declarations of deceased persons are not generally admissible, unless they are against the pecuniary interest of the party making them. There are two exceptions: first, where a declaration by word of mouth or by writing is made in the course of the business of the individual making it, there it may be received in evidence, though it is not against his interest; *Doe d Pattershall* v *Turford* (3 Barn and Ad 890). The service of a notice may thus be proved; and, in like manner, an entry by a notary's clerk that he had presented a bill, for that is in the ordinary discharge of his duty. But as to the point of interest, I have always understood the rule to be, that the declaration, to be admissible, must have been one which was contrary to the interests of the party making it, in a pecuniary point of view; and, with the exception of *Standen* v *Standen* (1 Peke's NP 45), I do not know any case which appears to break in upon that principle. I think it would lead to most inconvenient consequences, both to individuals and to the public, if we were to say that the apprehension of a criminal prosecution was an interest which ought to let in such declarations in evidence. But even if such a rule did exist, it would not permit the learned counsel here to bring in the statements of Mr Gunn, for how are your Lordships to know what state Mr Gunn's mind was in when he made the declarations? At that time of his conversation with his son, he might have entertained a very different belief from that which he laboured under when he demurred to the bill in Chancery, and refused to answer the interrogatories put to him there. He might have believed that the marriage having been celebrated abroad, the provisions of the Royal Marriage Act did not extend to it, and that he was in no danger whatever from what he had done.'

(LORDS DENMAN, COTTERHAM, and LANGDALE agreed)

The evidence tendered was rejected.

6.11 Commentary

R v *Coke and Littleton* at trial. In order to deal with Littleton's alibi, Mr Bunbury for the prosecution invites Holt J to take judicial notice (see 1.10.3 and 1.12 ante) of the area of the park and the surrounding streets in Oxbridge. For this purpose, Mr Bunbury tenders an Ordnance Survey map of the area and invites Holt J to examine it with a view to noticing judicially certain distances and the relationships between certain places, such as the park and Littleton's home.

6.12 Argument

Holt J: Am I permitted to examine the map?

Mr Bunbury: In my submission, My Lord, yes. This is a published public work, which can be used to show facts of public interest contained in it. I am in a position to prove, and my learned friends do not dispute, that this map is the official Ordnance Survey map for the area concerned. It can be used to enable Your Lordship to take judicial notice of facts of geographical notoriety in the area. It is part of a general rule of common law allowing facts contained in public documents to be proved. I would refer Your Lordship to:

Sturla v Freccia (1880) 5 App Cas 623 (HL)

One Mangini, the consul in London for the Genoese government, applied to his government to receive the rank of diplomatic agent. The application was referred to a committee. The committee's report contained a statement of Mangini's age and in a subsequent suit the report was tendered as evidence of that fact.

LORD BLACKBURN said: 'But, then, there comes another class of cases on which the argument principally rested; for it is only within that class of cases that the learned counsel for the Appellants in their able argument have made any serious struggle to shew that this document is admissible. It is an established rule of law that public documents are admitted for certain purposes. What a public document is, within that sense, is of course the great point which we have now to consider. Public documents are admissible, and I think I can hardly state it better than by quoting what Mr Baron *Parke* said in delivering the opinion of the Judges in the case of *The Irish Society* v *The Bishop of Derry* 12 Cl&F 641. His Lordship there says, "The fifth exception related to an entry in one of the books of the First Fruits Office of the collation and admission of *John Freeman* to the Rectory of *Camus*. Writs were issued from the Court of Exchequer to the bishops to ascertain the value of the first fruits and twentieths, and returns were made by the bishops. Search for the writs and returns was made, and the book was offered as secondary evidence of returns. We think the entry was properly received." That was the point decided — that the writs having been issued to the bishop to return the first fruits in his diocese, and the return of them being presumably lost, as it could not be found, the entry in the First Fruits Office (the copy of it) was good secondary evidence of the return. Of course, that involved in it that the return itself would be evidence. Then his Lordship says, "The writs related to a public matter — the revenue of the Crown, and the bishops in making the return discharged a public duty, and faith is given that they would perform their duty correctly; the return is therefore admissible on the same principle on which other public documents are received. It was contended that the bishop could not be permitted to make evidence for himself" (that is one objection which he meets) "and, therefore, that the entry though admissible between other parties was not to be received for the bishop; and the case was compared to an entry in the book of a union, of a surgeon's attendance, *Merrick* v *Wakley* 8 A&E 170, and the receipt of a certificate in a parish book, *R* v *Debenham* 2 B&Ald 185, which have been rightly held to be inadmissible for the surgeon in one case, or the parish keeping the book in the other. But neither of these was an entry of a public nature, in the proper sense of that word; the former was a memorandum, intended to operate as a sort of check to the surgeon, the latter a memorandum for the parish officer, concerning merely the *Holt J:* It may be that those matters are of less importance in relation to an documents made for the information of the Crown, or all the King's subjects who may require the information they contain, the entry by a public officer is presumed to be true when it is made, and is for that reason receivable in all cases, whether the officer or his successor may be concerned in such cases or not." Then he puts the case of the person who made a marriage register turning out to be interested, and says that would not prevent the register being received as evidence.

Now, my Lords, taking that decision, the principle upon which it goes is, that it should be a public inquiry, a public document, and made by a public officer. I do not think that "public" there is to be taken in the sense of meaning the whole world. I think an entry in the books of a manor is public in the sense that it concerns all the people interested in the manor. And an entry probably in a corporation book concerning a corporate matter, or something in which all the corporation is concerned, would be "public" within that sense. But it must be a public document, and it must be made by a public officer. I understand a public document there to mean a document that is made for the purpose of the public making use of it, and being able to refer to it. It is meant to be where there is a judicial, or *quasi*-judicial, duty to inquire, as might be said to be the case with the bishop acting under the writs issued by the Crown. That may be said to be *quasi*-judicial. He is acting for the public when that is done but I think the very object of it must be that it should be made for the purpose of being kept public, so that the persons concerned in it may have access to it afterwards.

In many cases, entries in the parish register, of births, marriages, and deaths, and other entries of that kind, before there were any statutes relating to them, were admissible, and they were "public" then, because the Common Law of *England* making it an express duty to keep the register, made it a public document in that sense kept by a public officer for the purpose of a register, and so made it admissible. I think as far as my recollection goes, although I will not pledge myself to its accuracy, and so far as I have ever heard anything cited, it will be found that, in every case in which a public document of that sort has been admitted, it has been made originally with the intent that it should be retained and kept, as a register to be referred to, ever after.

Taking that view of the matter, I think it becomes clear that this document is not evidence. (LORDS SELBORNE LC, HATHERLEY and WATSON agreed.)

Holt J: What conditions must be satisfied?

Mr Bunbury: My Lord, in the case of any public document, the document must first contain matters of public interest and be preserved for public use. And in relation to documents actually kept in some public office, the documents must be open to public inspection, the entry or record must have been made promptly after the events recorded, and the entry must have been made by a person having a duty to inquire into and satisfy himself of the truth of the facts recorded.

Holt J: It may be that those matters are of less importance in relation to an officially published map, which would clearly be issued only after having been verified by proper research.

Mr Bunbury: My Lord, yes. Of course in modern times public documents are no longer kept necessarily by one official, such as a local vicar, as was formerly the case. They are often a complex product of the work of many public servants. In such cases, in modern law the duty to inquire into the truth of the facts recorded may be undertaken by a number of people. I would refer Your Lordship to:

R v Halpin [1975] QB 907 (CA)

The defendant was charged with conspiring with others to cheat a local authority by means of putting in false claims for work allegedly done for the local authority by the defendant's limited company. The Crown sought to produce the file from the Companies Register containing the annual returns made under s.124 of the Companies Act 1948 to prove that the defendant and his wife were the sole shareholders and directors of the company during the relevant period. The defence objected to the file being produced on the ground that it was hearsay, for, although it was a public document, preserved for public use and open to the public for inspection, it was not a record made promptly after the events it recorded and the entry was made by an official who had no duty to inquire and satisfy himself as to the truth of the recorded facts. The judge ruled against the defence submission and the file was adduced in evidence. The defendant was convicted and appealed.

GEOFFREY LANE LJ, delivering the judgment of the court, said: 'Mr Anns contends that there are four conditions which must be satisfied before a document of this sort can be admitted in evidence. First, the document must be brought into existence and preserved for public use on a public matter. Secondly, it must be open to public inspection. Thirdly, the entry must be made promptly after the events which it purports to record. Fourthly, the entry must be made by a person having a duty to inquire and satisfy himself as to the truth of the recorded facts.

In the present case the first two conditions are clearly satisfied. There has been no dispute on either side as to that. As to the third, that is the matter of promptness, this court is of the view that that may affect the weight of the evidence but it does not affect its admissibility. It is as to the fourth point that the real dispute exists, namely, that the entry must be made, it is submitted, by a person having a duty to inquire and satisfy himself of the truth of the recorded facts.

It seems to be inescapable from the authorities that it was a condition of admissibility that the official making the record should either have had personal knowledge of the matters which he was recording or should have inquired into the accuracy of the facts.

There is no doubt that in a case such as the present the official in the Companies Registry has no personal knowledge of the matters which he is putting on the file or recording. There is equally no doubt that it would be most convenient if the identity of directors and so on could be established simply by production of the file from the company's register containing the returns made by the company. We do not, however, feel that convenience on its own is an adequate substitute for precedent, tempting though such a solution might be. The common law, as expressed in the earlier cases which have been cited, was plainly designed to apply to an uncomplicated community when those charged with keeping registers would, more often than not, be personally acquainted with the people whose affairs they were recording and the vicar, as already indicated, would probably himself have officiated at the baptism, marriage or burial which he later recorded in the presence of the churchwardens on the register before putting it back in the coffers. But the common law should move with the times and should recognise the fact that the official charged with recording matters of public import can no longer in this highly complicated world, as like as not, have personal knowledge of their accuracy.

What has happened now is that the function originally performed by one man has had to be shared between two: the first having the knowledge and the statutory duty to record that knowledge and forward it to the Registrar of Companies, the second having the duty to preserve that document and to show it to members of the public under proper conditions as required.

Where a duty is cast upon a limited company by statute to make accurate returns of company matters to the Registrar of Companies, so that those returns can be filed and inspected by members of the public, the necessary conditions, in the judgment of this court, have been fulfilled for that document to have been admissible. All statements on the return are admissible as prima facie proof of the truth of their contents.'

(Mr Atkyn and Mr Bacon having indicated that they had no objection, Holt J referred to the map, took judicial notice of certain facts and instructed the jury accordingly.)

6.13   Questions for Counsel

6.13.1   R v *Coke* and *Littleton:*   If Holt J had admitted Coke's evidence to the effect that he had been told that Margaret was promiscuous and wanted to have sexual relations with him, how should Holt J have directed the jury as to the use they were entitled to make of such evidence? Construct an appropriate passage for Holt J's summing up which fully and properly instructs the jury on this matter.

6.13.2   R v *Coke and Littleton:*   Argument 6.5:   Do you consider that Holt J was correct in rejecting this proposed evidence by Coke? If so, why? What arguments can be made for and against Holt J's decision?

6.13.3   R v *Coke and Littleton:*   In the light of the cases, what arguments are to be made for and against the admission of Margaret's conversation with Angela under the *res gestae* principle? Which way do you think Holt J should have decided?

6.13.4   *R* v *Coke and Littleton:*   Do you consider that Holt J was correct in refusing to admit evidence of Margaret's declaration before death? What arguments may be made for and against? If Holt J had admitted such a declaration, how should he have directed the jury with regard to the use they might make of it?

7　The Rule Against Hearsay: II

*ADMISSIONS AND CONFESSIONS; STATEMENTS IN
PRESENCE OF DEFENDANT*

A: ADMISSIONS

7.1 Introductory notes

7.1.1 As an exception to the rule against hearsay at common law, an admission by a
party adverse to his interest or to his asserted case is admissible evidence of the facts
admitted. The exception is based on the premise that a party is unlikely to make such
adverse admissions unless they are true, and consequently that admissions carry a
considerable degree of reliability. These admissions, styled 'informal', are no more
than pieces of *prima facie* evidence of the facts admitted, and may be challenged,
contradicted or explained away by other evidence. They should not be confused with
formal admissions made expressly for the purpose of proceedings, considered in
Chapter 1, which are generally conclusive unless withdrawn with leave of the court.
Admissions made by the defendant in a criminal case, relevant to the issue of his guilt,
are termed 'confessions' and are subject to special rules, dealt with in Section B of this
chapter.

7.1.2 Because admissions may be contradicted or explained away, and because their
weight is entirely a question of fact, the whole of a statement said to constitute an
admission should be placed before the court, unless exceptionally in a criminal case it
should be edited to exclude some inadmissible and prejudicial material, for example
references to bad character. An overall view of a statement may weaken or even
destroy the effect of an apparently damaging passage.

7.1.3 Where a party litigates in his personal capacity, an admission made by him
previously while litigating in some representative capacity may be admitted against
him. But where that party sues in a representative capacity, an admission made by him
in his personal capacity will not be admitted, as it would prejudice not only him, but
also the party he represents.

7.1.4 A party will be bound by admissions made by his agent acting within the scope
of his authority. Such admissions may therefore be used against him. Whether the
agent had authority and was acting within the scope of that authority is a question of
fact. Solicitors and counsel who have authority to conduct business or litigation on
behalf of clients, may be agents for this purpose, when acting properly within the
scope of their professional duties and powers.

7.1.5 At common law, it is a fundamental rule that an admission is evidence only against the maker (including a principal bound by the admission of his agent) and not against any other person implicated by it. This rule remains of great importance in criminal cases, but in civil cases it has been modified by the Civil Evidence Act 1968, by virtue of which such admissions are capable of being evidence for all purposes, though they may carry little weight against parties other than the maker.

7.1.6 Informal admissions may be made as to matters of fact or law, but their weight may not be great as to matters of law, especially where the point of law is complex or uncertain. Admissions as to matters of foreign law will usually be rejected altogether. Admissions of fact will similarly be rejected if they are based on nothing more substantial than hearsay, as to which the maker has no personal knowledge. (*A Practical Approach to Evidence,* pp 153-9.)

7.2 Commentary

Blackstone v *Coke* at trial. Mr Atkyn, on behalf of Coke, is making his closing speech to Hardwicke J. In the course of a review of the evidence, he refers to the letter of 3 March 1980, from Eldon & Co, Margaret Blackstone's solicitors, to Mansfield & Co, Coke's solicitors.

7.3 Argument

Mr Atkyn: In my submission, My Lord, this letter is most significant. It runs, in the second paragraph, entirely contrary to the plaintiff's case that she was unable to have an abortion for medical or psychiatric reasons. This letter is in effect an admission that she chose not to have an abortion. It is further an admission by conduct of the weakness of the plaintiff's case, because of the refusal to submit to a blood test.

Hardwicke J: I'm not sure I would be inclined to give much weight to those arguments. But first things first. Can the letter be admissible evidence in this action?

Mr Atkyn: Yes, My Lord. Admissions may be made in various ways — orally, in writing or by conduct, such as by refusing a blood test. The principle is similar to that in:

Moriarty v **London, Chatham and Dover Railway Co.** (1870) LR 5 QB 314

LORD COCKBURN CJ said: 'The conduct of a party to a cause may be of the highest importance in determining whether the cause of action in which he is plaintiff, or the ground of defence, if he is defendant, is honest and just; just as it is evidence against a prisoner that he has said one thing at one time and another at another, as shewing that the recourse to falsehood leads fairly to an inference of guilt. Anything from which such an inference can be drawn is cogent and important evidence with a view to the issue. So, if you can shew that a plaintiff has been suborning false testimony, and has endeavoured to have recourse to perjury, it is strong evidence that he knew perfectly well his cause was an unrighteous one. I do not say that it is conclusive; I fully agree that it should be put to the jury, with the intimation that it does not always follow, because a man, not sure he shall be able to succeed by righteous means, has recourse to means of a different character, that that which he desires, namely, the gaining of the victory, is not his due, or that he has good ground for believing that justice entitles him to it.'

(BLACKBURN and LUSH JJ agreed.)

Hardwicke J: What evidential value do you say the letter has?

Mr Atkyn: In the first place, My Lord, it contradicts the case presented to Your Lordship by the plaintiff in this case. But it goes somewhat further than that. By the Civil Evidence Act 1968, s.9, an admission is evidence of the facts admitted in civil cases.

Civil Evidence Act 1968, s.9

9.—(1) In any civil proceedings a statement which, if this Part of this Act had not been passed, would by virtue of any rule of law mentioned in subsection (2) below have been admissible as evidence of any fact stated therein shall be admissible as evidence of that fact by virtue of this subsection.

(2) The rules of law referred to in subsection (1) above are the following, that is to say any rule of law—

   (a) whereby in any civil proceedings an admission adverse to a party to the proceedings, whether made by that party or by another person, may be given in evidence against that party for the purpose of proving any fact stated in the admission....

Hardwicke J: Of course, this admission, if admission it be, was not made by Miss Blackstone, but by her solicitors.

Mr Atkyn: My Lord, yes. But a principal may be bound by admissions made by his or her agent, provided that there is evidence that the agent had authority to deal with the matter in hand and was acting within the scope of that authority. This agency may be inferred in a proper case, as in:

Edwards v *Brookes (Milk) Ltd* [1963] 1 WLR 795 (DC)

An inspector of weights and measures went to the defendant's depot to discuss deficiencies in the contents of milk cartons bought from a machine. He spoke to a man who said he was Norman Jones, the depot manager. Another person called at the inspector's office four days later and said that he was a representative of the company, whereupon a further conversation took place. The defendants were charged with an offence under weights and measures legislation. Objections were made to the inspector's evidence of the conversations with Norman Jones and the representative on the ground that the statements made by them were inadmissible against the company unless it was proved that they were agents of the company and were authorised by the company to make the statements. The justices excluded evidence of the statements and subsequently dismissed the summons.

LORD PARKER CJ said: 'When you get, as here, the full circumstances of going to the depot, trying to speak to someone in authority, finding someone who appears to be in authority, and then being told by him that he is the depot manager, that must in my judgment be evidence on which the justices can, if they so wish, infer than the man Norman Jones was an agent of the company.

So far as the second interview is concerned, the position is very much stronger, because having left the schedule with the alleged depot manager, four days later a man turns up claiming to be the representative of the company to discuss the matter.'
Appeal allowed.

In the case of legal representatives, the agency is, in my submission, a clear one which extends to the making of admissions of fact. I would also refer Your Lordship to:

Marshall and Another v *Cliff and Another* (1815) 4 Camp 133 (Nisi Prius)

This was an action against the defendants as owners of the ship 'Arundel,' for not properly carrying goods of the plaintiffs.

To prove the defendants to be owners of the vessel, there was put in an undertaking in the following form, given before the action was commenced, by the gentleman who was afterwards their attorney on the record.

'I hereby undertake to appear for Messrs Thompson and Marshall, joint owners of the sloop "Arundel," to any action you may think fit to bring against them.

Richard Corner.'

LORD ELLENBOROUGH said: 'I think this is sufficient *prima facie* evidence. The Court would have enforced the undertaking by attachment. I must presume that Mr Corner, who is now the attorney on the record, was then the agent of the defendants, and had authority from them to admit that they were joint owners of the vessel.

The plaintiffs had a verdict.

The same rule may apply to Counsel, when acting in a case in accordance with his instructions, as in:

R v *Turner and Others* (1975) 61 Cr App R 67 (CA)

The question arose, *inter alia,* as to whether an admission of an offence made by counsel in the course of mitigation of another offence, was admissible on the prosecution of the appellant for the offence so admitted.

LAWTON LJ, giving the judgment of the court, said: 'The problem before us must be considered in the light of a few elementary principles, which are as follows. First, a duly authorised agent can make admissions on behalf of his principal. Mr Waley did not dispute that proposition. Secondly, the party seeking to rely upon the admission must prove that the agent was duly authorised. Mr Mathew agreed that this was so. Thirdly, whenever a fact has to be proved, any evidence having probative effect and not excluded by a rule of law is admissible to prove that fact: circumstantial evidence is just as admissible as direct evidence. Whenever a barrister comes into Court in robes and in the presence of his client tells the judge that he appears for that client, the court is entitled to assume, and always does assume, that he has his client's authority to conduct the case and to say on the client's behalf whatever in his professional discretion he thinks is in his client's interest to say. If the Court could not make this assumption, the administration of justice would become very difficult indeed. The very circumstances provide evidence first, that the barrister has his client's authority to speak for him and secondly, that what the barrister says his client wants him to say. Counsel should never act without instructions, and they seldom do. What happened in this case was probably caused by inexperience: the barrister had only been in practice a short time. There is nothing to suggest that he was trying to mislead the Court. His dicomfiture arising from this case will ensure that he never makes the same mistake again and will provide a cautionary tale for generations of barristers to come. It follows that proof of the circumstances in which the barrister said what he did amounted to prima facie evidence that he was authorised by Shervill to say it. The contested evidence was admissible.'

Appeal dismissed.

Hardwicke J: So you would say that Miss Blackstone's case may be prejudiced by her solicitors, who must be presumed to be acting upon her instructions.

Mr Atkyn: Yes, My Lord. For not dissimilar reasons, a party may be bound by admissions made in one capacity, even when litigating in a different capacity. I would refer to:

Stanton v *Percival* (1855) 5 HL Cas 257

The appellants, who were litigants in their personal capacity, had on a previous occasion made admissions when representing a mentally disordered person against the respondents.

The question arose as to whether the admissions could be tendered in the later proceedings.

THE LORD CHANCELLOR said: 'In this case, one of the personal representatives of the lunatic, and the husbands of the other two, were themselves the committees whose answers are in question. Assuming that these answers could not be read against the lunatic, yet when the committees have themselves become defendants in her place, I can discover no reason whatever for doubting that, as against them, the answer may be read. It must be presumed that they would not have untruly stated anything adverse to the lunatic, whose interests they are bound to protect; and by what they have themselves stated, it is most reasonable that they should be bound. After the order to revive, the cause might properly be dealt with just as if the committees had been Defendants from the beginning, not as committees, but in the right in which they were made Defendants to the bill of revivor; and the question then is, whether the Plaintiff would have been entitled to the decree now appealed from if the lunatic had been dead before the filing of the original bill, and if that bill had been filed against the Defendants to the bill of revivor, and the proceedings which actually took place had been taken in a suit so constituted.'

Hardwicke J: It may be that Mr Noy will argue that an admission on such a question as this should not be admitted, because it is really based on no more than hearsay (see 6.5 ante). I shall consider the letter of course, but I am uncertain about its weight.

B: CONFESSIONS

7.4 Introductory notes

7.4.1 In criminal cases, admissions relevant to the issue of guilt, termed confessions, are admissible at common law to prove the truth of the facts admitted. But if a confession is made to a person in authority, its admissibility is subject to conditions relating to the way in which it was obtained. A person in authority is one who is concerned in the arrest, detention, interrogation or prosecution of the defendant and who therefore has, or may reasonably be thought by the defendant to have, some influence or control over the way in which the defendant is to be treated during the investigation or prosecution. Police officers are the usual, though not the only example of persons in authority. The term confession does not necessarily signify a complete or comprehensive recognition of guilt. A confession may be a partial admission only, and may be made orally or in writing, or in a combination of ways.

7.4.2 A confession made to a person in authority is admissible only if the prosecution prove beyond reasonable doubt that it was made voluntarily, and in the absence of any oppression. If this is disputed, the judge must resolve the question by hearing evidence and argument in the absence of the jury, on the voir dire.

7.4.3 'Voluntarily', in the context of confessions, means that the confession must have been obtained without causing the defendant either fear of prejudice or hope of advantage. There is no restriction on the conduct which may create such a fear or hope. Any threat or inducement, however slight, may have this effect as a matter of law, but ultimately, the question for the judge is whether the confession may, in fact, have been induced by the threat or inducement.

7.4.4 The absence of oppression means that there must be nothing to sap the free will of the defendant, or to cause him to speak when he would otherwise have remained silent. This too, is ultimately a question of fact, the question being whether the circumstances might have been oppressive to the individual defendant who made the confession.

7.4.5 Even where the confession is proved to be admissible in law, by reference to the above tests, the judge has a discretion to exclude it if admission would involve unfairness to the defendant because of some breach of the Judges' Rules by the investigating officers. These are rules of practice for the guidance of police officers, which deal with the conduct of investigations and interrogations. The most important safeguards built into the rules relate to the freedom of access of the defendant to a solicitor, and the need for the defendant to be cautioned about his right to remain silent at certain crucial stages of an inquiry.

7.4.6 A confession, properly proved, is sufficient evidence on which to convict if the jury are prepared to accord it sufficient weight. However, a confession is evidence only against its maker, and not against any other person, for example a co-defendant, who may be implicated by it. The co-defendant is not, for this reason alone, entitled to a separate trial, but failure on the part of the judge to direct the jury as to the value of the statement as evidence will be a ground of appeal. Where the confession contains material which may be prejudicial as well as inadmissible, for example a reference to bad character, a rule of practice calls for its editing to exclude those matters. Where this cannot be done without destroying the sense of the statement, the unedited statement may nevertheless have to be used with a strong warning to the jury to disregard the prejudicial parts.

7.4.7 Where the judge rules a confession to be inadmissible, no reference to it may be made in the presence of the jury, even in cross-examination of the defendant. If other evidence has come to light as a result of the confession, for example the recovery of a body or of stolen goods, such evidence will be admissible provided that it can be fully proved without reference to the confession.

7.4.8 Where the defendant makes a statement which is partly damaging to, and partly favourable to his case, the jury must look at the whole statement and decide whether it can be regarded as a confession, when looked at as a whole. The defence are entitled to suggest that the favourable passages nullify or weaken the force of the statement as a whole. If the jury find that it is a confession, they may act upon it according to its weight. They may, however, regard the confession as evidence of any inculpating facts contained therein (because it is an adverse admission), but they may not regard the statement as evidence of any facts consistent with the defendant's case (in relation to which it is self-serving; Chapter 12, Section C). However, such favourable passages are evidence of the defendant's reaction to the charge, or of the overall picture. (*A Practical Approach to Evidence,* pp 160–87.)

7.5 Commentary

R v *Coke and Littleton* at trial. During the evidence in chief of D/I Glanvil, Mr Bunbury indicates to Holt J that a question of law arises. The jury retire. Mr Atkyn has, before the start of the trial, indicated to Mr Bunbury that he objects to the admissibility of the oral and written confessions of which D/I Glanvil is about to give evidence. These confessions have therefore not been opened or referred to in the presence of the jury. Mr Atkyn explains to Holt J his objections, which are that the confessions were not obtained voluntarily, that the circumstances under which they were obtained were oppressive to Coke, and that breaches of the Judges' Rules occurred. Holt J hears evidence in the absence of the jury from D/I Glanvil, D/S Bracton and Coke himself. All these witnesses give evidence along the lines of their depositions and proof of evidence respectively, and are not materially shaken in cross-examination. Holt J invites Counsel to address him as to the admissibility of the confessions.

7.6 Argument: Person in authority

Mr Atkyn: My Lord, my first point is that these confessions were made to D/I Glanvil, who was a person in authority.

Holt J: It may be that there will be no dispute about that. But I would like to hear from you briefly on the point.

Mr Atkyn: My Lord, a police officer having a defendant in custody is the classic instance of a person in authority. Conversely, not every person who is a police officer, or who plays a part in dealing with a defendant in the course of an investigation or prosecution is a person in authority for the purposes of this rule. For example, a police surgeon who examines the defendant is not so, according to the decision in:

R v Nowell [1948] 1 All ER 794 (CCA)

The defendant was arrested on a charge of driving a motor car while under the influence of drink. He was taken to a police station where, following normal procedure, a police doctor was called. The defendant at first refused to be examined, but after being told that it might be to his advantage he underwent an examination as a result of which he was certified as being in an unfit state to drive a car owing to his consumption of alcohol. The defendant appealed against his conviction on the ground that the police doctor's evidence was inadmissible.

HUMPHREYS J, delivering the judgment of the court, said: 'I should add that during the argument we were referred, by counsel for the appellant, to the Scottish case, *Reid* v *Nixon, Dumigan* v *Brown* 1948 Sessions Notes 17. In reading the opinion of the court in that case, the Lord Justice-General made a number of general observations as to the principles on which police officers and doctors should act in examining persons who are charged with such an offence as this. According to the opinion, the Lord Advocate had conceded that in all such cases the police surgeon or other doctor summoned by the police to conduct an examination was acting as the hand of the police, and not as an independent medical referee. This court can only say that it does not agree that that state of things exists in this country, whether it exists in Scotland or not. Our view is that the evidence of a doctor, whether he be a police surgeon or anyone else, should be accepted, unless the doctor himself shows that it ought not to be, as the evidence of a professional man giving independent expert evidence with no other desire than to assist the court.'
Appeal dismissed.

Holt J: Presumably, it would not be enough that the person to whom the confession was made was later a witness for the prosecution.

Mr Atkyn: My Lord, no. The Privy Council held so in:

Deokinanan v *R* [1969] 1 AC 20 (PC)

The appellant was charged with murder. He had confessed to the murder to a friend who had been placed in custody with the appellant by the police in the hope of obtaining information from the appellant. The appellant was convicted and appealed on the ground that the friend's evidence about the conversation was inadmissible.

VISCOUNT DILHORNE, delivering the judgment of their Lordships, stated the facts and continued: 'Further, even if a promise by Balchand had induced the confession, Balchand was not and could not in their Lordships' opinion have been regarded by the appellant as a person in authority. It has long been established that a confession must be induced by a person in authority to be inadmissible in evidence (see *R* v *Row* (1809) Russ&Ry 153; *R* v *Gibbons* (1823) IC&P 97; *R* v *Moore* (1852) 2 Den 522).

In *R* v *Wilson (David); R* v *Marshall-Graham* [1967] 2 QB 406, Lord Parker CJ said:

> The first question that rises is whether Captain Birkbeck was a person in authority. There is no authority so far as this court knows which clearly defines who does and who does not come within this category. It is unnecessary to go through all the cases; it is clear, however, in *R* v *Thompson* [1893] 2 QB 12 that the chairman of a company whose money was said to have been embezzled by the prisoner was held to be a person in authority. It is also clear that in some cases it has been held that the prosecutor's wife is a person in authority, and in one case that the mother-in-law of a person whose house had been destroyed by arson was said to be a person in authority vis-a-vis a young girl employed by the owner of the house, in other words she was looked upon as a person in authority in relation to that girl.
>
> Mr Hawser in the course of the argument sought to put forward the principle that a person in authority is anyone who can reasonably be considered to be concerned or connected with the prosecution, whether as initiator, conductor or witness. The court finds it unnecessary to accept or reject the definition, save to say that they think that the extension to a witness is going very much too far.

In this case at the time of the confession Balchand was no more than a possible witness for the prosecution and their Lordships agree that the mere fact that a person may be a witness for the prosecution does not make him a person in authority.

Mr Kellock argued that a person in authority meant a person who could fulfil the promise made and that as Balchand could have done what he promised, he was a person in authority. He contended that in the cases where confessions induced by promises made by persons in authority had been excluded, the promisor always had power to fulfil the promise.

If this be the case, it does not follow that that is the meaning to be given to the words "person in authority." The fact that a person could have kept his promise may show the reality of the promise and that it was a real inducement, but it is not a definition of those words. Mr Kellock was unable to cite any case in support of his contention. In their Lordships' opinion his contention cannot be sustained.'
Appeal dismissed.

But on the other hand, a person who may appear to be capable of influencing the treatment of the defendant will be a person in authority, even though he is not a police officer. I would refer Your Lordship to:

R v *Moore* (1852) 2 Den CC 522 (CCR)

The defendant was tried for the murder of her new born child. There was received in evidence against her a confession made by her, in the presence of her mistress, to a surgeon, who was attending her. She was acquitted of murder but convicted of concealing the birth of her child.

PARKE B, delivering the judgment of the court, said: 'A rule has been laid down in different precedents by which we are bound, and that is, that if the threat or inducement is held out actually or constructively by a person in authority, it cannot be received, however slight the threat or inducement, and the prosecutor, magistrate, or constable, is such a person, and so the master or mistress may be...But in referring to the cases where the master or mistress have been held to be persons in authority, it is only when the offence concerns the master or mistress, that their holding out the threat or promise renders the confession inadmissible.

In *R* v *Upchurch*, R&M, CC 865, the offence was arson of the dwelling-house, in the management of which the mistress took a part. *R* v *Taylor*, 8 C&P 703, is to the like effect; so *R* v *Carrington*, 109; *R* v *Howell*, 534; so where the threat was used by the master of a ship to one of the crew, and the offence committed on board the ship by one of the crew towards another; and in that case also the master of the ship threatened to apprehend him, and the offence being a felony, and a felony actually committed, would have a power to do so, on reasonable suspicion that the prisoner was guilty. In *R* v *Warringham*, tried before me, Surrey Spring Assizes, 1851, the confession was in consequence of what was said by a mistress of the prisoner, she being in the habit of managing the shop, and the offence being larceny from the shop.

In the present case, the offence of the prisoner, in killing her child or concealing its dead body, was in no way an offence against the mistress of the house. She was not the prosecutrix then, and there was no probability of herself or the husband being the prosecutor of an indictment for that offence.

Conviction affirmed.

Holt J: I seem to recall that the person in authority need not actively initiate the threat or inducement. It is enough, is it not, if he is present when it is initiated, and does nothing to prevent or remove it?

Mr Atkyn: Your Lordship is quite right. Such a case was:

R v *Cleary* (1963) 48 Cr App R 116 (CCA)

The defendant, who was suspected of complicity in a murder was interviewed by police officers at a police station. During the interview the defendant's father arrived and after a conversation with his son he said to the defendant in the hearing of the police officers, 'Put your cards on the table. Tell them the lot. If you did not hit him, they cannot hang you.' The defendant subsequently made a statement to the police. The judge ruled that, as a matter of law, the father's words to the defendant could not amount to an inducement held out to him in the presence of a person in authority and that the statement was accordingly admissible. The defendant was convicted of manslaughter and appealed.

FINNEMORE J said: 'There are a number of cases on this matter which have been cited to us and which it is not necessary for us now to repeat. Suffice it to say this: first of all, the cases have gone a very long way in favour of the accused person and in favour of excluding a confession. There are cases very near the line on both sides. In view of the course which this case took, it seems unnecessary now to review those or to go through them in detail, though the court has had them drawn to their attention. What is plain is this, that any kind of inducement made by a person in authority will make the statement inadmissible. It has also been decided that, though the inducement be made by a person not in authority, if in fact it is made in the presence of persons in authority, the position is the same as if they had made it themselves unless they take steps to dissent from it.

In this case there is no doubt at all what was said by the father was in the presence of the two chief inspectors, who heard what was said. The inducement must, of course, act on the mind of the person who thereupon makes a statement, and it is to be noted here it was after this had been said by the father that the appellant said: "I will now make a statement."

The question is: was there an inducement? There is nothing wrong in a person saying to an accused person: "Tell the truth." Several cases were cited to us, in one of which [Reeves and Handcock (1872) LR ICCR 362] a mother had said to her two sons in the presence of a police officer "Now be good boys and tell the truth." That was held to be admissible. There are other cases very near the line where the alleged inducement was a phrase such as "You had better tell the truth," or "It will be better for you to tell the truth" where the inducement had been held to render a confession inadmissible as not being free and voluntary.

Two questions really arise in this case: first, are these words in law capable of being an inducement? Secondly, were they in fact an inducement and did the accused person, the present appellant, feel moved by them to make his statement, always remembering it is for the prosecution to prove that they were not affecting him? Indeed the onus of proof is on the prosecution all the way through. It would appear from the extracts that we have had read to us that the learned judge at the trial decided that these words were not capable of being an inducement, that they did not go past an exhortation to tell the truth. "I may be right or I may be wrong" the learned judge said in the discussion, "It seems to me what I have to decide is whether this goes beyond a mere exhortation to tell the truth." Then he said, after further argument, "I content myself by saying this evidence is admissible."

It seems to this Court that the learned judge decided as a matter of law that these words could not be an inducement. We have formed the view that, whatever precise meaning may be given to the words: "Put your cards on the table. Tell them the lot. If you did not hit him, they cannot hang you" — and different people can perhaps give different meanings — they are at least capable of being an inducement. It may well be that it was in the appellant's mind, knowing that two persons with whom he had been had already been charged with capital murder that he might find himself charged with capital murder and perhaps convicted of it and hanged. In that case the father's remark could be an inducement to him to make a statement in the belief, on what his father said, that, if he did make a statement, his chances of not being hanged would be better.

What we have to decide is whether the words were capable of being an inducement. In the view of this court, they were capable. It would then be for the jury to decide whether in fact there was an inducement, and whether in fact the prosecution had proved that the appellant was not affected by the inducement. Quite properly, if one may say so, the learned trial judge, having made a decision in law, did not direct the jury about that matter. All he said was "Members of the jury, here is the statement made. If you think this statement was made" — it must not be forgotten the appellant denied that he made the incriminating statement — "and made voluntarily, what do you make of it?" There should have been then a careful and full direction what, on another view of the matter, was a quite difficult question to determine, and no direction of any kind other than the words I have read was in fact given to the jury. The question whether in fact the prosecution had shown that the appellant was not affected by the inducement, if the jury found that there had been an inducement, was not dealt with at all. Conviction quashed.

Holt J: Yes, I am grateful for that exposition. Mr Bunbury?

Mr Bunbury: My Lord, I do not dispute this point.

7.7 Argument: Voluntariness and absence of oppression

(Mr Atkyn then directed the attention of Holt J to the evidence given by Coke on the voir dire.)

Mr Atkyn: If Your Lordship accepts that evidence, or even concludes that it may be right, then the confessions were involuntary, and were obtained by oppression. These are concepts which go back to:

R v *Thompson* [1893] 2 QB 12 (CCR)

The defendant was tried for embezzling the money of a company. It was proved that, on being taxed with the crime by the chairman of the company, he said, 'Yes, I took the money.' He afterwards made out a list of the sums which he had embezzled, and repaid to the company a part of the sums. The chairman stated that at the time of the confession no threat was used and no promise made as regards the prosecution of the defendant, but admitted that, before receiving it, he had said to the defendant's brother, 'It will be the right thing for your brother to make a statement.' The defendant, when he made the confession, knew that the chairman had spoken these words to his brother.

CAVE J said: 'To be admissible, a confession must be free and voluntary. If it proceeds from remorse and a desire to make reparation for the crime, it is admissible. If it flows from hope or fear, excited by a person in authority, it is inadmissible. On this point the authorities are unanimous. As Mr Taylor says in his Law of Evidence (8th ed Part 2, ch 15, s.872), "Before any confession can be received in evidence in a criminal case, it must be shewn to have been voluntarily made; for, to adopt the somewhat inflated language of Eyre, CB, 'a confession forced from the mind by the flattery of hope, or by the torture of fear, comes in so questionable a shape, when it is to be considered as the evidence of guilt, that no credit ought to be given to it, and, therefore, it is rejected:" *Warickshall's Case.'*
(LORD COLERIDGE CJ, HAWKINS, DAY and WILLS JJ concurred.)
Conviction quashed.

Holt J: It seems that either a threat or inducement may lead a particular defendant to make a confession. That is the effect of the rule, is it not?
Mr Atkyn: My Lord, it is. Either may render a confession involuntary. The principle is clearly stated in:

Ibrahim v *R* [1914] AC 599 (PC)

The appellant a serving soldier, was charged with murder. Evidence from his commanding officer was admitted that shortly after the murder he said to the appellant, who was then in custody, 'Why have you done such a senseless act?' to which the appellant replied, 'Some three or four days he has been abusing me; without a doubt I killed him.' There was a body of other evidence which clearly established the guilt of the appellant. He was convicted and appealed by special leave to the Privy Council.

LORD SUMNER, delivering the judgment of their Lordships, said: 'It has long been established as a positive rule of English criminal law, that no statement by an accused is admissible in evidence against him unless it is shewn by the prosecution to have been a voluntary statement, in the sense that it has not been obtained from him either by fear of prejudice or hope of advantage exercised or held out by a person in authority. The principle is as old as Lord Hale. The burden of proof in the matter has been decided by high authority in recent times in *R* v *Thompson* [1893] 2 QB 12, a case which, it is important to observe, was considered by the trial judge before he admitted the evidence. There was, in the present case, Major Barrett's affirmative evidence that the prisoner was not subjected to the pressure of either fear or hope in the sense mentioned. There was no evidence to the contrary. With *R* v *Thompson* before him, the learned judge must be taken to have been satisfied with the prosecution's evidence that the prisoner's statement was not so induced either by hope or fear, and, as is laid down in the same case, the decision of this question, albeit one of fact, rests with the trial judge. Their Lordships are clearly of opinion that the admission of this evidence was no breach of the aforesaid rule.'
Appeal dismissed.

I would also refer Your Lordship to *DPP* v *Ping Lin*, where the House of Lords examined in detail the law relating to the admissibility of confessions.

DPP v *Ping Lin* [1976] AC 574 (HL)

The appellant was convicted of conspiracy to contravene the Misuse of Drugs Act 1971. He was discovered by police officers smoking heroin in his flat, and substantial quantities of the drug were found there. The appellant, when questioned, maintained that he was user of, but not a dealer in, the drug, and offered to help the police to find those higher up in the chain of supply, in return for being 'let out' or helped by the police. The officer conducting the interview refused to make any such agreement, but on one occasion added, 'If you show the judge that you have helped the police to trace bigger drug people, I am sure he will bear it in mind when he sentences you.' The appellant then disclosed the name of his supplier.

LORD MORRIS OF BORTH-Y-GEST said: 'My Lords, in the judgment of the Privy Council (delivered by Lord Sumner) in *Ibrahim* v *The King* [1914] AC 599, it was said that it had long been established as a positive rule of English criminal law that no statement by an accused is admissible in evidence against him unless it is shown by the prosecution to have been a voluntary statement. If an objection is made to the admission of evidence as to a statement made by an accused it will be for the judge to decide as to its admissibility. He will generally, in the absence of the jury, have to hear the testimony of witnesses in regard to the impugned evidence and in regard to the relevant surrounding circumstances. He will then decide whether the prosecution have shown that the statement was a voluntary statement. Lord Sumner explained or illustrated what he meant by a voluntary statement. He meant a voluntary statement "in the sense" that it had not been obtained either by fear of prejudice or hope of advantage, the fear being as he put it "exercised" by or the hope being "held out" by someone whom he described as a person in authority. No occasion arises in the present case to consider the meaning or the significance of the phrase "person in authority." The police officers in the present case were clearly within the designation of persons whom Lord Sumner had in mind.

The guidance given by Lord Sumner's words is in my view clear. From them the sense and the spirit of the rule can be readily comprehended. Particular words are merely the instruments chosen to convey meaning. For this purpose words are but servants. If by their use a clear meaning has been conveyed then their purpose has been achieved.

In the circumstances posed a judge must decide whether the prosecution have shown that a statement was voluntary. His decision will generally be one of fact. He may perhaps in some cases before giving his decision derive help from a consideration or perusal of reported decisions but he will always remember that most of these reported decisions merely record what the ruling of another judge has been in another case and in the particular circumstances of that case and on the basis of its own particular facts. He will always remember also that considerations of space may often make it difficult to record in a report all the relevant circumstances and facts. A judge will often have to rule at times and in places which do not readily make it possible to consult copious authorities. This will be no disadvantage. What is a clear and straightforward rule need not be obscured by subtleties and complications. The rule is one which in a fair-minded way can readily be applied by a judge once he has clearly ascertained the facts.

The task of the judge will be to apply the spirit and intendment of the rule. Without being anchored to any particular words he will consider whether the statement of an accused was brought about by some hope or fear held out or caused by someone who could be classed as a person in authority. The judge will be ruling on admissibility and not (primarily at all events) on any question as to the propriety of the conduct of someone who conducted an interview or asked questions or as to the propriety or impropriety of something said or done. The judge will be ascertaining the facts as to what was said in an interview and not (primarily at all events) inquiring as to the motives or intentions of the person or persons who conducted an interview.

In my view it is not necessary, before a statement is held to be inadmissible because not shown to have been voluntary, that it should be thought or held that there was impropriety in the conduct of the person to whom the statement was made. Whether there was or whether there was not, what has to be considered is whether a statement is shown to have been voluntary rather than one brought about in one of the ways referred to. To this extent I would with respect diverge from what was said in *R* v *Isequilla* [1975] 1 WLR 716 though I consider that the decision in that case was entirely correct. The certified point of law poses therefore first a question as to which of two stated tests of admissibility is correct.

One stated alternative test is phrased as being whether what was said was capable of being an inducement and may on the evidence have been so regarded by the accused. The test is in my view much simpler than that. In considering whether the statement of an accused was brought about by hope or fear the judge will have to ascertain all the facts concerning the alleged and so-called "inducement." If it is said to have consisted in something said by a person conducting an interview then the facts must be ascertained as to what was said and as to what were the circumstances. Then what was said must be considered in a common sense way in the light of all the circumstances: and what was said must be given in a common sense way the meaning which it would rationally be understood to have by the person to whom it was said.

The other stated alternative test itself introduces an alternative and is phrased as being whether the Crown have proved that what was said by the person in authority either was not an "inducement" or was not intended by him to be one (he being guilty of no other relevant impropriety). Again the test is in my view much simpler. The test is simply whether the Crown have proved that a statement made by an accused was voluntary in the sense that it was not obtained from him either because some person in authority "exercised" fear or prejudice or "held out" hope of advantage. Stated otherwise, was it as a result of something said or done by a person in authority that an accused was caused or led to make a statement: did he make it because he was caused to fear that he would be prejudiced if he did not or because he was caused to hope that he would have advantage if he did. The prosecution must show that the statement did not owe its origin to such a cause.

As the rule of the criminal law was recognised as long ago as in 1914 as then being a long established "positive" rule I see no necessity to re-examine or to consider the reasons which have been assigned as its justification or its basis (as to this see the speech of Lord Reid in *R v Harz; R v Power* [1967] 1 AC 760, 820). The rule is clearly established. Though it was established in days long before an accused person could give evidence himself and in days when accused or convicted persons lacked many protections now available to them I do not think that a reconsideration or modification of the rule lies within the province of judicial decision.

Accepting that on its facts the case was perhaps near the boundary line I have not been persuaded either that the ruling of the learned judge or the conclusion of the Court of Appeal was wrong, or was based upon any wrong application of principle. I would therefore dismiss the appeal.'

LORD HAILSHAM OF ST. MARYLEBONE said: 'The evidence against the appellant, if, as happened, it was admitted and believed, was overwhelming and compelling. Its reliability was not challenged before your Lordships. The question raised was as to the admissibility of a significant part of it, and this in turn depends upon the application of the well known rule, peculiar to English law and its derivative systems, that to be admissible, confessions, however convincing, must be voluntary in the sense that the prosecution must prove, and prove beyond reasonable doubt, in the classical words of Lord Sumner in *Ibrahim v The King* [1914] AC 599, 609:

that it has not been obtained from him either by fear of prejudice or hope of advantage exercised (sic) or held out by a person in authority.

In passing, I must say that the word "exercised" in the above quotation though repeatedly reproduced, is, I believe, meaningless and corrupt in the report. I believe that Lord Sumner really said "excited" and that he was quoting from the almost equally well known and authoritative judgment of Cave J in *R v Thompson* [1893] 2 QB 12, 15. However that may be, the sense is obvious and unaffected.

But, on the subject of confessions, English law is not wholly rational. It is subject to the general rule, described by Lord Sumner as a "rule of policy" to which I have already referred, viz that, before a confession is to be admitted in evidence, it must be proved by the prosecution beyond reasonable doubt, "as a fundamental condition of its admissibility" that it is "voluntary in the sense that it has not been obtained by fear of prejudice or hope of advantage excited" (if I am right in my emendation) "or held out by a person in authority." The appellant's contention was, and is, that his confession was inadmissible on the basis that it was induced by a hope of advantage in that he had been led to believe that, if he led the police to find his supplier, the judge would bear it in mind deciding his sentence. Quite obviously, perverse and unacceptable as such a result would be, it is a contention which must be examined seriously in the light of the rule, and, if, on the above facts, it is found to be correct, effect must be given to it by your Lordships' House, unless it were prepared to overrule a line of authorities going back to the later half of the eighteenth century (cf *R* v *Rudd* (1775) 1 Leach 115, *R* v *Warickshall* (1783) 1 Leach 263, *R* v *Cass* (1784) 1 Leach 293, Note (a) recognised by the Privy Council in *Ibrahim* [1914] AC 599, and by your Lordships' House in *R* v *Harz; R* v *Power* [1967] 1 AC 760, 818, 821, and in numberless other cases in this country and the Commonwealth.

To my mind, the rule itself, though it has been repeatedly criticised (eg by Parke B, and Lord Campbell CJ in *R* v *Baldry* (1852) 2 Den 430 and *R* v *Scott* (1856) Dears & B 47 and perhaps by Lord Sumner in *Ibrahim*, and, more mildly, by Lord Reid in *Harz and Power*), is far too firmly established to be modified except by the legislature. By the judiciary, though it ought not to be extended, it must by no means be whittled down. It bears, it is true, all the marks of its origin at a time when the savage code of the eighteenth century was in full force. At that time almost every serious crime was punishable by death or transportation. The law enforcement officers formed no disciplined police force and were not subject to effective control by the central government watch committees or an inspectorate. There was no legal aid. There was no system of appeal. To crown it all the accused was unable to give evidence on his own behalf and was therefore largely at the mercy of any evidence, either perjured or oppressively obtained, that might be brought against him. The judiciary were therefore compelled to devise artificial rules designed to protect him against dangers now avoided by other and more rational means. Nevertheless, the rule has survived into the twentieth century, not only unmodified but developed, and only Parliament can modify it now from the form in which it was given classical expression by Lord Sumner.

I cannot myself help regarding the issue as basically one of fact. The trial judge should approach his task by applying the test enunciated by Lord Sumner in a common sense way to all the facts in the case in their context much as a jury would approach it if the task had fallen to them. In the light of all the facts in their context, he should ask himself this question, and no other:

> Have the prosecution proved that the contested statement was voluntary in the sense that it was not obtained by fear of prejudice or hope of advantage excited or held out by a person in authority (or, where it is relevant, as is not the case on appeal here), by oppression?

LORD SALMON said: 'The law relating to the admissibility in evidence of an alleged confession or statement by an accused is plain and simple. It has been clearly stated by many eminent judges and never doubted.

> By [the law of England], to be admissible, a confession must be free and voluntary... If it flows from hope or fear, excited by a person in authority, it is inadmissible." *R* v *Thompson* [1893] 2 QB 12 per Cave J at p 15.

The Rule laid down in *Russell on Crimes and Misdemeanours,* 5th ed, vol 3, pp 441, 442 is, that a confession, in order to be admissible, must be free and voluntary: that is, must not be extracted by any sort of threats or violence, nor obtained by any direct or implied promises, however slight, nor by the exertion of any improper influence. *R* v *Fennell* (1881) 7 QBD 147 per Lord Coleridge CJ at p 150.

It was re-stated in the celebrated judgment of Lord Sumner in *Ibrahim* v *The King* [1914] AC 599, 609:

> It has long been established as a positive rule of English criminal law, that no statement by an accused is admissible in evidence against him unless it is shown by the prosecution to have been a voluntary statement, in the sense that it has not been obtained from him either by fear of prejudice or hope of advantage exercised or held out by a person in authority.

This simple principle was affirmed in your Lordships' House in *R* v *Harz; R* v *Power* [1967] 1 AC 760.

It follows that a judge may allow evidence of an alleged confession or statement by an accused to go before the jury only if he is satisfied that the confession or statement has not been obtained in contravention of the principle laid down in the authorities to which I have referred. This is because of the risk that, unless the judge is so satisfied, to allow evidence of an alleged confession or statement to go before the jury might seriously prejudice the accused. Hence "the trial within a trial." The judge's decision is, in reality, a decision on the facts. He has to weigh up the evidence and decide whether he is satisfied that no person in authority has obtained the confession or statement, directly or indirectly, by engendering fear in the accused that he will be worse off if he makes no confession or statement or by exciting hope in the accused that he will be better off if he does make a confession or statement. If the judge is so satisfied, he may admit evidence of the confession or statement. If he is not so satisfied he must exclude it.

Unfortunately, there are far too many reported cases concerning appeals against decisions allowing evidence of confessions or statements to go before a jury. A whole body of case law seems to have been conjured up out of what are essentially decisions on questions of fact. This has, I fear, led to a geat deal of unnecessary confusion and complication in a branch of the law which is essentially clear and simple. I entirely agree with my noble and learned friend Lord Kilbrandon that in deciding whether an alleged confession or statement was free and voluntary and should be admitted in evidence, it is useless, just as it is in an accident case, to search for another case in which the facts seem to be similar and treat it as binding. Facts vary infinitely from case to case. The judge's task is to consider the evidence before him, to assess its implications and to decide the case on his view of that evidence in the light of the basic established principle.

The somewhat pedantic approach which seems to have been adopted in some of the cases to which we have been referred should be avoided. These cases are of doubtful validity and of little, if any, value. The Court of Appeal should not disturb the judge's findings merely because of difficulties in reconciling them with different findings of fact, on apparently similar evidence, in other reported cases, but only if it is completely satisfied that the judge made a wrong assessment of the evidence before him or failed to apply the correct principle — always remembering that usually the trial judge has better opportunities of assessing the evidence than those enjoyed by an appellate tribunal.

In the context of the question raised by this appeal it is difficult to understand the relevance of the references to impropriety in some of the cases to which we have been referred. No doubt, for anyone to obtain a confession or statement in breach of the established rule is ex hypothesi improper. Indeed, it is impossible to imagine how the rule could be breached with propriety. It would seem, therefore, that the references to impropriety add nothing. They may, however, have been intended to cover instances in which a person in authority has obtained a confession by subjecting an accused to inhuman treatment; but, in my view, the rule as stated by Lord Sumner already covers such cases. In any event, no authority can be needed for the self-evident proposition that a confession or statement so obtained could not be voluntary.

In my opinion, the intention of a person in authority who makes a threat or a promise or offers any inducement prior to an accused making a confession or statement is irrelevant. So is the fact that the threat is gentle or the promise or inducement slight save in so far as this may throw any light on the vital question — was the confession or statement procured by the express or implicit threat, promise or inducement.

The question as to whether the rule laid down in *Reg* v *Thompson* [1893] 2 QB 12, *Reg* v *Fennell,* 7 QBD 147 and *Ibrahim* v *The King* [1914] AC 599 is based on "the reliability principle" or "the disciplinary principle" (referred to in the Eleventh Report of the Criminal Law Revision Committee (1972) Cmnd 4991, para 56) is possibly an important philosophical question but for present purposes it is only of academic interest. It does not touch the effect or undoubted validity of the rule. No doubt it may be germane to any consideration as to whether the rule should be abolished by legislation — a matter with which your Lordships cannot be concerned when sitting in your judicial capacity. By some, the rule may be regarded as irrational; by others as salutory and indeed essential.

(LORD WILBERFORCE agreed LORD KILBRANDON delivered a concurring judgment.)
Appeal dismissed.

Holt J: The defendant Coke gave evidence that threats were made to him relating to a possible further charge, rather than to the actual charge of rape about which he was being question. How does that affect the matter?

Mr Atkyn: My Lord, it is the effect produced on the defendant's mind that is important, and not the precise nature of the threat or inducement. If Your Lordship would look at what was said in:

Commissioners of Customs and Excise v Harz and Another [1967] 1 AC 760 (HL)

The defendants were charged with conspiracy to cheat and defraud the Commissioners of purchase tax. At interviews with the defendants, customs officers told them that they would be prosecuted for breach of a statutory obligation to speak. No such obligation existed. As a result the defendants made confessions. The confessions were admitted by the trial judge and the defendants were convicted. The Court of Criminal Appeal quashed the convictions and the Commissioners appealed to the House of Lords.

LORD REID said: 'It is said if the threat or promise which induced the statement related to the charge or contemplated charge against the accused, the statement is not admissible; but that if it related to something else, the statement is admissible. This distinction does appear in some, but by no means all, modern textbooks and it has a very curious history. There is no mention of it in the earlier works of authority — Hale, Pleas of the Crown, Chap 38; Hawkins, Pleas of the Crown, Chap 46; East, Pleas of the Crown, Chap 16. Apparently it first appears in the 1840s. Joy states (Confessions (1842), p 13):

> But the threat or inducement held out must have reference *to the prisoner's escape from the charge,* and be such as would lead him to suppose, it will be better for him to admit himself to be guilty of an offence, which he never committed.

And Taylor (Evidence, 1st ed (1848), p 592) says:

> We come now to the nature of the inducement: and here it may be laid down as a general rule that in order to exclude a confession, the inducement whether it be in the shape of a promise, a threat, or mere advice must have reference to the prisoner's escape from the criminal charge against him....

There appears to have been no judicial consideration of this "rule" for more than a century after it was first formulated. But in *R* v *Joyce* [1958] 1 WLR 140. Slade J based his judgment on the rule as stated in Kenny (see Kenny's Criminal Law, 19th ed (1966), p 531). I doubt whether he need have done. The constable had only said: "I need to take a statement from you." Unless he misled the man into thinking that he would bound to make a statement and would suffer in some way if he refused, I would not regard that as involving any threat or inducement at all. The only case in the Court of Criminal Appeal brought to our notice was *R* v *Shuter* (1965) *The Times* 27 November p 12. There Fenton Atkinson J said: "In our view inducement will not vitiate a confession when the proffered benefit has no bearing on the course of the prosecution and on this point the textbook writers speak with one voice." Research in preparing the present case shows that there are notable exceptions. Then he quoted Kenny and other textbooks, *Lloyd* 6 C&P 393, and *Joyce* [1958] 1 WLR 140, being the only decided cases which he cited. And then he said: "That principle must have been acted upon times without number for very many years past." I would venture to doubt that. Appeal has been easy for nearly 60 years, and, unless counsel have been very much less astute that I would suppose, I can scarcely think that many opportunities to appeal on this matter can have been missed.

One suggested justification of this rule appears to be that the tendency to exclude confessions which followed on some vague threat or inducement had been carried much too far and that the formula set out in many textbooks affords a useful and time-honoured way of limiting this tendency. But the common law should proceed by the rational development of principles and not by the elaboration of rules or formulae. I do not think that it is possible to reconcile all the very numerous judicial statements on rejection of confessions but two lines of thought appear to underlie them: first, that a statement made in response to a threat or promise may be untrue or at least untrustworthy: and, secondly, that nemo tenetur se ipsum prodere. It is true that many of the so-called inducements have been so vague that no reasonable man would have been influenced by them, but one must remember that not all accused are reasonable men or women: they may be very ignorant and terrified by the predicament in which they find themselves. So it may have been right to err on the safe side. But if the tendency to reject confessions is thought to have been carried too far, it cannot be proper to try to redress the balance by engrafting on the general principle an illogical exception, which at best can only operate sporadically, leaving the mischief untouched in the great majority of cases.

That the alleged rule or forumula is illogical and unreasonable I have no doubt. Suppose that a daughter is accused of shop-lifting and later her mother is detected in a similar offence, perhaps at a different branch, where the mother is brought before the manager of the shop. He might induce her to confess by telling her that she must tell him the truth and it will be worse for her if she does not: or the inducement might be that if she will tell the truth he will drop proceedings against the daughter. Obviously the latter would in most cases be far the more powerful inducement and far the more likely to lead to an untrue confession. But if this rule were right the former inducement would make the confession inadmissible but the latter would not. The law of England cannot be so ridiculous as that.

In *R* v *Smith* [1959] 2 QB 35 a soldier was accused of murder during a barrack room fight. Soon after the fight the sergeant-major put his company on parade and said that they would be kept there until he learned who was responsible. After a time Smith confessed. The inducement clearly was that, if the culprit confessed, his comrades would be released. It had nothing to do with any impending charge. But it was held sufficient to make the confession inadmissible. Lord Parker CJ said [1959] 2 QB 35, 39:

> It has always been a fundamental principle of the courts, and something quite apart from the Judges' Rules of Practice, that a prisoner's confession outside the court is only admissible if it is voluntary. In deciding whether an admission is voluntary the court has been at pains to hold that even the most gentle, if I may put it that way, threats or slight inducements will taint a confession.

This case must have been wrongly decided if the alleged rule exists.

In the well-known statement of the general principle by Lord Sumner in *Ibrahim* v *The King* [1914] AC 500 this rule is omitted. And, perhaps more important, it is omitted from the passage from the Judges' Rules whioh I have already quoted. I do not think that these omissions are likely to have been due to mere oversight. So I come without hesitation to the conclusion that this alleged rule should not be adopted; indeed that it never has been part of the law of England.

(LORDS MORRIS of BORTH-Y-GEST, HODSON, PEARCE, and WILBERFORCE agreed.)

Appeal dismissed.

Indeed, My Lord, the proposition that the categories are not closed is firmly established. I would also refer to:

R v *Middleton* [1975] QB 191 (CA)

The defendant was told by a police officer that, unless he made a statement, it would be necessary to detain the woman in whose house he had sought to store stolen goods and to have her children put in care. He subsequently confessed. The recorder ruled that the confession was admissible because the alleged threat was not directed to the defendant personally or to any member of his family circle or to any intimate of his. The defendant was convicted of handling the goods and appealed.

EDMUND DAVIES LJ, giving the judgment of the court, said: 'The question that arises in this appeal is whether there is any authority for the proposition that the inducement or threat is relevant only if it impinges upon the small circle embracing the alleged offender and members of his family and possibily his very close intimates. Mr Mundy has frankly told the court today he can cite no authority for having so submitted below. We have to ask ourselves accordingly — Is it the law? Each member of this court (who, if we may say so, combine between us an extremely long experience of the criminal law and practice) does not so regard it. We do not think it accords with our own experience, nor do we think it accords with our principle, for underlying the basic rules about the admissibility of confessions is the need for fairness to an accused person.

The courts reprehend the resorting to threats or inducements in order to extort a confession. But if such extortion is used, what does it matter to whom the inducement or the threat relates? As a matter of common sense, of course, the more remote the person involved in the threat is from the person or close circle of the accused man the more difficult it may be to establish that the confession was improperly obtained; but that is a consideration which goes to the weight of the evidence that a threat was made and not to the admissibility of a confession if the threat was, in fact, established. To take a possibly absurd and far-fetched example, if a person suspected of a crime is told that someone who is a stranger to him will be grievously harmed unless he "comes clean" and makes a confession and he accordingly complies, is it the law that in those circumstances the admissibility of the confession is unimpaired? In a civilised country we think that question has only to be asked to answer itself. In our judgment it demands a negative answer.

The law, as we understand it, is not confined in the way submitted to and accepted by the recorder. The categories of inducement are not closed.

Appeal allowed.

Holt J: You have also referred to oppressive circumstances, and the defendant Coke has described, in his own words, the effect of what he says occurred as having 'taken all the wind out of my sails', which I suppose means that he felt somehow compelled to confess. Is that what you referred to?

Mr Atkyn: My Lord, precisely so. The term has been defined by Court of Appeal in:

R v Prager [1972] 1 WLR 260 (CA)

Police officers arrived at the defendant's home with a search warrant issued under s.9 of the Official Secrets Act 1911 and told him that they wanted to question him. They began to question him at 9.15 am but gave him no caution. The questioning continued until 12.30 pm and then from 5.40 pm to 7.40 pm. He was then cautioned and thereafter made oral admissions. He was further cautioned at 9.50 pm and he made a written confession. The defendant applied for leave to appeal against his conviction on the ground that the questioning amounted to oppression.

EDMUND DAVIES LJ, reading the judgment of the court, said: 'Was the voluntary nature of the alleged oral and written confessions established? In *R v Harz; R v Power* [1967] 1 AC 760, 818, Lord Reid, in a speech with which all the other Law Lords agreed, treated the test laid down in note (e) in the introduction to the Judges' Rules as a correct statement of the law. As we have already indicated, the criticism directed in the present case against the police is that their interrogation constituted "oppression." This word appeared for the first time in the Judges' Rules 1964, and it closely followed the observation of Lord Park CJ in *Callis* v *Gunn* [1961] 1 QB 495, 501, condemning confessions "obtained in an oppressive manner."

The only reported judicial consideration of "oppression" in the Judges' Rules of which we are aware is that of Sachs J in *R v Priestly* (1967) 51 Cr App R 1, where he said:

> ...to my mind, this word, in the context of the principles under consideration imports something which tends to sap, and has sapped, that free will which must exist before a confession is voluntary....Whether or not there is oppression in an individual case

depends upon many elements. I am not going into all of them. They include such things as the length of time of any individual period of questioning, the length of time intervening between periods of questioning, whether the accused person had been given proper refreshment or not, and the characteristics of the person who makes the statement. What may be oppressive as regards a child, an invalid or an old man or somebody inexperienced in the ways of this world may turn out not to be oppressive when one finds that the accused person is of a tough character and an experienced man of the world.

In an address to the Bentham Club in 1968, Lord MacDermott described "oppressive questioning" as

questioning which by its nature, duration, or other attendant circumstances (including the fact of custody) excites hopes (such as the hope of release) or fears, or so affects the mind of the subject that his will crumbles and he speaks when otherwise he would have stayed silent.

We adopt these definitions or descriptions and apply them to the present case. Application dismissed.

Holt J: Mr Bunbury, Mr Atkyn submits that you must prove beyond reasonable doubt that these confessions, oral and written, were given voluntarily, and without oppression. What do you say?

Mr Bunbury: My Lord, I accept that as a matter of law, but I say that the evidence has proved those facts.

(Mr Bunbury reminded Holt J of the evidence of the police officers.)

Mr Bunbury: My Lord, in addition, even if Your Lordship found some degree of impropriety, the question is, what effect did that actually have on Coke? He is a man with a previous conviction, who has been to police stations before. He does not appear noticeably nervous or hesitant. It may well be that any small suggestion of fear, if there was any, was removed before Coke made his written statement under caution. This would liken the case to:

R v *Smith* [1959] 2 QB 35 (CMAC)

The appellant, a private soldier, was convicted of the murder of another soldier. Immediately after the fight the appellant's regimental sergeant-major put his company on parade and indicated that the men would be kept there until a confession was forthcoming. At the trial the judge-advocate admitted in evidence a statement made by the appellant to the sergeant-major at the parade confessing to the killing. Evidence was also given of a confession the following day to an investigating officer.

LORD PARKER CJ, giving the judgment of the court, said: 'The court thinks that the principle to be deduced from the cases is really this: that if the threat or promise under which the first statement was made still persists when the second statement is made, then it is inadmissible. Only if the time-limit between the two statements, the circumstances existing at the time and the caution are such that it can be said that the original threat or inducement has been dissipated can the second statement be admitted as a voluntary statement.

In the present case the judge-advocate had to consider or rule on this second statement. Having admitted the first statement, there was no question on that basis but that the second statement must be also admissible. Accordingly, he never had to rule on the question of admissibility. He never had to exercise any discretion in the matter, and there was no occasion for his leaving it to the court as to the value or weight to be attached to the confession. This court, however, is of the clear opinion that the second statement was admissible.'

Appeal dismissed.

Mr Atkyn: There is no evidence here that any threat was removed.
(Holt J indicated that he was persuaded that the confessions were admissible in law.)

7.8 Argument: Discretion and the Judges' Rules

Mr Atkyn: In those circumstances, My Lord, I wish to submit that this would be a proper case for the exercise of Your Lordship's discretion to exclude confessions, notwithstanding that they may be technically admissible. I rely on the evidence of the defendant Coke to show that there were breaches of the Judges' Rules.

Holt J: That is something which I can consider, of course, but it goes only to my discretion, as you rightly say. I think Lord Goddard CJ made that clear in *R v May* (1952) 36 Cr App R 91 (CCA), when he said:

> The test of the admissibility of a statement is whether it is a voluntary statement. There are certain rules known as the Judges' Rules which are not rules of law but rules of practice drawn up for the guidance of police officers; and if a statement has been made in circumstances not in accordance with the Rules, in law that statement is not made inadmissible if it is a voluntary statement, although in its discretion the court can always refuse to admit it if the court thinks there has been a breach of the Rules.

Mr Atkyn: My Lord, yes. Indeed the Court of Appeal have re-affirmed that point more recently in *R v Prager:*

R v Prager [1972] 1 WLR 260 (CA) (For facts see 7.7 ante)

EDMUND DAVIES LJ, said: 'As the Rules of 1964 make clear, they were 'put forward as a guide to police officers conducting investigations. Non-conformity with these rules may render answers and statements liable to be excluded from evidence in subsequent criminal proceedings. Nevertheless, Mr Comyn insisted that the admissibility of an alleged confession must, in the first place (and, he seemed to be saying, in the last place also) depend upon whether the Rules have been complied with...

Mr Comyn submitted before us that it was imperative that Lord Widgery CJ decided first whether rule II had or had not been breached, for, if it had been, the confession should not have been admitted unless there emerged "some compelling reason why the breach should have been overlooked." He cited no authority for that proposition, which, he claimed, involved a point of law of very great importance. This "complex lack of authority" (to use Mr Comyn's phrase) is not surprising, for in our judgment, the proposition advanced involves no point of law and is manifestly unsound. Its acceptance would exalt the Judges' Rules into rules of law. That they do not purport to be, and there is abundant authority for saying that they are nothing of the kind. Their non-observance may, and at times does, lead to the exclusion of an alleged confession; but ultimately all turns on the judge's decision whether, breach or no breach, it has been shown to have been made voluntarily.'

Holt J: Well, let us look at the Rules. The introduction sets out some principles of law that are not affected by the Rules.

Practice Note (Judges' Rules) [1964] 1 WLR 152
INTRODUCTION
These Rules do not affect the principles
   (a)   That citizens have a duty to help a police officer to discover and apprehend offenders;
   (b)   That police officers, otherwise than by arrest, cannot compel any person against his will to come to or remain in any police station;
   (c)   That every person at any stage of an investigation should be able to communicate and

to consult privately with a solicitor. This is so even if he is in custody provided that in such a case no unreasonable delay or hindrance is caused to the processes of investigation or the administration of justice by his doing so;

(d)   That when a police officer who is making enquiries of any person about an offence has enough evidence to prefer a charge against that person for the offence, he should without delay cause that person to be charged or informed that he may be prosecuted for the offence;

(e)   That it is a fundamental condition of the admissibility in evidence against any person, equally of any oral answer given by that person to a question put by a police officer and of any statement made by that person, that it shall have been voluntary, in the sense that it has not been obtained from him by fear of prejudice or hope of advantage, exercised or held out by a person in authority, or by oppression.

The principle set out in paragraph (e) above is overriding and applicable in all cases. Within that principle the following Rules are put forward as a guide to police officers conducting investigations. Non-conformity with these Rules may render answers and statements liable to be excluded from evidence in subsequent criminal proceedings.

The last of these under (e) we have already considered, of course. Are any of the others relevant here?

Mr Atkyn: My Lord, the evidence of the defendant Coke suggested that there had been breaches of principles (b), (c) and (d). He told Your Lordship that he had not been arrested, that he had been denied access to his solicitor and that he was charged only the next morning, even though D/I Glanvil had sufficient evidence to justify a charge on the day of the arrest. The importance attached to these matters by the courts is shown by the case of:

R v *Lemsatef* [1977] 1 WLR 812 (CA)

The defendant was detained by officers of the Customs and Excise at about 12.40 am in connection with suspected drugs offences, and was interrogated until 4.20 am when he asked to see a solicitor, a request which was refused for reasons found by the court to be wholly inadequate. Although the defendant's wife later instructed a solicitor, the solicitor was not permitted by the officers to see the defendant until 6.18 pm that day, by which time the defendant had made both oral and written confessions. The trial judge, treating the question as one of discretion, since he found the confessions to be voluntary and therefore admissible in law, allowed them to go to the jury. The defendant was convicted and appealed.

LAWTON LJ, delivering the judgment of the court, said: 'The law is clear. Neither arrest nor detention can properly be carried out without the accused person being told the offence for which he is being arrested. There is no such offence as "helping police with their inquiries." This is a phrase which has crept into use, largely because of the need for the press to be careful about how they report what has happened when somebody has been arrested but not charged. If the idea is getting around amongst either Customs and Excise officers or police officers that they can arrest or detain people, as the case may be, for this particular purpose, the sooner they disabuse themselves of that idea, the better...

If detaining or arresting officers are going to refuse to allow solicitors to advise a man under detention or arrest, it is no use their mouthing the words of the Judges' Rules: they must be prepared, if asked, to justify what they are doing... This court wishes to stress that it is not a good reason for refusing to allow a suspect, under arrest or detention to see his solicitor, that he has not yet made any oral or written admission.
Appeal allowed on other grounds.

Holt J: I cannot say that I was impressed with Coke's evidence on those points. He admitted that he had never previously complained of being denied access to his solicitor. Let us come to the Rules themselves. Rule I

I.   When a police officer is trying to discover whether, or by whom, an offence has been committed he is entitled to question any person, whether suspected or not, from whom he thinks that useful information may be obtained. This is so whether or not the person in question has been taken into custody so long as he has not been charged with the offence or informed that he may be prosecuted for it.

Any complaint on that?
Mr Atkyn: No, My Lord.
Holt J: Rule II states:

II.   As soon as a police officer has evidence which would afford reasonable grounds for suspecting that a person has committed an offence, he shall caution that person or cause him to be cautioned before putting to him any questions, or further questions, relating to that offence.
The caution shall be in the following terms:

You are not obliged to say anything unless you wish to do so but what you say may be put into writing and given in evidence.

When after being cautioned a person is being questioned, or elects to make a statement, a record shall be kept of the time and place at which any such questioning or statement began and ended and of the persons present.

Mr Atkyn: My Lord, here I do have a complaint. Coke's evidence indicated a failure to caution at almost all stages. In my submission, a caution was required at the very outset, in view of the evidence available to the officers.
Holt J: According to the officers, that is what happened. There is a conflict of evidence, which I shall have to resolve. The cases seem to me to require a caution at the stage when some admissible evidence is available. I have in mind:

R v *Osbourne; R* v *Virtue* [1973] QB 678 (CA)

The defendants were arrested on suspicion of robbery, and were interrogated without caution. At the time of the interrogation, the officer had no admissible evidence against the defendants, but had reason to suspect their involvement in the robbery. Later, evidence was forthcoming when the defendants were identified on an identification parade. The defendants appealed against their conviction on the ground, *inter alia,* that evidence of the interrogation had been wrongly admitted because, in the absence of a caution, rule II of the Judges' Rules 1964 had not been complied with.

LAWTON LJ, giving the judgment of the court, said: 'It is important for the court to remind itself that the Judges' Rules are intended for the guidance of police officers. They have to comply with the rules. If a police officer looks at the rules and asks himself the question "What do they mean?" he would answer in the light of his own police experience. In police experience, evidence means information which can be put before a court.
There are other indications in the rules that that is the right way for them to be construed. The rules contemplate three stages in the investigations leaing up to somebody being brought before a court for a criminal offence. The first is the gathering of information, and that can be gathered from anybody, including persons in custody provided they have not been charged. At the gathering of information stage no caution of any kind need be administered. The final stage, the one contemplated by rule III of the Judges' Rules, is when the police officer has got enough (and I stress the word "enough") evidence to prefer a charge. That is clear from the introduction to the Judges' Rules which sets out the principle. But a police officer when carrying out an investigation meets a stage in between the mere gathering of information and the getting of enough evidence to prefer the charge. He reaches a stage where he has got the beginnings of evidence. It is at that stage that he must caution. In the judgment of this court,

he is not bound to caution until he has got some information which he can put before the court as the beginnings of a case.
Appeals dismissed.

Mr Atkyn: In my submission, the facts of this case dictated a caution at once, or almost at once. It is of course a matter for Your Lordship to accept or reject the officers' evidence that they did caution at the outset. If Coke is right, then there was a clear breach of Rule II in my submission.

Holt J: I think that is right. Have you any complaints about Rule III?

III.—(a) Where a person is charged with or informed that he may be prosecuted for an offence he shall be cautioned in the following terms:

Do you wish to say anything? You are not obliged to say anything unless you wish to do so but whatever you say will be taken down in writing and may be given in evidence.

(b) It is only in exceptional cases that questions relating to the offence should be put to the accused person after he has been charged or informed that he may be prosecuted. Such questions may be put where they are necessary for the purpose of preventing or minimising harm or loss to some other person or to the public or for clearing up an ambiguity in a previous answer or statement.
Before any such questions are put the accused should be cautioned in these terms:

I wish to put some questions to you about the offence with which you have been charged (or about the offence for which you may be prosecuted). You are not obliged to answer any of these questions, but if you do the questions and answers will be taken down in writing and may be given in evidence.

Any questions put and answers given relating to the offence must be contemporaneously recorded in full and the record signed by that person or if he refuses by the interrogating officer.

(c) When such a person is being questioned, or elects to make a statement, a record shall be kept of the time and place at which any questioning or statement began and ended and of the persons present.

Mr Atkyn: Again, My Lord, it is a matter for evidence. But if Coke's account of events be right, then he should have been cautioned at the time of charge.

Holt J: Yes, but he does not complain that he was interrogated subsequently. I think your only point would be if the officers had already made a decision to charge Coke, before interrogating him at the police station, and had informed him of their intention. Then you might bring the case within the rule laid down in:

Conway v Hotten [1976] 2 All ER 213 (DC)

The appellant was told that he would be charged with an offence relating to keys. He was put in a cell for 20 minutes to think about it. He was then questioned further about the offence, and he made certain admissions. It was contended at the appellant's trial, that those admissions should not be admissible in evidence, having been obtained in breach of Rule III of the Judges' Rules. The justices heard evidence of the admissions and convicted the appellant.

WATKINS J said: 'It is urged on us that since what was said here by the police officer was not, "you may be charged", but "you will be charged", that that is the same thing as saying that a charge had in fact been already preferred. Thus the same consequences should follow. Since this is not an exceptional case, that much, I think, must be conceded, the justices should have found that the police officers or officer were at any rate technically in breach of this particular rule.

In my view when a person is told that he will be charged he comes into the same category for the purpose of r.3(b) as a man finds himself in who has already been charged. But that does not mean that justices are by reason of a breach of one or even more than one of the rules bound to say that a statement before them is inadmissible. As is evident from what Lord Goddard CJ said, *R v May* (1952) 36 Cr App R 91, at 93, the justices taking account of all such matters are still enabled to reach a conclusion that a confession is admissible.

For these reasons I do not believe it possible to say that these justices, even if r.3 was broken or that what happened was an actual threat or was oppressive in any way, did not take account of these matters in reaching the conclusion they did on the question of admissibility.'

(KILNER BROWN J and LORD WIDGERY CJ agreed.)
Appeal dismissed.

Mr Bunbury: My Lord, may I just add that this is not a case to which the phrase 'informed that he might be prosecuted' applies, so as to preclude further questioning. The meaning of that phrase was explained in:

R v Collier and Stenning [1965] 1 WLR 1470 (CCA)

The defendants were arrested on suspicion of burglary and at the police station made damaging statements to the station sergeant. On appeal against conviction it was argued that the arrest was an intimation that they would be charged and so the statements were inadmissible under Rule III(a) of the Judges' Rules.

LORD PARKER CJ, giving the judgment of the court, stated the facts and continued: 'It was said...that in the circumstances of this case the arrest on suspicion of having committed an offence, a breaking and entering, was itself tantamount to informing the prisoners that they might be prosecuted for the offence. In the opinion of this court, however, those words "or informed that he may be prosecuted" are intended merely to cover a case where the suspect has not been arrested, and where, in the course of questioning, a time comes when the police contemplate that a summons may be issued. Those words have no application to such a case as this, where the suspect is arrested and may, on further consideration, be charged. In *R v Brackenbury* it was assumed without argument that these words did apply to such a case as this, but in the opinion of this court, they do not.'
Appeal dismissed.

Holt J: Yes. Mr Atkyn, have you any points on Rules IV, V and VI?

IV.   All written statements made after caution shall be taken in the following manner:
(a)   If a person says that he wants to make a statement he shall be told that it is intended to make a written record of what he says. He shall always be asked whether he wishes to write down himself what he wants to say; if he says that he cannot write or that he would like someone to write it for him, a police officer may offer to write the statement for him. If he accepts the offer the police officer shall, before starting, ask the person making the statement to sign, or make his mark to, the following:

I,..................., wish to make a statement. I want someone to write down what I say. I have been told that I need not say anything unless I wish to do so and that whatever I say may be given in evidence.

(b)   Any person writing his own statement shall be allowed to so so without any prompting as distinct from indicating to him what matters are material.
(c)   The person making the statement, if he is going to write it himself, shall be asked to write out and sign before writing what he wants to say, the following:

I make this statement of my own free will. I have been told that I need not say anything unless I wish to do so and that whatever I say may be given in evidence.

(d) Whenever a police officer writes the statement, he shall take down the exact words spoken by the person making the statement, without putting any questions other than such as may be needed to make the statement coherent, intelligible and relevant to the material matters: he shall not prompt him.

(e) When the writing of a statement by a police officer is finished the person making it shall be asked to read it and to make any corrections, alterations or additions he wishes. When he has finished reading it he shall be asked to write and sign or make his mark on the following certificate at the end of the statement:

I have read the above statement and I have been told that I can correct, alter or add anything I wish. This statement is true. I have made it of my own free will.

(f) If the person who has made a statement refuses to read it or to write the above mentioned certificate at the end of it or to sign it, the senior police officer present shall record on the statement itself and in the presence of the person making it, what has happened. If the person making the statement cannot read, or refuses to read it, the officer who has taken it down shall read it over to him and ask him whether he would like to·correct, alter or add anything and to put his signature or make his mark at the end. The police officer shall then certify on the statement itself what he has done.

V. If at any time after a person has been charged with, or has been informed that he may be prosecuted for an offence a police officer wishes to bring to the notice of that person any written statement made by another person who in respect of the same offence has also been charged or informed that he may be prosecuted, he shall hand to that person a true copy of such written statement, but nothing shall be said or done to invite any reply or comment. If that person says that he would like to make a statement in reply, or starts to say something, he shall at once be cautioned or further cautioned as prescribed by Rule III(a).

VI. Persons other than police officers charged with the duty of investigating offences or charging offenders shall, so far as may be practicable, comply with these rules.

Mr Atkyn: My Lord, just one.
(Mr Atkyn addresses Holt J on Coke's evidence of how the written statement was made, in the light of Rule IV.)

Holt J: I see no reason to exercise my discretion so as to exclude these confessions. I prefer the evidence of the officers, but in any case, I do not think that the breaches alleged would have justified exclusion in this case. Mr Atkyn, the confessions will go before the jury, but you may of course raise all these matters before them on the question of what weight should be accorded to them. And if new facts come to light, I can reconsider my ruling, in accordance with the decision in:

R v **Watson** [1980] 1 WLR 991 (CA)

The appellant challenged the admissibility of written statements made by him. At a 'trial within a trial' the judge ruled that the statements were voluntary and thus admissible. The judge later refused to reconsider his ruling in the light of subsequent evidence.

CUMMING-BRUCE LJ, reading the judgment of the court, said: 'In our view the judge was wrong to rule as he evidently did that he had no power to consider the relevance of evidence, given after the 'trial within a trial', upon the issue whether the written statements were not voluntary and therefore inadmissible. He should have allowed counsel to develop his submission and should have ruled upon its merits.

It is the duty of the judge to exclude from the jury's consideration evidence which is inadmissible. In the case of a written statement, made or signed by the accused, the judge must be satisfied that the prosecution have proved that the contested statement was voluntary, before allowing the jury to decide whether to act on it. Experience has shown that where the question of the voluntary character of a statement has been investigated and decided at a trial within a trial it is only in very rare and unusual cases that further evidence later emerges which may cause the judge to reconsider the question whether he is still satisfied that the statement was voluntary and admissible. But where there is such further evidence, the judge has power to consider the relevance of the admissibility of evidence upon which he has already ruled.'

Appeal dismissed on the facts.

7.9 Commentary

R v Coke and Littleton at trial. In the light of the above ruling, Mr Bacon makes an application to Holt J on behalf of Littleton.

7.10 Argument

Mr Bacon: My Lord, I am somewhat concerned about the written statement under caution made by Coke, which, in the light of Your Lordship's ruling, the prosecution now propose to place before the jury. That statement is, I accept, evidence against Coke. But it is not evidence against my client. Indeed, Your Lordship would no doubt direct the jury to that effect.

Holt J: If I did not, it would be a ground of appeal which would almost certainly succeed, as I understand it from the case of:

R v *Gunewardene* [1951] 2KB 600 (CCA)

The appellant was convicted of manslaughter together with one Hanson. At the trial, the prosecution put in a statement which Hanson had made to the police incriminating the appellant.

LORD GODDARD CJ, delivering the judgment of the court, said: 'We now turn to the second of the main questions argued on behalf of the appellant. As we have said, there is no doubt that the statement made by the prisoner Hanson incriminated the appellant in a high degree. This is a matter of very frequent occurrence where two or more prisoners are charged with complicity in the same offence. This state of affairs is no doubt a ground upon which the judge can be asked to exercise his discretion and order a separate trial, but no such application was made in the present case. If no separate trial is ordered it is the duty of the judge to impress on the jury that the statement of one prisoner not made on oath in the course of the trial is not evidence against the other and must be entirely disregarded, and that warning was emphatically given by Hilbery, J, in the present case. But it would be impossible to lay down that where two prisoners are being tried together counsel for the prosecution is bound, in putting in the statement of one prisoner, to select certain passages and leave out others.

As Alice Hanson had pleaded not guilty, counsel for the prosecution was bound to prove the case against her, and, so far as she was concerned, the evidence mainly consisted in the statement which she had made. The judge not only warned the jury that they must not regard her statement as evidence against the appellant but was at pains not to read, in his summing up, the whole of the statement which she made, confining himself to those parts which bore on her guilt and not on that of the appellant, though he did read one passage which implicated the appellant, again warning the jury that it was not evidence against him. He went so far as to advise the jury not to ask for the woman's statement when they retired, so that they should not have before them matters prejudicial to the appellant.

If we were to lay down that the statement of one prisoner could never be read in full because it might implicate, or did implicate, the other, it is obvious that very difficult and inconvenient situations might arise. It not infrequently happens that a prisoner, in making a statement, though admitting his or her guilt up to a certain extent, puts greater blame upon the co-prisoner, or is asserting that certain of his or her actions were really innocent and it was the conduct of the co-prisoner that gave them a sinister appearance or led to the belief that the prisoner making the statement was implicated in the crime. In such a case that prisoner would have a right to have the whole statement read and could, with good reason, complain if the prosecution picked out certain passages and left out others. The statement was clearly admissible against Hanson and was read against her, and although in many cases counsel do refrain from reading passages which implicate another prisoner and have no real bearing on the case against the prisoner making the statement, we cannot say that anything has been admitted in this case which was not admissible, and the judge gave adequate and emphatic directions to the jury on the subject.'

Appeal dismissed.

It seems to me that would always be a necessary direction, even, according to *R* v *Dibble* (1908) 1 Cr App Rep 155 (CCA) where the maker of the confession gave evidence for the prosecution.

Mr Bacon: My Lord, even if Your Lordship gives such a direction, the terms of the confession are quite explicit about my client, and there is a considerable risk of prejudice in allowing inadmissible material to go before them. In my submission, the evidential value of the statement against Coke would in no way be lessened if the second paragraph were to be edited to omit all of it except: 'After she went I was worried'.

Holt J: What authority is there for such a course?

Mr Bacon: My Lord, the case of:

R v *Rogers and Tarran* [1971] Crim LR 412 (Mold Crown Court)

The defendants were charged with corruption contrary to section 1 (1) of the Prevention of Corruption Act 1906. The defendant R was charged with corruptly giving and the defendant T with corruptly receiving, a sum of money as an inducement or reward for showing favour to R. During the course of the opening the prosecution wished to adduce a certain statement made by R in a police interview. It was argued, inter alia, by counsel on behalf of T that the admission of such evidence against R, although not evidence against T would nevertheless be adversely prejudicial to T.

Crichton J, in giving judgment on the admissibility of the statement, said: 'counsel for each defendant submits that the court should exclude certain evidence of R, in particular, answers to two questions put to him in an interview. These statements are clear admissions that R carries on a business of plant hire on the basis that he spends a considerable amount of money every year in bribes. The real question is whether the prejudice exceeds the probative value. These answers by R are admissible against R. Had R been tried alone, I would have admitted this evidence, it would have been unjust to the prosecution not to admit it. But this admission is not evidence against T. I take account of the fact that the initial interview includes a very broad question and a broad answer. It does not specifically refer to T, and I am mindful of the fact that R has admitted bribery with W at approximately the same period. I have already said that R's admission is not evidence against T, but I have come to the conclusion that it is manifestly prejudicial to T. This is a joint trial and it is quite right to say that the evidence must be treated quite separately, but I have come to the conclusion that it would be impossible to disabuse the jury from the belief that R was a man who conducts his business by giving bribes and if this evidence was admitted it would prejudice T. I have therefore come to the conclusion that the prejudice outweighs the probative value and have decided to exclude the questions and answers.'

Both defendants were eventually acquitted. No application was made on behalf of the defendants for separate trials.

The practice involved was laid down in:

R v *Weaver* [1968] 1 QB 353 (CA)

Two pieces of evidence, possibly prejudicial to the defendants, were inadvertently admitted during their trial.

SACHS LJ, said: 'The court recognises that according to current practice appropriate steps are in certain circumstances taken to avoid some fact prejudicial to the accused being mentioned. Thus a statement by the accused may be "edited" to avoid prejudicing the prisoner: an effort is made to eliminate matters which, it is thought, it would be better that the jury should not know. The best way for this to be done is for the evidence to appear unvarnished in the depositions taken before the magistrates: then at the trial counsel can confer and the judge can, if necessary, take his part in ensuring that any "editing" is done, if it is done at all, in the right way and to the right degree. Here that does not appear to have happened: in consequence the true facts came out in evidence by inadvertence, so far as counsel was concerned, and it was thus that difficulties arose.'

Holt J: Mr Bunbury, would you oppose that course?
Mr Bunbury: No,. My Lord.
Mr Atkyn: My Lord, I would oppose that course. It is relevant to my client's case as to how this statement came to be made to emphasise to the jury the repugnance he feels for offences against children, and the fear he had of being implicated in the offence against Angela Blackstone. If the statement is edited, the whole sense of that is lost.
Holt J: Yes, I think that is right. I shall not edit the statement, but I shall give the jury a careful direction as to its use.

7.11   Commentary

R v *Coke and Littleton* at trial.   Mr Atkyn makes a similar application.

7.12   Argument

Mr Atkyn: My Lord, I have an application to edit the oral replies attributed to Coke, to remove the phrase, 'With form for the same thing'. It adds nothing to the force of the reply, but is highly prejudicial, because it tends to reveal Coke's bad character to the jury. Your Lordship has been referred to *R* v *Weaver* (7.10 ante).
Mr Bunbury: My Lord, in *Turner* v *Underwood* the court held a reply in such terms to be admissible.

Turner v *Underwood* [1948] 2 KB 284 (DC)

The appellant was convicted of indecent behaviour in a railway carriage to the annoyance of a fellow passenger. On complaint being made, the appellant made a statement after caution in the course of which he said, 'I have done time for this before.' The whole statement was read out at the trial as part of the prosecution evidence.

LORD GODDARD CJ, said: 'In the first place, this is a statement made by the man at the time, and in strictness what a man says in relation to the charge is admissible against him. Any voluntary statement which a person makes is admissible in law. It is the practice as a rule in cases which are tried before juries that where the court knows that there is something said

by a man in his statement which admits a previous conviction, or shows other matters reflecting on his character, the court sees that that is not read out to the jury; but in this case the officer was giving evidence as to what the man himself said, and no one can say it is a rule of law that what a man says in relation to the charge is not evidence against him. The court must know what has been said before it can rule one way or another whether the evidence is admissible or not. It is not like a case where a judge or chairman or recorder is trying a case on depositions and can say: "I direct you to leave out this part of the evidence." This statement was also relevant and admissible because,I think, it goes to show that the man was admitting that what he had done was a deliberate and indecent act.
(HUMPHREYS and PRITCHARD JJ agreed.)
Appeal dismissed.

Mr Atkyn: My Lord, if such a fact has some relevance to the evidential value of the reply as a confession, that is one thing. But that is not the case here, and the general rule is that such prejudicial material should be edited out. I would refer Your Lordship to:

R v *Knight and Thompson* (1946) 31 Cr App R 52 (CCA)

The appellants, on being arrested, each made a voluntary confession admitting not only the offence charged, but also a series of other offences. Neither had put his character in issue. The prosecution desired that the statements should not be read *in toto* before the jury, but the Chairman ruled that they should be read.

LEWIS J, delivering the judgment of the Court, stated the facts and continued: 'The effect of that was that the jury had before them the fact that the two appellants, whose characters were not in issue, had been guilty of other crimes. That was contrary to the rules of evidence, and in this case was a matter of considerable importance because the question whether or not they were guilty of the offence with which they were charged depended solely on their evidence on the one hand and the evidence of Mr O'Brien on the other. No such charges were made, and no doubt could not have been made, against Mr O'Brien; but the position was that the jury, having heard the records of the two appellants on their own confession, would be inclined to say: "Here is a story told by two men who are self-confessed criminals, and here on the other hand is Mr O'Brien, a perfectly respectable, honest man; we prefer to believe him", which would be quite natural. We think that this trial was unsatisfactory in that those parts of the statements which admitted that they had committed other offences were allowed to be put before the jury.'
Convictions quashed.

Holt J: I shall order that phrase to be edited out. Mr Bunbury, please see that D/I Glanvil and any other officers involved give their evidence accordingly.

7.13 Commentary

R v *Coke and Littleton* at trial.   Before the jury return, Holt J makes one further observation to counsel.

7.14 Observation

Holt J: Before the jury return to court, may I make one general observation to counsel. The defendant Coke, as he was entitled to do, gave evidence on the *voir dire*. In *Wong Kam-ming* v *R* and in *R* v *Brophy* rulings were made as to the extent to which references to that evidence might be made subsequently during the trial. I shall expect those rulings to be followed.

Wong Kam-ming v *R* [1980] AC 247 (PC)

The defendant was charged with murder and malicious wounding arising from a violent attack by a group of men against a massage parlour. The only evidence against him was his own written confession that he had been present at the scene of the attack, and had 'chopped' someone with a knife. As a result of an objection by the defence, heard on the voir dire, the trial judge held the statement to be inadmissible and excluded it. But in the course of giving evidence on the voir dire, the defendant had admitted in cross-examination that the contents of his statement were in fact true. The Crown applied for, and were given, leave to prove before the jury the defendant's admissions on the voir dire, and later, when the defendant gave evidence before the jury, to cross-examine him with regard to discrepancies between his evidence before the jury and his evidence on the voir dire. The defendant was convicted and appealed.

LORD EDMUND DAVIES, delivering the majority decision, said: 'The conduct of the trial has been attacked in several respects, and these were conveniently summarised by counsel for the defendant in framing the following questions. 1. During the cross-examination of a defendant in the voir dire as to the admissibility of his challenged statement, may questions be put as to its truth? 2. If "Yes," has the court a discretion to exclude such cross-examination, and (if so) was it properly exercised in the present case? 3. Where, although the confession is held inadmissible, the answers to questions 1 and 2 are nevertheless in favour of the Crown, is the prosecution permitted, on resumption of the trial of the main issue, to adduce evidence of what the defendant said during the voir dire? 4. If "Yes," is there a discretion to exclude such evidence, and (if so) was it properly exercised here? 5. Even although it be held that the answer to question 3 is "No," may the defendant nevertheless be cross-examined upon what he said during the voir dire? Their Lordships proceed to consider these questions.
Questions 1 and 2: relevance of truth of extra-judicial statements
In *R* v *Hammond* [1941] 3 All ER 318 prosecuting counsel was held entitled to ask the accused, when cross-examining him during the voir dire, whether a police statement which the accused alleged had been extorted by gross maltreatment was in fact true, and elicited the answer that it was. Upholding the propriety of putting the question, Humphreys J said in the Court of Appeal, at p 321:

> In our view, [the question] clearly was not inadmissible. It was a perfectly natural question to put to a person, and it was relevant to the issue of whether the story which he was then telling of being attacked and ill-used by the police was true or false... it surely must be admissible, and in our view it is admissible, because it went to the credit of the person who was giving evidence. If a man says, 'I was forced to tell the story. I was made to say this, that and the other,' it must be relevant to know whether he was made to tell the truth, or whether he was made to say a number of things which were untrue. In other words, in our view, the contents of the statement which he admittedly made and signed were relevant to the question of how he came to make and sign that statement, and, therefore, the questions which were put were properly put."

Although much criticised, that decision has frequently been followed in England and Wales and in many other jurisdictions. Their Lordships were told by counsel that in England and Wales .it has become common practice for prosecuting counsel to ask the defendant in the voir dire whether his challenged statement was in fact true. It is difficult to understand why this practice is permitted, and impossible to justify it by claiming that in some unspecified way it goes to "credit."...
The sole object of the voir dire was to determine the voluntariness of the alleged confession in accordance with principles long established by such cases as *Ibrahim* v *The King* [1914] AC 599. This was emphasised by this Board in *Chan Wei Keung* v *The Queen* [1967] 2 AC 160, while the startling consequences of adopting the *Hammond* approach were well illustrated in the Canadian case of *R* v *Hnedish* (1958) 26 WWR 685, 688, where Hall CJ said:

Having regard to all the implications involved in accepting the full impact of the *Hammond* decision which can, I think, be summarised by saying that regardless of how much physical or mental torture or abuse has been inflicted on an accused to coerce him into telling what is true, the confession is admitted because it is in fact true regardless of how it was obtained, I cannot believe that the *Hammond* decision does reflect the final judicial reasoning of the English courts...I do not see how under the guise of 'credibility' the court can transmute what is initially an inquiry as to the 'admissibility' of the confession into an inquisition of an accused. That would be repugnant to our accepted standards and principles of justice; it would invite and encourage brutality in the handling of persons suspected of having committed offences.

It is right to point out that counsel for the Crown did not seek to submit that the prosecution could in every case properly cross-examine the defendant during the voir dire regarding the truth of his challenged statement. Indeed, he went so far as to concede that in many cases it would be wrong to do anything of the sort. But he was unable to formulate an acceptable test of its propriety, and their Lordships have been driven to the conclusion that none exists. In other words, in their Lordships's view, *R* v *Hammond* [1941] 3 All ER 318 was wrongly decided, and any decisions in Hong Kong which purported to follow it should be treated as overruled. The answer to question 1 is therefore "No," and it follows that question 2 does not fall to be considered.

Questions 3 and 4

In the instant appeal counsel for the Crown felt constrained to submit that, even were the trial judge to exclude a confession on the ground that torture had been used to extort it, any damaging statements made by the defendant on the voir dire could nevertheless properly by adduced as part of the prosecution's case. Boldness could go no further.

Fortunately for justice, their Lordships have concluded that, where the confession has been excluded, the argument against ever admitting such evidence as part of the Crown case must prevail. But what if the confession is held *admissible?* In such cases, it is unlikely that the prosecution will need to do more than rely upon the confession itself. Nevertheless, in principle should they be prevented from proving in addition any admission made by the defendant on the voir dire? This question has exercised their Lordships a great deal, but even in the circumstances predicated it is preferable to maintain a clear distinction between the issue of voluntariness, which is alone relevant to the voir dire, and the issue of guilt falling to be decided in the main trial. To blur this distinction can lead, as has already been shown, to unfortunate consequences, and their Lordships have therefore concluded that the same exclusion of evidence regarding the voir dire proceedings from the main trial must be observed, regardless of whether the challenged confession to be excluded or admitted. It followed that question 3 must be answered in the negative, and question 4 accordingly does not arise.

Question 5

In *R* v *Treacy* [1944] 2 All ER 229, where the defendant's answers under police interrogation were held inadmissible, it was held that he could not be cross-examined to elicit that he had in fact given those answers, Humphreys J saying, at p 236:

In our view, a statement made by a prisoner under arrest is either admissible or it is not admissible. If it is admissible, the proper course for the prosecution is to prove it...If it is not admissible, nothing more ought to be heard of it, and it is quite a mistake to think that a document can be made admissible in evidence which is otherwise in-admissible simply because it is put to a person in cross-examination.

In their Lordships' judgment, *R* v *Treacy* was undoubtedly correct in prohibiting cross-examination as to the *contents* of confessions which the court has ruled inadmissible. But what if during the voir dire the accused has made self-incriminating statements not strictly related to the confession itself but which nevertheless have relevance to the issue of guilt or innocence of the charge preferred? May the accused be cross-examined so as to elicit those matters? In the light of their Lordships' earlier conclusion that the Crown may not adduce as part of its case evidence of what the accused said during a voir dire culminating in the exclusion of an impugned confession, can a different approach here be permitted from that condemned in *R* v *Treacy?* Subject to what was said as to the court's discretion to exclude it in proper circumstances, counsel for the Crown submitted that it can be, citing in support section 13 of the Hong Kong Evidence Ordinance (c 8), which was based on the familiar provision in section 4 of the Criminal Procedure Act 1865 of the United Kingdom, relating to the confrontation of a witness with his previous inconsistent statements. But these statutory provisions have no relevance if the earlier statements cannot be put in evidence. And, having already concluded that the voir dire statements of the defendant are not admissible during the presentation of the prosecution's case, their Lordships find it impossible in principle to distinguish between such cross-examination of the defendant on the basis of the voir dire as was permitted in the instant case by the trial judge and upheld by the majority of the Court of Appeal and that cross-examination based on the contents of an excluded confession which, it is common ground, was rightly condemned in *R* v *Treacy* [1944] 2 All ER 229.

But what if the voir dire resulted in the impugned confession being *admitted,* and the defendant later elects to give evidence? If he then testifies to matters relating, for example, to the *reliability* of the confession (as opposed to its *voluntariness,* which ex hypothesi, is no longer in issue) and in so doing gives answers which are markedly different from his testimony given during the voir dire may he be cross-examined so as to establish that at the earlier stage of the trial he had told a different story? Great injustice could well result from the exclusion of such cross-examination, and their Lordships can see no justification in legal principle or on any other ground which renders it impermissible. As has already been observed, a defendant seeking to challenge the admissibility of a confession may for all practical purposes be *obliged* to testify in the voir dire if his challenge is to have any chance of succeeding, and his evidence is then (or certainly should be) restricted strictly to the issue of admissibility of the confession. But the situation is quite different where, the confession having been *admitted* despite his challenge, the defendant later elects to give evidence during the main trial and, in doing so, departs materially from the testimony he gave in the voir dire. Having so chosen to testify, why should the discrepancies not be elicited and demonstrated by cross-examination? In their Lordships' view, his earlier statements made in the voir dire provide acceptable a basis for his cross-examination to that end as any other earlier statements made by him — including, of course, his confession which, though challenged, had been ruled admissible. Indeed, for such purpose and in such circumstances, his voir dire statements stand on no different basis than, for example, the sworn testimony given by a defendant in a previous trial where the jury had disagreed. No doubt the trial judge has a discretion and, indeed, a duty to ensure that the right of the prosecution to cross-examine or rebut is not used in a manner unfair or oppressive to the defendant and no doubt the judge is under an obligation to see to it that any statutory provisions bearing on the situation (such as those earlier referred to) are strictly complied with. But, subject thereto, their Lordships hold that cross-examination in the circumstances predicated which is directed to testing the credibility of the defendant by establishing the inconsistencies in his evidence is wholly permissible.'

LORD HAILSHAM of ST. MARYLEBONE, dissenting, said: 'The reservations I feel about the opinion of the majority in this case are...confined to the views they express in relation to questions (1) and (2). In order to avoid prejudice to the defendant the voir dire normally takes place in the absence of a jury. It is therefore a trial on an issue of fact before a judge alone. It is open to the defendant (presumably under the provisions of the Criminal Evidence Act 1898 or its Hong Kong equivalent) to give evidence and there are limits imposed by that Act or the equivalent Ordinance on what may be asked him in cross-examination. Subject to these limitations, and to any other general rules of evidence (such as those relating to hearsay) it seems to me that the only general limitations on what may be asked or tendered ought to be relevance to the issue to be tried, as in any other case in which an issue of fact is to be tried by a judge alone, and as to this, subject to appeal, the judge is himself the arbiter on the same principles as in any other case in which he is the judge of fact. It appears to be the opinion of the majority that it is possible to say a priori that in no circumstances is the truth or falsity of the alleged confession relevant to the question at issue on the voir dire or admissible as to credibility of either the prosecution or defence witnesses. I disagree. It is common ground that the question at issue on the voir dire is the voluntary character of the statement. This is the factum probandum, and, since the burden is on the prosecution, the prosecution evidence is taken before that of the defence. The voir dire may take place, as in the instant appeal, at the beginning of the trial, when all that is known of the facts must be derived from the depositions, or from counsel's opening. More frequently, however, the voir dire takes place at a later stage in the trial when the prosecution tenders the evidence, usually of the police, in support of the voluntary character of the statement. By that time many facts are known and much of the evidence has been heard. I can conceive of many cases in which it is of the essence of the defence case on the voir dire that the confession, whose voluntary character is in issue, is in whole or part untrue, and, it may be, contrary to admitted fact. If the defence can succeed in establishing this or even raising a serious question about it either as the result of cross-examining the prosecution witnesses, or by evidence led by the defence itself, serious doubt can be raised as to the voluntary nature of the confession. How can it be said, counsel for the defence might wish to argue, that the defendant can have provided so much inaccurate information to his own detriment, unless he was forced to do so by some improper means? If the defence can be allowed to make the point, which seems to me to be a valid one, it must be open to the prosecution to cross-examine upon it when it is the turn of the defence witnesses to be scrutinised.

Appeal allowed.

R v *Brophy* [1981] 3 WLR 103 (HL)

The defendant was charged with forty nine counts, including twelve of murder, thirty six of causing explosions or illegal possession of explosives or firearms, and one (Count 49) of belonging to the IRA, an organisation proscribed by statute. He was tried in Northern Ireland, by a judge sitting alone under a special statutory provision applicable to that province. The only evidence against him was a number of written and oral statements that he was alleged to have made to the police after his arrest. The defendant challenged the admissibility of these statements on the basis that they had been obtained by torture or inhuman treatment. In the course of his evidence in chief, on the voir dire, the defendant admitted in terms that he had been a member of the IRA during the greater part of the period charged in Count 49. The trial judge excluded the statements and accordingly acquitted the defendant on Counts 1-48, but convicted him on Count 49 on the evidence of his own admission on the voir dire. The Court of Appeal for Northern Ireland allowed the defendant's appeal, and the Crown appealed to the House of Lords.

LORD FRASER of TULLYBELTON said: 'I do not overlook or minimise the risk that accused persons may make false allegations of ill-treatment by the police; some of them undoubtedly do. But the detection of dishonest witnesses on this, as on other matters, is part of the ordinary duty of the courts and it should be left to them. The possibility, indeed the practical certainty, that some accused will give dishonest evidence of ill-treatment does not justify inhibiting their freedom to testify at the voir dire. The importance of the principle was explained by Lord Hailsham of St. Marylebone in the recent Privy Council case of *Wong Kam-ming* v *The Queen* [1980] AC 247, 261, where he said this:

> ...any civilised system of criminal jurisprudence must accord to the judiciary some means of excluding confessions or admissions obtained by improper methods. This is not only because of the potential unreliability of such statements, but also, and perhaps mainly, because in a civilised society it is vital that persons in custody or charged with offences should not be subjected to ill-treatment or improper pressure in order to extract confessions. It is therefore of very great importance that the courts should continue to insist that before extra-judicial statements can be admitted in evidence the prosecution must be made to prove beyond reasonable doubt that the statement was not obtained in a manner which should be reprobated and was therefore in the truest sense voluntary. For this reason it is necessary that the defendant should be able and feel free either by his own testimony or by other means to challenge the voluntary character of the tendered statement. If, as happened in the instant appeal, the prosecution were to be permitted to introduce into the trial the evidence of the defendant given in the course of the voir dire when the statement to which it relates has been excluded whether in order to supplement

the evidence otherwise available as part of the prosecution case, or by way of cross-examination of the defendant, the important principles of public policy to which I have referred would certainly become eroded, possibly even to vanishing point.

The case of *Wong Kam-ming* differs from the present in two respects. First, the trial there was by a judge and jury. Secondly, the accused's admission had been elicited in cross-examination at the voir dire. The decision is therefore not directly in point, but neither of these features was essential to the observations by Lord Hailsham of St. Marylebone in the passage which I have quoted, which were quite wide enough to apply to the facts of this appeal. In my opinion they are applicable here also.

A submission was made by counsel for the Crown that the position of the accused could be adequately safeguarded if his evidence at the voir dire were admissible at the substantive trial, provided that the judge had a discretion to exclude at the trial any such evidence which would prejudice him unfairly. This was the approach favoured by Bray CJ in *R v Wright* [1969] SASR 256 — a South Australian case, the actual decision in which cannot stand with *Wong Kam-ming* and was not supported by counsel for the Crown in this appeal. With all respect, I cannot regard that as a satisfactory solution. The right of the accused to give evidence at the voir dire without affecting his right to remain silent at the substantive trial is in my opinion absolute and is not to be made conditional on an exercise of judicial discretion.

(LORDS DIPLOCK, RUSSELL of KILLOWEN, KEITH of KINKEL and ROSKILL agreed.)

Appeal dismissed.

7.15 Commentary

R v Coke and Littleton on appeal against conviction. At the trial, Littleton elected not to give evidence, but to make an unsworn statement from the dock. In the course of this statement, he said to the jury: 'I told the police the truth when they arrested me; that they had made a mistake. That is the truth, and I have nothing to add to it.' In the course of summing up to the jury, Holt J said of this statement:

The important thing to bear in mind in relation to Littleton's asserted alibi is that there is no defence evidence of it before you. That of itself does not mean he must be guilty, and you must not regard it in that way. But a statement from the dock cannot prove facts in issue in a case[1]. It is true that the prosecution put before you what Littleton had said to the police when he was arrested, and it is also true that he then denied his guilt, and said that they had got the wrong man. By all means take that into account as part of the general picture. But when a defendant makes a statement out of court, which generally supports his case, that is not evidence that his story is true. It may be evidence that he has been consistent, and you are entitled to consider that. But it is not evidence of his alibi unless he confirms it from the witness box, and this he has chosen not to do. That is why I say that there is no defence evidence of the alibi, so you must look to see whether the prosecution has proved his guilt to you, on the evidence you have.

Mr Bacon appeals on the ground that this was a misdirection.

7.16 Argument

Leach LJ: That seems to me to be a model direction. The defendant cannot rely upon self-serving statements to prove his case — it is not the same as the prosecution adducing a confession, which is evidence of the facts confessed to. Take for example:

---

[1]As to the effect of unsworn statements from the dock, see 11.12.4 et seq.

R v McGregor [1968] 1 QB 371 (CA)

At the defendant's trial on a charge of receiving he gave evidence in the presence of a police officer. The jury disagreed and a new trial was ordered. At the second trial the court admitted evidence from the police officer that, at the first trial the defendant had made admissions that he had possession of the goods but had given explanations of how he did not know they were stolen. The defendant did not give evidence at the second trial. The jury were directed that they were to consider the defendant's explanations given at the first trial but that they could not be tested because he had not given evidence at the second trial. The defendant was convicted and appealed.

LORD PARKER CJ, giving the judgment of the court, said: 'As we understand it, Mr Dovener says, and says rightly, that if the prosecution are minded to put in an admission or a confession they must put in the whole and not merely a part of it. He then goes on from that as the next stage to rely on an old case — not necessarily the worse for that — in 1827, *R* v *Jones* (1827) 2 C&P 629, in which Sergeant Bosanquet ruled in the following terms:

> There is no doubt that if a prosecutor uses the declaration of a prisoner, he must take the whole of it together, and cannot select one part and leave another...

So far that seems quite correct. But he then went on:

> ...and if there be either no other evidence in the case, or no other evidence incompatible with it, the declaration so adduced in evidence must be taken as true.

Accordingly, Mr Dovener submits, as I understand it, that not only must the admission as to possession be taken to be true, the defendant not having gone into the box and denied it, but also that his explanation must be taken to be true. In the opinion of this court, *R* v *Jones* is no longer authority. It was an old case, long before 1898, and as stated in Archbold, Criminal Pleading, Evidence and Practice, 36th ed (1966), para 1128:

> The better opinion seems to be that, as in the case of all other evidence, the whole should be left to the jury, to say whether the facts asserted by the prisoner in his favour be true.

The court is satisfied that that passage in Archbold sets out the true position...
Finally, Mr Dovener submits that the jury ought to have been told in fact that they should give equal weight to that part of the evidence of the defendant at the previous hearing which dealt with his admission of possession and with his explanations. The court cannot conceive why the jury should attach equal weight to both. The defendant not having given evidence, not having gone into the box to deny the truth of his statement earlier that he had put the goods into his wife's shopping bag, and not having gone into the witness box to verify the explanations he had given on the previous occasions, it was only natural and proper that the jury should attach greater weight to the admission than to the explanations.'
Appeal dismissed.

Mr Bacon: My Lord, the defendant is entitled to have what he said to the police considered.

East LJ: The learned judge said that they were to consider it, but not as evidence of the truth of what he said to the police. That is the critical distinction between a confession adduced by the prosecution and a self-serving statement, even when the two are contained in the same statement. This is how I read:

R v Donaldson and Others (1976) 64 Cr App R 59 (CA)

The defendant was charged, *inter alia,* with handling stolen goods. He made a statement to the police partly denying, party admitting the charge against him. At his trial he did not give evidence, and the jury were directed that the statement was only evidence to the extent that it might represent an admission. He was covicted and appealed.

JAMES LJ, giving the judgment of the court, said: 'In our view there is a clear distinction to be made between statements of admission adduced by the Crown as part of the case against the defendant and statements entirely of a self serving nature made and sought to be relied upon by a defendant. When the Crown adduce a statement relied upon as an admission it is for the jury to consider the whole statement including any passages that contain qualifications or explanations favourable to the defendant, and bear upon the passages relied upon by the prosecution as an admission, and it is for the jury to decide whether the statement viewed as a whole constitutes an admission. To this extent the statement may be said to be evidence of the facts stated therein. If the jury find that it is an admission they may rely upon it as proof of the facts admitted. If the defendant elects not to give evidence then in so far as the statement contains explanations or qualifications favourable to the defendant the jury, in deciding what, if any, weight to give to that part of the statement, should take into account that it was not made on oath and has not been tested by cross-examination.

When the Crown adduce evidence in the form of a statement by the defendant which is not relied on as an admission of the offence charged such a statement is evidence in the trial in that it is evidence that the defendant made the statement and of his reaction which is part of the general picture which the jury have to consider but it is not evidence of the facts stated.'
[The court held that although there had been a misdirection, it had not affected the verdict and no miscarriage of justice had occurred.]
Appeal dismissed.

Mr Bacon: My Lord, might I also refer you to a recent unreported decision of the Court of Appeal:

R v Duncan, unreported, 7 May 1981 (CA)

The appellant made statements admitting the killing of a woman with whom he was living. At his trial for murder the appellant elected not to give evidence or call witnesses. The trial judge raised the question of provocation and invited submissions. The judge ruled that, in so far as the appellant's statements were self-serving, they could not be evidence of the facts and therefore provocation would not be left to the jury. The appellant was convicted and appealed on the ground that the ruling was wrong.

LORD LANE CJ, delivering the judgment of the Court, said: 'The basic rules are as follows: (1) What a person says out of Court is, generally speaking, not admissible to prove the truth of what he says. (2) It may be admissible if — (a) it is an exception to the hearsay rule, in which case it is evidence of the truth of what is stated; (b) it falls outside the hearsay rule, that is to say if it is adduced for a purpose other than proving the truth of the statement — an example of this is to be found in *Subramaniam* v *Public Prosecutor* [1956] 1 WLR 965, where a statement was relevant to the question of whether there had been duress or not. The only relevant exception to the hearsay rule in the present circumstances is that relating to admissions against interest or confessions.

The issue between the parties here is the extent to which confessions are properly to be regarded as evidence of the truth of the facts which they state. Both parties are agreed that if a statement is adduced as an admission against interest, the whole of the statement must be admitted. Any other course would obviously be unfair.

It is contended on behalf of the Crown that this rule does not however make the contents of the statement evidence of the facts contained therein except in so far as those statements are admissions against interest. Mr Judge, on the other hand, on behalf of the appellant, contends that the whole statement is evidence of the truth of the facts contained therein. He however concedes that the Judge is entitled to explain to the jury, if indeed it needs explanation, that the weight to be given to those parts of the statement which contain admissions against interest may be very different from the weight to be given to the parts which are self-exculpatory.

One is bound to observe that if the contentions of the Crown are correct, the Judge would be faced with a very difficult task in trying to explain to the jury the difference between those parts of a "mixed" statement (if we may call it such) which were truly confessions and those parts which were self-exculpatory. It is doubtful if the result would be readily intelligible. Suppose a prisoner had said "I killed X. If I had not done so, X would certainly have killed me there and then." If the Judge tells the jury that the first sentence is evidence of the truth of what it states but that the second sentence is not; that it is merely something to which they are entitled to have regard as qualifying the first sentence and affecting its weight as an admission, they will either not understand or disregard what he is saying. Judges should not be obliged to give meaningless or unintelligible directions to juries.

We turn to examine the authorities. In *McGregor* (1967) 51 Cr App R 338, Lord Parker, Chief Justice, at page 341 said this: "As we understand it, Mr Dovener says and says rightly that, if the prosecution are minded to put in an admission or a confession, they must put in the whole and not merely part of it." He later cited with approval a passage from the then current edition of Archbold: "....the better opinion seems to be that as in the case of all other evidence the whole should be left to the jury to say whether the facts asserted by the prisoner in his favour be true." Lord Parker went on to consider and reject out of hand a submission by counsel for the appellant that the jury should have been directed to give equal weight to both parts of the appellant's statement, those containing admissions and those containing excuses or explanations.

This case is clear authority for the proposition that in the case of a "mixed" statement both parts are evidence of the facts they state, though they are obviously not to be regarded as having equal weight.

R v Sparrow (1973) 57 Cr App R 352 seems to be inconsistent with the primary ruling in *McGregor,* which was not cited to the Court, because Lord Justice Lawton at page 357 says this: "The trial judge had a difficult task in summing up that part of the case which concerned the appellant. First, he had to try to get the jury to understand that the appellant's exculpatory statement to the police after arrest, which he had not verified in the witness box, was not evidence of the facts in it save in so far as it contained admissions. Many lawyers find difficulty in grasping this principle of the law of evidence. What juries make of it must be a matter of surmise, but the probabilities are they make very little." He then turned to consider the extent to which the Judge should comment on the way in which the case has been conducted and upon the failure of the accused man to go into the witness box.

R v Donaldson and Others (1977) 64 Cr App R 59 was another example of a "mixed" statement. At page 65 Lord Justice James says this:

> In our view there is a clear distinction to be made between statements of admission adduced by the Crown as part of the case against the defendant and statements entirely of a self-serving nature made and sought to be relied upon by a defendant. When the Crown adduce a statement relied upon as an admission it is for the jury to consider the whole statement including any passages that contain qualifications or explanations favourable to the defendant, that bear upon the passages relied upon by the prosecution as an admission, and it is for the jury to decide whether the statement viewed as a whole constitutes an admission. To this extent the statement may be said to be evidence of the facts stated therein.

Finally in *Pearce* (1979) 69 Cr App R 365, the Court gave directions on how three different factual situations should be approached. We are in this case only concerned with the first: "(1) A statement which contains an admission is always admissible as a declaration against interest and is evidence of the facts admitted. With this exception a statement made by an accused person is never evidence of the facts in the statement." It is not clear from this what standing is to be given to the exculpatory parts of a "mixed" statement, but since the Court expressly based themselves upon the principles in *Donaldson,* one can assume that the statement is to be viewed as a whole by the jury.

We should add that we were referred to a number of other decisions: *Storey* 52 Cr App R 334 in which *McGregor* was not cited and which concerned the question of a purely exculpatory statement and its evidential weight upon a submission of no case; *Thompson* (1975) Cr LR 34; *Barbery* (1975) 62 Cr App R 248 — which were cases of purely exculpatory statements.

Where a "mixed" statement is under consideration by the jury in a case where the defendant has not given evidence, it seems to us that the simplest, and therefore the method most likely to produce a just result, is for the jury to be told that the whole statement, both the incriminating parts and the excuses or explanations, must be considered by them in deciding where the truth lies. It is, to say the least, not helpful to try to explain to the jury that the exculpatory parts of the statement are something less than evidence of the facts they state. Equally, where appropriate, as it usually will be, the Judge may, and should, point out that the incriminating parts are likely to be true (otherwise why say them?), whereas the excuses guide in matters of this sort.'

(The court held on the facts that there was nothing in the appellant's statements which amounted to a claim of provocation.)

Appeal dismissed.

Leach LJ: Yes, thank you. Mr Bacon.

Mr Bacon: My Lord, it is submitted that in that case, as in Donaldson, the Court of Appeal was considering the position with regard to a 'mixed' statement, one which contained both admissions and passages which were self-serving. In the present case, it is submitted that the court is concerned with a purely exculpatory statement. I would refer Your Lordships to *R v Storey* (1968) 52 Cr App R 334, a decision of the Court of Appeal, which was not doubted in Duncan.

R v Storey (1968) 52 Cr App R 334 (CA)

The police found on entering the defendant's flat a very large quantity of cannabis resin. In a voluntary statement not on oath the defendant gave the police the explanation that it belonged to a man who had brought it into her flat against her will, and the explanation, if true, would have afforded a complete answer to the charge. At the close of the prosecution case a submission was made by the defence that there was no case to answer, but the submission was overruled by the judge. The defendant was convicted and applied for leave to appeal.

WIDGERY LJ, delivering the judgment of the court, said: 'The question which arises in this case is whether the fact that she gave shortly afterwards an explanation which, if true, would provide a completely innocent explanation is enough to produce a situation in which the learned judge's duty was to say that there was no case to answer.

The Court has given careful consideration to this important point. We think it right to recognise that a statement made by the accused to the police, although it always forms evidence in the case against him, is not in itself evidence of the truth of the facts stated. A statement made voluntarily by an accused person to the police is evidence in the trial because of its vital relevance as showing the reaction of the accused when first taxed with the incriminating facts. If, of course, the accused admits the offence, then as a matter of shorthand one says that the admission is proof of guilt, and, indeed, in the end it is. But if the accused makes a statement which does not amount to an admission, the statement is not strictly evidence of the truth of what was said, but is evidence of the reaction of the accused which forms part of the general picture to be considered by the jury at the trial.

Accordingly, in our judgment, in this case the fact that the cannabis was on the applicant's bed in her flat was in itself some evidence of possession to go to the jury. Her unsworn explanation, although, if true, it would have been a complete answer to the charge, did not cancel out or nullify the evidence which was provided by the presence of the cannabis. It was ultimately for the jury to decide whether that explanation was or might be true, and it was not for the judge necessarily to accept it at the stage when he was considering the submission. In the event therefore, we have come to the conclusion that the learned judge was entitled to and right to leave this matter to the jury and not to withdraw it from them merely because the accused's unsworn explanation would, if true, have been a complete answer to the charge. Application refused.

7.17 Commentary

R v Coke and Littleton at trial. After hearing evidence on the voir dire, Holt J
excludes Coke's confessions. The effect of this is that the confessions may not be
referred to in the presence of the jury (see *R v Treacy*) [1944] 2 All ER 229 (CCA) (see
13.20 post). Mr Bunbury nonetheless wishes to lead evidence of the finding of articles
of Margaret Blackstone's underwear at Coke's flat. This discovery was made on the
basis of the information provided in Coke's written statement under caution. Mr
Atkyn objects to the evidence.

7.18 Argument

Mr Atkyn: My Lord, in my submission, the evidence is tainted by the
inadmissibility of the confession itself, because its discovery cannot be explained to the
jury without introducing the contents of the statement which Your Lordship has ruled
to be inadmissible. The case is similar to that of:

R v Barker [1941] 2 KB 381 (CCA)[1]

The appellant was convicted of conspiracy to defraud. Because of inducements held out by
officers of the Inland Revenue, the appellant produced books which contained evidence of
fraud. The appellant's actual confession of fraud was excluded because of the inducements,
but it was argued that the books were admissible in their own right.

TUCKER J, delivering the judgment of the court, said: '[Counsel for the Crown] cited a
passage setting out what he submitted was the law on this matter as summarised in
Archbold's Criminal Pleading, Evidence and Practice, 30th ed, p 402: Although a confession
for the above or any other reasons may not be receivable in evidence, yet any discovery that
takes place in consequence of such confession, or any act done by the defendant, if it is
confirmed by the finding of the property, will be admitted. The court accepts that statement
of the law and does not desire to question that there may be cases in which evidence can be
given of facts the existence of which have come to the knowledge of the police as the result of
an inadmissible confession. But in the present case the promise or inducement which was
implied in this extract from Hansard expressly related to the production of business books
and records, and the court is of opinion that if, as a result of a promise, inducement or threat,
such books and documents are produced by the person or persons to whom the promise or
inducement is held out, or the threat made, those documents stand on precisely the same
footing as an oral or a written confession which is brought into existence as the result of such
a promise, inducement or threat.
    The result is that, in the opinion of the court, these vital documents and books, namely, the
ledgers and the working papers of the appellant, were wrongly admitted in evidence.'
Appeal allowed.

Holt J: Mr Bunbury, what do you say?
Mr Bunbury: My Lord, the discovery is an independent one, which stands in its
own right without reference to the confession. It is accordingly admissible under the
principle in:

R v Warickshall (1783) 1 Leach 263 (Old Bailey)

The defendant was charged with receiving stolen goods. As a result of her improperly induced

---

[1]The precise facts, but not the principle, of Barker, would now be governed by statute: Taxes
Management Act, 1970 s.105.

confession the property was found hidden in her bed.

NARES J: 'It is a mistaken notion, that the evidence of confessions and facts which have been obtained from prisoners by promises or threats, is to be rejected from a regard to public faith: no such rule ever prevailed. The idea is novel in theory, and would be as dangerous in practice as it is repugnant to the general principles of criminal law. Confessions are received in evidence, or rejected as inadmissible, under a consideration whether they are or are not intitled to credit. A free and voluntary confession is deserving of the highest credit, because it is presumed to flow from the strongest sense of guilt, and therefore it is admitted as proof of the crime to which it refers; but a confession forced from the [264] mind by the flattery of hope, or by the torture of fear, comes in so questionable a shape when it is to be considered as the evidence of guilt, that no credit ought to be given to it; and therefore it is rejected. This principle respecting confessions has no application whatever as to the admission or rejection of facts, whether the knowledge of them be obtained in consequence of an extorted confession, or whether it arises from any other source; for a fact, if it exist at all, must exist invariably in the same manner, whether the confession from which it is derived be in other respects true or false. Facts thus obtained, however, must be fully and satisfactorily proved, without calling in the aid of any part of the confession from which they may have been derived; and the impossibility of admitting any part of the confession as a proof of the fact, clearly shews that the fact may be admitted on other evidence; for as no part of an improper confession can be heard, it can never be legally known whether the fact was derived through the means of such confession or not; and the consequences to public justice would be dangerous indeed; for if men were enabled to regain stolen property, and the evidence of attendant facts were to be suppressed, because they had regained it by means of an improper confession, it would be holding out an opportunity to compound felonies.

Mindful of the reproach addressed to counsel by Erle J in *R v Berriman* I do not seek to refer to the confession, even in part.

R v Berriman (1854) 6 Cox CC 388 (Surrey Assizes)

The prisoner was charged with concealment of birth. Counsel for the Crown wished to ask a witness whether, in consequence of an answer improperly elicited from the prisoner by the examining magistrate, the remains of a child were found.

ERLE J said: 'No! *Not in consequence of what she said.* You may ask him what search was made, and what things were found, but under the circumstances, I cannot allow that proceeding to be connected with the prisoner.'

Holt J: Provided that no reference is made to any part of the confession I shall admit the evidence.

C: STATEMENTS MADE IN THE PRESENCE OF THE DEFENDANT

7.19 Introductory notes

7.19.1 Where statements relevant to the issues are made in the presence of a party, the reaction of that party to those statements may be of some evidential value. Accordingly, the statements may be admitted in order to show, in context, what that reaction was. The important application of the rule in contemporary practice is in criminal cases, where almost always the defendant is interrogated extensively about the alleged offence. If the defendant admits the allegations, then the interrogation becomes, in effect, a confession and is admissible as such. But if the defendant denies the allegations, or elects to remain silent, problems arise as to whether any part of the interrogation should be admitted.

7.19.2   Where the defendant denies the allegations, although arguably the questions put to him might remain admissible for the purpose of showing his reaction to them, they have no evidential value in and of themselves. Generally, if the defence so request, fairness will dictate the exclusion of an interrogation consisting of no more than a series of denials. The case is of course quite different where the manner of denial, including perhaps a false story, is relevant. In practice, the defence often have no objection to evidence of denials, which may assist by showing the defendant's consistency in his account of events. But this may be outweighed where the questions are a detailed and hearsay statement of the prosecution case, punctuated only by monosyllabic denials.

7.19.3   Where the defendant remains silent in the face of the allegations, his silence cannot be held against him. Hence, although it is arguable that his silence is a part of the 'overall picture' which the jury should consider, the interrogation as a whole lacks evidential value, and should be excluded where the hearsay nature of the questions may prejudice the defence. However, where the defendant is questioned or accused 'on even terms', there is some authority that his failure to deny or rebut the charge when he might reasonably be expected to do so may be regarded as evidence that he admits the charge. Generally, this would seem to apply to cases of spontaneous challenge by the complainant of some person closely involved in the offence, but it has also been held that a defendant may be on even terms with a police officer, in the rare cases where questioning takes place in the presence of his solicitor. It is inappropriate under normal circumstances to speak of even terms during a formal interrogation by police officers, and ordinarily no adverse inference can be drawn from the defendant's silence.

7.19.4   Despite the observations made above, evidence such as that described in 7.19.2 and 7.19.3 above is generally admitted in practice as part of the 'overall picture', unless the defence specifically object. (*A Practical Approach to Evidence*, pp 185–91.)

7.20   Commentary

R v *Coke and Littleton* at trial.   Mr Bacon, on behalf of Littleton, applies to Holt J in the absence of the jury and at the proper moment during the evidence in chief of Angela Blackstone to exclude the evidence of Angela's words of identification and the conversation between Littleton and the officers on the street immediately thereafter.

7.21   Argument

   Mr Bacon: My Lord, the depositions show that my client consistently denied his guilt when questioned by the police, and eventually refused to answer their questions because he was not allowed to see his solicitor. The accusation by Angela and the questions of the officers are mere hearsay in themselves. Unless my client adopted them and thereby made a confession, they are of no evidential value against him. The case may be compared to that of:

R v Norton [1910] 2 KB 496 (CCA)

The appellant was convicted of having sexual intercourse with a girl under thirteen. At the trial statements made in the presence of the appellant by the girl (who was not called as a witness) charging him with having committed the offence were narrated to the jury. There was no evidence that the appellant had in any way accepted the statement.

PICKFORD J, reading the judgment of the court, said: 'As a general rule, statements as to the facts of a case under investigation are not evidence unless made by witnesses in the ordinary way, but to this rule there are exceptions. One is that statements made in the presence of a prisoner upon an occasion on which he might reasonably be expected to make some observation, explanation, or denial are admissible under certain circumstances. We think it is not strictly accurate, and may be misleading, to say that they are admissible in evidence against the prisoner, as such an expression may seem to imply that they are evidence of the facts stated in them and must be considered upon the footing of other evidence. Such statements are, however, never evidence of the facts stated in them; they are admissible only as introductory to, or explanatory of, the answer given to them by the person in whose presence they are made. Such answers may, of course, be given either by words or by conduct, e.g. by remaining silent on an occasion which demanded an answer.

If the answer given amounts to an admission of the statements or some part of them, they or that part become relevant as shewing what facts are admitted; if the answer be not such an admission, the statements are irrelevant to the matter under consideration and should be disregarded. This seems to us to be correctly and shortly stated in Taylor on Evidence, s.814, p 574: "The statements only become evidence when by such acceptance he makes them his own statements."

No objection was taken in this case to the admission of the statements in evidence, but as the prisoner may be tried again on an indictment on which that question may arise, we think it well to state in what cases such statements can be given in evidence. We think that the contents of such statements should not be given in evidence unless the judge is satisfied that there is evidence fit to be submitted to the jury that the prisoner by his answer to them, whether given by word or conduct, acknowledged the truth of the whole or part of them. If there be no such evidence, then the contents of the statement should be excluded; if there be such evidence, then they should be admitted, and the question whether the prisoner's answer, by words or conduct, did or did not in fact amount to an acknowledgment of them left to the jury.

In trials of prisoners on indictment, in which the most numerous and important of these cases arise, there is, as a rule, no difficulty in deciding whether there be such evidence or not, as the prisoner's answer appears upon the depositions, and the chance that the evidence with regard to it may be different on the trial is so small that it may be disregarded. When, however, the evidence of the prisoner's answer does not appear, there does not seem to be any practical difficulty in applying the rule above stated. The fact of a statement having been made in the prisoner's presence may be given in evidence, but not the contents, and the question asked, what the prisoner said or did on such a statement being made. If his answer, given either by words or conduct, be such as to be evidence from which an acknowledgment may be inferred, then the contents of the statement may be given and the question of admission or not in fact left to the jury; if it be not evidence from which such an acknowledgment may be inferred, then the contents of the statement should be excluded. To allow the contents of such statements to be given before it is ascertained that there is evidence of their being acknowledged to be true must be most prejudicial to the prisoner, as, whatever directions be given to the jury, it is almost impossible for them to dismiss such evidence entirely from their minds. It is perhaps too wide to say that in no case can the statements be given in evidence when they are denied by the prisoner, as it is possible that a denial may be given under such circumstances and in such a manner as to constitute evidence from which an acknowledgment may be inferred, but, as above stated, we think they should be rejected unless there is some evidence of an acknowledgment of the truth. Where they are admitted we think the following is the proper direction to be given to the jury: — That if they come to the conclusion that the prisoner had acknowledged the truth of the whole or any part of the facts stated they might take the statement, or so much of it as was acknowledged to be true (but no

more), into consideration as evidence in the case generally, not because the statement standing alone afforded any evidence of the matter contained in it, but solely because of the prisoner's acknowledgment of its truth; but unless they found as a fact that there was such an acknowledgement they ought to disregard the statement altogether.'
Conviction quashed.

I would refer Your Lordship also to:

R v Christie [1914] AC 545 (HL)

The defendant was convicted of indecent assault on a small boy. Shortly after the alleged offence, the boy, together with his mother and a police officer, approached the defendant, and the boy said, 'That is the man,' and went on to describe what had been done to him. The defendant said in reply, 'I am innocent', and the issue was one of identification. The boy, giving evidence unsworn, identified the defendant in court. He was not asked about the identification at the time of the defendant's arrest, but evidence to that effect was elicited from the other witnesses. The Court of Criminal Appeal quashed the conviction and the Crown appealed to the House of Lords.

LORD ATKINSON said: 'The rule of law undoubtedly is that a statement made in the presence of an accused person, even upon an occasion which should be expected reasonably to call for some explanation or denial from him, is not evidence against him of the facts stated save so far as he accepts the statement, so as to make it, in effect, his own. If he accepts the statement in part only, then to that extent alone does it become his statement. He may accept the statement by word or conduct, action or demeanour, and it is the function of the jury which tries the case to determine whether his words, action, conduct, or demeanour at the time when a statement was made amounts to an acceptance of it in whole or in part. It by no means follows, I think, that a mere denial by the accused of the facts mentioned in the statement necessarily renders the statement inadmissible, because he may deny the statement in such a manner and under such circumstances as may lead a jury to disbelieve him, and constitute evidence from which an acknowledgment may be inferred by them.

Of course, if at the end of the case the presiding judge should be of opinion that no evidence has been given upon which the jury could reasonably find that the accused had accepted the statement so as to make it in whole or in part his own, the judge can instruct the jury to disregard the statement entirely. It is said that, despite this direction, grave injustice might be done to the accused, inasmuch as the jury, having once heard the statement, could not, or would not, rid their mind of it. It is, therefore, in the application of the rule that the difficulty arises. The question then is this: Is it to be taken as a rule of law that such a statement is not to be admitted in evidence until a foundation has been laid for its admission by proof of facts from which, in the opinion of the presiding judge, a jury might reasonably draw the inference that the accused had so accepted the statement as to make it in whole or in part his own, or is it to be laid down that the prosecutor is entitled to give the statement in evidence in the first instance, leaving it to the presiding judge, in case no such evidence as the above mentioned should be ultimately produced, to tell the jury to disregard the statement altogether?

In my view the former is not a rule of law, but it is, I think, a rule which, in the interest of justice, it might be most prudent and proper to follow as a rule of practice....

LORD READING said: 'A statement made in the presence of one of the parties to a civil action may be given in evidence against him if it is relevant to any of the matters in issue. And equally such a statement made in the presence of the accused may be given in evidence against him at his trial.

The principles of the laws of evidence are the same whether applied at civil or criminal trials, but they are not enforced with the same rigidity against a person accused of a criminal offence as against a party to a civil action....

That there is danger that the accused may be indirectly prejudiced by the admission of such a statement as in this case is manifest, for however carefully the judge may direct the jury, it is often difficult for them to exclude it altogether from their minds as evidence of the facts contained in the statement.

In general, such evidence can have little or no value in its direct bearing on the case unless the accused, upon hearing the statement, by conduct and demeanour, or by the answer made by him, or in certain circumstances by the refraining from an answer, acknowledged the truth of the statement either in whole or in part, or did or said something from which the jury could infer such an acknowledgment, for if he acknowledged its truth, he accepted it as his own statement of the facts. If the accused denied the truth of the statement when it was made, and there was nothing in his conduct and demeanour from which the jury, notwithstanding his denial, could infer that he acknowledged its truth in whole or in part, the practice of the judges has been to exclude it altogether. In *R* v *Norton* [1910] 2 KB 496 Pickford J, in delivering the judgment of the Court of Criminal Appeal, said at p 500: "If there be no such evidence" (that is of acknowledgment by the accused), "then the contents of the statement should be excluded; if there be such evidence, then they should be admitted." If it was intended to lay down rules of law to be applied whenever such a statement is tendered for admission, I think the judgment goes too far; they are valuable rules for the guidance of those presiding at trials of criminal cases when considering how the discretion of the Court, with regard to the admission of such evidence, should be exercised, but it must not be assumed that the judgment in *R* v *Norton* exhausts all the circumstances which may have to be taken into consideration by the Court when exercising its judicial discretion.

It might well be that the prosecution wished to give evidence of such a statement in order to prove the conduct and demeanour of the accused when hearing the statement as a relevant fact in the particular case, notwithstanding that it did not amount either to an acknowledgment or some evidence of an acknowledgment of any part of the truth of the statement. I think it impossible to lay down any general rule to be applied to all such cases, save the principle of strict law to which I have referred.

Upon the whole, therefore, I come to the conclusion that the rules formulated in *R* v *Norton* and followed in this and other cases, must be restricted in their application as above indicated, and cannot be regarded as strict rules of law regulating the admissibility of such evidence.

(VISCOUNT HALDANE LC and LORDS DUNEDIN, PARKER of WADDINGTON and MOULTON delivered concurring judgments.)

Appeal dismissed.

Holt J: Mr Bunbury, what do you say?

Mr Bunbury: My Lord, firstly, the case is not the same as *R* v *Christie*, where the child victim was not called to give evidence, and where the evidence of others as to what he had said was hearsay. Angela's words were a part of the act of identification. Secondly, it is alleged that Littleton did at length make a confession, albeit to his wife, so that his denials have not been consistent. The jury must consider his reaction as a whole, and assess the overall picture.

Holt J: Let us assume for a moment that Littleton had elected to remain silent from the outset, instead of later at the police station. As I understand what was said in *Hall* v *R*, no adverse inference could be drawn from that silence.

Hall v R [1971] 1 WLR 298 (PC)

The appellant was convicted of unlawful possession of a controlled drug. The evidence against him was that the drug was found on premises which he occupied jointly with others, but not in his room. He was told by an officer that another defendant had said that the drug belonged to him, but made no reply to this allegation.

LORD DIPLOCK, delivering the judgment of their Lordships, said: 'It is not suggested in the instant case that the appellant's acceptance of the suggestion of Daphne Thompson which was repeated to him by the police constable was shown by word or by any positive conduct, action or demeanour. All that is relied upon is his mere silence.

It is a clear and widely known principle of the common law...that a person is entitled to refrain from answering a question put to him for the purpose of discovering whether he has committed a criminal offence. A fortiori he is under no obligation to comment when he is informed that someone else has accused him of an offence. It may be that in very exceptional circumstances an inference may be drawn from a failure to give an explanation or a disclaimer but in their Lordships' view silence alone on being informed by a police officer that someone else has made an accusation against him cannot give rise to an inference that the person to whom this information is communicated accepts the truth of the accusation...The caution merely serves to remind the accused of a right which he already possesses at common law. The fact that in a particular case he has not been reminded of it is no ground for inferring that his silence was not in exercise of that right, but was an acknowledgment of the truth of the accusation.'

Appeal allowed.

Mr Bunbury: With respect, My Lord, even in that case, Angela's accusation would be admissible, on the basis of what Cave J said about accusations made 'on even terms' in:

R v *Mitchell* (1892) 17 Cox CC 503 (Nottingham Assizes)

The defendant was charged with murder. A statement made by the deceased woman was held not to be admissible as a dying declaration, and the taking of her deposition by a magistrate had to be stopped when the deceased became too ill to continue, and before the defendant's solicitor had had any opportunity to cross-examine her; it was therefore inadmissible in evidence. It was sought to admit what there was of the deposition as a statement made in the presence of the defendant.

CAVE J said: 'Now the whole admissibility of statements of this kind rests upon the consideration that if a charge is made against a person in that person's presence it is reasonable to expect that he or she will immediately deny it, and that the absence of such a denial is some evidence of an admission on the part of the person charged, and of the truth of the charge. Undoubtedly, when persons are speaking on even terms, and a charge is made, and the person charged says nothing, and expresses no indignation, and does nothing to repel the charge, that is some evidence to show that he admits the charge to be true. But, where a statement is made in such circumstances that the prisoner cannot repel the charge, it is absurd to say that his remaining silent is any evidence of the truth of the charge. In this case, where a woman was lying on her deathbed, and her evidence was being formally taken, the last thing in the world to be expected is that the prisoner should have started up and denied it, and said that all the woman was saying was untrue, especially when she was represented by a solicitor, and knew that her solicitor would be allowed to ask questions in turn, and that everything would be done for her which could be done. It would in my opinion be simply monstrous to say that because she did not do so, that is to be taken as evidence of her guilt.'

This principle has been adopted more recently in:

R v *Chandler* [1976] 1 WLR 585 (CA)

The defendant was convicted of conspiracy to defraud. He had been interviewed by the police in the presence of his solicitor. Both before and after being cautioned he answered some questions, but in relation to others either remained silent or refused to answer them. At the trial the judge in summing up said that a person who had been cautioned had a right to remain silent, but it was for the jury to decide whether the defendant remained silent before caution because of this right or because he might have thought, if he had answered, he would have incriminated himself.

LAWTON LJ, reading the judgment of the court, referred to two dicta of Lord Diplock in

Hall v *R* and continued: 'We have reservations about these two statements of law because they seem to conflict with *R* v *Christie* [1914] AC 545 and with earlier cases and authorities. For reasons which will appear later in this judgment, it is not necessary in this case to review the law relating to the so-called right of silence. The law has long accepted that an accused person is not bound to incriminate himself; but it does not follow that a failure to answer an accusation or question when an answer could reasonably be expected may not provide some evidence in support of an accusation. Whether it does will depend upon the circumstances.

This principle was applied in *Bessela* v *Stern* (1877) 2 CPD 265. In that case, which was an action for breach of promise of marriage, evidence from the plaintiff's sister was accepted as corroboration for the purpose of the statute 32 & 33 Vict c 68. This evidence was to the effect that the defendant had made no denial when the plaintiff had upbraided him for having promised to marry her and failing to do so. In *R* v *Mitchell* (1892) 17 Cox CC 503, 508, Cave J said:

> Undoubtedly, when persons are speaking on even terms, and a charge is made, and the person charged says nothing, and expresses no indignation, and does nothing to repel the charge, that is some evidence to show that he admits the charge to be true.

As Professor Sir Rupert Cross commented in his book, *Evidence,* 4th ed, p 189, in reference to *R* v *Mitchell,* this "is a broad principle of common sense." Indeed it is.... It would be unfortunate if the law of evidence was allowed to develop in a way which was not in accordance with the common sense of ordinary folk. We are bound by *R* v *Christie,* not by *Hall* v *The Queen. R* v *Christie,* in our judgment, does accord with common sense.

When the judge's comments are examined against the principles enunciated in both *R* v *Mitchell* and *R* v *Christie* we are of the opinion that the defendant and the detective sergeant were speaking on equal terms since the former had his solicitor present to give him any advice he might have wanted and to testify, if needed, as to what had been said. We do not accept that a police officer always has an advantage over someone he is questioning. Everything depends upon the circumstances. A young detective questioning a local dignitary in the course of an inquiry into alleged local government corruption may be very much at a disadvantage. This kind of situation is to be contrasted with that of a tearful housewife accused of shoplifting or of a parent being questioned about the suspected wrongdoing of his son. Some comment on the defendant's lack of frankness before he was cautioned was justified provided the jury's attention was directed to the right issue, which was whether in the circumstances the defendant's silence amounted to an acceptance by him of what the detective sergeant had said. If he accepted what had been said, then the next question should have been whether guilt could reasonably be inferred from what he had accepted. To suggest, as the judge did, that the defendant's silence could indicate guilt was to short-circuit the intellectual process which has to be followed.
Appeal allowed.

Holt J: It may be that the case of *Parkes* v *R* is factually closer to the present case.

Parkes v *R* [1976] 1 WLR 1251 (PC)

The defendant was charged with the murder of a woman who had died from stab wounds. At his trial the deceased's mother gave evidence that she had found her daughter injured and had gone to the defendant and said, 'What she do you — Why you stab her?'; that the defendant had made no answer and had tried to stab her when she threatened to hold him until the police came. The judge directed the jury that the defendant's failure to reply to the mother's accusation coupled with his conduct immediately afterwards was evidence from which the jury could infer that the defendant had accepted the truth of the accusation. The defendant was convicted and appealed.

LORD DIPLOCK, delivering the judgment of their Lordships, said: 'In the instant case, there is no question of an accusation being made by or in the presence of a police officer or any other person in authority or charged with the investigation of the crime. It was a spontaneous charge made by a mother about an injury done to her daughter. In circumstances such as these, their Lordships agree with the Court of Appeal of Jamaica that the direction given by Cave J in *R* v *Mitchell* (1892) 17 Cox CC 503, 508 is applicable....

Here Mrs Graham and the defendant were speaking on even terms. Furthermore, as the Chief Justice pointed out to the jury, the defendant's reaction to the twice-repeated accusation was not one of mere silence. He drew a knife and attempted to stab Mrs Graham in order to escape when she threatened to detain him while the police were sent for.

Appeal dismissed.

You would not say that there was a case of 'even terms' at the police station, presumably? I understand that Littleton was not permitted to see his solicitor.

Mr Bunbury: My Lord, that is correct.

Holt J: Mr Bacon, I shall undoubtedly admit the identifying words spoken by Angela Blackstone. I rather incline to admit the whole of your client's conversation with the officers which I do not regard as prejudicial, so that the jury may weigh it against the alleged confession to his wife. It may even assist your case. You may want to consider that, and raise the issue again if you wish, when the officers give evidence.

Mr Bacon: I am much obliged to Your Lordship.

7.22 Questions for Counsel

7.22.1 Blackstone v *Coke:* Do you agree with Mr Atkyn that the letter of 3 March 1980 from Eldon & Co contains admissions in writing or by conduct adverse to Margaret Blackstone's case? Assuming that Margaret's evidence was that she refused an abortion only on medical advice, what would be the weight of such an admission?

7.22.2 R v *Coke and Littleton:* Devise appropriate questions for use on the voir dire, based on the depositions and proofs of evidence:

(a) to put to D/I Glanvil in order to establish that Coke's confessions are admissible:

(b) to put to Coke in order to establish the converse proposition.

7.22.3 Consider what arguments, if any, may be open to Littleton in law or as a matter of discretion, to exclude his conversations with his wife or the police officers.

7.22.4 Analyse, giving your reasons, whether you would apply on behalf of Littleton, to exclude any of the questions put to him to which he made denials. What arguments may be made, from a tactical point of view, for and against making such an application? Given that Mr Bacon chose to make an application, do you agree with Holt J's ruling, firstly as to Angela's identifying words and secondly as to Littleton's conversations with the officers?

7.23 Note

Guidance to courts on applying the principles relating to the admissibility of confessions was given recently by the Court of Appeal in *R* v *Rennie* (1981) *The Times,* 7 Nov. The defendant objected at his trial for conspiracy to obtain a pecuniary advantage by deception to the admissibility of evidence of an oral confession and to a statement under caution made by him. There was a trial within a trial. The grounds of the objection were that the interviewing officer led the defendant to believe that unless he made the admissions other members of his family might be arrested and charged. The officer denied telling the defendant that he was going to bring the rest of his family into it. He admitted, however, that the defendant was afraid that they would be involved. He relied upon the decision in *DPP* v *Ping Lin* (7.7 ante).

In the course of a reserved judgment the Lord Chief Justice offered the following general guidance:

> Very few confessions were inspired solely by remorse. Often the motives of an accused person were mixed and included a hope that an early admission might lead to an earlier release or a lighter sentence. If it were the law that the mere presence of such a motive, even if prompted by something said or done by a person in authority, led inexorably to the exclusion of a confession, nearly every confession would be rendered inadmissible.
>
> That was not the law. In some cases the hope might be self-generated. If so, it was irrelevant even if it provided the dominant motive for making the confession. In such a case the confession would not have been obtained by anything said or done by a person in authority.
>
> More commonly the presence of such a hope would, in part at least owe its origin to something said or done by such a person. There could be few prisoners who were being firmly but fairly questioned in a police station to whom it did not occur that they might be able to bring both their interrogation and their detention to an earlier end by confessing.
>
> Their Lordships did not understand the speeches delivered in the House of Lords in *DPP* v *Ping Lin* to require the exclusion of every such confession. The essence of their Lordships' opinions in that case could be summarised as follows:
>
> The law relating to the admissibility of confessions was much simpler than appeared to have been thought in the years immediately preceding 1975.
>
> It was, as stated by Lord Sumner in *Ibrahim* v *The King* ([1914] AC 599, 609): '... no statement of an accused is admissible in evidence against him unless it is shown by the prosecution to have been a voluntary statement in the sense that it had not been obtained from him either by fear or prejudice or hope of advantage exercised or held out by a person in authority' or, as had now to be added, by oppression.
>
> It was unnecessary and undesirable to complicate that question by considerations of whether conduct was 'improper' or constituted an 'inducement'.
>
> The sense and spirit of the principle were more important than the particular wording in which it was expressed. Above all it was to be applied with common sense.
>
> The person best able to get the flavour and effect of the circumstances in which the confession was made was the trial judge, and his findings of fact and reasoning were entitled to respect.
>
> How was the principle to be applied where a prisoner, when deciding to confess, not only realised the strength of the evidence known to the police and the hopelessness of escaping conviction, but was conscious at the same time, of the fact that it might well be advatageous to him, or as might have been so in the present case, to someone close to him, if he confessed?
>
> How, in particular, was the judge to approach the question when those different thoughts might all, to some extent at least, have been prompted by something said by the police officer questioning the prisoner?
>
> The answer would not be found from any refined analysis of the concept of causation nor from too detailed attention to any particular phrase on Lord Sumner's formulation. Although the question was for the judge, he should approach it much as would a jury were it for them. In other words he should understand the principle and the spirit behind it and apply his common sense. Their Lordships would add, he should remind himself that 'voluntary' in ordinary parlance meant of one's own free will.

8 The Rule Against Hearsay: III

A: STATUTORY EXCEPTIONS IN CRIMINAL CASES

8.1 Introductory notes

8.1.1 The decision in *Myers* v *DPP* [1965] AC 1001, showed that the courts were not prepared to accord judicial recognition to a new exception to the hearsay rule. This prompted Parliament to consider some statutory reform of the rule. There had, even before this, existed a number of specific statutory provisions allowing the admission of pieces of hearsay evidence in particular cases. The Criminal Evidence Act 1965 introduced for the first time a rule of wider application, which applies to any criminal case provided the statutory conditions are met. In summary, the Act provides that hearsay evidence can be introduced where it is in documentary form and is or forms part of a record relating to any trade or business, and is compiled from a basis of personal knowledge of the facts dealt with, and provided also that the supplier of the information is for good reason unable to attend to give evidence.

8.1.2 In addition to this general provision, there remain a number of important individual statutory provisions permitting the use of hearsay in certain cases. Some, like the Theft Act 1968, s.27(4), deal with very narrow cases. Others, relating to the taking of depositions from persons who are dangerously ill, or from children and young persons in certain cases apply in a variety of situations, but are usually circumscribed by stringent conditions designed to avoid injustice to the defendant. Typically, such provisions permit the defence to object to the admission of the evidence and require the taking of direct oral evidence.

8.1.3 Of particular importance in practice are the provisions of s.9 of the Criminal Justice Act 1967 and s.102 of the Magistrates' Courts Act 1980. Both sections, subject to somewhat different conditions, permit the use as evidence of written statements made by a person for the purpose of criminal proceedings. Both sections require that the defence have no objection to the admission of the evidence, and are therefore much used for saving the time of witnesses where evidence is undisputed. Section 102 of the Magistrates' Courts Act 1980 applies to committal proceedings in the magistrates' court, and s.9 of the Criminal Justice Act 1967 to all other criminal proceedings. (*A Practical Approach to Evidence,* pp 192-201.)

8.2 Commentary

R v *Coke and Littleton* at trial. Having received notice of alibi on behalf of the defendant Littleton, Mr Bunbury proposes to seek to refute that alibi by proving that Littleton was not at home until 4.15 pm on 8 July 1979, as he claimed, but instead had been working at a public house called the King's Head in Oxbridge where he was casually employed between 10.00 am and 2.00 pm. Mr Bunbury explains to Holt J in the absence of the jury what course he proposes to take.

8.3 Argument

Mr Bunbury: My Lord, I propose to call the manager of the King's Head public house to produce a book kept in the public house for accounting purposes which shows the hours worked by and wages paid to casual bar staff. There is an entry which appears to show that the defendant Littleton was working in the bar on the morning in question, which is inconsistent with his alibi.

Holt J: Yes. Mr Bacon, have you any objection to that evidence?

Mr Bacon: My Lord, yes. Simply that it is hearsay. As I understand it, my learned friend intends to use this entry to prove the truth of the facts stated in it. In my submission, he ought to call a witness who can say that he saw the defendant Littleton at that time and place.

Mr Bunbury: My Lord, in my submission, the evidence is admissible as forming part of a business record within the meaning of Section 1 of the Criminal Evidence Act 1965, which reads:

Criminal Evidence Act 1965, s.1

1. — (1) In any criminal proceedings where direct oral evidence of a fact would be admissible, any statement contained in a document and tending to establish that fact shall, on production of the document, be admissible as evidence of that fact if:—

(a) the document is, or forms part of, a record relating to any trade or business and compiled, in the course of that trade or business, from information supplied (whether directly or indirectly) by persons who have, or may reasonably be supposed to have, personal knowledge of the matters dealt with in the information they supply; and

(b) the person who supplied the information recorded in the statement in question is dead, or beyond the seas, or unfit by reason of his bodily or mental condition to attend as a witness, or cannot with reasonable diligence be identified or found, or cannot reasonably be expected (having regard to the time which has elapsed since he supplied the information and to all the circumstances) to have any recollection of the matters dealt with in the information he supplied.

(2) For the purpose of deciding whether or not a statement is admissible as evidence by virtue of this section, the court may draw any reasonable inference from the form or content of the document in which the statement is contained, and may, in deciding whether or not a person is fit to attend as a witness, act on a certificate purporting to be a certificate of a fully registered medical practitioner.

(3) In estimating the weight, if any, to be attached to a statement admissible as evidence by virtue of this section regard shall be had to all the circumstances from which any inference can reasonably be drawn as to the accuracy or otherwise of the statement, and, in particular, to the question whether or not the person who supplied the information recorded in the statement did so contemporaneously with the occurrence or existence of the facts stated, and to the question whether or not that person, or any person concerned with making or keeping the record containing the statement, had any incentive to conceal or misrepresent the facts.

(4) In this section 'statement' includes any representation of fact, whether made in words or otherwise, 'document' includes any device by means of which information is recorded or

stored and 'business' includes any public transport, public utility or similar undertaking carried on by a local authority and the activities of the Post Office.

Holt J: Mr Bunbury, I note that the section has a number of conditions as to which I shall need to be satisfied. What course do you suggest we adopt?

Mr Bunbury: My Lord, I would respectfully invite Your Lordship to hear evidence about those conditions in the absence of the jury. Indeed, the defence are entitled to have the matter investigated if they so desire. I would refer Your Lordship to:

R v Nichols (1976) 63 Cr App R 187 (CA)

The appellant was convicted of handling stolen motor vehicle tyres. During the trial the prosecution attempted to admit certain documents, for example a driver's delivery sheet, under s.1 of the Criminal Evidence Act 1965, arguing that the judge was entitled to draw an inference from the general circumstances in which such a document is likely to come into existence. The documents were admitted.

JAMES LJ, delivering the judgment of the court, said: 'In the judgment of this Court the judge did fall into the errors which Mr Wedmore argues were present in the conduct of this trial. It is our view that the documents in the pages of exhibit 6 were wrongly admitted in evidence at the stage they were admitted, and that there had not been created sufficient foundation for the judge to draw the reasonable inference which he is required to draw, or may draw, from the face of the documents in order to satisfy himself that those requirements of section 1(1)(b) are satisfied. There was nothing to indicate in the state of the evidence whether those who might have been called as witnesses in relation to the information compiled on the document were alive or dead, whether in this country or beyond the seas, whether unfit or fit to attend as witnesses or would or would not have a reasonable expectation of being able to recollect the information which they provided and which was contained in the documents. Further, the objection having been raised by counsel for the then defendant, the defendant was entitled to have the matter investigated as in a trial within a trial in order to ascertain whether or not the evidence could properly be admitted pursuant to the Act. That is sufficient to dispose of the crucial issue involved in this appeal.

It may be found useful if we add that the course that this trial took in relation to this point of admissibility of evidence pursuant to the Criminal Evidence Act 1965, is not a course which inevitably follows whenever the Crown seek to rely upon the provisions of the Act. A great deal of time was spent in this case. From what we have been told — and there is no indication given to the contrary so we accept it — the documents in question apparently were not available until the trial started and it does appear from the transcript that Mr Wedmore was in a position in which he was making objections without having had an opportunity of seeing the documents to which he was objecting — a position which did not find favour with the trial judge and gave rise to some exchanges between the judge and counsel in the case. But it is no fault of the appellant or his counsel if the documents were not available until a late stage. This particular Act was passed in order to simplify the course of a trial, in order to provide a means of establishing facts without the necessity of calling a large body of witnesses or making detailed investigations and obtaining statements from a considerable number of persons who would then have to come to the trial to give evidence in respect of those facts which were within their personal knowledge and it is important that the Act is operated to the end that its purpose is achieved — the simplification of proceedings. In many cases where evidence is sought to be adduced as admissible pursuant to the terms of section 1 of the Criminal Evidence Act 1965, it may have been possible for the facts to be agreed as between prosecution and defence provided the proper preparation and presentation of the case was followed.

It occurs to us that one sensible step would be the service of a notice to admit facts in the early stages of the case. The accused is not bound to admit facts but if he does admit facts then those admitted facts can form part of the evidence. If he does not admit the facts stated in the notice then witness statements can be taken and served upon him on the basis that those witnesses need not attend the trial unless the Crown or the accused desire their attendance, in which case notice should be served, and at that stage the accused has an opportunity of deciding whether to challenge the evidence or not. If he does not challenge the evidence and seek the attendance of the witnesses, then their witness statements can be read in the course of the trial. If he does challenge the evidence then the Crown can take advantage, in the proper case, of the provisions of the Act and it is for the Crown then to lay the foundation by which the Court can be satisfied that the evidence that they seek to adduce can properly be adduced by reason of that enactment. It may be that these few observations will serve to obviate troubles that beset the trial in this particular case.

Reverting to the present appeal, for the reasons expressed, that evidence was improperly admitted for the prosecution, there was an irregularity in the course of the trial resulting from the misdirection of the judge as to admissibility of evidence and the conviction cannot stand.' Appeal allowed.

Holt J: Yes, very well.

(Mr Bunbury called evidence in the absence of the jury showing that the licensee of the King's Head, who supplied the information contained in the book relating to 8 July 1979, had subsequently been incapacitated by a stroke and was unable to attend court to give evidence. The evidence further showed that the book was kept for accounting purposes in connection with the operation of the business of the King's Head.)

Holt J: Well, Mr Bacon, in the light of that, is there any reason why the entry in the book should not be placed before the jury under the statute as evidence of the facts contained in it? It seems to me to be a statement contained in the document within the meaning of the section, and, if the jury accept it, would seem to tend to establish the fact of Littleton's attendance for work. It seems to me plainly to fall within the definition of statement and document cotained in Section 1(4), and to tend to establish the facts contained within it.

Mr Bacon: My Lord, with respect I agree. I would submit there are two reasons why this evidence is not admissible in the present case. The first is that this is a book obviously kept in a haphazard fashion, in rather bad handwriting, apparently containing contributions from a number of people and not maintaining a regular sequence from day to day. In my submission, it is impossible to regard this as a record within the meaning of the section. I refer to the observations of the Court of Appeal in:

R v *Tirado* (1974) 59 Cr App R 80 (CA)

The appellant who was convicted of obtaining property by deception, ran an employment agency in Oxford. He wrote to Moroccans in Morocco stating that he had work for them and inviting them to post their fees to the agency or to do so through a Moroccan bank. The latter method was used in all the examples before the court. The appellant, in the course of his defence, maintained that his business was wholly honest, although muddled and inefficient. He said that on occasions he had made refunds of the sums which he had received and produced a number of cheque stubs from his office in connection with the alleged repayments as evidence of honest conduct. To rebut this the prosecution produced, from a series of files kept by the appellant, various unanswered letters of complaint addressed to the persons aggrieved to the appellant's firm.

LORD WIDGERY CJ, giving the judgment of the court said: 'If the appellant was running his defence in that way, and was putting forward these cheque stubs found on his premises as evidence of the honest conduct of the business, it seems to us that there cannot possibly have been any objection to the prosecution producing the appropriate file, putting it before the appellant in the witness box and saying: "In view of what you now tell us what do you say about the file, and what do you say about those letters of complaint?" If the matter had been handled in that way, there would, we think, have been no possible reason for saying that the documents had been improperly let in, regardless of any view which might have been formed of their admissibility under the Act of 1965.

The procedure, no doubt, did not precisely follow that which I have described, and one of the reasons may have been the judge's ruling in regard to the effect of the 1965 Act, and even assuming for the moment that the judge was wrong in his view on the 1965 Act and that these documents were not let in in evidence on that account, we can see no possible reason for thinking that the use of the documents in the manner which I have described could give rise to a miscarriage of justice and thus result in a decision in this case going in favour of the appellant. Thus in the end it seems to us that, although the documents were not handled in the conventional manner having regard to their nature, yet the result cannot give rise to a miscarriage of justice which would cause us to think that this appeal should be allowed.

But before leaving this point, of course I must return to this decision on the Act of 1965. We do not find it necessary to give a detailed definition of the words used in the section which I have read and which have not, so far as we know, been the subject of judicial comment before, but although we will leave the matter for final decision on another day, we have at least some hesitation in saying that a file of correspondence, maintained simply as a file of correspondence, and added to from time to time as letters come in, is or can be a record relating to any trade or business and compiled from information supplied within the meaning of section 1 of the Act of 1965. The language of section 1 seems on its face to contemplate the making or compilation of a record. That means the keeping of a book or a file, or a card index, into which information is deliberately put in order that it may be available to others another day. A cash book, a ledger, a stock book: all these may be records because they contain information deliberately entered in order that the information may be preserved. We think it at least widely open to question whether a file of the kind referred to in this case, either as a whole or when its individual documents are looked at, can come within the definition of a record within the meaning of the Act.

Appeal dismissed.

Mr Bunbury: My Lord, I accept my learned friend's point in principle. But this is a very different case. One is not dealing here with a miscellaneous collection of documents. It may be that the jury will find the record unimpressive and be inclined to place less weight on it for that reason. But Your Lordship has heard evidence that this book was maintained as a record of a trade or business. The most my learned friend can say is that it is not a good record. In my submission, the right way to regard this is that adopted by the Court of Appeal in *R* v *Jones; R* v *Sullivan,* in which it was pointed out that even single documents having a limited life span could amount to a record if they were properly kept for commercial purposes.

R v *Jones; R* v *Sullivan* [1978] 1 WLR 195 (CA)

The defendants, who ran a transport business, were charged with conspiracy to steal goods from containers. One of the containers broken into had been packed with cartons of cotton goods in Hong Kong and from there shipped to Southampton. To prove the number of cartons originally placed in the container, the prosecution put in evidence under s.1(1) of the Criminal Evidence Act 1965 a bill of lading and a cargo manifest both made out in Hong Kong, being the 'record' of a trade or business made by a person beyond the seas. The defendants were convicted and appealed.

GEOFFREY LANE LJ, giving the judgment of the court, related the facts and the relevant parts of s.1 of the Criminal Evidence Act 1965 and continued: 'It is not in dispute that all the necessary ingredients of that section are fulfilled in this case, apart from the one matter, namely, can it be said that the documents to which I have referred were a record or form part of a record relating to the trade or business? Mr Harvey has, if we may say so, very ably argued before us that on the plain construction of the words they do not form part of a record and what he says is this. He submits that in order to be a record the documents must have some permanence. It must be something which can be referred to as a record in the future although he concedes he is there using the word which he is seeking to define. He goes on to submit that it must not be a document which is used merely to service an individual transaction; it must be going to be kept beyond the limit of that one single transaction; something to be kept, he says, as a record available beyond the immediate transaction, deliberately done with an eye to its use in the future — something which is merely brought into existence to service the one transaction is not enough. Those were the various ways he put the matter although he was in some difficulty in explaining to us the precise degree of permanence which the document must have before it becomes a record.

He drew our attention to the definition of "record" contained in the *Shorter Oxford English Dictionary*, 3rd ed (1944), vol II p 1675. There were two passages to which he referred, the first was:

> The fact or condition of being preserved as knowledge, especially by being put into writing; knowledge or information preserved or handed down in this way.

The second was as follows:

> An account of some fact or event preserved in writing or other permanent form; a document, monument, etc, on which such an account is inscribed; also anything or person serving to indicate or give evidence of, or preserve the memory of, a fact or event; a memorial.

It seems to this court that the documents in the present case fall precisely within those definitions.

Although it is not an exhaustive definition of the word, 'record' in this context means a history of events in some form which is not evanescent. How long the record is likely to be kept is immaterial: it may be something which will not survive the end of the transaction in question, it may be something which is indeed more lasting that bronze, but the degree of permanence does not seem to us to make or mar the fulfilment of the definition of the word 'record'. The record in each individual case will last as long as commercial necessity may demand.

The documents in the present case seem to us to fall precisely into that category. They are the written records of the particular transaction. They are documents containing the history of this particular transaction, where the goods started from, the method of transport, the name of the ship, the port of arrival and the container depot destination on the one hand and the final consignee's destination on the other. They are carefully and deliberately compiled for the information of those in this country who are going to be the recipients of the goods. There is no necessity, as we see it, for the contents of these documents to be entered into a book or a ledger as was suggested in one of the cases; indeed these very documents themselves might have been copied into a ledger but how, one asks, could that make them any more or less a record than they are at the moment?

We have come to the conclusion, despite Mr Harvey's argument, quite plainly that these documents were records or part of records within the meaning of the section of the Act which I have read and that particular part of his argument therefore fails.'

Appeal dismissed.

I do not understand my learned friend to dispute that the King's Head is a trade or business within the meaning of the section. It is of course true that a trade or business imports some commercial operation. Your Lordship will be aware of the decision in *R v Gwilliam* dealing with goverment departments.

R v Gwilliam [1968] 1 WLR 1839 (CA)

At the trial of the defendant for driving with an excessive proportion of alcohol in the blood contrary to s.1(1) of the Road Safety Act 1967, evidence was admitted to the effect that boxes of 'Alcotest 80' devices had been accompanied by a consignment note from the Head Office Supplies and Transport branch, and that a box containing devices used for breath tests on the defendant bore a label stating that they had been approved by the Secretary of State for the Home Department for the purpose of the Road Safety Act 1967. The jury were directed that the label was evidence on which they could hold that the device was of a type approved by the Secretary of State in accordance with s.7(1), and the defendant was convicted.

LORD PARKER CJ, giving the judgment of the court, stated the facts, referred to s.1 of the Criminal Evidence Act 1965, and continued: 'The sole point in this case and the point upon which the recorder gave a certificate was whether there was admissible evidence from which the jury were entitled to hold that this "Alcotest" equipment which had been used was a type approved by the Secretary of State for the Home Department. The necessity for that is founded on the decision of the Divisional Court in *Scott v Baker,* that being a case decided on May 14 this year and accordingly long after the trial in the present case.

At the very outset counsel for the defendant took the point that proof was required of the approval by the Secretary of State of the "Alcotest" equipment. It was submitted by the prosecution that that was proved, or that there was evidence from which the jury could find that it was proved, from a label which was inside the lid of the testing set. That label read:

Alcotest 80. Approved by the Secretary of State for the Home Department for the purpose of the Road Safety Act, 1967.

That was admitted by the recorder and left to the jury as evidence on which they could hold that there had been such approval. It is now conceded by Mr Barnes (and, in the opinion of this court, right conceded) that that label was not admissible evidence of approval at all. Accordingly one starts with this: that something was left to the jury which was not evidence of approval.

Notwithstanding that, it is said that this is a case for the application of the proviso in that approval was proved from two other matters. At the trial a Superintendent Westwood was called who was in charge of the traffic department at the police divisional headquarters at that time and he gave evidence, first, that equipment of this kind was issued in large quantities to the police, and secondly and more important he produced, and was allowed to produce, a consignment note covering the equipment used in the present case which equipment had been delivered to police headquarters and indeed had been signed for by Superintendent Westwood. That consignment note was in this form. It was headed: "Consignment Note. Road Transport, Home Office, S & T Branch liability" and it recited that the goods were sent (this appears in a rubber stamp) from the Head Office Supply and Transport Store, Arbury Road, Nuneaton, Warwickshire. Mr Barnes submits that that evidence by Superintendent Westwood and the consignment note itself were admissible evidence to prove the approval by the Secretary of State. He relies primarily for that on the provisions of the Criminal Evidence Act, 1965, and in particular section 1(1) which reads as follows:

In any criminal proceedings where direct oral evidence of a fact would be admissible, any statement contained in a document and tending to establish that fact shall, on production of the document, be admissible as evidence of that fact if — (a) the document is, or forms part of, a record relating to any trade or business and compiled, in the course of that trade or business, from information supplied (whether directly or indirectly) by persons who have, or may reasonably be supposed to have, personal knowledge of the matters dealt with in the information they supply...

Mr Barnes puts it in this way: that evidence of the fact of the Secretary of State's approval could be given by direct oral evidence and accordingly any statement contained in a document of the type there described which tends to establish that approval would be admissible.

This court is quite satisfied that that submission fails. It may be (and the court is not deciding this case on that basis) that it is quite impossible to say that the consignment note itself is a record or forms part of a record within the meaning of section 1(1). It may also be that one could not reasonably suppose that the clerk, whoever it was, who prepared that consignment note could have personal knowledge of the matter. But what is quite clear, in the judgment of this court, is, that the document, even if a record, was not a record relating to any trade or business. It is to be observed that section 1(4) defines "business" as including

> any public transport, public utility or similar undertaking carried on by a local authority and the activities of the Post Office.

In the judgment of this court the Home Office S & T Branch does not carry on a business within the meaning of that subsection.

Appeal allowed.

A similar approach was taken with regard to Home Office records in *R* v *Patel* (1981) 73 Cr App R 117 (CA). Your Lordship will also know the following case which deals with a hospital run by the National Health Service.

R v *Crayden* [1978] 1 WLR 604 (CA)

At his trial, on two counts of burglary, the defendant alleged that oral admissions and a written statement made by him to the police on 17 April 1976, had been obtained by the use of violence. On the evening of 17 April he had gone to a National Health Service hospital and been examined by a casualty officer, who had made notes of the examination. A radiologist at the hospital had also made a report on an X-ray taken of the defendant's jaw. The police denied that they had used violence, and the prosecution sought to put in evidence the records made by the casualty officer and the radiologist, under s.1 of the Criminal Evidence Act 1965, as being records related to a business and compiled in the course of that business. The judge ruled that the records were admissible and the defendant was convicted.

LAWTON LJ, giving the judgment of the court, stated the facts and continued: 'The sole question for consideration in this appeal is whether the judge should have admitted the medical record in evidence. Without the provisions of section 1 of the Criminal Evidence Act 1965, they could not have been admitted: they contained hearsay...

In the Act of 1965 the word 'business' cannot, in our judgment, have been intended to have the wide meaning ascribed to it by Lindley LJ in *Rolls* v *Miller* (1884) 26 Ch D 71, and by the House of Lords in *Town Investments Ltd* v *Department of the Environment* [1977] 2 WLR 450. Had it been intended to have this wide meaning it would have been unnecessary to enlarge its meaning by bringing in public transport, public utilities and the activities of the Post Office. And why the records relating to these activities rather than those relating to government business generally, to local government activities such as the social services and direct building, and the records kept by the armed services and the police, all of which would have been included in a wide meaning? Had the Act of 1965 been intended to make government records generally admissible we would have expected to find some words of limitation in the Act, otherwise confidential documents which in the past would not have been admissible in evidence would have become admissible. An example of a class of such documents is provided by *Lilley* v *Pettit* [1946] KB 401 which related to the regimental records of a serving soldier. The Division Court adjudged that they were not admissible in evidence as public documents. The absence of any words of limitation points towards a narrower construction of the word "business."

Every one of the activities specified by the enlarging words in the Act of 1965 relates to an activity which has an element in it of supplying services or goods although it may not be the only element. The supply of goods or services by the bodies specified in section 1(4) is a form of commercial activity carried on for the public benefit, but not for the private profit. It follows, in our judgment, that the word "business" as used in this Act has a commercial connotation. We do not find it necessary to construe this word in more precise terms since our only task is to say whether the medical records of the Brook Hospital produced by Miss Sherlock related to a trade or business. Whether a hospital outside the National Health Service should be adjudged to be a business for the purposes of the Act of 1965 does not arise for decision in this appeal.

Miss Goddard submitted that even if the word "business" in the Act of 1965 should be construed more narrowly than in such cases as *Rolls* v *Miller* and *Town Investments Ltd.,* the Brook Hospital would still be within a narrower definition. This was because running such a hospital involves many activities which are far removed from medical treatment. They include appointing staff, maintaining premises and acquiring and maintaining equipment, furniture and other movable property: see section 12 of the National Health Service Act 1946. All these activities, however, are ancillary to the main purpose of the hospital which is to provide for the area in which it is situated a service "designed to secure improvement in the physical and mental health of the people [of that area] and the prevention, diagnosis and treatment of illness…": see section 1 of the National Health Service Act 1946. In our judgment the provision of such a service cannot be a business with the meaning of that word as used in this Act.

Finally we note that the restricted meaning which we have put upon the word "business" in the Act of 1965 is in line with a ruling given by Judge Buzzard at the Central Criminal Court in *R* v *O'Dowd* (unreported) August 15, 1977. That judge, however, did not, so we were told, have his attention invited to the authorities cited in argument in this court.

It follows that the defendant's hospital record should not have been admitted in evidence. Appeal allowed.

Nothing of that sort applies here.

Mr Bacon: My Lord, of course I concede that point.

Holt J: I think on balance that I shall leave this document to the jury as being a record. What they make of it in terms of weight is of course a matter for them.

Mr Bacon: My Lord, I do have a second objection, that the section requires a showing that the supplier of the information should be a person who has or may reasonably be supposed to have personal knowledge of the matters with which he deals. In my submission, the evidence adduced by the prosecution does not go so far. There was no evidence as to where the licensee obtained his information, and of course he is unfortunately unable to assist us.

Mr Bunbury: In my submission, My Lord, the section is satisfied. Your Lordship has heard evidence from the manager that the licensee made his entry in the book on the same day, 8 July 1979. It is true that there is no direct evidence that the licensee was personally on the premises, or if so for how long. Nonetheless, it is a reasonable inference to be drawn in the circumstances.

Holt J: I do not see why in any event the evidence should be objectionable, even on the assumption that the licensee obtained the information from someone whom he knew to be present in the public house at the material times, and who may reasonably be supposed to have had personal knowledge.

Mr Bacon: My Lord, with respect, the answer to that is that there is no evidence that anyone other than the licensee is unfit to attend this court to give evidence.

Holt J: Yes, I think that is right.

Mr Bunbury: My Lord, this is not a case where there is a real difficulty about personal knowledge as there was in:

R v *Pettigrew* (1980) 71 Cr App R 39 (CA)

Shortly after a burglary in which some £650 in new £5 notes was stolen from a house, the appellant was found in possession of three new £5 notes. The prosecution wished to prove that the three notes could have come from the sequence of notes stolen, which could be traced by a series of steps from the Bank of England to the loser. In order to do this the prosecution tendered in evidence a print-out from a computer operated by an employee of the Bank of England. The operator fed into the machine bundles of printed and serially numbered notes, and himself noted the first number of the series. The machine then recorded the number of each note in the bundle and rejected any notes which were defective.

BRIDGE LJ, giving the judgment of the court, said: 'Mr McHale's perfectly short and simple submission is that, in those circumstances it cannot be said that anyone — if it were to be anyone, it would have to be the machine operator — had personal knowledge of that which emerges from the machine at the end of the day in a computer print-out recording the serial numbers of every note in each bundle to which the print-out relates.

Mr Williamson, in an attractive argument for the Crown, submits that the operator of the machine can fairly be said to have personal knowledge of the serial numbers of the notes in each bundle which he feeds into the machine. Although he has not mentally recorded them, he has the means of knowledge of the bundle of notes he has fed into the machine, which bear consecutive serial numbers, and he records on a card the first number of each bundle which he feeds into the machine.

This is a most attractive argument, and if the machine did nothing but record the totality of the numbers of notes in each bundle fed into it, it may well be — it is not necessary for present purposes to decide the point finally — that the argument for the Crown should prevail. But what at the end of the day has convinced us that we cannot accept it is the recognition that the machine has the important dual function of separating out the defective notes and rejecting them and recording the numbers of those rejected and recording the serial numbers of the notes at the beginning and end of each bundle.

The numbers of the notes which have been rejected can never be said to be in the personal knowledge of the operator or in the mind of anybody. They are recorded purely by the operation of the machine. The operator could never be said to have personal knowledge of those rejected notes, and knowledge of the numbers of the rejected notes is essential to know the serial numbers of the notes in the bundles to which the computer print-out relates.

Accordingly, although the point is highly technical, and one which may be thought to expose a lacuna in the Criminal Evidence Act 1965, the point is one on which the argument for the appellant Pettigrew is entitled to prevail.'
Appeal allowed.

Holt J: I agree that that difficulty does not arise in thise case,· but I think there is some force in what Mr Bacon says. I shall consider the evidence I heard in the absence of the jury, and then give my ruling as to whether I am satisfied that I can reasonably suppose the licensee to have had personal knowledge in the circumstances presented to me.

B: STATUTORY EXCEPTIONS IN CIVIL CASES

8.4 Introductory notes

8.4.1 The Civil Evidence Act 1968 effectively reversed the common law rule against hearsay for the purpose of civil proceedings. In place of the rule and its common law exceptions, the Act provides that in civil proceedings, hearsay statements may be admissible by virtue of the Act itself, by virtue of any other statutory provision or by agreement between the parties, but not otherwise. Civil proceedings are defined as including, in addition to civil proceedings in any of the ordinary courts of law, civil proceedings before any other tribunal in relation to which the strict rules of evidence apply and arbitrations or references.

8.4.2 Within this framework, ss.2, 4 and 5 of the Act apply to the admissibility of different kinds of statements. The principal provision is that of s.2, which deals with statements of fact, whether made orally or in a document or otherwise by any person, whether called as a witness in the proceedings or not. Where the party desiring to put in the hearsay statement also intends to call the maker as a witness, the admissibility of the hearsay statement is subject to certain requirements of leave, and as to the timing of the putting in of the statement. In the case of statements made otherwise than in documents, the statement must be proved by the direct oral evidence of the maker of the statement or a person who perceived it being made, except where the statement consists of oral evidence given in other legal proceedings which may be proved in any manner authorised by the court.

8.4.3 Under s.4, statements contained in documents are admissible as evidence of the facts stated therein, if the document is or forms part of a record compiled by a person acting under a duty, and from information which was supplied by a person who had, or may reasonably be supposed to have had, personal knowledge of the matters dealt with in that information, where the information was supplied to the compiler of the record either directly or indirectly through one or more intermediaries each acting under a duty. The section provides similar conditions, where the party desiring to put in the hearsay statement has called or intends to call as a witness the person who originally supplied the information from which the record containing the statement was compiled.

8.4.4 Under s.5 of the Act, provision is made for the admissibility of statements produced by computers, subject to complicated provisions designed to ensure the reliability and accuracy of such statements.

8.4.5 Section 8 of the Act provides statutory authority for rules of court to govern the admission of statements under the Act. These rules have been enacted in RSC Order 38, Rules 21–31. In essence, the Rules provide that a party wishing to adduce a hearsay statement under ss.2, 4 or 5 must serve, within certain time limits, notice of his intention to do so. On receipt of such notice, any other party may serve a counter-notice requiring the first named party to call the maker of the statement as a witness. Counter-notice may, however, be ineffective, in cases where, for one of the reasons set out in Rule 25, it is impossible or pointless to call the maker of the statement as a witness, for example, where he is dead or incapacitated by illness. Such a reason should be alleged by the party giving notice of intention to adduce the statement and, if disputed, the question must be decided by the court. Notwithstanding these provisions, the court has an overriding discretion under Rule 29 to permit evidence to be given, notwithstanding any failure to comply with the rules.

8.4.6 The Civil Evidence Act 1972 applies to statements of opinion, the 1968 Act relating to statement of fact. Except in relation to expert opinion evidence, the notice procedure described above applies also to statements admitted under this Act. However, in relation to expert opinion evidence, further rules of court are provided in RSC Order 38, Rules 36–44, and these are dealt with in Chapter 9. (*A Practical Approach to Evidence,* pp 202–224.)

8.5 Commentary

Blackstone v *Coke* at trial. Mr Noy on behalf of the plaintiff wishes to call evidence from Mrs Helen Blackstone as part of his case. Unfortunately, shortly after giving evidence for the prosecution in the criminal case, Mrs Blackstone suffered a serious stroke. Although she has recovered some mobility, her memory and powers of concentration have been very drastically reduced. After Mrs Blackstone has been sworn, Mr Noy attempts to examine her in chief, only to find that she is almost entirely unable to assist him. In those circumstances, Mr Noy makes an application to Hardwicke J.

8.6 Argument

Mr Noy: My Lord, in the circumstances that have arisen, I propose to ask Your Lordship to consider hearsay evidence from Mrs Blackstone, consisting of the evidence given by her at the criminal trial of the defendant Mr Coke, about which Your Lordship has already heard something.

Hardwicke J: I am not sure whether this is the course I ought to take. You have called this witness, and unfortunately she has been unable to help as much as you had wished. But on what basis can I consider what she has said on another occasion?

Mr Noy: Your Lordship may do so under Section 2 of the Civil Evidence Act 1968. If Your Lordship will look at that Act, it may be convenient to start with Section 1.

Civil Evidence Act 1968, s.1

1. — (1) In any civil proceedings a statement other than one made by a person while giving oral evidence in those proceedings shall be admissible as evidence of any fact stated therein to the extent that it is so admissible by virtue of any provision of this Part of this Act or by virtue of any other statutory provision or by agreement of the parties, but not otherwise.

(2) In this section "statutory provision" means any provision contained in, or in an instrument made under, this or any other Act, including any Act passed after this Act.

These are of course civil proceedings within the meaning of the Act. If Your Lordship looks at the definition of that section in Section 18(1).

Civil Evidence Act 1968, s.18(1)

18. — (1) In this Act 'civil proceedings' includes, in addition to civil proceedings in any of the ordinary courts of law —
(a) civil proceedings before any other tribunal, being proceedings in relation to which the strict rules of evidence apply; and
(b) an arbitration or reference, whether under an enactment or not,
but does not include civil proceedings in relation to which the strict rules of evidence do not apply.

My Lord, from there, the Act goes on to provide for the admissibility of statements by virtue of Section 2.

Civil Evidence Act 1968, s.2

2. — (1) In any civil proceedings a statement made, whether orally or in a document or

otherwise, by any person, whether called as a witness in those proceedings or not, shall, subject to this section and to rules of court, be admissible as evidence of any fact stated therein of which direct oral evidence by him would be admissible.

(2) Where in any civil proceedings a party desiring to give a statement in evidence by virtue of this section has called or intends to call as a witness in the proceedings the person by whom the statement was made, the statement—

(a)   shall not be given in evidence by virtue of this section on behalf of that party without the leave of the court; and

(b)   without prejudice to paragraph (a) above, shall not be given in evidence by virtue of this section on behalf of that party before the conclusion of the examination-in-chief of the person by whom it was made, except—

(i)   where before that person is called the court allows evidence of the making of the statement to be given on behalf of that party by some other person; or

(ii)   in so far as the court allows the person by whom the statement was made to narrate it in the course of his examination-in-chief on the ground that to prevent him from doing so would adversely affect the intelligibility of his evidence.

(3) Where in any civil proceedings a statement which was made otherwise than in a document is admissible by virtue of this section, no evidence other than direct oral evidence by the person who made the statement or any person who heard or otherwise perceived it being made shall be admissible for the purpose of proving it:

Provided that if the statement in question was made by a person while giving oral evidence in some other legal proceedings (whether civil or criminal), it may be proved in any manner authorised by the court.

Hardwicke J: Yes. Looking again at Section 2(2), it seems to me that this is a case where you require leave, because you have called Mrs Blackstone as a witness. Mr Atkyn, do you have any objection to leave being granted?

Mr Atkyn: My Lord, I do. What is happening here is that my learned friend is seeking to bolster an unsatisfactory part of his case by using a hearsay statement. I would refer Your Lordship to the observations made by Lawton J in:

Harvey v Smith-Wood [1964] 2 QB 171

A witness, an elderly man called for the plaintiff, gave evidence which appeared to conflict with the evidence given by the plaintiff. The plaintiff's counsel thereupon sought to put in evidence a written statement made by the witness some six years before, submitting that the statement was admissible under s.1(1) of the Evidence Act 1938. (The 1938 Act was the first general major inroad into the common law of hearsay evidence. It was confined to civil proceedigs and applied only to documentary evidence. In general terms it rendered documentary hearsay admissible subject to certain conditions. The substantive parts of the 1938 Act are repealed by the Civil Evidence Act 1968, in respect of all proceedings to which the latter applies. The 1968 Act has not yet been extended to civil proceedings in magistrates' courts, and in such proceedings, the 1938 Act may still be resorted to.)

LAWTON J, said: 'I have come to the conclusion, with some regret, that on the proper construction of section 1(1) of the Act of 1938, the document which Mr Ackner seeks to have admitted in evidence can be so admitted. I say that I have come to that conclusion with some regret because it seems to me that it is an unfortunate situation if counsel can call a witness and, when that witness does not come up to proof, counsel should be allowed to produce some earlier document which shows that on some other occasion the witness made a different statement. I appreciate — and I have borne it in mind in coming to my decision as to the proper construction of the Act — that the object of the Act is to see that the relevant evidence is before the court; and it may well be in the sort of situation which has arisen in this case, it is right, in case one side or the other seeks to rely on evidence given by a particular witness,

that the court should have full information as to what the witness has said on some previous occasion. Nevertheless, it seems to me that the use of this provision should be one which counsel should hesitate to adopt except in very special circumstances. Having myself observed this witness in the witness box, I will content myself by saying at this stage that I can well understand counsel thinking that this is such a special case. The witness is an elderly man, and it may well be that he is not as fit now as he was at the time when he made the statement that is sought to be admitted in evidence.'
Ruling accordingly.

Hardwicke J: What do you say about that, Mr Noy?

Mr Noy: My Lord, that was a decision on the Evidence Act 1938 which took a much narrower view of the use of hearsay statements. Even under that statute, the learned judge felt constrained to allow the statement to be put in, his expressions of reluctance notwithstanding. In my submission, the 1968 Act goes much further than its predecessor, and it is expressly envisaged by Section 2 that statements should be admissible even where the maker is called to give evidence. Of course, the weight of such statement is a matter for Your Lordship.

Hardwicke J: Yes, I think that is right. I am inclined to give leave. I must also consider the provisions of Section 2(2)(b) as to the timing of this statement. Ordinarily it should not be put in evidence before the conclusion of examination-in-chief. I suppose the reason for that is to allow the other side a reasonable opportunity to cross-examine on the oral evidence given in court.

Mr Noy: My Lord, that is right. I have in fact finished my examination-in-chief of Mrs Blackstone, although it may be that Your Lordship would have been inclined to hold that the statement should be admitted at this point in any event, on the ground that to delay it would adversely effect the intelligibility of Mrs Blackstone's evidence.

Hardwicke J: Yes. I see that Section 2(3) specifically refers to hearsay evidence consisting of evidence given in some other legal proceedings.

Mr Noy: My Lord, yes. Ordinarily, in the case of an oral statement, I would have to call a person who perceived the statement being made, since Mrs Blackstone's evidence would clearly be useless for the purpose under the circumstances. However, Your Lordship may authorise any manner of proof for this evidence. I would refer Your Lordship to the course approved by the Court of Appeal in:

Taylor v Taylor [1970] 1 WLR 1148 (CA)

In September 1969, the wife petitioned for divorce on the ground of her husband's adultery alleging incest with their 14-year-old daughter for which the husband had been tried and convicted in November 1962. The husband denied the adultery and cross prayed for a divorce on the ground of the wife's adultery. At the hearing of the suit the commissioner, relying solely on the depositions of witnesses at the criminal trial and without reference to a transcript of the criminal proceedings, found that the husband had been wrongly convicted of of incest and dismissed the wife's petition. He granted the husband a decree nisi of divorce on the ground of the wife's adultery. The wife appealed on the question whether a transcript of the criminal proceedings was admissible under ss.2(1) and 4(1) of the Civil Evidence Act 1968.

DAVIES LJ, after stating the facts and dealing with another ground of appeal, read ss.2(1) and 4(1) of Civil Evidence Act 1968 and continued: 'In my view, the transcript would be admissible under either of those sections. It may be, though I express no direct opinion on this, that the summing up of the judge might not be covered by section 2(1) because that is dealing with a statement in evidence, and of course the judge cannot give evidence. But I think that the transcript of the summing up would probably be admissible under section 4(1), since that is a record compiled by the shorthand writer in his capacity as such.

Mr Roger Gray referred us to the Rules of the Supreme Court (Amendment) 1969, the rules made under the Act to which I have just referred. The relevant rules are as follows. Rule 21 provides that notice of intention to give such statements in evidence shall be given at certain times prior to the hearing. Rule 29 provides that

> ...the court may, if it thinks it just to do so, allow a statement falling within section 2(1), 4(1) or 5(1) of the Act to be given in evidence at the trial or hearing of a cause or matter notwithstanding — (a) that the statement is one in relation to which rule 21(1) applies and that the party desiring to give the statement in evidence has failed to comply with that rule....

In other words, the court can waive the necessary requirement of giving notice in advance. Then, importantly, rule 28:

> Where a party to a cause or matter has given notice in accordance with rule 21 that he desires to give in evidence at the trial or hearing of the cause or matter — (a) a statement falling within section 2(1) of the Act which was made by a person, whether orally or in a document, in the course of giving evidence in some other legal proceedings (whether civil or criminal), or (b) a statement falling within section 4(1) of the Act which is contained in a record of direct oral evidence given in some other legal proceedings (whether civil or criminal), any party to the cause or matter may apply to the court for directions under this rule, and the court hearing such an application may give directions as to whether, and if, so on what conditions, the party desiring to give the statement in evidence will be permitted to do so and (where applicable) as to the manner in which that statement and any other evidence given in those other proceedings is to be proved.

It was contended by Mr Gray that in those circumstances the transcript was not admissible or ought not to be admitted. But I have not the least doubt, especially in view of the terms of rule 28, which I have just quoted, that the transcript is admissible; and we accordingly decided to admit the transcript of the criminal proceedings, some parts of which were referred to by Mr Campbell, for the wife, and one part of the summing up was referred to by Mr Gray for the husband.

(FENTON ATKINSON and PHILLIMORE LJJ agreed.)

Appeal allowed.

Hardwicke J: That seems a very satisfactory method of proceeding. Is the transcript available?

Mr Noy: Yes, my Lord.

Mr Atkyn: My Lord, I have one further objection to the admissibility of this evidence. As Your Lordship knows, the Rules of the Supreme Court provide for certain steps to be taken with regard to the giving of notice, before hearsay evidence can be adduced under Section 2. As Your Lordship knows, provision was made by Section 8(1) for the making of rules:

Civil Evidence Act 1968, s.8(1)

8. — (1) Provision shall be made by rules of court as to the procedure which, subject to any exceptions provided for in the rules, must be followed and the other conditions which, subject as aforesaid, must be fulfilled before a statement can be given in evidence in civil proceedings by virtue of section 2, 4 or 5 of this Act.

My Lord, the principal provisions of the Rules is to be found in RSC Order 38, Rule 21.

Rules of the Supreme Court, Ord. 38, Rule 21

21. — (1) Subject to the provisions of this rule, a party to a cause or matter who desires to give in evidence at the trial or hearing of the cause or matter any statement which is admissible in evidence by virtue of section 2, 4 or 5 of the Act must —

(a) in the case of a cause or matter which is required to be set down for trial or hearing or adjourned into court, within 21 days after it is set down or so adjourned, or within such other period as the Court may specify, and

(b) in the case of any other cause or matter, within 21 days after the date on which an appointment for the first hearing of the cause or matter is obtained, or within such other period as the Court may specify,

serve on every other party to the cause or matter notice of his desire to do so, and the notice must comply with the provisions of rule 22, 23 or 24, as the circumstances of the case require.

(2) Paragraph (1) shall not apply in relation to any statement which is admissible as evidence of any fact stated therein by virtue not only of the said section 2, 4 or 5 but by virtue also of any other statutory provision within the meaning of section 1 of the Act.

(3) Paragraph (1) shall not apply in relation to any statement which any party to a probate action desires to give in evidence at the trial of that action and which is alleged to have been made by the deceased person whose estate is the subject of the action.

I need not trouble Your Lordship with the detail required by Rule 22 in the case of Section 2 statements, because my learned friend will concede that no notice has in fact been served in this case.

Hardwicke J: What do you say about that, Mr Noy?

Mr Noy: My Lord, I say that the objection is quite without merit. The only purpose of service of such notice is to enable an opponent to require the attendance as witness of the makers of hearsay statements whose attendance at court is possible and practicable. My learned friend presumably has in mind the provisions of Rule 26, which states:

Rules of the Supreme Court, Order 38, Rule 26

26. — (1) Subject to paragraphs (2) and (3), any party to a cause or matter on whom a notice under rule 21 is served may within 21 days after service of the notice on him serve on the party who gave the notice or a counter notice requiring that party to call as a witness at the trial or hearing of the cause or matter any person (naming him) particulars of whom are contained in the notice.

(2) Where any notice under rule 21 contains a statement that any person particulars of whom are contained in the notice cannot or should not be called as a witness for the reason specified therein, a party shall not be entitled to serve a counter notice under this rule requiring that person to be called as a witness at the trial or hearing of the cause or matter unless he contends that that person can or, as the case may be, should be called, and in that case he must include in his counter notice a statement to that effect.

(3) Where a statement to which a notice under rule 21 relates is one to which rule 28 applies, no party on whom the notice is served shall be entitled to serve a counter notice under this rule in relation to that statement, but the foregoing provision is without prejudice to the right of any party to apply to the Court under rule 28 for directions with respect to the admissibility of that statement.

(4) If any party to a cause or matter by whom a notice under rule 21 is served fails to comply with a counter notice duly served on him under this rule, then, unless any of the reasons specified in rule 25 applies in relation to the person named in the counter notice, and without prejudice to the powers of the Court under rule 29, the statement to which the notice under rule 21 relates shall not be admissible at the trial or hearing of the cause or matter as evidence of any fact stated therein by virtue of section 2, 4 or 5 of the Act, as the case may be.

Not only would this procedure be entirely inappropriate, since it was always the plaintiff's intention to call Mrs Blackstone, but in fact the applicable rule here is Rule 28 which deals with hearsay statements in the form of evidence given in other legal proceedings.

Rules of the Supreme Court, Order 38, Rule 28

28. Where a party to a cause or matter has given notice in accordance with rule 21 that he desires to give in evidence at the trial or hearing of the cause or matter —
(a) a statement falling within section 2(1) of the Act which was made by a person, whether orally or in a document, in the course of giving evidence in some other legal proceedings (whether civil or criminal), or
(b) a statement falling within section 4(1) of the Act which is contained in a record of direct oral evidence given in some other legal proceedings (whether civil or criminal),
any party to the cause or matter may apply to the Court for directions under this rule, and the Court hearing such an application may give directions as to whether, and if so on what conditions, the party desiring to give the statement in evidence will be permitted to do so and (where applicable) as to the manner in which that statement and any other evidence given in those other proceedings is to be proved.

Hardwicke J: In any case, if I take the view that you could not reasonably have foreseen being put into this position because of Mrs Blackstone's unfortunate indisposition, I would imagine that I could admit the evidence notwithstanding any requirement of notice.

Mr Noy: Your Lordship could. Rule 29 gives the court a broad discretion.

Rules of the Supreme Court, Order 38, Rule 29

29. — (1) Without prejudice to section 2(2)(a). and 4(2)(a) of the Act and rule 28, the Court may, if it thinks it just to do so, allow a statement falling within section 2(1), 4(1) or 5(1) of the Act to be given in evidence at the trial or hearing of a cause or matter notwithstanding —
(a) that the statement is one in relation to which rule 21(1) applies and that the party desiring to give the statement in evidence has failed to comply with that rule, or
(b) that that party has failed to comply with any requirement of a counter notice relating to that statement which was served on him in accordance with rule 26.
(2) Without prejudice to the generality of paragraph (1), the Court may exercise its power under that paragraph to allow a statement to be given in evidence at the trial or hearing of a cause or matter if a refusal to exercise that power might oblige the party desiring to give the statement in evidence to call as a witness at the trial or hearing an opposite party or a person who is or was at the material time the servant or agent of an opposite party.

Hardwicke J: In what way should this discretion be exercised?

Mr Noy: Your Lordship should exercise it judicially having regard to the conduct of the parties and the need to do justice between them. May I first refer Your Lordship to:

Ford v Lewis [1971] 1 WLR 623 (CA)

The infant plaintiff, who was attempting to cross a road, was struck by a van driven by the defendant. The plaintiff was at the material time in the charge of her parents. By the time of the trial the defendant had become a patient in a mental hospital and it was agreed that he was unfit to be called as a witness. At the trial his counsel sought to put in evidence, under s.2(1) of the Civil Evidence Act 1968, a photostat copy of a written statement, proved by the guardian *ad litem* to be in the defendant's handwriting, giving his version of the accident, and also, under s.4(1) of the Act, hospital records relating to the plaintiff's father which stated that he had been in a state of intoxication when admitted to hospital after the accident. No notice of intention to put those documents in evidence had been served on the plaintiff's advisers as required by RSC, Ord 38, rr.21(1), 22 and 23, and the reason for non-compliance was not disclosed to the judge. Plaintiff's counsel refused an adjournment offered by the judge who thereupon, in the exercise of his discretion under RSC, Ord 38, r.29(1), admitted the documents. He found that the statement attributed to the defendant rang true, acquitted him of negligence and dismissed the claim. During the hearing of the plaintiff's appeal, on the ground that the judge had wrongly exercised his discretion in admitting the documents, leading counsel for the defendant informed the court that he had taken the decision not to serve the notices, as required by the rules, because he had formed the view that disclosure of the contents of the documents to the plaintiff and her parents before the trial might have affected their evidence; further, that no notice in the prescribed form could have been given in regard to the hospital notes, since they had only been obtained on the day of the trial.

EDMUND DAVIES LJ said: 'In these most unfortunate circumstances, it seems to me impossible that the defendant should be permitted to rely upon the judge's purported exercise of his discretion under rule 29. I hold that there can be no valid exercise of such discretion if there has (for any reason) been a deliberate withholding from the court of the reason of non-compliance. Had Veale J known that this was the result of a deliberate decision based upon the tactical value of surprise, I regard it as inconceivable that he would have ruled in favour of admitting the statement. But, with the profoundest respect to Davies LJ I go so far as to say that, even if he had, such an attitude ought not to be countenanced by this court. A suitor who deliberately flouts the rules has no right to ask the court to exercise in his favour a discretionary indulgence created by those very same rules. Furthermore, a judge who, to his knowledge, finds himself confronted by such a situation would not, as I think, be acting judicially if he nevertheless exercised his discretion in favour of the recalcitrant suitor. The rules are there to be respected, and those who defy them should not be indulged or excused. Slackness is one thing; deliberate disobedience another. The former may be overlooked; the latter never, even though, as here, it derives from mistaken zeal on the client's behalf. To tolerate it would be dangerous to justice.
(DAVIES LJ also delivered a judgment. Whilst condemning the course adopted on behalf of the defendant, His Lordship was against the granting of a new trial on the ground of the already considerable delay and because it seemed to him that the ultimate result must be the same. KARMINSKI LJ agreed with EDMUND DAVIES LJ.)
Appeal allowed. New trial ordered.

My Lord, that was a case where it would have been improper to exercise discretion. But in *Morris* v *Stratford-on-Avon RDC* the facts were in some ways not dissimilar to those of this case, and a proper basis existed to exercise a discretion, as follows:

Morris v *Stratford-on-Avon RDC* [1973] 1 WLR 1059 (CA)

The plaintiff was struck by a lorry driven by an employee of the defendants. At the trial, which took place five years after the event, the driver gave evidence for the defendants. His evidence was inconsistent and confused, and at the end of his examination in chief counsel for the defendants applied for leave to put in evidence, under s.2 of the Civil Evidence Act 1968, a proof of evidence given by the driver to the defendants' insurers some nine months after the accident. Although prior notice had not been given to the other side as required by RSC, Ord 38, r.21(1) and despite objections made by the plaintiff's counsel, the judge exercised his discretion and admitted the statement. He found on the evidence that the plaintiff had failed to establish that the defendants had been in any way negligent and dismissed the claim. The plaintiff appealed.

MEGAW LJ said: 'Nothing that I say must be taken in any way as suggesting that non-compliance with the rules as to notice is a matter that can be lightly overlooked. On the other hand, there must be cases in which there is, sensibly and reasonably, no ground for supposing that a statement which is in existence is going to be used by a party. It would perhaps be unfortunate if the matter were to be so interpreted that, in every case, those who are advising a party felt it necessary to advise him that, if there is any possibility, however remote, that, as a result of something which may happen hereafter, an application might be sought to be made, then notice should be given in advance. But, quite clearly, if there is reason to suppose, on proper consideration of the evidence, that such an application may be made, then care must be taken that the proper notice should be given.

As I say, it is important that the notices should be given. We were told by counsel for the defendant, and I have no doubt whatever but that it is correct, that in the present case it had not crossed his mind that this statement would be one which there would be occasion to put in in evidence, and that it was only when the evidence of Mr Pattison came to be taken that it occurred to him that it would be desirable that application should be made. In my judgment, no blame whatever attaches to counsel for making the application at that stage.

Let me say that the present case is, in my judgment, totally different from the case in this court of *Ford* v *Lewis* [1971] 1 WLR 623, to the judgment in which we were referred....

It is perfectly apparent that that is not this case, and that this case bears no conceivable relationship to the matters that motivated the court to take the course that it did in that case. However, it is right that careful consideration should always be given, on an application of this sort, to matters such as those that were stressed before us by counsel for the plaintiff: for example, that the statement was taken as a proof of evidence and that it was not closely contemporary with the time of the accident but was taken some nine months later. Those are matters which of course go to weight; but they can also be relevant on the question of a decision as to the exercise of discretion. Another matter which in my judgment must always be carefully watched, when an application of this sort is made under the Civil Evidence Act 1968 without proper notices having been given, is for the judge to make sure, so far as he can, that no injustice will be done to the other party by reason of the statement being allowed to be put in evidence. If there is ground to suppose that there will be any injustice caused, or that the other party will be materially prejudiced or embarrassed, then the judge should either refuse to allow the document to be admitted or, in his discretion, allow it on terms, such as an adjournment at the cost of the party seeking to put in the statement.

If I thought that in the present case there was any possibility that the plaintiff was prejudiced or that injustice might have been done by reason of the admitting of this statement when it was admitted, I should have had no hesitation in saying that the judge would have been wrong in admitting it. But, having regard to all the circumstances of which we have heard in this case, I am satisfied that there has been no such prejudice and that no injustice resulted. Accordingly, I take the view that Stirling J was not wrong in the manner in which he exercised his discretion.'

(DAVIES LJ and WALTON J agreed.)

Appeal dismissed.

Hardwicke J: ·Yes, those cases are very clear. I do not think that the service of notice would have had any purpose in this case, even if it were required. I shall admit the evidence in the form of the transcript of Mrs Blackstone's evidence in the criminal case, and since examination-in-chief has been concluded, this appears to be the appropriate moment to adduce it.

8.7 Commentary

Blackstone v *Coke* at trial.   Mr Atkyn for the defence proposes to adduce in evidence the hearsay statement of Anthony Henneky. Before trial, Mr Coke's solicitors, Mansfield & Co, served a notice under RSC Order 38, Rule 21, that it was intended to adduce the evidence of Mr Henneky in the form of his hearsay statement. This notice was in the proper form prescribed by Rule 22. At the same time, the notice stated that Mr Henneky should not be called as a witness at the trial because: 'He is beyond the seas, to wit in the State of California in the United States of America'. Margaret Blackstone's solicitors, Eldon & Co, served no counter-notice under Rule 26.

However, Mr Noy, on behalf of the plaintiff now objects to the admission of Mr Henneky's statement.

8.8 Argument

Mr Noy: My Lord, the ground of the objection is that it has not been shown that Mr Henneky should not be called as a witness. This is not a case where those instructing my learned friend have no idea of the whereabouts of Mr Henneky. The simple truth is that he could have returned from the United States to give evidence, but has not done so.

Hardwicke J: Mr Atkyn, what do you say?

Mr Atkyn: My Lord, factually my learned friend is correct. I am in a position to call evidence that Mr Henneky has refused to return from the United States, and of course there is no machinery whereby those instructing me could have compelled him. But I rest my application on more substantial ground. Firstly, from a procedural point of view, the defendant gave notice in proper form under Rule 21, and that notice specified that Mr Henneky should not be called as a witness for one of the reasons laid down in Rule 25.

Rules of the Supreme Court, Order 38, Rule 25

25. The reasons referred to in rules 22(3), 23(2) and 24(3) are that the person in question is dead, or beyond the seas or unfit by reason of his bodily or mental condition to attend as a witness or that despite the exercise of reasonable diligence it has not been possible to identify or find him or that he cannot reasonably be expected to have any recollection of matters relevant to the accuracy or otherwise of the statement to which the notice relates.

In such case, My Lord, Rule 26(2) contains a mandatory provision that the plaintiff serve a counter-notice putting in dispute the allegation that Mr Henneky should not be called. This has not been done.

But even leaving that aside, it is not incumbent on the defendant to make efforts to bring Mr Henneky back from the United States, even assuming such efforts are possible. In *Rasool* v *West Midlands Passenger Transport Executive* exactly that situation arose, and it was held that any one of the reasons specified in Rule 25, standing alone, would be sufficient.

Rasool v *West Midlands Passenger Transport Executive* [1974] 3 All ER 638 (QBD)

The plaintiff commenced an action against the defendants for damages in respect of personal injuries sustained by him as a result of the negligence of a bus driver employed by the defendants. The defendants served notice on the plaintiff under RSC, Ord 38, r.21(1), of their intention to give in evidence at the trial a statement made by C who had been an eye-witness to the plaintiff's accident. C's statement was to the effect that the bus driver was in no way to blame for the accident. The defendant's notice asserted that C could not be called as a witness since 'she has left her former address in Birmingham and cannot at present be found. It is understood that she is now beyond the seas and is probably resident in Jamaica.' On the available evidence, this account appeared to be accurate, although the defendants had made no effort to trace C there. It was contended for the plaintiff that C's statement was inadmissible since, although C was beyond the seas, it was still necessary under s.8(2)(b) of the Civil Evidence Act 1968 for the defendants to prove that despite the exercise of reasonable diligence she could not be found.

FINER J said: '…as I read s.8(2)(b) of the 1968 Act and the rules which reflect it, the five reasons that may be relied on for not calling a witness are disjunctive reasons. If the maker of the statement is beyond the seas it does not have to be proved also that he cannot by reasonable diligence be found. His whereabouts abroad may be precisely known, yet if it be established that he is indeed abroad that is in itself a sufficient reason for admitting the statement. It would follow that the application in this case (the terms of which were followed in the order) should not have been based on the ground that Mrs Collum had left her former address and could not be found. The real ground was that she was beyond the seas.

In finding, however, that the absence of the maker beyond the seas is a sufficient reason in itself for admitting the statement, even if no effort is made to trace the precise whereabouts of the proposed witness, or even if those whereabouts are known, I have deliberately elided the question whether the court nevertheless has any discretion to exclude it. At first sight it seems peculiar that there should be no such discretion. Take the case of a witness who has been party to a conversation in which it is common ground that the plaintiff and defendant make a contract, but they dispute the terms they agreed. The witness lives at a known address in Paris, despite which the plaintiff seeks to adduce his evidence in the form of a statement, relying on the fact the witness is beyond the seas. Or in the present case, one may imagine that it was Mrs Collum, a professed eye-witness to a serious accident whose statement may damn the plaintiff, who lived at a known address in Paris. Nevertheless, I find it a clear conclusion from the provisions of the statute and the rules which I have earlier mentioned that if the court is satisfied on any of the five specified reasons the statement becomes admissible, and there is no residuary discretion to exclude it by reference to other circumstances. The relevant provisions leave no room for such a discretion. The scheme of the law is that the counter-notice is ineffectual unless it raises an issue regarding the reason alleged in the notice which is ultimately determined in favour of the giver of the counter-notice. If the counter-notice is ineffectual, the notice takes effect. I consider that this would be the result even apart from s.8(3)(a), but that provision clinches the point by providing in terms that the rules cannot — with the exceptions provided for in s.8(3)(b), which has no application to the present case — confer on the court a discretion to exclude a statement where the requirements of the rules affecting its admissibility have been complied with.

The weight to be attached to the statement admitted in evidence remains a matter for the court. In the circumstances postulated in the examples I gave, where the whereabouts abroad of an important witness in a substantial case are known or can be easily ascertained, but the party relying on his evidence nevertheless adopts a method of adducing it which does not permit of cross-examination, no doubt the court would pay little attention to it. It may be that this is a risk which the defendants run if they make no efforts to find Mrs Collum in Jamaica, so as to permit at least the possibility of evidence being taken on commission. But all that will be a matter for the trial judge.'

Appeal dismissed.

My Lord, this decision was approved by the Court of Appeal in *Piermay Shipping Co, S.A. and another* v *Chester* [1978] 1 WLR 411.

This is a matter which Your Lordship is being asked to determine now, because of my learned friend's client's failure to serve counter-notice as required by the rules. This has prevented the matter from being decided at a pre-trial stage, as the rules envisage. (Hardwicke J held the evidence to be admissible.)

8.9 Commentary

Blackstone v *Coke* at trial. Mr Noy for the plaintiff wishes to place before the court voluminous written medical and psychiatric records dealing with Margaret Blackstone. These reports were compiled by a number of doctors and nurses, some of whom have now gone abroad, and one or two of whom are unidentifiable. Mr Noy wishes to tender these reports to show both the medical and psychiatric condition of Margaret after the rape and the reasons why she could not reasonably have been expected to undergo an abortion.

8.10   Argument

Mr Noy: My Lord, in my submission, these documents are admissible by virtue of Section 4 of the Civil Evidence Act 1968. Your Lordship will be familiar with its provisions:

Civil Evidence Act 1968, s.4

4. — (1) Without prejudice to section 5 of this Act, in any civil proceedings a statement contained in a document shall, subject to this section and to rules of court, be admissible as evidence of any fact stated therein of which direct oral evidence would be admissible, if the document is, or forms part of, a record compiled by a person acting under a duty from information which was supplied by a person (whether acting under a duty or not) who had, or may reasonably be supposed to have had, personal knowledge of the matters dealt with in that information and which, if not supplied by that person to the compiler of the record directly, was supplied by him to the compiler of the record indirectly through one or more intermediaries each acting under a duty.

(2) Where in any civil proceedings a party desiring to give a statement in evidence by virtue of this section has called or intends to call as a witness in the proceedings the person who originally supplied the information from which the record containing the statement was compiled, the statement —

(a)   shall not be given in evidence by virtue of this section on behalf of that party without the leave of the court;
and
(b)   without prejudice to paragraph (a) above, shall not without the leave of the court be given in evidence by virtue of this section on behalf of that party before the conclusion of the examination-in-chief of the person who originally supplied the said information.

(3) Any reference in this section to a person acting under a duty includes a reference to a person acting in the course of any trade, business, profession or other occupation in which he is engaged or employed or for the purposes of any paid or unpaid office held by him.

My Lord, in my submission, these reports are clearly in documentary form and form part of a record compiled by persons acting under a duty.

Hardwicke J: They certainly would seem to be records. And of course under this section, there is no such limitation as there is under the Criminal Evidence Act 1965, which requires the records to be those of a trade or business.

Mr Noy: My Lord, that is right. And as Your Lordship will know, the Act does not in any way limit the kind of duty under which the compiler of the records should be acting.

Mr Atkyn: My Lord, the only observation I make is that there seems to be some doubt as to the requirement of personal knowledge. Since there is no evidence as to who made many of the entries in these reports, it is difficult to see how Your Lordship can be satisfied that those who supplied the information directly or indirectly had personal knowledge.

Hardwicke J: Mr Noy, that does trouble me.

Mr Noy: My Lord, in the cases where the doctors and nurses are available of course I can produce direct evidence. But in my submission, even in the other cases where witnesses are not available, Your Lordship is entitled to draw an inference. The statute specifically refers to a person who had or may reasonably be supposed to have had personal knowledge. If Your Lordship would look at *Knight and others* v *David and others,* Your Lordship will see an example of this sort of inference:

Knight and others v David and others [1971] 1 WLR 1671 (ChD)

A claim by the plaintiffs to certain land depended upon events which occurred in 1886, and for the purpose of establishing that claim, the plaintiffs sought to put in evidence a tithe map and tithe apportionment survey, made under the provisions of the Tithe Act 1836.

GOULDING J said: '...the plaintiffs rely on Section 4 of the Civil Evidence Act 1968, the material part of which is contained in subsection (1)...

Mr Francis argued that the tithe document is not within that subsection on either or both of two grounds: First, he says that the statements therein are statements relating to title, and direct oral evidence of title would not be admissible. I find this perhaps the most difficult point in the question I am considering, but, on the whole, I conclude that Mr Francis's argument must fail if a living person could state in evidence that the machinery of the Act was carried out, and that a certain person was, and another was not, entered as proprietor of certain land. In my judgment, such a statement would be admissible.

Mr Francis's second point was that it was not established that the record compiled by the officers under the Act of 1836 was compiled from information supplied by persons who had, or might be supposed to have had, personal knowledge of the matters dealt with. In my judgment, having regard to the nature of the document and the lapse of time, it is right for the court to infer that this condition is satisfied. Therefore...I should also be prepared to admit this evidence under Section 4 of the Act of 1968.

Hardwicke J: I think I would be inclined to follow that reasoning. Certainly medical records are compiled for important purposes, and I am entitled to infer that they were made by persons having knowledge of what they recorded. I will admit the evidence.

8.11   Questions for counsel

8.11.1   Blackstone v *Coke:* Are there any further arguments that Mr Atkyn might have made to Hardwicke J with regard to the admissibility of Mrs Blackstone's evidence in the criminal case? What arguments might Mr Atkyn address to Hardwicke J relating to the ·weight to be attached to such evidence?

8.11.2   R v *Coke and Littleton.* Should Holt J admit in evidence the records of the King's Head? What factors would govern their weight, if admitted?

8.11.3   Blackstone v *Coke.* Do you agree with the decision of Hardwicke J to admit the statement of Anthony Henneky into evidence under Section 2 of the Act? What arguments might Mr Noy address to Hardwicke J relating to the weight of such evidence? Are there any steps open to Mr Noy to attack or discredit such evidence?

9 Opinion Evidence and Previous Judgments

A: OPINION EVIDENCE

9.1 Introductory notes

9.1.1 At common law, the opinions, beliefs and inferences of a witness are inadmissible to prove the truth of the matters believed or inferred. The function of witnesses is to relate facts, and the function of the court to form opinions about those facts. Opinions, beliefs and inferences are nonetheless admissible for the purpose of proving the state of mind of the holder of an opinion or the drawer of an inference at the relevant time. The same rule applies to evidence of general reputation or public opinion, which is an extended form of opinion evidence. Such evidence is inadmissible to prove the truth of the matters generally reputed or believed to be true, but will be admissible to prove what the general reputation of a matter or the state of public opinion on that matter in fact was at the relevant time.

9.1.2 This general rule at common law is subject to three exceptions, as follows:
    9.1.2.1 As a matter of last resort, general reputation will be admissible to prove matters of public concern that would otherwise be impossible or very difficult to prove.
    9.1.2.2 Expert opinion evidence is admissible to prove matters of specialised knowledge, on which the court would be unable, unaided, to reach a proper conclusion.
    9.1.2.3 Non-expert opinion evidence may be received on matters within the competence and experience of people generally, as a way of receiving their observation of facts.

9.1.3 Where opinion evidence is admissible, it may be admitted in civil cases in the form of hearsay statements by virtue of s.1 of the Civil Evidence Act 1972. This section applies the provisions of the Civil Evidence Act 1968 to hearsay statements of opinion, except that statements produced by computers (which would be admissible on matters of fact by virtue of s.5 of the 1968 Act) are inadmissible in so far as they are relied upon for matters of opinion. Where a hearsay statement is to be admitted under s.4 of the 1968 Act as extended, and the original supplier of the information is or was qualified to give expert opinion evidence to that effect, s.4 applies without the requirement of personal knowledge. Such hearsay statements are subject to the notice provisions of RSC Order 38, Rules 21–31, except that in the case of expert opinion evidence, separate provision is made by s.2 of the Civil Evidence Act 1972.

9.1.4 Evidence of general reputation is of lesser importance in modern practice, because many matters formerly the subject of such evidence may now be proved by records. Such evidence is nonetheless employed where necessary, to establish matters of pedigree or the existence of a marriage, to identify or show a reference to a person or thing, to prove the existence of a public or general right, and to prove good or bad character. In civil cases all these uses of evidence of general reputation are expressly provided for by s.9(3) of the Civil Evidence Act 1968. The section does not change the rules of common law substantively, but provides that the evidence of general reputation shall be admissible by virtue of s.9(3) in any case where previously it would have been admissible at common law. The section also provides for the admissibility of evidence of 'family tradition', which is a more specific version of general reputation relevant in cases of pedigree and marriage.

9.1.5 Expert opinion evidence is admissible within a subject requiring special knowledge and expertise. The evidence may be given from a witness who has acquired, by study or practice, the necessary knowledge and expertise. The function of such witnesses is to assist the court to draw proper inferences and form proper opinions from evidence concerning such specialised facts. The question of the qualification of a witness to give expert evidence is one of competence, and should be investigated by the court before permitting the witness to give evidence as an expert. The court is concerned with actual expertise, and not with the means by which that expertise is acquired, so that experience is just as important as paper qualifications. An expert witness is compellable, and while not entitled to have his evidence accepted without question, the tribunal of fact should not capriciously disregard expert evidence in favour of unaided lay opinion, or content itself with unaided observation on a matter calling for expert evidence. Nevertheless the function of the tribunal of fact is to weigh expert evidence, and to decide between conflicting expert opinions.

9.1.6 The function of an expert is to assist the court by giving his opinion on the matters of specialised knowledge that require it. At common law, there was a rule that the expert might not be asked his opinion on the 'ultimate question', that is to say his opinion on an issue in the case. The rule is almost certainly obsolete in modern practice, and in civil cases has been expressly reversed by s.3 of the Civil Evidence Act 1972. Expert evidence is not admissible on any question upon which the lay opinion of the tribunal of fact would be equally valid. An expert may relate to the court his investigation of the facts of the case and his familiarity with the exhibits, in order to explain his opinion. There is no objection to an expert basing his opinion on his findings or conclusions in cases with which he has previously dealt, provided that his evidence is not taken as proving any matters of fact relating to such previous cases. There was at common law a rule that the expert might not state the reasons for his opinion in chief, though he might be asked for them in cross-examination. This rule is now obsolete and the universal practice is for evidence to be presented in any convenient form, including a full explanation during the course of evidence in chief of the expert's reasoning. An expert witness may further be asked any hypothetical question, or asked to refer to a work of authority on his subject, and may relate to the court the results of any tests or experiments made for the purposes of the case or generally. He may also, with the permission of the court, demonstrate any matter during the trial or during a view of the *locus in quo,* subject to the discretion of the judge to ensure proper control of such demonstrations.

9.1.7 In civil cases, rules of court made under the Civil Evidence Act 1972, provide for disclosure of the expert evidence which it is intended to call at trial, in the interests of saving time and costs. The court may give directions as to the degree of disclosure in any given case. Whether or not such evidence must be disclosed depends on the nature of the evidence to be adduced, and the rules provide separately for different kinds of expert evidence. The question of disclosure is one to be dealt with by the master on summons for directions, unless in special circumstances, the direction should be given at some other time.

9.1.8 In certain cases, the court may of its own motion appoint an independent expert to inquire and report upon any question of fact or opinion where the assistance of such an expert appears to be needed. Either party may apply for leave to cross-examine the court expert, and may with leave call evidence to contradict him.

9.1.9 Non-expert opinion evidence is admissible on matters of general competence, and in circumstances where it is essentially a way of relating the witness's observation of facts. The rule applies to such every day observations as questions of identity and resemblance, mental or physical condition, age, speed or value. The rationale of this rule is that many matters of observation are ultimately questions of opinion, but nonetheless permit a witness to state coherently observations that would otherwise be difficult or impossible to explain. In civil cases, the reception of non-expert opinion evidence on these matters is specifically provided for by s.3(2) of the Civil Evidence Act 1972. (*A Practical Approach to Evidence.* pp 225–39.)

9.2 Commentary

R v *Coke and Littleton* on appeal against conviction. At trial, Mr Bacon on behalf of Littleton proposed to adduce evidence from Mrs Littleton and other witnesses to the effect that Littleton was a man of good reputation in Oxbridge. (As to the evidential value of such evidence, and its purpose when called for the defence, see 4.3 ante.) Holt J held the evidence to be inadmissible. Mr Bacon complains to the Court of Appeal that the evidence should have been admitted.

9.3 Argument

Leach LJ: As I understand the law, Mr Bacon, evidence of opinion is not admissible at common law to prove the truth of matters believed, although I can quite see that you might adduce it in order to prove the state of mind of the person holding an opinion.
Mr Bacon: My Lord, I would certainly agree that evidence of opinion is admissible to prove state of mind. Your Lordship will be familiar with the decision in:

Sheen v Bumpstead (1863) 2 H&C (Ex Ch)

In an action for falsely representing that W, a tradesman was trustworthy, the defendant called as a witness the counterman, who was acquainted with the transactions between the defendant and W, and asked him: 'Was W at the time of the representation trustworthy to your belief?' The defendant also called four tradesmen of the same town, who were asked as to the general reputation of W for trustworthiness. The defendant appealed on the ground of the improper reception of the evidence.

COCKBURN CJ said: '...the plaintiff, in order to shew that Watson was not only trustworthy at the time mentioned, but not trustworthy to the knowledge of the defendant, gave evidence of certain circumstances from which the jury were asked to infer that at the time the defendant wrote the letter of the 24th October, 1860, he knew that Watson was not trustworthy. In answer to the plaintiff's case the witness Adams is called, and in order to rebut the inference sought to be raised, is asked whether, knowing of all the transactions between the defendant and Watson, he believed that Watson was trustworthy. It is in effect, "What impression did these transactions produce on your mind?" In my judgment, that was a legitimate question, and one which the defendant had a right to put.
    With regard to the question put to the other witnesses respecting the general reputation of Watson for trustworthiness as a tradesman, I think it also admissible. It was important to ascertain the state of mind of the defendant at the time he made the representation complained of, and that could only be shewn by inference. A plaintiff may not be able to bring home to the defendant by direct and positive evidence a knowledge of the falsehood of his representation; the plaintiff may, however, prove certain facts which necessarily lead to that inference. Now, suppose the plaintiff had called every tradesman in the town to say, not only that Watson was insolvent, but that his insolvency was notorious, would it not have been a fair and obvious remark to the jury, that the defendant must have known what was the common knowledge of every other tradesman? On the other hand, if, after the plaintiff has established a prima facie case against the defendant, the latter calls a number of tradesmen, who have had dealings with Watson, and they say that at the time the defendant made the representation, they believed that Watson was perfectly solvent, is not that strong evidence [morally at least] from which the jury may infer that what was the common opinion of tradesmen in the neighbourhood was shared by the defendant, and that in making the representation he acted in good faith. I should hesitate before I held such evidence inadmissible in point of law. It would clearly have been admissible if it had tended to shew that every tradesman, who had contracted with Watson, believed him to be solvent. It is true that the defendant only called four or five persons who had dealings with Watson, but that is a matter for the jury, and goes only to the weight of the evidence and not to its admissibility.'
(The rest of court concurred.)
Judgment affirmed.

Nonetheless, My Lords, evidence of general reputation has long been generally recognised as admissible for certain purposes, of which the proof of character is one. If Your Lordships would look at the case of *R* v *Rowton* (1865) Le & Ca 520 (CCR) (see 4.3 ante).
    East LJ: It might assist us to know for what other purposes evidence of general reputation has been held to be admissible.
    Mr Bacon: My Lord, certainly. In the first place, it has frequently been used in older cases to establish pedigree or the existence of a marriage. Of course, these questions are nowadays proved by reference to official records admissible under the public document rule (see 6.11 and 6.12 ante). Secondly, evidence of general reputation has frequently been admitted to show a reference to some person or thing, or to prove the existence of some public or general right. These are cases in which, as a matter of last resort, the courts permit matters of evident public concern to be proved by the general belief or reputation prevalent in the public mind. Perhaps I might cite as an example:

Re Steel, Wappett v Robinson [1903] 1 Ch 135

By her will made in 1899 the testatrix, after appointing the plaintiffs to be executors and trustees of her will, devised 'my freehold land and hereditaments at Morland Field, in the said parish of Morland,' unto and to the use of the defendant and her heirs, with a substitutionary gift to other persons in the event of the defendant predeceasing her. And the testatrix devised and bequeathed the residue of her real and personal estate to her trustees on trust for sale and conversion, the proceeds to be held on the trusts therein declared. The testatrix died in January 1902. It appeared that in 1886 she had inherited four fields adjoining one another at Morland Field from her brother. Two of these fields were of freehold tenure, but the other two, though commonly called customary freeholds, or simply freeholds, in the locality, were in fact privileged copyholds held of the lords of the manor of Morland at fixed customary rents with fixed fines on death or alienation. The testatrix had never paid the customary rents, and it did not appear that she was aware of any distinction in the tenure of the four fields. An originating summons was issued to determine whether the defendant was entitled to these customary freeholds.

SWINFEN EADY J said: 'The case is not free from doubt, but on the whole I am of opinion that the customary freeholds passed under the specific devise...

Although the testatrix was not only heiress-at-law but also customary heiress to her brother, it does not appear that she was aware of any distinction of tenure in the four fields she inherited, or that they had devolved on her in two different capacities. The fields in dispute are not strictly freeholds, but they are usually known as freeholds or customary freeholds in the locality, and in devising her "freehold land and hereditaments at Morland" the testatrix was not, I think, using the word "freehold" in the strict technical sense of tenure. I am of opinion that both the freeholds and the customary freeholds passed to the defendant.'

Cox LJ: That of course was a civil case. Are the rules different in respect of criminal cases?

Mr Bacon: My Lord, they are not different. It is true that the basis of admissibility has been changed somewhat, because these areas of reputation evidence are now admissible by statute. If Your Lordships would look at Section 9(3) and (4) of the Civil Evidence Act 1968, Your Lordships will find that it has effectively adopted these common law rules regarding evidence of general reputation and given them a statutory basis:

Civil Evidence Act 1968, s.9

9(3) In any civil proceedings a statement which tends to establish reputation or family tradition with respect to any matter and which, if this Act had not been passed, would have been admissible in evidence by virtue of any rule of law mentioned in subsection (4) below:—

(a) shall be admissible in evidence by virtue of this paragraph in so far as it is not capable of being rendered admissible under section 2 or 4 of this Act; and

(b) if given in evidence under this Part of this Act (whether by virtue of paragraph (a) above or otherwise) shall by virtue of this paragraph be admissible as evidence of the matter reputed or handed down;

and, without prejudice to paragraph (b) above, reputation shall for the purposes of this Part of this Act be treated as a fact and not as a statement or multiplicity of statements dealing with the matter reputed.

(4) The rules of law referred to in subsection (3) above are the following, that is to say any rule of law:—

(a) whereby in any civil proceedings evidence of a person s reputation is admissible for the purpose of establishing his good or bad character;

(b) whereby in any civil proceedings involving a question of pedigree or in which the existence of a marriage is in issue evidence of reputation or family tradition is admissible for the purpose of proving or disproving pedigree or the existence of the marriage, as the case may be; or

(c) whereby in any civil proceedings evidence of reputation or family tradition is admissible for the purpose of proving or disproving the existence of any public or general right or of identifying any person or thing.

Nonetheless, the Act makes no change in the substance of the common law rules themselves.

Cox LJ: Yes.

9.4 Commentary

R v *Coke and Littleton* on appeal. At the trial, the prosecution called no handwriting expert to deal with the Exhibits GG1 and GG3. The prosecution nonetheless asserted as part of their case that Coke was the author of Exhibit GG1. During the defence case, Mr Atkyn on behalf of Coke called his instructing solicitor, Mr Mansfield, who gave evidence that he was a long time student of calligraphy although he had not received formal training, and had never acted as a professional handwriting expert. Mr Mansfield then gave evidence that in his opinion, Mr Coke was not the author of Exhibit GG1, and illustrated that opinion by detailed comparisons between Exhibits GG1 and GG3. Mr Atkyn complains to the Court of Appeal about the following passage in the summing up of Holt J to the jury dealing with the subject of the handwriting evidence:

Members of the jury, I must now deal with the subject of the handwritten exhibits GG1 and GG3. As you will recall, the prosecution called no evidence from any handwriting expert in order to prove to you that the defendant Coke is the author of Exhibit GG1. The defence on the other hand called a witness, Mr Mansfield, in order to prove the contrary. Now you may think that the reason why the prosecution did not call such a witness is that the documents speak for themselves. You have already seen them more than once in this court, and when you retire to consider your verdict, you will be at liberty to take them with you into the jury room. There you can examine them at your leisure, bearing in mind that it is the prosecution who have set out to prove that the authorship of these documents is one and the same. If necessary, you will be provided with a magnifying glass, which may enable you to look at the exhibits more closely. But with regard to Mr Mansfield, let me just say this. He claimed for himself some expertise in the field of handwriting, but his profession is that of solicitor. He has, it is true, purely out of interest, spent much time examining documents over the last fifteen years. You may think that he has inevitably acquired some degree of expertise through that. For that reason I permitted him to give evidence as an expert witness. But you may think that in this case no expert witness can do more than you can. Mr Mansfield stated that he was sure that Coke was not the author of Exhibit GG1. But that is entirely a matter for you. And if you all follow my advice, you will not place too much emphasis on opinion evidence in this kind of case. There is no reason why you should not trust your own obvservation.

9.5 Argument

Mr Atkyn: My Lords, the first point I take is that this was eminently a matter for expert evidence. The need for expert evidence in a field so specialised that the court could not reach a proper conclusion unaided has long been recognised at common law. It goes back at least as far as:

Folkes v Chadd and Others (1782) 3 Doug 157 (KB)

In an action for trespass the question was whether an embankment erected by the plaintiff caused silting in the defendant's harbour. Mr Smeaton, a distinguished engineer, testified to his opinion as an expert that the silting was not caused by the embankment. The trial judge rejected the evidence on the ground that it was a matter of opinion and not of facts.

LORD MANSFIELD, delivering the opinion of the court, said: 'It is objected that Mr Smeaton is going to speak, not as to facts, but as to opinion. That opinion, however, is deduced from facts which are not disputed — the situation of banks, the course of tides and of winds, and the shifting of sands. His opinion, deduced from all these facts, is, that, mathematically speaking, the bank may contribute to the mischief, but not sensibly. Mr Smeaton understands the construction of harbours, the causes of their destruction, and how remedied. In matters of science no other witnesses can be called. An instance frequently occurs in actions for unskilfully navigating ships. The question then depends on the evidence of those who understand such matters; and when such questions come before me, I always send for some of the brethren of the Trinity House. I cannot believe that where the question is, whether a defect arises from a natural or an artificial cause, the opinions of men of science are not to be received. Hand-writing is proved every day by opinion; and for false evidence on such questions a man may be indicted for perjury. Many nice questions may arise as to forgery, and as to the impressions of seals; whether the impression was made from seal itself, or from an impression in wax. In such cases I cannot say that the opinion of seal-makers is not to be taken. I have myself received the opinion of Mr Smeaton respecting mills, as a matter of science. The cause of the decay of the harbour is also a matter of science, and still more so, whether the removal of the bank can be beneficial. Of this such men as Mr Smeaton alone can judge. Therefore we are of opinion that his judgment, formed on facts, was very proper evidence.'
Rule for a new trial made absolute.

Leach LJ: I appreciate that there are times when expert evidence is called for, Mr Atkyn. But surely there are also cases where the observation of the jury is just as valuable. The judge made every concession to the jury in terms of aiding them to reach their conclusion, for example by providing them with a magnifying glass.

Mr Atkyn: My Lord, that is so. But at the same time, the scientific comparison of handwriting evidence is a specialised study (see also 15.6). In my submission, it is quite wrong for the jury to be left to form their own unaided view on a matter on which expert evidence is called for. I refer Your Lordships to:

R v Tilley; R v Tilley [1961] 1 WLR 1309 (CCA)

The appellants, G and L, were both charged with the larceny of a car. Their case was that they had bought it from a person claiming to be the owner and from whom they had obtained a receipt, which they produced. At the trial, in cross-examination, each appellant was asked to write out the words of the receipt. G's handwriting was plainly different, but there were similarities between L's writing and that on the receipt. Counsel for the prosecution did not pursue the matter, as it was the prosecution case that the receipt was a document devised by the appellants in order to explain their possession of the car if questioned, and that it was not of great importance whether they or someone else had written it. The matter was not mentioned again until the summing up, when the deputy chairman commented upon the similarities and invited the jury to decide whether or not the receipt was genuine, giving the jury the receipt and the handwriting exhibits to examine. G and L were convicted and appealed.

ASHWORTH J, giving the judgment of the court, stated the facts and continued: '...criticism is now made by Mr Simpson on behalf of the two appellants that it was not right or fair that the defence should suddenly be met with this kind of address to the jury on a topic which had never been ventilated throughout the trial. Moreover, it was said that the topic was one on which the Crown had not relied, and in regard to it, if the defendants had had an opportunity they might have been in a position to call expert evidence. Those criticisms were, we think, of considerable force. But the matter goes even further. The question arises whether in any case it was proper for the deputy chairman to indulge in comments himself about these documents and then hand them to the jury for their consideration and decision without any evidence having been called to assist them on that issue.

The matter has come before the court in more than one previous case. One to which our attention was called was *R* v *Harvey* (1869) 11 Cox CC 546. The matter was also raised in *R* v *Rickard* (1918) 13 Cr App R 140. In that case Salter J, giving the judgment of this court, said this, after referring to section 8 of the Criminal Procedure Act, 1865 (Lord Denman's Act) Ibid, 143: "That case [*R* v *Crouch* (1850) 4 Cox CC 163] does not decide what degree of preparation is necessary to constitute an expert, but it does decide that a person is not entitled to give such evidence if his only knowledge on the subject is that acquired in the course of the case. That was the position of the police officer, and the position of Busby is less satisfactory. Therefore no expert evidence at all was given in the case. This court does not decide that expert evidence in such cases is necessary, and the observations of Blackburn J in *Harvey* 11 Cox CC 546 do not so decide, but it is clear from the nature of things that to leave a question of handwriting to a jury without assistance is a somewhat dangerous course."

In the present case there was no evidence, not even questions directed to alleged similarities, and the matter only arose in the course of the summing up. This court endorses and reaffirms the statement of principle to be found in Salter J's judgment on behalf of this court in *Rickard's* case. A jury should not be left unassisted to decide questions of disputed handwriting on their own.

It is also to be noted that, although *R* v *Day* [1940] 1 All ER 402 raised in the main an utterly different issue, the question of handwriting did occur, and Croom-Johnson J ruled that the jury could not be asked to compare handwriting, without some assistance by way of expert evidence, and that ruling was once again in conformity with the decision in *Rickard's* case.

In these circumstances, in the view of this court, it is right to say that the course pursued by the deputy chairman was not in accordance with the principles previously laid down, and should not be followed in any other case.

Appeals allowed.

East LJ: You say that the learned judge allowed the jury to reach their conclusion unaided. But he did refer in his summing up to the evidence of Mr Mansfield.

Mr Atkyn: My Lord, he did, but in such terms as to invite the jury to prefer their own visual appreciation of the exhibits to the categorical opinion which Mr Mansfield expressed.

Cox LJ: Is that not a matter of legitimate comment for a judge in his summing up?

Mr Atkyn: My Lord, with respect, no. If Your Lordships make the assumption that handwriting evidence is a proper subject for expert opinion, then the jury should not be invited to reach their own conclusion contrary to the view of an expert without good reason. I would refer Your Lordships to:

Anderson v *R* [1972] AC 100 (PC)

The appellant was charged with murder. He put forward a defence of alibi but was convicted chiefly on circumstantial evidence and sentenced to death. He appealed against conviction to the Appeal Court of Jamaica on the ground, *inter alia*, that there had been a misdirection by the trial judge. The Court of Appeal held that there had been a misdirection but that no substantial miscarriage of justice had occurred and they applied the proviso to s.13(1) of the Judicature (Appellate Jurisdiction) Law 1962 and dismissed the appeal. A further appeal was made to the Judicial Committee.

LORD GUEST, delivering the reasons for the judgment of their Lordships, said: 'The complaint which formed the basis of the Court of Appeal's judgment related to the trial judge's summing up in regard to the condition of the accused's boots. It should be explained that when the accused was arrested on December 25, his water boots were found and also a piece of cardboard from inside the boots. He admitted wearing the boots on the night of December 23. Mr Garriques a forensic expert examined the water boots and the cardboard on December 28. He found no human blood on the water boots. In his summing up the trial judge referred to the water boots in this way:

> He [Mr Garriques] says there was no blood on the shoes — well, that is merely his opinion, members of the jury, you are not bound to accept it because he happens to be an expert in this particular field. An expert is brought before you merely to guide and assist you in evaluating evidence of a particular nature, he being trained in that particular field therefor. You will weigh well what an expert has said before you discard his evidence because neither you nor I is trained in that particular field in the same way that Mr Garriques would weigh well what I would have to say in the field of law, because he is not trained in that particular field. But you are still judges of the facts and you may accept or reject evidence of the expert.

The Court of Appeal considered that this was a serious misdirection because the judge was inviting the jury to disregard the evidence of the expert to the effect that there was no blood on the boots and form their own opinion as to whether there was blood upon the boots.

So far as the piece of cardboard is concerned this was found by Detective Constable Dwyer on his visit to the accused's home on December 25. It was in the right foot of the water boots which the accused said he was wearing on December 23. It had brown marks resembling blood stains. Mr Garriques said that on his examination on December 28 he found that those marks were human blood stains. The stains must have been about two weeks old but they could have been there before two weeks. In his opinion it was not more recent than two weeks. It might have been older. It was definitely not a fresh stain.

The trial judge in his summing up to the jury when dealing with Mr Garriques' evidence said that the witness found human blood. "In his opinion they were then about two weeks old." There is no doubt that in the summing up a confusion might have arisen in the jury's mind as to whether blood on the cardboard could have been of more recent origin than two weeks. Their Lordships are prepared to accept, following the Court of Appeal, that there was misdirections by the trial judge in regard to the boots and in regard to the cardboard.

Their Lordships do not agree with counsel for the respondent that these were subsidiary matters. These were serious misdirections as the Court of Appeal have held. There was no evidence of blood on the boots or the cardboard that could have implicated the accused.' (His Lordship went on to consider the question of the proviso and affirmed the judgment of the Court of Appeal of Jamaica.)

Appeal dismissed.

Leach LJ: Nor, of course, should the jury be told that they must automatically accept expert evidence.

Mr Atkyn: My Lords, I accept that entirely. That would seem to follow from the decision in:

R v Lanfear [1968] 2 QB 77 (CA)

The appellant was charged with driving a motor vehicle on a road while unfit to drive through drink. The doctor who had examined him at the police station after the offence gave evidence at his trial. The appellant was convicted and appealed on the ground, *inter alia,* that the deputy recorder misdirected the jury in telling them that the doctor's evidence must be accepted unless the doctor showed by his own conduct that it ought not to be accepted.

DIPLOCK LJ, reading the judgment of the court, stated the facts and continued: 'In his notice of appeal he makes a number of complaints about the summing up by the deputy recorder. As regards all of the complaints but one I need say no more than that there is, in the view of this court, no substance in them. But he did complain, with justification, about the terms in which the deputy recorder instructed the jury about the attitude they should adopt towards the medical evidence. There is considerable excuse for the deputy recorder because he read out to them a passage which appears in the current volume of Archbold's Criminal Pleadings, Evidence and Practice 36th ed (1966) para 2849, under the heading "Medical Witness," which is in the following terms:

The evidence of any doctor, whether a police surgeon or not, should be accepted as the evidence of a professional man giving independent expert evidence with the sole desire of assisting the court, unless the doctor himself shows that his evidence ought not to be accepted.

The deputy recorder paraphrased that slightly. He said this:

Let me say immediately about medical evidence in general — this again, members of the jury, is a matter of law. The evidence of any doctor, whether a police surgeon or not, is to be accepted as the evidence of a professional man giving independent evidence with the sole desire of assisting the court unless the doctor by his own conduct shows that his evidence ought not to be accepted.

I think the only difference is that instead of "himself" he has substituted the words "by his own conduct." Then he goes on subsequently to say this:

...his evidence is to be accepted as the evidence of a professional man giving independent expert evidence with the sole desire of helping the court. This, then, puts him into a position in which, in the absence of reasons for rejecting his evidence, his evidence ought to be accepted.

In the view of this court that is an incorrect statement of the law and the passage which is cited in Archbold, which comes from *R v Nowell* (1948) 64 TLR 277, 278 is taken out of its context. In that case the argument before the court was based on the fact that a doctor who had examined a defendant had explained to him that it might be in his own interests to allow the doctor to examine him. The defendant eventually agreed to be examined and was examined by the doctor, who certifed that owing to his consumption of alcohol, the defendant was unfit to drive a car. The argument was that the doctor should be treated as if he were an arm of the police and that there was an inducement held out to the defendant which made the evidence of the doctor as to the result of his examination inadmissible. That argument was sought to be supported by a decision of the Scots court, *Reid v Nixon* and *Dumigan v Brown* 1948 SC(J) 68, and the passage now incorporated in Archbold appeared at the end of the judgment in the Court of Criminal Appeal where they were dealing with that. After referring to the two cases, the court said (1948) 64 TLR 277, 278:

It is not necessary to read the judgment of the court which was given by the Lord Justice-General, who made a number of general observations with regard to the principles on which he suggested police officers and doctors should act in examining persons who are charged with such an offence as this. The Lord Advocate, according to the judgment of the Lord Justice-General, had stated that in all such cases the police surgeon or other doctor summoned by the police to conduct an examination was acting as the hand of the police and not as an independent medical referee. This court can only say that it does not agree that that state of affairs, whether it exists in Scotland or not, exists in this country. Our view is that the evidence of a doctor, whether he be a police surgeon or anyone else, should be accepted, unless the doctor himself shows that it ought not to be, as the evidence of a professional man giving independent expert evidence with the sole desire of assisting the court.

What that passage meant in that context was that the evidence should be treated, as regards admissibility and other matters of that kind, like that of any other independent witness. But taken out of its context, the use of the word "accepted" may well, we think, give to the jury a false impression of the weight to be given to a doctor's evidence. It is therefore desirable that in subsequent editions of Archbold that passage, which was read by the deputy recorder in this case, should be corrected.

Having said that, however, this, in the view of this court, is the clearest possible case in which to apply the proviso. On the evidence before the jury no jury properly directed could have possibly found the appellant otherwise than guilty of the offence.

Appeal dismissed.

But this was not a case where the jury had to decide between two conflicting expert opinions, and in my submission the learned judge should have invited the jury to place far more reliance upon the evidence given by Mr Mansfield, which was not shaken substantially in cross-examination.

East LJ: No doubt what the learned judge was seeking to do was to remind the jury that Mr Mansfield had no formal qualification in the field of document examination.

Mr Atkyn: My Lords, it is true that Mr Mansfield is not formally qualified in that field and that his profession is that of solicitor. However, that was a matter of competence. If the learned judge did not think that Mr Mansfield had the necessary qualities to be an expert witness, then it was his duty to refuse to permit his evidence to be given at all. I would submit to Your Lordships that qualification as an expert is not necessarily a matter of paper qualification, but may very often be one of actual expertise. There is indeed authority on very similar facts for that view. I refer Your Lordships to:

R v *Silverlock* [1894] 2 QB 766 (CCR)

The defendant was charged with obtaining a cheque by false pretences. It became necessary to prove that certain documents were in the defendant's handwriting and the solicitor for the prosecution was called as an expert witness for this purpose. It was objected that the solicitor was not an expert, and could not give evidence as to his opinion. The solicitor said that he had since 1884, quite apart from his professional work, given considerable study and attention to handwriting and had on several occasions professionally compared evidence in handwriting. The objection was overruled, and the evidence was admitted. The jury convicted the defendant, who appealed.

LORD RUSSELL OF KILLOWEN CJ, after stating the facts and dealing with another ground of appeal, continued: 'We now come to the second objection, as to the proof of the handwriting which affords a good illustration of that class of evidence called evidence of opinion. It is true that the witness who is called upon to give evidence founded on a comparison of handwritings must be peritus; he must be skilled in doing so; but we cannot say that he must have become peritus in the way of his business or in any definite way. The question is, is he peritus? Is he skilled? Has he an adequate knowledge? Looking at the matter practically, if a witness is not skilled the judge will tell the jury to disregard his evidence.

There is no decision which requires that the evidence of a man who is skilled in comparing handwriting, and who has formed a reliable opinion from past experience, should be excluded because his experience has not been gained in the way of his business. It is, however, really unnecessary to consider this point; for it seems from the statement in the present case that the witness was not only peritus, but was peritus in the way of his business. When once it is determined that the evidence is admissible, the rest is merely a question of its value or weight, and this is entirely a question for the jury, who will attach more or less weight to it according as they believe the witness to be peritus.

(MATHEW, DAY, VAUGHAN, WILLIAMS and KENNEDY JJ concurred.)
Conviction affirmed.

Cox LJ: Was Mr Mansfield asked to give a direct opinion as to the authorship of Exhibit GG1?

Mr Atkyn: Yes, My Lord. Your Lordship will see on page 87 of the transcript that Mr Mansfield was asked exactly that question and gave it as his opinion that Coke was not the author of that exhibit.

Cox LJ: I always understood it to be a rule that an expert witness might not be asked directly the question upon which the jury had to pronounce.

Mr Atkyn: My Lord, there was certainly a rule of the common law at one time to that effect. But as Your Lordship will appreciate, its force has been much eroded in modern times. Indeed for civil cases, Your Lordship will know that the rule was expressly reversed by:

Civil Evidence Act 1972, s.3

3(1) Subject to any rules of court...where a person is called as a witness in any civil proceedings, his opinion on any relevant matter on which he is qualified to give expert evidence, shall be admissible in evidence...
(3) In this section 'relevant matter' includes an issue in the proceedings in question.

Leach LJ: Certainly in my experience, that subsection is declaratory of the common law in its modern form. I certainly see no reason why Mr Mansfield should not have been asked that question.

Mr Atkyn: My Lord, I am much obliged. I do appreciate of course that the court will not be assisted by expert evidence at all, where the question is one within the general expertise of laymen such as jurors. Thus, on a simple question of the intent with which the defendant performs an act in a criminal case, no amount of expert psychiatric evidence will assist the jury. It is a matter for them to determine on the basis of their experience of every day affairs. The same rule would seem to apply for example to whether or not the defendant was provoked. I would refer Your Lordship to the decision in:

R v Turner [1975] QB 834 (CA)

The defendant, who was charged with murder, admitted that he had killed his girl friend by hitting her with a hammer, but pleaded that he had been provoked by her statement that she had had affairs with other men and that he was not the father of her expected child. The defence sought to call a psychiatrist to give his opinion that the defendant was not suffering from a mental illness, that he was not violent by nature but that his personality was such that he could have been provoked in the circumstances and that he was likely to be telling the truth. The judge ruled the psychiatric evidence inadmissible. The defendant was convicted and appealed.

LAWTON LJ related the facts and continued: 'Before this court Mr Mildon submitted that the psychiatrist's opinion as to the defendant's personality and mental make-up as set out in his report was relevant and admissible for three reasons: first, because it helped to establish lack of intent; secondly, because it helped to establish that the defendant was likely to be easily provoked; and thirdly, because it helped to show that the defendant's account of what had happened was likely to be true. We do not find it necessary to deal specifically with the first of these reasons. Intent was not a live issue in this case. The evidence was tendered on the issues of provocation and credibility. The judge gave his ruling in relation to those issues. In any event the decision which we have come to on Mr Mildon's second and third submissions would also apply to his first.

The first question on both these issues is whether the psychiatrist's opinion was relevant. A man's personality and mental make-up do have a bearing upon his conduct. A quick-tempered man will react more aggressively to an unpleasing situation than a placid one. Anyone having a florid imagination or a tendency to exaggerate is less likely to be a reliable witness than one who is precise and careful. These are matters of ordinary human experience. Opinions from knowledgeable persons about a man's personality and mental make-up play a part in many human judgments. In our judgment the psychiatrist's opinion was relevant. Relevance, however, does not result in evidence being admissible; it is a condition precedent to admissibility. Our law excludes evidence of many matters which in life outside the courts sensible people take into consideration when making decisions. Two broad heads of exclusion are hearsay and opinion. As we have already pointed out, the psychiatrist's report contained a lot of hearsay which was inadmissible. A ruling on this ground, however, would merely have trimmed the psychiatrist's evidence: it would not have excluded it altogether. Was it inadmissible because of the rules relating to opinion evidence?

The foundation of these rules was laid by Lord Mansfield in *Folkes* v *Chadd* (1782) 3 Doug KB 157 and was well laid: the opinion of scientific men upon proven facts may be given by men of science within their own science. An expert's opinion is admissible to furnish the court with scientific information which is likely to be outside the experience and knowledge of a judge or jury. If on the proven facts a judge or jury can form their own conclusions without help, then the opinion of an expert is unnecessary. In such a case if it is given dressed up in scientific jargon it may make judgment more difficult. The fact that an expert witness has impressive scientific qualifications does not by that fact alone make his opinion on matters of human nature and behaviour within the limits of normality any more helpful than that of the jurors themselves; but there is a danger that they may think it does.

What, in plain English, was the psychiatrist in this case intending to say? First, that the defendant was not showing and never had shown any evidence of mental illness, as defined by the Mental Health Act 1959, and did not require any psychiatric treatment; secondly, that he had had a deep emotional relationship with the girl which was likely to have caused an explosive release of blind rage when she confessed her wantonness to him; thirdly, that after he had killed her be behaved like someone suffering from profound grief. The first part of his opinion was within his expert province and outside the experience of the jury but was of no relevance in the circumstances of this case. The second and third points dealt with matters which are well within ordinary human experience. We all know that both men and women who are deeply in love can, and sometimes do, have outbursts of blind rage when discovering unexpected wantonness on the part of their loved ones; the wife taken in adultery is the classical example of the application of the defence of "provocation"; and when death or serious injury results, profound grief usually follows. Jurors do not need psychiatrists to tell them how ordinary folk who are not suffering from any mental illness are likely to react to the stresses and strains of life. It follows that the proposed evidence was not admissible to establish that the defendant was likely to have been provoked. The same reasoning applies to its suggested admissibility on the issue of credibility. The jury had to decide what reliance they could put upon the defendant's evidence. He had to be judged as someone who was not mentally disordered. This is what juries are empanelled to do. The law assumes they can perform their duties properly. The jury in this case did not need, and should not have been offered, the evidence of a psychiatrist to help them decide whether the defendant's evidence was truthful.

Mr Mildon submitted that such help should not have been rejected by the judge because in *Lowery* v *The Queen* [1974] AC 85 the Privy Council had approved of the admission of the evidence of a psychologist on the issue of credibility. We had to consider that case carefully before we could decide whether it had in any way put a new interpretation upon what have long been thought to be the rules relating to the calling of evidence on the issue of credibility, viz that in general evidence can be called to impugn the credibility of witnesses but not led in chief to bolster it up. In *Lowery* v *The Queen* evidence of a psychologist on behalf of one of two accused was admitted to establish that his version of the facts was more probable than that put forward by the other. In every case what is relevant and admissible depends on the issues raised in that case. In *Lowery* v *The Queen* the issues were unusual; and the accused to whose disadvantage the psychologist's evidence went had in effect said before it was called that he was not the sort of man to have committed the offence. In giving the judgment of the Board, Lord Morris of Borth-y-Gest said, at p 103:

> The only question now arising is whether in the special circumstances above referred to it was open to King in defending himself to call Professor Cox to give the evidence that he gave. The evidence was relevant to and necessary for his case which involved negativing what Lowery had said and put forward; in their Lordships' view in agreement with that of the Court of Criminal Appeal the evidence was admissible.

We adjudge *Lowery* v *The Queen* [1974] AC 85 to have been decided on its special facts. We do not consider that it is an authority for the proposition that in all cases psychologists and psychiatrists can be called to prove the probability of the accused's veracity. If any such rule was applied in our courts, trial by psychiatrist would be likely to take the place of trial by jury and magistrates. We do not find that prospect attractive and the law does not at present provide for it.

In coming to the conclusion we have in this case we must not be taken to be discouraging the calling of psychiatric evidence in cases where such evidence can be helpful within the present rules of evidence... We have not overlooked what Lord Parker CJ said in *Director of Public Prosecutions* v *A and BC Chewing Gum Ltd.* [1968] 1 QB 159, 164 about the advance of science making more and more inroads into the old common law principle applicable to opinion evidence; but we are firmly of the opinion that psychiatry has not yet become a satisfactory substitute for the common sense of juries or magistrates on matters within their experience of life.

Appeal dismissed.

On the other hand, where the nature of the defence goes beyond what might be termed the ordinary everyday experience of jurors, then expert evidence is proper and necessary. Such a case was:

R v *Smith* [1979] 1 WLR 1445 (CA)

The applicant occupied rooms in the same house as the victim and his wife. The victim arrived home late one evening, having been drinking heavily, and was told by his wife that she had had an altercation with the applicant. The victim went up to the room where the applicant was asleep. A quarrel and fight took place during which the applicant stabbed the victim to death with a knife. While in custody the applicant was examined by two psychiatrists. At his trial for murder the applicant raised the defence of automatism while asleep. The prosecution, who contended that the applicant had recently thought of that defence, sought and obtained leave to cross-examine him about his interviews with the psychiatrists and to call the psychiatrists to give their views on automatism. The applicant was convicted of murder and applied for leave to appeal against conviction on the ground, *inter alia*, that the judge erred in allowing the psychiatrists to give their opinions as to whether the applicant's evidence was consistent with a defence of automatism.

GEOFFREY LANE LJ, giving the judgment of the court, stated the facts, considered another submission and continued: 'The next point Mr Blom-Cooper made is this: as a matter of discretion these reports should not be admitted. In effect, he says this: that in order to be admissible at all the reports must be relevant; that is to say, relevant to some issue which the jury have to determine. He submits that since there was no question of insanity or diminished responsibility, automatism or not was a matter which could and should be decided by the jury in the light of their own experience and they should not be assisted by medical or expert evidence as to the state of mind of the defendant. That being so, he suggests the doctors' evidence was irrelevant and, on that basis, should not have been admitted. Here, again, he cites a number of authorities. First was the decision of this court in *R* v *Chard* (1971) 56 Cr App R 268:

> Where no issue of insanity, diminished responsibility or mental illness has arisen, and it is conceded on the medical evidence that the defendant is entirely normal, it is not permissible to call a medical witness to state how, in his opinion, the defendant's mind operated at the time of the alleged crime with regard to the question of intent.

He referred to a passage of Roskill LJ's judgment, at p 270:

> Mr Back was unable to cite any authority in support of that proposition, not altogether surprisingly, for with the greatest respect to his argument, it seems to this court that his submission, if accept, would involve the court admitting medical evidence in other cases not where there was an issue, for example, of insanity or diminished responsibility but where the sole issue which the jury had to consider, as happens in scores of different kinds of cases, was the question of intent.... One purpose of jury trials is to bring into the jury box a body of men and women who are able to judge ordinary day-to-day questions by their own standards, that is, the standards in the eyes of the law of theoretically ordinary reasonable men and women. That is something which they are well able by their ordinary experience to judge for themselves. Where the matters in issue go outside that experience and they are invited to deal with someone supposedly abnormal, for example, supposedly suffering from insanity or diminished responsibility, then plainly in such a case they are entitled to the benefit of expert evidence.

> There is a further decision very much to the same effect which we do not find it necessary to cite in detail. I mention it simply for the purpose of completeness. That is *R* v *Turner (Terence)* [1975] QB 834. So, the question seems to be whether or not the applicant exhibited the type of abnormality in relation to automatism that would render it proper and, indeed, desirable for the jury to have expert help in reaching their conclusion. It seems to us without the benefit of authority that that is clearly the case. This type of automatism — sleepwalking — call it what you like, is not something, we think, which is within the realm of the ordinary juryman's experience. It is something on which, speaking for ourselves as judges, we should like help were we to have to decide it and we see not why a jury should be deprived of that type of help....
> Accordingly, it seems to us this was a case where the jury were entitled to have the benefit of medical evidence and the judge was right on that basis at any rate to admit the evidence in question as he did.
> (His Lordship decided that there was no reason to exclude the evidence because of possible unfairness to the applicant. The court granted leave to appeal, treating the hearing as the appeal.)
> Appeal dismissed.

East LJ: I see from the transcript that Mr Mansfield was asked a number of questions regarding previous cases in which he had given evidence, and his experience of cases where some deliberate attempt had been made to conceal a person's handwriting. Did the prosecution object to those questions?

Mr Bunbury: My Lord, I represented the prosecution at the trial and we did not object. The prosecution would concede that it is proper to put to an expert questions relating to his past experience, because it is on his past experience that his expertise and his opinion will be founded. Of course, nothing the expert says with regard to past cases can introduce any such facts into evidence, but he may make use of those cases in order to formulate his opinion. This seems to the prosecution to follow from the decision in:

English Exporters (London) Limited v *Eldonwall Limited* [1973] Ch 415

By an originating summons the plaintiff tenants applied, pursuant to Part II of the Landlord and Tenant Act 1954, for the grant by the defendant landlords of a new tenancy of certain premises. By a summons the landlords applied under s.24(A) of the Act for the determination of an interim rent while the tenancy continued under the provisions of the Act. During the hearing two valuers gave evidence as expert witnesses.

MEGARRY J said: 'As an expert witness, the valuer is entitled to express his opinion about matters within his field of competence. In building up his opinions about values, he will no doubt have learned much from transactions in which he has himself been engaged, and of which he could give first-hand evidence. But he will also have learned much from many other sources, including much of which he could give no first-hand evidence. Textbooks, journals, reports of auctions and other dealings, and information obtained from his professional brethren and others, some related to particular transactions and some more general and indefinite, will all have contributed their share. Doubtless much, or most, of this will be accurate, though some will not; and even what is accurate so far as it goes may be incomplete, in that nothing may have been said of some special element which affects values. Nevertheless, the opinion that the expert expresses is none the worse because it is in part derived from the matters of which he could give no direct evidence. Even if some of the extraneous information which he acquires in this way is inaccurate or incomplete, the errors and omissions will often tend to cancel each other out; and the valuer, after all, is an expert in this field, so that the less reliable the knowledge that he has about the details of some reported transaction, the more his experience will tell him that he should be ready to make some discount from the weight that he gives it in contributing to his overall sense of values. Some aberrant transactions may stand so far out of line that he will give them little or no weight. No question of giving hearsay evidence arises in such cases; the witness states his opinion from his general experience.

   On the other hand, quite apart from merely expressing his opinion, the expert often is able to give factual evidence as well. If he has first-hand knowledge of a transaction, he can speak of that. He may himself have measured the premises and conducted the negotiations which led to a letting of them at £x, which comes to £y per square foot; and he himself may have read the lease and seen that it contains no provisions, other than some particular clause, which would have any material effect on the valuation; and then he may express his opinion on the value. So far as the expert gives factual evidence, he is doing what any other witness of fact may do, namely, speaking of that which he has perceived for himself. No doubt in many valuation cases the requirement of first-hand evidence is not pressed to an extreme: if the witness has not himself measured the premises, but it has been done by his assistant under his supervision, the expert's figures are often accepted without requiring the assistant to be called to give evidence. Again, it may be that it would be possible for a valuer to fill a gap in his first-hand knowledge of a transaction by some method such as stating in his evidence that he has made diligent enquiries of some person who took part in the transaction in question, but despite receiving full answers to his enquiries, he discovered nothing which suggested to him that the transaction had any unusual features which would affect the value as a comparable. But basically, the expert's factual evidence on matters of fact is in the same position as the factual evidence of any other witness. Further, factual evidence that he cannot give himself is sometimes adduced in some other way, as by the testimony of some other witness who was himself concerned in the transaction in question, or by proving some document which carried the transaction through, or recorded it; and to the transaction thus established, like the transactions which the expert himself has proved, the expert may apply his experience and opinions, as tending to support or qualify his views.

   That being so, it seems to me quite another matter when it is asserted that a valuer may give factual evidence of transactions of which he has no direct knowledge, whether per se or whether in the guise of giving reasons for his opinion as to value. It is one thing to say "From my general experience of recent transactions comparable with this one, I think the proper rent should be £x": it is another thing to say "Because I have been told by someone else that the premises next door have an area of x square feet and were recently let on such-and-such terms for £y a year, I say the rent of these premises should be £z a year." What he has been told about the premises next door may be inaccurate or misleading as to the area, the rent, the terms and much else besides. It makes it no better when the witness expresses his confidence in the reliability of his source of information: a transparently honest and careful witness cannot make information reliable if,instead of speaking of what he has seen and heard for himself, he is merely retailing what others have told him. The other party to the litigation is entitled to have a witness whom he can cross-examine on oath as to the reliability of the facts deposed to, and not merely as to the witness's opinion as to the reliability of information which was given to him not on oath, and possibly in circumstances tending to inaccuracies and slips. Further, it is often difficult enough for the courts to ascertain the true facts from witnesses giving direct evidence, without the added complication of attempts to evaluate a witness's opinion of the reliability, care and thoroughness of some informant who has supplied the witness with the facts that he is seeking to recount.

It therefore seems to me that details of comparable transactions upon which a valuer intends to rely in his evidence must, if they are to be put before the court, be confined to those details which have been, or will be, proved by admissible evidence, given either by the valuer himself or in some other way. I know of no special rule giving expert valuation witnesses the right to give hearsay evidence of facts: and notwithstanding many pleasant days spent in the Lands Tribunal while I was at the Bar, I can see no compelling reasons of policy why they should be able to do this. Of course, the long-established technique in adducing expert evidence of asking hypothetical questions may also be employed for valuers. It would, I think, be perfectly proper to ask a valuer "If in May 1972 No. 3, with an area of 2,000 sq ft, was let for £10,000 a year for seven years on a full repairing lease with no unusual terms, what rent would be appropriate for the premises in dispute?" But I cannot see that it would do much good unless the facts of the hypothesis are established by admissible evidence; and the valuer's statement that someone reputable had told him these facts, or that he had seen them in a reputable periodical, would not in my judgment constitute admissible evidence...

Putting matters shortly, and leaving on one side the matters that I have mentioned, such as the Civil Evidence Act 1968 and anything made admissible by questions in cross-examination, in my judgment a valuer giving expert evidence in chief (or in re-examination): (a) may express the opinions that he has formed as to values even though substantial contributions to the formation of those opinions have been made by matters of which he has no first-hand knowledge; (b) may give evidence as to the details of any transactions within his personal knowledge, in order to establish them as matters of fact; and (c) may express his opinion as to the significance of any transactions which are or will be proved by admissible evidence (whether or not given by him) in relation to the valuation with which he is concerned; but (d) may not give hearsay evidence stating the details of any transactions not within his personal knowledge in order to establish them as matters of fact.'

Mr Atkyn: I am very much obliged to my learned friend. Your Lordships will also see from the transcript that Mr Mansfield was asked to look at works of authority regarding the comparison of documents, and was also allowed to produce enlargements of photographs he had taken of both exhibits. In my submission, those were proper matters to assist the court in following the opinion which Mr Mansfield was giving.

Leach LJ: But you would say that in any event, the learned judge's summing up was defective in tending to invite the jury to reach some unaided opinion with regard to this evidence.

Mr Atkyn: Yes, my Lords.

9.6 Commentary

Blackstone v *Coke* on summons for directions. Mr Noy has disclosed to the Master that two psychiatrists examined Margaret Blackstone during the period between the alleged rape and the delivery of her child, and monitored her psychiatric condition during that period. Mr Noy further states that the first expert, Dr Burke is in the United Kingdom and available to give evidence but the second, Dr Hare, has gone abroad and cannot be contacted. Mr Noy therefore proposes to adduce the evidence of Dr Hare by way of his admissible hearsay statement under s.2 of the Civil Evidence Act 1968 as applied to statements of opinion by s.1 of the Civil Evidence Act 1972. Mr Atkyn applies for a direction that the plaintiff disclose to his instructing solicitors the subject matter of the reports of these two experts in written form.

9.7 Argument

Mr Atkyn: Master, my learned friend has indicated that he intends to adduce the evidence of these two witnesses at the trial. In my submission, I am entitled to a direction that the subject matter of their reports be disclosed in writing to those instructing me. I would refer you to the Civil Evidence Act 1972, Section 2(3) which provides:

Civil Evidence Act 1972, s.2(3)

2(3) Notwithstanding any enactment or rule of law by virtue of which documents prepared for the purpose of pending or contemplated civil proceedings or in connection with the obtaining or giving of legal advice are in certain circumstances privileged from disclosure, provision may be made by rules of court:—

(a) for enabling the court in any civil proceedings to direct, with respect to medical matters or matters of any other class which may be specified in the direction, that the parties or some of them shall each by such date as may be so specified (or such later date as may be permitted or agreed in accordance with the rules) disclose to the other or others in the form of one or more expert reports the expert evidence on matters of that class which he proposes to adduce as part of his case at the trial; and

(b) for prohibiting a party who fails to comply with a direction given in any such proceedings under rules of court made by virtue of paragraph (a) above from adducing in evidence by virtue of Section 2 of the Civil Evidence Act 1968 (admissibility of out-of-court statements), except with the leave of the court, any statement (whether of fact or opinion) contained in any expert report whatsoever in so far as that statement deals with matters of any class specified in the direction.

The purpose of such a direction would be that, by virtue of Section 2(5), the rules made in pursuance of Section 2 of the Act may prohibit the adducing, without leave, of any expert oral evidence, if any direction given under Section 2(3) is not complied with.

The Master: Yes. I believe the place to start is RSC Order 38, Rule 36, which gives effect to those statutory provisions;

Rules of the Supreme Court, Order 38, Rule 36

36(1) Except with the leave of the Court or where all parties agree, no expert evidence may be adduced at the trial or hearing of any cause or matter unless the party seeking to adduce the evidence —

(a) has applied to the Court to determine whether a direction should be given under rule 37, 38 or 41 (whichever is appropriate) and has complied with any direction given on the application....

(2) Nothing in paragraph (1) shall apply to evidence which is permitted to be given by affidavit...

Which of the three rules refered to in Rule 36(1) do you say is appropriate to this case?

Mr Atkyn: In the case of Dr Burke, Master, Rule 37 seems to apply.

Rules of the Supreme Court, Order 38, Rule 37

37(1) This rule applies to any action for personal injuries, except:—
(a) any Admiralty action; and
(b) any action where the pleadings contain an allegation of a negligent act or omission in the course of medical treatment.
(2) Where an application is made under rule 36(1) in respect of oral expert evidence, then, unless the Court considers that there is sufficient reason for not doing so, it shall direct that the substance of the evidence be disclosed in the form of a written report or reports to such other parties and within such period as the Court may specify.
(3) Where the expert evidence relates to medical matters the Court may, if it thinks fit, treat the following circumstances as sufficient reason for not giving a direction under paragraph (2), namely that the expert evidence may contain an expression of opinion:—
(i) as to the manner in which the personal injuries were sustained; or
(ii) as to the genuineness of the symptoms of which complaint is made...

This rule is mandatory in the case of oral medical expert evidence in actions of personal injuries, and in my submission that phrase covers the present case.

The Master: Well, let us deal with that first. Mr Noy, what do you say?

Mr Noy: Master, firstly we are dealing with material to which legal professional privilege applies (see also 10.9 et seq).

The Master: The rules do not oblige you to waive your privilege. It is true that Section 2(3) of the Act states that privilege shall not interfere with the working of the procedure for disclosure. But at the same time, you are entitled to insist on the privilege, at the cost of not calling the evidence. You know of course the decision in:

Causton v *Mann Egerton Limited* [1974] 1 WLR 162 (CA)

In a personal injuries action, an order was made for the agreement of a medical report if possible. At the defendants' solicitors' request, the plaintiff's solicitors sent them the plaintiff's medical report. Later, however, the defendants' solicitors refused to send theirs to the plaintiff's solicitors. The judge refused to order the defendants to disclose their medical reports about the plaintiff. The plaintiff appealed.

LORD DENNING MR (dissenting) said: 'It was suggested in the course of the argument that the medical reports were privileged from discovery and on that account the defendants could not be compelled to produce them. That would be correct if there were no agreement or understanding on the matter: see *In re Saxton, decd* [1962] 1 WLR 968 and *Worrall* v *Reich* [1955] 1 QB 296. But here there was an understanding which amounted to a waiver of the privilege. It was suggested that the solicitor could not waive the privilege on behalf of his client. To this there is a short answer: a solicitor, like counsel, has complete authority over the suit, the mode of conducting it and all this is incident to it. Unless his client has expressly withdrawn that authority or any part of it, the other party is entitled to assume that he is acting within his authority. This is certainly the case when he enters into an agreement to compromise the action itself (see *Chown* v *Parrott* (1863) 14 CBNS 74 and In *re Newen; Carruthers* v *Newen* [1903] 1 Ch 812); a fortiori when he makes a reasonable agreement to disclose medical reports, thereby waiving any privilege in respect of it. The other side must be able to rely on what the solicitor says. It would be impossible to conduct litigation otherwise.

In my opinion, therefore, there was an implied understanding that the defendants, on getting the plaintiff's reports, would act with reciprocity, that is to say, they would show the plaintiff their medical reports. In view of this understanding I think the court should order the defendants to produce them and take any necessary measures to enforce the production. It seems to me most unfair that the defendants should insist on seeing all the plaintiff's medical reports — as they did — and yet refuse to show the reports that they themselves obtained.

STAMP LJ said: '*Worrall* v *Reich* [1955] 1 QB 296, which is a decision of this court, appears to me to be clear authority that medical reports made on behalf of either party on the advice of their legal advisers and for the purposes of preparing their case at the trial are privileged documents. Such documents are by well recognised principles privileged. However desirable it may be that there should be agreements between the parties for the disclosure and exchange of such documents, in the absence of an agreement or waiver of the privilege which would otherwise attach to them, they remain in my judgment privileged. Reading the correspondence in this case as carefully as I can, I can find no agreement for the exchange of reports, and nothing which could be said to amount to a waiver by the defendants of their privilege for the reports in question. Even if such a waiver can be effected by a solicitor without the authority of his client — a question on which I express no view, because on my view of the case it does not arise for decision — I cannot agree with Lord Denning MR that such an agreement or waiver should be implied in the way it was done in *Devine* v *British Transport Commission* [1954] 1 WLR 686. That case was decided before *Worrall* v *Reich* [1955] 1 QB 296, and the point of privilege, if taken, was not discussed in the judgment. If it had been, I venture to think that *Devine* v *British Transport Commission* [1954] 1 WLR 686 would have been relevant authority for the consideration of this court in *Worrall* v *Reich* [1955] 1 QB 296. Nor was the report in *Devine* v *British Transport Commission* [1954] 1 WLR 686 one upon which the party obtaining it did not intend to rely at the trial; and I would be slow to imply an agreement to disclose such a document.'

(ROSKILL LJ delivered a judgment agreeing with STAMP LJ.)

Appeal dismissed.

appreciate this is not always a popular choice with counsel, but the courts have directed that the code shall be strictly enforced. I am thinking of:

Ollett v *Bristol Aerojet Ltd* [1979] 1 WLR 1197 (QBD)   Practice Note

ACKNER J having given judgment for the plaintiff on the issue of liability in a personal injuries action, continued: 'Before leaving this case I would like to make two observations with regard to expert reports...

The first point I make is this. There has been in the past some suggestion that, when an order is made under RSC, Ord 38, r 38 that the *substance* of the experts' reports be exchanged, then that order is satisfied by the experts merely setting out factual descriptions of the machine and the alleged circumstances in which the accident happened and leaving out any conclusions as to the defects in the machine, the system of work or other relevant opinion evidence. This seems to me to be a total misconception of the ordinary meaning of the word "substance." It is also a misconception of the function of an expert. An expert, unlike other witnesses, is allowed, because of his special qualifications and/or experience to give *opinion* evidence. It is for his opinion evidence that he is called, not for a factual description of the machine or the circumstances of the accident, although that is often necessary in order to explain and/or justify his conclusions. When the substance of the expert's report is to be provided, that means precisely what it says, both the substance of the factual description of the machine and/or the circumstances of the accident and his expert opinion in relation to that accident, which is the very justification for calling him.

Secondly, there appears to be a tendency to make orders which do not involve any obligation to disclose experts' reports, other than medical reports. It is true that the court has to be satisfied that it is desirable for experts' reports to be exchanged but, as *The Supreme Court Practice* (1976), p 604 indicates, the court will ordinarily make such an order.

The whole purpose of Order 38 is, in relation to expert evidence, to save expense by dispensing with the calling of experts when there is in reality no real dispute and, where there is a dispute, by avoiding parties being taken by surprise as to the true nature of the dispute and thereby being obliged to seek adjournments.

This case was the simplest of industrial accidents, without the slightest justification for the withholding of expert reasons. It was exactly the sort of case where exchange of experts' reports would have highlighted the only potential issue. The exchange, if it had been ordered, as should have been the case, would have resulted in the amendment sought at the trial causing no surprise to the defendants, and probably it would have resulted in the action not being fought. I trust that in future registrars will in practice ordinarily make an order for the exchange of expert reports.

Mr Noy: Master, yes. I would say in any event that because of Rule 37(3), the court should find a 'sufficient reason' for not ordering disclosure in this case, because the evidence expresses an opinion as to Miss Blackstone's symptoms.

Mr Atkyn: Master, even if that is the case, you have power under Rule 39 to order that some of the expert evidence be disclosed, and if you find that the expression of an opinion in this case is enough to amount to a special reason, then I invite you to use your powers under this rule.

Rules of the Supreme Court, Order 38, Rule 39

39. Where the Court considers that any circumstances rendering it undesirable to give a direction under rule 37 or 38 relate to part only of the evidence sought to be adduced, the Court may, if it thinks fit, direct disclosure of the remainder.

The Master: Yes, that is something that I shall have to consider. Of course, although Rule 37 is mandatory, it is open to me to find that there are sufficient reasons not to disclose, or as you point out to use my limiting power under Rule 39. I was contrasting that in my own mind with the provisions of the other rules to which we sometimes have to refer. For example, under Rule 38 which relates to the case of oral expert evidence outside Rule 37, disclosure should only be made if I am satisfied that it is desirable to do so.

Rules of the Supreme Court, Order 38, Rule 38

38(1) Where an application is made under rule 36(1) in respect of oral expert evidence to which rule 37 does not apply, the Court may, if satisfied that it is desirable to do so, direct that the substance of any expert evidence which is to be adduced by any party be disclosed in the form of a written report or reports to such other parties and within such period as the Court may specify...

I will reserve my opinion for a moment on the matters addressed to me.

Mr Atkyn, what do you say about the evidence of Dr Hare who is abroad and cannot be contacted?

Mr Atkyn: My Lord, his evidence comes under Rule 41.

Rules of the Supreme Court, Order 38, Rule 41

41. Where an application is made under rule 36 in respect of expert evidence contained in a statement and the applicant alleges that the maker of the statement cannot or should not be

called as a witness, the Court may direct that the provisions of rules 20 to 23 and 25 to 33 shall apply with such modifications as the Court thinks fit.

As I understand it, my learned friend is saying Dr Hare cannot or should not be called as a witness. He is of course entitled to take that position, but I would invite you, Master, to make a direction under the rule that this doctor's evidence be subject to the notice procedure under RSC Order 38, Rules 21–31 (see also 8.7, 8.8 ante).

The Master: Mr Noy?

Mr Noy: Master, I do not oppose that application. But I would make the same observation as I did in the case of Dr Burke, namely that I should not be compelled to disclose to the other side the substance of Dr Hare's opinion regarding the genuineness of Miss Blackstone's symptoms. Master, you have power under the rule to make any necessary modification to the operation of the notice procedure, and I would invite you to exercise that power by removing from the requirement of notice that part of Dr Hare's statement dealing with his opinion.

The Master: No, I am against you. I think it is only fair, if this witness is not to be called at trial, that Mr Atkyn should have the opportunity of advising as to what evidence may have to be called to contradict him. Even if I am with you under Rule 37 in the case of Dr Burke, I do not think I should make any limitation. In my opinion, notice should be given of your intention to adduce Dr Hare's evidence accompanied by a statement of the reason why he cannot or should not be called.

Mr Atkyn: Master, there is one more matter. There was some indication, I think in the course of correspondence between solicitors, that the plaintiffs intended to call a third expert in respect of whom no application for directions has been made.

Mr Noy: My Lord, a third expert has been mentioned. It is not the intention of the plaintiffs to call him at trial, and the content of his expert reports are of course the subject of legal professional privilege.

The Master: Yes, Mr Atkyn, I think your remedy in his case, if you deem it necessary, is to issue a subpoena ordering that doctor to attend on your behalf. You will be aware of course that, like any other witness, an expert is compellable to the extent that he is competent. The authority for that is:

Harmony Shipping Co, S.A. v Saudi Europe Line Limited and Others [1979] 1 WLR 1380 (CA)

A handwriting expert, who had had a consultation with those advising the plaintiffs in an action concerning a charter-party, was later approached by the solicitors acting for the defendants in the action. After giving them an opinion on certain documents the expert realised that they concerned the same matter in which he had already been consulted by the plaintiffs. He then informed the defendants' solicitors that he could not accept further instructions from them as it was not his practice, once consulted by one party to an action, to accept instructions from another party. The defendants, anxious to secure the expert's evidence, served him with a *subpoena ad testificandum*. The plaintiffs sought to have the subpoena set aside and the expert excluded from giving evidence for the defendants. The judge refused to set the subpoena aside or to restrain the expert from giving evidence. The plaintiffs appealed.

LORD DENNING MR stated the facts and continued: 'So we have before us a question of principle. If an expert witness has been consulted by one side and has given his opinion to that side, can he thereafter be consulted and subpoenaed by the other side to give his opinion on the facts of the case? That is the issue which this court has to decide.

So far as witnesses of fact are concerned, the law is as plain as can be. There is no property in a witness. The reason is because the court has a right to every man's evidence. Its primary duty is to ascertain the truth. Neither one side nor the other can debar the court from ascertaining the truth either by seeing a witness beforehand or by purchasing his evidence or by making communication to him. In no way can one side prohibit the other side from seeing a witness of fact, from getting the facts from him and from calling him to give evidence or from issuing him with a subpoena. That was laid down by the Law Society in 1944 and published in the "Short Guide to Professional Conduct and Etiquette." It was affirmed and approved in 1963 by the then Lord Chief Justice and the judges and republished in *The Law Society's Gazette* for February 1963. It says:

> ...the Council have always held the view that there is no property in a witness and that so long as there is no question of tampering with the evidence of witnesses it is open to a solicitor for either party to civil or criminal proceedings to interview and take a statement from any witness or prospective witness at any stage of the proceedings, whether or not that witness has been interviewed or called as a witness by the other party.

That principle is established in the case of a witness of fact: for the plain, simple reason that the primary duty of the court is to ascertain the truth by the best evidence available. Any witness who has seen the facts or who knows the facts can be compelled to assist the court and should assist the court by giving that evidence.

The question in this case is whether or not that principle applies to expert witnesses. They may have been told the substance of a party's case. They may have been given a great deal of confidential information on it. They may have given advice to the party. Does the rule apply to such a case?

Many of the communications between the solicitor and the expert witness will be privileged. They are protected by legal professional privilege. They cannot be communicated to the court except with the consent of the party concerned. That means that a great deal of the communications between the expert witness and the lawyer cannot be given in evidence to the court. If questions were asked about it, then it would be the duty of the judge to protect the witness (and he would) by disallowing any questions which infringed the rule about legal professional privilege or the rule protecting information given in confidence — unless, of course, it was one of those rare cases which come before the courts from time to time where in spite of privilege or confidence the court does order a witness to give further evidence.

Subject to that qualification, it seems to me that an expert witness falls into the same position as a witness of fact. The court is entitled, in order to ascertain the truth, to have the actual facts which he has observed adduced before it and to have his independent opinion on those facts...

In this particular case Mr Davies has been subpoenaed by the defendants. It seems to me that that is very right and proper.

(WALLER and CUMMING-BRUCE LJJ delivered judgments agreeing with LORD DENNING.)

Appeal dismissed.

Mr Atkyn: Master, I am very much obliged.

9.8 Commentary

R v *Coke and Littleton* at trial. Mr Bunbury for the prosecution is examining Angela Blackstone in chief. During the course of this examination, Mr Bunbury asks Angela for a description of the man who indecently assaulted her at Coke's flat on 8 July 1979. His intention is to ask Angela thereafter whether she identified anyone in particular as being that man on 8 July 1979, and whether she could identify him now. Mr Bacon objects to the admissibility of the evidence.

9.9 Argument

Mr Bacon: My Lord, I object to this evidence on the ground that Miss Blackstone is being asked to give her opinion. Matters of appearance, resemblance and identity are matters of opinion evidence and in my submission should be rejected.

Mr Bunbury: My Lord, with great respect to my learned friend, this point is entirely without merit. Opinion evidence is admissible from any witness on matters within the competence of people generally. At common law, witnesses have always been permitted to give evidence of such matters, and the rule has been codified for civil proceedings by:

Civil Evidence Act 1972, s.3(2)

> 3(2) It is hereby declared that where a person is called as a witness in any civil proceedings, a statement of opinion by him on any relevant matter on which he is not qualified to give expert evidence, if made as a way of conveying relevant facts personally perceived by him, is admissible as evidence of what he perceived.

In my submission, Miss Blackstone is doing no more than relate what she perceived on this occasion.

Holt J: What sort of matters are within the competence of people generally?

Mr Bunbury: My Lord, certainly identity and resemblance, which are both matters of personal observation. The rule would also apply to the mental and physical condition of a person. I accept, of course, that there are some matters where expert opinion evidence would be required on such a matter. For example, in *R* v *Davies* [1962] 1 WLR 1111 (CMAC), although a lay witness could state that a person had been drinking, he could not say that the person was unfit to drive through drink which was a matter of expert evidence.

Similarly, my Lord, a witness is able to give evidence of the apparent age, speed or value of a person or object, subject again to the obvious comment that where the value of some antique or some specialised item is involved, expert evidence would be required.

But in my submission, in the present case, the evidence I propose to call from Miss Blackstone goes no further than her telling the court what she perceived on that day. (Holt J admitted the evidence.)

B: PREVIOUS JUDGMENTS

9.10 Introductory notes

9.10.1 A judgment is in effect merely a specialised kind of opinion: the opinion of the court. At common law, the balance of authority lay against the admissibility of previous judgments as evidence of the facts on which they were based, for or against strangers to the judgment (i.e. all those other than the parties or their privies). To admit such judgments as evidence was seen as an improper use of opinion evidence. The rule was crystallised in *Hollington* v *F Hewthorn and Co Limited* [1943] KB 587, and became known as the rule in *Hollington* v *Hewthorn*. In certain civil cases, the rule has been reversed by the Civil Evidence Act 1968, ss.11–13. These sections render admissible certain previous criminal convictions and findings or adultery or paternity for the purpose of civil proceedings in which they may be relevant. Other than provided for by these sections, the rule in *Hollington* v *Hewthorn* remains good law, and this of course includes criminal proceedings.

9.10.2 The Civil Evidence Act 1968, s.13, which applies to evidence of previous convictions in subsequent defamation proceedings, renders the evidence conclusive on the question whether the subject committed the offence of which he was convicted. But where evidence is admissible by virtue of ss.11 and 12, which relate to previous convictions and findings of adultery or paternity relevant to other kinds of civil action, the party against whom such evidence is offered may disprove the conviction or finding. The effect of the evidence admitted under the section is, however, to shift the burden of proof onto the party seeking to disprove the conviction or finding, and the better view is that the fact of the conviction or finding by a competent court is a matter of very considerable weight which will not be lightly held to be disproved. A party must plead his intention to adduce evidence under ss.11 or 12. (*A Practical Approach to Evidence*, pp 260–265.)

9.11 Commentary

Blackstone v *Coke* at trial. In accordance with the pleading in paragraph 3 of the statement of claim, Mr Noy on behalf of plaintiff proposes to introduce evidence of Coke's conviction of rape at the Oxbridge Crown Court.

9.12 Argument

Mr Noy: My Lord, I now propose to adduce evidence of the conviction of the defendant Mr Coke on 10 January 1980 at the Oxbridge Crown Court of the rape which is the subject of this action. As Your Lordship will see, this conviction has been properly pleaded in section 3 of the statement of claim, as required by RSC Order 18, Rule 7A.

Hardwicke J: Yes. Perhaps you would remind me of the principles of admissibility of evidence of this kind. My recollection is that at common law, such evidence is not admissible.

Mr Noy: Your Lordship is quite right. Various decisions for and against admissibility were to be found at common law, but the Court of Appeal came down decisively against admissibility in:

Hollington v F. Hewthorn and Co. Ltd [1943] KB 587 (CA)

In an action arising out of a collision between two cars on the highway in which the plaintiff alleged negligence on the part of the defendant driver, the plaintiff sought to give evidence of a conviction of the defendant driver of careless driving at the time and place of the collision. Hilbery J ruled that this evidence was inadmissible.

GODDARD LJ, reading the judgment of the court, said: Is it, then, relevant to an issue whether the defendant, by negligent driving, collided with and thereby injured the plaintiff, to prove that he had been convicted of driving without due care and attention on the occasion when the plaintiff was injured? As stated above, Mr Denning admits that he would have to identify the negligent driving which formed the subject of the charge with that which caused the injury to the plaintiff, for the record of the conviction itself would show no more than that the defendant was convicted for so driving on a certain day and in a certain parish or place. In truth, the conviction is only proof that another court considered that the defendant was guilty of careless driving. Even were it proved that it was the accident that led to the prosecution, the conviction proves no more than what has just been stated. The court which has to try the claim for damages knows nothing of the evidence that was before the criminal court. It cannot know what arguments were addressed to it, or what influenced the court in arriving at its decision. Moreover, the issue in the criminal proceedings is not identical with that raised in the claim for damages. Assume that evidence is called to prove that the defendant did collide with the plaintiff, that has only an evidential value on the issue whether the defendant, by driving carelessly, caused damage to the plaintiff. To link up or identify the careless driving with the accident, it would be necessary in most cases, probably in all, to call substantially the same evidence before the court trying the claim for personal injuries, and so proof of the conviction by itself would amount to no more than proof that the criminal court came to the conclusion that the defendant was guilty. It is admitted that the conviction is in no sense an estoppel, but only evidence to which the court or a jury can attach such weight as they think proper, but it is obvious that once the defendant challenges the propriety of the conviction the court, on the subsequent trial, would have to retry the criminal case to find out what weight ought to be attached to the result. It frequently happens that a bystander has a complete and full view of an accident. It is beyond question that, while he may inform the court of everything that he saw, he may not express any opinion on whether either or both of the parties were negligent. The reason commonly assigned is that this is the precise question the court has to decide, but, in truth, it is because his opinion is not relevant. Any fact that he can prove is relevant, but his opinion is not. The well recognised exception in the case of scientific or expert witnesses depends on considerations which, for present purposes, are immaterial. So, on the trial of the issue in the civil court, the opinion of the criminal court is equally irrelevant...

Hilbery J rejected the conviction on the ground that it was res inter alios acta, which is the reason generally given for not admitting that class of evidence. No doubt, it is difficult for a layman to understand why it is that if A prosecutes B, say, for doing him grievous bodily harm, and subsequently brings an action against him for damages for assault, this doctrine should apply so that he cannot use the conviction as proof that B did assault him. The "alios" can only be the Crown who, in the case of what is commonly called a private prosecution, is no more than the nominal prosecutor. It is for this reason that we have stressed the question of relevancy, and, indeed, it is relevancy that lies at the root of the objection to the admissibility of the evidence. Other reasons can, of course, be given for the rule, and in other cases would have great force. A judgment obtained by A against B ought not to be evidence against C, for, in the words of the Chief Justice in the *Duchess of Kingston's Case* (1776) 2 Sm LC, 13th ed, 644, it would be unjust to bind any person who could not be admitted to make a defence, or to examine witnesses or to appeal from a judgment he might think erroneous: and therefore...the judgment of the court upon facts found, although evidence against the parties, and all claiming under them, are not, in general, to be used to the prejudice of strangers. This is true, not only of convictions, but also of judgments in civil actions. If given between the same parties they are conclusive, but not against anyone who was not a party. If the judgment is not conclusive we have already given our reasons for holding that it ought not to be admitted as some evidence of a fact which must have been found owing mainly to the impossibility of determining what weight should be given to it without retrying the former case. A judgment, however, is conclusive as against all persons of the existence of the state of things which it actually affects when the existence of that state is a fact in issue. Thus, if A sues B alleging that owing to B's negligence he has been held liable to pay *xl* to C, the judgment obtained by C is conclusive as to the amount of damages that A has had to pay C, but it is not evidence that B was negligent: see *Green* v *New River Co.* (1792) 4 TR 589, and B can show, if he can, that the amount recovered was not the true measure of damage.

This decision has been reversed for civil cases of certain kinds, of which the present case is one.

Hardwicke J: So that in other cases, the rule in *Hollington* v *Hewthorn* remains undisturbed?

Mr Noy: My Lord, yes. For example, in a criminal case, to which the statute does not apply, where a defendant is being prosecuted for handling stolen goods, the mere fact that someone has been convicted of theft is not evidence that the goods are stolen.

But in civil cases, the matter is now governed by Section 11 of the Civil Evidence Act 1968, which provides:

Civil Evidence Act 1968, s.11

11(1) In any civil proceedings the fact that a person has been convicted of an offence by or before any court in the United Kingdom or by a court-martial there or elsewhere shall... be admissible in evidence for the purpose of proving, where to do so is relevant to any issue in those proceedings, that he committed that offence, whether he was so convicted upon a plea of guilty or otherwise and whether or not he is a party to the civil proceedings; but no conviction other than a subsisting one shall be admissible in evidence by virtue of this section.

(2) In any civil proceedings in which by virtue of this section a person is proved to have been convicted of an offence by or before any court in the United Kingdom or by a court-martial there or elsewhere:—

(a) he shall be taken to have committed that offence unless the contrary is proved; and

(b) without prejudice to the reception of any other admissible evidence for the purpose of identifying the facts on which the conviction was based, the contents of any document which is admissible as evidence of the conviction, and the contents of the information, complaint, indictment or charge-sheet on which the person in question was convicted, shall be admissible in evidence for that purpose.

Hardwicke J: It may be helpful to observe as I do, looking down the Act, that Sections 12 and 13 appear to contain similar provisions.

Mr Noy: My Lord, that is right. Section 12 provides for the admissibility of findings of adultery and paternity:

Civil Evidence Act 1968, s.12

12(1) In any civil proceedings:—

(a) the fact that a person has been found guilty of adultery in any matrimonial proceedings; and

(b) the fact that a person has been adjudged to be the father of a child in affiliation proceedings before any court in the United Kingdom,

shall... be admissible in evidence for the purpose of proving, where to do so is relevant to any issue in those civil proceedings, that he committed the adultery to which the finding relates or, as the case may be, is (or was) the father of that child, whether or not he offered any defence to the allegation of adultery or paternity and whether or not he is a party to the civil proceedings; but no finding or adjudication other than a subsisting one shall be admissible in evidence by virtue of this section.

(2) In any civil proceedings in which by virtue of this section a person is proved to have been found guilty of adultery as mentioned in subsection (1)(a) above or to have. been adjudged to be the father of a child as mentioned in subsection (1)(b) above:—

(a) he shall be taken to have committed the adultery to which the finding relates or, as the case may be, to be (or have been) the father of that child, unless the contrary is proved; and

(b) without prejudice to the reception of any other admissible evidence for the purpose of identifying the facts on which the finding or adjudication was based, the contents of any document which was before the court, or which contains any pronouncement of the court, in the matrimonial or affiliation proceedings in question shall be admissible in evidence for that purpose.

Section 13 provides for the admissibility of previous convictions in defamation actions.

Civil Evidence Act 1968, s.13

13(1) In an action for libel or slander in which the question whether a person did or did not commit a criminal offence is relevant to an issue arising in the action, proof that, at the time when that issue falls to be determined, that person stands convicted of that offence shall be conclusive evidence that he committed that offence; and his conviction thereof shall be admissible in evidence accordingly.

Your Lordship will observe that unlike Section 11 and 12, Section 13 provides that evidence of a subsisting criminal conviction is to be conclusive evidence of the commission of the offence for the purpose of defamation proceedings.

Hardwicke J: Of course, you rely upon Section 11 in this case. I note that the section requires that any such conviction should be 'subsisting'. What is the significance of that?

Mr Noy: My Lord, it means merely that the conviction has not been overturned on appeal.

Hardwicke J: Mr Atkyn, has there been or is there to be an appeal against conviction?

Mr Atkyn: My Lord, no. And I would concede that even if such an appeal were pending, the conviction would still subsist, although the right course would be for Your Lordship to adjourn the matter pending the outcome of the criminal appeal, a course adopted by Golding J in *Re Raphael, Raphael* v *D'Antin and another* [1973] 1 WLR 998 (Ch D).

Mr Noy: I am obliged to my learned friend. Your Lordship will see that by virtue of Section 11(2) because there is a subsisting conviction, the defendant Coke shall be taken to have committed the offence unless the contrary is proved.

Hardwicke J: What is the effect of that provision?

Mr Noy: My Lord, in my submission, it operates to shift the burden of proof onto the defendant. The rule is neatly illustrated in the case of *Wauchope* v *Mordecai* [1970] 1 WLR 317 (CA):

Wauchope v Mordecai [1970] 1 WLR 317 (CA)

The plaintiff was knocked off his bicycle when the defendant opened the door of a car as the plaintiff was passing. The defendant was later convicted of the offence of opening the door so as to cause injury or danger. By an oversight, the trial judge was not referred to s.11 of the Civil Evidence Act 1968 and found for the defendant, basing his decision on the incidence of the legal burden of proof. The plaintiff appealed.

LORD DENNING MR said: 'The judge, unfortunately, was not told by anyone that the Civil Evidence Act, 1968, s.11, was already in operation. It comes in Part II, which was brought into force by an Order in Council on October 25, 1968. Under that section, the conviction of Mr Mordecai by the magistrate was admissible in evidence. Not knowing of it, the judge went by the old law in *Hollington* v *F Hewthorn & Co Ltd* [1943] KB 587. He ignored the conviction altogether. He said:

It has nothing to do with me whether a magistrate heard it; it has nothing to do with me whether the magistrate thought it right.... It does not matter to me one iota whether the magistrate thought you were to blame or thought the motorist was to blame. It does not matter.

That was wrong. Section 11(1) of the Civil Evidence Act, 1968, says:

In any civil proceedings the fact that a person has been convicted of an offence...shall...be admissible in evidence for the purpose of proving, where to do so is relevant to any issue in those proceedings, that he committed that offence...

So the conviction was admissible in evidence.

Eventually the judge rested his decision on the burden of proof. He came down against Mr Wauchope saying:

> I think he was riding down that road in the twilight pretty fast, and I think that as he rode down pretty fast he just failed to give Mr Mordecai just those few inches of room. The net result was that his shoulder hit Mr Mordecai's car and the result of that is that he fell on the road. I am not saying that I am altogether certain that that is true, but I am not satisfied that the other story is true. It could have happened either way, but, on the whole, I think Mr Mordecai's story rings just a little more truly that the plaintiff's."

The judge was wrong on the burden of proof. Unknown to him, section 11(2) had been brought into force...

So in this case, in view of the conviction, it was to be taken that Mr Mordecai had opened the door of the car so as to cause injury, unless the contrary was proved. The burden of proof in this civil case was altered. Instead of the burden being on Mr Wauchope to prove that Mr Mordecai was negligent, it was for Mr Mordecai to prove that he had not opened the door so as to cause injury. If the judge had been reminded of this new Act, I think that he would have held in favour of Mr Wauchope.'

(SALMON and EDMUND DAVIS LJJ agreed.)

Appeal allowed. •

Hardwicke J: Even given that provision, I seem to recall that there is some difference of opinion in the Court of Appeal as to whether the section goes any further than merely shifting the burden of proof.

Mr Noy: My Lord, that is correct. No doubt Your Lordship has in mind the decision in:

Stupple v *Royal Insurance Company* [1971] 1 QB 50 (CA)

In 1963 a bullion van was robbed. In 1964 the plaintiff, S, was convicted of the robbery. The main evidence against him was of the finding by the police of banknotes in his flat after the robbery. The banknotes were subsequently claimed by the plaintiffs, S and his wife. The defendants, the insurance company who had paid to the bank the amount they had lost be reason of the robbery, counterclaimed against S that as a participant in the robbery he owed them their net loss. The two cases were tried together and S sought to show that he was not guilty of the robbery. After considering the effect of s.11 of the Civil Evidence Act 1968, the judge gave judgment for the defendants on the claim and the counterclaim, after asking himself the question, what his views would have been if he had sat as a juryman on the criminal trial.

LORD DENNING MR said: 'Mr Hawser, for Mr Stupple, submitted that the only effect of the Act was to shift the burden of proof. He said that, whereas previously the conviction was not admissible in evidence at all, now it was admissible in evidence, but the effect was simply to put on the man the burden of showing, on the balance of probabilities, that he was innocent. He claimed that Mr Stupple had done so.

I do not accept Mr Hawser's submission. I think that the conviction does not merely shift the burden of proof. It is a weighty piece of evidence of itself. For instance, if a man is convicted of careless driving on the evidence of a witness, but that witness dies before the civil action is heard (as in *Hollington* v *F Hewthorn & Co Ltd* [1943] 1 KB 587) then the conviction itself tells in the scale in the civil action. It speaks as clearly as the witness himself would have done, had he lived. It does not merely reverse the burden of proof. If that was all it did, the defendant might well give his own evidence negativing want of care, and say: "I have discharged the burden. I have given my evidence and it has not been contradicted." In answer to the defendant's evidence, the plaintiff can say to him: "But your evidence is contradicted. It is contradicted by the very fact of your conviction."

In addition, Mr Hawser sought, as far as he could, to minimise the effect of shifting the burden. In this, too, he did not succeed. The Act does not merely shift the evidential burden, as it is called. It shifts the legal burden of proof. I explained the difference long ago, in 1945, in an article in the Law Quarterly Review 61 LQR 379. Take a running-down case where a plaintiff claims damages for negligent driving by the defendant. If the defendant has not been convicted, the legal burden is on the plaintiff throughout. But if the defendant has been convicted of careless driving, the legal burden is shifted. It is on the defendant himself. At the end of the day, if the judge is left in doubt the defendant fails because the defendant has not discharged the legal burden which is upon him. The burden is, no doubt, the civil burden. He must show, on the balance of probabilities, that he was not negligent: see *Public Prosecutor* v *Yuvaraj* [1970] 2 WLR 226, 231, in the Privy Council quite recently. But he must show it nevertheless. Otherwise he loses by the very force of the conviction.

How can a man, who has been convicted in a criminal trial, prove his innocence in a subsequent civil action? He can, of course, call his previous witnesses and hope that the judge will believe them now, even if they were disbelieved before. He can also call any fresh witnesses whom he thinks will help his case. In addition, I think he can show that the witnesses against him in the criminal trial were mistaken. For instance, in a traffic accident he could prove that a witness who claimed to have seen it was miles away and committed perjury. This would not, of course, prove his innocence directly, but it would do so indirectly by destroying the evidence on which he was convicted. So in this case Mr Stupple could prove that Mr Ford was mistaken.

In any case, what weight is to be given to the criminal conviction? This must depend on the circumstances. Take a plea of guilty. Sometimes a defendant pleads guilty in error: or in a minor offence he may plead guilty to save time and expense, or to avoid some embarrassing fact coming out. Afterwards, in the civil action, he can, I think, explain how he came to plead guilty.

Take next a case in the magistrates' court when a man is convicted and bound over or fined a trifling sum, but had a good ground of appeal, and did not exercise it because it was not worth while. Can he not explain this in a civil court? I think he can. He can offer any explanation in his effort to show that the conviction was erroneous: and it is for the judge at the civil trial to say how far he has succeeded.

In my opinion, therefore, the weight to be given to a previous conviction is essentially for the judge at the civil trial. Just as he has to evaluate the oral evidence of a witness, so he should evaluate the probative force of a conviction.

If the defendant should succeed in throwing doubt on the conviction, the plaintiff can rely, in answer, on the conviction itself; and he can supplement it, if he thinks it desirable, by producing (under the hearsay sections) the evidence given by the prosecution witnesses in the criminal trial, or, if he wishes, he can call them again. At the end of the civil case, the judge must ask himself whether the defendant has succeeded in overthrowing the conviction. If not, the conviction stands and proves the case.'

WINN LJ said: 'In my opinion the judge was right to hold that this enactment meant that, unless the defendant proved on a balance of probability, viz, by a civil standard of proof, that he was innocent, he must be treated for all relevant purposes as having committed the offence of which he was convicted. I do not myself think that it was any requisite, or, indeed, any proper, part of the function of the judge to consider what view he himself might have taken of the case had he sat on it either as juryman or judge: nor was it on a correct view relevant to his decision whether there had been an unsuccessful application to the Court of Appeal for leave to appeal against the conviction. Notwithstanding that the judge gave himself a great deal of avoidable trouble, effort and anxiety, he reached a conclusion which the Act of 1968 justified, and I see no reason to suppose that his decision, which was of a very limited scope, was wrong.'

BUCKLEY LJ said: 'There remains, however, the problem of what weight, if any, should be accorded to the proved fact of conviction in deciding whether any other evidence adduced is sufficient to discharge the onus resting on B. In my judgment no weight is in this respect to be given to the mere fact of conviction.

If, as seems to be the case, I differ from Lord Denning MR in this respect, I do so with the greatest diffidence.

The effect of the bare proof of conviction is, I think, spent in bringing section 11(2)(a) into play. But very much weight may have to be given to such circumstances of the criminal proceedings as are brought out in the evidence in the civil action. Witnesses called in the civil proceedings may give different evidence from that which they gave in the criminal proceedings. Witnesses may be called in the civil proceedings who might have been but were not called in the criminal proceedings, or vice versa. The judge may feel that he should take account of the fact that the judge or jury in the criminal proceedings disbelieved a witness who is called in the civil proceedings, or that the defendant pleaded guilty or not guilty, as the case may be. Many examples could be suggested of ways in which what occurred or did not occur in the criminal proceedings may have a bearing on the judge's decision in the civil proceedings: but the judge's duty in the civil proceedings is still to decide that case on the evidence adduced to him. He is not concerned with the evidence in the criminal proceedings except as far as it is reproduced in the evidence called before him, or is made evidence in the civil proceedings under the Civil Evidence Act, 1968, section 2, or is established before him in cross-examination. He is not concerned with the propriety of the conviction except so far as his view of the evidence before him may lead him incidentally to the conclusion that the conviction was justified or is open to criticism: but even if it does so, this must be a consequence of his decision and cannot be a reason for it. The propriety or otherwise of the conviction is irrelevant to the steps leading to his decision.

It was suggested in argument that so to view Section 11 would result in the issues in the criminal proceedings being retried in the civil proceedings, and that this would be contrary to an intention on the part of the legislature to avoid this sort of duplication.

I do not myself think that this would be the result in most cases, and I do not discern any such general intention in the section. If the fact of conviction were meant to carry some weight in determining whether the convicted man has successfully discharged the onus under Section 11(2)(a) of proving that he did not commit the offence, what weight should it carry? I cannot accept that this should depend on such considerations as, for instance, the status of the court which convicted, or whether the decision was a unanimous or a majority verdict of a jury. I cannot discover any measure of the weight which the unexplored fact of conviction should carry. Although the section has made proof of conviction admissible and has given proof of conviction a particular statutory effect under Section 11(2)(a), it remains, I think, as true today as before the Act that mere proof of conviction proves nothing relevant to the plaintiff's claim, and it clearly cannot be intended to shut out or, I think, to mitigate the effect of any evidence tending to show that the convicted person did not commit the offence. In my judgment, proof of conviction under this section gives rise to the statutory presumption laid down in Section 11(2)(a), which, like any other presumption, will give way to evidence establishing the contrary on the balance of probability, without itself affording any evidential weight to be taken into account in determining whether that onus has been discharged.'
[The court upheld the judge's view that the conviction and its affirmation by the Court of Criminal Appeal were 'from a practical point of view...conclusive']

In my submission, the better view is that of Lord Denning MR.

Hardwicke J: Well, it may be that Mr Atkyn will not agree with that view. Mr Atkyn, is it the defendant's intention to seek to disprove this conviction?

Mr Atkyn: My Lord, it is.

Hardwicke J: Well, you are entitled to do that by virtue of the section. Mr Noy, in those circumstances, what evidence do you propose to adduce?

Mr Noy: My Lord, I propose to follow the course advocated by the Court of Appeal in *Taylor v Taylor* [1970] 1 WLR 1148 (CA), and adduce a certified transcript of the trial.

Hardwicke J: Yes. I am anxious in light of the Court of Appeal's comments there to investigate the matter thoroughly, for which purpose I shall need the transcript including the depositions, a note of the evidence and, of course the summing up.

Mr Noy: My Lord, those will all be available. Your Lordship will have noted from the judgments of the Court of Appeal that the transcript is admissible under Section 2 of the Civil Evidence Act 1968, and the text of the summing up in particular under Section 4 of the same Act, as being a record compiled by the shorthand writer acting under a duty. (For the operation of ss.2 and 4 of the Civil Evidence Act 1968, see 8.9, ante.)

Hardwicke J: Mr Atkyn, how do you propose to proceed?

Mr Atkyn: My Lord, by referring to the transcript also and by calling my client to give evidence in due course.

Hardwicke J: Yes, very well. Let us proceed.

9.13   Questions for Counsel

9.13.1 R v Coke and Littleton. Compose a direction to be included in Holt J's summing up to the jury, which would be adequate to direct their attention to:

(a)   the failure of the prosecution to call a handwriting expert to deal with exhibits GG1 and GG3, and the possible views the jury might take about that,

(b)   the evidence of Mr Mansfield and how it should be regarded, and

(c)   the use that the jury might themselves make of the original Exhibits GG1 and GG3 during their retirement.

9.13.2 Blackstone v Coke. What factors would you weigh, acting on behalf of Margaret Blackstone, in deciding what expert evidence should be disclosed to the defence and used at trial, and on the other hand what expert evidence should be retained under the legal professional privilege for use in preparation of the case? Do you agree with the Master's decision to order a Rule 21 notice to be served on the defence in respect of the evidence of Dr Hare?

9.13.3 Blackstone v Coke. If Mr Noy intends to call expert handwriting evidence at trial, what application ought he make to the Master on summons for directions and what directions do you think the Master should give about that evidence?

9.13.4 Blackstone v Coke. Assume that you are to call Mr Hale on behalf of the plaintiff in order to prove the defendant Coke's authorship of Exhibit GG1. Mr Hale has available an enlarged photographic chart showing what he alleges to be the similarities in the detailed handwriting in Exhibits GG1 and GG3. What questions would you ask of Mr Hale in chief, in order to allow him fully to explain his opinion to the judge?

9.13.5 Blackstone v Coke. Would the plaintiff be entitled to call evidence from Mrs Helen Blackstone to the effect that

(a)   following the incident involving Coke, her daughter was extremely depressed, occasionally hysterical and given to fits of weeping?

(b)   following the same incident, her daughter was subject to serious psychiatric disturbance as a result of which it would have been inadvisable for her to undergo an abortion? If the answer to either question is 'no', by what evidence should these matters be proved?

10   Public Policy and Privilege

A: PUBLIC POLICY

10.1 Introductory notes

10.1.1 In general, the parties to litigation should be free to present to the court all available relevant evidence that supports their cases. To this end, each party is, in general, entitled to disclosure of relevant evidence in the possession of the other parties. This rule is, however, subject to certain limitations imposed by the policy of the law. Those limitations which are based upon the personal rights of the parties themselves are referred to as private evidential privileges, and are considered in Section B. But other restrictions apply which are founded upon consideration of public policy and demand that certain evidence, however relevant and cogent, be excluded because of the fear that disclosure might damage the national interest or seriously impair the working of some aspect of the public service. In these cases, there must be a balancing of the interest of the public in exclusion against the interest of the litigants in disclosure. Ordinarily, great weight will be given to the view of the relevant minister or senior public servant who advocates exclusion, but in the last resort, the matter is one to be decided by the court, which will if necessary review the documents concerned before reaching a decision. More weight will be given to a claim to exclude directed at individual documents (a 'contents claim') than to an indiscriminate attack on all documents of certain kind (a 'class claim') particularly where the documents are of a routine nature.

10.1.2 The public policy factor applies to evidence in any form and regardless of the nature of the proceedings. It is generally considered that no waiver of an objection based on public policy is possible, and that such objection may be taken not only by a representative of the public service involved but by any of the parties or by the court of its own motion. It also follows that where facts are excluded by public policy, the objection affects not only the original documents which are the immediate subject of exclusion, but also means that those facts cannot be proved by secondary evidence such as copies of such documents, or oral evidence of their contents. Furthermore, such documents may not be used by a witness to refresh his memory while giving evidence. Private evidential privileges, conversely, may be lost or waived, and such facts proved by secondary evidence.

10.1.3 The most obvious category of public policy objections is that of affairs of state in the sense of matters that directly affect national security or the innermost workings of government. Such grounds are particularly potent in time of war.

However, governmental and administrative matters generally, including important affairs of local government, may equally be protected, although in such cases, a great burden lies upon the party asserting the objection.

10.1.4   By an old rule of the common law, in any public prosecution or in any information for fraud against the revenue laws or in any civil proceedings arising from these, no evidence may be given that would tend to reveal the identity of any person who has given information leading to the institution of the prosecution or proceedings. There is a public interest in preserving the anonymity of informants. This rule applies in all cases, except where the identity of an informant is a necessary piece of evidence to show the innocence of an accused person. In modern law, this rule of public policy applies not only to police informers, but to other professional investigators or members of the public who give information regarding crime, or regarding other misconduct that may be of interest to statutory bodies such as the Gaming Board or the NSPCC.

10.1.5   There is no rule of public policy excluding documents or evidence merely because they have been supplied under a promise of confidentiality. However, the confidentiality of a document or other piece of evidence will be an important factor in the court's consideration of the question whether it comes within the heading of public policy or not. The court recognises that there is a public interest in the free exercise of confidential relationships, and will seek to preserve these where it can be done without undue damage to the rights of litigants. Once again, this is a process of balancing competing interests.

10.1.6   It is contrary to public policy to compel judges to make any disclosure of a matter affecting the substance of any proceeding in which they have been judicially engaged. While the rule applies strictly only to superior judges, the evidence of any judge should be taken only as a last resort. The rule does not strictly apply to matters collateral to the proceedings, for example the events surrounding the escape of a prisoner from court during a trial. No inquiry may be made of jurors with regard to the proceedings in the jury room during deliberation, though the court can inquire into any matter concerning the jury which takes place in open court. (*A Practical Approach to Evidence*, pp 267–85.)

10.2   Commentary

Blackstone v *Coke* at trial.   In response to the subpoena issued on behalf of the defendant, the director of the Oxbridge City Children's Department attends in person and with counsel and is sworn. In response to questions by Mr Atkyn on behalf of Coke, the director agrees that Margaret Blackstone approached his department with regard to the question of long-term fostering for her child. When questioned as to the contents of his files, including reports on Margaret and details of conversations between her and the department's officers, the director declines to answer questions or to produce his files on the ground of public policy. He places before Hardwicke J an affidavit, which sets forth that it is the policy of the Oxbridge City Children's Department to withhold as confidential all conversations and reports dealing with persons with whom the department is concerned, and that in the opinion of the director the work of the department would be rendered impracticable unless a guarantee of confidentiality could be offered to those who communicate with it. Hardwicke J calls on Mr Erskine, counsel for the director, to address him on the question of public policy.

10.3 Argument

Hardwicke J: I have difficulty in seeing why this case should fall within the category of public policy. It seems quite unlike the situations envisaged in the cases.

Mr Erskine: Possibly Your Lordship has in mind the more dramatic cases dealing with affairs of state. I would concede that these are perhaps the most obvious example of public policy cases. For example, may I refer Your Lordship to:

Asiatic Petroleum Company Limited v Anglo Persian Company Limited [1916] 1 KB 822 (CA)

The defendants, acting under the direction of the Board of Admiralty, refused to produce a letter to their agents on the ground that it contained information concerning the government's plans for the campaign in Persia during the First World War.

SWINFEN EADY LJ said: 'The foundation of the rule is that the information cannot be disclosed without injury to the public interests, and not that the documents are confidential or official, which alone is no reason for their non-production...'
The defendant's objection was upheld.

Hardwicke J: Am I to take it that the concept of public policy extends beyond the somewhat dramatic circumstances of those cases? And, if so, am I bound by the affidavit submitted by the director, or is it my function to decide whether the evidence sought by Mr Atkyn should be admitted or excluded?

Mr Erskine: Perhaps I can answer both Your Lordship's questions by reference to the leading decision of The House of Lords in:

Conway v Rimmer [1968] AC 910 (HL)

The plaintiff, a probationary police constable, was prosecuted for theft by the defendant, a superintendent in the same force. The jury stopped the case. The plaintiff now brought an action for malicious prosecution against the defendant. In the course of discovery, the defendant disclosed a list of documents in his possession, admittedly relevant to the plaintiff's action, which included four reports made by him about the plaintiff during his period of probation, and a report in connection with his prosecution. The Home Secretary objected to production of all five documents on the grounds that each fell within a class of documents the production of which would be injurious to the public interest.

LORD REID set out the affidavit of the Home Secretary and continued: 'The question whether such a statement by a Minister of the Crown should be accepted as conclusively preventing any court from ordering production of any of the documents to which it applies is one of very great importance in the administration of justice. If the commonly accepted interpretation of the decision of this House in *Duncan v Cammell, Laird & Co Ltd* [1942] AC 624 is to remain authoritative the question admits of only one answer — the Minister's statement is final and conclusive. Normally I would be very slow to question the authority of a unanimous decision of this House only 25 years old which was carefully considered and obviously intended to lay down a general rule. But this decision has several abnormal features.

Events have proved that the rule supposed to have been laid down in *Duncan's* case is far from satisfactory. In the large number of cases in England and elsewhere which have been cited in argument much dissatisfaction has been expressed and I have not observed even one expression of whole-hearted approval. Moreover a statement made by the Lord Chancellor in 1956 on behalf of the Government, to which I shall return late, makes it clear that that Government did not regard it as consonant with public policy to maintain the rule to the full extent which existing authorities had held to be justifiable.

I have no doubt that the case of *Duncan* v *Cammell, Laird & Cò Ltd* was rightly decided. The plaintiff sought discovery of documents relating to the submarine *Thetis* including a contract for the hull and machinery and plans and specifications. The First Lord of the Admiralty had stated that "it would be injurious to the public interest that any of the said documents should be disclosed to any person." Any of these documents might well have given valuable information, or at least clues, to the skilled eye of an agent of a foreign power. But Lord Simon LC took the opportunity to deal with the whole question of the right of the Crown to prevent production of documents in a litigation. Yet a study of his speech leaves me with the strong impression that throughout he had primarily in mind cases where discovery or disclosure would involve a danger of real prejudice to the national interest. I find it difficult to believe that his speech would have been the same if the case had related, as the present case does, to discovery of routine reports on a probationer constable.

I find it difficult to believe that he would have put these three examples on the same level if he had intended the third to cover such minor matters as a routine report by a relatively junior officer. And my impression is strengthened by the passage at the very end of the speech:

> ...the public interest is also the interest of every subject of the realm, and while, in these exceptional cases the private citizen may seem to be denied what is to his immediate advantage, he, like the rest of us, would suffer if the needs of protecting the interests of the country as a whole were not ranked as a prior obligation.

Would he have spoken of "these exceptional cases" or of "the needs of protecting the interests of the country as a whole" if he had intended to include all manner of routine communications? And did he really mean that the protection of such communications is a "prior obligation" in a case where a man's reputation or fortune is at stake and withholding the document makes it impossible for justice to be done?

It is universally recognised that here there are two kinds of public interest which may clash. There is the public interest that harm shall not be done to the nation or the public service by disclosure of certain documents, and there is the public interest that the administration of justice shall not be frustrated by the withholding of documents which must be produced if justice is to be done. There are many cases where the nature of the injury which would or might be done to the nation or the public service is of so grave a character that no other interest, public or private, can be allowed to prevail over it. With regard to such cases it would be proper to say, as Lord Simon did, that to order production of the document in question would put the interest of the state in jeopardy. But there are many other cases where the possible injury to the public service is much less and there one would think that it would be proper to balance the public interests involved. I do not believe that Lord Simon really meant that the smallest probability of injury to the public service must always outweigh the gravest frustration of the administration of justice.

It is to be observed that, in a passage which I have already quoted, Lord Simon referred to the practice of keeping a class of documents secret being "*nècessary* [my italics] for the proper functioning of the public interest." But the certificate of the Home Secretary in the present case does not go nearly so far as that. It merely says that the production of a document of the classes to which it refers would be "injurious to the public interest": it does not say what degree of injury is to be apprehended. It may be advantageous to the functioning of the public service that reports of this kind should be kept secret — that is the view of the Home Secretary — but I would be very surprised if anyone said that that is necessary.

There are now many large public bodies, such as British Railways and the National Coal Board, the proper and efficient functioning of which is very necessary for many reasons including the safety of the public. The Attorney-General made it clear that Crown privilege is not and cannot be invoked to prevent disclosure of similar documents made by them or their servants even it if were said that this is required for the proper and efficient functioning of the that public service. I find it difficult to see why it should be *necessary* to withhold whole classes of routine "communications with or within a public department" but quite unnecessary to withhold similar communications with or within a public corporation. There the safety of the public may well depend on the candour and completeness of reports made by subordinates whose duty it is to draw attention to defects. But, so far as I know, no one has ever suggested that public safety has been endangered by the candour or completeness of such reports having been inhibited by the fact that they may have to be produced if the interests of the due administration of justice should ever require production at any time....

I would therefore propose that the House ought now to decide that courts have and are entitled to exercise a power and duty to hold a balance between the public interest, as expressed by a Minister, to withhold certain documents or other evidence, and the public interest in ensuring the proper administration of justice. That does not mean that a court would reject a Minister's view: full weight must be given to it in every case, and if the Minister's reasons are of a character which judicial experience is not competent to weigh, then the Minister's view must prevail. But experience has shown that reasons given for withholding whole classes of documents are often not of that character. For example a court is perfectly well able to assess the likelihood that, if the writer of a certain class of document knew that there was a chance that his report might be produced in legal proceedings, he would make a less full and candid report than he would otherwise have done.

I do not doubt that there are certain classes of documents which ought not to be disclosed whatever their content may be. Virtually everyone agrees that Cabinet minutes and the like ought not to be disclosed until such time as they are only of historical interest. But I do not think that many people would give as the reason that premature disclosure would prevent candour in the Cabinet. To my mind the most important reason is that such disclosure would create or fan ill-informed or captious public or political criticism. The business of government is difficult enough as it is, and no government could contemplate with equanimity the inner workings of the government machine being exposed to the gaze of those ready to criticise without adequate knowledge of the background and perhaps with some axe to grind. And that must, in my view, also apply to all documents concerned with policy making within departments including, it may be, minutes and the like by quite junior officials and correspondence with outside bodies. Further it may be that deliberations about a particular case require protection as much as deliberations about policy. I do not think that it is possible to limit such documents by any definition. But there seems to me to be a wide difference between such documents and routine reports. There may be special reasons for withholding some kinds of routine documents, but I think that the proper test to be applied is to ask, in the language of Lord Simon in *Duncan's* case, whether the withholding of a document because it belongs to a particular class is really "necessary for the proper functioning of the public service."

It appears to me that, if the Minister's reasons are such that a judge can properly weigh them, he must, on the other hand, consider what is the probable importance in the case before him of the documents or other evidence sought to be withheld. If he decides that on balance the documents probably ought to be produced, I think that it would generally be best that he should see them before ordering production and if he thinks that the Minister's reasons are not clearly expressed he will have to see the documents before ordering production. I can see nothing wrong in the judge seeing documents without their being shown to the parties. Lord Simon said (in *Duncan's* case) that "where the Crown is a party...this would amount to communicating with one party to the exclusion of the other." I do not agree. The parties see the Minister's reasons. Where a document has not been prepared for the information of the judge, it seems to me a misuse of language to say that the judge "communicates with" the holder of the document by reading it. If on reading the document he still thinks that it ought to be produced he will order its production.

It appears to me to be most improbable that any harm would be done by disclosure of the probationary report on the appellant or of the report from the police training centre. With regard to the report which the respondent made to his chief constable with a view to the prosecution of the appellant there could be more doubt, although no suggestion was made in argument that disclosure of its contents would be harmful now that the appellant has been acquitted. And, as I have said, these documents may prove to be of vital importance in this litigation.

In my judgment, this appeal should be allowed and these documents ought now to be required to be produced for inspection. If it is then found that disclosure would not, in your Lordships' view be prejudicial to the public interest, or that any possibility of such prejudice is, in the case of each of the documents, insufficient to justify its being withheld, then disclosure should be ordered.
(LORDS MORRIS of BORTH-Y-GEST, HODSON, PEARCE and UPJOHN delivered concurring judgments.)
Documents ordered to be produced.

Hardwicke J: This seems to me to be a 'class claim' rather than a 'contents claim', yet that is but one matter to be weighed in the balance . What concerns me more is that the documents in the director's possession are not governmental documents.

Mr Erskine: My Lord, neither were they governmental documents in *Conway* v *Rimmer*. Nonetheless, the public policy rule applies to governmental and administrative matters generally. For example, it has been recognised that the workings of government extend beyond political questions into other legitimate areas of governmental concern, for example the regulation of the economy. This is clear from the House of Lords in:

Burmah Oil Company Limited v Bank of England [1980] AC 1090 (HL)

The company sought a declaration against the Bank that a sale by the company to the Bank of certain stock at a price required by the government, pursuant to an agreement made in 1975, was inequitable and unfair, and claimed an order for the transfer back of the stock at the 1975 price. The company had, at the time of the agreement, been in dire financial straits because of an international oil crisis, and the agreement had been designed to 'rescue' the company, under the very close control of the government, working through the Bank. The company sought discovery of all relevant documents. The Crown intervened and objected to the production of some sixty-two documents, which for this purpose were divided into three categories. Categories A and B both related to the formulation of government economic policy, at ministerial level and at a lower level. By a majority, the Court of Appeal upheld the Crown's objection. The company appealed.

LORD SCARMAN said: 'My Lords, at the beginning of his long and careful argument on behalf of the Attorney-General, Mr Silkin QC reminded the House that this is an interlocutory appeal from a decision of the Court of Appeal refusing (by a majority) to interfere with decisions reached by Foster J in the exercise of his discretion. Of course, he was correct. But it would be wrong to infer either that the appeal lacks importance because it is interlocutory or that no question of law arises because upon questions as to discovery of documents the judge exercises his discretion. The truth is that the appeal raises a question of law of great importance. Your Lordships are asked to determine the respective spheres of the executive and the judiciary where the issue is whether documents for which "public interest immunity" is claimed are to be withheld from disclosure in litigation to which they are relevant. More specifically, the House has to decide whether *Conway* v *Rimmer* [1968] AC 910 is definitive of the law, i.e. sets limits statute-wise to the power of the court, or is an illustration upon its particular facts of a broader principle of judicial review....
It becomes necessary, therefore, to analyse closely the public interest immunity objection made by the minister and to determine the correct approach of the court to a situation in which there may be a clash of two interests — that of the public service and that of justice.
In *Conway* v *Rimmer* [1968] AC 910 this House had to consider two questions. They were formulated by Lord Reid in these terms, at p 943:

...first, whether the court is to have any right to question the finality of a minister's certificate and, secondly, if it has such a right, how and in what circumstances that right is to be exercised and made effective.

The House answered the first question, but did not, in my judgment, provide, nor was it required to provide, a complete answer to the second.

As I read the speeches in *Conway* v *Rimmer* the House answered the first question by establishing the principle of judicial review. The minister's certificate is not final. The immunity is a rule of law: its scope is a question of law: and its applicability to the facts of a particular case is for the court, not the minister, to determine. The statement of Lord Kilmuir LC of June 6, 1956 (all that is relevant is quoted in *Conway* v *Rimmer* at p 922) that: "The minister's certificate on affidavit setting out the ground of the claim must in England be accepted by the court..." is no longer a correct statement of the law. Whether *Conway* v *Rimmer* be seen as a development of or a departure from previous English case law is a matter of no importance. What is important is that it aligned English law with the law of Scotland and of the Commonwealth. It is the heir apparent not of *Duncan* v *Cammell, Laird & Co Ltd* [1942] AC 624 but of *Robinson* v *State of South Australia* (No. 2) [1931] AC 704 and of *Glasgow Corporation* v *Central Land Board,* 1956 SC (HL) 1.

Having established the principle of judicial review, the House had in *Conway* v *Rimmer* [1968] AC 910 a simple case on the facts to decide....

In reaching its decision the House did indicate what it considered to be the correct approach to the clash of interests which arises whenever there is a question of public interest immunity. The approach is to be found stated in two passages of Lord Reid's speech: pp 940C–F and 952C–G. The essence of the matter is a weighing, on balance, of the two public interests, that of the nation or the public service in non-disclosure and that of justice in the production of the documents. A good working, but not logically perfect, distinction is recognised between the contents and the classes of documents. If a minister of the Crown asserts that to disclose the contents of a documents would, or might, do the nation or the public service a grave injury, the court will be slow to question his opinion or to allow any interest, even that of justice, to prevail over it. Unless there can be shown to exist some factor suggesting either a lack of good faith (which is not likely) or an error of judgment or an error of law on the minister's part, the court should not (the House held) even go so far as itself to inspect the document. In this sense, the minister's assertion may be said to be conclusive. It is, however, for the judge to determine whether the minister's opinion is to be treated as conclusive. I do not understand the House to have denied that even in "contents" cases the court retains it power to inspect or to balance the injury to the public service against the risk of injustice, before reaching its decision.

In "class" cases the House clearly considered the minister's certificate to be more likely to be open to challenge. Undoubtedly, however, the House thought that there were certain classes of documents, which ought not to be disclosed however harmless the disclosure of their contents might be, and however important their disclosure might be in the interest of justice. Cabinet minutes were cited as an example. But the point did not arise for decision. For the documents in *Conway* v *Rimmer* [1968] AC 910, though confidential, were "routine," in no way concerned with the inner working of the government at a high level; and their production might well be indispensable to the doing of justice in the litigation.

The point does arise in the present case. The documents are "high level." They are concerned with the formulation of policy. They are part of the inner working of the government machine. They contain information which the court knows does relate to matters in issue in the action, and which may, on inspection, prove to be highly material. In such circumstances the minister may well be right in his view that the public service would be injured by disclosure. But is the court bound by his view that it is *necessary* for the proper functioning of the public service that they be withheld from production? And, if non-disclosure is necessary for that purpose, is the court bound to hold that the interest in the proper functioning of the public service is to prevail over the requirements of justice?

If the answer to these two questions is to be in the affirmative as Lord Reid appears to suggest in *Conway* v *Rimmer*, I think the law reverts to the statement of Lord Kilmuir. A properly drawn minister's certificate, which is a bona fide expression of his opinion, becomes final. But the advance made in the law by *Conway* v *Rimmer* was that the certificate is not final. I think, therefore, that it would now be inconsistent with principle to hold that the court may not — even in a case like the present — review the certificate and balance the public interest of government to which alone it refers, against the public interest of justice, which is the concern of the court.

I do not therefore accept that there are any classes of document which, however harmless their contents and however strong the requirement of justice, may never be disclosed until they are only of historical interest. In this respect I think there may well be a difference between a "class" objection and a "contents" objection — though the residual power to inspect and to order disclosure must remain in both instances. A Cabinet minute, it is said, must be withheld from production. Documents relating to the formulation of the policy at a high level are also to be withheld. But is the secrecy of the "inner workings of the government machine" so vital a public interest that it must prevail over even the most imperative demands of justice? If the contents of a document concern the national safety, affect diplomatic relations or relate to some state secret of high importance, I can understand an affirmative answer. But if they do not (and it is not claimed in this case that they do), what is so important about secret government that it must be protected even at the price of injustice in our courts?

The reasons given for protecting the secrecy of government at the level of policy-making are two. The first is the need for candour in the advice offered to ministers: the second is that disclosure "would create or fan ill-informed or captious public or political criticism." Lord Reid in *Conway* v *Rimmer* [1968] AC 910, 952, thought the second "the most important reason." Indeed, he was inclined to discount the candour argument.

I think both reasons are factors legitimately to be put into the balance which has to be struck between the public interest in the proper functioning of the public service (i.e. the executive arm of government) and the public interest in the administration of justice. Sometimes the public service reasons will be decisive of the issue: but they should never prevent the court from weighing them against the injury which would be suffered in the administration of justice if the document was not to be disclosed. And the likely injury to the cause of justice must also be assessed and weighed. Its weight will vary according to the nature of the proceedings in which disclosure is sought, the relevance of the documents, and the degree of likelihood that the document will be of importance in the litigation. In striking the balance, the court may always, if it thinks it necessary, itself inspect the documents.

Inspection by the court is, I accept, a power to be exercised only if the court is in doubt, after considering the certificate, the issues in the case and the relevance of the documents whose disclosure is sought. Where documents are relevant (as in this case they are), I would think a pure "class" objection would by itself seldom quieten judicial doubts — particularly if, as here, a substantial case can be made out for saying that disclosure is needed in the interest of justice.

Something was made in argument about the risk to the nation or the public service of an error at first instance. Injury to the public interest — perhaps even very serious injury — could be done by production of documents which should be immune from disclosure before an appellate court could correct the error. The risk is inherent in the principle of judicial review. The House in *Conway* v *Rimmer* [1968] AC 910 recognised its existence, but, nevertheless, established the principle as part of our law. Gibbs J also mentioned it in *Sankey* v *Whitlam*, 53 ALJR 11. I would respectfully agree with Lord Reid's observations on the point in *Conway* v *Rimmer* [1968] AC 910, 953D: "...it is important that the minister should have a right to appeal before the document is produced."

In cases where the Crown is not a party — as in the present case — the court should ensure that the Attorney-General has the opportunity to intervene before disclosure is ordered.

For these reasons I was one of a majority of your Lordships who thought it necessary to inspect the 10 documents. Having done so, I have no doubt that they are relevant and, but for the immunity claim, would have to be disclosed, but their significance is not such as to override the public service objections to their production. Burmah will not suffer injustice by their non-disclosure, while their disclosure would be, in the opinion of the responsible minister, injurious to the public service. I would, therefore, dismiss the appeal.

(LORDS WILBERFORCE, SALMON, EDMUND-DAVIES and KEITH delivered concurring speeches.)

Appeal dismissed.

Hardwicke J: Well, that is an example of central government branching out. But apart from *Conway* v *Rimmer,* are there other examples of local government or other administrative bodies being entitled to assert a public policy objection?

Mr Erskine: My Lord, there are. As an example, perhaps I might cite Your Lordship the decision in:

D v National Society for the Prevention of Cruelty to Children [1978] AC 171 (HL)

The plaintiff claimed damages for injury to her health caused by false allegations that she had ill-treated her daughter. The allegation had been made by a representative of the Society acting on information given in confidence. The plaintiff sought discovery of, *inter alia,* the identity of the informant and the society claimed that the identity ought to be withheld on the ground of public policy. The Court of Appeal held that the plaintiff was entitled to discovery of the identity. The Society appealed to the House of Lords.

LORD SIMON OF GLAISDALE said 'Counsel for the appellants relied on *Conway* v *Rimmer* [1968] AC 910, where conflicting public interests were indeed weighed. But your Lordships' House was really there concerned with the validity of claims by the Crown (based on *Duncan* v *Cammell, Laird and Co Ltd* [1942] AC 624) that the executive could procure the exclusion of evidence by a conclusive ministerial certificate that the evidence belonged to a class the disclosure of any part of which would be detrimental to the public interest. Your Lordships' House overruled *Duncan* v *Cammell, Laird and Co Ltd* in this respect and further laid down that if in doubt the court could itself look at a document in the light of any ministerial certificate in order to ascertain whether its forensic publication could really affect the public interest adversely. I do not think that *Conway* v *Rimmer* provides any real foundation for the appellants' wide proposition.

That proposition does, on the other hand, reflect the general principles underlying this branch of the law, as I endeavoured to state them near the outset of this speech. Nevertheless, your Lordships are here concerned with public policy, with all the circumspection which such concern enjoins.

The first question on such a circumspect approach is not so much to canvass general principle as to ascertain whether the law has recognised an existing head of public policy which is relevant to this case. Of that there can be no doubt. The need of continuity in society; the legal application to children of the traditional role of the Crown as parens patriae; its exercise in the Court of Chancery in such a way as to make the welfare of a child the first and paramount consideration in ·matters of custody and guardianship (*In re Thain (An Infant)* [1926] Ch 676); a vast code of legislation starting with the Prevention of Cruelty to Children Act 1889 and culminating in the Children Act 1975; *In re D (Infants)* [1970] 1 WLR 599, decided in this very branch of the law — all this attests beyond question a public interest in the protection of children from neglect or ill-usage.

The patria potestas in respect of children in need of help has been largely devolved on local authorities. But the appellants, not only by royal charter but also by statutory recognition, have an important role to play. Apart from the police and the local authority, they are the only persons authorised to take care proceedings in respect of a child or young person (Children and Young Persons Act 1969, Section 1; Children and Young Persons Act 1969 (Authorisation for the purposes of Section 1) Order 1970). They have, of course, other important functions for the protection of children from neglect or ill-usage; my noble and learned friends who have preceded me have set them out.

Before passing to the next question I must deal with an argument on behalf of the respondent which arises at this point. Counsel emphasised that the appellants have legal and other powers and functions, but no legal duties in this field. Only the local authority has a duty to take care proceedings and, for example, provide places of safety. The law, it was argued, will only exclude sources of information from disclosure in court if the informaltion is given to someone who has a *duty* to act. No authority was cited in support of this assertion, and, with all respect, I cannot agree with it. First, it is the performance of the *function* of safeguarding children who may be in peril which is the concern of society; enjoining a legal *duty* is merely a way of ensuring that the *function* is performed. Secondly, the police too have only a function (not a duty) as regards care proceedings; but it is accepted that police sources of information about children who may be in peril cannot be investigated in court.

Hardwicke J: Having read those cases, I would accept that the director is entitled to make the assertion, and it follows that I must weigh the public interest in preserving the secrecy of the workings of the children's department against Mr Atkyn's interest on behalf of the defendant in having access to what may be important and relevant evidence. One matter which concerns me is the statement in the director's affidavit that these reports are confidential. Is it said that confidentiality is in itself a ground for asserting public policy?

Mr Erskine: In itself, my Lord, no. I would refer Your Lordship to what was said in:

Alfred Crompton Amusement Machines Limited v *Commissioners of Customs and Excise (No. 2)* [1974] AC 405 (HL)

The commissioners had obtained information from customers of the company and others, relevant to assessments of the company's liability for purchase tax, which were the subject of an intended arbitration. The commissioners, in an affidavit sworn by their chairman, Sir Louis Petch, claimed privilege for the documents containing the information.

LORD CROSS of CHELSEA said: 'I turn now to the question of "Crown privilege" or rather privilege on the ground of "public interest." Sir Louis Petch first submits that the commissioners have no power to disclose documents obtained from or containing information obtained from third parties in pursuance of the powers conferred by Section 24(6) of the Act unless they have express statutory authority for so doing. Lord Denning MR rightly rejected this contention which your Lordships have held to be ill-founded in *Norwich Pharmacal Co* v *Customs and Excise Commissioners* [1974] AC 133. But then Sir Louis says that even if they have power to do so the commissioners think that it is contrary to the public interest for them to disclose such documents or any other documents which contain references to the contents of documents obtained under Section 24(6) because such documents were obtained in confidence from the third parties concerned on the understanding that the commissioners would not disclose them to anyone else. Such disclosure, it is said, would be unfair to the third parties and would be harmful to the proper working of the department. So far as I can see the Court of Appeal did not deal with this argument at all. It is true, as Lord Denning MR points out, that the 2(c) documents are documents of an ordinary character — invoices and so on — such as are normally disclosed by parties to litigation; but Sir Louis' objection to their disclosure is not based on their character but on the manner in which they were obtained. "Confidentiality" is not a separate head of privilege, but it may be a very material consideration to bear in mind when privilege is claimed on the ground of public interest. What the court has to do is to weigh on the one hand the considerations which suggest that it is in the public interest that the documents in question should be disclosed and on the other hand those which suggest that it is in the public interest that they should not be disclosed and to balance one against the other. Plainly there is much to be said in favour of disclosure. The documents in question constitute an important part of the material on which the commissioners based their conclusion that the appellants sell to retailers. That is shown by the reply which the commissioners made to the request for particulars under paragraph 5(h) of the defence. Yet if the claim to privilege made by the commissioners is upheld this information will be withheld from the arbitrator. No doubt it will form part of the brief delivered to counsel for the commissioners and may help him to prove the appellants' evidence in cross-examination; but counsel will not be able to use it as evidence to controvert anything which the appellants' witnesses may say. It is said, of course, that the appellants cannot reasonably complain if the commissioners think it right to tie their own hands in this way. But if the arbitrator should decide against them the appellants may feel — however wrongly — that the arbitrator was unconsciously influenced by the fact that the commissioners stated in their pleadings that they had this further evidence in support of their view which they did not disclose and which the appellants had no opportunity to controvert. Moreover, whoever wins it is desirable that the arbitrator should have all the relevant material before him. On the other hand, there is much to be said against disclosure. The case is not, indeed, as strong as the case against disclosing the name of an informer — for the result of doing that would be that the source of information would dry up whereas here the commissioners will continue to have their powers under Section 24(6). Nevertheless, the case against disclosure is, to my mind, far stronger than it was in the *Norwich Pharmacal* case. There it was probable that all the importers whose names were disclosed were wrongdoers and the disclosure of the names of any, if there were any, who were innocent would not be likely to do them any harm at all. Here, on the other hand, one can well see that the third parties who have supplied this information to the commissioners because of the existence of their statutory powers would very much resent its disclosure by the commissioners to the appellants and that it is not at all fanciful for Sir Louis to say that the knowledge that the commissioners cannot keep such information secret may be harmful to the efficient working of the Act. In a case where the considerations for and against disclosure appear to be fairly evenly balanced the courts should I think uphold a claim to privilege on the ground of public interest and trust to the head of the department concerned to do whatever he can to mitigate the ill-effects of non-disclosure. Forbes J was so impressed by those possible ill-effects that he failed to appreciate how reasonable Sir Louis' objections to disclosure were and dismissed them with the remark "We are not living in the early days of the Tudor administration." I do not regard Sir Louis as a modern Cardinal Morton. His objections to disclosure were taken in the interest of the third parties concerned as much as in the interests of the commissioners and if any of them is in fact willing to give evidence, privilege in respect of any documents or information obtained from him will be waived.'

(VISCOUNT DILHORNE, and LORDS REID, MORRIS of BORTH-Y-GEST and KILBRANDON agreed.)

It appears from this that confidentiality is an important matter which must be borne in mind, but which is not in itself conclusive. I would refer Your Lordship also to the decisions in:

Science Research Council v Nasse; Leyland Card v Vyas [1979] QB 144 (CA); [1980] AC 1028 (HL)

The two appeals were heard together. The complainants alleged that refusal of promotion by their employers was motivated by unlawful discrimination. They sought discovery of confidential reports by their employers concerning both themselves and the other employees who were considered for promotion at the same time. The employers in each case did not object to disclosure of the reports relating to the applicants, but did object to discovery of those dealing with the rivals. The Employment Appeal Tribunal ordered disclosure in both cases. The employers appealed to the Court of Appeal.

BROWNE LJ, in the Court of Appeal said: 'It is well established that the mere fact that information or opinions have been given in confidence does not in itself confer any privilege or immunity from discovery if such disclosure is necessary in the interests of justice: see, for example, *Wheeler v Le Marchant* (1881) 17 ChD 675, 681, *per* Sir George Jessel MR: *R v Lewes Justices* [1973] AC 388, *per* Lord Salmon at pp 411–412; *Alfred Crompton Amusement Machines Ltd v Customs and Excise Commissioners* [1974] AC 405, 433–434, *per* Lord Cross of Chelsea, with whom all the other members of the House agreed on this point; and *D v NSPCC* [1978] AC 171, *per* Lord Diplock at p 218A–C, Lord Hailsham at p 230C–E, Lord Edmund-Davies at p 245 (Proposition I). But confidentiality may be relevant in deciding whether there exists some wider public interest which should give protection from disclosure: see Lord Diplock and Lord Hailsham in the *NSPCC* case. Also, I have no doubt that the courts should and will do all they can to uphold the moral and social duty not to break confidences: see *per* Lord Denning MR in the Court of Appeal in *D v NSPCC* [1978] AC 171, 190; Lord Hailsham at p 227, quoting the Sixteenth Report of the Law Reform Committee (1967) (Cmnd 3472); and Lord Edmund-Davies at p 245, Proposition II.

(LORD DENNING MR and LAWTON LJ delivered judgments allowing the appeals.) Appeals allowed.

The complainants appealed to the House of Lords.

LORD WILBERFORCE, in the House of Lords, said: 'On these points my conclusions are as follows:

1. There is no principle of public interest immunity, as that expression was developed from *Conway* v *Rimmer* [1968] AC 910, protecting such confidential documents as those with which these appeals are concerned. That such an immunity exists, or ought to be declared by this House to exist, was the main contention of Leyland. It was not argued for by the SRC; indeed that body argued against it.

2. There is no principle in English law by which documents are protected from discovery by reason of confidentiality alone. But there is no reason why, in the exercise of its discretion to order discovery, the tribunal should not have regard to the fact that documents are confidential, and that to order disclosure would involve a breach of confidence. In the employment field, the tribunal may have regard to the sensitivity of particular types of confidential information, to the extent to which the interests of third parties (including their employees on whom confidential reports have been made, as well as persons reporting) may be affected by disclosure, to the interest which both employees and employers may have in preserving the confidentiality of personal reports, and to any wider interest which may be seen to exist in. preserving the confidentiality of systems of personal assessments.

3. As a corollary to the above, it should be added that relevance alone, though a necessary ingredient, does not provide an automatic sufficient test for ordering discovery. The tribunal always has a discretion. That relevance alone is enough was, in my belief, the position ultimately taken by counsel for Mrs Nasse thus entitling the complainant to discovery subject only to protective measures (sealing up, etc). This I am unable to accept.

4. The ultimate test in discrimination (as in other) proceedings is whether discovery is necessary for disposing fairly of the proceedings. If it is, then discovery must be ordered notwithstanding confidentiality. But where the court is impressed with the need to preserve confidentiality in a particular case, it will consider carefully whether the necessary information has been or can be obtained by other means, not involving a breach of confidence.

5. In order to reach a conclusion whether discovery is necessary notwithstanding confidentiality the tribunal should inspect the documents. It will naturally consider whether justice can be done by special measures such as "covering up" substituting anonymous references for specific names, or, in rare cases, hearing in camera.

6. The procedure by which this process is to be carried out is one for tribunals to work out in a manner which will avoid delay and unnecessary applications. I shall not say more on this aspect of the matter than that the decisions of the Employment Appeal Tribunal in *Stone* v *Charrington & Co Ltd* (unreported), February 15, 1977, *per* Phillips J, *Oxford* v *Department of Health and Social Security* [1977] ICR 884, 887, *per* Phillips J and *British Railways Board* v *Natarajan* [1979] ICR 326 *per* Arnold J well indicate the lines of a satisfactory procedure, which must of course be flexible.

7. The above conclusions are essentially in agreement with those of the Court of Appeal. I venture to think however that the formula suggested, namely [1979] QB 144, 173, 182:

> The industrial tribunals should not order to permit the disclosure of reports or references that have been given and received in confidence except in the very rare cases where, after inspection of a particular document, the chairman decides that it is essential in the interests of justice that the confidence should be overridden: and then only subject to such conditions as to the divulging of it as he shall think fit to impose — both for the protection of the maker of the document and the subject of it.

may be rather too rigid. For myself I prefer to rest such rule as can be stated upon the discretion of the court....

LORD EDMUND-DAVIES said: 'Learned counsel for the appellants went so far as to submit that the confidential nature of the documents here in question is totally irrelevant to the matter of discovery, and that the tribunal or court should therefore wholly ignore the protests of third parties against the disclosure of information furnished by them in the belief that neither it nor its sources would ever be revealed. Reliance for that submission was placed on cases ranging from *Hopkinson* v *Lord Burghley* (1867) LR 2 Ch App 477 to *McIvor* v

Southern Health and Social Services Board [1978] 1 WLR 757; and the Industrial Relations
Act 1971, Section 158(1), and the Employment Protection Act 1975, Section 18, were
adverted to as illustrating Parliament's ability to provide express safeguards for the
preservation of confidences when it thinks this is desirable. But for myself I am wholly unable
to spell out from the absence of corresponding statutory provisions applicable to the present
cases the conclusion that confidentiality is an irrelevance. It is true that it cannot of itself
ensure protection from disclosure (*Alfred Crompton Amusement Machines Ltd v Customs
and Excise Commissioners* [1974] AC 405; *D v National Society for the Prevention of Cruelty
to Children* [1978] AC 171), but confidentiality may nevertheless properly play a potent part
in the way in which a tribunal or court exercises its discretion in the matter of discovery.

There was ample evidence supporting the view expressed by the Court of Appeal that the
disclosure to inspection of confidential reports could well create upsets and unrest which
would have a general deleterious effect. And a court, mindful of that risk, may
understandably — and properly — think it right to scrutinise with particular care a request
for their inspection. That is not to say, however, that the fear of possible unrest should deter
the court from ordering discovery where the demands of justice clearly require it, but it serves
to counsel caution in such cases....

LORD FRASER of TULLYBELTON said: 'The argument based on the need for candour
in reporting echoes the argument which was presented in *Conway v Rimmer* [1968] AC 910
and I do not think that it has any greater weight now than it had then. The objections by and
on behalf of employees other than the complainers to having their confidential reports
disclosed, readily understandable as they are, do not create a public interest against
disclosure. They are based on a private interest which must yield, in accordance with well-
established principles, to the greater public interest that is deemed to exist in ascertaining the
truth in order to do justice between the parties to litigation. I am not satisfied that disclosure
of the contents of confidential reports of the kind in question here would have serious
consequences upon the efficiency of British industry. In any event, the possibility of industrial
unrest is not a sufficient reason for the courts to fail to give full effect to the intentions of
Parliament; the courts cannot refuse to apply the law between litigants because of threats by
third parties. Much reliance was placed in argument on a passage in the speech of Lord
Hailsham of St Marylebone in *D v National Society for the Prevention of Cruelty to
Children* [1978] AC 171, 230 as follows:

> The categories of public interest are not closed, and must alter from time to time whether
> by restriction or extension as social conditions and social legislation develop.

Speaking for myself I fully accept that proposition, but any extension can only be made by
adding new categories analogous to those already existing, just as in that case immunity was
extended to a new category of informers to the NSPCC by analogy with informers to the
police who were already entitled to immunity. There is no analogy between the suggested
public interest in the present cases and the kinds of public interest that have so far been held
to justify immunity from disclosure. Such public interest as there is in withholding the
documents from disclosure is not enough to justify the creation of a new head of immunity
for a whole class of documents.

Two other considerations point against immunity. One is that in some cases immunity
would make it impossible for an employee to enforce his rights under the Acts. The
confidential information is almost always in the possession of the employer, and, in cases
where discrimination cannot be inferred from the bare fact that someone other than the
complainer has been selected for preferment, it may be of vital importance to the complainer
to have access to the reports on the preferred individual. This is particularly true where the
complaint is based on discrimination on grounds of race or sex, because in those cases the
onus of proof is on the complainer. But even where the complaint is of discrimination for
trade union activities, and the onus is on the employer, disclosure may be essential in order to
do justice between the parties.

The second consideration is that, if public interest immunity applied, it could not be waived
either by the employer alone, or by the employer with the consent of the individual who is the
subject of a report and of the person who made it. That would be inconvenient, and, in my
opinion, quite unnecessarily restrictive.

(LORDS SALMON and SCARMAN delivered judgments dismissing the appeals.)
Appeals dismissed.

Hardwicke J: It seems to me, as Lord Reid said in *Conway* v *Rimmer,* the test is whether the withholding of this evidence is really necessary for the proper functioning of the public service. That is something that I must weigh. Does any counsel invite me to inspect these documents before giving my ruling?

Mr Atkyn: In my submission, Your Lordship should inspect them in order to test the strength of the claim being made.

Mr Erskine: My Lord, while I agree that Your Lordship has power to inspect the documents, it has been said that this power should be sparingly exercised.

Mr Noy: I agree with my learned friend, Mr Erskine.

Hardwicke J: I do not find it necessary to examine these documents. I accept that the objection taken by the director is made in good faith. But Miss Blackstone went to the department for her own personal benefit and it is not suggested that any question of the welfare of her child is directly involved in these documents. I do not think the working of this department will be adversely affected by disclosure of these files. But I think that serious injustice might result to the defendant in this action if the objection is upheld. Weighing the competing interests in this way, I shall order the director to answer Mr Atkyn's questions.

10.4   Commentary

R v *Coke and Littleton* at trial.   Under persistent cross-examination by Mr Bacon on behalf of Littleton, D/I Glanvil reveals for the first time that quite apart from Angela Blackstone's identification of Littleton on the street, he had received information that Littleton was in the area of Coke's flat at about the material time, contrary to his alibi. He is pressed by Mr Bacon for details which would indicate the reliability or otherwise of this information.

10.5   Argument

Mr Bacon: Inspector, from whom did this information emanate?

Mr Bunbury: My Lord, that is an improper question. The identity of informants on such matters is protected by public policy.

Holt J: Well, let the jury retire while the matter is discussed. (The jury retire.)

Mr Bunbury: My Lord, in any public prosecution, a rule of public policy restrains the revealing of the identity of informants, based on the simple consideration that sources of information would be likely to dry up were this not so. I would refer Your Lordship to:

Marks v *Beyfus* (1890) 25 QBD 494 (CA)

The plaintiff, who had brought an action alleging a conspiracy to prosecute maliciously, sought to elicit from the Director of Public Prosecutions the name of his informant. The refusal of the Director to answer was upheld by the trial judge, and the plaintiff was nonsuited. The Divisional Court refused a new trial, and the plaintiff appealed.

LORD ESHER MR said: 'What, then, is the rule as to the disclosure of the names of

informants, and the information given by them in the case of a public prosecution? In the case of *Attorney General* v *Briant* 15 M&W 169, Pollock, CB, discussing the case of *R* v *Hardy* 24 St Tr 199, says that on all hands it was agreed in that case that the informer, in the case of a public prosecution, should not be disclosed; and later on in his judgment, Pollock, CB, says: "The rule clearly established and acted on is this, that in a public prosecution a witness cannot be asked such questions as will disclose the informer, if he be a third person...and we think the principle of the rules applies to the case where a witness is asked if he himself is the informer." Now, this rule as to public prosecutions was founded on grounds of public policy, and if this prosecution was a public prosecution the rule attaches; I think it was a public prosecution, and that the rules applies. I do not say it is a rule which can never be departed from if upon the trial of a prisoner the judge should be of opinion that the disclosure of the name of the informant is necessary or right in order to shew the prisoner's innocence, then one public policy is in conflict with another public policy, and that which says that an innocent man is not to be condemned when his innocence can be proved is the policy that must prevail. But except in that case, this rule of public policy is not a matter of discretion; it is a rule of law, and as such should be applied by the judge at the trial, who should not treat it as a matter of discretion whether he should tell the witness to answer or not. The learned judge was, therefore, perfectly right in the present case in applying the law, and in declining to let the witness answer the questions.'
(LINDLEY and BOWEN LJJ delivered concurring judgments.)
Appeal dismissed.

Holt J: No doubt Mr Bacon will say that this is a case where the information is necessary to show the prisoner's innocence.

Mr Bacon: My Lord, I do say so.
(Both counsel then addressed Holt J as to whether the identity of the informant or merely the substance of the earlier identification was necessary to the proper conduct of the defence.)

Holt J: Mr Bunbury, I must of course accord great weight to the task of ensuring that the defendant Littleton has a fair trial. He must have every opportunity to present his defence fully to the jury.

Mr Bunbury: My Lord, with respect I agree. But Your Lordship should also give great weight to the importance of maintaining the confidentiality of informants, who give information on the basis that the police and the courts are able to protect their identity. Because of the importance of a free flow of information, the rule has been extended beyond informers in criminal cases involving the police, to cases where information is given to various other public bodies who have duties of investigation. I would refer Your Lordship for example to the case of *Alfred Crompton Amusement Machines Ltd* v *Commissioners of Customs and Excise* (No. 2) [1974] AC 405 [10.3 ante] a case concerning taxation which, like the detection of crime, has always been recognised as an area in which confidentiality of informants should be maintained.

The matter has been taken beyond matters of taxation, and applies to information given for the proper working of public bodies such as the Gaming Board. I would refer to:

Rogers v *Home Secretary; Gaming Board for Great Britain* v *Rogers* [1973] AC 388 (HL)

The Gaming Board refused applications by Rogers for certificates of consent to the grant to him of licences under the Gaming Act 1968 to operate certain gaming establishments. The refusal followed a letter to the board from the Assistant Chief Constable of Sussex concerning Rogers. In some unexplained way, Rogers obtained a copy of the letter, and laid an information against the Assistant Chief Constable, alleging criminal libel. The proceedings resulted from the issue by Rogers of witness summonses against the Chief Constable of

Sussex and the secretary of the board, to attend at the magistrates' court and produce documents, including copies of the letter.

LORD REID said: 'The ground put forward has been said to be Crown privilege. I think that that expression is wrong and may be misleading. There is no question of any privilege in the ordinary sense of the word. The real question is whether the public interest requires that the letter shall not be produced and whether that public interest is so strong as to override the ordinary right and interest of a litigant that he shall be able to lay before a court of justice all relevant evidence. A Minister of the Crown is always an appropriate and often the most appropriate person to assert this public interest, and the evidence or advice which he gives to the court is always valuable and may sometimes be indispensable. But, in my view, it must always be open to any person interested to raise the question and there may be cases where the trial judge should himself raise the question if no one else has done so. In the present case the question of public interest was raised by both the Attorney-General and the Gaming Board. In·my judgment both were entitled to raise the matter. Indeed I think that in the circumstances it was the duty of the board to do as they have done.

The claim in the present case is not based on the nature of the contents of this particular letter. It is based on the fact that the board cannot adequately perform their statutory duty unless they can preserve the confidentiality of all communications to them regarding the character, reputation or antecedents of applicants for their consent.

Claims for "class privilege" were fully considered by this House in *Conway* v *Rimmer* [1968] AC 910. It was made clear that there is a heavy burden of proof on any authority which makes such a claim. But the possibility of establishing such a claim was not ruled out. I venture to quote what I said in that case, p 952:

> There may be special reasons for withholding some kinds of routine documents, but I think that the proper test to be applied is to ask, in the language of Lord Simon in *Duncan* v *Cammell Laird & Co Ltd* [1942] AC 624, 642, whether the withholding of a document because it belongs to a particular class is really "necessary for the proper functioning of the public service."

I do not think that "the public service" should be construed narrowly. Here the question is whether the withholding of this class of documents is really necessary to enable the board adequately to perform its statutory duties. If it is, then we are enabling the will of Parliament to be carried out.

There are very unusual features about this case. The board require the fullest information they can get in order to identify and exclude persons of dubious character and reputation from the privilege of obtaining a licence to conduct a gaming establishment. There is no obligation on anyone to give any information to the board. No doubt many law-abiding citizens would tell what they know even if there was some risk of their identity becoming known, although many perfectly honourable people do not want to be thought to be mixed up in such affairs. But it is obvious that the best source of information about dubious characters must often be persons of dubious character themselves. It has long been recognised that the identity of police informers must in the public interest be kept secret and the same considerations must apply to those who volunteer information to the board. Indeed, it is in evidence that many refuse to speak unless assured of absolute secrecy.

The letter called for in this case came from the police. I feel sure that they would not be deterred from giving full information by any fear of consequences to themselves if there were any disclosure. But much of the information which they can give must come from sources which must be protected and they would rightly take this into account. Even if information were given without naming the source, the very nature of the information might, if it were communicated to the person concerned, at least give him a very shrewd idea from whom it had come.

It is possible that some documents coming to the board could be disclosed without fear of such consequences. But I would think it quite impracticable for the board or the court to be sure of this. So it appears to me that, if there is not to be very serious danger of the board being deprived of information essential for the proper performance of their difficult task, there must be a general rule that they are not bound to produce any document which gives information to them about an applicant.

We must then balance that fact against the public interest that the course of justice should not be impeded by the withholding of evidence. We must, I think, take into account that these documents only came into existence because the applicant is asking for a privilege and is submitting his character and reputation to scrutiny. The documents are not used to deprive him of any legal right. The board have a wide discretion. Not only can they refuse his application on the ground of bad reputation although he may say that he has not deserved that reputation; it is not denied that the board can also take into account any unfavourable impression which he has made during an interview with the board.

Natural justice requires that the board should act in good faith and that they should so far as possible tell him the gist of any grounds on which they propose to refuse his application so that he may show such grounds to be unfounded in fact. But the board must be trusted to do that; we have been referred to their practice in this matter and I see nothing wrong in it.

In the present case the board told the appellant nothing about the contents of this letter because they say that they had sufficient grounds for refusing his application without any need to rely on anything in the letter. Their good faith in this matter is not subject to any substantial challenge. If the appellant had not by someone's wrongful act obtained a copy of the letter there was no reason why he should ever have known anything about it.

In my judgment on balance the public interest clearly requires that documents of this kind should not be disclosed, and that public interest is not affected by the fact that by some wrongful means a copy of such a document has been obtained and published by some person. I would therefore dismiss the appellant's appeal.'

(LORDS MORRIS of BORTH-Y-GUEST, PEARSON, SALMON and SIMON of GLAISDALE delivered separate judgments agreeing that the witness summonses should be set aside.)

The rule has also been applied to persons who give information to societies concerned with the welfare of children. I refer to:

D v NSPCC [1978] AC 171 (HL) (for facts see 10.3 ante)

LORD DIPLOCK said: 'The public interest which the NSPCC relies upon as obliging it to withhold from the plaintiff and from the court itself material that could disclose the identity of the society's informant is analogous to the public interest that is protected by the well established rule of law that the identity of police informers may not be disclosed in a civil action, whether by the process of discovery or by oral evidence at the trial: *Marks v Beyfus* (1890) 25 QBD 494.

The rationale of the rule as it applies to police informers is plain. If their identity were liable to be disclosed in a court of law, these sources of information would dry up and the police would be hindered in their duty of preventing and detecting crime. So the public interest in preserving the anonymity of police informers had to be weighed against the public interest that information which might assist a judicial tribunal to ascertain facts relevant to an issue upon which it is required to adjudicate should be withheld from that tribunal. By the uniform practice of the judges which by the time of *Marks v Beyfus*, 25 QBD 494 had already hardened into a rule of law, the balance has fallen upon the side of non-disclosure except where upon the trial of a defendant for a criminal offence disclosure of the identity of the informer could help to show that the defendant was innocent of the offence. In that case, and in that case only, the balance falls upon the side of disclosure.

My Lords, in *R v Lewes Justices, Ex parte Secretary of State for the Home Department* [1973] AC 388 this House did not hesitate to extend to persons from whom the Gaming Board received information for the purposes of the exercise of their statutory functions under the Gaming Act 1968 immunity from disclosure of their identity analogous to that which the law had previously accorded to police informers. Your Lordships' sense of values might well be open to reproach if this House were to treat the confidentiality of information given to those who are authorised by statute to institute proceedings for the protection of neglected or ill-treated children as entitled to less favourable treatment in a court of law than information given to the Gaming Board so that gaming may be kept clean. There are three categories of persons authorised to bring care proceedings in respect of neglected or ill-treated children: local authorities, constables and the NSPCC. The anonymity of those who tell the police of their suspicions of neglect or ill-treatment of a child would be preserved without any extension of the existing law. To draw a distinction in this respect between information given to the police and that passed on directly to a local authority or to the NSPCC would seem much too irrational a consequence to have been within the contemplation of Parliament when enacting the Children and Young Persons Act 1969. The local authority is under an express statutory duty to bring care proceedings in cases where this is necessary if neither the police nor the NSPCC have started them, while, as respects the NSPCC, the evidence shows that, presumably because it is not associated in the public mind with officialdom, the public are readier to bring information to it than to the police or the welfare services of the local authority itself.'

Holt J: This is a difficult matter which I shall have to consider carefully, bearing in mind that the evidence to which D/I Glanvil has referred is in effect evidence of visual identification.

B: PRIVATE EVIDENTIAL PRIVILEGES

10.6 Self-incrimination: introductory notes

10.6.1 No witness is bound to answer any question if the answer thereto would, in the opinion of the judge, have a tendency to expose the witness to any criminal charge, penalty or criminal forfeiture which the judge regards as reasonably likely to be preferred or sued for. In practice, it is exposure to possible criminal charges that is of importance. There is no privilege with regard to questions, the answer to which would tend to expose the witness to the risk of civil proceedings, even at the suit of the Crown, except in the rare instance of proceedings for a penalty. There is no longer any privilege with regard to questions the answer to which would tend to implicate the witness in the commission of adultery. If the witness is wrongly compelled to answer in breach of his privilege, his answer will be inadmissible in subsequent proceedings.

10.6.2 Where the privilege exists, it operates to allow the witness not only to refuse to answer questions which are directly incriminating but also questions, the answers to which would be capable of providing evidence against him. No adverse inference may be drawn from the proper invoking of the privilege.

10.6.3 Whether the privilege may properly be invoked is a matter of law for the judge, who must decide not only whether answering the question might tend to expose the witness to a criminal charge, but also that there is a real risk of such charge being instituted. The mere forbearance of the prosecuting authorities in the past is not always a reliable guide as to whether proceedings will be instituted in the future, perhaps partly as a result of the witness's answer.

10.6.4 In civil proceedings, it is now provided by s.14(1)(a) of the Civil Evidence Act 1968 that the risk of prosecution applies only as regards criminal offences under the law of any part of the United Kingdom (including the law of the EEC). It is generally thought, though undecided, that in criminal cases the common law would now follow the same rule.

10.6.5 Similarly, in civil cases it is now provided by s.14(1)(b) of the Civil Evidence

Act, 1968 that the privilege extends with equal scope to questions, the answer to which would tend to incriminate the witness's spouse. In criminal cases, it is also thought, but undecided that the same rule would apply at common law. (*A Practical Approach to Evidence,* pp 285-90.)

10.7 Commentary

Blackstone v *Coke* at trial. Contrary to the expectations of Coke, the witness Anthony Henneky has returned from the United States voluntarily to give evidence on Coke's behalf. In chief, Mr Henneky gives evidence that he first met Margaret Blackstone during 1977, early in that year. He is unable to be more precise about the date. He has described Margaret in the witness box as somewhat promiscuous and has given evidence that at her behest they started to have sexual intercourse together. In answer to Mr Atkyn in chief, he further gave evidence that he had sexual intercourse with Margaret during 1979, and particularly on frequent occasions during May and June of that year, shortly before Mr Henneky went to the United States. Dealing with the weekend of the alleged rape, he gave evidence specifically that he and Margaret had had sexual intercourse on the Friday and Saturday nights in the back of Mr Henneky's car. In cross-examination, Mr Henneky refuses to answer a question put by Mr Noy on behalf of Margaret as to the first date on which sexual intercourse took place between them.

10.8 Argument

Hardwicke J: Mr Atkyn, I am minded to direct the witness to answer the question, upon pain of being in contempt.

Mr Atkyn: My Lord, the witness has asked to raise through me the privilege against self-incrimination. As Your Lordship knows, Margaret Blackstone was born on 3 May 1962, which would mean that she was just fifteen years of age early in 1977. In those circumstances, it may be that Mr Henneky's answer, if given, would tend to implicate him in an offence of having sexual intercourse with a girl under the age of sixteen years.

Hardwicke J: Mr Henneky, are you claiming the privilege against self-incrimination?

Mr Henneky: Yes, My Lord.

Mr Atkyn: As Your Lordship will be aware, an answer given on oath in any judicial proceedings is generally admissible as evidence in a subsequent criminal prosecution, because it represents an adverse admission or confession.

Hardwicke J: Is it a matter for me to decide whether the privilege is well taken?

Mr Atkyn: Yes, My Lord. You should, My Lord, first satisfy yourself that the answer to the question would tend to expose the witness to a criminal charge. Your Lordship is entitled to do this in camera if necessary so that the precise nature of the answer may be heard without the fear of its transmission to the prosecuting authorities. Secondly, Your Lordship must be satisfied that there is a real risk of prosecution. I would refer Your Lordship to:

R v *Boyes* (1861) 1 B&S 311 (QB)

A witness claiming the privilege against self-incrimination had been handed a pardon under the Great Seal. The effect of this was to prevent his prosecution for the offence. In theory he might still have been impeached for the offence because a pardon cannot be pleaded in answer to an impeachment, though this would have been very unlikely.

LORD COCKBURN CJ said: 'We are of opinion that the danger to be apprehended must be real and appreciable, with reference to the ordinary operation of law in the ordinary course of things — not a danger of an imaginary and unsubstantial character, having reference to some extraordinary and barely possible contingency, so improbable that no reasonable man would suffer it to influence his conduct. We think that a merely remote and naked possibility, out of the ordinary course of the law and such as no reasonable man would be affected by, should not be suffered to obstruct the administration of justice. The object of the law is to afford to a party, called upon to give evidence in a proceeding inter alios, protection against being brought by means of his own evidence within the penalties of the law. But it would be to convert a salutary protection into a means of abuse if it were to be held that a mere imaginary possibility of danger, however remote and improbable, was sufficient to justify the withholding of evidence essential to the ends of justice.

Now, in the present case, no one seriously supposes that the witness runs the slightest risk of an impeachment by the House of Commons. No instance of such a proceeding in the unhappily too numerous cases of bribery which have engaged the attention of the House of Commons has ever occurred, or, so far as we are aware, has ever been thought of. To suppose that such a proceeding would be applied to the case of this witness would be simply ridiculous...it was therefore the duty of the presiding Judge to compel him to answer.'

And I would also refer Your Lordship to a case on somewhat different facts but to which the same principle applied:

Blunt v Park Lane Hotel Limited and Briscoe [1942] 2 KB 253 (CA)

This was an action for slander based on an allegation that the plaintiff had committed adultery. The plaintiff objected to answering interrogatories which the defendants wished to administer in support of their plea of justification. The defendants were given leave to administer the interrogatories. The plaintiff appealed.

GODDARD LJ said: '...the rule is that no one is bound to answer any question if the answer thereto would, in the opinion of the judge, have a tendency to expose the deponent to any criminal charge, penalty, or forfeiture which the judge regards as reasonably likely to be preferred or sued for. This rule was laid down by the Queen's Bench in *R v Boyes* 1 B&S 311, and the words in which I have stated it are those of Stephen J in *Lamb v Munster (1882) 10 QBD* 110. A party can also claim privilege against discovery of documents on the like ground: see *Hunnings v Williamson* (1883) 10 QBD 459. Is there, then, except in a case of a clerk in holy orders, any reasonable likelihood that such interrogatories would expose a person to ecclesiastical penalties? It is purely fantastic to suppose anything of the sort. When Lord Hardwicke decided *Finch v Finch* 2 Ves Sen 493 and *Chetwynd v Lindon* 2 Ves Sen 450, there was, no doubt, a real risk of such proceedings. In those days the courts of the Church exercised a very active jurisdiction over the laity in criminal causes. Heresy, simony, defamation, brawling in church or churchyard, and all forms of immorality and not merely adultery were within their cognisance, *pro reformatione morum et pro salute animae....* Such jurisdiction has long been obsolete, so far as the laity are concerned, when it has not been expressly taken away by legislation.

...One other argument that was adduced was that an admission of adultery might result in the refusal of the sacrament to the offender. There is a complete air of unreality about such an argument in a case of this sort, and I will only say that, assuming that acts of adultery (of which the offender may have repented) as distinct from living in adultery would furnish "lawful cause" within the Statute 1 Edward 6, C 1, for a minister's refusal to administer the sacrament, that is not a penalty within the rule to which I referred at the beginning of this judgment.'

(LORD CLAWSON delivered a judgment to the same effect.)

Appeal dismissed.

Hardwicke J: It has always seemed to me that the prosecuting authorities are reluctant to prosecute these days where the girl is already aged fifteen.

Mr Atkyn: My Lord, I take Your Lordship's point. But it cannot be said that there is not a real danger to Mr Henneky, and of course forbearance as such is not always a guarantee of safety from prosecution. I would refer Your Lordships to the observations of the House of Lords in:

Rio Tinto Zinc Corporation and others v Westinghouse Electric Corporation [1978] AC 547 (HL)

The appellants claimed privilege in respect of certain documents which they were ordered to produce on the basis that their production might render the appellants liable to fines under the EEC Treaty which was part of English law.

VISCOUNT DILHORNE said: 'It was argued that the discovery of the document would not in the circumstances tend to expose the appellant companies to such proceedings. It was said that as the Commission had knowledge from the Friends of the Earth documents for a considerable time of the existence of the cartel and had taken no action, there was no real risk of such proceedings if the documents in the possession of the companies were disclosed.

In *Triplex Safety Glass Co Ltd* v *Lancegaye Safety Glass (1934) Ltd* [1939] 2 KB 395 the judgment of the Court of Appeal, of which Sir Wilfrid Greene MR was a member, was delivered by du Parcq LJ. He said at p 404 that it was not in doubt that the power of the court to insist on an answer to interrogatories extended to any case in which it was not made to appear to the court "that there is reasonable ground to apprehend danger to the witness from his being compelled to answer: *R* v *Boyes* per cur (1861) 1 B&S 330." That was the test applied in the *Triplex* case and the same test is to be applied in relation to the discovery of documents. In the present case Lord Denning MR said (ante, p 573F–G) that he doubted whether that case would be decided in the same way today. It may be that it would not be held that answering interrogatories as to libel would not be a reasonable ground for apprehending a prosecution for criminal libel. I do not read Lord Denning as criticising the reasoning in the *Triplex* case but only its application.

Lord Denning MR went on to say at p 574 that if it appears that a witness's answer could be used against him in criminal proceedings, his objections should be upheld; and that if it appears that a witness is at risk "great latitude should be allowed to him in judging for himself the effect of any particular question." He went on to say:

It may be improbable that they (proceedings) will be taken, but nevertheless, if there is some risk of their being taken — a real and appreciable risk — as distinct from a remote or insubstantial risk, then he should not be made to answer or to disclose the documents.

With these observations I respectfully agree. It was suggested that the reasoning in the *Triplex* case had reduced the burden which formerly lay on a person claiming privilege but I do not think that that is the case. In his judgment du Parcq LJ reviewed the earlier cases and based his conclusions on them. Lord Denning contrasted a real and appreciable risk with a remote or insubstantial one, and once it appears that the risk is not fanciful, then it follows that it is real. If it is real, then there must be a reasonable ground to apprehend danger, and, if there is, great latitude is to be allowed to the witness and to a person required to produce documents.

If the appellant companies are compelled to produce the documents which they were asked to produce, I cannot reach the conclusion that it would be fanciful to suppose that that would expose them to no greater risk than at present of proceedings for the recovery of a penalty being brought against them. The documents might well authenticate and support the information now in the hands of the Commission. They might afford conclusive proof of a breach of article 85 and, when in possession of such evidence, the Commission might decide to take action.'

Hardwicke J: It is a matter which I must consider carefully, and I think that I shall hear Mr Henneky's answer in camera before deciding. Of course, anything that he might say would in any case be inadmissible against him in subsequent proceedings, if he is wrongly compelled to answer. I have in mind:

R v *Garbett* (1847) 1 Den CC 236 (Central Criminal Court)

The defendant was convicted of forgery. At his trial he was wrongly compelled to answer a question in breach of the privilege against self-incrimination.

The majority of the judges were of opinion, that if a witness claims the protection of the court, on the ground that the answer would tend to incriminate himself, and there appears reasonable ground to believe that it would do so, he is not compellable to answer; and if obliged to answer, notwithstanding, what he says must be considered to have been obtained by compulsion, and cannot be given in evidence against him.

Mr Atkyn: My Lord, that is right. May I just add before Your Lordship hears the evidence, that it would of course would be quite wrong that an adverse inference should be drawn against Mr Henneky or any witness simply by reason of his insistence on a recognised privilege, if the privilege is well taken. I would refer Your Lordship to:

Wentworth v *Lloyd* (1864) 10 HL Cas 589

The appellant instituted proceedings to set aside a sale of his property made on his behalf by one of the respondents to the others. Evidence was given by a Mr Wright, who had acted for some years as the appellant's solicitor. He was prevented from answering a question on the ground that it was the subject of legal professional privilege.

THE MASTER OF THE ROLLS said: 'The Plaintiff no doubt had a right to prevent Mr Wright from stating what the Plaintiff had told him about Mr Mort. It is the client's privilege to prevent the solicitor from divulging confidential communications. But if the client chooses to adopt this conduct, he must be subject to the rule laid down in *Armory* v *Delamirie* (Str 505), where the keeping back of evidence must be taken most strongly against the person who does so. When I say this I wish to distinguish between the case of the suppression of evidence by a witness, and the case where he declines to answer the question on the ground that he is not bound to criminate himself; in which case no presumption of guilt can be fairly drawn from his refusal to answer, or the privilege would be at once destroyed. This is no case of crimination. By the terms of the obligation he is under in this suit he is bound to supply every species of evidence, written or parol, that he can, and I must treat his refusal to allow a witness to answer a question in the same light as if he had kept a material witness out of the way, or refused or prevented the production of a document in his possession.'

LORD CHELMSFORD said: 'The use which the Master of the Rolls made of the exercise of the Plaintiff's right to prevent the disclosure of confidential communications seems to me so entirely at variance with principle, and so utterly in contradiction to the well-known and invariably recognised privilege of professional confidence, that I cannot pass it by in silence; and, without dwelling upon the contrasted case, I think it would be found upon examination that the presumptions in the two instances to which his Honor referred, are exactly the reverse of what he assumed them to be. I confess that I am unable to conceive the analogy between a client closing the mouth of his solicitor upon a question as to professional communications, and the conduct of the jeweller in *Armory* v *Delamirie,* who, upon a mounted jewel which had been found being brought to him, took out the stones and returned the empty socket to the finder, and not producing the jewel at the trial of the action brought to recover its value, was made to pay in damages the value of a jewel of the finest water, which would fit the socket, upon the rule *omnia praesumuntur contra spoliatorem.* But a person who refuses to allow his solicitor to violate the confidence of the professional relation cannot be regarded in that odious light. The law has so great a regard to the preservation of the secrecy of this relation, that even the party himself cannot be compelled to disclose his own statements made to his solicitor with reference to professional business.

As Lord Brougham says, when speaking, in *Bolton* v *The Corporation of Liverpool* (1 Myl and K 94, 95), of the supposed right to compel the disclosure of such communications, "It is plain that the course of justice must stop if such a right exists. No man will dare to consult a professional adviser with a view to his defence, or to the enforcement of his rights. The exclusion of such evidence is for the general interest of the community, and therefore to say that when a party refuses to permit professional confidence to be broken, everything must be taken most strongly against him, what is it but to deny him the protection which, for public purposes, the law affords him, and utterly to take away a privilege which can thus only be asserted to his prejudice.'

Hardwicke J: I accept that entirely.

(Hardwicke J heard evidence in camera as to the date of the first sexual intercourse between Henneky and Margaret Blackstone and ruled that the privilege was well taken.)

10.9 Legal professional privilege: Introductory notes

10.9.1 Two rules of privilege apply to the relationship between lawyer and client. The first is that communications between lawyer and client, made in the course of seeking and giving advice within the normal scope of legal practice, are privileged in all cases at the instance of the client. The second is that communications between a client, or his legal adviser, and third parties in contemplation of actual litigation are privileged, provided that use for the purposes of litigation is at least the dominant purpose of the communication. The rule applies to solicitor and counsel alike and extends to lawyers or advisers in England or elsewhere, and to litigation contemplated or pending in England or elsewhere. It is unclear whether the privilege extends to laymen who appear in front of some statutory tribunal on behalf of a friend or colleague.

10.9.2 Other confidential communications, such as that between clergyman and penitent or social worker and client are not the subject of any privilege in English law. Consequently, communications passing between such persons even though confidential, may be ordered to be disclosed. A limited form of privilege exists in relation to patent agents under s.104 of the Patents Act 1977. (*A Practical Approach to Evidence*, pp 290–93.) Further, by s.10 of the Contempt of Court Act 1981 a court may not require a person to disclose, and a person is not guilty of contempt for refusing to disclose, the source of information contained in a publication for which he is responsible unless it is established that disclosure is necessary in the interests of justice or national security or for the prevention of disorder or crime.

10.10 Commentary

Blackstone v *Coke* at trial.   Mr Noy on behalf of the plaintiff wishes to introduce into evidence a copy of the letter to Coke from his solicitor, Mr Mansfield, dated 20 February 1980, which was inadvertently sent to Eldon and Co. Although Eldon and Co returned to Mr Mansfield the original of this letter, they made a copy thereof and notified Mansfield and Co of their intention to make use of his copy by letter dated 3 March 1980. Mr Atkyn on behalf of Coke objects to admissibility of the letter.

10.11   Argument

Mr Atkyn: My Lord, this is the clearest possible example of a document protected by legal professional privilege. It is a direct communication between my client and his solicitor, fairly referable to the solicitor-client relationship, and in the course of that relationship, as the court adumbrated in:

Minster v *Priest* [1930] AC 558 (HL)

The respondent refused to act as a solicitor in a transaction relating to land, and was alleged to have defamed the plaintiff in the course of giving his reasons for so refusing. The respondent pleaded that the slander was uttered on a privileged occasion and under such circumstances as to make it a privileged communication. The jury found for the appellant, but the Court of Appeal upheld the claim of privilege and set aside the judgment.

LORD BUCKMASTER said: 'I am not prepared to assent to a rigid definition of what must be the subject of discussion between a solicitor and his client in order to secure the protection of professional privilege. That merely to lend money, apart from the existence or contemplation of professional help, is outside the ordinary scope of a solicitor's business is shown by the case of *Hagart and Burn-Murdoch* v *Inland Revenue Commissioners* [1929] AC 386. But it does not follow that, where a personal loan is asked for, discussions concerning it may not be of a privileged nature.

The relationship of solicitor and client being once established, it is not a necessary conclusion that whatever conversation ensued was protected from disclosure. The conversation to secure this privilege must be such as, within a very wide and generous ambit of interpretation, must be fairly referable to the relationship, but outside that boundary the mere fact that a person speaking is a solicitor, and the person to whom he speaks is his client affords no protection.'

LORD ATKIN said: 'It is I think apparent that if the communication passes for the purpose of getting legal advice it must be deemed confidential. The protection of course attaches to the communications made by the solicitor as well as by the client. If therefore the phrase is expanded to professional communications passing for the purpose of getting or giving professional advice, and it is understood that the profession is the legal profession, the nature of the protection is I think correctly defined. One exception to this protection is established. If communications which otherwise would be protected pass for the purpose of enabling either party to commit a crime or a fraud the protection will be withheld. It is further desirable to point out, not by way of exception but as a result of the rule, that communications between solicitor and client which do not pass for the purpose of giving or receiving professional advice are not protected. It follows that client and solicitor may meet for the purpose of legal advice and exchange protected communications, and may yet in the course of the same interview make statements to each other not for the purpose of giving or receiving professional advice but for some other purpose. Such statements are not within the rule: see per Lord Wrenbury *O'Rourke* v *Darbishire* [1920] AC 581, 629.'
(VISCOUNT DUNEDIN, and LORDS THANKERTON and WARRINGTON of CLIFFE agreed.)
Appeal allowed.

Hardwicke J: Of course, if your client has no privilege for any reason, then he is no better off merely because a document happens to be in the hands of his solicitors. You are, of course, familiar with the decision in:

R v *Peterborough Justices, ex parte Hicks* [1977] 1 WLR 1371 (DC)

Solicitors acting for two clients (Hicks and Trotter) charged with offences involving fraud, forgery and theft, had in their possession a file of papers relating to the clients' defence including a power of attorney purporting to have been made in favour of one of the clients. A police officer applied for and obtained a search warrant under s.16 of the Forgery Act 1913, empowering him to enter the solicitors' premises and to search for the power of attorney as being a forgery. The clients and their solicitors applied for an order of *certiorari* to quash the order for the search warrant.

EVELEIGH J said: 'If the document in the present case had been in the hands of the second applicant, Trotter, it is not suggested that an order could not be made under Section 16 for its seizure. But Sir Michael says that the lawful excuse put forward by the solicitor is an excuse peculiar to him, namely, that he has had it in the course of his profession, dealing as a professional man with the affairs of his client, and if privilege in the strict sense does not apply, nonetheless there is an analogous position which gives rise to an explanation of lawful authority or excuse. He also argues, if need be, that the claim of professional privilege itself applies to documents in the hands of a solicitor for this purpose.

The claim of privilege, it is true, applies to documents in the hands of solicitors in a great variety of circumstances; but it is the privilege of the client. When one looks at Section 16 there is nothing to indicate that an exception shall be made in the case of documents in the hands of solicitors, which could have been done had Parliament so intended. Right in the forefront of one's consideration of this point is that the solicitor holds the document in the right of his client and can assert in respect of its seizure no greater authority than the client himself or herself possesses. The client in this case would have possessed no lawful authority or excuse that would prevent the document's seizure. In my view the solicitor himself can be in no better position. The solicitor's authority or excuse in a case like this is the authority or the excuse of the client.'

WIEN J said: 'Counsel on behalf of the applicants said that he could not argue that if the lay client was served with a search warrant, then she could say that there was any lawful excuse. Once that concession is made, I think, it exposes the dilemma in which counsel for the applicants is placed. The solicitor has no greater protection than the lay client. The question of privilege or bona fide belief in privilege as amounting to lawful excuse does not arise.' (LORD WIDGERY CJ agreed.)
Application refused.

Mr Atkyn: I accept that, My Lord, but the privilege is that of the client, and in my submission existed in this letter. It is not the kind of case where any dishonest or underhand arrangement operated to destroy the privilege as was the case in:

R v Cox and Railton (1884) 14 QBD 153 (CCR)

The defendants were convicted of a conspiracy to defraud. At the trial a solicitor was called by the prosecution to prove that the defendants had consulted him with reference to drawing up a bill of sale that was alleged to be fraudulent. The reception of this evidence was objected to one the ground that it was privileged.

STEPHEN J, delivering the judgment of the court, said: 'The question, therefore is, whether, if a client applies to a legal adviser for advice intended to facilitate or to guide the client in the commission of a crime or fraud, the legal adviser being ignorant of the purpose for which his advice is wanted, the communication between the two is privileged? We expressed our opinion at the end of the argument that no such privilege existed. It it did, the result would be that a man intending to commit treason or murder might safely take legal advice for the purpose of enabling himself to do so with impunity, and that the solicitor to whom the application was made would not be at liberty to give information against his client for the purpose of frustrating his criminal purpose. Consequences so monstrous reduce to an absurdity any principle or rule in which they are involved. Upon the fullest examination of the authorities we believe that they are not warranted by any principle or rule of the law of England, but it must be admitted that the law upon the subject has never been so distinctly and fully stated as to shew clearly that these consequences do not follow from principles which do form part of the law, and which it is of the highest importance to maintain in their integrity....The case which has always been regarded as the great leading authority on the question of the privilege of legal advisers is *Greenough* v *Gaskell* 1 My & K 98 decided by Lord Brougham in 1833....In this case the rule as to professional communications was laid down in the following words:— "If, touching matters that come within the ordinary scope of professional employment, they" (legal advisers) "receive a communication in their professional capacity, either from a client or on his account, and for his benefit in the transaction of his business, or, which amounts to the same thing, if they commit to paper in the course of their employment on his behalf, matters which they know only through their professional relation to the client, they are not only justified in withholding such matters, but bound to withhold them, and will not be compelled to disclose the information or produce the papers in any court of law or equity, either as party or as witness."

....This rule has been accepted and acted upon ever since,and we fully recognise its authority, but we think that the present case does not fall either under the reason on which it rests, or within the terms in which it is expressed. The reason on which the rule is said to rest cannot include the case of communications, criminal in themselves, or intended to further any criminal purpose, for the protection of such communications cannot possibly be otherwise than injurious to the interests of justice, and to those of the administration of justice. Nor do such communications fall within the terms of the rule. A communication in furtherance of a criminal purpose does not "come into the ordinary scope of professional employment." A single illustration will make this plain. It is part of the business of a solicitor to draw wills. Suppose a person, personating some one else, instructs a solicitor to draw a will in the name of the supposed testator, executes it in the name of the supposed testator, gives the solicitor his fee, and takes away the will. It would be monstrous to say that the solicitor was employed in the "ordinary scope of professional employment." He in such case is made an unconscious instrument in the commission of a crime.'
Conviction affirmed.

Hardwicke J: Mr Noy, what do you say about the privilege?

Mr Noy: My Lord, I say that the privilege has been lost. I accept of course that those instructing my learned friend were entitled to the return of the original document and this was done in accordance with the rule in *Lord Ashburton* v *Pape* [1913] 2 Ch 469 (CA).

Even in relation to the original, there are certain cases in which its use will not be restrained, for example use by the Crown in a public prosecution. I refer to:

Butler v Board of Trade [1971] Ch 680

Among papers at a solicitor's office handed over to the Official Receiver of a company in compulsory liquidation was a copy of a letter written to the plaintiff by the solicitor in which she volunteered a warning that he might incur serious consequences if he did not take care. In criminal proceedings under s.332(3) of the Companies Act 1948 the Board of Trade intended to adduce the copy in evidence. The plaintiff sought the opinion of the court whether there was any equity to prevent the Board of Trade from doing so on the ground that the original of the letter was privileged and the copy confidential.

GOFF J said: 'The plaintiff relies on the decision of the Court of Appeal in *Ashburton* v *Pape* [1913] 2 Ch 469, where a party to certain bankruptcy proceedings, having by a trick obtained a copy of a privileged letter, Neville J granted an injunction restraining him and his solicitors from publishing or making use of it, save for the purposes of these proceedings, and the Court of Appeal varied the order by striking out the exception, so that the injunction was unqualified.

Before I consider that further, I can dispose briefly of the argument advanced by counsel for the defendants that the plaintiff cannot be entitled to any relief in equity because he does not come with clean hands. That seems to me to beg the question. If the letter was part of a criminal project then the copy is not protected anyhow. If, however, it was not such a part then the mere fact, if it be so, that it may help the defendants prove their case on the criminal charge does not soil the hands of the plaintiff with respect to his proprietary interests in the copy.

I turn back to *Ashburton* v *Pape*. In the present case there was no impropriety on the part of the defendants in the way in which they received the copy, but that, in my judgment, is irrelevant because an innocent recipient of information conveyed in breach of confidence is liable to be restrained. I wish to make it clear that there is no suggestion of any kind of moral obliquity on the part of the solicitors, but the disclosure was in law a breach of confidence. Nevertheless, *Ashburton* v *Pape* does differ from the present case in an important particular, namely, that the defendants are a department of the Crown and intend to use the copy letter in a public prosecution brought by them.

As far as I am aware, there is no case directly in point on the question whether that is merely an immaterial difference of fact or a valid distinction, but in my judgment it is the. latter because in such a case there are two conflicting principles, the private right of the individual and the interest of the state to apprehend and prosecute criminals: see *per* Lord Denning MR in *Chic Fashions (West Wales) Ltd* v *Jones* [1968] 2 QB 299, 313 and in *Ghani* v *Jones* [1970] 1 QB 693, 708.

In my judgment it would not be a right or permissible exercise of the equitable jurisdiction in confidence to make a declaration at the suit of the accused in a public prosecution in effect restraining the Crown from adducing admissible evidence relevant to the crime with which he is charged. It is not necessary for me to decide whether the same result would obtain in the case of a private prosecution, and I expressly leave that point open.'
Action dismissed.

Hardwicke J: Well, as you say, you have returned the original. What use do you say you can make of the copy? Is that not also privileged?

Mr Noy: My Lord, no. I would refer Your Lordship to *Calcraft* v *Guest* [1898] 1 QB 759 (CA), which is authority for the proposition that secondary evidence may be used, even though the original is privileged. In other words, My Lord, privilege must be guarded or else it will be lost. I would refer also to *R* v *Tompkins* (1977) 67 Cr App R 181 (CA), in which the question of admissibility was considered.

Hardwicke J: Well, this is an unfortunate situation. I am quite sure that this document was originally privileged as being a communication between solicitor and client. But it seems equally clear that the privilege has been lost by its actual disclosure to the other side, whether one thinks in terms of a waiver or loss of the privilege. For what it is worth, I think that Mr Noy is entitled to put the copy letter in evidence.

10.12 Commentary

Blackstone v *Coke* at trial. Eldon and Co, Margaret Blackstone's solicitors, have subpoenaed Father Wigmore, the Roman Catholic priest referred to in Mansfield and Co's letter of 20 February 1980, to attend to give evidence at the trial. In answer to Mr Noy, Father Wigmore states that he is Coke's parish priest and that he has from time to time seen him in confession. Father Wigmore refuses to answer any further questions put by Mr Noy as to matters revealed to the priest in the confessional. Mr Noy requests Hardwicke J to order Father Wigmore to answer.

10.13 Argument

Mr Noy: My Lord, the law gives no effect to confidential relationships other than

that between lawyer and client in terms of privilege. Your Lordship is entitled to direct
Father Wigmore to answer.

Hardwicke J: Mr Atkyn, subject to anything you say, I think that position is
correct.

Mr Atkyn: My Lord, I must accept that this relationship is not one which is
privileged, or the confidence of which entitles the priest to refuse to answer. But I
would invite Your Lordship's attention to the judgment of Browne LJ, in *Science
Research Council* v *Nasse* (see 10.3 ante), and to the opinion of the Court of Appeal
in:

Attorney General v Mulholland and Foster [1963] 2 QB 477 (CA)

The defendants were journalists who commented in their newspapers on the Vassall spy case
by suggesting that high ranking officials of the Admiralty should have known that Vassall
was more than a mere clerk, and perhaps had known of Vassall's spying but had kept quiet. A
tribunal of inquiry was set up with the same powers to compel witnesses as a court of law.
Both journalists refused to answer questions asking them to name their sources and were
imprisoned for contempt.

LORD DENNING MR said: 'But then it is said that however relevant these questions were
and however proper to be answered for the purpose of the inquiry, a journalist has a privilege
by law entitling him to refuse to give his sources of information. The journalist puts foward as
his justification the pursuit of truth. It is in the public interest, he says, that he should obtain
information in confidence and publish it to the world at large, for by so doing he brings to the
public notice that which they should know. He can expose wrongdoing and neglect of duty
which would otherwise go unremedied. He cannot get this information, he says, unless he
keeps the source of it secret. The mouths of his informants will be closed to him if it is known
that their identity will be disclosed. So he claims to be entitled to publish all his information
without ever being under any obligation, even when directed by the court or a judge, to
disclose whence he got it. It seems to me that the journalists put the matter much too high.
The only profession that I know which is given a privilege from disclosing information to a
court of law is the legal profession, and then it is not the privilege of the lawyer but of his
client. Take the clergyman, the banker or the medical man. None of these is entitled to refuse
to answer when directerd to by a judge. Let me not be mistaken. The judge will respect the
confidences which each member of these honourable professions receives in the course of it,
and will not direct him to answer unless not only it is relevant but also it is a proper and,
indeed, necessary question in the course of justice to be put and answered. A judge is the
person entrusted, on behalf of the community, to weigh these conflicting interests — to weigh
on the one hand the respect due to confidence in the profession and on the other hand the
ultimate interest of the community in justice being done or, in the case of a tribunal such as
this, in a proper investigation being made into these serious allegations.'

DONOVAN LJ said: 'While the journalist has no privilege entitling him as of right to refuse
to disclose the source, so I think the interrogator has no absolute right to require such
disclosure. In the first place the question has to be relevant to be admissible at all: in the
second place it ought to be one the answer to which will serve a useful purpose in relation to
the proceedings in hand. I prefer that expression to the term "necessary." Both these matters
are for the consideration and, if need be, the decision of the judge. And over and above these
two requirements, there may be other considerations, impossible to define in advance, but
arising out of the infinite variety of fact and circumstance which a court encounters, which
may lead a judge to conclude that more harm than good would result from compelling a
disclosure or punishing a refusal to answer.'
(DANCKWERTS LJ agreed.)

Further, My Lord, that statement of Lord Denning MR was approved by the House of Lords in *British Steel Corporation* v *Granada Television Ltd* [1980] 3 WLR 774.[1]

Hardwicke J: Mr Noy, while accepting your point as to privilege, I think Mr Atkyn has a point with regard to the balancing of interests in such cases. It is a matter for you, but I am not sure I would be impressed by the need to break such an inportant confidence in a case such as this even though I may be entitled to do so. (Mr Noy conferred with his solicitors and client, withdrew the question and terminated his examination of Father Wigmore, who was released.)

10.14 Commentary

Blackstone v *Coke* at trial. In her list of documents, the plaintiff disclosed a psychiatric report prepared by one Dr Watson, very shortly after the alleged rape. The list of documents claimed privilege for this report on the ground that it was a communication between Miss Blackstone and her medical adviser made for the purposes of and in contemplation of litigation. Mr Atkyn, on behalf of Coke, applies for the report to be disclosed and put in evidence. Hardwicke J having heard evidence on the question, finds as a question of fact that the report was made at a stage when litigation was not directly in Miss Blackstone's contemplation.

10.15 Argument

Mr Atkyn: My Lord, this is not a case where the plaintiffs have disclosed a report prior to calling the doctor concerned to give evidence, as provided for by RSC, Order 38, Rules 36–44 (see 9.7 ante). Despite the claim of privilege made, no privilege can be maintained in this case, in the light of Your Lordship's finding that litigation was not seriously contemplated. I refer Your Lordship to:

Wheeler v *Le Marchant* (1881) 17 Ch D 675 (CA)

In an action for specific performance of a building contract to take on lease building land from the defendants, the defendants sought to protect from production letters which had passed between their solicitors and their surveyors. The judge held that the letters were privileged.

JESSEL MR said: 'The actual communication to the solicitor by the client is of course protected, and it is equally protected whether it is made by the client in person or is made by an agent on behalf of the client, and whether it is made to the solicitor in person or to a 'clerk or subordinate of the solicitor who acts in his place and under his direction. Again, the evidence obtained by the solicitor, or by his direction, or at his instance, even if obtained by the client, is protected if obtained after litigation has been commenced or threatened, or with a view to the defence or prosecution of such litigation. So, again, a communication with a solicitor for the purpose of obtaining legal advice is protected though it relates to a dealing which is not the subject of litigation, provided it be a communication made to the solicitor in that character and for that purpose. But what we are asked to protect here is this. The solicitor, being consulted in a matter as to which no dispute has arisen, thinks he would like to know some further facts before giving his advice, and applies to a surveyor to tell him what the state of a given property is, and it is said that the information given ought to be protected because it is desired or required by the solicitor in order to enable him the better to give legal advice. It appears to me that to give such protection would not only extend the rule beyond

---

[1]With regard to journalists, see Contempt of Court Act 1981, 10.9.2 ante.

what has been previously laid down, but beyond what necessity warrants.'
(BRETT and COTTON LJJ delivered concurring judgments.)
Appeal allowed.

Hardwicke J: What test should be applied to this question?
Mr Atkyn: I would refer Your Lordship on that point to the case of:

Waugh v British Railways Board [1980] AC 521 (HL)

The plaintiff's husband, who was employed by the defendants, was killed in a collision between two trains, and she brought an action under the Fatal Accidents Act 1976 in respect of his death. The board denied negligence and alleged contributory negligence on the part of the deceased. The plaintiff sought discovery of an internal report, prepared by the board for submission to the railway inspectorate and the ministry. There was also the intention that the report be placed before the board's solicitors. The board claimed that it was a privileged document.

LORD WILBERFORCE said: 'I think it desirable to attempt to discern the reason why what is (inaccurately) called legal professional privilege exists. It is sometimes ascribed to the exigencies of the adversary system of litigation under which a litigant is entitled within limits to refuse to disclose the nature of his case until the trial. Thus one side may not ask to see the proofs of the other side's witnesses or the opponent's brief or even know what witnesses will be called: he must wait until the card is played and cannot try to see it in the hand. This argument cannot be denied some validity even where the defendant is a public corporation whose duty it is, so it might be thought, while taking all proper steps to protect its revenues, to place all the facts before the public and to pay proper compensation to those it has injured. A more powerful argument to my mind is that everything should be done in order to encourage anyone who knows the facts to state them fully and candidly — as Sir George Jessel MR said, to bare his breast to his lawyer: *Anderson* v *Bank of British Columbia* (1876) 2 Ch D 644, 699. This he may not do unless he knows that his communication is privileged.

But the preparation of a case for litigation is not the only interest which call for candour. In accident cases "...the safety of the public may well depend on the candour and completeness of reports made by subordinates whose duty it is to draw attention to defects": *Conway* v *Rimmer* [1968] AC 910, *per* Lord Reid, at p 941. This however does not by itself justify a claim to privilege since, as Lord Reid continues:

> ...no one has ever suggested that public safety has been endangered by the candour or completeness of such reports having been inhibited by the fact that they may have to be produced if the interests of the due administration of justice should ever require production at any time.

So one may deduce from this the principle that while privilege may be required in order to induce candour in statements made for the purposes of litigation it is not required in relation to statements whose purpose is different — for example to enable a railway to operate safety.

It is clear that the due administration of justice strongly requires disclosure and production of this report: it was contemporary; it contained statements by witnesses on the spot; it would be not merely relevant evidence, but almost certainly the best evidence as to the cause of the accident. If one accepts that this important public interest can be overridden in order that the defendant may properly prepare his case, how close must the connection be between the preparation of the document and the anticipation of litigation? On principle I would think that the purpose of preparing for litigation ought to be either the sole purpose or at least the dominant purpose of it: to carry the protection further into cases where that purpose was secondary or equal with another purpose would seem to be excessive, and unnecessary in the interest of encouraging truthful revelation. At the lowest such desirability of protection as might exist in such cases is not strong enough to outweigh the need for all relevant documents to be made available.

There are numerous cases in which this kind of privilege has been considered. A very useful review of them is to be found in the judgment of Haver J in *Seabrook* v *British Transport Commission* [1959] 1 WLR 509 which I shall not repeat. It is not easy to extract a coherent principle from them....

It appears to me that unless the purpose of submission to the legal adviser in view of litigation is at least the dominant purpose for which the relevant document was prepared, the reasons which require privilege to be extended to it cannot apply. On the other hand to hold that the purpose, as above, must be the sole purpose would, apart from difficulties of proof, in my opinion, be too strict a requirement, and would confine the privilege too narrowly.'
(LORDS RUSSELL of KILLOWEN and KEITH of KINKEL agreed. LORDS EDMUND DAVIES and SIMON of GLAISDALE delivered judgments to the same effect.)
Disclosure ordered.

Hardwicke J: In the light of that case, it would seem that the purpose of litigation must be 'at least the dominant purpose' for which the document was prepared. In the light of my findings of fact, the plaintiff cannot maintain that position. The claim of privilege seems to me to be unfounded and I shall order the report to be produced.

10.16 Matrimonial communications: Introductory notes

10.16.1 The common law recognises no privilege for communications passing between spouses during the marriage. A statutory privilege was enacted by the Evidence Amendment Act 1853 and restated in succeeding statutes concerned with the evidence of spouses. The privilege still exists in relation to criminal cases but has been abolished for civil cases by the Civil Evidence Act 1968. Even where the privilege exists, it does not survive the dissolution of the marriage, so that a widow or divorced spouse is compellable to testify as to communications made during the marriage. (*A Practical Approach to Evidence,* pp 293–4.)

10.17 Commentary

R v *Coke and Littleton* at trial. Mr Bunbury is examining D/I Glanvil in chief and has arrived at the point where the Inspector would deal with the conversation between Littleton and Mrs Littleton recorded by D/I Glanvil at the police station. Mr Bacon having indicated to Mr Bunbury before the trial began that an objection would be made to the admissibility of this evidence, it was not opened to the jury, and at Mr Bunbury's request Holt J asks the jury to retire so that argument may take place in their absence.

10.18 Argument

Mr Bacon: My Lord, this conversation is plainly privileged. While I concede that there is no rule of privilege at common law, such privilege is provided by Section 3 of the Evidence Amendment Act 1853.

Evidence Amendment Act 1853, s.3

3. No husband shall be compellable to disclose any communication made to him by his wife during the marriage, and no wife shall be compellable to disclose any communication made to her by her husband during the marriage.

It has also been reaffirmed in subsequent statutes dealing with the competence of spouses generally[1].

It is true that the privilege has been abolished in relation to civil cases by the Civil Evidence Act 1968, s.16(3), but as Your Lordship knows the privilege still applies to criminal proceedings.

Civil Evidence Act 1968, s.16

16(3) Section 3 of the Evidence (Amendment) Act 1853 (which provides that a husband or wife shall not be compellable to disclose any communication made to him or her by his or her spouse during the marriage) shall cease to have effect except in relation to criminal proceedings.

Holt J: Yes.

Mr Bacon: My Lord, it is only right Your Lordship should know that Mrs Littleton has instituted divorce proceedings against her husband. Had the marriage actually been dissolved, the privilege would no longer exist. I would refer to:

Shenton v *Tyler* [1939] Ch 620 (CA)

The appellant brought an action against the respondent, claiming a declaration that the respondent's husband had, in his lifetime, created a secret trust in her favour. The appellant sought to put interrogatories to the respondant concerning communications between the respondent and her husband. The judge held that the communications were privileged.

LUXMOORE LJ said: 'The conclusion at which I have arrived is that, before the passing of the Evidence Act, 1851, there was a rule of the common law that communications between husband and wife were not admissible in evidence; and since the evidence was itself inadmissible, no question of privilege arose; and there was, therefore, no rule dealing with this aspect of the case. It was not until the evidence of the husband or wife became admissible by reason of the Evidence Act, 1851, and the Evidence Amendment Act, 1853, that the question of compellability arose, and was met by the express provisions of s.3 of the last mentioned Act. The privilege, therefore, appears to me to rest entirely on the provisions of s.3 of the 1853 Act; and I am satisfied that there was and is no rule of common law, apart from those provisions, conferring or recognising any such privilege.

The question arises, how far does this statutory privilege extend? The section is silent as to a widower or widow, or divorced person. None of the cases cited have in my opinion any bearing on this question…In Stephen's Digest of the Law of Evidence, 12th ed, p 146, it is stated that it is doubtful whether s.3 of the Act of 1853 has any application to a widower or divorced person, questioned after the dissolution of the marriage, as to what had been communicated whilst it lasted: a statement which must apply with equal force to a widow.

Plainly, the words of the section do not include the case of any persons other than husbands and wives: and since I have come to the conclusion that the privilege is statutory, I am unable to find any warrant for extending the words of the section by construction so as to include widowers and widows and divorced persons.'
(SIR WILFRED GREENE MR delivered a judgment to the same effect. FINLAY LJ agreed.)
Appeal allowed.

But the marriage is still subsisting and so the privilege also subsists.

Holt J: Mr Bunbury, what do you say about that?

Mr Bunbury: My Lord, I accept what my learned friend says about the law. But the fact is that the privilege has been lost by virtue of its being communicated to D/I

---

[1]See Criminal Evidence Act 1898, s.1(d); Sexual Offences Act 1956, s.39; Theft Act 1968, s.30 and generally 11.6.

Glanvil. I would refer Your Lordship to:

Rumping v *DPP* [1964] AC 814 (HL)

The appellant was charged with murder. A letter written by the appellant to his wife, confessing to the murder, was handed by him to a third party for posting, but the latter passed it to the police. The trial judge allowed the letter to be given in evidence and the appellant was convicted. The ruling was upheld, and a further appeal was made to the House of Lords.

LORD REID stated the facts and continued: 'The case for the appellant is that there is a rule or principle of the common law which protects communications between husband and wife which are not intended to be disclosed to others. It was argued that, if a third person overhears such a conversation or intercepts or obtains possession of a letter or other writing from one spouse to the other, the law will not require or permit him to disclose that communication in evidence in any case, civil or criminal. The Solicitor-General on the other hand submitted that there is no such rule and that such a third person can be required to disclose any such communication in evidence, if it is relevant, no matter how he came to overhear the conversation or gain possession of the writing. The only protection, he said, is that in a criminal case the judge has discretion to exclude the evidence if he thinks it proper to do so...

Before the enactment of a series of statutes beginning in 1851 it had been a long-standing rule that no party to a civil action, no accused person, and no husband or wife of such a party or person could give evidence at all. So the question now before your Lordships could only arise either where a third party had overheard a conversation or obtained possession of a written communication between the spouses, or where a communication between spouses would be relevant evidence in a case to which neither spouse was a party. No doubt such cases might not occur very often, but even so the authorities are surprisingly meagre and inconclusive.

There is no clear and specific statement that the rule for which the appellant contends ever existed. But there are a number of expressions of opinion which are inconsistent with or difficult to reconcile with the existence of such a rule. And, perhaps more important, there are several cases where I would have expected such a rule to have been founded on in argument and in the judgments if it existed. I refer in particular to the cases which decided that a widow or a divorced woman could not give evidence about conversations with her husband during their marriage: the rule now contended for would have afforded a much simpler ground of judgment than the somewhat illogical reasons given by the judges.

On the other hand there are many clear and forcible expressions of opinion that it is contrary to public policy to require disclosure of confidential communications between husband and wife: it is better that injustice should sometimes be done by preventing such disclosure than that the fear of possible future disclosure should be a general embarrassment to marital relations. It is true that most if not all of these opinions were expressed with regard to direct disclosure by one of the spouses. But it would be almost as embarrassing to marital relations if spouses had to fear possible future disclosure by a witness who was an eavesdropper or who had intercepted or stolen a letter from one spouse to the other.

Any legal principle based on such considerations would demand that communications between husband and wife should be equally protected both in civil and criminal proceedings against disclosure by one of the spouses or by some third person. So, if I could be satisfied that these considerations had been generally accepted as a basis of a doctrine of public policy, I would not be deterred from applying them to this case by the mere fact that no rule regarding disclose of such communications by third persons had ever been formulated. The rarity of cases involving such disclosure by third persons would sufficiently explain the absence of any such rule.

But I find it impossible to hold that any general principle based on public policy had become established....

The Evidence Amendment Act, 1853 (Lord Brougham's Act) made husbands and wives of parties competent and compellable witnesses in civil proceedings, and then provided with regard to communications between husband and wife: "3. No husband shall be compellable to disclose any communication made to him by his wife during the marriage, and no wife shall be compellable to disclose any communication made to her by her husband during the marriage."

I find it impossible to suppose that this section could have been framed in this manner if Parliament, or those who advised Parliament, had thought for a moment that there was any such rule as that now contended for. The protection given by this section is narrower than and of a different character from that which would have been given by the supposed rule or principle. The argument for the appellant is that in 1853 it was incompetent to ask any witness to disclose communications between husband and wife, at least if intended to be confidential. If that had been the case the natural course would have been to extend that rule to husbands and wives themselves when they were made competent witnesses. It might have been amended if that were thought desirable, but why pass it over in silence and adopt quite a different scheme. Under section 3 disclosure of these communications is not made incompetent. On the contrary, the husband or wife who is a witness can disclose them if he or she chooses to do so and the other spouse has no right to object. It is a mystery to me why it was decided to give this privilege to the spouse who is a witness: it means that if that spouse wishes to protect the other he or she will disclose what helps the other spouse but use this privilege to conceal communications if they would be injurious, but on the other hand a spouse who has become unfriendly to the other spouse will use this privilege to disclose communications if they are injurious to the other spouse but conceal them if they are helpful.

But one thing does appear quite clearly from section 3. Parliament cannot have thought that disclosure of such communications is contrary to public policy, because it has authorised a spouse giving evidence to disclose them if he or she so wishes whether or not the other spouse objects. Moreover, nothing is said in the Act about disclosure by a third party who is a witness, and I cannot believe that any competent draftsman, believing there was or might be a rule preventing third parties from making such disclosures, would have failed to take notice of it. For the question would at once arise whether Section 3 was intended to abrogate or supersede the old rule or to leave it standing for third parties alongside the new rule for spouses.

I can state my conclusion in this way. Before 1853 there was no established rule or principle which would have enabled this appeal to succeed. There were, however, statements with regard to public policy which would have carried the appellant a very long way. But public policy is essentially a matter for Parliament, and the terms of Section 3 of the Act of 1853 show that the Parliament of that time did not regard it as contrary to public policy to permit disclosure of communications between husband and wife. I cannot find in anything that has happened since that date sufficient ground to entitle the court now to take a different view as to public policy, and I can find no other basis on which this appeal could succeed. I therefore move that this appeal should be dismissed....'

VISCOUNT RADCLIFFE (dissenting) said: 'No one, I think, supposes that the Criminal Evidence Act, 1898, contains any prescription that can be applied to the facts now before us. Under that Act husband and wife became for the first time generally competent as witnesses, but neither could be called except upon the application of the accused and neither, even if called, was to be compellable to disclose any communication made to him or her during marriage. Thus the consequence of giving evidence was not permitted to be that a marriage confidence could be extracted by the prosecution. It follows that the wife here, if she had received the letter intended for her eyes, could not have been made to produce it in court as evidence against the appellant and, if she had retained it or destroyed it, there the matter would have rested and the husband's confidence remained inviolate.

Ought the law to apply a different rule merely because the letter has miscarried and has come into the hands of the police? Considering the history and the nature of the principle that lies behind the special rules governing testimony of husband and wife in criminal trials, I do not think that it should. If it does, we must recognise the implications that, personally, I find overwhelmingly distasteful. A husband may gasp or mutter to his wife some agonised self-incrimination, intended for no ear in the world but hers: yet the law will receive and proceed upon the evidence of the successful eavesdropper, professional, amateur or accidental. It is free, I suppose, to entertain the testimony of the listening device, if properly proved. An incriminating letter may be intercepted by any means: it may be snatched from the wife's hand after receipt, taken into custody if she has mislaid it accidentally, withdrawn from her possession by one means or another: in all these cases, it is said, the trophy may be carried into court by the prosecution and, given proof that the prisoner is its author, the law has no rule that excludes it from weighing against him as a confession.

I do not for a moment suppose, of course, that any of your Lordships is indifferent to these implications or that by this decision you desire to countenance them. But the only alternative to admitting them is to rely, as the learned Solicitor-General did in argument, upon the exercise of an inherent discretion in the judge who presides at the trial to exclude evidence which he regards as unfairly prejudicial to the accused. Certainly, there is such discretion, and there are, for instance, judges' rules. But I cannot agree that a matter of this sort is a proper subject for so vague and uncontrollable a thing as judicial discretion.

My conclusion is that there exists a principle of law which calls for the exclusion of this letter, whatever may be the form in which it is tendered as evidence.'

LORD MORRIS of BORTH-Y-GEST said: 'My Lords, a survey of the authorities and of the statutory provisions leads me to the view that there has never been a rule at common law that no evidence may be given by anyone as to communications made between husband and wife during marriage. There has, however, been a recognition of the feeling or public sentiment that in ordinary circumstances it is seemly that the confidences of married life should be respected and protected. That recognition found expression as one of the various reasons which were assigned for the old general rule as to the incompetence of husbands and wives as witnesses. That general rule may have made it unnecessary to consider the desirability of some such rule as is suggested in the argument for the appellant and no occasion arose to assess or to define, as a matter of public policy, the extent to which or the circumstances under which, the confidences of married life should as a matter of law be protected. When, however, by the Act of 1853 the general rule was changed no rule was enacted to the effect that no evidence could be given of any inter-marital communications: nor was it so enacted when the Act of 1898 was passed.

In the present case the stage of a confidence between husband and wife was never reached but the case can be decided without regard to that circumstance. The wife was not a witness. No question of any statutory privilege arose. There was no doubt as to the competency as witnesses of those who gave evidence. In my judgment there was neither rule of law nor requirement of public policy which precluded the reception in evidence of what the appellant had written.

I would dismiss the appeal.'

LORD HODSON said: 'I would dismiss the appeal, not upon the narrow ground that the communication in question did not reach the appellant's wife, but upon the ground that the common law rule contended for is not shown to have been established as a separate principle apart from the competency of witnesses, and that the admission of evidence is, as the Court of Criminal Appeal held, governed by the statute of 1898, which gives a privilege to a spouse to refuse to disclose communications between husband and wife but does not affect the proof of such statements being given by admissible evidence.'

(LORD PEARCE concurred in dismissing the appeal.)

Appeal dismissed.

Holt J: In those circumstances, I think that the detail of the conversation is admissible, the privilege having been lost.

10.19 Questions for Counsel

10.19.1 Blackstone v Coke. How would you have argued for the Director of the Oxbridge City Children's Department? Which of the matters raised by Mr Erskine would you have emphasised?

10.19.2 R v Coke and Littleton. Analyse, giving your reasons, the question whether

Holt J should direct D/I Glanvil to disclose the identity of his informant.

10.19.3 Blackstone v *Coke.* In view of Hardwicke J's ruling as to Mr Henneky's privilege against self-incrimination, what questions may Mr Noy ask him in cross-examination so as to test his evidence effectively while avoiding privileged matters?

10.19.4 Blackstone v *Coke.* Do you agree with Mr Noy's decision not to press Father Wigmore? If so, why? Would his decision necessarily have been the same in front of a jury?

11 Competence and Compellability: Oaths and Affirmations

11.1 Introductory notes

A witness is said to be competent if his evidence is receivable by the court in the proceedings in which he is called. A witness is said to be compellable if he is not only competent, but may lawfully be required by the court, under sanction of penalty as a contemnor, to give his evidence. It follows that a witness may only be compellable if he is first shown to be competent. The general rule is that all witnesses are both competent and compellable in the absence of some rule of law providing to the contrary. Historically, a variety of witnesses to whom suspicion attached, such as the parties to proceedings, their spouses, children of tender years, persons of defective intellect, convicts and non-Christians, were held not to be competent at common law. These incompetences have been gradually repealed. In modern law, the parties and their spouses are competent and compellable, subject to special provisions for the defendant in criminal cases and his or her spouse. Children of tender years are competent subject to judicial investigation of their understanding of the importance of telling the truth. Persons of defective intellect are competent co-extensively with their understanding of the case and of the duty of telling the truth. All other incompetences have been abolished by statute. The rule that all competent witnesses are also compellable is subject to one important exception in favour of the defendant in a criminal case and his or her spouse, and a number of miscellaneous exceptions.

11.1.1 Parties: The incompetence of parties was abolished by statute during the last century. Consequently, the parties to the proceedings are both competent and compellable. To this rule, Parliament provided one notable and important exception in the Criminal Evidence Act 1898. This Act rendered the defendant in a criminal case competent to give evidence for the defence, but provided that he should not be called 'except on his own application'. The defendant, though competent, is consequently not compellable. The Act provides for the defendant's competence only as a witness for the defence, and he is accordingly incompetent as a witness for the prosecution. Where the prosecution wish to call a person who is charged in any proceedings to give evidence against a co-defendant, they must, therefore, ensure that he first ceases to be a defendant, either by pleading guilty or by having no evidence offered against him or otherwise. (*A Practical Approach to Evidence*, pp 299–305.)

11.2 Commentary

R v Coke and Littleton at trial. At the outset of the trial, Mr Bunbury on behalf of the prosecution indicates to Holt J what course the trial is to take.

11.3 Argument

Mr Bunbury: My Lord, before pleas are taken, may I indicate the course which the prosecution propose to take. My learned friend, Mr Atkyn, has intimated that his client will tender a plea of guilty to the charge of rape. Should this be the case, the prosecution would seek a short adjournment in order to take a statement from Coke with a view to calling him as witness for the prosecution in the case against Littleton.

Holt J: You propose to call one defendant to help prove the guilt of the other?

Mr Bunbury: With respect, My Lord, not a defendant. I accept of course that while Coke is a defendant, he is not a competent witness for the prosecution. As Your Lordship knows, the defendant was wholly incompetent until the Criminal Evidence Act 1898. That Act rendered the defendant competent only as a witness for the defence.

Criminal Evidence Act 1898, s.1

1 Every person charged with an offence...shall be a competent witness for the defence at every stage of the proceedings, whether the person so charged solely or jointly with any other person. Provided as follows:

(a) A person so charged shall not be called as a witness in pursuance of this Act except on his own application.

Any attempt to call a defendant at trial in breach of this rule would, I accept, lead to the quashing of any conviction.

Holt J: I take it that if Mr Coke does not plead guilty, then you would be unable to call him for the prosecution unless you offered no evidence against him or otherwise removed him from the case entirely.

Mr Bunbury: My Lord, that is correct. The matter would not be cured simply by severing the indictment, because I accept that as a matter of practice it would be wrong to call for the prosecution a person who has been charged and against whom proceedings are pending. I would refer to the case of:

R v *Pipe* (1966) 51 Cr App R 17 (CA)

The prosecution called at the trial of the appellant an accomplice against whom proceedings had been brought, but had not been concluded.

LORD PARKER CJ, giving the judgment of the court, said: 'In the judgment of this court, the course taken here was wholly irregular. It may well be, and indeed it is admitted, that in strict law Swan was a competent witness, but for years now it has been the recognised practice that an accomplice who has been charged, either jointly charged in the indictment with his co-accused or in the indictment though not under a joint charge, or indeed has been charged though not brought to the state of an indictment being brought against him, shall not be called by the prosecution, except in limited circumstances. Those circumstances are set out correctly in *Archbold,* in paragraph 1297 of the current edition, where it is said that where it is proposed to call an accomplice at the trial, it is the practice (a) to omit him from the indictment or (b) take his plea of Guilty on arraignment or before calling him either (c) to offer no evidence and permit his acquittal or (d) to enter a *nolle prosequi....*

In the judgment of this court, it is one thing to call for the prosecution an accomplice, a witness whose evidence is suspect, and about whom the jury must be warned in the recognised way. It is quite another to call a man who is not only an accomplice, but is an accomplice against whom proceedings have been brought which have not been concluded.' Conviction quashed.

Holt J: Mr Bacon, have you any observations on behalf of LIttleton?

Mr Bacon: Only this. In my submission, it would be right that if Coke does plead guilty, he should be sentenced immediately, and not at the end of the trial. I would refer to:

R v *Payne* [1950] 1 All ER 102 (CCA)

The appellant and two other men were indicted on a charge of housebreaking. On arraignment the appellant pleaded guilty and the other men not guilty. The appellant was sentenced at once, before the other men had been tried.

LORD GODDARD CJ:...'It may be a very convenient course to sentence on the first day prisoners who plead Guilty, but that ought not to apply where two or more men are indicted together. If one pleads Guilty and the others Not Guilty, the proper course is to postpone sentence on the man who has pleaded Guilty until the others have been tried and then to bring up all the prisoners to be dealt with together because by that time the court will be in possession of the facts relating to all of them and will be able to assess properly the degree of guilt of each. This man received a heavier sentence than the other two because he was tried in a different court on a different day. This is a most inconvenient practice and it ought to cease. I hope that sessions will discontinue such a practice. It can only lead to different sentences being passed, and will, naturally, leave a sense of grievance in the minds of prisoners.

What I have said does not apply in the exceptional case where a man who pleads Guilty is going to be called as a witness. In those circumstances it is right that he be sentenced there and then so that there can be no suspicion that his evidence is coloured by the fact that he hopes to get a lighter sentence. I do not throw doubt on that very proper practice. I am only speaking of the cases in which those circumstances do not arise.'

Holt J: I see the force of that. Clearly Coke's evidence would be more satisfactory if he were no longer under expectation of any particular leniency. But I am not sure that would be a satisfactory course in this case. The matter is entirely one of practice. I do not feel that I would have sufficient information as to the role played by Coke to enable me to sentence properly at this stage. But this is academic until we see how Coke elects to plead. Let the indictment be put.

11.4 Commentary

R v *Coke and Littleton* on appeal against conviction. At the trial, Coke elected not to give evidence in his defence and was subsequently convicted. Coke now complains to the Court of Appeal of the following passage in the summing up of Holt J to the jury:

Members of the jury, so far as the defendant Coke is concerned, it cannot have escaped you that he was conspicuously absent from the witness box. You may have thought, in view of the matters put to the complainant Margaret Blackstone on Coke's behalf in cross-examination, that he would have been anxious to provide you with some evidence of his side of the case. But there has been none. What you make of that is entirely a matter for you. But you may think it not without significance, as Mr Bunbury observed to you in his closing speech, that Coke has chosen to avoid the risk of cross-examination on the detail of his story.

11.5   Argument

Mr Atkyn: My Lords, the defect in the summing up is that it treats Mr Coke as a compellable witness.

Leach LJ: He is of course competent by virtue of Section 1 of the Criminal Evidence Act 1898. Indeed, he would be entitled to give evidence at the committal proceedings before the Justices, on the voir dire, and during the course of mitigation. The statute says that he is competent 'at every stage of the proceedings.' Perhaps the learned judge was seeking to draw attention to that point. It was made in:

R v *Wheeler* [1917] 1 KB 283 (CCA)

The appellant, having pleaded guilty to a charge under the Sale of Food and Drugs Act 1875, was then sworn as a witness and wilfully made a false statement in order to influence the court as to the punishment to be inflicted. He was subsequently convicted of perjury in respect of that statement.

VISCOUNT READING CJ, delivering the judgment of the court, said: 'The first point taken on behalf of the appellant is that he was called after the issue in the case had been determined, that is, after he had pleaded guilty, and that the statement which he then made was one which he was not competent to make. In other words, the contention is that he was not a competent witness when he was sworn....

On the first point it has been ingeniously argued that the Criminal Evidence Act, 1898, which for the first time, at any rate in most cases, allowed the accused to give evidence, only allows him to give evidence at a particular time during the proceedings. It is, therefore, desirable to consider the provisions of that Act. Section 1 provides: [His Lordship read the section.] Now the words of that section are of very wide import. It is said that the accused, when he has pleaded guilty, cannot be a "witness for the defence" because the defence is then at an end; but those words obviously mean on behalf of the defendant. Then it was argued that the words "at every stage of the proceedings" must be limited to the proceedings in the different Courts, that is, before magistrates or at the trial by a jury. We see no reason for so limiting the meaning of those words. We think that those words are intended to enable an accused person to give evidence at every stage of the proceedings where evidence can properly be given; in other words, that wherever the defence can be heard evidence can be given by the defendant. It was further argued that the appellant was not a "competent witness for the defence," by reason of the provision of s.2 that where the accused is the only person called by the defence as a witness to the facts of the case he shall be called "immediately after the close of the case for the prosecution," and that as he was not called as a witness at that time he was not a competent witness when he was called and could not be lawfully sworn. That argument, however, loses all force when the true meaning is given to s.2. That section does no more than prescribe what is to happen in the circumstances therein described. Nowhere in that section or in the Act can we find any words to the effect that the accused can only be called as a witness at that time. It is very difficult to say that it was the intention of an enabling Act like this that the accused should not be entitled to give any evidence himself except in the particular way prescribed in s.2. When once we have arrived at that conclusion as to the meaning of the Act the whole argument for the appellant on this point fails.'
Appeal dismissed.

Mr Atkyn: My Lord, I accept that the appellant Coke was a competent witness. By Section 1(a) of the 1898 Act there is a proviso that: 'A person so charged shall not be called as a witness in pursuance of this Act except on his own application.' But the Act goes further than that. As the summing up reveals, my learned friend, Mr Bunbury, was improperly permitted to refer to Coke's absence from the witness box during the course of his closing speech. This is directly contrary to the provisions of Section 1(b) of the Criminal Evidence Act 1898 which provides: 'The failure of any person charged with an offence or of the wife or the husband, as the case may be, of the person so charged, to give evidence shall not be made the subject of any comment by the prosecution.'

Cox LJ: As I understand your argument, you also complain about the way in which the learned judge commented on the appellant's absence from the witness box. How do you put that part of your case?

Mr Atkyn: My Lord, I accept that the learned judge was entitled to comment on that fact. But he should have done so in a balanced way, stressing to the jury that the defendant is not obliged to give evidence and that he is not compellable. I would refer Your Lordships to:

R v Mutch [1973] 1 All ER 178 (CA)

The appellant was arrested and charged with robbery in a grocer's shop. The appellant denied the charge, claiming that he was not in the shop at the time of the incident. No formal identification parade was held by the police as it was alleged by the prosecution that, whilst on bail and for the purpose of confusing anyone attending an identification parade of which he was the suspect member, the appellant tried to alter his appearance by tinting his hair and moustache, and by reshaping the latter. At his trial, an assistant in the shop at the time of the incident identified the appellant, but he elected not to give evidence. He did, however, call two witnesses to prove that he had not altered his appearance as alleged. The trial judge, in summing up, told the jury that they were entitled to draw inferences unfavourable to the appellant because he was not called to establish an innocent explanation of facts, proved by the prosecution which, without such an explanation, told for his guilt. The appellant was convicted.

LAWTON J, reading the judgment of the court, said: 'Since the first decade of this century, there have been many cases in which this court and its predecessor have had to rule whether comments about an accused's absence from the witness box or a failure to disclose a defence when questioned by the police were permissible, and as Salmon LJ pointed out in *R v Sullivan* (1966) 51 Cr App R 102:

The line dividing what may be said and what may not be said is a very fine one, and it is perhaps doubtful whether in a case like the present it would be even perceptible to the members of any ordinary jury.

Nevertheless, as long as the law recognises the so called right to silence, judges must keep their comments on the correct side of the line even though the differences between what is permissible and what is not may have little significance for many jurors. In the circumstances of this case there would be no point in reviewing the cases, some of which are not easy to reconcile, as we are firmly of the opinion that the trial judge used a form of words which was inappropriate to the case and the evidence which he was summing up. The words he used might have been permissible if the evidence had established a situation calling for 'confession and avoidance'; they were not proper for one of flat denial as this case was.

Judges who are minded to comment on an accused's absence from the witness box should remember, first, Lord Oaksey's comment in *Waugh v R* [1950] AC 203:

It is true that it is a matter for the judge's discretion whether he shall comment on the fact that a prisoner has not given evidence; but the very fact that the prosecution are not permitted to comment on that fact shows how careful a judge should be in making such comment;

and, secondly, that in nearly all cases in which a comment is thought necessary (the *R v Corrie* (1904) 68 JP 294 and *R v Bernard* (1908) 1 Cr App R 218 type of cases being rare exceptions) the form of comment should be that which Lord Parker CJ described in *R v Bathurst,* as the accepted form, namely that:

> the accused is not bound to give evidence, that he can sit back and see if the prosecution have proved their case, and that, while the jury have been deprived of the opportunity of hearing his story tested in cross-examination, the one thing that they must not do is to assume that he is guilty because he has not gone into the witness box.

Appeal allowed.

My Lord, a detailed review of the case law was undertaken in:

R v Sparrow [1973] 1 WLR 488 (CA)

A policeman was shot in the course of a car theft by the appellant and his co-accused. At his trial for murder, the defendant did not give evidence to support his plea that the gun used was only intended to frighten anyone attempting to apprehend them. In his summing up the judge, commenting on the appellant's failure to give evidence, said that if he never contemplated that any shooting would take place it was essential that he should give evidence which could be tested in cross-examination. The appellant was convicted of murder.

LAWTON LJ, reading the judgment of the court said: '...Mr Brown, on behalf of the appellant, submitted with his usual incisiveness that that comment could have and would have been understood by the jury as a direction that they should assume that there was nothing in the appellant's defence and that he was guilty because he had not given evidence. In our judgment that is how the trial judge's comment would have been understood, but we think that that is how the jury would have assessed the situation if the judge's comment had not been been made. In our experience of trials, juries seldom acquit persons who do not give evidence when there is a clear case for them to answer and they do not answer it. Lord Goddard CJ recognised that, as one would have expected him to do, in his judgment in *R v Jackson* [1953] 1 WLR 591, 595:

> ...whatever may have been the position immediately after the Criminal Evidence Act 1898 came into operation, everybody knows that absence from the witness box requires a very great deal of explanation...

The reason lies in common sense. An innocent man who is charged with a crime, or with any conduct reflecting upon his reputation, can be expected to refute the allegation as soon as he can by giving his own version of what happened. Juries know this, and they must often be perplexed as to why they should be told by judges, as they often have been since the passing of the Criminal Evidence Act 1898, that when considering their verdict they should not take into account the fact that the accused has said not a word in his own defence even though the case against him is a strong one. The law, however, has set limits upon what judges may say about an accused's election not to give evidence. Our task is to adjudge whether the trial judge went too far in this case.

The limits have been set by the judges, and the experience of this court is that in recent years many judges at first instance have come to think that their right to comment on the absence of the defendant from the witness box has been restricted by the report of the Judicial Committee of the Privy Council in *Waugh v The King* [1950] AC 203 and the judgment of this court in *R v Bathurst* [1968] 2 QB 99, to which I have referred above. Sometimes judges stress the right of the defendant not to give evidence, as Devlin J did in *R v Adams* (unreported), April 9, 1957, and what he said in that case, taken out of context, is often used by defending counsel as an excuse for not calling the defendant.

Two propositions founded on *Waugh v The King* [1950] AC 203 and *R v Bathurst* [1968] 2 QB 99 are argued from time to time: first, that if a judge does decide to comment he should do so once only and that if he makes any more comments he is acting unfairly, and secondly, that any substantial variation from the form of comment suggested by Lord Parker CJ in *R* v *Bathurst* [1968] 2 QB 99, 107 is unfair. Present day doubts about what a judge can and cannot say by way of comment have led us to examine what principles, if any, apply.

Before the passing of the Criminal Evidence Act 1898 there was no problem of this kind because the defendant had no right to give evidence. As soon as that Act came into operation, the question arose as to whether a judge had any right to comment on the election of the defendant not to give evidence on his own behalf. It was answered in *R* v *Rhodes* [1899] 1 QB 77 by Lord Russell CJ in these words, at p 83:

> There is nothing in the Act that takes away or even purports to take away the right of the court to comment on the evidence in the case, and the manner in which the case has been conducted. The nature and degree of such comment must rest entirely in the discretion of the judge who tries the case; and it is impossible to lay down any rule as to the cases in which he ought or ought not to comment on the failure of the prisoner to give evidence, or as to what those comments should be. There are some cases in which it would be unwise to make any such comment at all; there are others in which it would be absolutely necessary in the interests of justice that such comments should be made. That is a question entirely for the discretion of the judge; and it is only necessary now to say that that discretion is in no way affected by the provisions of the Criminal Evidence Act 1898.

That clear statement of the law has never been questioned; it is the law. From 1899 until *Waugh* v *The King* [1950] AC 203 it was the practice of judges when justice required them to do so to comment in robust terms upon a defendant's absence from the witness box. An example of such comments which has been remembered at the Bar is provided by *R* v *Nodder* (unreported), 1937. The defendant had been indicted for the murder of a small girl. Swift J began his summing up by reminding the jury that they had heard evidence from several witnesses at to where the murdered girl had been up to a certain time when the defendant had been with her but none from the defendant himself, although he alone could·have given evidence of where she had been afterwards. The justice of that case called for that comment, and at the time when it was made informed opinion at the Bar did not question the propriety of it. It would, however, be questioned today. Why?

Many would say that the change in judicial practice resulted from *Waugh* v *The King* [1950] AC 203. There the appellant had been convicted of murder. The case against him was weak, so weak, indeed, that the police authorities, after they had completed their investigations, accepted his explanation as to what had happened and decided not to prosecute him. A coroner, however, ordered his prosecution. The only evidence of any strength against him was provided by a statement which the deceased had made shortly before his death. At the trial the appellant did not give evidence. In his summing up the trial judge commented nine times on that fact and on two of those occasions he made comments in much the same terms as Swift J had done in *R* v *Nodder* (unreported). The Judicial Committee of the Privy Council disapproved of those comments. Lord Oaksey delivered the reasons for the Board's report. He said, at p 211:

> Whilst much of the summing up is unexceptionable, there are certain parts of it which, in their Lordships' view, do constitute a grave departure from the rules that justice requires, and they are therefore of opinion that the conviction must be quashed. It is true that it is a matter for the judge's discretion whether he shall comment on the fact that a prisoner has not given evidence; but the very fact that the prosecution are not permitted to comment on that fact shows how careful a judge should be in making such comment.

He went on to point out how weak the prosecution's case had been and continued, at p 212:

> *In such a state of the evidence* — the italics are ours — the judge's repeated comments on the appellant's failure to give evidence may well have led the jury to think that no innocent man could have taken such a course... in the present case their Lordships think that the prisoner's counsel was fully justified in not calling the prisoner, and that the judge, if he made any comment on the matter at all, ought at least have pointed out to the jury that the prisoner was not bound to give evidence and that it was for the prosecution to make

out the case beyond reasonable doubt.

Lord Oaksey went on to find that the dying declaration had been wrongly admitted and inaccurately commented upon.

In our judgment *Waugh* v *The King* [1950] AC 203 establishes nothing more than this: it is a wrongful exercise of judicial discretion for a judge to bolster up a weak prosecution case by making comments about a defendant's failure to give evidence, and implicit in the report is the concept that failure to give evidence has no evidential value. We can find nothing in it which qualifies the statement of principle in *R* v *Rhodes* [1899] 1 QB 77. Our view of *Waugh* seems to have been that of Lord Goddard CJ in *R* v *Jackson* [1953] 1 WLR 591 when he said, at p 594:

> ...I do not want in the least to appear to be whittling down what their Lordships in the Judicial Committee said on these matters, but each case on·such a point as this must depend on its own facts...It has to be remembered, among other things, that the charge against the appellant was one of receiving stolen property...if ever there was a case in which one would expect him to give evidence to explain his possession of the property that is the case.

In the present case, the charge was murder, and the evidence went to establish that when the police officer was shot by the co-defendant the appellant was standing close by and that after the shooting the pair of them drove off together and that one them within a short time in the presence of the other reloaded the pistol; there has to be added to that the submission of the appellant's counsel that the prosecution's evidence was consistent with the possibility that the joint enterprise between the co-defendant and the appellant was merely to frighten the police officer with a pistol (which the appellant knew was loaded) and that the co-defendant departed from it by pressing the trigger a number of times.

In the judgment of this court, if the trial judge had not commented in strong terms upon the appellant's absence from the witness box he would have been failing in his duty. The object of a summing up is to help the jury and in our experience a jury is not helped by a colourless reading out of the evidence as recorded by the judge in his notebook. The judge is more than a mere referee who takes no part in the trial save to intervene when a rule of procedure or evidence is broken. He and the jury try the case together and it is his duty to give them the benefit of his knowledge of the law and to advise them in the light of his experience as to the significance of the evidence, and when an accused person elects not to give evidence, in most cases but not all the judge should explain to the jury what the consequences of his absence from the witness box are, and if, in his discretion, he thinks that he should do so more than once he may, but he must keep in mind always his duty to be fair. As A T Lawrence J pointed out in *R* v *Voisin* [1918] 1 KB 531, 536:

> Comments on the evidence which are not misdirections do not by being added together constitute a misdirection.

How should this be done? in *R* v *Bathurst* [1968] 2 QB 99 Lord Parker CJ gave judges some guidance, but what he said was, as he appreciated, obiter. It was in these terms, at p 107:

> ...as is well known, the accepted form of comment is to inform the jury that, of course, he — the defendant — is not bound to give evidence, that he can sit back and see if the prosecution have proved their case, and that while the jury have been deprived of the opportunity of hearing his story tested in cross-examination, the one thing they must not do is to assume that he is guilty because he has not gone into the witness box.

In many cases, a direction in some such terms as these will be all that is required; but we are sure that Lord Parker CJ never intended his words of guidance to be regarded as a judicial directive to be recited to juries in every case in which a defendant elects not to give evidence. What is said must depend upon the facts of each case and in some cases the interests of justice call for a stronger comment. The trial judge, who has the feel of the case, is the person who must exercise his discretion in this matter to ensure that a trial is fair. A discretion is not to be fettered by laying down rules and regulations for its exercise: see *R* v *Selvey* [1970] AC 304, *per* Lord Hodson, at p 364. What, however, is of the greatest importance in Lord Parker CJ's advice to judges is his reference to the need to avoid telling juries that absence from the witness box is to be equated with guilt. As we have already said, this was implicit in *Waugh* v *The King* [1950] AC 203 and Lord Parker CJ's dictum on this point has been accepted by this court as the law in *R* v *Pratt* [1971] Crim LR 234 and *R* v *Mutch* [1973] Crim LR 111.

How should these principles be applied in this case? In our judgment there is nothing in the complaint about the cumulative effects of the comments, particularly as the trial judge at the beginning of his summing up explained accurately and clearly that the appellant had a right to remain silent and to rest his defence on the presumption that he was innocent until proved guilty. The interests of justice required that the trial judge should get the jury to understand that an exculpatory statement, unverified on oath, such as the appellant had made after arrest, was not evidence save in so far as it contained admissions, and his task was not made easier by the present state of the law which required the Attorney-General to say nothing about the appellant's silence but allowed the co-defendant's counsel to say what he liked and, were he so minded, to put into words what it is almost certain the majority of the jurors were asking themselves, viz., having regard to the strength of the evidence, if the appellant was innocent why had he not gone into the witness box to say so? Our law, however, does not require a defendant to give evidence and a judge must not either by express words or impliedly give jurors to understand that a defence cannot succeed unless the defendant gives evidence. Unfortunately, probably by a slip of the tongue, that is what the trial judge did when he said to the jury:

Is it not essential that he should go into the witness box and tell you that himself and be subject to cross-examination about it? Well, he did not do so and there it is.

He did overstep the limits of justifiable comment; he should not have said what he did.
How far did these few words in a long summing up effect the jury's verdict? This must always be a matter of speculation, but we are confident on the facts of this case that the jury would have come to the same verdict if the trial judge had not said what he did. There has been no miscarriage of justice.'
Appeal dismissed.

(The court indicated that subject to hearing Mr Bunbury, they considered the summing up to be in error.)

11.6 Spouses: Introductory notes

11.6.1 As in the case of parties to proceedings themselves, the incompetence of their spouses was gradually removed during the 19th Century. And as in the case of the parties themselves, spouses are now competent and compellable in all cases, subject to special provisions regarding the spouse of the defendant in a criminal case. The defendant's spouse was regarded as incompetent as a witness for the prosecution at common law, save in the exceptional cases of high treason and offences of violence against the spouse or children of the family. To these cases of competence at common law, Parliament added a succession of statutory exceptions in which a spouse may be competent and today the range of such offences is a wide one. It is now settled that even where a spouse is a competent witness for the prosecution, he or she is nonetheless not compellable.

11.6.2 Under the Criminal Evidence Act 1898, a spouse is a competent witness for the defence but may only be called on the application of the defendant. This means, in effect, whether the spouse is called for the defendant to whom he or she is married or on behalf of another defendant, the consent of the former is required. There are, however, statutory exceptions to this rule, which may well be more significant than the rule itself.

11.6.3 At common law, the incompetence of a spouse survived the termination of the marriage by death or divorce, but only in respect of matters that occurred during the marriage. In civil cases, the rule is subject to grave doubt in an age when present spouses are undoubtedly both competent and compellable. In criminal cases, where the spouse is in general an incompetent witness for the prosecution, it is still thought that the spouse remains incompetent after dissolution of the marriage, in respect of matters occurring during the marriage. (*A Practical Approach to Evidence,* pp 305–15.)

11.7 Commentary

R v *Coke and Littleton* on appeal against conviction. At trial, over the objection of both defendants, Mr Bunbury called Mrs Littleton to give evidence for the prosecution. Mrs Littleton proved reluctant to give evidence, but on being told by Holt J that she would otherwise be in contempt, gave certain evidence which supported the case against both defendants. Both Coke and Littleton were in due course convicted. Both defendants appealed on the grounds that firstly, Mrs Littleton was not a competent witness for the prosecution, and secondly, even if she were, she was wrongly compelled to give evidence.

11.8 Argument

Leach LJ: It will be convenient to deal first with the question of competence. Mr Bunbury, we feel we should call on you to explain how the defendant Littleton's wife could be a competent witness for the prosecution against her husband. At common law, she is certainly incompetent, is she not?

Mr Bunbury: In general, My Lord, yes. But even at common law there are some exceptional cases. The older writers cite high treason as being one, but it is also clear that the spouse is a competent witness for the prosecution in a case involving violence against the spouse or the children of the family.

Cox LJ: I think some difficulty has arisen over the interpretation of the phrase 'offence of violence'.

Mr Bunbury: Your Lordship is quite right. Some of the difficulty is reflected in the decision in:

R v *Verolla* [1963] 1 QB 285 (Bedford Assizes)

The defendant was charged with attempting to cause a poison to be taken by his wife with intent to murder her. During the prosecution case, the trial judge expressed doubts as to the competence of the defendant's wife as a witness and adjourned the trial for that point to be argued.

MELFORD STEVENSON J said: 'If the evidence is to be admitted it necessarily involves my differing from the view expressed by Gorman J in *R* v *Yeo* [1951] 1 All ER 864n. I have now, after an adjournment of the hearing, had the advantage of a very full argument and presentation of the authorities from the case of *R* v *Lord Audley* 3 St Tr 401, HL onwards. That was a case where the husband was charged, amongst other things, with aiding and abetting a rape upon his wife which quite obviously involved physical violence towards her and the application of force, but in the course of discussion there is recorded a resolution of the judges "that in civil cases a wife may not; but in a criminal case of this nature where the wife is the party aggrieved and on whom the crime is committed she is to be admitted a witness against her husband."

It is quite plain on the facts of *Lord Audley's* case that physical violence was, as I said, an ingredient in the offence charged and that case does not appear to me to advance very far the argument on either side in the present case.

In *Reeve* v *Wood* (1864) 5 B&S 364, which was a case stated by petty sessions arising out of a complaint that a man was able to maintain his wife and children and that he neglected or refused to do so, so that they became chargeable to the parish, it was determined that the wife of the accused was not a competent witness against him. Blackburn J said Ibid 369: "The general rule is that the wife is not admissible as a witness against her husband; but in civil cases — with which, however, we have at present no immediate concern — various statutory exceptions have been made; and in criminal matters from an early period — I believe the case of *Lord Audley* is the earliest on record — an exception was admitted to the rule; which went on the principle that where the offence charged touched the person of the wife, and where, therefore, she must be cognisant of it, and might perhaps be the only person cognisant of it, she was an admissible witness." The words "the only person cognisant of it," suggest that the basis of admission of such evidence, at least in part, is that it is in many instances essential to admit it if the offence is to be proved at all.

In *Director of Public Prosecutions* v *Blady* [1912] 2 KB 89 the Divisional Court of the King's Bench Division had to consider a case stated by a metropolitan magistrate on a charge under Section 1 of the Vagrancy Act, 1898, of knowingly living wholly or in part on the earnings of prostitution. The person on whose earnings the defendant was supposed to be living was the wife, and she started the prosecution but it was apparently taken over by the Director of Public Prosecutions. Pickford and Avory JJ, with Lush J dissenting, held that the wife was not an admissible witness for the prosecution. Mr Travers Humphries, who appeared for the appellants, cited in his argument *Reeve* v *Wood* to which I have just referred, and particularly the judgment of Blackburn J. He also cited *R* v *Wakefield* (1827) 2 Lew CC1, to which I have also been referred, and *Lord Audley's* case. He cited those cases to support the proposition that the exception at common law to the rule which forbids the husband to give evidence against the wife is that such evidence may be admitted on a charge which affected the liberty or person of the wife.

The language in which Avory J expressed the matter was as follows [1912] 2 KB 89, 91: "To the general rule of law that in the case of husband and wife one is not a competent witness against the other on a criminal charge, there is, so far as I know, only one exception at common law, namely, that either is a competent witness on any charge which affects his or her liberty or person. The cases cited to us by Mr Humphreys in support of his argument are cases in which the liberty or person of the wife has been affected by force or fraud."

Pickford J said Ibid 90: "At common law the rule, whatever its origin might be, was that a wife could not give evidence against her husband. There were exceptions, but they were confined to cases in which the offence itself concerned the liberty, health or person of the wife. If we were to extend the exception beyond those limits we should be legislating."

Pickford J, and, indeed, the majority of the court, took the view that the offence of living on immoral earnings does not necessarily involve the liberty, health or person of the wife and therefore the evidence was inadmissible. I have to consider whether the exception to the general rule which excludes a wife's evidence in a criminal case is as wide as it is said to be in the language adopted by Pickford and Avory JJ; that is to say, can one properly admit the evidence, not only in cases where the husband is charged with assault or with an offence involving assault, but also in a case where the liberty or person of the wife is affected.

This, as I have said, is a charge of attempting to murder the wife by poisoning. I cannot think that for this purpose there can be any distinction between an attempt and the completed offence. It is quite true that an attempt to murder by poisoning does not necessarily, at any rate does not on the evidence presented to this court, involve any force or offer of force but it is in my view plainly an offence which affects the person of the wife. I think that the language chosen by Avory J although merely by obiter dictum in *Blady's* case is justified by the earlier authorities to which I have referred and others to which I have been referred in the course of argument.'

(The trial proceeded and the defendant was found Not Guilty.)

East LJ: You say that the present charges fell within the common law exception?

Mr Bunbury: No, My Lord. But a number of statutory provisions have been enacted dealing with the subject of competence. The earliest of these was under the Criminal Evidence Act 1898, s.1, which held the spouse of the defendant to be a competent witness for the defence. My Lords, Section 1(c) went on to provide:

Criminal Evidence Act, 1898 s.1(c)

The wife or husband of the person charged shall not, save as in this Act mentioned, be called as a witness in pursuance of this Act except on the application of the person so charged.

But this provision must be read together with Section 4 of the same Act.

Criminal Evidence Act 1898, s.4

4(1) The wife or husband of a person charged with an offence under any enactment mentioned in the schedule to this Act may be called as a witness either for the prosecution or defence and without the consent of the person charged.

(2) Nothing in this Act shall affect a case where the wife or husband of a person charged with an offence may at common law be called as a witness without the consent of that person.

This section, therefore, contemplates some cases in which the spouse should be a competent witness for the prosecution.

Leach LJ: What offences are mentioned in the schedule of the Act?

Mr Bunbury: My Lord, the contents of the schedule have changed from time to time. Before the passing of the Sexual Offences Act 1956, sexual offences were by and large comprised in the schedule. But I referred to the 1898 Act by way of background, because it provides the basis for the provision under Section 39 of the Sexual Offences Act 1956 which in my submission applies to the present case. The section provides:

Sexual Offences Act 1956, s.39

39(1) Where this section applies, the wife or husband of the accused shall be competent to give evidence at every stage of the proceedings, whether for the defence or for the prosecution, and whether the accused is charged solely or jointly with any other person: Provided that:—

(a)   the wife or husband shall not be compellable either to give evidence or, in giving evidence, to disclose any communication made to her or him during the marriage by the accused; and

(b)   the failure of the wife or husband of the accused to give evidence shall not be made the subject of any comment by the prosecution.

(2) Subject to the following subsection, this section applies on a charge of any offence under this Act, except in so far as it is excluded in the case of section twelve (buggery), section fifteen (indecent assault on a man) and section sixteen (assault with intent to commit buggery).

(3) This section shall not affect section one of the Criminal Evidence Act, 1898, or any case where the wife or husband of the accused may at common law be called as a witness without the consent of the accused.

Cox LJ: That section certainly appears to apply to the charges in the present case. I seem to remember that there is some provision also under the Theft Act 1968. *Mr Bunbury:* My Lord, there is. Your Lordship no doubt has in mind:

Theft Act 1968, s.30

30(2)...a person shall have the same right to bring proceedings against that person's wife or husband for any offence (whether under this Act or otherwise) as if they were not married, and a person bringing any such proceedings shall be competent to give evidence for the prosecution at every stage of the proceedings.

(3) Where a person is charged in proceedings not brought by that person's wife or husband with having committed any offence with reference to that person's wife or husband or to property belonging to the wife of husband, the wife or husband shall be competent to give evidence at every stage of the proceedings, whether for the defence or for the prosecution, and whether the accused is charged solely or jointly with any other person:

Provided that:—

(a) the wife or husband (unless compellable at common law) shall not be compellable either to give evidence or, in giving evidence, to disclose any communication made to her or him during the marriage by the accused; and

(b) her or his failure to give evidence shall not be made the subject of any comment by the prosecution.

Leach LJ: Those provisions seem to be very wide.

Mr Bunbury: My Lord, they are. Your Lordship will notice that they are not confined to offences under the Theft Act 1968. The breadth of the expression 'with reference to' the spouse is considerable as appears from the decision in:

R v *Noble* [1974] 1 WLR 894 (CA)

The defendant was charged on indictment with the forgery of her husband's signature on documents. At the trial the judge ruled that by virtue of s.30(3) of the Theft Act 1968 the husband was a competent witness for the Crown and could give evidence for the prosecution that he had not given the defendant authority to sign his name. The defendant was convicted and appealed on the ground that the husband's evidence was inadmissible.

MOCATTA J, reading the judgment of the court, said: 'When one comes to the language of subsection (3) itself the wide and somewhat vague phrase "with reference to" is immediately noticeable in contrast to the use of word "against" in subsection (2) and also in the Married Women's Property Acts. Prima facie it would seem that the words "with reference to" have been intentionally used in preference to "against" in order to widen the category of criminal proceedings against a spouse in which the other spouse shall be competent to give evidence. Whether this be right or not, the words in fact used are ordinary non-technical English words carrying a wider meaning than the word "against" had it appeared in this context in their stead.

As against the argument for the Crown, it was sought to limit the construction to be placed on "any offence with reference to that person's wife or husband" in two ways. The first was by reference to the long title to the Act to which it was argued that the ejusdem generis rule applied so as to limit the ambit of the words "and for other purposes connected therewith." We have been unable to derive any assistance from this argument, since we cannot discern a relevant genus covering the preceding words in the long title. It was further argued that "any offence" in subsection (3) meant any offence under the Theft Act and therefore did not include offences under the Forgery Act. The words "any offence" are very wide and since they are made applicable not only to property belonging to the husband or wife, we can find no justification for limiting their application to proceedings in respect of offences under the Theft Act 1968.'

Appeal dismissed.

Leach LJ: Mr Atkyn, I can well understand Mr Bacon's complaint on behalf of Littleton, with regard to the admission of Mrs Littleton's evidence. But what complaint does your client have?

Mr Atkyn: My Lord, it is clear law that where a spouse's evidence is wrongly admitted and bears on the guilt or innocence of any other defendant, the convictions of both defendants must be quashed. I would refer Your Lordships to:

R v Mount (1934) 24 Cr App R 135 (CCA)

Three defendants were charged jointly with shopbreaking, and all were convicted. The wife of one of the defendants was called as a witness for the Crown, and, after stating that she was willing to give evidence, gave evidence which was vital to the case against the other two defendants. These two defendants appealed.

CHARLES J, giving the judgment of the court, said: 'All that evidence was absolutely inadmissible. It has long been held that at common law a wife is not only not a compellable, but not even a competent, witness against her husband. That principle was enunciated with regard to a case where prisoners are charged jointly in *Thompson* (1872) LR 1 CCR 887, where it was made quite clear that, where two or more persons are indicted jointly, the wife or husband of any such defendant is not an available witness against any co-defendant. Indeed, save for certain exceptional cases which are to be found in the Schedule to the Criminal Evidence Act, 1898, that rule of common law is absolute and undisturbed.'
Convictions quashed.

(The court indicated that it had formed a provisional view that Mrs Littleton was a competent witness for the prosecution under Section 39 of the Sexual Offences Act 1956.)

Mr Atkyn: My Lords, even if that is so, she was wrongly compelled to give evidence. In relation to the statutory competence of a spouse under the 1898 Act, to which Section 39 of the 1956 Act refers, question was decided by the House of Lords in:

Leach v R [1912] AC 305 (HL)

The appellant was convicted of incest. At the trial his wife was called by the prosecution, but she raised the objection that under s.4 of the Criminal Evidence Act 1898 she could not be compelled to give evidence against her husband. The trial judge ruled that the wife was a compellable witness and directed her to give evidence, which she did. This ruling was affirmed by the Court of Criminal Appeal, and an appeal was made to the House of Lords.

EARL LOREBURN LC said: 'My Lords, I do not pretend to conjecture whether the decision which your Lordships, I think, will arrive at, is pro bono publico or not. It is very desirable that in a certain class of cases justice should not be thwarted by the absence of the necessary evidence, but upon the other hand it is a fundamental and old principle to which the law has looked, that you ought not to compel a wife to give evidence against her husband in matters of a criminal kind. It is not our duty today to consider consequences at all. What we have to consider is the meaning of the law that has been laid down in the Act of 1898.

Now, my Lords, if it had not been for that 4th section the wife could not have been allowed to give evidence, and the result of that was that the wife could not have been compelled to do so and was protected against compulsion. The difference between leave to give evidence and compulsion to give evidence is recognised in a series of Acts of Parliament. Does then the 4th section, which I have read, deprive the wife of this protection? It is capable of being construed in different ways, and it may hereafter lead, for all I know, to various other difficulties, but the present question is, does it deprive this woman of this protection? My Lords, it says in effect that the wife can be allowed to give evidence, even if her husband objects. It does not say she must give evidence against her own will. It seems to me that we must have a definite change of the law in this respect, definitely stated in an Act of Parliament, before the right of this woman can be affected, and therefore I consider that this appeal ought to be allowed, with what consequences, or how that may be conformable to what is in the true interests of society or the public in this particular case, we are not concerned and are not at liberty to inquire.'

LORD HALSBURY said: 'I should have thought that it would occur not only to a lawyer, but to almost every Englishman, that a wife ought not to be allowed to be called against her husband, and that those who are under the responsibility of passing Acts of Parliament would recognise a matter of that supreme importance as one to be dealt with specifically and definietely and not to be left to inference.'

LORD ATKINSON said: 'My Lords, I concur. The principle that a wife is not to be compelled to give evidence against her husband is deep seated in the common law of this country, and I think if it is to be overturned it must be overturned by a clear, definite, and positive enactment, not by an ambiguous one such as the section relied upon in this case.'
(LORDS MACNAGHTEN, SHAW of DUNFERMLINE, and ROBSON agreed.)
Appeal allowed.

In relation to cases which were not covered by the statute, the same result was reached by the House of Lords more recently in:

Hoskyn v Commissioner of Police of the Metropolis [1979] AC 474 (HL)

The appellant was charged with wounding one Janis Scrimshaw with intent to do her grievous bodily harm. Two days before the start of the trial, the appellant and Janis Scrimshaw were married. Mrs Hoskyn, as she now was, was reluctant to give evidence and being compelled to do so by the judge, was treated as hostile. Her evidence nonetheless assisted in the conviction of the appellant. The appellant's conviction was upheld by the Court of Appeal and he appealed to the House of Lords.

LORD WILBERFORCE, having referred to the decision in *Leach* v *R* (see above), continued: 'My Lords, it is certain that their Lordships were dealing with a point of statutory construction (of Section 4 of the Act of 1898), that they were not called upon to pronounce upon the position at common law, and that anything they said, expressly or by implication, as to the latter would be outside what they were called on to decide. Nevertheless I cannot believe that they would have used the strong and unqualified expressions which they did, if they had thought that there were special cases, outside the ambit of the statute, in which a wife was compellable. If they had so thought they would surely have thought it necessary to deal with the argument by analogy: "...it is true that the principle we are stating is not absolute: there are exceptions at common law, when the wife is competent and compellable, but that does not affect the position under statute," or at least to qualify in some way their general statements. And if they had been asked: "What about the case where a wife was competent at common law — does not the ordinary rule make her compellable" they would surely have answered: "No, because the considerations which led the law to treat her as competent do not in any way weaken the force of the principle we have stated that a wife ought not to be forced into the witness box, a principle of general application and fundamental importance."

My Lords, when *R* v *Lapworth* [1931] 1 KB 117 came to be decided in 1931 the Court of Criminal Appeal was content to distinguish *R* v *Leach* as a case on a point of statutory construction. This they were formally entitled to do. Their own judgment as to the common law rests upon two arguments, first the general argument that, in English law, all competent witnesses are compellable — this of course is true but it does not resolve the particular question whether the wife of an accused person, who clearly enjoys a special status, is within or without this rule.

Secondly they found upon an observation during argument attributed by the Criminal Appeal Reports to the Earl of Halsbury, 7 Cr App R 157, 166:

> I should have thought that if the known state of the law was that in order to confer competency you had to enact it, the fact that you simply used the word 'competent' did not necessarily mean 'against his or her will'

and they argue [1931] 1 KB 117, 122 "I read that as meaning: if the known state of the law is such as to confer competency without a statute, then compellability follows as a matter of course from that fact" — with all respect a complete non sequitur. I respect the view of these experienced judges as to the practice, but against this they give no weight to such authority as can be found which I have cited, which, in the view of one respected author, led him to think that the "better opinion" is against compellability. Nor do they examine in any depth, or indeed at all, the fundamental question which I think to be this: a wife is in principle not a competent witness on a criminal charge against her husband. This is because of the identity of interest between husband and wife and because to allow her to give evidence would give rise to discord and to perjury and would be, to ordinary people, repugnant. Limited exceptions have been engrafted on this rule, of which the most important, and that now relevant, relates to cases of personal violence by the husband against her. This requires that, as she is normally the only witness and because otherwise a crime would go without sanction, she be permitted to give evidence against him. But does this permission, in the interest of the wife, carry the matter any further, or do the general considerations, arising from the fact of marriage and her status as a wife, continue to apply so as to negative compulsion? That argument was in just this form put to the House of Lords and in a general form answered in the affirmative. It was not faced in *R v Lapworth* at all.

My Lords, after careful consideration I have reached the conclusion that *R v Lapworth* was wrongly decided and must be overruled, that the general principles stated in *R v Leach* [1912] AC 305 apply and that the wife should be held non-compellable.'

LORD SALMON, after referring to *Leach v R*, continued: 'It seems to me that the finding that you could not infer into a statute a power to compel a wife to give evidence against her husband in a criminal matter was based on their Lordship's opinion that it was contrary to the common law to compel a wife to give such evidence and that such compulsion could be introduced into a statute only by plain and express words. Although their Lordships were only construing a statute, their ratio decidendi was based largely on their opinion as to the effect of the common law and therefore cannot in my view be regarded as merely obiter dicta. I regard *Leach's* case [1912] AC 305 as a binding authority for the proposition that a wife can never be a compellable witness against her husband unless expressly made so by statute. To suppose as Avory J did in *Lapworth's* case [1931] 1 KB 117 that this House cannot have had in mind the common law principle which permitted a wife to give evidence against her husband charged with inflicting injuries upon her seems strange — particularly as that principle was clearly spelt out to their Lordships by counsel in opening the appeal: see p 306.

My Lords, for the reasons I have explained, I respectfully disagree with Avory J when in delivering the judgment of the court, he said, at p 121: "Once it is established that she [the wife] is a competent witness, it follows that she is a compellable witness." I also disagree with him when he said, at p 122:

> An observation made by Lord Halsbury in that case confirms me in the view of the law that I have expressed when I said (quoting from the report of *Leach's* case, 7 Cr App R 157, 166): I should have thought that if the known state of the law was that in order to confer competency you had to enact it, the fact that you simply used the word "competent" did not necessarily mean "against his or her will."

I should have thought that that observation of Lord Halsbury to which Avory J alluded, far from confirming the view he stated in *Lapworth's* case completely destroys it.

I have no doubt that the decision in *Lapworth's* case has been followed by trial judges, the Court of Criminal Appeal and the Court of Appeal (Criminal Division) in such cases as may have come before them since 1931 and were covered by *R v Lapworth*. *R v Algar* [1954] 1 QB

279 in which that great judge, Lord Goddard CJ, presided is an example of such a case. But it must be remembered that the courts which decided those cases were bound by the decision in *R* v *Lapworth*. This however is the first time that your Lordships' House has had an opportunity of considering *Lapworth's* case. For my part I strongly disapprove of it for the reasons I have attempted to explain.

I have already said that in the instant case the Court of Appeal was bound by *Lapworth's* case and was therefore compelled to follow it. I cannot however agree with the Court of Appeal when it sought to justify the decision in *Lapworth's* case by saying:

> It must be borne in mind that the court of trial in circumstances such as this where violence is concerned...is not dealing merely with a domestic dispute between husband and wife, but it is investigating a crime. It is in the interests of the state and members of the public that where that is the case, evidence of that crime should be freely available to the court which is trying the crime."

If such a consideration could have been a justification for the decision in *Lapworth's* case still more would it be a justification for making the wife a competent and compellable witness against her husband were he to be charged with murder — which clearly she is not.'

LORD EDMUND-DAVIES (dissenting) said: 'As appears from the speeches I have had the advantage of reading, your Lordships are all of the opinion that the question demands a negative answer, and some of your Lordships have described the idea that an affirmative answer is called for as "repugnant" to the married state and, as such, entirely unacceptable. This attitude may be contrasted with that adopted in the instant case by Geoffrey Lane LJ who, after reviewing most of the legal authorities brought to light by the admirable researches of appellant's counsel, said:

> It must be borne in mind that the court of trial in circumstances such as this where personal violence is concerned (and this case is a good example where wounding with a knife is concerned) is not dealing merely with a domestic dispute between husband and wife, but it is investigating a crime. It is in the interests of the state and members of the public that where that is the case evidence of that crime should be freely available to the court which is trying the crime. It may very well be that the wife or the husband, as the case may be, is the only person who can give evidence of that offence. In those circumstances it seems to us that there is no reason in this case for saying that we should in any way depart from the ruling...in *R* v *Lapworth*...

What is the proper attitude and what, accordingly, the proper answer to the certified question? Such legal learning as has a bearing (however remote) on the matter has been extensively reviewed by your Lordships, and no purpose would be served by my attempting it all over again, though I naturally propose to comment on the views expressed by your Lordships in the light of the available material. There is common agreement that there exists only one authority directly in point, *R* v *Lapworth*, and it follows that, as far as this House is concerned, we are engaged in an act of lawmaking. I have the misfortune to think that the law as your Lordships conceive it to be is inimical to the public weal, and particularly so at a time when disturbing disclosures of great violence between spouses are rife. Nor am I able to accept, as your Lordships have in fact said, that if spouses subjected to violence are to become compellable witnesses against their attackers it must be left to Parliament to say so. On the contrary, it is open to your Lordships to declare here and now that such is already the law, were you minded to do so.

In a scene of great confusion, what stand rock-like are two unchallengeable propositions about the common law. They are:

(1) That all competent witnesses are, virtually without exception, also compellable witnesses. As Willes J said in *Ex parte Fernandez* (1861) 10 CBNS 3, 39:

> Every person in the kingdom except the sovereign may be called upon and is bound to give evidence to the best of his knowledge upon any question of fact material and relevant to an issue tried in any of the Queen's courts, unless he can show some exception in his

favour, such, for instance, as that suggested to exist in this case, namely, that to answer might put him in peril of criminal proceedings.

As my noble and learned friend, Lord Wilberforce, has said, the only recognised exceptions to that proposition "provide no analogy for the treatment of a wife."

(II) That although in earliest times spouses were wholly incompetent to give evidence against each other in any case, ever since *Lord Audley's Case* (1631) 3 St Tr 402, where a wife was raped by a footman at her husband's instigation and in his presence, the common law has unquestionably been that a spouse is a competent prosecution witness in cases of assault or infringement of liberty perpetrated by the other party to the marriage. That this was a momentous development which was felt to undermine one of the most basic legal concepts is deducible from such writers as Gilbert CJ, who claimed with manifest (but, as it turned out, misplaced) relief that the decision

...hath since been exploded...because it may be improved to dreadful purposes, to get rid of husbands that prove uneasy, and must be a cause of implacable quarrels if the husband chance to be acquitted: *Gilbert on Evidence*, 6th ed (1801), p 120.

My Lords, the fundamental question is whether, as the appellant contends, one spouse who, though physically attacked by the other, is unwilling to testify for the prosecution, can lawfully claim to be within any exception to the general rule that, being competent, he or she is therefore compellable. In my judgment the case law, the statutory history and the textbooks do not establish that the question must receive an affirmative answer. The epoch-making decision in *Lord Audley's Case,* 3 St Tr 402 is sought to be explained away as arising simply *ex necessitate,* a spouse assaulted in secret having no redress were she denied a hearing in the courts. But the criminal law serves a dual purpose: to render aid to citizens who themselves seek its protection, and itself to take active steps to protect those other citizens who, though grievously in need of protection, for one reason or another do not themselves set the law in motion. And it does not follow that their failure should mean that, proceedings having nevertheless been instituted, the injured spouse should be less compellable as a Crown witness than one unrelated by marriage to the alleged assailant. I readily confess to a complete absence of any feeling of "repugnance" that, in the circumstances of the instant case, Mrs Hoskyn was compelled to testify against the man who had three days earlier become her husband. And, agreeing as I do with the attitude of Geoffrey Lane LJ, I am regretfully unable to accept the view expressed by my noble and learned friend, Lord Salmon, that "...if she does not want to avail herself of [the law's] protection, there is, in my view, no ground for holding that the common law forces it upon her."

...My Lords, if the proper conclusion is that the law upon the certified question has hitherto been uncertain, this House has now an opportunity to declare what that law is. In that event, I end as I began by inviting your Lordships to consider what decision is likely to advance the public good. This House had only a few years ago to deal with a case arising from events as horrible as those which led to Lord Audley's conviction in 1631. Indeed, the facts in *R v Morgan* [1976] AC 182 were startling similar, for there too a husband had procured other men to rape his wife. It would surely have created a revulsion going far beyond "repugnance" if the wronged wife at the last moment declined to testify against her husband and, in consequence, he and the four other accused were acquitted, so inextricably did her evidence involve all five accused. The noble and learned Lord, Viscount Dilhorne, has spoken of the repugnance created by a wife being compelled "...to testify against her husband on a charge involving violence, no matter how trivial and no matter the consequences to her and to her family." For my part I regard as extremely unlikely any prosecution based on trivial violence being persisted in where the injured spouse was known to be a reluctant witness. Much more to the point, as I think, are cases such as the present, as *R v Morgan,* and as others arising from serious physical maltreatment by one spouse to the other.

Such cases are too grave to depend simply upon whether the injured spouse is, or is not, willing to testify against the attacker. Reluctance may spring from a variety of reasons and does not by any means necessarily denote that domestic harmony has been restored. A wife who has once been subjected to a "carve-up" may well have more reasons than one for being an unwilling witness against her husband. In such circumstances, it may well prove a positive boon to her to be directed by the court that she has no alternative but to testify. But, be that as it may, such incidents ought not to be regarded as having no importance extending beyond the domestic hearth. Their investigations and, where sufficiently weighty, their prosecution is a duty which the agencies of law enforcement cannot dutifully neglect. In *R* v *Algar* [1954] 1 QB 279, Lord Goddard CJ said, at p 285:

> At common law one spouse could not give evidence against the other except in the case of offences against the person or liberty of the other party to the marriage. In such cases a spouse is both competent and compellable.

These words should not be regarded as being merely conforming to *R* v *Lapworth* [1931] 1 KB 117, which was never cited in the case. And even if it had been, Lord Goddard CJ was never content to apply without explicit remonstrance decisions with which he disagreed. In expressing himself as he did, he was, I believe, drawing upon his immense reservoirs of knowledge of the common law and of the long-standing practice of the courts. *R* v *Lapworth* is the only authority cited to your Lordships which bears directly on the facts of this case, and Avory J claimed to be doing no more than asserting what had long been the law. The decision itself must surely have since been applied in countless cases without any known expressions of outrage or resentment. It is, with respect, a decision which should find favour with this House today.

My Lords, for these reasons I would dismiss this appeal.'
(VISCOUNT DILHORNE and LORD KEITH of KINKEL agreed with LORD WILBERFORCE.)
Appeal allowed.

Cox LJ: I observe from the transcript that evidence was given that Mrs Littleton was separated from her husband. Is this of significance?

Mr Bacon: My Lord, no. The mere fact that the parties are living apart does not bring any incompetence to an end. I would refer Your Lordship to:

Moss v Moss [1963] 2 QB 799 (DC)

A husband preferred an information against his wife that she persistently telephoned him with intent to cause annoyance. The justices rejected a submission on behalf of the wife that, since the parties were man and wife, the husband was not a competent witness against the wife. The wife appealed.

HAVERS J, said: 'Mr Drinkwater contended that the common law rule only applied while the wife was under coverture and that she was only under coverture while she was sub potestate viri. He further contended that a decree of judicial separation brought the coverture to an end and that thereafter the husband or wife was a competent witness against the other in respect of any matters which arose after the date of the decree.

Mr Drinkwater sought to derive some assistance for this argument from the fact that Lord Alvanley said in *Monroe* v *Twistleton* Peake, Add Cas 219, 220, that the divorced wife was competent to prove any fact after the divorce but not to prove a contract or anything else which happened "during the coverture." He also relied upon the use by Lord Goddard CJ of similar words in *R* v *Algar* [1954] 1 QB 279, 287.

It is clear, however, that both Lord Alvanley and Lord Goddard were speaking of cases in which there had been a divorce and were using the words "during the coverture" as a convenient phrase to describe the period of time when the marriage was subsisting.

Mr Drinkwater also referred to *Dawes* v *Creyke* (1885) 30 Ch D 500 (cited without disapproval in *Waite* v *Morland* (1888) 38 Ch D 135, 137). This case, however, was merely a decision upon the construction of the words "during the...coverture" in a marriage settlement.

Further, Mr Drinkwater contended that if regard is paid to the reason for the common law rule, given in *O'Connor* v *Marjoribanks* 4 Man & G 435, namely, to preserve the confidence of the conjugal relation, there is no room for the application of the rule after a decree for judicial separation.

He contended that a decree of judicial separation under which the spouses lived apart caused just as much a disruption of the conjugal relationship as a decree absolute of divorce, and that there was no reason why thereafter one spouse should not be competent to give evidence against the other in criminal proceedings in respect of matters which arose after the decree.

If this argument is correct, it would apply also to spouses who were living apart under non-cohabitation orders made by justices under the Matrimonial Proceedings (Magistrates' Courts) Act, 1960, and to spouses living apart under a separation agreement.

I am unable to accept the argument of Mr Drinkwater though it is not lacking in attraction.

The common law rule has existed at any rate since 1628.

Prior to the Matrimonial Causes Act, 1857, the Ecclesiastical Courts had for centuries granted decrees of divorce a mensa et thoro which did not dissolve the marriage and were equivalent to the modern decree of judicial separation.

I know of no authority and none was cited to us in which it was held that after the pronouncement of such a decree either by an Ecclesiastical Court before 1857 or thereafter by the Court for Divorce and Matrimonial Causes or its successor the Probate, Divorce and Admiralty Division of the High Court of Justice one spouse had been held a competent witness against the other in criminal proceedings (apart from the common law and statutory exceptions).

It has also to be borne in mind that after a decree for judicial separation there still remains the opportunity for reconciliation, which it is the policy of the law to encourage.

In my judgement, the common law rule applies to the spouses notwithstanding a decree of judicial separation and neither spouse is a competent witness against the other in criminal proceedings so long as the marriage subsists.'

(LORD PARKER CJ and WIDGERY J agreed.)

Appeal allowed.

Indeed, My Lords, at common law the incompetence of a spouse survives the termination of the marriage, at least in respect of matters that occurred during the marriage, as the events in this case did. I would refer Your Lordships to:

Monroe v *Twistleton* (1802) Peake Add Cas 219 (Nisi Prius)

In order to prove a contract the plaintiff called Mrs Sandon, who, at the time of making it, was the wife of the defendant, but had since been divorced from him. The defendant objected to her competence.

LORD ALVANLEY said: 'To prove any fact arising after the divorce this lady is a competent witness, but not to prove a contract or anything else which happened during the coverture. She was at that time bound to secrecy; what she did might be in consequence of the trust and confidence reposed in her by her husband; and miserable indeed would the condition of a husband be, if, when a woman is divorced from him, perhaps for her own misconduct, all the occurrences of his life, entrusted to her while the most perfect and unbounded confidence existed between them, should be divulged in a court of justice. If she might be a witness in a civil proceeding, she might equally be so in a criminal prosecution; and it never shall be endured that the confidence which the law has created while the parties remained in the most intimate of all relations, shall be broken whenever, by the misconduct of one party' (for misconduct alone can have that effect), the relation has been dissolved.'

(The plaintiff called other witnesses, and obtained a verdict.)

East LJ: It strikes me as rather surprising that the rule has survived in civil cases, because as I understand it the parties and their spouses have long been competent and compellable witnesses in such cases. Yet *Monroe* v *Twistleton* implies that former spouses may not be.

Mr Bacon: My Lord, I respectfully agree. However, in criminal cases the rule corresponds with the general incompetence of spouses for the prosecution, and appears to survive. I refer Your Lordships to:

R v *Algar* [1954] I QB 279 (CCA)

A wife who had been lawfully married obtained a decree of nullity on the ground of her husband's impotence. After the decree had been pronounced she was called as a witness for the prosecution at her former husband's trial for alleged criminal offences, committed while the parties had been living together. The former husband appealed against conviction.

LORD GODDARD CJ, giving the judgment of the court, said: 'So we now have to inquire whether the incompetency in a criminal case extended beyond the actual period of coverture. *Monroe v Twistleton* (1802) Peake Add Cas 219, a case approved again and again, lays down in terms that a divorced wife cannot be called to testify against her husband in respect of any matters arising or conversations which had passed during the marriage. The same rule was applied in the case of a widow: *Doker v Hasler* Ry&M. Both of those cases were decided at nisi prius, the first by Alvanley CJ, the second by Best CJ, afterwards Lord Wynford. They were approved by the Court of Common Pleas in *O'Connor v Marjoribanks* (1842) 4 Man&G 435, where the incompetence was extended to the widow's personal representatives. The reason for the rule was stated in that case both by Tindal CJ and Maule J to be the necessity of preserving the confidence of the conjugal relation, and this reason for the rule has been stated in much the same terms by other judges of eminence. In *O'Connor's* case Maule J said ibid 445: "A rule may be a very good rule, though the reason on which it is founded may not be applicable to every case which is governed by the rule." As Lord Sumner once observed in *Jones v Jones* [1916] 2 AC 481: "principles are like that."

All those cases were cited without criticism or dissent by the Court of Appeal as recently as *Shenton v Tyler* [1939] Ch 620.... In a criminal case, therefore, subject to the common law and modern statutory exceptions mentioned above, a spouse remains incompetent to give evidence against the other, and the incompetence continues after divorce in respect of matters which arose during the coverture.

We have now to consider whether the same incompetency attaches after a decree of nullity. In our opinion this depends solely on whether the marriage annulled was void or merely voidable. A marriage is void where there is bigamy, consanguinity, non-age or where it has been celebrated contrary to the requirements of the law now collected and enacted in sections 25 to 49 of the Marriage Act, 1949. In those cases the court will regard the marriage as never having taken place and no status of matrimony as ever having been conferred. Consequently, the parties never having been husband and wife either is competent to be called against the other: *Wells v Fisher* (1831) 1M&Rob 99...

But impotence only makes a marriage voidable. Until it has been avoided at the suit of the aggrieved party it will be regarded by every court as valid and subsisting. The parties are husband and wife till a decree has been pronounced, and if one party dies before one was, or without one being, obtained the other is the widow or widower of the deceased.

...We think it clear that the reason for the incompetency applies to these persons with force at least equal to the case of divorced persons. It would be artificial in the highest degree to apply a different rule in the two cases....

The result is that the evidence of the appellant's former wife was inadmissible.'
Conviction quashed.

Leach LJ: Well, in this case, the marriage was still subsisting.
(The court indicated its view that Mrs Littleton had been wrongly compelled.)

11.9 Children: Introductory notes

11.9.1 At common law, children of tender years were incompetent to give evidence.

The designation of a child as being of tender years was not a matter of set age, but had to be determined by an inquiry made by the judge as to the child's ability to give evidence on oath. In the older cases, the inquiry was primarily directed to the child's religious state of mind and therefore his or her ability to be properly sworn. But the present day test is concerned with the understanding of the child of the duty of telling the truth in relation to the proceedings in court (over and above the normal social duty to tell the truth). The judge must conduct this inquiry by means of questions to the child in open court and in the presence of the jury.

11.9.2 In criminal cases, where in the opinion of the judge the child is not competent to give evidence on oath, the child may give evidence unsworn, provided the court finds that he or she is of sufficient intelligence to justify the reception of the evidence, and that the child understands the duty of speaking the truth. Where such evidence is given for the prosecution, the defendant may not be convicted of the offence unless the evidence is corroborated. (*A Practical Approach to Evidence*, pp 315–18.)

11.10   Commentary

R v *Coke and Littleton* at trial.   Mr Bunbury, on behalf of the prosecution, proposes to call Angela Blackstone to give evidence. Before doing so, he invites Holt J to investigate Angela's competence as a witness in the presence of the jury.

11.11   Course of Evidence and Argument

Holt J (having asked Angela her name and address):   Angela, how old are you?
Angela: Thirteen, sir.
Holt J: Do you live at home with your mother and father and your sister, Margaret?
Angela: Yes.
Holt J: Do you understand why your mother and father have brought you here today?
Angela: Yes, I do.
Holt J: Why?
Angela: To tell you about what happened when Margaret and I were at the man's flat.
Holt J: Do you understand the difference between telling the truth and telling lies?
Angela: Yes, sir.
Holt J: Do you think it is important to tell the truth?
Angela: Yes. I learned at school and in the Girl Guides always to tell the truth and my mother and father told me how important it is today.
Holt J: Do you believe in God?
Angela: No, not really. I went to Sunday School when I was younger, but I don't really believe it.
Holt J: Do you think that people who tell lies are punished when they die?
Angela: No. I know sometimes they are punished here on earth, but I don't believe in hell.
(Holt J invited counsel to ask any questions they wished. No counsel asked questions.)

Holt J: Does any counsel have any objection to the evidence of Angela Blackstone being received?

Mr Atkyn: My Lord, I would make the observation that Angela's religious state does not equip her to take a meaningful oath. As Your Lordship knows, the court has a duty to inquire into this matter and I would refer in this connection to:

R v Brasier (1779) 1 Leach 199, 1 East PC 443 (CCR)

The defendant was convicted of assaulting a child under seven years of age with intent to rape. The judges were unanimously of opinion that no testimony whatever can be legally received except upon oath, and that an infant, though under the age of seven years, may be sworn in a criminal prosecution, provided such infant appears, on strict examination by the court, to possess a sufficient knowledge of the nature and consequences of an oath...for there is no precise or fixed rule as to the time within which infants are excluded from giving evidence; but their admissibility depends upon the sense and reason they entertain of the danger and impiety of falsehood, which is to be collected from their answers to questions propounded to them by the court; but if they are found incompetent to take an oath, their testimony cannot be received.

Holt J: You are surely not saying that in this day and age a court must be deprived of the evidence of a child simply because of some defect in his or her religious education?

Mr Atkyn: My Lord, no. In a criminal case, Your Lordship has power to order that the evidence of the witness be taken unsworn. May I ask Your Lordship to look at:

Children and Young Persons Act 1933, s.38

38(1) Where, in any proceedings against any person for any offence, any child of tender years called as a witness does not in the opinion of the court understand the nature of an oath, his evidence may be received, though not given upon oath, if, in the opinion of the court, he is possessed of sufficient intelligence to justify the reception of the evidence, and understands the duty of speaking the truth...[1]

Holt J: I am mindful of my powers under this section, but of course it would be preferable for Angela to give evidence on oath if that course could be taken. Mr Bunbury, what do you say about that?

Mr Bunbury: My Lord, I would say that the test referred to by my learned friend in the case of *R v Brasier* has been superseded by the more modern approach of the Court of Appeal in:

R v Hayes [1977] 1 WLR 234.(CA)

The defendant was charged with inciting three young boys to commit acts of gross indecency, and with committing an act of gross indecency with one of the boys. He denied that he was the man involved. At the time of the trial the boys were aged 12, 11 and 9. The youngest boy was permitted to give unsworn evidence. The judge, after questioning the older boys, allowed the oath to be administered to them although the eldest had said that he was ignorant of the existence of God but he did understand the importance of telling the truth, particularly on that occasion. The defendant was convicted. He applied for leave to appeal on the ground

---

[1]As to the requirement for evidence of corroboration for evidence admitted under this section, see 14.4 post.

that, in the light of the boys' answers to his questions, the judge had exercised his discretion wrongly in permitting them to be sworn.

BRIDGE LJ, giving the judgment of the court, said: 'It is unrealistic not to recognise that, in the present state of society, amongst the adult population the divine sanction of an oath is probably not generally recognised. The important consideration, we think, when a judge has to decide whether a child should properly be sworn, is whether the child has a sufficient appreciation of the solemnity of the occasion and the added responsibility to tell the truth, which is involved in taking an oath, over and above the duty to tell the truth which is an ordinary duty of normal social conduct.

Against the background of those general considerations of principle, we think it right also to approach the matter on the footing that this is very much a matter within the discretion of the trial judge and we think that this court, although having jurisdiction to interfere if clearly satisfied that the trial judge's discretion was wrongly exercised, should hesitate long before doing so. The judge sees and hears the boy or girl, which means very much more than the bare written word, and it may easily be that the judge comes to the conclusion that the way in which he has initially been phrasing his questions has been such that the child to whom the questions are directed has not sufficiently understood them, and he may then attempt to phrase his questions in a different way.'
Application refused.

In my submission, Angela's answers to Your Lordship indicate that she does understand the duty of telling the truth and is therefore capable of being sworn.

Holt J: It seems to me from the judgment in that case, that the Court of Appeal regarded the understanding of the child as more important than actual age.

Mr Bunbury: My Lord, yes. Although the court ventured the view that a minimum of age of between eight and ten was indicated for the purposes of being sworn, the court did stress that the child's understanding was the decisive factor. (Holt J permitted Angela to give evidence on oath.)

B: *OATHS AND AFFIRMATIONS*

11.12 Introductory notes

11.12.1 It is a fundamental rule that evidence given to the court for any purpose should be sworn, that is to say that prior to giving evidence the witness should take a lawful oath or affirmation to tell the truth, the whole truth and nothing but the truth. In certain very limited cases, evidence may be given unsworn. These cases are:

11.12.1.1 Where the evidence of children may be given unsworn by virtue of s.38(1) of the Children and Young Persons Act 1933 (see 11.11, ante).

11.12.1.2 The evidence of witnesses called merely to produce documents may be received unsworn, unless the identity of the document is in dispute.

11.12.1.3 On licensing applications, evidence may be received unsworn in the discretion of the court, but where the application is opposed, the evidence is generally required to be sworn.

11.12.1.4 A judge or counsel asked to explain some aspect of a case in which he has been judicially or professionally engaged, may appear and speak unsworn from his proper place in court.

11.12.2 Evidence given unsworn in a case where none of the above exceptions applies is a nullity and may lead to the verdict or judgment being set aside on appeal.

11.12.3 Statute provides forms of oath and affirmation and allows any witness the choice of affirming as an alternative to being sworn. Oaths and affirmations have the same effect in law, which is that the sanction of perjury for false evidence in judicial proceedings is available in either case. The judge may insist on a witness affirming, and this power is used in cases where the witness seeks to be sworn in a manner that would cause embarrassment, delay or inconvenience.

11.12.4 The Criminal Evidence Act 1898 preserved the right of the defendant in a criminal case to make an unsworn statement from the dock regarding the facts and merits of the case, and this is in modern practice regarded as an alternative to giving evidence. Although counsel may advise the defendant as to the emphasis that should be placed on various matters, the statement should be made in the defendant's own words. It is still undecided whether the statement has an evidential value as to the facts stated in it, or whether it is merely a persuasive argument akin to the arguments of counsel. The latter seems to be the preferred view under modern law. It appears that evidence in rebuttal of an unsworn statement may not generally by given by a co-defendant whose case is affected by it, but it has been held that the prosecution may offer evidence in rebuttal of a false statement of good character made from the dock. (*A Practical Approach to Evidence*, pp 319–24.)

11.13 Commentary

R v *Coke and Littleton* at trial. After Coke has given evidence in his defence, Littleton elects not to give evidence on oath but to make an unsworn statement from the dock. In the course of this statement, while asserting his own innocence, he states facts damaging to Coke's defence. In the absence of the jury, Mr Atkyn makes an application to call evidence in rebuttal.

11.14 Argument

Mr Atkyn: My Lord, I am not entitled to cross-examine the defendant Littleton with regard to what he has said from the dock. Nevertheless, parts of his statement were extremely damaging to the defence of the defendant Coke and I ask that I be permitted to call evidence in rebuttal.

Holt J: I am not sure whether that course is appropriate. It seems to me that I shall have to direct the jury that the statement is not evidence against your client. As I recall, the Criminal Evidence Act 1898, s.1(h) provides that: 'Nothing in this Act shall affect…any right of the person charged to make a statement without being sworn.' It seems to me that Parliament was saying that the right to make an unsworn statement was somehow different from evidence but should co-exist with a defendant's right to give evidence.

Mr Atkyn: My Lord, I accept that position. Indeed that view was naturally taken when the defendant was not entitled to give evidence. In modern cases, the unsworn statement may have somewhat more effect. I refer to:

R v *Frost;* **R** v *Hale* (1964) 48 Cr App R 284 (CCA)

The appellants were convicted of receiving stolen property. At the trial neither went into the witness box and gave evidence, but Hale exercised his right to make an unsworn statement from the dock. In his summing up the Commissioner made no reference to the statement, though at the end of the statement he had told the jury that it was not evidence because not made on oath.

LORD PARKER CJ, giving the judgment of the court, said: 'In connection with this point Mr Nicholls says in the first instance that the learned Commissioner was wrong in telling the jury that the statement was not evidence. In the opinion of this court, it is quite unnecessary to consider what is really an academic question, whether it is called evidence or not. It is clearly not evidence in the sense of sworn evidence that can be cross-examined to; on the other hand, it is evidence in the sense that the jury can give it it such weight as they think fit.... It is quite clear today that it has become the practice and the proper practice for a judge not necessarily to read out to the jury the statement made by the prisoner from the dock, but to remind them of it, to tell them that it is not sworn evidence which can be cross-examined to, but that nevertheless they can attach to it such weight as they think fit, and should take it into consideration in deciding whether the prosecution have made out their case so that they feel sure that the prisoner is guilty.

The Commissioner went a long way in complying with what this court thinks is the proper practice, but he did go on to say that the statement was mere comment and may be analogous to counsel's speeches. In the opinion of the court, whatever the statement is called, it is certainly more than mere comment, and in so far as it is stating facts, it is clearly something more and different from the comments in counsel's speeches. In these circumstances, this court feels that there was a misdirection.'
Conviction quashed.

Mr Bacon: My Lord, may I invite Your Lordship's attention to a case which seems to bear on the question Your Lordship is asked to decide:

R v Coughlan (1976) 64 Cr App R 11 (CA)

The appellant was charged with a co-accused, MacLochlain, with conspiracy to cause explosions. The appellant gave evidence on oath, whereas the co-accused only made a statement from the dock. The jury were directed to decide the case on the sworn evidence given in the witness box, but were told to bear in mind the co-accused's statement from the dock when considering the evidence. Both the appellant and his co-accused were convicted.

SHAW LJ, giving the judgment of the court, said: 'It was argued for the appellant that his direction denied to MacLochlain's statement any evidential value, and that its true legal status was that it was evidence in the trial. Mr Blom-Cooper went on to submit that as the tenor of the statement gave support to the appellant's evidence that there had been no complicity, the undue disparagement of the weight and importance of MacLochlain's statement deprived the appellant of the benefit of that support and so caused prejudice to him.

When the Criminal Evidence Act 1898 made it possible for a person charged with an offence to be a witness in his own defence, it expressly preserved by section 1(h) what had until then been the only right of such a person, namely, to make a statement without being sworn. The section makes a clear distinction between the position where an accused person elects to assume the role of a witness in his defence and the situation where he makes an unsworn statement. In the latter case, he is not a witness and he does not give evidence. Nonetheless, in preserving his right to make an unsworn statement, the statute tacitly indicated that something of possible value to the person charged was being retained. What is said in such a statement is not to be altogether brushed aside; but its potential effect is persuasive rather than evidential. It cannot prove facts not otherwise proved by the evidence before the jury, but it may make the jury see the proved facts and the inferences to be drawn from them in a different light. Inasmuch as it may thus influence the jury's decision they should be invited to consider the content of the statement in relation to the whole of the evidence. It is perhaps unnecessary to tell the jury whether or not it is evidence in the strict sense. It is material in the case. It is right, however, that the jury should be told that a statement not sworn to and not tested by cross-examination has less cogency and weight than sworn evidence.

Mr Blom-Cooper cited a number of cases by which he sought to fortify his submission that the content of an unsworn statement from the dock was evidence in the case. The first was a decision of Cave J in Shimmin (1882) 15 Cox 122. That was, of course, before an accused could give evidence from the witness-box. There was then no other way in which a prisoner could assert any facts in a trial. Stronger support was to be found in *The People (Att.-Gen.)* v *Riordan* [1948] IR 416, an Irish case in which the President of the Court of Criminal Appeal in the Irish Republic, Gavin Duffy P, at p 417, described a statement from the dock as "an integral part of the evidence upon which the jury had to find its verdict."...

The controversial question is in the end reduced to a mere logomachy. Whatever status may be assigned to an unsworn statement, it can hardly vie with sworn evidence in cogency and weight.'

Appeal dismissed.

I would also refer Your Lordship to:

R v George (1978) 68 Cr App R 210 (CA)

The applicant and his co-accused, Gilpin, were convicted of murder and burglary. The main ground of appeal was whether the judge wrongly refused to allow the applicant's father to be recalled in order to rebut the statement from the dock made by Gilpin implicating the applicant in the offences charged.

LORD WIDGERY CJ, stated the facts and continued: 'The situation in regard to statements from the dock is less defined in the books than one would expect, having regard to the fact that it is a very age-old and respectable institution. But one thing which can be said with certainty is that the problem of a statement from the dock so far as a co-accused is concerned is exactly the same as the problem which arises when a co-accused has made some statement not in Court which damages a co-accused.

We think, as submitted by Mr Jeffreys, that we should treat these two situations alike. In each case the handicap imposed upon the defendant is that he cannot cross-examine the so-called witness. The more one looks at these two situations the more obvious it becomes that they are on a par.

Therefore, it seems to us that the proper approach to this case is to say that the statement made from the dock by Gilpin was not evidence at all against George. If that is a proper first step, and we think it is, then it becomes quite clear that such a statement which implicates a co-accused should be put before a jury as a statement which is wholly ineffective to weigh in the scales against the co-accused.

That, in effect, is what the learned judge did at the trial, and he instructed the jury in the clearest terms that they were not to regard Gilpin's statement as being evidence against George.

For the reasons which I have endeavoured to give, that seems to us to have been exactly the right way to deal with this problem in this case.'

Application refused.

Holt J: What do you say to that, Mr Atkin?

Mr Atkyn: In my submission, Your Lordship should also look at a case where the prosecution were held to be entitled to rebut statements as to the defendant's character made from the dock:

R v Campbell (1978) 69 Cr App R 221 (CA)

The appellant was convicted of fraudulent trading. At the trial the appellant made an unsworn statement from the dock representing himself to be an honest business man. The prosecution successfully applied to the judge to call rebutting evidence to show that the appellant was a person of bad character.

BRIDGE LJ said: 'How far is it permissible, when an unsworn statement from the dock has been made, for the Crown in rebuttal to lead evidence to controvert a matter which has been raised for the first time in the course of the statement from the dock and so may be said to arise *ex improviso* and not to have been foreseeable by those presenting the prosecution case in the first instance?

A statement from the dock is not, of course, evidence. It is, as many think — the fact that a defendant is still at liberty to make a statement of fact from the dock, invite a jury to consider his version of the facts without taking the oath and without subjecting himself to cross-examination — an anomalous historical survival from the days before the Criminal Evidence Act 1898 when a person could not give evidence on his own behalf. There it is, anomaly or not; the courts have to grapple with it and a statement from the dock unsworn now seems to have taken on in current practice a somewhat shadowy character half-way in value and weight between sworn evidence and mere hearsay. A jury cannot be told to disregard it altogether. They must be told to give it such weight as they think fit, but it can be properly pointed out to them that it cannot have the same value as sworn evidence which has been tested by cross-examination.

The first question one asks is whether, as a matter of law, if a statement of fact relevant to the issues in the trial is made in the course of an unsworn statement from the dock which would, if given in evidence by the defendant or witnesses called on his behalf, give rise to an opportunity to call rebutting evidence, the same opportunity arises in a case where the evidence is unsworn.

There is no authority on this point in this country. The current edition of *Archbold*, para 583a, observes: "In principle there can be no objection to the Crown being allowed to call evidence in rebuttal of an assertion made during the course of a statement from the dock where, had such a statement been made during the course of sworn evidence, rebuttal evidence would properly be admissible." Reliance is placed for that proposition on certain Australian cases which have said that if the law were otherwise it would be a manifest absurdity. We are urged in this case to say that that is a correct principle which ought to be applied in English law and for present purposes we are content to assume that this is correct.

The next question then arises. If the statement of fact — which has come for the first time in the course of the statement from the dock — relates not to any matter directly in issue in the proceedings but to the character or credibility of the defendant who is making the statement, does that let his character in and does that enable the prosecution to lead evidence of his bad character? Again, we are content to assume that the answer to that question is in the affirmative. It would seem to be so from a passage in the judgment of Lord Goddard, CJ in *Butterwasser* (1947) 32 Cr App R 81; [1948] 1 KB 4.

It was said at p 84 and p 6 of the respective reports: "It is elementary law that during the last 150 or perhaps 200 years, ever since the practice has grown up of allowing a prisoner to call evidence of good character, or where he has put questions to witnesses for the Crown and obtained or attempted to obtain admissions from them that he is a man of good character, in other words, where the prisoner puts his character in issue, evidence in rebuttal can be given by the prosecution to show that he is in fact a man of bad character."'
Appeal allowed.

In my submission, Your Lordship can draw some analogy from this case. Further more, a similar approach has been taken recently in another decision. I refer Your Lordship to:

R v De Vere [1981] 3 All ER 473 (CA)

The appellant was charged with obtaining property and services by deception. He did not give evidence himself from the witness box but made an unsworn statement from the dock, attacking the character of prosecution witnesses and setting himself up as a man of good character. After prosecution submissions the trial judge ruled that, under s.1(f)(ii) of the Criminal Evidence Act 1898, they were entitled to prove previous convictions, because the nature or conduct of the defence was such as to involve imputation on the character of the witnesses. However, he also ruled that the appellant had not given evidence of his own good character since the unsworn statement was not evidence, and he would have excluded the rebutting evidence on that ground. The appellant was convicted and appealed on the ground, *inter alia,* that the evidence was wrongly admitted.

LORD LANE CJ, delivering the judgment of the court, stated that if the appellant did not give evidence s.1(f)(ii) did not apply to enable the prosecution to adduce evidence of his bad character. The trial judge therefore had erred in admitting the evidence under s.1(f)(ii) (on this point see *R* v *Butterwasser* [1948] 1 KB 4, 4.00 ante). His Lordship continued: 'Therefore one has to turn to the question of whether, that being a material irregularity, it is right or proper that the proviso to s.2(1) of the Criminal Appeal Act 1968 should be applied and that the conviction should nevertheless stand. In order to determine this question, one has to ask oneself whether the judge was right in excluding evidence of bad character of the defendant because a statement from the dock was not evidence strictly so called, because that is what the judge did.

We have been referred to authority on this matter and the first, and possibly the most important, is *R* v *Campbell* (1979) 69 Cr App R 221, a judgment of this court. [His Lordship referred to the judgment of Bridge LJ in that case (above) and continued:]

'We respectfully agree with those suggestions. It would be indeed an extraordinary state of affairs if a defendant were to be allowed in an unsworn statement from the dock to set himself up as a man of good character, of unblemished record, who has had no trouble with the police, a man of substance, highly thought of by his friends and neighbours, immune from any contradiction, if the fact were that he was a man with a long string of convictions, whom nobody trusted. It cannot be right that such a state of affairs should exist and we agree whole-heartedly and respectfully with what Bridge LJ said on that occasion. The simple question is whether the defendant has made his character an issue in the case. If he states from the dock that he is of good character it seems to us that he clearly does make that an issue, whether the statement is classified as evidence or as a mere averment.

We are reinforced in that view by an Australian judgment to which we have been referred, namely *R* v *Macecek* [1960] Qd R 247, a decision of the Court of Criminal Appeal in Queensland. It was a majority judgment to the effect of what Bridge LJ was saying, but there are certain passages which are so striking that they can be read and incorporated in this judgment to the benefit of all.

The first passage is in the judgment of Wanstall J, one of the majority. He said (at 258):

I think that the drawing of analogies and comparisons on the procedural level cannot assist to elucidate this matter. The difficulty arises because the position is anomalous and it must be treated as an anomaly. It would be fallacious to argue that because statements of facts from the dock "are not evidence of the facts stated" (*R* v *McKenna* ([1951] QSR 299 at 307)) there is no evidence to be rebutted, and therefore such statements may not be contradicted by evidence in reply. It is true that both in form and in timing such a statement is an address or speech, but it nevertheless adds factual matter to the material for consideration by the jury, and in that sense has an evidentiary character and effect.

It seems to this court that that last sentence at any rate precisely encapsulates the effect, or the possible effect, of the statement from the dock and is a very happy exposition of the difficulty. Wanstall J then said (at 259):

In *Brown* v *The King* ((1913) 17 CLR 570 at 588) Issacs J and Powers J quoted the remark of Windeyer J in *R* v *Chantler* ((1891) 12 NSWLR 116) that the object of the provision which allowed a prisoner to make an unsworn statement from the dock "was not to enable a guilty man to escape from justice but to enable the court to discover the true facts of the case", and went on to say: "And so the court held in that case that the prisoner's statements might be contradicted by ordinary testimony in reply. If not, said Innes J it would encourage fabrication".

The final passage is from Stable J, the other judge in the majority (at 271):

So, even though the unsworn statement may be less than "evidence", its factual content —
apart from argumentative content — may have a profound effect upon the mind of the
jury. It may well provide that upon which a reasonable doubt is founded so that a guilty
man may go free, perhaps through his skill in lying fortified by the knowledge that his lie
will not be tested, or perhaps even questioned beyond a direction to the jury as to the
weight to be given it.

These pronouncements are weighty support for the view which this court has taken, namely
that in a proper case where, as here, the defendant in a statement from the dock puts his
character in issue, in the sense of setting himself up as being a man of good repute, that
evidence may, on the judge exercising his discretion, be rebutted by the prosecution calling
evidence to the contrary. So up to that point the judge having been wrong in his exclusion of
rebutting evidence on that ground, the foundation is laid for the application of the proviso,
because, quite plainly, if the judge had acted in the way which we think is correct, the
evidence which was admitted wrongly would have been properly admitted on the other
ground.
Appeal dismissed.

Holt J: I must say that the cases are not easy to follow. I think that in the case of a
statement implicating a co-defendant the balance lies against admitting evidence in
rebuttal. However, I shall give a strong direction to the jury in summing up that
nothing in Littleton's statement can prove facts not otherwise proved by evidence
against the defendant Coke.

11.15   Questions for Counsel

11.15.1   R v *Coke and Littleton.*   What considerations should Mr Bunbury have in
mind in deciding whether or not to call Coke as a witness for the prosecution if he
should plead guilty? Is Holt J correct in declining to sentence Coke before the end of
the trial?

11.15.2   R v *Coke and Littleton.*   Construct a passage to be included in Holt J's
summing up to the jury that would properly deal with Coke's election not to give
evidence in his defence.

11.15.3   R v *Coke and Littleton.*   Do you agree with the Court of Appeal that Mrs
Littleton was a competent witness for the prosecution? Had she been called as a
witness for the defence, would there have been any restrictions on the questions which
might have been asked of her in chief or in cross-examination?

11.15.4   R v *Coke and Littleton.*   Do you agree with Holt J's decision to permit
Angela to give evidence on oath? Why do you think Holt J thought it 'preferable' for
her to be sworn, as opposed to giving unsworn evidence under Section 38(1) of the
Children and Young Persons Act, 1933?

11.15.5   R v *Coke and Littleton.*   Assuming that Holt J is correct in refusing Mr
Atkyn leave to call evidence in rebuttal of Littleton's unsworn statement from the
dock, construct a passage for his summing up which would properly deal with the
effect of that statement on the case for Coke.

12 Evidence in Chief

A: INTRODUCTION

12.1 Examination in chief is the process whereby a party elicits, from a witness called by him, evidence that he anticipates will be favourable to his case. Examination in chief should be conducted on the basis of the witness's deposition or signed proof of evidence, but need not be limited to the matters therein.

With the exception of the parties themselves and of expert witnesses, the judge may order that a witness withdraw from court until called to give evidence. In criminal cases, withdrawal until this stage is the usual rule although the officer in charge of the case is habitually permitted to remain in court until at least the start of the police evidence, unless the defence specifically object. In civil cases, the rule is that witnesses remain in court unless the judge orders otherwise. In any case, the matter is one for the discretion of the judge, and the evidence of a witness who has wrongly remained in court before giving evidence is not for that sole reason inadmissible.

Because it is important that evidence be given in the words of the witness and not of counsel, evidence in chief must be conducted without recourse to leading questions. A leading question is one which suggests the answer required of the witness in direct terms, or puts words into the witness's mouth. However, for reasons of convenience, leading questions may be asked with the agreement of one's opponent, which may be limited to certain facets of the case, on preliminary matters, on matters which are not in dispute, where the witness is asked about facts already in evidence, and where the witness is ruled to be hostile (12.20 et seq). Evidence elicited by means of leading questions is not rendered inadmissible, but may lack weight. (*A Practical Approach to Evidence*, pp 325-6.)

B: REFRESHING THE MEMORY

12.2 Introductory notes

12.2.1 Before giving evidence, any witness may review his deposition or proof of evidence, or refer to any document in order to refresh his recollection of the case. There is probably no duty in law to inform an opponent that one's witnesses have referred to documents outside court. This is a proper subject for cross-examination, as affecting the weight of the witness's evidence, but a document used outside court probably cannot be called for or inspected by the cross-examiner.

12.2.2 Once in the witness-box, a witness's right to refresh his memory is more restricted. While giving evidence, a witness may refresh his memory only by referring

to a document made or verified by the witness contemporaneously with the events to
which it relates. Verification means that the witness, if he did not actually make the
document, must have read it at or promptly after the time it was made, and
acknowledged the accuracy of the relevant facts contained in it. Contemporaneity is a
matter of fact and degree in every case. A document need not have been literally
contemporaneous, but must have been made while the relevant events were fresh in
the witness's memory. Whether these conditions have been fulfilled is a matter to be
decided by the judge.

12.2.3   The cross-examiner is entitled to call for and inspect any document used by a
witness to refresh his memory while giving evidence. He may further cross-examine on
any part of the document referred to by the witness without making the document
evidence in the case. But where he cross-examines upon any other part of the
document, he opens up a new line of evidence and his opponent may insist that the
document be put in evidence. In such a case he has gone beyond cross-examination on
the evidence in chief (which was aided by the document).

12.2.4   At common law a memory-refreshing document put in evidence because of
cross-examination is not evidence of the truth of any fact stated therein. Generally, the
document will be hearsay and self-serving. What is evidence is what the witness states
orally, having refreshed his memory from the document, though in many cases where
the witness reads the document to the court but cannot actually recollect the events,
the distinction almost vanishes. The only use that the jury are entitled to make of the
document is as evidence of the consistency or inconsistency of the witness. They may
not substitute the document for his evidence. This is the position in criminal cases.

12.2.5   In civil cases, the common law rule has been abrogated by statute. The judge
may treat the document as evidence of any fact stated in it of which direct oral
evidence by the witness would be admissible. This does not rule out its use as affecting
consistency, but allows the judge to accept the whole or part of the document as
evidence of the facts stated in addition to or in substitution for the oral evidence of the
witness. (*A Practical Approach to Evidence,* pp 326–31.)

12.3   Commentary

R v *Coke and Littleton* at trial.   Mr Bunbury for the prosecution calls D/I Glanvil,
who enters the witness box and produces a note book.

12.4   Course of evidence

  D/I Glanvil: I swear by Almighty God that the evidence I shall give shall be the
truth, the whole truth and nothing but the truth. Geoffrey Glanvil, detective inspector,
attached to Oxbridge police station, My Lord.
  Mr Bunbury: Inspector, I see you are looking at a note book. Are you asking to
be allowed to refresh your memory?
  D/I Glanvil: I am, My Lord.
  Mr Bunbury: When were your notes made?
  D/I Glanvil: At Oxbridge police station after the events of the day had ended, sir.

Mr Bunbury: Were the events fresh in your mind at that time?

D/I Glanvil: They were, My Lord, and the notes were made at the first practicable opportunity during the inquiry which occupied the afternoon and evening.

Holt J: Any questions, Mr Atkyn? Mr Bacon?

Mr Atkyn: Yes, My Lord. Inspector, how long after the events did you make your notes?

D/I Glanvil: Well, sir, Mrs Littleton did not leave the police station until about 10pm and I would say it was about two hours after that. D/S Bracton and I took a meal break and attended to other matters first. The notes relating to the formal charge the next day were made immediately afterwards.

Mr Atkyn: Did you make your notes together with D/S Bracton?

D/I Glanvil: Yes, sir. In fact, after we had discussed the matter, I wrote the notes and D/S Bracton then read them over and signed them as being correct.

Mr Atkyn: So there is just the one notebook?

D/I Glanvil: Yes, sir.

Mr Bacon: I have nothing further to that, my Lord.

Holt J: Any objections?

Mr Atkyn: Yes, My Lord. On the inspector's evidence, the notes could not have been made earlier than about midnight, in so far as they refer to the events of 8 July. Of course, I make no objection to the notes of the formal charges. But the important notes would seem not to be very close in time to all the events. According to the inspector's deposition, he was called from the police station at about 4.15pm, so that from that moment, it might have been almost eight hours before any note was made.

Holt J: How should I view that interval of time?

Mr Atkyn: Your Lordship is not considering the actual length of time as such, but the likelihood of accuracy. In my submission, this length of time is unacceptable. On the evidence of the inspector, there was an avoidable delay of some two hours.

Mr Bunbury: My Lord, in my submission, that is not the way to approach this case. The question is whether the events were fresh in the inspector's mind. (Mr Bunbury dealt with the facts and continued.) The courts have permitted reference after considerably greater delay. In *R* v *Langton* the relevant document had been compiled over a period of two weeks.

R v *Langton* (1876) 2 QBD 296 (CCR)

The defendant was a timekeeper, and C a pay clerk, in the employment of a colliery company. It was the duty of the defendant every fortnight to give a list of the days worked by the workmen to a clerk who entered the days and the wages due in respect of them in a time book. At pay time it was the duty of the defendant to read out from the time book the number of days worked by each workman to C, who paid the wages accordingly. C saw the entries in the time book while the defendant was reading them out. The defendant was convicted of obtaining money by false pretences from the company. The question was whether C should have been permitted to refresh his memory from the time book.

LORD COCKBURN CJ: 'With regard to the first point, the propriety of allowing the witness to refresh his memory by means of the time book, I think he was rightly allowed to do so. If the witness had only seen the entries in the absence of the prisoner, the case might be different. There would then be obvious dangers in admitting such a use of the book, which do not exist in the present case. Here the entries were read aloud by the prisoner himself, and seen by the witness at the time of reading, and he made payments in accordance with them.'
(LORD COLERIDGE CJ, CLEASBY B, POLLOCK B, and FIELD J concurred.)

Conviction affirmed.

And in more recent times in *R* v *Fotheringham* [1975] Crim LR 710 (CA), a witness was permitted to refer to his statement to the police made twenty-two days after the event, even though he was an accomplice. In my submission, the delay here is not abnormal, and is perfectly consistent with a clear recollection. The officers had the advantage of their combined recollections and had been continuously involved with this inquiry during the afternoon and evening.

Holt J: The collaboration in making the notes, of course, is quite usual and to be encouraged.

Mr Bunbury: My Lord, in *R* v *Bass* this practice was specifically endorsed by the Court of Criminal Appeal.

R v **Bass** [1953] 1 QB 680 (CCA)

The appellant was convicted of shopbreaking and larceny. The only evidence against him was contained in statements amounting to a confession of guilt which he was alleged to have made, before he was charged, during an interrogation by two police officers at a police station. At the trial the officers gave evidence and read their accounts of the interview from their notebooks. As these accounts appeared to be identical, and the officers denied that they had been prepared in collaboration, the defendant asked that the jury should be allowed to inspect the notebooks, but the application was refused.

BYRNE J, delivering the judgment of the court, said: 'With regard to the second ground of appeal, the matter stood in this way. The officers' notes were almost identical. They were not made at the time of the interview. One officer made his notes after the appellant had been charged, and the other officer made his an hour later. Mr Crowder suggested to the officers in cross-examination that they had collaborated. They denied that suggestion. This court has observed that police officers nearly always deny that they have collaborated in the making of notes, and we cannot help wondering why they are the only class of society who do not collaborate in such a matter. It seems to us that nothing could be more natural or proper when two persons have been present at an interview with a third person than that they should afterwards make sure that they have a correct version of what was said. Collaboration would appear to be a better explanation of almost identical notes than the possession of a superhuman memory...
The deputy chairman's desire to preserve the confidential nature of the notebooks could probably quite easily have been achieved with the assistance of a pin or a piece of sticking plaster so that only the relevant pages could be read. Be that as it may, however, the jury should have been permitted to see the notebooks. The credibility and accuracy of the two police officers was a vital matter, for it was upon their evidence, and their evidence alone, that the whole of the case against the appellant rested, and as they had denied collaboration in the making of their notes, the jury should have been given the opportunity of examining them.'
Appeal allowed.

Finally, My Lord, contemporaneity is a question of fact and degree in every case and is a matter for Your Lordship.
(Holt J heard argument from Mr Bacon, and on the facts before him held that the notes were sufficiently contemporaneous, and permitted D/I Glanvil to refresh his memory from them.)

12.5 Commentary

R v *Coke and Littleton* at trial. D/I Glanvil's evidence in chief has progressed to the point where he is ready to deal with the conversation which he overheard between Mr and Mrs Littleton. The inspector seeks leave to refresh his memory from the transcript of the tape-recording as to what was said.

12.6 Argument

Holt J: How did the transcript come to be made?

D/I Glanvil: My Lord, it was made from a handwritten note of the recording made by a secretary the day after the conversation. I personally checked that note against the recording and found it to be accurate. I then caused a typed transcript to be prepared.

Mr Bunbury: My Lord, in my submission there is no reason why the transcript cannot be referred to. First, the recording is itself a contemporaneous record, and the fact that it is in the form of a cassette rather than a written document does not matter, as was pointed out in *R v Mills; R v Rose* [1962] 1 WLR 1152 (CCA). Second, where an original contemporaneous record is shown to exist, it is proper to refer to a later copy, provided that it is shown to be a true copy, as D/I Glanvil has proved by his evidence in this case. This not infrequently occurs where officers take a rough note of an interview and write it up in fuller form afterwards. I would invite Your Lordship's attention to:

Attorney-General's Reference (No. 3 of 1979) (1979) 69 Cr App R 411 (CA)

The defendants were charged on two counts of criminal deception. As the complainant was a senile witness the prosecution relied upon answers given by the defendants to the police at interviews. The first police officer to give evidence at the trial told the court that he had made brief jottings of questions and answers during interviews with the defendants and within two hours had compiled his notebook with the assistance of the jottings. The judge ruled that the officer could only refresh his memory from the original jottings and not from his notebook. As the officer could not decipher many of the jottings or recollect the full content of the questions and answers there was insufficient evidence to support a conviction. The Attorney-General referred for the opinion of the court the questions:

(a) Whether a police officer who has taken brief jottings in the course of interviewing an accused person, and within a short time thereafter made a full note in his notebook incorporating not only those brief jottings, but expanding thereon from his then recollection, should be permitted to refresh his memory from that notebook at the accused person's subsequent trial?

(b) Whether in the aforementioned circumstances the police officer is bound to retain the original jottings and disclose their existence to the court of trial?

(c) Whether in the above circumstances it is the duty of the prosecution in such circumstances to make available to the court of trial and the defence copies of the police officer's original brief jottings?

LORD WIDGERY CJ, giving the judgment of the court, said: 'Why the learned judge took this attitude, we confess we do not know. Looking at paragraph 515 of *Archbold* (40th ed), a book available to all the judges, one finds this: "The rule may be stated as follows: a witness may refresh his memory by reference to any writing made or verified by himself concerning and contemporaneously with, the facts to which he testifies. 'Contemporaneously' is a somewhat misleading word in the context of the memory refreshing rule. It is sufficient, for the purposes of the rule, if the writing was made or verified at a time when the facts were still fresh in the witness's memory." That, in our view, is the correct rule...As a side issue one might bear in mind that the judge says it has always been the practice to make the normal note, if I may so describe it, available to the defence on cross-examination. So one must make a two-stage note. Counsel for the defence is entitled to examine the police officer's notebook to see whether his entries are consistent with his evidence or not. That is exactly the same thing as saying whether the note has been made in two stages rather than one. That is only a subsidiary point.'

(Mr Atkyn and Mr Bacon indicated that having heard these authorities cited, they had no objection, and Holt J allowed D/I Glanvil to refresh his memory from the transcript.)

12.7 Commentary

R v *Coke and Littleton* at trial.   Mr Bunbury for the prosecution calls D/S Bracton to give evidence.

12.8 Course of evidence

D/S Bracton: I swear by Almighty God that the evidence I shall give shall be the truth, the whole truth and nothing but the truth. Dennis Bracton, detective sergeant, attached to Oxbridge police station, my Lord. May I refresh my memory from the note made by D/I Glanvil?
Mr Bunbury: Were you present when that note was made?
D/S Bracton: I was, sir.
Mr Bunbury: Was the note the product of your joint recollections?
D/S Bracton: That is correct, sir.
Mr Bunbury: What did you do after the note had been made?
D/S Bracton: I read the note and signed it to indicate my agreement that the contents were accurate, My Lord.
Holt J: Have you looked at the note since then?
D/S Bracton: I read it over again today outside court before the trial began, My Lord.
Holt J: Any objections?
Mr Atkyn: My Lord, I will not pursue again the question of contemporaneity, as Your Lordship was against me in the case of D/I Glanvil, and the issue is the same. And I would accept that this officer properly verified the note, as occurred for example in:

Anderson v **Whalley** (1852) 3 Car & Kir 54 (CP)

(Before TALFOURD J)
Case for the negligent navigation of a vessel, whereby the vessel was injured. In the course of the cause the captain of the defendant's vessel was put into the witness box. He deposed that the ship's log, which he produced, was written by the mate, and that the mate was and had been for some time serving abroad on the coast of Portugal; that he had himself read the log about a week after it was written; that the matters to which it referred were then fresh in his mind, and he at that time thought the narrative it contained to be correct. It was then proposed that the witness should refresh his memory by looking at the log-book. Byles, Serjt, for the plaintiffs, objected. The witness had not himself written the log-book, and therefore could not be allowed to refresh his memory by it. The absence of the mate was not an excuse...The learned judge overruled the objection.

But I am concerned that this witness has been looking at documents before giving evidence and submitting himself to the court's ruling on how his memory might be refreshed.

Mr Bunbury: My Lord, D/S Bracton looked at the note on my instructions, so that his evidence might be more helpful to the jury. There is the clear authority of the Court of Appeal for the practice in:

R v *Richardson* [1971] 2 QB 484 (CA)

Before the trial of the defendant on two charges of burglary and attempted burglary relating to offences which had taken place about 18 months earlier, four prosecution witnesses were shown the statements which they had made to the police a few weeks after the offences. Two of those witnesses had positively identified the defendant, and identification was the sole issue at the trial. The defence submitted that the evidence of all four witnesses was, in the circumstances, inadmissible. The trial judge rejected those submissions. The defendant was convicted and appealed.

SACHS LJ, giving the judgment of the court said: '...it is...necessary to consider what should be the general approach of the court to there being shown in this way to witnesses their statements — which were not "contemporaneous" within the meaning of that word as normally applied to documents used to refresh memory.

First, it is to be observed that it is the practice of the courts not to allow a witness to refresh his memory in the witness-box by reference to written statements unless made contemporaneously. Secondly, it has been recognised in a circular issued in April 1969 with the approval of the Lord Chief Justice and the judges of the Queen's Bench Division (the repositories of the common law) that witnesses for the prosecution in criminal cases are normally (though not in all circumstances) entitled, if they so request, to copies of any statements taken from them by police officers. Thirdly, it is to be noted that witnesses for the defence are normally, as is known to be the practice, allowed to have copies of their statements and to refresh their memories from them at any time up to the moment when they go into the witness-box — indeed, Mr Sedgemore was careful not to submit that there was anything wrong about that. Fourthly, no one has ever suggested that in civil proceedings witnesses may not see their statements up to the time when they go into the witness-box. One has only to think for a moment of witnesses going into the box to deal with accidents which took place five or six years previously to conclude that it would be highly unreasonable if they were not allowed to see them.

Is there, then, anything wrong in the witnesses in this case having been offered an opportunity to see that which they were entitled to ask for and to be shown on request? In a case such as the present, is justice more likely to be done if a witness may not see a statement made by him at a time very much closer to that of the incident?...

It is true that by the practice of the courts of this country a line is drawn at the moment when a witness enters the witness-box; when giving evidence there in chief he cannot refresh his memory except by a document which, to quote the words of *Phipson on Evidence,* 11th ed (1970), p 634, para 1528: "must have been written either at the time of the transaction or so shortly afterwards that the facts were fresh in his memory." (Incidentally, this definition does provide a measure of elasticity and should not be taken to confine witnesses to an over-short period.) This is, moreover, a practice which the courts can enforce: when a witness is in the box the court can see that he complies with it.

The courts, however, must take care not to deprive themselves by new, artificial rules of practice of the best chances of learning the truth. The courts are under no compulsion unnecessarily to follow on a matter of practice the lure of the rules of logic in order to produce unreasonable results which would hinder the course of justice. Obviously it would be wrong if several witnesses were handed statements in circumstances which enabled one to compare with another what each had said. But there can be no general rule (which, incidentally, would be unenforceable, unlike the rule as to what can be done in the witness-box) that witnesses may not before trial see the statements which they made at some period reasonably close to the time of the event which is the subject of the trial. Indeed, one can imagine many cases, particularly those of a complex nature, where such a rule would militate very greatly against the interests of justice.

On the basis of this general approach, this court now returns to the facts of the present case. There had been great delay in the matter coming before the court and it appears to this court that nothing unreasonable was done in the particular circumstances.'
Appeal dismissed.

Holt J: Did you inform Mr Atkyn or Mr Bacon that you had given those instructions to D/S Bracton?
Mr Bunbury: No, My Lord. I took the view that it was unnecessary to do so in this case, where the witness had verified the note contemporaneously. Had the document not been contemporaneously verified, I would have done so. But I would observe that there is no duty to do so beyond a duty of appropriate conduct by counsel. I would refer Your Lordship to:

R v Westwell [1976] 2 All ER 812 (CA)

The appellant was charged with assault occasioning actual bodily harm. Before the trial, which took place 11 months after the fight which was the subject of the charge, certain prosecution witnesses asked if they could see their written statements and they were allowed to do so. The prosecution did not inform the defence that this had been done, but the fact that it had became known to the defence, who submitted that in consequence the jury ought to be directed to acquit. The judge refused and the appellant was convicted.

BRIDGE LJ, delivering the judgment of the court, stated the facts and continued: 'There is no general rule that prospective witnesses may not, before giving evidence at a trial, see the statements which they made at or near the time of the events of which they are to testify. They may see them whether they make a request to do so or merely accept an offer to allow them to do so. On the other hand, there is no rule that witnesses must be allowed to see their statements before giving evidence. There may be cases where there is reason to suppose that the witness has some sinister or improper purpose in wanting to see his statement and it is in the interests of justice that he should be denied the opportunity. Examples are suggested in the Home Office circular and in the judgment of this court in *R v Richardson* [1971] 2 QB 484. However, in most cases and particularly where, as often happens, there is a long interval between the alleged offence and the trial, the interests of justice are likely to be best served and witnesses will be more fairly treated if, before giving evidence, they are allowed to refresh their recollection by reference to their own statements made near the time of the events in question. As was said by the Supreme Court of Hong Kong in 1966 [in *Lau Pak Ngam v The Queen* [1966] Crim LR 443] in passages quoted with approval by this court in *R v Richardson,* if a witness is deprived of this opportunity his testimony in the witness box becomes more a test of memory than truthfulness; and refusal of access to statements would tend to create difficulties for honest witnesses but would be likely to do little to hamper dishonest witnesses.. We have all, from time to time, seen the plight of an apparently honest witness, subjected to captious questioning about minor differences between his evidence in the witness box and the statement he made long ago and has never seen since, although his tormentor has it in his hand and has studied it in detail. Although such cross-examination frequently generates in the jury obvious sympathy with the witness and obvious irritation with the cross-examiner, it must leave a witness who has come to court to do his honest best with a smarting sense of having been treated unfairly.

Neither in the approved statement in the Home Office circular, nor in the judgment of the court in *R v Richardson,* is it laid down that the Crown must inform the defence that a prosecution witness has been allowed to look at his written statement before giving evidence. In *R v Richardson* the defence first discovered the fact for themselves in the course of cross-examination of a prosecution witness. The court made no criticism of the Crown on that account, nor was it invited to do so. Moreover, the decision of the trial judge, refusing to allow previous witnesses to be recalled for cross-examination about their statements, was upheld because in the particular facts of that case no prejudice was thereby caused to the defence.

Since hearing the argument in this appeal, our attention has been called to the decision of the Division Court in *Worley* v *Bentley* [1976] 2 All ER 449 in which the same point arose. The court held that it was desirable but not essential that the defence should be informed that witnesses have seen their statements. We agree. In some cases the fact that a witness has read his statement before going into the witness box may be relevant to the weight which can properly be attached to his evidence and injustice might be caused to the defendant if the jury were left in ignorance of that fact.

Accordingly, if the prosecution is aware that statements have been seen by witnesses it will be appropriate to inform the defence. But if, for any reason, this is not done, the omission cannot of itself be a ground for acquittal. If the prosecution tell the defence that the witness has been allowed to see his statement the defence can make such use of the information as it thinks prudent, but in any event the defence, where such a fact may be material, can ask the witness directly when giving evidence whether the witness has recently seen his statement. Where such information is material it does not ultimately matter whether it is volunteered by the prosecution or elicited by the defence. If the mere fact that the prosecution had not volunteered the information were a bar to conviction, this would be an artificial and arbitrary rule more appropriate to a game or a sporting contest than to a judicial process. The question for the court is whether, in the event, the trial can be continued without prejudice or risk of injustice to the defendant.

In the present case the defence knew, before the prosecution case was concluded, that the witnesses had seen their statements. The defence could have applied to recall the witnesses if they thought cross-examination about the statements worthwhile. They could have made whatever points they wished to make with the jury about the weight to be attached to the prosecution evidence.'

Appeal dismissed.

(Holt J held that no irregularity had occurred on the facts before him, and allowed D/S Bracton to refresh his memory from the note.)

12.9 Commentary

R v *Coke and Littleton* at trial. Mr Bunbury for the prosecution calls WPC Raymond to give evidence. Mr Bunbury indicates that he has a special application to make in her case.

12.10 Argument

Mr Bunbury: My Lord, I am instructed that this officer's notebook cannot be found, and in those circumstances, I ask that she be permitted to refer to her deposition. I propose to ask WPC Raymond to give evidence as to how her witness statement came to be made. If it was made by copying from her contemporaneous note, then the decision in *Attorney-General's Reference* (No. 3 of 1979) to which Your Lordship was referred at an earlier stage of the trial would permit her to use the statement. But My Lord, there is also direct authority in the case of:

R v Cheng (1976) 63 Cr App R 20 (CA)

Police officers kept observation on a number of men, including the defendant, who were suspected of peddling heroin. The defendant was later charged with unlawfully supplying a preparation of a dangerous drug, and at his trial one of the officers who had kept observation was called as a prosecution witness. He no longer had the relevant notebook and sought to refresh his memory from a statement he had prepared from his notebook and used at the committal proceedings. The defence objected to the use of the statement because it did not contain the notes about the other men who had been under surveillance and was thus a partial not an exact copy of the notebook. The trial judge ruled that the officer could refer to his statement and the defendant was convicted.

LAWTON LJ, giving the judgment of the court, said: 'In *Burton* v *Plummer* (1834) 2 A&E 341, the question before the Court was whether a witness could look at a copy of an original note which he had made. The Court adjudged that he could; but he had to be able to say that the copy was an accurate copy of the original note.
It was almost inevitable after that case that some lawyer would raise the question as to what was an accurate copy. That very problem was considered by the House of Lords in *Horne* v *MacKenzie* (1839) 6 Cl & Fin 628. The point arose in this way: I read from the headnote: "A, a surveyor, made a survey or report, which he furnished to his employers: being afterwards called as a witness, he produced a printed copy of this report, on the margin of which he had, two days before, to assist him in giving his explanations as a witness, made a few jottings. The report had been made up from his original notes, of which it was in substance, though not in words, a transcript...." In other words, as appears clear when one looks at the details of the case what he was looking at in the witness box was not strictly a copy at all of his original note. He was allowed to refresh his memory from it and the House of Lords seems to have taken the view, albeit *obiter*, that there was nothing wrong in his doing so.
The judgment of the House was delivered by Lord Cottenham: he said at p 645: "If your Lordships think that there should be a new trial on this ground, it will be unnecessary to give any decision on the question of evidence. But I may say that in my opinion the witness was, under the circumstances of this case, entitled to refer to the paper to refresh his memory."
In our judgment that opinion of the Lord Chancellor resolves this case. What the police constable was doing in this case was what the surveyor had done in that case. He had transcribed that part of his note which he thought was relevant. We can see nothing wrong in that. Indeed if we had felt bound to say that it was wrong for him to refresh his memory from his statement, we would have brought about an absurdity, because it is now established by Richardson (1971) 55 Cr App R 244; [1971] 2 QB 484...that a witness can see his original statement outside court. If he could read it right up to the court door and learn it off by heart, but was forbidden in the witness box to look at it at all, this would be a triumph of legalism over common sense.
What seems to us to be the position is this. If the statement in this case, or any other transcription of notes in other cases, is substantially what is in the notes and there is evidence to that effect, then the judge should allow the witness to refresh his memory from the statement or transcription as the case may be. But if, after investigation, it turns out that the statement or transcription bears little relation to the original note, then a different situation arises. The judge in the exercise of his discretion would be entitled to refuse to allow a witness to refresh his memory from such an imperfect source of information.
In this case we are satisfied, as the trial judge was, that the statement was a reliable source of information.'
Appeal dismissed.

(WPC Raymond gave evidence that her original note had been made immediately after the events, that her witness statement dated 16 July 1979 had been made by copying out her notes, and that her notebook had been lost following an administrative error at Oxbridge police station. Holt J permitted her to refresh her memory from the witness statement.)

12.11 Commentary

R v *Coke and Littleton* on appeal against conviction. At trial, Mr Atkyn for Coke cross-examined D/I Glanvil extensively as to the contents of his notebook, having first called for and inspected the book. At the end of cross-examination, Mr Bunbury applied to Holt J that the notebook should be admitted into evidence and placed before the jury. Over the objection of defence counsel, this was done. Mr Atkyn contends that Holt J erred in admitting the notebook. He further complains of the following passage in the summing-up:

Members of the jury, there were times during the cross-examination of Inspector Glanvil when, as you may think, he appeared hesitant. On some occasions, discrepancies between what he had said and the corresponding entries in his notebook were pointed out to him. The inspector agreed that he was unable to account for these discrepancies beyond saying that if something was in his notebook, it must be correct. Well, members of the jury, all witnesses forget things — it is just human nature with all of us, isn't it? And you may think especially so with a busy senior police officer who has to deal with and give evidence in many different cases. Happily, however, that notebook has been admitted into evidence, and you are able to fill in many of the gaps left in the evidence. You may think that by putting the notebook and the inspector's present recollection of the events together, you are able to form a pretty coherent and full picture of what occurred. Of course, it is open to you, if you wish, to say that the lack of recollection causes you to give little weight to the inspector's evidence. It is entirely a matter for you.

12.12 Argument

Leach LJ: Mr Atkyn, I am not sure I understand why this document should not have been admitted. If you call for and inspect a document in the possession of your opponent, he is entitled to have it admitted into evidence.

Mr Atkyn: With respect, I think Your Lordship has in mind a rather different rule applying to evidentiary documents, which if called for from the possession of an opposite party must be made evidence if that opposite party so desires (see 13.22 post). But what the learned judge had here was a memory-refreshing document. In my submission, My Lord, I was entitled to cross-examine on the notebook, because I went no further than the facts concerning which D/I Glanvil had refreshed his memory from the book, and about which he had given evidence. There is authority for this in:

Senat v *Senat* [1965] P 172

In a defended suit for divorce involving charges of adultery between the husband and several women, two of the women gave evidence. The wife also sought to rely upon entries in Miss H's address book. The address book was identified by Miss H and put in evidence. Counsel for the husband, to whom it had been shown, did not object, but he did not call for and inspect it; he did, however, cross-examine Miss H on it.

SIR JOCELYN SIMON P said: 'In my view the mere inspection of a document does not render it evidence which counsel inspecting it is bound to put in. I think that the true rules are as follows: Where a document is used to refresh a witness's memory, cross-examining counsel may inspect that document in order to check it, without making it evidence. Moreover he may cross-examine upon it without making it evidence provided that his cross-examination does not go further than the parts which are used for refreshing the memory of the witness: *Gregory* v *Tavernor* (1833) 6 C&P 280. But if a party calls for and inspects a document held by the other party, he is bound to put it in evidence if he is required to do so: *Wharam* v *Routledge* (1805) 5 Esp 235. The distinction is shown clearly in the ruling of Sir Cresswell Cresswell, who had, of course, great experience both in the courts of common law and in the divorce court, in *Palmer* v *Maclear and M'Grath* (1858) 1 Sw & Tr 149, 151.'

(Mr Atkyn and Mr Bunbury were then invited to address the court on the question whether Mr Atkyn's cross-examination had gone beyond the facts about which D/I Glanvil had refreshed his memory. The court indicated that they had formed the preliminary view that the notebook should not have been placed before the jury.)

Leach LJ: Mr Atkyn, we should, however, like to hear you on the summing-up. Assuming that the notebook was rightly admitted, why do you say the learned judge's direction was at fault?

Mr Atkyn: My Lords, the learned judge implied that the jury were entitled to make use of the notebook as evidence of the truth of its contents, whereas in a criminal case, they are entitled to use it to assess the consistency or otherwise of the witness, and so to assess the weight of his evidence, but for no further purpose. They may not substitute the notebook for the evidence for the purpose of proving the facts in issue.

East LJ: Why do you say in a criminal case?

Mr Atkyn: My Lord, because for civil cases, Parliament has expressly altered the rule by statute. If Your Lordship would look at:

Civil Evidence Act 1968, s.3(2)

Nothing in this Act shall affect any of the rules of law relating to the circumstances in which, where a person called as a witness in any civil proceedings is cross-examined on a document used by him to refresh his memory, that document may be made evidence in those proceedings; and where a document or any part of a document is received in evidence in any such proceedings by virtue of any such rule of law, any statement made in that document or part by the person using the document to refresh his memory shall by virtue of this subsection be admissible as evidence of any fact stated therein of which direct oral evidence by him would be admissible.

But in criminal cases, the position is still governed by the common law rules. Your Lordships will observe that even in civil cases, the common law rules governing the admission of such documents were left intact; only their evidential value, if admitted, was provided for. In criminal cases, the position remains wholly unchanged. Your Lordships' court had occasion quite recently to re-affirm this in:

R v *Virgo* (1978) 67 Cr App R 323 (CA)

The defendant, the head of the Obscene Publications Squad, was convicted of conspiracy and corruptly accepting bribes. At his trial the judge granted the prosecution permission to allow a leading prosecution witness — a self-confessed dealer in pornography and a very unsavoury character — to use his diaries to refresh his memory while giving evidence, and copies of the diaries were before the jury. The object of the diaries was to assist the witness to give accurate dates. In summing up, the judge directed the jury that the diaries were the most important documents in the case against the defendant, that the entries were powerful evidence, pointing to a corrupt relationship between him and the witness, and that although they did not amount to corroboration in law, they were very important in relation to the witness' evidence.

GEOFFREY LANE LJ said: 'There is always a danger in circumstances such as these when attention has been focussed on a particular document for a long period of time, and when the document has been subjected to a minute and line by line analysis, as these diaries were that the document will achieve an importance which it does not warrant. It was most important in this case that the status of these diaries should be clearly understood throughout the trial and particularly at the end of the trial when the learned judge came to sum up the matter to the jury.

Those diaries were never more, at best, than a means whereby Humphreys might be able to give accurate dates and accurate chapter and verse for the incidents in respect of which he was giving evidence. They were never more than documents prepared by Humphreys and Humphreys was a self-confessed dealer in pornography. He was an accomplice and he was, on any view, a highly unsavoury character in many other ways. His evidence, par excellence, required corroboration.

The learned judge made perfectly plain to the jury, in impeccable language at the outset of his direction, the general law relating to corroboration. No one complained about that for a moment, nor could they complain. So far as Humphreys' diaries were concerned, not only did his evidence in general require corroboration, but by the same token, the answers which he gave about his diaries required corroboration. At the very highest, if the jury were convinced that the diaries were genuine, they showed a degree of consistency in Humphreys which otherwise might have been lacking, just as a complaint by the victim of a sexual assault, if made at the first reasonable opportunity thereafter, may show consistency in his or her evidence, though that analogy, one concedes, is not altogether apt. What the diaries could not under any circumstances do, was to support the oral evidence of Humphreys other than in a very limited way which we have already endeavoured to describe. In no way were they evidence of the truth of their contents.

Taking the two steps as set out in the decision in *Turner* (1975) 61 Cr App R 67, to which we have been referred, the diaries might assist the jury to say, in the first instance, that the witness in question was not wholly devoid of credit but what they could in no circumstances do was to contribute to the second stage of *Turner (supra),* namely the search for corroboration.'

Appeal allowed.

My Lords, while the learned judge did call attention to the use of the notebook on the question of weight, he also gave the jury the clear impression that they could make use of the book as evidence of the facts recorded in it by D/I Glanvil. In my submission, this was a serious misdirection.

C: PREVIOUS CONSISTENT STATEMENTS

12.13 Introductory notes

12.13.1 At common law, a witness is not permitted to relate his own statements on previous occasions consistent with his present evidence, either as evidence of any fact stated by him or to prove his consistency. The rule extends to evidence of previous consistent conduct.

12.13.2 The common law rule no longer applies to civil cases, because previous consistent statements (which have a hearsay character) are admissible as evidence of the facts stated by virtue of and subject to the provisions of Part 1 of the Civil Evidence Act 1968, (see 8.4 et seq). In criminal cases, the common law rules continue to apply, subject to the following exceptional instances, in which previous consistent statements are admitted for good reason, and usually for a limited purpose.

12.13.2.1 Statements admissible under the *res gestae* rule are not objectionable merely because they confirm the evidence of the witness who made them. (See 6.6.2 and 6.8 ante).

12.13.2.2 Statements made by the defendant in criminal cases when taxed with or questioned about the offence charged are usually admitted, even where consistent with his defence at trial, though the evidential value of such statements presents difficulties (see 7.1.9 ante).

12.13.2.3 A witness may relate his previous identification of the defendant as the perpetrator of the offence charged, even though this is consistent with his evidence at trial. It seems that such evidence is admissible to prove the guilt of the defendant as charged, and not merely for the purpose of confirming the evidence of the witness. Where the prosecution case depends wholly or substantially on evidence of visual identification, the judge should withdraw the evidence from the jury if the evidence is of poor quality and unsupported by other evidence implicating the defendant. If it is of good quality, the judge should nonetheless warn the jury in clear terms of the dangers of identification evidence, and should direct their attention specifically to any weaknesses in it, and to the circumstances in which the identification was made. The jury should in every case be warned to exercise caution in evaluating such evidence. In general, a witness should not be permitted to identify the defendant in court (a 'dock identification') unless the witness has previously identified the defendant in controlled circumstances at a properly conducted identification parade.

12.13.2.4   In sexual cases (whether the offence charged is alleged to be committed against a male or a female) but not in other cases, the complainant is permitted to state that at the first practicable opportunity after the commission of the offence, he or she made a complaint to another person and to relate the terms of the complaint. The other person may also give evidence to the same effect. What amounts to the first practicable opportunity is a question of fact and degree in every case. The complaint must have been spontaneous, and while it is not objectionable merely because given in response to questioning by the hearer, it will be inadmissible if it is induced by leading or suggestive questions from a reluctant complainant. A recent complaint is admissible only for either or both of two purposes: to confirm the evidence of the complainant and as relevant to the issue of consent, if applicable. If the complainant does not give evidence and consent is not in issue, the complaint is inadmissible. The complaint is never capable of corroborating the evidence of the complainant, because it does not come from an independent source. (see 14.3 post)

12.13.2.5   Where it is suggested to a witness in cross-examination that he has fabricated his evidence since a specific date or period, the witness is permitted to prove that on an occasion prior to that date or period, he made a statement consistent with his evidence. This exception does not apply to a general suggestion of untruthfulness without reference to a time scale. In criminal cases, the previous statement is evidence which goes only to rebut the charge of recent fabrication, and no further. But in civil cases, statute specifically provides that the statement may be used as evidence of any fact stated in it of which direct oral evidence by the witness would be admissible. (*A Practical Approach to Evidence*, pp 331–43.)

12.14   Commentary

R v *Coke and Littleton* on appeal against conviction.   At trial, Angela Blackstone identified Littleton as her assailant only with nervousness and great hesitation. Mr Bacon for Littleton complains that evidence of Angela's ·previous identification of Littleton in Plowden Drive was inadmissible. This evidence was called from Angela herself, and from the police officers and Mrs Blackstone who were also present. Mr Bacon further complains that even if the evidence was admissible, Holt J should have withdrawn it from the jury as being too unreliable, or failing this should have directed the jury specifically to consider the circumstances of the identification with care and caution and should have expressly directed their attention to any weaknesses in it. The passage in the summing up relating to this identification is as follows:

> Members of the jury, the defendant Littleton says, and has from the very first said, that Angela had identified the wrong man. He has presented you with an alibi. He says simply, 'I was not there, it must have been someone else'. So obviously, the question whether Angela's identification of him was correct or not is crucial to his defence. And you will bear in mind what I have said already regarding the burden and standard of proof. You may think that you must look with great care at the circumstances in which the identification was made. But bear in mind also that very little time had elapsed since the commission of the offence, and that Angela had a considerable time in which to make her observation. The rest depends on the weight which you are prepared, having seen her in the witness box, and having seen her cross-examined, to attach to her evidence.

12.15 Argument

Leach LJ: Mr Bacon, how do you support your ground based on admissibility? Is it not rather late in the day to be taking this particular point?

Mr Bacon: My Lords, this case involves a previous consistent statement, which both on authority and principle ought not to be admitted unless some clearly warranted exception can be found. I would refer Your Lordships, for example, to:

R v Roberts [1942] 1 All ER 187 (CCA)

The defendant was convicted of murdering a girl by shooting her. His defence was that the gun went off accidentally while he was trying to make up a quarrel with the girl. Two days after the event he told his father that the defence would be accident. The trial judge would not allow this conversation to be proved.

HUMPHREYS J, delivering the judgment of the court, said: 'In our view the judge was perfectly right in refusing to admit that evidence, because it was in law inadmissible. It might have been, and, perhaps, by some judges would have been, allowed to be given on the ground that it was the evidence which the defence desired to have given, was harmless, and there was no strenuous opposition on the part of the prosecution. Such evidence might have been allowed to be given, but the judge was perfectly entitled to take the view which he did, that in law that evidence was inadmissible. The law upon the matter is well-settled. The rule relating to this is sometimes put in this way, that a party is not permitted to make evidence for himself. That law applies to civil cases as well as to criminal cases. For instance, if A and B enter into an oral contract, and some time afterwards there is a difference of opinion as to what were the actual terms agreed upon and there is litigation about it, one of those persons would not be permitted to call his partner to say: "My partner a day or two after told me what his view of the contract was and that he had agreed to do" so and so. So, in a criminal case, an accused person is not permitted to call evidence to show that, after he was charged with a criminal offence, he told a number of persons what his defence was going to be, and the reason for the rule appears to us to be that such testimony has no evidential value. It is because it does not assist in the elucidation of the matters in dispute that the evidence is said to be inadmissible on the ground that it is irrelevant. It would not help the jury in this case in the least to be told that the appellant said to a number of persons, whom he saw while he was waiting his trial, or on bail if he was on bail; that his defence was this, that or the other. The evidence asked to be admitted was that the father had been told by his son that it was an accident. We think the evidence was properly refused. Of course, if the statement had been made to the father just at the time of the shooting, that would have been a totally different matter, because it has always been regarded as admissible that a person should be allowed to give in evidence any statement accompanying an act so that it may explain the act. It was put by counsel for the appellant that the statement might be admissible on the ground that the accused had been asked in cross-examination, and it had been suggested to him in cross-examination that this story of accident was one which he had recently concocted. If any such question had been put, undeniably the evidence would have been admissible as showing it was not recently concocted, because the accused had said so on the very day the incident occurred. The answer is that no such question had been put, and no suggestion made, to the accused.' [The defendant's appeal was allowed on other grounds.]

My Lords, it is no answer to this submission to say that Angela's identification was an act or conduct rather than a statement. The following case shows that self-serving conduct is treated in law in the same way:

Corke v Corke and Cooke [1958] P 93 (CA)

A husband petitioned for divorce on the ground of adultery. The wife had been in the co-respondent's bedroom, and, when challenged by the husband a few minutes later, they denied adultery. Shortly after that, the wife phoned her doctor requesting him to come at once and examine them with a view to establishing that recent intercourse had not taken place. The doctor declined to examine them, being of opinion that any negative evidence which he might obtain would be valueless. At the hearing of the husband's petition the judge admitted the evidence of the wife, the co-respondent and the doctor as to the phone conversation and dismissed the petition. The husband appealed, contending that the judge had misdirected himself in law in admitting evidence of the contents of the telephone conversation.

HODSON LJ said: 'A good illustration of the rule as to the rejection of statements not amounting to admissions is contained in *Jones v South Eastern & Chatham Railway Co* (1918) 87 LJKB 775. A woman's hand was injured by blood poisoning. She alleged that the injury was caused by pinching her thumb on a nail while working on her employers' premises. They alleged that the injury was received at her home. Evidence was heard of statements made by her to certain persons that she had done it at home and evidence to the contrary effect of statements made by her, inter alia, to a doctor was rejected as inadmissible. It was argued on her behalf that such evidence should be received to substantiate the consistency of her story as to the accident and to show that it was not subsequently fabricated, especially as evidence of statements adverse to her interest had been admitted. This argument was not accepted. It was held by the Court of Appeal that the statements in the appellant's favour were rightly rejected as inadmissible. Swinfen Eady LJ said ibid 777: "It was argued that there is in certain cases a rule under which a witness may be asked to give particulars of what a person has said shortly after an occurrence, and the complaint that such a person may have made shortly after an occurrence, not as being evidence of the facts complained of but as being evidence of the consistency of the story of the complainant from beginning to end, and it is said that such a question ought to have been admitted in the present case on that principle. The answer is twofold; first, that the principle has no application to a case of this kind. No doubt in cases especially of violence upon women and girls the rule is established under which a question of that kind is allowed to be put, and a recent statement is allowed to be given in evidence — see *R v Lillyman* [1896] 2 QB 167 — that is to say, that upon the trial of an indictment for offences against women and girls involving violence, the fact that complaint is made by the prosecutrix shortly after the occurrence, with the particulars of the complaint made, so far as they relate to the charge against the prisoner, are allowed to be given in evidence on the part of the prosecution, not as being evidence of the facts complained of, but as evidence of the consistency of the conduct of the prosecutrix with the story told by her in the box, and as tending to negative any consent of hers. That is a special class of case in which such evidence has for a very long time been allowed to be admitted, but it has nothing to do with such a case as the present..."

Different considerations may well apply where the state of a person's mind is in issue (for example, domicile cases), but those considerations do not, in my judgment, apply to this case which involves the straight issue of adultery. This offence could be proved by admissions tending to show that it had been committed but cannot be disproved by statements of the person charged afterwards made to third persons tending to show that it had not been committed.

It appears from the authorities that the rule is justified by the risk of fabrication by a person who, in the words of Eyre CJ, might be in a difficulty. Take this case. The respondent seeks to support her defence by showing that she was ready to submit to a scientific investigation to show that the charge made against her must be untrue. If she had submitted to an examination evidence as to her condition would, of course, be relevant and admissible, but the statement that she made to the doctor that she was willing to be examined to this end, is of no value. Persons who are unjustly charged will often react in different ways. Some may protest their innocence to all and sundry, others may be so stunned by the allegation that they refrain from so doing or from taking any prompt steps to assert their freedom from guilt. There is no reason, in my opinion, why justices requires the admissibility of such evidence in favour of an accused person for it seems the fundamental basis of the rule is that such evidence has no probative value.

Since, on the view which I have formed upon the facts found by the commissioner, who heard and carefully considered the evidence, the conclusion ought to be that adultery is not proved, quite apart from the admissibility of the evidence I have just discussed, the result should therefore be not that there should be a new trial but that the judgment of the commissioner should be affirmed and the appeal dismissed.'

(SELLERS LJ agreed; MORRIS LJ dissented.)

Appeal dismissed.

East LJ: I have always understood that rule to be subject to a number of exceptions, for example statements forming part of the *res gestae* or made by an accused in answer to questions about the charge. Is not *R* v *Christie* authority for the proposition that a witness may relate his previous identifications? It may be an exception, but the modern practice of identification parades depends upon it:

R v *Christie* [1914] AC 545 (HL) (For the facts, see 7.21 ante)

LORD ATKINSON said: '...it cannot, I think, be open to doubt that if the boy had said nothing more, as he touched the sleeve of the coat of the accused, than "That is the man," the statement was so closely connected with the act which it accompanied, expressing, indeed, as it did, in words little if anything more than would have been implied by the gesture simpliciter, that it should have been admitted as part of the very act of identification itself. It is on the admissibility of the further statement made in answer to the question of the constable that the controvery arises. On the whole, I am of opinion, though not without some doubt, that this statement only amplifies what is implied by the words "That is the man," plus the act of touching him.

A charge had been made against the accused of the offence committed on the boy. The words "That is the man" must mean "That is the man who has done to me the thing of which he is accused." To give the details of the charge is merely to expand, and express in words what is implied under the circumstances in the act of identification. I think, therefore, that the entire statement was admissible on these grounds, even although the boy was not asked at the trial anything about the former identification. The boy had in his evidence at the trial distinctly identified the accused. If on another occasion he had in the presence of others identified him, then the evidence of these eye witnesses is quite as truly primary evidence of what acts took place in their presence as would be the boy's evidence of what he did, and what expressions accompanied his act. It would, I think, have been more regular and proper to have examined the boy himself as to what he did on the first occasion, but the omission to do so, while the bystanders were examined on the point, does not, I think, violate the rule that the best evidence must be given. His evidence of what he did was no better in that sense than was their evidence as to what they saw him do.'

LORD MOULTON said: 'Speaking for myself, I have great difficulty in seeing how this evidence is admissible on the ground that it is part of the evidence of identification. To prove identification of the prisoner by a person, who is, I shall assume, an adult, it is necessary to call that person as a witness. Identification is an act of the mind, and the primary evidence of what was passing in the mind of a man is his own testimony, where it can be obtained. It would be very dangerous to allow evidence to be given of a man's words and actions, in order to shew by this extrinsic evidence that he identified the prisoner, if he was capable of being called as a witness and was not called to prove by direct evidence that he had thus identified him. Such a mode of proving identification would, in my opinion, be to use secondary evidence where primary evidence was obtainable, and this is contrary to the spirit of the English rules of evidence.'

LORD READING said: 'No objection was raised by Mr Dickens, for the respondent, to the admission of the first part of the statement, namely, "That is the man." It implied that Christie was the man designated by the boy as the person who had committed the offence, and meant little, if anything, more than the act of touching the sleeve of Christie or pointing to him. The importance is as to the admission of the additional words, describing the various acts done by Christie. These were not necessary to complete the identification or to explain it. There was no dispute that in the presence of his mother and the police constable the boy designated Christie as the man who had committed the offence. According to the constable's evidence the additional statement was made in answer to his question to the boy, "What did he do to you?" (Question 138). At the trial, and before the statement was admitted, the boy identified Christie in Court, and was not cross-examined. The additional statement was not required by the prosecution for the purpose of proving the act of identification by the boy. The statement cannot, in my judgment, be admitted as evidence of the state of the boy's mind when in the act of identifying Christie, as that would amount to allowing another person to give in evidence the boy's state of mind, when he was not asked, and had not said anything about it in his statement to the Court.

If the prosecution required the evidence as part of the act of identification it should have been given by the boy before the prosecution closed their case. In my judgment it would be a dangerous extension of the law regulating the admissibility of evidence if your Lordships were to allow proof of statements made, narrating or describing the events constituting the offence, on the ground that they form part of or explain the act of identification, more particularly when such evidence is not necessary to prove the act, and is not given by the person who made the the statement. I have found no case in which any such statement has been admitted.'

VISCOUNT HALDANE LC said: 'The only point on which I desire to guard myself is the admissibility of the statement in question as evidence of identification. For the boy gave evidence at the trial, and if his evidence was required for the identification of the prisoner that evidence ought, in my opinion, to have been his direct evidence in the witness-box and not evidence of what he said elsewhere. Had the boy, after he had identified the accused in the dock, been asked if he had identified the accused in the field as the man who assaulted him, and answered affirmatively, then that fact might also have been proved by the policeman and the mother who saw the identification. Its relevancy is to shew that the boy was able to identify at the time and to exclude the idea that the identification of the prisoner in the dock was an afterthought or a mistake. But beyond the mere fact of such identification the examination ought not to have proceeded.'

Mr Bacon: My Lords, there is no doubt that that case bears a strong similarity to the present case. But there, the boy identified the accused in court, and his previous identification really did no more than confirm what happened in court.

Cox LJ: That is essentially what happened here. I can understand the point that her hesitancy ought to have influenced the judge in the way in which he approached the evidence of identification, but I cannot see why it was inadmissible, that she had recognised the man before.

Leach LJ: Suppose she had been unable to identify him at all. This court held that the officers might have given the same evidence in:

R v *Osbourne; R* v *Virtue* [1973] QB 678 (CA)

The defendants were convicted of robbery. Both defendants had been picked out at an identification parade, Osbourne by Mrs B and Virtue by Mrs H. At the trial, some seven months after the parade, Mrs B said that she could not remember having picked out anyone at a parade; and Mrs H first said that she thought one of the defendants to be a man she had picked out at a parade, and then said that she did not think that that man was in court. The police inspector in charge of the parade was then called and gave evidence that the women had identified the defendants.

LAWTON LJ, giving the judgment of the court, said: 'Out attention was drawn to the Criminal Law Procedure Act 1865. The situation envisaged by section 3 of the Act of 1865 did not arise in this case at all because nobody suggested that those two ladies were acting in the way envisaged by that Act, namely, adversely, or, to use the modern term, hostilely, but it was said that the trial judge allowed the prosecution to call evidence to contradict them, which is not admissible.

We do not agree that Chief Inspector Stevenson's evidence contradicted their evidence. All that Mrs Brookes had said was that she did not remember, and, as I have already indicated, that is very understandable after a delay of seven months and a half months. She had, however, done something. Within four days of the robbery she had attended an identification parade. She had been told in the presence and hearing of the defendant Osbourne, as is the usual practice, what she was to do, namely, point out anybody whom she had seen at the time of the raid. She did point somebody out and it was the defendant Osbourne. One asks oneself as a matter of conmonsense why, when a witness has forgotten what she did, evidence should not be given by another witness with a better memory to establish what, in fact, she did when the events were fresh in her mind. Much the same situation arises with regard to Mrs Head. She said in the witness box that she had picked somebody out. She did not think that the man she had picked out was in court, but that again is understandable because appearances can change after seven and half months, and if the experience of this court is anything to go by, accused persons often look much smarter in the dock than they do when they are first arrested. This court can see no reason at all in principle why evidence of that kind should not be admitted.

It was submitted that the admission of that evidence was contrary to a decision of the House of Lords in *R* v *Christie* [1914] AC 545. That case has long been regarded as a difficult one to understand because the speeches of their Lordships were not directed to the same points, but this can be got from the speeches: that evidence of identification other than identification in the witness box is admissible. All that the prosecution were seeking to do was to establish the fact of identification at the identification parades held on November 20. This court can see no reason why that evidence should not have been admitted....

It is pertinent to point out that in 1914 when the House of Lords came to consider *R* v *Christie* [1914] AC 545 the modern practice of identity parades did not exist. The whole object of identification parades is for the protection of the suspect, and what happens at those parades is highly relevant to the establishment of the truth. It would be wrong, in the judgment of this court, to set up artificial rules of evidence, which hinder the administration of justice. The evidence was admissible.'
Appeal dismissed.

Mr Bacon: In that case, My Lords, the position of the defendants was protected by the mechanism of a properly controlled identification parade.
East LJ: There would hardly have been much point in holding a parade in the circumstances of this case.
Leach LJ: In the time of *R* v *Christie* I don't think they used parades at all. It is surely a question of weight here, Mr Bacon, as to how much reliance the jury could properly be invited to put on the previous identification and what happened in court. I think it is much too late to argue in terms of admissibility of previous identifications

generally.

(East and Cox LJJ indicated their concurrence in this view, and Mr Bacon was invited to address the court on his alternative grounds.)

Mr Bacon: My Lords, there are very great dangers in evidence of visual identification. Because of the concern that such evidence generates and the possibilities of inaccuracy and prejudice, this court comprising five members of the bench especially convened for the purpose, laid down new rules of practice for cases which depend wholly or substantially on evidence of this kind. I refer of course to:

R v Turnbull [1977] QB 224 (CA)

The Court of Appeal considered four separate appeals against conviction, all on the ground that the identification of the defendant was unsatisfactory.

LORD WIDGERY CJ, reading the judgment of the court, said: 'Each of these appeals raises problems relating to evidence of visual identification in criminal cases. Such evidence can bring about miscarriages of justice and has done so in a few cases in recent years. The number of such cases, although small compared with the number in which evidence of visual identification is known to be satisfactory, necessitates steps being taken by the courts, including this court, to reduce that number as far as is possible. In our judgment the danger of miscarriages of justice occurring can be much reduced if trial judges sum up to juries in the way indicated in this judgment.

First, whenever the case against an accused depends wholly or substantially on the correctness of one or more identifications of the accused which the defence alleges to be mistaken, the judge should warn the jury of the special need for caution before convicting the accused in reliance on the correctness of the identification or identifications. In addition he should instruct them as to the reason for the need for such a warning and should make some reference to the possibility that a mistaken witness can be a convincing one and that a number of such witnesses can all be mistaken. Provided this is done in clear terms the judge need not use any particular form of words.

Secondly, the judge should direct the jury to examine closely the circumstances in which the identification by each witness came to be made. How long did the witness have the accused under observation? At what distance? In what light? Was the observation impeded in any way, as for example by passing traffic or a press of people? Had the witness ever seen the accused before? How often? If only occasionally, had he any special reason for remembering the accused? How long elapsed between the original observation and the subsequent identification to the police? Was there any material discrepancy between the description of the accused given to the police by the witness when first seen by them and his actual appearance? If in any case, whether it is being dealt with summarily or on indictment, the prosecution have reason to believe that there is such a material discrepancy they should supply the accused or his legal advisers with particulars of the description the police were first given. In all cases if the accused asks to be given particulars of such descriptions, the prosecution should supply them. Finally, he should remind the jury of any specific weaknesses which had appeared in the identification evidence.

Recognition may be more reliable than identification of a stranger; but even when the witness is purporting to recognise someone whom he knows, the jury should be reminded that mistakes in recognition of close relatives and friends are sometimes made.

All these matters go to the quality of the identification evidence. If the quality is good and remains good at the close of the accused's case, the danger of a mistaken identification is lessened; but the poorer the quality, the greater the danger.

In our judgment when the quality is good, as for example when the identification is made after a long period of observation, or in satisfactory conditions by a relative, neighbour, a close friend, a workmate and the like, the jury can safely be left to assess the value of the identifying edvidence even though there is no other evidence to support it: provided always, however, that an adequate warning has been given about the special need for caution. Were the courts to adjudge otherwise, affronts to justice would frequently occur....

When, in the judgment of the trial judge, the quality of the identifying evidence is poor, as for example when it depends solely on a fleeting glance or on a longer observation made in difficult conditions, the situation is very different. The judge should then withdraw the case from the jury and direct an acquittal unless there is other evidence which goes to support the correctness of the identification. This may be corroboration in the sense lawyers use that word; but it need not be so if its effect is to make the jury sure that there has been no mistaken identification: for example, X sees the accused snatch a woman's handbag; he gets only a fleeting glance of the thief's face as he runs off but he does see him entering a nearby house. Later he picks out the accused on an identity parade. If there was no more evidence than this, the poor quality of the identification would require the judge to withdraw the case from the jury; but this would not be so if there was evidence that the house into which the accused was alleged by X to have run was his father's. Another example of supporting evidence not amounting to corroboration in a technical sense is to be found in *R* v *Long* (1973) 57 Cr App R 871. The accused, who was charged with robbery, had been identified by three witnesses in different places on different occasions but each had only a momentary opportunity for observation. Immediately after the robbery the accused had left his home and could not be found by the police. When later he was seen by them he claimed to know who had done the robbery and offered to help to find the robbers. At his trial he put forward an alibi which the jury rejected. It was an odd coincidence that the witnesses should have identified a man who had behaved in this way. In our judgment odd coincidences can, if unexplained, be supporting evidence.

The trial judge should identify to the jury the evidence which he adjudges is capable of supporting the evidence of identification. If there is any evidence or circumstances which the jury might think was supporting when it did not have this quality, the judge should say so. A jury, for example, might think that support for identification evidence could be found in the fact that the accused had not given evidence before them. An accused's absence from the witness box cannot provide evidence of anything and the judge should tell the jury so. But he would be entitled to tell them that when assessing the quality of the identification evidence they could take into consideration the fact it was uncontradicted by any evidence coming from the accused himself.

Care should be taken by the judge when directing the jury about the support for an identification which may be derived from the fact that they have rejected an alibi. False alibis may be put forward for many reasons: an accused, for example, who has only his own truthful evidence to rely on may stupidly fabricate an alibi and get lying witnesses to support it out of fear that his own evidence will not be enough. Further, alibi witnesses can make genuine mistakes about dates and occasions like any other witnesses can. It is only when the jury is satisfied that the sole reason for the fabrication was to deceive them and there is no other explanation for its being put forward can fabrication provide any support for identification evidence. The jury should be reminded that proving the accused has told lies about where he was at the material time does not by itself prove that he was where the identifying witness says he was.

In setting out these guidelines for trial judges, which involve only changes of practice, not law, we have tried to follow the recommendations set out in the Report which Lord Devlin s Committee made to the Secretary of State for the Home Department in April 1976. We have not followed that report in using the phrase "exceptional circumstances" to describe situations in which the risk of mistaken identification is reduced. In our judgment the use of such a phrase is likely to result in the build up of case law as to what circumstances can properly be described as exceptional and what cannot. Case law of this kind is likely to be a fetter on the administration of justice when so much depends upon the quality of the evidence in each case. Quality is what matters in the end. In many cases the exceptional circumstances to which the report refers will provide evidence of good quality, but they may not: the converse is also true.

A failure to follow these guidelines is likely to result in a conviction being quashed and will do so if in the judgment of this court on all the evidence the verdict is either unsatisfactory or unsafe.

Having regard to public disquiet about the possibility of miscarriages of justice in this class of case, some explanation of the jurisdiction of this court may be opportune. That jurisdiction is statutory: we can do no more than the Criminal Appeal Act 1968 authorises us to do. It does not authorise us to re-try cases. It is for the jury in each case to decide which witnesses should be believed. On matters of credibility this court will only interfere in three circumstances: first, if the jury has been misdirected as to how to assess the evidence; secondly, if there has been no direction at all when there should have been one; and thirdly, if on the whole of the evidence the jury must have taken a perverse view of a witness, but this is rare.

The limitations, such as they are, upon our jurisdiction do not mean that we cannot interfere to prevent miscarriages of justice. In 1966 Parliament released appellate jurisdiction in criminal cases tried on indictment from the limitations which the Criminal Appeal Act 1907 and the case law based upon it had put upon the old Court of Criminal Appeal. The jurisdiction of this court is wider. We do not hesitate to use our extended jurisdiction whenever the evidence in a case justifies our doing so. In assessing a case, however, it is our duty to use our experience of the administration of justice. In every division of this court that experience is likely to be extensive and helps us to detect the specious, the irrelevant and what is intended to deceive.'

I have to submit to Your Lordships here that the learned judge made no real attempt to follow these guidelines in relation to the evidence which he described correctly as 'crucial to the defence'.

East LJ: What do you say the judge should have done?

Mr Bacon: Firstly, My Lords, I would contend that he should have withdrawn the evidence from the jury as being of poor quality. This girl was young, and very distressed. She no doubt felt that she was expected to identify someone for the police officers and there she was in Plowden Drive, where Coke's flat is situated, and where she had been not long before.

Leach LJ: As against that, Mr Bunbury might say that she had had ample opportunity to observe her assailant at very close quarters. In fact the circumstances of identification seem particularly favourable in that respect.

East LJ: There is also surely a good deal of the supporting evidence for which the Lord Chief Justice said the jury should look. Why could they not take into account Coke's evidence that Littleton was there, or the recorded conversation with Mrs Littleton?

Mr Bacon: My Lords, those are the points which the learned judge should in any event have drawn to the jury's attention, if he proposed to leave the evidence to them. Yet the summing-up contains no warning as to the dangers of this kind of evidence. None of the weaknesses were indicated to the jury; and there is no guidance as to what supporting evidence existed or what weight it should be given. The jury were left more or less without assistance on this question, which vitally affected my client's defence.

Leach LJ: I think this is by far your best point. We will hear what Mr Bunbury has to say about it. (The court proceeded to hear argument from Mr Bunbury.)

12.16 Commentary

R v *Coke and Littleton* at trial.   Mr Bunbury for the prosecution has called Margaret Blackstone to give evidence in chief. Having dealt with the rape itself and the girls' return home, Mr Bunbury asks for the jury to retire and indicates his intention to call evidence from Margaret and subsequently from her mother as to the conversation in which Margaret told her mother what had happened. Mr Atkyn having indicated his objection to this evidence before the trial, it was not opened to the jury.

12.17 Argument

Mr Bunbury: My Lord, it is a well recognised exception to the rule against previous consistent statements that in a sexual case, recent complaints may be given in evidence.

Holt J: For what purposes can such evidence be admitted? Are not the purposes of a recent complaint limited?

Mr Bunbury: My Lord, they are. I would concede that a recent complaint is not evidence of the truth of what the complainant said, standing alone. Nor can it corroborate the complainant's evidence, because it does not come from an independent source. But it has two effects that are pertinent here. Firstly, it may confirm the complainant's evidence, and secondly, it is evidence which can rebut any suggestion of consent. If these purposes were not germane to the case, the recent complaint would be wholly inadmissible, as occurred in:

R v Wallwork (1958) 42 Cr App R 153 (CCA)

The defendant was convicted of incest with his daughter, aged five. At the trial the child was put in the witness box by the prosecution, but was unable to give any evidence. However, evidence by her grandmother of a complaint made by the child to her, in which she named the defendant as her assailant, was admitted.

LORD GODDARD CJ, giving the judgment of the court, said: '...in our opinion, in this particular case that evidence was not admissible. In cases of rape or indecent assault it has always been held that evidence of a complaint and the terms of the complaint may be given, but they may be given only for a particular purpose, not as evidence of the fact complained of, because the fact that the woman says not on oath: "So-and-so assaulted me" cannot be evidence against the prisoner that the assault did take place. The evidence may be and is tendered for the purpose of showing consistency in her conduct and consistency with the evidence she has given in the box. It is material, for instance, where a question of identity is concerned, that she made an immediate complaint or a complaint as soon as she had a reasonable opportunity of making it and made the complaint against the particular man. It is also material, and most material, very often on the point whether the girl or woman was a consenting party. None of these matters arise in this case. The child had given no evidence because when the poor little thing was put into the witness box, she said nothing and could not remember anything. The learned judge had expressly told the jury to disregard her evidence altogether. Therefore, there was no evidence given by her with regard to which it was necessary to say what she had said to her grandmother was consistent; not could there be any question of the identity of the prisoner or any question of consent. The learned judge, having once admitted that evidence ought — and he omitted to do this — to have told the jury that it was no evidence of the facts complained of by the child.'
(The court dismissed the appeal on the ground that no substantial miscarriage of justice was caused by the irregularities).

Holt J: Yes. The complainant has given evidence here, and consent is in issue. Can you call evidence of the terms of the complaint? I can see that the fact that it was made might be significant, but adducing what she said goes much further.

Mr Bunbury: My Lord, in my submission I can. The older cases were unclear, but the law has been settled since:

R v Lillyman [1896] 2 QB 167 (CCR)

The defendant was charged with attempted unlawful intercourse with a girl between the ages of thirteen and sixteen; with assault upon her with intent to ravish; and with an indecent assault upon her. The girl gave evidence that the acts complained of had been done without her consent. The prosecution also tendered evidence in chief of a complaint made by her to her mistress, in the absence of the defendant, shortly after the commission of the acts, and proposed to ask the details of the complaint as made by the girl. The defence objected to the admission of the evidence, but the trial judge admitted it. The mistress then deposed to all that the girl had said respecting the defendant's conduct towards her. The defendant was convicted.

HAWKINS J, delivering the judgment of the court, stated the facts and continued: 'It is necessary, in the first place, to have a clear understanding as to the principles upon which evidence of such a complaint, not on oath, nor made in the presence of the prisoner, nor forming part of the *res gestae,* can be admitted. It clearly is not admissible as evidence of the facts complained of: those facts must therefore be established, if at all, upon oath by the prosecutrix or other credible witness, and, strictly speaking, evidence of them ought to be given before evidence of the complaint is admitted. The complaint can only be used as evidence of the consistency of the conduct of the prosecutrix with the story told by her in the witness box, and as being inconsistent with her consent to that of which she complains....

We proceed to consider the second objection, which is, that the evidence of complaint should be limited to the fact *a complaint* was made without giving any of the particulars of it. No authority binding upon us was cited during the argument, either in support of or against this objection. We must therefore determine the matter upon principle...

After very careful consideration we have arrived at the conclusion that we are bound by no authority to support the existing usage of limiting evidence of the complaint to the bare fact that a complaint was made, and that reason and good sense are against our doing so. The evidence is admissible only upon the ground that it was a complaint of that which is charged against the prisoner, and can be legitimately used only for the purpose of enabling the jury to judge for themselves whether the conduct of the woman was consistent with her testimony on oath given in the witness box negativing her consent, and affirming that the acts complained of were against her will, and in accordance with the conduct they would expect in a truthful woman under the circumstances detailed by her. The jury, and they only, are the persons to be satisfied whether the woman's conduct was so consistent or not. Without proof of her condition, demeanour, and verbal expressions, all of which are of vital importance in the consideration of that question, how is it possible for them satisfactorily to determine it? Is it to be left to the witness to whom the statement is made to determine and report to the jury whether what the woman said amounted to a real complaint? And are the jury bound to accept the witness's interpretation of her words as binding upon them without having the whole statement before them, and without having the power to require it to be disclosed to them, even though they may feel it essential to enable them to form a reliable opinion? For it must be borne in mind that if such evidence is inadmissible when offered by the prosecution, the jury cannot alter the rule of evidence and make it admissible by asking for it themselves.

In reality, affirmative answers to such stereotyped questions as these, "Did the prosecutrix make a complaint" (a very leading question, by the way) "of something done to herself?" "Did she mention a name?" amount to nothing to which any weight ought to be attached; they tend rather to embarrass than assist a thoughtful jury, for they are consistent either with there having been a complaint or no complaint of the prisoner's conduct. To limit the evidence of the complaint to such questions and answers is to ask the jury to draw important inferences from imperfect materials, perfect materials being at hand and in the cognisance of the witness box. In our opinion, nothing ought unnecessarily to be left to speculation or surmise.

It has been sometimes urged that to allow the particulars of the complaint would be calculated to prejudice the interests of the accused, and that the jury would be apt to treat the complaint as evidence of the facts complained of. Of course, if it were so left to the jury they would naturally so treat it. But it never could be legally so left; and we think it is the duty of the judge to impress upon the jury in every case that they are not entitled to make use of the complaint as any evidence whatever of those facts, or for any other purpose than that we have stated. With such a direction, we think the interests of an innocent accused would be more protected than they are under the present usage. For when the whole statement is laid before the jury they are less likely to draw wrong and adverse inferences, and may sometimes come to the conclusion that what the woman said amounted to no real complaint of any offence committed by the accused...

In the result, our judgment is that the whole statement of a woman containing her alleged complaint should, so far as it relates to the charge against the accused, be submitted to the jury as a part of the case for the prosecution, and that the evidence in this case was, therefore, properly admitted.'
Conviction affirmed.

Holt J: Mr Atkyn, what is your objection?

Mr Atkyn: My Lord, I accept what my learned friend has said about the law. But there is a further requirement that the complaint should have been made at the first practicable opportunity, and should have been spontaneous and unrehearsed. It is not just a matter of the length of time that elapsed. But may I refer Your Lordship to:

R v Osborne [1905] 1 KB 551 (CCR)

The defendant was convicted of an indecent assault on a girl under the age of thirteen years, whose consent to the act was therefore immaterial. At the trial evidence was admitted of the answer given by the girl to a question put by another child, in the absence of the defendant, as to why the girl had not waited for the other child at the defendant's house. The girl's reply was a complaint of the defendant's conduct to her.

RIDLEY J, reading the judgment of the court, said: 'It appears to us that the mere fact that the statement is made in answer to a question in such cases is not of itself sufficient to make it inadmissible as a complaint. Questions of a suggestive or leading character will, indeed, have that effect, and will render it inadmissible; but a question such as this, put by the mother or other person, "What is the matter?" or "Why are you crying?" will not do so. These are natural questions which a person in charge will be likely to put; on the other hand, if she were asked, "Did So-and-so" (naming the prisoner) "assault you?" "Did he do this and that to you?" then the result would be different, and the statement ought to be rejected. In each case the decision on the character of the question put, as well as other circumstances, such as the relationship of the questioner to the complainant, must be left to the discretion of the presiding judge. If the circumstances indicate that but for the questioning there probably would have been no voluntary complaint, the answer is inadmissible. If the question merely anticipates a statement which the complainant was about to make, it is not rendered inadmissible by the fact that the questioner happens to speak first... We are, at the same time, not insensible of the great importance of carefully observing the proper limits within which such evidence should be given. It is only to cases of this kind that the authorities on which our judgment rests apply; and our judgment also is to them restricted. It applies only where there is a complaint not elicited by questions of a leading and inducing or intimidating character, and only when it is made at the first opportunity after the offence which reasonably offers itself. Within such bounds, we think the evidence should be put before the jury, the judge being careful to inform the jury that the statement is not evidence of the facts complained of, and must not be regarded by them, if believed, as other than corroborative of the complainant's credibility, and, when consent is in issue, of the absence of consent.'
Conviction affirmed.

Holt J: Well, those are matters which I had better investigate in evidence, before inviting you to address me.
(Holt J then heard evidence in the absence of the jury from Margaret and her mother about the circumstances in which Margaret's complaint was made. He then invited counsel to address him.)

Mr Atkyn: My Lord, the evidence suggests not only questioning but that the complaint was more or less dragged out of this girl by her mother. Miss Blackstone had at least one perfectly sound opportunity to report what she says occurred. Instead, she went to her room. There was ample opportunity and indeed motive for concoction, and the evidence does not disclose an intent to make a spontaneous, outraged complaint.

(Mr Bunbury replied, pointing out that Margaret's extreme distress must be considered. Holt J held with some hesitation, and describing the decision as 'close', that the complaint was admissible. He indicated that the jury would be directed to weigh it with care.)

12.18 Commentary

R v Coke and Littleton at trial.   Mr Atkyn for Coke is cross-examining Margaret Blackstone. No recent complaint has been admitted in chief. He has suggested to her that she consented to have sexual intercourse with Coke, and that she has made up the story of rape in order to protect herself against criticism of her behaviour while with her younger sister, including allowing Angela to be indecently assaulted without trying to intervene. Margaret denies all these matters. Mr Atkyn prepares to conclude his cross-examination on what he anticipates will be a ringing note, only to receive a rebuff in re-examination by Mr Bunbury.

12.19 Course of evidence

Q: Miss Blackstone, I do not want you to be in any doubt of what I am suggesting. You felt guilty about misbehaving in the presence of your younger sister, isn't that right?

A: No.

Q: And it was only when the police needed a statement from you, that you thought up this story of rape?

A: That isn't true.

Q: You worked out a story to match your sister's account of things, so that it was ready when the police needed your statement on the 12 July.

A: No.

Mr Atkyn: No further questions.

(Mr Bacon then cross-examined on behalf of Littleton)

Holt J: Mr Bunbury?

Mr Bunbury: You got home after your visit to Henry Coke's flat. What time was that?

A: I'm not quite sure. Probably about 4 o'clock.

Q: Do you know what time the police were called?

A: Not exactly, no.

Q: Who called them?

A: My mother. She telephoned from an extension just outside my room, on the landing.

Q: Before your mother made that telephone call, had you spoken to her?

A: Yes. She came into my room. I was lying on the bed, crying. She asked me what the matter was.

Mr Atkyn: My Lord, I don't know how far my learned friend proposes to take this matter. If he intends to explore it, I would object most strongly.

Mr Bunbury: My Lord, perhaps the jury might retire?

(Holt J asked the jury to withdraw)

Mr Bunbury: My Lord, in my submission, I would be entitled to ask Miss Blackstone to deal with this conversation, in order to rebut the clear suggestion made in cross-examination that she invented a story of rape when she knew the police had been called and would want a statement from her. I anticipate the evidence would show that she had already complained specifically of rape. I would refer your Lordship to:

R v *Oyesiku* (1971) 56 Cr App R 240 (CA)

The defendant was convicted of assault occasioning actual bodily harm and assaulting a police officer. At the trial the defendant's wife gave evidence that the police officer was the aggressor. During cross-examination it was put to her that her evidence was a late invention and concocted with a view to helping the defendant. The trial judge refused to admit in evidence an earlier statement made by the wife to a solicitor before she had seen her husband after his arrest. This statement was to the same effect as the evidence she gave in court.

KARMINSKI LJ, giving the judgment of the court, said: 'It was argued with great force before us by Mr Hazan that this decision to exclude the evidence was wrong in law...In *Coll* (1889) 25 LR Ir 522 at p 541, Holmes J said: "It is I think clear that the evidence of a witness cannot be corroborated by proving statements to the same effect previously made by him; nor will the fact that his testimony is impeached in cross-examination render such evidence admissible. Even if the impeachment takes the form of showing a contradiction or inconsistency between the evidence given at the trial and something said by the witness on a former occasion it does not follow that the way is open for proof of other statements made by him for the purpose of sustaining his credit. There must be something either in the nature of the inconsistent statement, or in the use made of it by the cross-examiner, to enable such evidence to be given." We regard that statement of the law as correct, and applicable to the present case.

Our attention has also been drawn to a recent decision in the High Court of Australia, *Nominal Defendant* v *Clement* (1961) 104 CLR 476. I desire to read only one passage from the full judgment of Dixon CJ. He said this (at p 479): "The rule of evidence under which it was let in is well recognised and of long standing. If the credit of a witness is impugned as to some material fact to which he deposes upon the ground that his account is a late invention or has been lately devised or reconstructed, even though not with conscious dishonesty, that makes admissible a statement to the same effect as the account he gave as a witness, if it was made by the witness contemporaneously with the event or at a time sufficiently early to be inconsistent with the suggestion that his account is a late invention or reconstruction. But, inasmuch as the rule forms a definite exception to the general principle excluding statements made out of court and admits a possibly self-serving statement made by the witness, great care is called for in applying it. The judge at the trial must determine for himself upon the conduct of the trial before him whether a case for applying the rule of evidence has arisen and, from the nature of the matter, if there be an appeal, great weight should be given to his opinion by the appellate court. It is evidence however that the judge at the trial must exercise care in assuring himself not only that the account given by the witness in his testimony is attacked on the ground of recent invention or reconstruction or that a foundation for such an attack has been laid by the party, but also that the contents of the statement are in fact to the like effect as his account given in his evidence and that having regard to the time and circumstances in which it was made it rationally tends to answer the attack. It is obvious that it may not be easy sometimes to be sure that counsel is laying a foundation for impugning the witness's account of a material incident or fact as a recently invented, devised or reconstructed story. Counsel himself may proceed with a subtlety which is the outcome of caution in pursuing what may prove a dangerous course. That is one reason why the trial judge's opinion has a importance."

Dealing with the last paragraph of that quotation from Dixon CJ, there is no doubt at all that in this case counsel was making an attack, becuase it was clear from what he said at the trial and indeed what he said to us today. That judgment of the Chief Justice of Australia, although technically not binding upon us, is a decision of the greatest persuasive power, and one which this Court gratefully accepts as a correct statement of the law applicable to the present appeal.

That is the position in law, and in our view the learned trial judge was wrong to refuse to allow that evidence to be given. The value of it, of course, was a matter for the jury to assess.' Conviction quashed.

Holt J: Mr Atkyn, I think, subject to what you say, that this is a proper line of questioning.

Mr Atkyn: My Lord, I have made a general attack on Miss Blackstone's truthfulness and credibility, which in my submission does not allow my learned friend to invoke the recent fabrication rule. If Your Lordship would look at:

Fox v General Medical Council [1960] 1 WLR 1017 (PC)

A doctor was found guilty by the General Medical Council of infamous conduct, in relation to his adulterous association with a woman patient, who subsequently committed suicide. He appealed to the Privy Council.

LORD RATCLIFFE, giving the judgment of their Lordships said: 'The remaining objection taken relates to what was said to be the wrongful refusal to admit a piece of relevant evidence for the appellant. It was sufficiently apparent that the appellant's solicitor wished to call a Mr Frampton — an old friend of the appellant — to confirm that on April 15 the appellant had told him the same general story about his relations with Mrs Thomas, in particular that her outburst of the previous day was not induced by any improper conduct of his, that constituted his defence to the charge before the committee. The purpose of such evidence of a witness's previous statement is and can only be to support his credit, when his veracity has been impugned, by showing a consistency in his account which adds some probative value to his evidence in the box. Generally speaking, as is well known, such confirmatory evidence is not admissible, the reason presumably being that all trials, civil and criminal, must be conducted with an effort to concentrate evidence upon what is capable of being cogent and, as was remarked by Humphreys J in *R v Roberts* [1942] 1 All ER 187 it does not help to support the evidence of a witness, who is the accused person, to know that he has frequently told other persons before the trial what his defence was. Evidence to that effect is therefore in a proper sense immaterial.

There are, however, certain special exceptions, or at any rate one head of exception, from this general rule. If in cross-examination a witness's account of some incident or set of facts is challenged as being a recent invention, thus presenting a clear issue as to whether at some previous time he said or thought what he has been saying at the trial, he may support himself by evidence of earlier statements by him to the same effect. Plainly the rule that sets up the exception cannot be formulated with any great precision, since its application will depend on the nature of the challenge offered by the course of cross-examination and the relative cogency of the evidence tendered to repel it. Its application must be, within limits, a matter of discretion, and its range can only be measured by the reported instances, not in themselves many, in which it has been successfully invoked.

Thus, in *R v Cole* (1889) 24 LR Ir 522, a police witness who identified an accused in his trial evidence as being present at and party to the crime charged, being cross-examined on an earlier information sworn by him that did not mention the name of that accused, was allowed to give evidence to the effect that he had mentioned the name in an information of still earlier date. The admission of his evidence seems to be have been treated by the court as coming within the "recent invention" exception. That apart, it seems to have been little more than a permissible exercise of the right of re-examination to ask him in effect whether or not the second of the two informations may not have been due to inadvertence, and thus to displace the inference which the cross-examination had sought to draw from its contents....

Perhaps the best example of the way in which the exception can be properly invoked and applied is offered by *Flanagan v Fahy* [1918] Ir 2 KB 361. There a witness who had testifed to the forging of a will was cross-examined to the effect that he had invented his story because of enmity between him and the accused, the beneficiaries under the propounded will. He was allowed to call confirmatory evidence to show that before the cause of this enmity had arisen he had told a third party the story he was now telling. In that situation the issue raised by the cross-examination was clearly defined: a recent invention due to a specified cause, and if the witness could show that his account had been the same before the cause existed he was certainly adding a relevant fact in support of his credibility.

Did Mr Frampton's evidence, as tendered, come within the exception? In their Lordships' opinion it did not. It is impossible to say that its exclusion was wrongful in the legal sense.'
Appeal dismissed.

My Lord, those words describe the position in this case.

Holt J: I am against you, Mr Atkyn. I think there was a specific allegation of recent fabrication, and I shall allow the evidence in rebuttal. Mr Bunbury, how should I direct the jury to view this evidence in due course?

Mr Bunbury: My Lord, in a criminal case, it will be evidence going only to rebut the actual suggestion made. It is not the same position as the statutory rule governing civil cases under section 3(1)(b) of the Civil Evidence Act, 1968:

'Where in any civil proceedings — ...
(b) a previous statement made by a person called [as a witness in those proceedings] is proved for the purpose of rebutting a suggestion that his evidence has been fabricated, that statement shall by virtue of this subsection be admissible as evidence of any fact stated therein of which direct oral evidence by him would be admissible.'

D: UNFAVOURABLE AND HOSTILE WITNESSES

12.20 Introductory notes

12.20.1 A witness who proves unfavourable to the party calling him may be freely contradicted by the calling of any other admissible evidence available to that party, including, where proper, a hearsay statement of the witness admissible in a civil case under Part 1 of the Civil Evidence Act 1968. The unfavourable evidence must stand alongside such other evidence.

12.20.2 However, a party may not directly impeach a witness called by him by cross-examination, or by introducing the witness's previous statements inconsistent with his evidence, except where the judge has ruled that the witness is hostile. This means that the witness is displaying an animus inimical to the party calling him, or evinces no desire to give evidence fairly or to tell the truth.

12.20.3 The introduction of previous inconsistent statements is possible only after obtaining the judge's ruling, and is governed by statute, except that the judge still has power at common law to permit any questioning that seems necessary to him in order to ensure a fair trial.

12.20.4 Where the witness's previous inconsistent statements are introduced in order to impeach him, the statements are at common law evidence only of the consistency or inconsistency of the witness, and cannot be used to prove facts stated therein. This rule applies to criminal cases. In civil cases, statute provides that such statements may be used as evidence of any facts stated of which direct oral evidence by the witness would be admissible. (*A Practical Approach to Evidence*, pp 343–47.)

12.21 Commentary

R v *Coke and Littleton* at trial. Margaret Blackstone is called to give evidence for the prosecution. After being sworn, she declines to answer questions from Mr Bunbury or the judge dealing with the offences charged. Mr Bunbury applies to Holt J for leave to treat her as a hostile witness.

12.22 Argument

Holt J: I am a little concerned about that course. It is not as though she has given any evidence against the interests of the prosecution. Presumably you could proceed by calling other evidence.

Mr Bunbury: My Lord, I do have other evidence, of course and could call it following the rule in:

Ewer v Ambrose (1825) 3 B & C 746 (KB)

In an action of assumpsit for money had and received, B was called as a witness by the defendant to prove a partnership, but he proved the contrary.

LITTLEDALE J said: 'Where a witness is called by a party to prove his case, and he disproves that case, I think the party is still at liberty to prove his case by other witnesses. It would be a great hardship if the rule were otherwise, for if a party had four witnesses upon whom he relied to prove his case, it would be very hard, that by calling first the one who happened to disprove it, he should be deprived of the testimony of the other three. If he had called the three before the other who had disproved the case, it would have been a question for the jury upon the evidence whether they would give credit to the three or to the one. The order in which the witnesses happen to be called ought not therefore to make any difference.'

But in my submission, it is unsatisfactory to dispense with the evidence of the complainant on a charge of this kind, if it can be avoided. But even where a witness remains wilfully silent, she may be treated as hostile. My Lord, the law is founded on the Criminal Procedure Act 1865, s.3, which states:

A party producing a witness shall not be allowed to impeach his credit by general evidence of bad character; but he may, in case the witness shall prove adverse, contradict him by other evidence, or, by leave of the judge prove that he has made at other times a statement inconsistent with his present testimony; but before such last-mentioned proof can be given, the circumstances of the supposed statement sufficient to designate the particular occasion, must be mentioned to the witness, and he must be asked whether or not he has made such statement.

My Lord, in *Greenough* v *Eccles* it was held that the word 'adverse' used in the identically worded precursor of this section meant 'hostile'.

Greenough v Eccles (1859) 5 CB (NS) 786 (CP)

In an action on a bill of exchange, a witness called by the defendants supported the evidence of the plaintiff. The witness was then asked by the defendant's counsel about a previous statement inconsistent with his present testimony. The defence also proposed to put in evidence the statement. The judge ruled that the witness was not hostile and that therefore he had no power under s.22 of the Common Law Procedure Act 1854 to admit such evidence.

WILLIAMS J said: 'The section [s.22 of the Common Law Procedure Act 1854] lays down three rules as to the power of a party to discredit his own witness, first, he shall not be allowed to impeach his credit by general evidence of his bad character, — secondly, he may contradict him by other evidence, — thirdly, he may prove that he has made at other times a statement inconsistent with his present testimony.

These three rules appear to include the principal questions that have ever arisen on the subject; as may be seen by referring to the chapter in Phillipps on Evidence which treats "of the right of a party to disprove or impeach the evidence of his own witness." And it will there be further seen that the law relating to the first two of these rules was settled before the passing of the act, while, as to the third, the authorities were conflicting: that is to say, the law was clear that you could not discredit your own witness by general evidence of bad character, but you might nevertheless contradict him by other evidence relevant to the issue. Whether you could discredit him by proving that he had made inconsistent statements, was to some extent an unsettled point.

In favour of construing the word "adverse" to mean merely "unfavourable," the main arguments are, that, taking the words of the section in their natural and ordinary sense, its object appears to be to declare the whole law on the subject by negativing the right as to the first, and affirming it both on the second and third points; but that it proceeds to fetter the right as to both the latter; for, the right is declared to exist in the former as well as the latter of these two instances, "in case the witness shall, in the opinion of the judge, prove adverse," — with the additional qualification, as to the latter, that the leave of the judge must be obtained. The right, it is argued, according to this enactment, is not to exist in either instance, if the judge is not of that opinion. The fetter thus imposed, it is further said, would be harmless in its operation, if "adverse" be construed "unfavourable," but most oppressive if it means "hostile"; because the party producing the witness would be fixed with his evidence, when it proved pernicious, in case the judge did not think the witness "hostile," which might often happen; whereas, he could not in such a case fail to think him "unfavourable"...

But there are two considerations which have influenced my mind to disregard these arguments. The one is, that it is impossible to suppose the legislature could have really intended to impose any fetter whatever on the right of a party to contradict his own witness by other evidence relevant to the issue, — a right not only fully established by authority, but founded on the plainest good sense. The other is, that the section requires the judge to form an opinion that the witness is adverse, before the right to contradict, or prove that he has made inconsistent statements, is to be allowed to operate. This is reasonable, and indeed necessary, if the word "adverse" means "hostile," but wholly unreasonable and unnecessary if it means "unfavourable."

On these grounds, I think the preferable construction is, that, in case the witness shall, in the opinion of the judge, prove "hostile," the party producing him may not only contradict him by other witnesses, as he might heretofore have done, and may still do, if the witness is unfavourable, but may also, by leave of the judge, prove that he has made inconsistent statements...

Whatever is the meaning of the word "adverse," the mere fact of the witness being in that predicament is not to confer the right of discrediting him in this way. The section obviously contemplates that there may be cases where the judge may properly refuse leave to exercise the right, though in his opinion the witness prove "adverse." And, as the judge's discretion must be principally, if not wholly, guided by the witness's behaviour and language in the witness box (for, the judge can know nothing, judicially, of his earlier conduct), it is not improbable that the legislature had in view the ordinary case of a judge giving leave to a party producing a witness who proves hostile, to treat him as if he had been produced by the opposite party, so far as to put to him leading and pressing questions; and that the purpose of the section is, to go a step further in this direction, by giving the judge power to allow such a witness to be discredited, by proving his former inconsistent statements, as if he were a witness on the other side.'

(COCKBURN CJ and WILLES J agreed with WILLIAMS J.)

I apprehend that I have a duty, prosecuting in a criminal case, to show Your Lordship Miss Blackstone's deposition and to ask for leave. I refer to:

R v Fraser; R v Warren (1956) 40 Cr App R 160 (CCA)

LORD GODDARD CJ said: 'If the prosecution have information in their possession which shows that the evidence which a witness called for the prosecution has given is in flat contradiction of a previous statement which he has made and so entitles the prosecution to cross-examine, they should apply for leave to cross-examine and not leave it to the judge to do so, because it is counsel's duty to cross-examine in such circumstances. If he has not done so, the judge has to do it. That is not right, because it may look as if the judge is taking sides, but he cannot help intervening in such circumstances, because it is his duty to see that the justice is done.'

Holt J: Accepting that, Mr Bunbury, she has given no evidence with which her deposition could be said to be inconsistent under the section.

Mr Bunbury: My Lord, in such a case, Your Lordship has power at common law to ensure fairness. The question arose in:

R v Thompson (1976) 64 Cr App R 96 (CA)

The appellant was charged, *inter alia,* with incest with one of his daughters, A. She was called for the prosecution, and after she had been sworn and answered certain preliminary questions, she refused to give evidence. The trial judge said she had to unless she wished to spend some time in prison. He then allowed her to be treated as hostile and be cross-examined about a statement made by her to the police, and the appellant was convicted.

LORD WIDGERY CJ, delivering the judgment of the court, said: 'Thus, one comes from there to Mr Mylne's main point today, his best point as he described it, which is that the girl Anne ought never to have been treated as hostile. He concedes that she was a hostile witness and that the provisions of section 3 of the Criminal Procedure Act 1865 applied to her, but he says, for a reason which I will endeavour to explain in a moment, that that section did not apply to this case...

It is to be observed in the text of that section that the party producing a witness is permitted in certain circumstances to contradict, and that he may produce a statement inconsistent with present testimony. The argument of Mr Mylne is that in order to get the benefit of section 3 it is not enough to show, as in this case, that the girl was hostile and stood mute of malice. It is essential, so the argument goes, that there should be a contradiction of a previous statement and an inconsistent current statement, and since in this case there was no such contradiction, the previous statement standing alone and the girl refusing to produce a second statement either consistent or otherwise, it is contended that the section has no application.

We do not find it necessary to express any view upon the section as applied to cases where there is an inconsistent statement. We think this matter must be dealt with by the provisions of the common law in regard to recalcitrant witnesses. Quite apart from what is said in section 3, the common law did recognise that pressure could be brought to bear upon witnesses who refused to co-operate and perform their duties. We have had the advantage of looking at one or two of the earlier cases prior to the Act to which I have already referred and their treatment of this matter.

The first is *Clarke v Saffery* (1824) Ry & M 126, and the issue before the Vice-Chancellor does not require to be considered in any detail. But it is to be observed that in the course of the trial the plaintiff's counsel called the defendant, who was also one of the assignees, as a witness, and objection was taken by the defendant's counsel to the mode of examining the defendant. There does not seem to be a second statement contradicting the earlier one there, yet Best CJ said, at p 126: "there is no fixed rule which binds the counsel calling a witness to a particular mode of examining him. If a witness, by his conduct in the box, shows himself decidely adverse, it is always in the discretion of the judge to allow a cross-examination...."

I pause there because the rest of Best CJ's judgment is subject to comment in the later cases, but that part which I have read seems to me to stand uncontradicted. That is what we are dealing with here. We are dealing here with a witness who shows himself decidedly adverse, and whereupon, as Best CJ says, it is always in the discretion of the judge to allow cross-examination. After all, we are only talking about the asking of leading questions. If the hostile witness declines to say anything at all that was inconsistent with his or her duty as making a second and inconsistent statement about the facts, Best CJ is recognising as a feature of the common law the right in the discretion of the judge always to allow cross-examination in those circumstances.

Then in the case of *Bastin v Carew* (1824) Ry & M 127 Lord Abbott CJ said, at p 127: "I mean to decide this, and no further. But in each particular case there must be some discretion in the presiding judge as to the mode in which the examination should be conducted, in order best to answer the purposes of justice."

The statement, which is consistently supported in later authorities, again seems to us to cover this case admirably. The short question after all is: was the judge right in allowing counsel to cross-examine in the sense of asking leading questions? On the authority of *Clarke v Saffrey* and *Bastin v Carew* it seems to us that he was right and there is no reason to suppose that the subsequent statutory intervention into this subject has in any way destroyed or removed the basic common law right of the judge in his discretion to allow cross-examination when a witness proves to be hostile.'

Appeal dismissed.

(Holt J declared Margaret to be a hostile witness. Mr Bunbury asked her to read her deposition and questioned her about it. Margaret answered that she had made that statement, but that its contents were not wholly true. She declined to elaborate or to say anything further.)

Mr Bunbury: My Lord, there it is. I do not propose to take it any further.

Mr Atkyn: My Lord, in those circumstances, the statement should not go to the jury. It is not evidence of any fact stated in it at common law, and the jury cannot use it as a substitute for evidence. I would refer to:

R v Golder [1960] 1 WLR 1169 (CCA)

The defendants were charged with burglary and larceny. A witness, whose evidence on deposition at the committal proceedings incriminated the defendants, repudiated her statement at the trial and, although treated as hostile by the prosecution, refused to admit that her deposition was true. The trial judge, in effect, directed that it was open to the jury to act upon the evidence contained in the deposition and the jury convicted.

LORD PARKER CJ said: 'A long line of authority has laid down the principle that while previous statements may be put to an adverse witness to destroy his credit and thus to render his evidence given at the trial negligible, they are not admissible evidence of the truth of the facts stated therein. It is unnecessary to refer to the cases in detail; the following extract from the judgment of this court in *R v Harris* (1927) 20 Cr App R 144, 147 is a sufficient statement of the principle: "It was permissible to cross-examine this girl upon the assertions she had previously made, not for the purpose of substituting those unsworn assertions for her sworn testimony, but for the purpose of showing that her sworn testimony, in the light of those unsworn assertions, could not be regarded as being of importance. It is upon that matter that confusion has sometimes arisen. It has undoubtedly sometimes been thought that where a witness is cross-examined upon a previous unsworn statement and admits that the statement was made, but says that the statement was untrue, that unsworn statement may sometimes be treated as if it could be accepted by the jury in preference to the sworn statement in the witness box...That of course is all wrong, as has been pointed out on various occasions by this court, and not least in the case of *White* (1922) 17 Cr App R 59."

In both *Harris* and *White* the previous statement was unsworn and not made in the presence of the accused. It could not, therefore, on any view be evidence against him. The principle, however, is equally applicable to earlier statements made on oath as it is to unsworn statements: cf *R v Birch* (1924) 18 Cr App R 26...

In the judgment of this court, when a witness is shown to have made previous statements inconsistent with the evidence given by that witness at the trial, the jury should not merely be directed that the evidence given at the trial should be regarded as unreliable; they should also be directed that the previous statements, whether sworn or unsworn, do not constitute evidence upon which they can act.'

Appeals allowed.

The situation is not the same as in civil cases, where statute, section 3(1) of the Civil Evidence Act, 1968 has modified the common law rule. This provides that:

'Where in any civil proceedings —
(a) a previous inconsistent or contradictory statement made by a person called as a witness in those proceedings is proved by virtue of section 3 of the Criminal Procedure Act, 1865... that statement shall by virtue of this subsection be admissible as evidence of any fact stated therein of which direct oral evidence by him would be admissible.'

Here, Miss Blackstone has given no evidence that could really assist the jury, and there is no issue to which her deposition can properly be directed. It is not as though she had given evidence which differed from the deposition. It would be wholly prejudicial to allow the jury to see it.

Holt J: Yes, I agree with that.

12.23 Questions for Counsel

12.23.1 R v Coke and Littleton: Frame a series of questions to take Margaret and Angela through their evidence without leading.

12.23.2 R v Coke and Littleton: Course of evidence 12.4. What other questions might have been asked of D/I Glanvil in chief or in cross-examination about the making of his notes? Argument 12.12. What points should Mr Bacon make for Littleton about the admissible of the notebook because of Mr Atkyn's cross-examination?

12.23.3 R v Coke and Littleton: Argument 12.14. Could you improve on Mr Bacon's argument on admissibility? Can anything be made of the fact that the procedure adopted by the police officers in conducting the search of the neighbourhood rendered it impracticable to hold a meaningful identification parade? Do you agree with Mr Bacon's points on the judge's treatment of the identification evidence?

12.23.4 R v Coke and Littleton: Argument 12.17. Do you think that the recent complaint should be admitted, assuming that Margaret and her mother give evidence along the lines of their depositions? What arguments for and against the admission as recent complaints of (a) Margaret's complaint to WPC Raymond, and (b) Angela's complaint to her mother, could be made on the analogous assumption?

12.23.5 R v Coke and Littleton: Course of evidence 12.19. Could you improve on

Mr Atkyn's argument on the facts? If not, how might Mr Atkyn have made his point equally cogently in cross-examination without risking the admission of the previous statement?

13   Cross-Examination and Beyond

A: CROSS-EXAMINATION GENERALLY

13.1   Introductory notes

13.1.1   Any witness who has been sworn on behalf of a party is liable to cross-examination by any other party. This applies even though the witness has not been examined in chief, except where it is clear that he is unable to give any relevant evidence at all (both rare cases). Where a witness who has given evidence in chief becomes unavailable for cross-examination, his evidence does not become inadmissible, but is likely to carry little weight, particularly if the witness has deliberately made himself unavailable. In the limited cases where evidence is permitted to be given unsworn (e.g. children of tender years) cross-examination is also available, with one or two unimportant exceptions.

13.1.2   Omission to cross-examine as to any relevant matter amounts to acceptance of such unchallenged evidence given in chief. In such a case, the evidence in chief may not be impugned in a closing speech and no explanation may be offered for the failure to cross-examine. If cross-examination on a point is inadvertently omitted, the judge may, and usually will, allow a witness to be recalled for the purpose. This does not prevent counsel from agreeing to dispense with repetitive cross-examination of purely corroborative witnesses, or to curtail cross-examination of vulnerable witnesses such as children, nor does it affect counsel's discretion to omit matters of marginal relevance which in his view would waste the time of the court.

13.1.3   A witness may be cross-examined as to any relevant matter, whether or not one of which he has given evidence in chief. With the exception of the defendant in criminal cases, for whom special statutory provisions exist (see 4.4. et seq) a witness may also be cross-examined freely about his credit as a witness. However, a complainant in a rape case may be cross-examined about sexual experience with persons other than the defendant only with the leave of the judge.

13.1.4   Leading questions may be employed in cross-examination, as may any form of question that is not a disguised comment or attempt to provoke or argue with the witness. Cross-examination is subject to rules of professional conduct, which generally provide that the cross-examiner has both a duty fearlessly to present his case, and a discretion and duty to avoid unnecessary allegations, especially as to credit, and especially affecting absent third parties. Cross-examination is subject to the rules of evidence just as much as evidence in chief. Thus, it is improper to cross-examine on the contents of an inadmissible document, in such a way as to expose them to the tribunal of fact. Nonetheless, matter raised in cross-examination that was not raised in chief because it was inadmissible in chief, may become admissible by reason of being cross-examined on, and may then be further explored in re-examination. Cross-examination may lend relevance to a matter that previously was irrelevant. (*A Practical Approach to Evidence*, pp 349-54.)

13.2 Commentary

R v *Coke and Littleton* at trial. Mr Atkyn on behalf of Coke is cross-examining. Margaret Blackstone. He has suggested to her that she consented to have sexual intercourse with Coke on 8 July 1979. Margaret denies this. Mr Atkyn asks for the jury to retire, and applies to Holt J for leave to cross-examine as to Margaret's previous sexual experience with others.

13.3 Argument

Holt J: In general, of course, cross-examination as to credit does not require leave, though I think a judge may always restrain excessive cross-examination. I have in mind:

R v *Sweet-Escott* (1971) 55 Cr App R 316 (Derbyshire Assizes)

The defendant had given evidence for the prosecution in 1970 on the preliminary investigation into a charge of blackmail. The solicitor for the alleged blackmailer, in the course of cross-examination as to credit, cross-examined the defendant on previous convictions between the years 1947 and 1950, which he then denied, but subsequently admitted. The defendant had not been convicted since 1950. The defendant was subsequently charged with perjury relating to his evidence.

LAWTON J said: 'How far back is it permissible for advocates when cross-examining as to credit to delve into a man's past and to drag up such dirt as they can find there? That is the problem which arises in this case, because the solicitor for the alleged blackmailer saw fit to dig up matters which had occurred when this defendant was a young man straight out of the Army after war service, who from 1950 onwards has had no convictions of any kind.

What, then, is the principle upon which the judge should draw the line? It seems to me that it is this. Since the purpose of cross-examination as to credit is to show that the witness ought not to be believed on oath, the matters about which he is questioned must relate to his likely standing after cross-examination with the tribunal which is trying him or listening to his evidence. In this case the tribunal was a bench of magistrates. One must assume, and I am glad to assume, that the Okehampton magistrates before whom the present defendant gave evidence were reasonable, fair-minded people. The question arises whether this cross-examination would have affected the decision of the Okehampton Magistrates to commit Miss X for trial had this defendant admitted that he had had those convictions. In my judgment, it is inconceivable that they would have refused to commit because over twenty years before as a young man he had got into trouble and had had no further convictions since.

In these circumstances I adjudge first, that no reasonably minded bench of magistrates could have taken an adverse view of this defendant's credit in the year 1970 because of these convictions, and secondly, that the cross-examination of the present defendant out of which this prosecution arose was not material in the proceedings because it offended against the principle which, in my judgment, is the right one for deciding whether cross-examination as to credit is material.

It follows that the prosecution have failed to establish one of the matters which has to be established, namely, that the answers, albeit they were untrue answers, were material in the proceedings. Accordingly, I shall direct the jury to acquit this defendant on this indictment.' Verdict: Not guilty.

Of course, no judge would interfere with cross-examination on behalf of a defendant, except for very good reason.

Mr Atkyn: My Lord, indeed. Of course, counsel is bound to cross-examine with due discretion and judgment, as witness the rules promulgated by the Bar Council. But in this particular instance, I require Your Lordship's leave because of the specific statutory provision of:

Sexual Offences (Amendment) Act 1976, s.2(1)

2(1) 'If at a trial any person is for the time being charged with a rape offence to which he pleads not guilty, then, except with the leave of the judge, no evidence and no question in cross-examination shall be adduced or asked at the trial, by or on behalf of any defendant at the trial, about any sexual experience of a complainant with a person other than that defendant.'

Holt J: Yes. Is there any assistance to be derived from the Act as to the circumstances in which leave should or should or not be given?

Mr Atkyn: My Lord, yes. By section 2(2) of the Act, it is provided that:

The judge shall not give leave in pursuance of the preceding subsection for any evidence or question except on an application made to him in the absence of the jury by or on behalf of a defendant; and on such an application the judge shall give leave if and only if he is satisfied that it would be unfair to that defendant to refuse to allow the evidence to be adduced or the question to be asked.

My Lord, that subsection was considered by the Court of Appeal in *R* v *Mills* when the court indicated that the material to be cross-examined on must be such as to lead the jury to take a very different view of the evidence of the complainant.

R v *Mills* (1978) 68 Cr App R 327 (CA)

The defendant was charged with rape. At the trial an application was made to cross-examine the complainant as to her previous sexual experience with other men. The application was refused and the defendant was subsequently convicted. He applied for leave to appeal.

ROSKILL LJ, giving the judgment of the court, said: 'This section [s.2 of the Sexual Offences (Amendment) Act 1976] has not yet, as far as this Court is aware, been considered by this Court. It was however considered by May J a few months before the present trial, in *Lawrence and Another* [1977] Crim LR 492, which that learned judge heard at Nottingham Crown Court on May 10, 1977. There is a brief report of the learned judge's ruling at pp 492 and 493, which reads thus: "The following passage is taken verbatim from the transcript of the ruling:

The important part of the statute which I think needs construction are the words "if and only if he [the judge] is satisfied that it would be unfair to that defendant to refuse to allow the evidence to be adduced or the question to be asked. And, in my judgment, before a judge is satisfied or may be said to be satisfied that to refuse to allow a particular question or a series of questions in cross-examination would be unfair to a defendant he must take the view that it is more likely than not that the particular question or line of cross-examination, if allowed, might reasonably lead the jury, properly directed in the summing up, to take a different view of the complainant's evidence from that which they might take if the question or series of questions was or were not allowed."

This comment follows:

On the facts of the case the learned judge ruled that cross-examination designed to form a basis for the unspoken comment, "Well, there you are, members of the jury, that is the sort of girl she is," was not permissible; distinguishing between cross-examination designed to blacken the complainant's sexual character so as to leave such a comment and cross-examination as to the trustworthiness of her evidence, the learned judge ruled that only the latter going to credit properly so called was permissible.

This is, as we pointed out to Mr Hunt in the course of argument, essentially a matter for the exercise of discretion by the trial judge within the framework of the Act, bearing in mind that that statutory provision is designed to secure protection for complainants. The learned judge here exercised his discretion after having had that decision of May J quoted to him.
Mr Hunt found himself unable to say that this was not a matter for the exercise of the learned judge's discretion, but argued that this Court should substitute its own discretion for that of the learned judge.
With respect, it would be entirely wrong for us to do so. In our view the approach adopted by May J in *Lawrence and Another (supra)* was entirely right and Boreham J, following that ruling of May J, exercised his discretion properly.'
Application refused.

Holt J: As I understand your application, you say that you want to put it to Miss Blackstone that she has had sexual relations with young men other than the defendant Coke. In what way is that permissible under this section as interpreted by the Court of Appeal in *R* v *Mills?*
(Mr Atkyn addressed Holt J on this question, with particular reference to the allegation that Margaret had previously threatened to accuse Kevin of raping her, without justification. Mr Bunbury replied. Holt J gave leave limited to the question of relations between Margaret and Kevin solely because of its relevance to the subsequent alleged threat, and refused it as to Margaret's sexual relations with anyone else other than Coke.)

13.4 Commentary

R v *Coke and Littleton* at trial. Mr Atkyn has apparently concluded his cross-examination of Margaret Blackstone. After cross-examination by Mr Bacon and re-examination by Mr Bunbury, Margaret is asked to take a seat at the back of the court. After the next adjournment of the court, at a stage when further evidence is being taken, Mr Atkyn asks to make an application in the absence of the jury, before the trial resumes in their presence.

13.5 Argument

Mr Atkyn: My Lord, entirely because of my inadvertence, I omitted to put to Miss Margaret Blackstone while she was in the witness box an important matter. This is that it is part of my client's case that Margaret Blackstone has on a previous occasion made an unfounded allegation of rape against a young man called Kevin. My Lord, the charge was made and later abandoned, and Kevin was not prosecuted. May she be recalled so that it may be put?

Mr Bunbury: My Lord, I object to that course. It involves an attack on character, and should have been made at the proper time.

Mr Atkyn: My Lord, it is entirely within Your Lordship's discretion. I would invite Your Lordship's attention to:

R v *Wilson,* unreported, 5 May 1977 (CA)

The appellant, with others, was charged in an indictment containing 11 counts. It was alleged that a gang of armed men had broken into a jeweller's shop but had fled when an alarm sounded. The appellant was arrested and interrogated, and admitted having taken part in the break-in. This admission was challenged by the appellant's counsel in cross-examination of the police. Consequently, the prosecution applied for and were granted leave to cross-examine the appellant about his character. This the prosecution then omitted, through inadvertence, to do. The trial judge allowed the appellant to be recalled for this purpose, and he was subsequently convicted.

SCARMAN LJ, delivering the judgment of the court, said: 'It is to be noted that the trial began on 4th October and did not finish until 20th of that month. As soon as Wilson's case was closed, the trial moved on to the cases of other co-defendants. Overnight Mr Locke for the Crown, reviewing the progress of the case, realised that, although he had been given leave, he had not in fact cross-examined the appellant to his criminal record. Accordingly he made application on the 15th October for leave to have Wilson recalled, so that he could cross-examined as to his record. That was a very unusual application and perhaps somewhat surprisingly the learned Judge acceded to it. Wilson was therefore recalled, so that, after the close of his defence and after the jury had heard the apparently favourable alibi evidence, he had questions to put to him about his record.

Since the real issue in the case was as to credibility, namely, were the jury satisfied with the evidence of the police officers who spoke to the admissions or did the case for the defendant raise a real doubt in their minds, the credibility of Wilson was of extreme importance in the case. By an irregularity, as Mr Clark would submit, the most damning evidence as to Wilson's credibility was admitted after the close of his case and after the apparently favourable alibi evidence had been given.

Mr Clark manfully sought to stop the Judge exercising his discretion in these circumstances, but failed and he now submits that it was a wrong exercise of the discretion of the Judge to recall his client for the purpose of that cross-examination and that in the circumstances it constituted a material irregularity giving him a ground for appeal under section 2 of the Criminal Appeal Act 1968.

We have been troubled by this exercise of discretion, not because it led to any injustice in the result, but because it is very unusual for a trial Judge to allow a defendant to be recalled after he has completed his evidence and after his case has been completed as well. Furthermore, it must be very exceptional in the history of trials for a defendant to be recalled so that he can be cross-examined as to his character. But we have come to the conclusion that it is not possible for us to say that it was a wrong exercise of discretion in the circumstances. The circumstances were those of a long and complicated trial with a number of co-defendants and a great body of evidence which had to be called in respect of the separate case of each defendant. It was a trial in which it was very difficult to keep to a coherent and consistent course. Counsel for the Crown was, as he said, darting about from one topic to another according to the stage that the trial had reached. Therefore the recall of Wilson was not quite as stark an event as it would have been if Wilson alone had been on trial and if all the evidence had been completed when the application was made.

Moreover the Judge's duty at all stages of a criminal trial is to exercise his discretion in a way which he thinks most advantageous for justice. A criminal trial is not a game and, if the prosecution makes a mistake, as they plainly did make in this case by failing to cross-examine Wilson at the appropriate time as to his record, then it is not for the Judge to say "Well, the prosecution lose out, because they have made a mistake". It is for the Judge to say, when application is made to recall a witness, "what will best serve the interests of justice?" bearing in mind that justice includes the interest of the defendant as well as the interest of the prosecution.

In the present case, where the Judge had already indicated perfectly properly, as Mr Clark concedes, that this was a case in which the defendant could be properly cross-examined as to his character, and when the main issue for the jury was to make up their minds as to who was telling the truth, the witnesses for the Crown or for the defence, (bearing in mind of course that there is no burden of proof upon the defence), it is really not possible to say that the learned Judge erred in the exercise of his discretion. Certainly the case against Wilson was overwhelming, if the jury came to the conclusion that the police witnesses were worthy of belief. Those being the circumstances, we are unable to accede to the submission of Mr Clark that there was a material irregularity in the trial.

Each one of us however has asked himself the question whether, on what we know of the trial, we would have allowed the recall of Wilson for this purpose after the conclusion of the case. Each one of us is very doubtful whether we would have done so. But that does not mean that the Judge was wrong. But it does mean, in our judgement, that this is a situation which all concerned with the administration of justice should strive officiously to ensure never occurs again.'

Appeal dismissed.

My Lord, cross-examination is of course such an important matter that it is generally permitted of every witness, even where as here, it is directed to matters outside the scope of evidence in chief. Indeed, it is allowed even where the witness is sworn in error and gives no evidence in chief, as long as it appears that he could give some relevant evidence I refer to:

Wood v MacKinson (1840) 2 Mood & R 273 (Nisi Prius)

A witness was called for the plaintiffs because of a mistake of counsel as to his being able to speak to a transaction. The mistake was discovered before any question was put and the witness was about to retire when the defendants claimed the right to cross-examine him.

COLERIDGE J said: '...it appears to me that the more satisfactory principle to lay down is this, that if there really be a mistake, whether on the part of counsel or officer, and that mistake be discovered before the examination in chief has begun, the adverse party ought not to have the right to take advantage of this mistake by cross-examining the witness. Here the learned counsel explains that there has been a mistake, which consists in this, that the witness is found not to be able to speak at all as to the transaction which was supposed to be within his knowledge. This is, I think, such a mistake as entitles the party calling the witness to withdraw him without his being subject to cross-examination. If, indeed, the witness had been able to give evidence of the transaction which he was called to prove, but the counsel had discovered that the witness, besides that transaction, knew other matters inconvenient to be disclosed, and therefore attempted to withdraw him, that would be a different case. I think the defendants have here no right to cross-examine the witness.'

(The witness accordingly withdrew without being cross-examined, and was afterwards called and examined by the defendants, as one of their witnesses.)

Holt J: Is it a matter of importance to your case?

Mr Atkyn: Yes, My Lord. Of course, unless that matter was put in cross-examination, my learned friend might well object to my calling evidence on the matter, and to my referring to it in my closing speech. It is a well known principle that one's case should be put to the witness, whether the part of the case relates to substantive issues or credit. I would refer Your Lordship to:

Browne v Dunn [1894] 6 R 67 (HL)

LORD HERSCHELL LC said: 'Now, my Lords, I cannot help saying that it seems to me to be absolutely essential to the proper conduct of a cause, where it is intended to suggest that a witness is not speaking the truth on a particular point, to direct his attention to the fact by some questions put in cross-examination showing that that imputation is intended to be made, and not to take his evidence and pass it by as a matter altogether unchallenged, and then, when it is impossible for him to explain, as perhaps he might have been able to do if such questions had been put to him, the circumstances which it is suggested indicate that the story he tells ought not to be believed, to argue that he is a witness unworthy of credit. My Lords, I have always understood that if you intend to impeach a witness you are bound, whilst he is in the box, to give him an opportunity of making any explanation which is open to him; and, as it seems to me, that is not only a rule of professional practice in the conduct of a case, but is essential to fair play and fair dealing with witnesses.'

LORD HALSBURY said: 'To my mind nothing would be more absolutely unjust than not to cross-examine witnesses upon evidence which they have given, so as to give them notice, and to give them an opportunity of explanation, and an opportunity very often to defend their own character, and, not having given them such an opportunity, to ask the jury afterwards to disbelieve what they have said, although not one question has been directed either to their credit or to the accuracy of the facts they have deposed to.'

At this stage, no-one else can be prejudiced by the exercise of Your Lordship's power to recall Miss Blackstone.

Holt J: That appears to me to be clearly the proper course. I shall recall her after the present witness has finished giving evidence.

B: *PREVIOUS INCONSISTENT STATEMENTS*

13.6 Introductory notes

13.6.1 A witness may be cross-examined as to statements made by him on previous occasions inconsistent with his evidence. The rule applies to any statement whether made orally or in writing, and is governed by statute. In each case, the statement must be relative to the indictment or proceeding. If the statement is in writing, the witness may be cross-examined without being shown the statement, unless and until it is proposed to use the statement to contradict him, when his attention must be called to the relevant part or parts.

13.6.2 At common law which governs criminal cases, a previous inconsistent statement introduced into evidence to contradict a witness cannot be used as evidence of the facts stated therein, and goes only to credit. However in civil cases, statute provides that such a statement may be used in evidence of any fact stated therein of which direct oral evidence by the witness would be admissible. (*A Practical Approach to Evidence*, pp 354–8.)

13.7 Commentary

R v *Coke and Littleton* at trial.   Mrs Helen Blackstone has given evidence in chief for the prosecution. Her evidence contained one matter which has taken the defence by surprise. She stated that in the course of Margaret's recent complaint to her (see 12.19 ante) Margaret mentioned that Coke threatened her with a knife, in order to force Margaret to have sexual intercourse with him. This is the first time that a knife has been mentioned in connection with this case. Mr Atkyn for Coke proceeds to cross-examine on this issue.

13.8 Course of evidence

Q: Do you say your daughter told you that Coke had threatened her with a knife?
A: Yes.
Q: Is your evidence today the first time you have ever made any mention of a knife?
A: What do you mean?
Q: Did you make a written statement to the police in connection with this matter on 12 July 1979?
A: I did make a statement, yes.
Q: Did you make any mention in that statement of a knife?
Mr Bunbury: Perhaps she might see her statement, My Lord?
Mr Atkyn: With respect, My Lord, I am entitled to her answer without her being shown the statement.
Holt J: Should she not be shown it?
Mr Atkyn: My Lord, at this stage, no. At common law under the rule in *Queen Caroline's Case* (1820) 2 B & B 287 this would certainly have been the position. But the law is now to be found in section 5 of the Criminal Procedure Act 1865, which states:

> A witness may be cross-examined as to previous statements made by him in writing or reduced into writing, relative to the subject-matter of the indictment or proceeding, without such writing being shown to him; but if it is intended to contradict such witness by the writing, his attention must, before such contradictory proof can be given, be called to those parts of the writing which are to be used for the purpose of so contradicting him: Provided always, that it shall be competent for the judge, at any time during the trial to require the production of the writing for his inspection, and he may thereupon make such use of it for the purpose of the trial as he may think fit.

Holt J: The first question, of course, is whether Mrs Blackstone's statement was made relative to the indictment or proceeding. There can hardly be much doubt of it, but I suppose that is strictly a matter which I have to decide as one of law, as Veale J pointed out in *R v Bashir; R v Manzur* [1969] 1 WLR 1303. Have you not contradicted her?
Mr Atkyn: Not yet, My Lord. I may do so, but I am entitled to await her reply.
Holt J: Yes, I think that is right. Very well.
(Mr Atkyn continued his cross-examination.)
Q: Mrs Blackstone, do you remember ever mentioning a knife before?
A: I really cannot remember.
Mr Atkyn: Then My Lord, may she see her statement?
Holt J: Certainly.
(Mrs Blackstone was shown and read her statement.)
Q: Mrs Blackstone, is that your statement bearing your signature?
A: Yes.
Q: Did you read it carefully before signing it, including the declaration at the top of the consequences of its being false?
A: Yes.

Q: Having read that statement today, do you still say there was talk of a knife?

A: Yes.

Q: That statement was made just four days after this alleged offence occurred?

A: Yes, on the 12th.

Q: Do you think your memory was better on 12 July, just four days after the conversation with your daughter, than it is today?

A: I suppose it would be.

Q: If Margaret had said something about a knife, that would have been something fairly dramatic which would have impressed itself upon you, wouldn't it?

A: I think so.

Q: Yet there is no mention of it in your statement, is there? Can you explain why not? Just look at the third paragraph, would you?

A: I must have forgotten about it. I was very upset by what happened.

Q: The truth is that there never was any mention of a knife, isn't it? The whole complaint was as you stated on 12 July, just four days after the conversation took place.

A: I think there was some mention of it.

Mr Bunbury: My Lord, I now apply for that statement to be shown to the jury.

Holt J: Well, that is a matter for me, as I read the section. Mr Atkyn has quite correctly called the witness's attention to the part of the statement concerned, and the witness has not denied that she made no mention of a knife. But I imagine Mr Atkyn would wish the jury to see it?

Mr Atkyn: Yes, My Lord. I accept that I have contradicted the witness, and I would wish to put the statement before the jury for that purpose. Since Your Lordship referred by implication to the purposes for which Your Lordship might call for and use the statement during the trial, it may be appropriate to refer Your Lordship to authority on the evidential use of the statement. The use referred to in the section does not extend to using it as evidence of the facts stated.

(Mr Atkyn referred the judge to the authorities set out in 12.22.)

13.9 Commentary

Blackstone v *Coke* at trial. Margaret Blackstone has given evidence in chief that Coke is the father of her child. Mr Atkyn for Coke cross-examines. He suggests that on a previous occasion, Margaret had told Anthony Henneky that he (Henneky) was the father.

13.10 Argument

Hardwicke J: Is that a proper question?

Mr Atkyn: Yes, My Lord. It is specifically allowed by:

Criminal Procedure Act 1865, s.4

s.4 If a witness upon cross-examination as to a former statement made by him relative to the subject-matter of the indictment or proceeding, and inconsistent with his present testimony, does not distinctly admit that he has made such statement, proof may be given that he did in fact make it; but before such proof can be given the circumstances of the supposed statement, sufficient to designate the particular occasion, must be mentioned to the witness, and he must be asked whether or not he has made such statement.

Hardwicke J: It may, I suppose, assist me as to credit.

Mr Atkyn: Your Lordship would be entitled to regard such a statement as evidence of the facts stated in it, in addition to any value it may have for purposes of impeachment. At common law, this would not have been the position.

(Mr Atkyn referred Hardwicke J to *R* v *Harris* (1927) 20 Cr App R 144 and *R* v *Golder and others* [1960] 1 WLR 1169; see 12.22 ante.)

But while that rule continues to apply to criminal cases, Your Lordship sitting in a civil case has a statutory power to make use of the statement as evidence of the facts stated. If your Lordship looks at:

Civil Evidence Act 1968, s.3(1)(a)

Where in any civil proceedings —
(a) a previous inconsistent or contradictory statement made by a person called as a witness in those proceedings is proved by virtue of section 3, 4 or 5 of the Criminal Procedure Act, 1865...that statement shall by virtue of this subsection be admissible as evidence of any fact stated therein of which direct oral evidence by him would be admissible.

Hardwicke J: The section appears to apply to written or oral statements because both section 4 and section 5 are referred to, and also to statements put to hostile witnesses under section 3. We had better hear first whether or not this witness will distinctly admit the statement put to her, or not. Then we shall see whether any proof is necessary.

Mr Atkyn: My Lord, yes.

(Mr Atkyn continued his cross-examination.)

C: FINALITY OF ANSWERS ON COLLATERAL ISSUES

13.11 Introductory notes

13.11.1 Cross-examination may properly be directed to 'collateral' issues, that is to say matters not directly relevant to the facts in issue, such as the credit of a witness. However, to avoid the undue proliferation of side issues, the cross-examiner must accept as final any answer given by the witness on a collateral issue. This does not connote that the cross-examiner must cease to cross-examine on the subject or that he is obliged to accept the answer as true. It means merely that the cross-examiner is not permitted to rebut the answer by calling evidence to the contrary.

13.11.2 The rule as to finality on collateral issues is subject to four important exceptions, in which the answers may be rebutted by the cross-examiner. The exceptions are:

13.11.2.1 Where a witness denies or refuses to admit that he has been convicted of a criminal offence.

13.11.2.2 Where an allegation is made and denied that the witness is biased or partial.

13.11.2.3 Where it is sought to introduce evidence that an adverse witness has a reputation for untruthfulness.

13.11.2.4 Where it is sought to introduce medical evidence bearing upon the reliability of an adverse witness. (*A Practical Approach to Evidence,* pp 358–63.)

13.12 Commentary

R v *Coke and Littleton* on appeal against conviction. During cross-examination of Margaret Blackstone, Mr Atkyn for Coke suggested to her, (a) that Margaret indulged in consensual sexual intercourse with Coke on two occasions prior to 8 July 1979[1]; (b) that Margaret had on various occasions prior to 8 July 1979 had consensual sexual intercourse with Coke's friend Kevin; and (c) that Margaret had previously threatened to complain falsely that Kevin had raped her. During the presentation of the defence case for Coke, Mr Atkyn proposed to lead evidence tending to support each of these allegations, which had been denied by Margaret during cross-examination. Holt J refused to allow any of this evidence to be given, on the ground that the answers were collateral and that Mr Atkyn was obliged to accept them as final. Mr Atkyn complains to the Court of Appeal that the evidence was admissible and should have been permitted.

13.13 Argument

Leach LJ: Mr Atkyn, what test do you say should be applied to determine whether an answer relates to a collateral matter or not? It seems to me that these were mere questions of credit.

Mr Atkyn: My Lords, in my submission they were matters which were directly relevant to the issues before the jury, about which I might have led evidence in chief as part of my case.

Perhaps Your Lordships' would first look at:

Attorney-General v *Hitchcock* (1847) 1 Exch 91

The defendant, a maltster, was charged with using a cistern in breach of certain statutory requirements. A prosecution witness was asked in cross-examination whether he had not previously said that he had been offered £20 by officers of the Crown, if he would state in evidence that the cistern had been so used. The witness denied the allegation, whereupon the defence proposed to call a witness of their own to state that the prosecution witness had said this. The judge held that the question tended to raise a collateral issue and ruled that it could not be put. The defence obtained a rule for a new trial on the ground that this evidence was improperly rejected.

POLLOCK·CB said: '...the test, whether the matter is collateral or not, is this: if the answer of a witness is a matter which you would be allowed on your part to prove in evidence — if it have such a connection with the issue, that you would be allowed to give it in evidence — then it is a matter on which you may contradict him. Or it may be as well put, or perhaps better, in the language of my Brother Alderson this morning, that, if you ask a witness whether he has not said so and so, and the matter he is supposed to have said would, if he had said it, contradict any other part of his testimony, then you may call another witness to prove that he had said so, in order that the jury may believe the account of the transaction

---

[1] Mr Atkyn would not, of course, have made such a suggestion on the basis of the instructions provided to him in chapter 2, but this re-writing of the facts will illustrate an important point.

which he gave to that other witness to be the truth, and that the statement he makes on oath in the witness box is not true.'
(His Lordship held that under the circumstances the evidence was properly excluded.)
(ALDERSON and ROLFE BB delivered concurring judgments.)
Rule discharged.

East LJ: Perhaps we should look separately at these pieces of evidence which you tendered to the trial judge. I certainly do not see why you could not have called evidence from your client that he had previously had consensual sexual intercourse with the complainant.

Mr Atkyn: My Lord, yes. That goes directly to the issue of consent, which was the basis of the defence. If Your Lordship would refer to:

R v Riley (1887) 18 QBD 481 (CCR)

The defendant was charged with assault with intent to commit rape. The defence was that whatever was done by the defendant to the complainant was done with her consent. She was cross-examined as to previous repeated acts of intercourse with the defendant at specified times and places before the time of the commission of the alleged offence, which she denied, and swore that she never had had intercourse with the defendant. Counsel for the defendant proposed to call several witnesses to prove these alleged acts of intercourse, but the trial judge refused to allow the witnesses to be called on the ground that such evidence was not admissible. The defendant was subsequently convicted.

LORD COLERIDGE CJ said: ' 'I think it is clear that the evidence of those witnesses should have been received. It has been held that evidence to shew that the woman has previously had connection with persons other than the accused, when she has denied that fact, must be rejected, and there are very good reasons for rejecting it. It should in my view be rejected, not only upon the ground that to admit it would be unfair and a hardship to the woman, but also upon the general principle that it is not evidence which goes directly to the point in issue at the trial. The question in issue being whether or not a criminal attempt has been made upon her by A, evidence that she has previously had connection with B and C is obviously not in point. It is obvious, too, that the result of admitting such evidence would be to deprive an unchaste woman of any protection against assaults of this nature. But to reject evidence of her having had connection with the particular person charged with the offence is a wholly different matter, because such evidence is in point as making it so much the more likely that she consented on the occasion charged in the indictment. This line of examination is one which leads directly to the point in issue. Take the case of a woman who has lived, without marriage, for years with the accused before the alleged assault was committed. Can it be reasonably contended that the proof of that fact, or evidence tending to prove that fact, is not material to the issue, and if material to the issue that such evidence should not be admitted?'
(POLLOCK B, STEPHEN, MATHEW and WILLS JJ agreed.)
Conviction quashed.

Cox LJ: Yes. Of course, that does not assist you on the question whether you were entitled to call evidence from this young man, Kevin. I appreciate that the learned judge gave you leave to cross-examine her on that subject,[1] but it seems to me that on the authorities you have cited, it was a collateral issue. Is not the case of *R v Holmes and Furness* against you?

R v Holmes and Furness (1871) LR 1 CCR 334

The complainant in an indictment for indecent assault, which on the facts alleged amounted,

---

[1]For the requirement of leave, see 13.2 and 13.3 ante.

in substance, to an attempt to rape, was asked in cross-examination whether she had not previously had intercourse with a man other than the defendants, and denied it. The defendants' counsel then called the man referred to and asked him if the complainant had ever had intercourse with him, but the trial judge refused to allow the question to be answered. The defendants were convicted.

KELLY CB said: 'The question is, whether on an indictment for rape, or for attempt at rape, or for an indecent assault, amounting in substance to an attempt at rape, if the prosecutrix is asked in cross-examination whether she has had connection with another person not the prisoner, and denies it, evidence can be called to contradict her. We are all of opinion that it cannot. In the first place, the general rule of evidence is that if a question be put in cross-examination as to a collateral point, the answer must be taken for better or for worse. And the reason is obvious. If such evidence as that here proposed were admitted, the whole history of the prosecutrix's life might be gone into; if a charge might be made as to one man, it might be made as to fifty, and that without notice to the prosecutrix. It would not only involve a multitude of collateral issues, but an inquiry into matters as to which the prosecutrix might be wholly unprepared, and so work great injustice. Upon principle, therefore, we must hold that the answer is binding.
     When we look at the authorities the case is still clearer. The first case on the subject is *R* v *Hodgson* R & R 211. That case was heard first before eight of the judges, and afterwards before the whole number. It was an actual decision that the prosecutrix on a charge of rape was not bound to answer such a question as that here put. That seems, as a matter of principle, to involve that, if the question had been answered, the answer would have been binding. But, further, the second objection taken in that case seems to raise the very point; and upon that the judges lay down the law distinctly, in accordance with the view which we take. That case is therefore an actual decision involving in principle the point now in question, and a dictum, at the least, by some of the most learned judges who ever sat, upon the very point. *R* v *Cockroft* 11 Cox CC 410 was an indictment for rape, and was tried first before Martin, B, and again before Willes, J, and both of those learned judges held that such evidence as that here tendered was inadmissible. So far all the decisions entirely support that view which we think to follow clearly from the settled principles of the law of evidence. We are asked to abandon that view upon the authority of *R* v *Robins* 2 Moo & R 512. That was no doubt a decision of Coleridge, J, after consulting Erskine, J, upon the very point now in dispute. But we cannot follow that ruling in opposition to the whole current of authority upon the question. In *R* v *Barker* 3 C & P 589 the question was as to evidence shewing the prosecutrix to be a common prostitute; and such evidence has long been held material. In *R* v *Martin* 6 C & P 562 the evidence was as to the prosecutrix having previously had connection with the prisoner. And such evidence is undoubtedly admissible, for it has a direct bearing upon the question of consent. These are really all the cases upon the subject. But from *R* v *Clarke* 2 Stark NPC 241 it may be collected that Holroyd, J, held the same view in the case of an indictment for an attempt at rape. We have, therefore, a deliberate judgment of the twelve judges, the decisions of Martin, B, and Willes, J, and the opinion of Holroyd, J, against the ruling of Coleridge, J.'
(PIGOTT B, BYLES, LUSH and HANNEN JJ agreed.)
Conviction affirmed.

Mr Atkyn: My Lord, if the evidence stopped at her sexual relationship with Kevin, I would respectfully agree. But there was further evidence of a false accusation resulting from the sexual relationship, and this was the matter which the defence was anxious to explore, for obvious reasons. The defence said throughout that this was a false accusation made to help the complainant explain away an otherwise embarrassing incident, and it was relevant to prove that the same thing had occurred before. It was not simply collateral, in my submission. (As to the admissibility of the previous accusation see 5.6 and 5.7 ante.)
(Leach LJ indicated that the court agreed that the evidence of Margaret's previous intercourse with Coke was admissible and that, subject to hearing Mr Bunbury as to whether the matter was collateral in so far as it related to a previous false accusation,

the court also felt that the remaining evidence was relevant to the issues before the jury, and should have been admitted.)

13.14 Commentary

R v Coke and Littleton at trial. During cross-examination of Margaret Blackstone, Mr Atkyn for Coke suggests to her that she has admitted orally to Coke's friend Kevin that she decided to allege rape because of her embarrassment at having Angela molested while supposedly in her charge. Margaret denies this. Margaret also refuses to admit or deny that she has been found guilty of theft in the juvenile court. Mr Atkyn now proposes to lead evidence to contradict her on both these matters, by calling Kevin and by producing a certificate of Margaret's finding of guilt. Mr Bunbury objects, and the jury retire.

13.15 Argument

Mr Atkyn: My Lord, my learned friend is correct in saying that these matters are, strictly, collateral. But the rule of finality is subject to well-recognised exceptions, and in my submission, these pieces of evidence fall into exceptional categories. The previous finding of guilt is perhaps the clearest, because it is provided for by statute. If Your Lordship looks at:

Criminal Procedure Act 1865, s.6

6. A witness may be questioned as to whether he has been convicted of any misdemeanour, and upon being so questioned, if he either denies or does not admit the fact, or refuses to answer, it shall be lawful for the cross-examining party to prove such conviction...

My Lord, Miss Blackstone was over the age of fourteen at the time of the conviction, and nothing in s.16(2) of the Children and Young Persons Act 1963 prevents its admission. There is no question, of course, of its being spent under the Rehabilitation of Offenders Act 1974.

Holt J: That seems to be right. You will no doubt wish to prove the finding of guilt by producing a certificate or certified extract from the register in the normal way[1]. But I am not so sure about the prospect of calling the witness Kevin to prove Miss Blackstone's alleged admissions. Is that not a collateral matter which you must accept?

Mr Atkyn: My Lord, it is true that there is no statutory basis for such evidence. But there is a sound basis at common law, where I seek to prove that a witness is biased or partial; or in other words that a witness is prepared to lie in order to serve some personal interest. Sometimes, that bias or partiality arises from some relationship between the parties, as was the case in:

Thomas v David (1836) 7C & P 350 (Nisi Prius)

In an action against the maker of a promissory note, a witness called for the plaintiff was

---

[1]See the remaining portion of s.6; Prevention of Crimes Act, 1871 s.18; Magistrates' Courts Rules 1981 r. 68.

asked in cross-examination if she did not constantly sleep with her employer, the plaintiff. She said that she did not. The defendant proposed to call a witness to contradict her. The defendant's case was that he was not the maker of the note: in effect that it was a forgery.

COLERIDGE J said: 'Is it not material to the issue, whether the principal witness who comes to support the plaintiff's case is his kept mistress? If the question had been, whether the witness had walked the streets as a common prostitute, I think that that would have been collateral to the issue, and that, had the witness denied such a charge, she could not have been contradicted; but here the question is, whether the witness had contracted such a relation with the plaintiff, as might induce her the more readily to conspire with him to support a forgery, just in the same way as if she had been asked if she was the sister or daughter of the plaintiff, and had denied that. I think that the contradiction is admissible.'
(The witness was examined, and stated that the witness in question slept constantly with her master.)
Verdict for the defendant.

Holt J: Yes, but here, the relationship this witness has is with her sister, who is not an adverse party, and not with the defendant Coke.
Mr Atkyn: My Lord, that is quite right. But witnesses may be partial or biased for other personal reasons. A case not dissimilar to the present case is:

R v Phillips (1936) 26 Cr App R 17 (CCA)

The appellant was charged with incest with his daughter B, the case for the prosecution resting mainly on the evidence of B and her younger sister I. The defence was that the charge was a fabrication, and that the two children had been schooled by their mother, with whom the appellant was on bad terms, into giving false evidence against him. Some months previously the appellant had been convicted of indecently assaulting B, and bound over. I had given evidence against the appellant on that occasion also. Each of the children denied a suggestion put to them in cross-examination by the appellant's counsel that on separate occasions they had each admitted to another person that their evidence at the previous trial was false and that they were repeating what their mother had told them to say. Counsel sought to call as witnesses for the appellant the two persons to whom the above statements by the children were said to have been made, but the judge, taking the view that the cross-examination of the children on this matter had been directed to credit only, declined to admit their evidence. The appellant was convicted.

LORD HEWART CJ, delivering the judgment of the court, said: 'The purpose and effect of those questions was to raise the defence on which the appellant sought to rely. The substantive part of his defence was that the children, upon whose evidence alone the case for the prosecution rested, were not speaking for themselves, but for the designer and controller of the whole matter, their mother.
Whatever the merits of that defence might have been proved to be, it was, at any rate, a defence which the appellant was entitled to raise. The questions were directed not to the credibility of the two witnesses, but to the very foundation of the appellant's answer to the charge. It was not denied by counsel for the Crown, and it appears to us, that the evidence was wrongly excluded, because a mis-apprehension arose from the brevity of the manner in which the matter was dealt with. If the evidence had been admitted, it is impossible to say what effect it would have produced. The witnesses might not have produced a favourable effect upon the jury, and even if they had done so, the jury might not have disbelieved the story of the two girls. On the other hand, the jury might have taken the view that the charge was a pure invention. That being so, it seems to this Court, especially in a case which exhibits an unpleasant atmosphere of a suspicious kind, impossible to say that, if the evidence excluded had been allowed to be heard, the jury must certainly or would inevitably have arrived at the same verdict.'
Conviction quashed.

In my submission, here too, the question goes to the root of the defence.

Holt J: So you would contend that there is here such bias as goes beyond mere credit?

Mr Atkyn: Yes, My Lord. I would also rely on the observations of the Court of Appeal in:

R v *Mendy* (1976) 64 Cr App R 4 (CA)

The appellant was charged with assault. At her trial all the witnesses were kept out of court in accordance with normal practice. While a detective was giving evidence about the assault, a constable in court noticed a man in the public gallery taking notes. This man was then seen to leave court and the same constable and a court officer saw him discussing the case with the appellant's husband, apparently describing the detective's evidence to him. The husband then gave evidence and in cross-examination denied that the incident with the man had occurred and the prosecution was given leave to call evidence by the constable and the court officer in rebuttal. The appellant was convicted and appealed on the ground that this evidence in rebuttal had been wrongly admitted, as the husband's answers in cross-examination were answers as to credit and the prosecution was not entitled to call evidence to contradict them.

GEOFFREY LANE LJ, reading the judgment of the court, said: 'Was the evidence admissible? A party may not, in general, impeach the credit of his opponent's witnesses by calling witnesses to contradict him on collateral matters, and his answers thereon will be conclusive — see *Harris* v *Tippett* (1811) 2 Camp 637, and *Phipson on Evidence*, 11th ed, paragraph 1553. The rule is of great practical use. It serves to prevent the indefinite prolongation of trials which would result from a minute examination of the character and credit of witnesses. It seems to have caused very little trouble in operation, judging by the paucity of authority on the subject. Difficulties may sometimes arise in determining what matters are merely collateral, see *Phillips* (1938) 26 Cr App R 17, but no one seriously suggests that the issue in the present case was other than collateral. On the other hand, it seems strange, if it be the case, that the Court and jury have to be kept in ignorance of behaviour by a witness such as that in the present case. The suggestion which lay behind the evidence in question was that Mr Mendy was prepared to lend himself to a scheme designed to defeat the purpose of keeping prospective witnesses out of Court;...

The truth of the matter is, as one would expect, that the rule is not all-embracing. It has always been permissible to call evidence to contradict a witness's denial of bias or partiality towards one of the parties and to show that he is prejudiced so far as the case being tried is concerned.

Pollock CB in *Attorney-General* v *Hitchcock* (1847) 1 Ex 9 puts the matter thus at p 101: "It is no disparagement to a man that a bribe is offered to him; it may be a disparagement to the man who makes the offer. If therefore the witness is asked about the fact and denies it or if he is asked whether he said so and so and he denies it he cannot be contradicted as to what he has said. *Lord Stafford's Case* [(1680) 7 How St Tr 1400] was totally different. There the witness himself had been implicated in offering a bribe to some other person. That immediately affected him as proving that he had acted the part of a suborner for the purpose of preventing the truth. In that case the evidence was to show that the witness was offered a bribe in a particular case, and the object was to show that he was so far affected towards the party accused as to be willing to adopt any corrupt course in order to carry out his purposes." In *Lord Stafford's Case, (supra)* the evidence was admitted.

Those words apply almost precisely to the facts in the present case. The witness was prepared to cheat in order to deceive the jury and help the defendant. The jury were entitled to be apprised of that fact.'

Appeal dismissed.

13.16 Commentary

R v *Coke and Littleton* at trial. During the presentation of the defence case for

Coke, Mr Atkyn tenders evidence from one Dr Johnson, who has for some years been
the Blackstone family's general physician and who has attended court under subpoena.
Mr Atkyn explains to Holt J that he anticipates that the doctor will say that (a) from
his long acquaintance with Margaret, he considers her prone to lying and being
dishonest, and that she has a reputation for untruthfulness (b) he has in the past
known her to be subject to outbursts of hysteria or extreme distress when under strain,
similar to the condition perceived by Dr Vesey during her examination, which tend to
make her unreliable and irrational until they subside.

13.17   Argument

Holt J: If you wish to ask Dr Johnson what Miss Blackstone's reputation is in the
community, then I do not see how you overcome Mr Bunbury's objection that it is a
collateral matter.

Mr Atkyn: My Lord, I first wish to ask the doctor for any evidence he may be
able to give as to her reputation for untruthfulness. I also seek to ask him about his
own opinion on that subject, as a long-standing acquaintance. My Lord, it is a form of
evidence which is little used, but which has been held by the Court of Appeal to be
proper. I refer to:

R v Richardson; R v Longman [1969] 1 QB 299 (CA)

The defendants were tried on indictment with conspiring together to pervert the course of
justice by trying to influence a jury and by suborning witnesses at a trial at which the brother
of one of the defendants was among those tried. At the trial the chief prosecution witness
gave evidence, and in order to discredit her the defence called a witness (a doctor) who was
asked whether he would believe the prosecution witness on her oath and he replied that in
certain particulars she could be believed on oath. The judge refused to allow the witness to be
asked the further question whether from his personal knowledge of her he would believe the
prosecution witness on her oath nor was the witness permitted to qualify his previous answer.
The defendants were convicted and appealed.

EDMUND DAVIES LJ, giving the judgment of the court, said: 'The legal position may be
thus summarised:
  1. A witness may be asked whether he has knowledge of the impugned witness's general
reputation for veracity and whether (from such knowledge) he would believe the impugned
witness's sworn testimony.
  2. The witness called to impeach the credibility of a previous witness may also express his
individual opinion (based upon his personal knowledge) as to whether the latter is to be
believed upon his oath and is *not* confined to giving evidence merely of general reputation.
  3. But whether his opinion as to the impugned witness's credibility be based simply upon
the latter's general reputation for veracity or upon his personal knowledge, the witness cannot
be permitted to indicate during his examination-in-chief the particular facts, circumstances or
incidents which formed the basis of his opinion, although he may be cross-examined as to
them...it is said that, while Mr Lassman was permitted to ask Dr Hitchens whether, in the
light of Mrs Clemence's general reputation for veracity, he would be prepared to believe her
on her oath, the question was never allowed to be answered in its entirety. It is submitted that
the form of such answer as Dr Hitchens gave showed that he desired to qualify it in some way
and was prevented by the judge from uttering more than the single qualifying word,
"But——."
  It is clear from the transcript that Mr Lassman also desired to ask another question of Dr
Hitchens, and we were told (and we accept) that it would have been in this form: "From your
personal knowledge of Mrs Clemence would you believe her on her oath?" That question, in

our judgment, he should have been permitted to put, but we have some sympathy with the trial judge suddenly confronted as he was with a situation which so rarely arises that not one of the learned Lords who decided *Toohey's* case [1965] AC 595 had throughout their extensive careers ever experienced it. Nevertheless, we are obliged to hold that the trial judge was technically wrong in ruling out that further question. As to whether he was also wrong in cutting short Dr Hitchens' attempt to qualify his earlier answer is far less clear: for it looks very much as though the witness was proceeding to adduce his reasons for qualifying it, and we know of no authority which permits that to be done.
(The court applied the proviso to s.4(1) of the Criminal Appeal Act 1907.)
Appeal dismissed.

Holt J: I see that the Court of Appeal said that the doctor could not give reasons for his opinion, at least in chief, though no doubt Mr Bunbury might investigate that, if he wishes.

Mr Atkyn: My Lord, yes.

Holt J: That being so, you may think it more appropriate to concentrate on the medical evidence, but of course that is entirely a matter for you.

Mr Atkyn: My Lord, in my submission, the doctor is entitled to state his opinion as to Margaret's reliability during a period of hysteria, based on his past observation and treatment of her. He may also substantiate that opinion by giving his reasons, even in chief, as Your Lordship is aware from the decision of the House of Lords in:

Toohey v Commissioner of Police of the Metropolis [1965] AC 595 (HL)

The defendant and two others were charged with assault with intent to rob. The victim's evidence was that they had demanded money and cigarettes, taken him up an alley and assaulted him in the course of searching him. The defence was that the alleged victim had been drinking and was behaving very strangely, and that while they were taking him home, he had become hysterical and had imagined that he was going to be robbed. A police surgeon gave evidence for the defence and said that when he examined the alleged victim there were no signs of injury on him, that he smelt of alcohol, and that throughout the examination he was weeping and hysterical. The judge refused to allow the doctor to be asked his opinion of the part played by alcohol in the victim's hysteria, and whether he was more prone to hysteria than a normal person. The defendant was convicted. His appeal to the Court of Criminal Appeal was dismissed, and he further appealed to the House of Lords.

LORD PEARCE said: 'The only general principles which can be derived from the older cases are these. On the one hand, the courts have sought to prevent juries from being beguiled by the evidence of witnesses who could be shown to be, through defect of character, wholly unworthy of belief. On the other hand, however, they have sought to prevent the trial of a case becoming clogged with a number of side issues, such as might arise if there could be an investigation of matters which had no relevance to the issue save in so far as they tended to show the veracity or falsity of the witness who was giving evidence which *was* relevant to the issue. Many controversies which might thus obliquely throw some light on the issues must in practice be discarded because there is not an infinity of time, money and mental comprehension available to make use of them.
There is one older case (*R* v *Hill* (1851) 20 LJMC 222) in which the Court for Crown Cases Reserved considered how it should deal with the evidence of a lunatic who was rational on some points. Evidence was given by doctors as to his credibility. Alderson B in argument made the sensible observation ibid, 224–225: "It seems to me almost approaching to an absurdity to say that a jury may, by hearing the statement of doctors, be able to say whether a man was insane when he made his will, and yet that they should not be competent to say whether a man be in a state of mind to enable him to give credible evidence when they see him before them." Lord Campbell CJ in giving judgment said ibid, 225: "The true rule seems to me to be that it was for the judge to see whether the witness understands the nature of an

oath and, if he does, to admit his testimony. No doubt, before he is sworn, the lunatic may be cross-examined, and evidence may be called to show that he labours under such a diseased mind as to be inadmissible; but, in the absence of such evidence he is prima facie admissible, and the jury may give such credit as they please to his testimony." The point was not quite the same as that which is before your Lordships, since the question was whether the lunatic should be allowed to give evidence at all. But there is inherent, I think, in the judgments an intention that the jury should have the best opportunity of arriving at the truth and that the medical evidence with regard to the witness's credibility should be before them.

Human evidence shares the frailties of those who give it. It is subject to many cross-currents such as partiality, prejudice, self-interest and, above all, imagination and inaccuracy. Those are matters with which the jury, helped by cross-examination and common sense, must do their best. But when a witness through physical (in which I include mental) disease or abnormality is not capable of giving a true or reliable account to the jury, it must surely be allowable for medical science to reveal this vital hidden fact to them. If a witness purported to give evidence of something which he believed that he had seen at a distance of 50 yards, it must surely be possible to call the evidence of an oculist to the effect that the witness could not possibly see anything at a greater distance than 20 yards, or the evidence of a surgeon who had removed a cataract from which the witness was suffering at the material time and which would have prevented him from seeing what he thought he saw. So, too, must it be allowable to call medical evidence of mental illness which makes a witness incapable of giving reliable evidence, whether through the existence of delusions or otherwise.

It is obviously in the interest of justice that such evidence should be available. The only argument that I can see against its admission is that there might be a conflict between the doctors and that there would then be a trial within a trial. But such cases would be rare and, if they arose, they would not create any insuperable difficulty, since there are many cases in practice where a trial within a trial is achieved without difficulty. And in such a case (unlike the issues relating to confessions) there would not be the inconvenience of having to exclude the jury since the dispute would be for their use and their instruction....

Medical evidence is admissible to show that a witness suffers from some disease or defect or abnormality of mind that affects the reliability of his evidence. Such evidence is not confined to a general opinion of the unreliability of the witness but may give all the matters necessary to show, not only the foundation of and reasons for the diagnosis, but also the extent to which the credibility of the witness is affected.'

(LORDS REID, MORRIS of BORTH-Y-GEST, HODSON and DONOVAN concurred.)
Appeal allowed.

(Holt J permitted the questions to be put to Dr Johnson.)

D: CROSS-EXAMINATION ON DOCUMENTS

13.18 Introductory notes

13.18.1 Documents are subject to the rules of evidence, and are not made admissible merely because they are referred to in cross-examination, if they are inadmissible in themselves for some reason such as hearsay. It is therefore not permissible to raise in cross-examination the contents of a document which has been ruled to be inadmissible, such as an involuntary confession.

13.18.2 Where a cross-examiner calls for and inspects a document in the possession of an adverse party or a witness called by an adverse party, the adverse party may insist that the document be put in evidence as part of the cross-examiner's case. The evidential value of documents so admitted has never been finally decided. (*A Practical Approach to Evidence*, pp 363–5.)

13.19 Commentary

R v *Coke and Littleton* at trial. During a hearing on the voir dire in the absence of the jury, Holt J ruled that the oral and written confessions alleged to have been made by Coke were inadmissible because they had not been made voluntarily (see also 7.4 et seq). At the conclusion of the prosecution case, Mr Atkyn calls Coke to give evidence. After examination in chief and cross-examination by Mr Bacon on behalf of Littleton, Mr Bunbury cross-examines Coke on behalf of the Crown. Mr Bunbury cross-examines generally about the events of 8 July 1979, and continues as below.

13.20 Course of evidence

Mr Bunbury: Is it your case that you used no force at all?
Coke: Yes.
Mr Bunbury: Have you ever told anyone that you were a bit forceful with Margaret?
Mr Atkyn: Well, before the defendant answers that question, My Lord, may the jury retire, because a point of law arises.
Holt J: Yes.
(The jury retires.)
Mr Atkyn: My Lord, I do not know what my learned friend intends by that question, but it seems to me that he is about to ask Coke about the contents of his statement under caution, which of course the jury have not seen because of Your Lordship's ruling.
Mr Bunbury: My Lord, the defendant Coke has told the jury that he used no force in having sexual intercourse with Miss Blackstone. It is only right that they should know that he has made an inconsistent statement on a previous occasion.
Holt J: My ruling was, of course, that the statement was not admissible as part of the prosecution case, but the question now is whether it can be used to contradict the defendant's evidence before the jury. Mr Atkyn, what do you say about that?
Mr Atkyn: As Your Lordship knows, cross-examination of a defendant is technically part of the prosecution case. There is abundant authority that inadmissible documents cannot be cross-examined upon. If it were not so, Your Lordship's ruling would be ineffective. I would refer Your Lordships to:

R v *Treacy* [1944] 2 All ER 229 (CCA)

The defendant was convicted of murder. At the trial he was cross-examined upon answers he made in an inadmissible statement and those answers were contrasted with certain answers he had made in the witness box.

HUMPHREYS J, giving the judgment of the court said: 'I say with regard to that statement as I said with regard to the two previous documents: either it was admissible in evidence or it was not. Counsel for the Crown did not think that he could have put in that statement against the appellant in the circumstances, seeing that the charge was one of murder. The statement, therefore, must be taken to be one that is inadmissible. But counsel for the Crown took the view:

When this man had made some statement in the witness box as to his movements on that morning which in my view did not agree with the statements which he had made in those inadmissible written answers to questions, I was entitled to put those to him.

We entirely disagree. In our view, a statement made by a prisoner under arrest is either admissible or it is not admissible. If it is admissible, the proper course for the prosecution is to prove it, give it in evidence, let the statement if it is in writing be made an exhibit, so that everybody knows what it is and everybody can inquire into it and do what they think right about it. If it is not admissible, nothing more ought to be heard of it, and it is quite a mistake to think that a document can be made admissible in evidence which is otherwise inadmissible simply because it is put to a person in cross-examination.'
Appeal allowed. Conviction quashed.

Nor is my learned friend entitled to read into evidence a document which is clearly inadmissible in law. I would refer Your Lordship in that context to:

R v Gillespie and Simpson (1967) 51 Cr App R 172 (CA)

The appellants, who were respectively the manageress and the cashier of a shop, were convicted of larceny, falsification of accounts and forgery. The substance of the charges against them was that they entered on a day-sheet against items of sale, smaller sums of money than had been received by the sales girls who took the money and handed it in at the cash desk. Five of the sales girls were called as witnesses by the prosecution to prove dockets issued by them, but in addition a number of other dockets, made out by sales girls who were not called as witnesses, were produced and the appellants were cross-examined on them, with a view to destroying a defence of mistakes by them in copying. The appellants did not accept what these dockets purported to record as true.

WINN LJ, delivering the judgment of the court, said: 'As it seems to this court, if a document is produced to a witness and the witness is asked: "Do you see what that document purports to record?" the witness may say: "I see it, I accept it as true," in which case the contents of the document become evidence against him: or he may say: "I see what is there written, I do not accept that as true," whereupon that which is purported to be recorded in the document is not evidence against that person who has rejected the contents; it becomes what one might call non-evidence, the document itself being nothing but hearsay.'
Convictions quashed.

Holt J: Mr Bunbury, that seems to me to be right.
Mr Bunbury: If Your Lordship pleases. In that case, I shall restrict myself to asking the witness to look at his statement and tell the jury whether he wishes to alter anything he has told them.
Mr Atkyn: My Lord, I would not object to that, on the clear understanding that no part of the contents of the statement are referred to in the presence of the jury, and that my learned friend must accept the defendant's answer as final, be it yes or no.
Mr Bunbury: My Lord, I accept that position.
Holt J: Very well, I shall allow that question but no more. Let the jury return.

13.21 Commentary

Blackstone v Coke at trial.   Margaret Blackstone, having given evidence in chief, is being cross-examined by Mr Atkyn on behalf of Coke. Mr Atkyn has been exploring the subject of her relationships with various boyfriends over a period of some months leading up to July 1979. During the course of cross-examination, Mr Atkyn notices that Margaret appears to be referring to some document.

13.22 Course of evidence

Mr Atkyn: Miss Blackstone, I see you looking at what appears to be a book. Would you please tell His Lordship and myself what that is.

Margaret: It is my diary relating to the period you have been asking me about.

Mr Atkyn: May I see it please?

Hardwicke J: Mr Noy?

Mr Noy: I have no objection, My Lord.

(Mr Atkyn inspects the diary and cross-examines Margaret extensively about references to Anthony Henneky on various dates during June and July 1979. After turning to other topics, Mr Atkyn concludes his cross-examination, and Mr Noy rises to re-examine.)

Mr Noy: Before I re-examine, my Lord, I formally apply for Miss Blackstone's diary to be admitted in evidence and exhibited. I think it will be Exhibit P4.

Mr Atkyn: My Lord, I object to that course. There has been discovery in this case, and my learned friend is not entitled to seek to put in evidence documents which were not disclosed.

Mr Noy: My Lord, this was a document which Miss Blackstone referred to in the witness box, and which my learned friend very properly inspected. But if I may refer Your Lordship to the case of *Stroud* v *Stroud* the consequences of his doing so is that the diary must go into evidence as part of my learned friend's case.

Stroud v *Stroud* [1963] 1 WLR 1080 (P)

A wife petitioned for divorce on the ground of cruelty. A doctor was called as a witness on her behalf. In the course of cross-examining that witness, the husband's counsel called for certain documents in the possession of the witness. The documents, which were medical reports relating to the wife, were handed to counsel who read them. The question arose whether his doing so had the effect of putting the documents in evidence.

WRANGHAM J said: 'It was then submitted by Mr Law that by calling for these documents, and by himself reading their contents, Mr Lawson had made them part of his evidence. In support of this contention Mr Law relied primarily upon *Calvert* v *Flower* (1836) 7 C & P 386. In that case counsel for the defendant called for a ledger under a notice to produce and after some controversy between counsel Lord Denman CJ said: "If the intestate's ledger is called for under a notice to produce, and it is not produced, Mr Kelly may cross-examine as to its contents; but if it is produced and given to Mr Kelly, it will be for me to decide whether Mr Kelly makes such use of it as will compel him to use it as his evidence." The book was produced and Mr Kelly turned over several pages of it so as to look at the contents of them. Lord Denman then said: "I ought now to say, that if Mr Kelly looks at the book he will be bound to put it in as his evidence," and Mr Kelly (who, I assume, was ultimately to become the Chief Baron of that name) said: "Certainly, I am fully aware that I must do so." Lord Denman went on: "I have mentioned this because it has been supposed by some, that an opposite counsel may look at papers or books called for under a notice to produce, and then not use them." It is plain, therefore, that at that stage Lord Denman was laying down in no uncertain terms that where a document is called for under a notice to produce and is read by the counsel who calls for the document that counsel by that conduct is putting in the document as part of his evidence....

It was contended by Mr Lawson that this rule had been laid down at a time when there was no discovery in the courts of common law and had now become virtually obsolete, since the procedure of inspection of the documents of the other party, subject to such limitations as privilege, now enables a litigant to do just what the rule was supposed to prevent; but though it may be that now the occasions for the practical application of the rule are fewer, because each party ordinarily knows the relevant documents in the possession of the other, the rule itself has never been abrogated, and it may still be of practical importance, for example, in criminal proceedings, where there is no discovery.

It was further contended that in this particular case the documents should be excluded from evidence because they ought to have been disclosed and not regarded, as they had been, as documents covered by privilege, and that if they had been disclosed they would have been inspected. There is nothing in any of the documents to show that they were prepared for the purpose of submission to the wife's legal advisers in connection with her divorce suit. Mr Law informed me that these statements were at the material time in the possession of the wife's solicitors. In those circumstances it may well be that these documents ought to have been disclosed. Nevertheless, it was open to Mr Lawson to investigate at the hearing what the documents were without actually calling for them, and to ask to be allowed to inspect such as should have been disclosed and inspected beforehand under the right of inspection given by the Rules of the Supreme Court. As he did not do that but chose to call for and read through these documents in court. I think the consequences as specified by Lord Denman and Sir Creswell must follow.'

(His Lordship ruled that the documents be put in evidence.)

Hardwicke J: Mr Atkyn, that appears to be correct.

Mr Atkyn: If Your Lordship so rules.

Mr Noy: My Lord, so that my position will not be misunderstood, I urge Your Lordship to admit the whole of the diary into evidence in accordance with the rule stated by Wrangham J in *Stroud* v *Stroud,* because there are certain references beyond those referred to by my learned friend in cross-examination, to which I want to refer in re-examination.

Hardwicke J: Yes.

(Mr Noy then re-examines, referring Miss Blackstone to entries in the diary referring to Coke and to the events of 8 July 1979. At the conclusion of re-examination, the following discussion ensues.)

Hardwicke J: Perhaps counsel can assist me. I am not sure that I am entitled to regard the contents of this diary, which I have now seen, as evidence of the facts recorded in it, or whether I should confine myself to regarding it as evidence of consistency.

Mr Noy: My Lord, in my submission, Your Lordship can regard it as evidence of the facts stated in it. It is precisely the same as if a memory–refreshing document had been admitted into evidence by reason of cross-examination, in which case Section 3(2) of the Civil Evidence Act 1968 makes the document evidence in the case[1].

Mr Atkyn: My Lord, in my submission this document was not admitted as a memory–refreshing document. Although Professor Cross in his book on evidence, fifth edition at page 262, points out that this question has never been decided in England, I would respectfully submit that since the date of *Stroud* v *Stroud* the position has been affected by:

Civil Evidence Act 1968, s.1(1)

1(1) In any civil proceedings a statement other than one made by a person while giving oral evidence in those proceedings shall be admissible as evidence of any fact stated therein to the extent that it is so admissible by virtue of any provision of this part of this Act or by virtue of any other statutory provision or by agreement of the parties, but not otherwise.

---

[1]As to the admission of memory refreshing documents and previous consistent or inconsistent statements, see 12.12 et seq.

In my submission, none of the three conditions for admissibility postulated by that subsection applies to the document before Your Lordship.

Hardwicke J: This is a difficult question. I incline to the view that this document must have an evidential value similar to memory refreshing documents and previous consistent or inconsistent statements. Of course, in a criminal case the matter might very well be different. I shall consider this matter and give judgment on it in due course.

E: BEYOND CROSS-EXAMINATION

13.23 Introductory notes

13.23.1 Following cross-examination, the party calling the witness is entitled to re-examine in order to explain or clarify any matters arising in cross-examination which appear unfavourable to his case. Re-examination may only take place where there has been cross-examination, and is restricted to matters dealt with by the cross-examiner. Re-examination may be used to explain any apparent contradiction exposed by cross-examination, or to re-establish the witness's credit if it has been attacked. As with examination in chief, re-examination must be conducted without reference to leading questions.

13.23.2 In general, all evidence that supports a party's case must be presented by means of evidence in chief. Evidence in rebuttal at a later stage will generally be permitted only where it is calculated to deal with a matter that arose unexpectedly and which could not reasonably have been foreseen. It is a course which will be permitted by the court where a party has been taken by surprise by some unexpected development of evidence. Where evidence could and should have been foreseen as necessary to the presentation of the case, that evidence should be presented in chief and may not be adduced by means of evidence in rebuttal.

13.23.3 Under the Civil Evidence Act 1968 s.7, evidence may be given to attack or support the credibility of the maker of an admissible hearsay statement who is not called as a witness. Similarly, evidence suggesting that the maker of such a statement has made inconsistent statements on other occasions may be admitted by virtue of s.7. The section is designed to simulate the cross-examiner's weapons of attack on credit and the use of previous inconsistent statements. Exploration of collateral matters are restricted as they would be in cross-examination of a live witness. Statements admitted by virtue of this section (which applies only to civil cases) may be treated as evidence of the facts stated in them.

13.23.4 Although the working of the adversarial system requires that the judge should not ordinarily interfere with the decision of the parties to call or to forbear from calling evidence, the judge may of his own motion call a witness where he thinks it necessary to the administration of justice. The power is principally of importance in criminal cases, where the judge has a general discretion over evidential matters in the interests of ensuring a fair trial. It is properly exercised where the prosecution failed to call a witness who on the face of it ought to be called in fairness to the defence. The power should be exercised sparingly. Such a witness may, with leave of the judge, be cross-examined by all parties, and in practice leave will invariably be given. (*A Practical Approach to Evidence,* pp 365–69.)

13.24   Commentary

R v *Coke and Littleton* at trial. Mr Bunbury calls the evidence on behalf of the prosecution and closes his case. Subsequently, the defence cases for Coke and Littleton are presented and closed. Mr Bunbury then applies to call evidence in rebuttal in an attempt to show that Coke was the author of Exhibit GG1. The evidence proposed to be called is that of the handwriting expert, Mr Hale, who was not called for the prosecution as part of the prosecution case. Mr Atkyn on behalf of Coke objects.

13.25   Argument

Mr Atkyn: My Lord, in my submission this is not a proper subject for evidence in rebuttal. It was clearly foreseeable that evidence of handwriting might be required, if the prosecution intended to rely upon an allegation that the defendant Coke was the author of Exhibit GG1.

Holt J: It is certainly a most unusual application. Mr Bunbury, what do you say about it?

Mr Bunbury: My Lord, the prosecution are always in the difficulty that the defence are not obliged to reveal the nature of their case before trial, except in the case where they must serve notice of alibi and this does not apply in the case of the defendant Coke.

Holt J: I accept that there are cases where matters arise which have not been pleaded or which take a party by surprise. I would also accept that this is particularly true of criminal cases, where pleadings are virtually non-existent. However, am I not right in thinking that every party both in civil and criminal cases is obliged to foresee the matters which he needs to prove his case?

Mr Atkyn: My Lord, if I might assist, the cases clearly support the view Your Lordship has taken. The classic statement of the rule was that laid down by Tindal CJ in *R* v *Frost* (1840) 9 C&P 129, and was cited in:

R v *Day* [1940] 1 All ER 402 (CCA)

The appellant was convicted of forging a cheque. As part of its case the prosecution produced two letter-cards and it was admitted that the handwriting upon these was the genuine handwriting of the appellant. The appellant gave evidence which amounted to a complete denial that he had written the cheque or signed it. Subsequently, the judge, on the application of the prosecution, admitted evidence of a handwriting expert to say that there were similarities between the known genuine handwriting of the appellant and the handwriting of the signature on the cheque.

HILBERY J, delivering the judgment of the court, stated the facts and continued: 'We think that the law is now well decided. It is true to say that, if a question as to the time at which evidence is to be received arises in the course of the trial, it may be that the judge may be called upon to decide the appropriate time, and, in so doing, exercise a judicial discretion. However, this was not such a case. This was a case where all that was being done was to seek to remedy an obvious deficiency in the evidence in support of the case for the prosecution, not only after the case for the prosecution had been closed, but also after the evidence for the defence had been heard, and it was an endeavour to call that supplementary evidence, although the material upon which that evidence was to be given had been in the hands of the prosecution from the beginning. It was evidence upon one branch of the prosecution's case, upon which it must have been realised that they must give positive evidence.

The law has been laid down and expounded in *R* v *Harris* [1927] 2 KB 587, where it is said, at p 594:

> But it is obvious that injustice may be done to an accused person unless some limitation is put upon the exercise of that right, and for the purpose of this case, we adopt the rule laid down by Tindal, CJ, in *R* v *Frost* (1840) 9 C & P 129 where Tindal, CJ, said: "There is no doubt that the general rule is that where the Crown begins its case like a plaintiff in a civil suit, they cannot afterwards support their case by calling fresh witnesses, because they are met by certain evidence that contradicts it. They stand or fall by the evidence they have given. They must close their case before the defence begins; but if any matter arises *ex improviso,* which no human ingenuity can foresee, on the part of a defendant in a civil suit, or a prisoner in a criminal case, there seems to me no reason why that matter which so arose *ex improviso* may not be answered by contrary evidence on the part of the Crown." That rules applies only to a witness called by the Crown and on behalf of the Crown, but we think that the rule should also apply to a case where a witness is called in a criminal trial by the judge after the case for the defence is closed.

Counsel for the prosecution sought to say that the rule relied upon for the appellant was confined to cases in which the fresh evidence was being called by the judge, but that passage answers that contention and makes the rule apply to evidence called on behalf of the Crown and by the judge. The judge continued, at p 595:

> and that the practice should be limited to a case where a matter arises *ex improviso,* which no human ingenuity can foresee, on the part of a prisoner, otherwise injustice would ensue.

In other words, the principle is to be applied whether the witness is called by the court or by the Crown....

> If those words are applied to the case which we have now under consideration, it becomes manifest, I think, that those conditions were not fulfilled in this case. First, the matter whether this handwriting was the handwriting of the appellant — that is, whether his was the hand which wrote the forgery with which he was charged — was a question about which from the outset the burden had been upon the prosecution to show that the handwriting was that of the appellant. It was, therefore, evidence concerning material which had been in the hands of the prosecution before the case was heard, and it was evidence the necessity of which was obvious from the start. Indeed, the judge had no hesitation in saying that, without it, it was impossible to ask the jury to act as handwriting experts and to pass a verdict which might be a conviction. It cannot be said, in the circumstances, that this evidence was evidence upon any matter which arose *ex improviso,* if those Latin words are given the meaning which was originally attributed to them. Nor can it be said that it was evidence the necessity of which no human ingenuity could foresee. It was evidence the necessity of which was obvious.'

Appeal allowed and conviction quashed.

(Holt J disallowed the evidence.)

13.26 Commentary

Blackstone v *Coke* at trial. The statement of Anthony Henneky has been put in evidence by Mr Atkyn on behalf of Coke under the Civil Evidence Act 1968, s.2, (see 8.7, ante). Mr Atkyn proposes to rely on the contents of this statement as showing that Mr Henneky may be the father of Margaret Blackstone's child and as pointing to acts of sexual intercourse between the two of them at about the time of conception.

Mr Noy on behalf of the plaintiff now wishes to introduce the letter from Mr Henneky's American attorney asserting that Mr Henneky denies being the father of the child. Mr Atkyn objects that this letter is inadmissible.

13.27 Argument

Hardwicke J: How do you say this letter can be admitted, Mr Noy?
Mr Noy: My Lord, Section 7 of the Civil Evidence Act 1968 provides:

(1)...Where in any civil proceedings a statement made by a person who is not called as a witness in those proceedings is given in evidence by virtue of Section 2 of this Act —
(a) Any evidence which, if that person had been so called, would be admissible for the purpose of destroying or supporting his credibility as a witness shall be admissible for that purpose in those proceedings; and
(b) Evidence tending to prove that, whether before or after he made that statement, that person made (whether orally or in a document or otherwise) another statement inconsistent therewith shall be admissible for the purpose of showing that that person has contradicted himself:...

My Lord, this is a case where the maker of an admissible hearsay statement has not been called, and where evidence is available to the plaintiff which would tend to show that he has made a statement inconsistent with that produced to the court. This is no more than I would have been entitled to put to him in cross-examination, had he been called as a witness. I should also draw Your Lordship's attention to the proviso to Section 7(1):

Provided that nothing in this subsection shall enable evidence to be given of any matter of which, if the person in question had been called as a witness and had denied that matter in cross-examination, evidence could not have been adduced by the cross-examining party.

My Lord, this is not a collateral matter because it goes directly to one of the facts in issue in the case, namely whether Mr Coke is proved to be the father of Miss Blackstone's child.
Hardwicke J: Yes. I think you are entitled to put the letter in. What evidential value do you say it has?
Mr Noy: If Your Lordship would look at Section 7(3), your Lordships will see that the provisions of Section 3(1)(a) are expressly applied to statements admitted under this section. In effect, therefore, Your Lordship will appreciate that statements admitted under this section are in the same category as those admitted in civil cases as previous inconsistent statements, and may therefore be regarded as evidence of the facts stated in them[1].

13.28   Questions for Counsel

13.28.1   R v Coke and Littleton: Do you agree with the decision of Holt J to give leave to Mr Atkyn to cross-examine Margaret Blackstone with regard to her sexual relationship with Kevin?

13.28.2   R v Coke and Littleton: What arguments can be made for and against the

---
[1]As to the evidential value of previous inconsistent statements, see 13.10, ante.

the view that the allegation of Margaret's previous threat to accuse Kevin of rape is collateral to the issues in the present case?

13.28.3 Blackstone v *Coke:* What arguments can be made for and against the view that the inconsistency between Anthony Henneky's hearsay statement and the letter from his American attorney is a purely collateral issue, so that the letter should be inadmissible under the terms of Section 7(1) of the Civil Evidence Act 1968?

14 Corroboration

14.1 Introductory notes

14.1.1 The term corroboration refers to support or confirmation offered by one piece of evidence to another. Thus, evidence may be confirmed in its tenor and effect by other admissible and independent evidence (the corroborating evidence) and is then said to be corroborated. Corroborated evidence is naturally likely to carry more weight than uncorroborated evidence. However, the main question for the law of evidence is whether a tribunal of fact is entitled to act on uncorroborated evidence, or whether corroboration should be required in all or some cases. At common law, the rule is that in the absence of some specific rule to the contrary, the tribunal of fact may always act upon the uncorroborated evidence of a single witness or document.

14.1.2 The common law rule is subject to two groups of exceptions which differ considerably in their nature and effect. Despite these differences, the two groups share the common justification that certain kinds of evidence are inherently unreliable, and that accordingly some form of support for them should be looked for if they are to be acted on in safety. Such unreliability may arise from the personal characteristics of a witness, from personal interest in the outcome of the case or in the acceptance of one's evidence, from personal motives in giving evidence or simply from the nature of the evidence in the case itself. The groups of exceptions are as follows:

14.1.2.1 Cases where corroboration is required as a matter of law. These cases are statutory· and the requirement of corroboration is mandatory, so that if there is no evidence capable of amounting to corroboration the judge must withdraw the case from the jury or dismiss the claim as the case may be. A conviction or judgment obtained in breach of this requirement will be set aside on appeal. The cases to which this rule applies are of high treason, perjury, personation at elections, speeding, offences of procurement under the Sexual Offences Act 1956, affiliation cases and most importantly the unsworn evidence of children tendered under the Children and Young Persons Act 1933, s.38(1).

14.1.2.2 Cases where corroboration is to be looked for as a matter of practice. These are cases at common law where the tribunal of fact must be warned of the danger of acting on uncorroborated evidence. It will be a ground of appeal if the jury is not warned of this danger in the course of summing up or in a civil case if the judge manifestly fails to warn himself of the danger. But, provided such warning is conveyed, the tribunal of fact may convict or act upon uncorroborated evidence and no appeal will lie solely because it does so. Kinds of evidence falling within this category are the sworn evidence of children, the evidence of accomplices, the evidence of complainants of sexual misconduct and the evidence of claimants to the property of deceased persons. In cases which turn wholly or substantially upon evidence of visual identification, as a matter of practice the courts require such evidence to be supported by other evidence capable of confirming the identification, but the requirement stops short of calling for corroborative evidence in the legal sense.

14.1.3 The assessment of corroboration falls into two parts. The first, the question whether evidence is capable in law of amounting to corroboration, is a matter of law for the judge. The second, the question whether on the assumption that evidence is capable in law of amounting to corroboration it does in fact amount to corroboration on the facts of the case, is one of fact for the jury. The judge must of course direct the jury as to what evidence, if any, is capable in law of amounting to corroboration, and then must leave the factual question to them.

14.1.4 In order to be capable in law of amounting to corroboration, evidence must be (a) admissible in itself; (b) from a source independent of the evidence requiring corroboration; and (c) such as to tend to show by confirmation of some material particular, not only that the offence charged was committed but also that it was committed by the defendant.

14.1.5 Where two or more witnesses each require corroboration as a matter of law or practice, the evidence of each may corroborate that of the other and is sufficient to satisfy the requirement in respect of each. This rule in favour of 'mutual corroboration' does not apply to (a) the unsworn evidence of two or more children; (b) the evidence of two or more accomplices who are *participes criminis* in the offence charged.

14.1.6 In certain cases, corroboration of a prosecution case may be afforded by the defendant himself, as where he is proved to have fabricated an 'innocent' account of his conduct. Where the defendant gives evidence in his defence, corroboration may be sought in the substance of the defendant's evidence (i.e. in what he actually says in the witness box on oath). However, the mere fact that the jury may disbelieve the defendant cannot amount to corroboration of the prosecution evidence. The defendant's failure to give evidence is not capable of amounting to corroboration. (*A Practical Approach to Evidence*, pp 370–86.)

14.2 Commentary

R v Coke and Littleton on appeal against conviction. At trial, Margaret Blackstone gave evidence of the alleged rape of her by Coke. As the complainant of a sexual offence, her evidence requires to be corroborated as a matter of practice. Mr Atkyn for Coke appeals on the ground that Holt J misdirected the jury with regard to the evidence that they could properly regard as corroborative. The passage in the summing-up complained of is as follows:

'Members of the jury, now that I have told you what corroboration means, you will naturally expect some guidance as to whether there is any evidence in this case which you could regard as corroborative of Margaret's evidence. Certainly there is. Whether you do find it corroborative in the circumstances is entirely a question of fact for you. But you may think that there was an abundance of evidence given which you could regard as corroborating her evidence. Let me give you two examples. You will recall that Margaret related to you a conversation she had with her mother on returning home from Coke's flat shortly after the commission of the alleged rape. That complaint was allowed to be given in evidence because it had the effect of confirming what Margaret said in evidence. Indeed, had it not possessed that confirming quality, it could not have been given in evidence at all because it would be what we lawyers call a mere self-serving statement. Or take another example. You heard evidence given that Dr Vesey took a vaginal swab from Margaret very shortly after the alleged offence, and that examination of that swab by Dr Espinasse showed that Margaret had had sexual intercourse within a recent time of its taking and definitely within forty-eight hours before. Now those are the sort of matters which you may think go to support Margaret's evidence and therefore corroborate it. But as I say, that is entirely a matter for you.'

14.3   Argument

Leach LJ: Mr Atkyn, you would probably concede at least that the learned judge was correct in taking upon himself the decision as a decision of law whether certain evidence was capable of amounting to corroboration.

Mr Atkyn: Yes, My Lord. That is of course a matter of law for the judge. I would also concede that the learned judge was correct in directing the attention of the jury to those parts of the evidence which he considered potentially corroborative. That being done, the value of the evidence was entirely a matter for the jury. Your Lordships will be familiar with the observations made by this Court in:

R v *Charles and others* (1976) 68 Cr App R 334 (CA)

LAWTON LJ said: 'There was a time some 20 years ago when the old Court of Criminal Appeal ruled that it was unnecessary for a judge to direct the jury as to what evidence was capable of being corroboration. Since that time the general practice has changed and it is now generally accepted, certainly in cases of any complication, that the judge should indicate to the jury what evidence is and what evidence is not capable of being corroboration.'

My Lords, my complaint is that the learned judge drew the attention of the jury to two matters that were incapable in law of amounting to corroboration.

East LJ: For what reasons?

Mr Atkyn: My Lords, corroborative evidence must satisfy certain requirements which were set out in the judgment of Lord Reading CJ in:

R v *Baskerville* [1916] 2 KB 658 (CCA)

The defendant was convicted of having committed acts of gross indecency with two boys. The only direct evidence of the commission of the acts charged was that of the boys themselves, who on their own statement were accomplices in the offences. However, a letter was proved to have been sent to one of the boys by the defendant in his handwriting signed by him with his initial B, enclosing a 10s note for both boys, and making an appointment for them to meet the defendant 'as arranged'. The judge told the jury that the letter afforded evidence which they would be entitled to find was sufficient corroboration of the boys' evidence.

LORD READING CJ, delivering the judgment of the court, said: 'We hold that evidence in corroboration must be independent testimony which affects the accused by connecting or tending to connect him with the crime. In other words, it must be evidence which implicates him, that is, which confirms in some material particular not only the evidence that the crime has been committed, but also that the prisoner committed it. The test applicable to determine the nature and extent of the corroboration is thus the same whether the case falls within the rule of practice at common law or within that class of offences for which corroboration is required by statute. The language of the statute, "implicates the accused," compendiously incorporates the test applicable at common law in the rule of practice. The nature of the corroboration will necessarily vary according to the particular circumstances of the offence charged. It would be in high degree dangerous to attempt to formulate the kind of evidence which would be regarded as corroboration, except to say that corroborative evidence is evidence which shows or tends to show that the story of the accomplice that the accused committed the crime is true, not merely that the crime has been committed, but that it was committed by the accused.

The corroboration need not be direct evidence that the accused committed the crime; it is sufficient if it is merely circumstantial evidence of his connection with the crime. A good instance of this indirect evidence is to be found in *R* v *Birkett* 8 C & P 732. Were the law otherwise many crimes which are usually committed between accomplices in secret, such as incest, offences with females, or the present case, could never be brought to justice.'
Appeal dismissed.

The test, My Lords, therefore is whether the evidence was admissible, from an independent source and tending to implicate the defendant in the commission of the offence charged.

Cox LJ: You would presumably not dispute that the evidence was admissible?

Mr Atkyn: My Lord, no. But in my submission both pieces of evidence referred to by the learned judge were lacking in the other two necessary qualities. So far as independance is concerned, it is well settled that a witness cannot corroborate himself. A situation on all fours with the present case arose in:

R v *Whitehead* [1929] 1 KB 99 (CCA)

On the trial of the appellant for having had unlawful sexual intercourse with a girl under sixteen, the judge directed the jury that although what the girl said to her mother several months after the offence was committed was not evidence, yet the jury could infer what the girl said, namely, that the appellant was responsible for her condition, from what the mother did, because the appellant was at once accused, and that that amounted to corroboration of the girl's story. The appellant was convicted.

LORD HEWART, delivering the judgment of the court, said: 'This is not a case like *R* v *Lillyman* [1896] 2 QB 167 or *R* v *Osborne* [1905] 1 KB 551, because in those cases the complaint was made at the first opportunity which reasonably offered itself after the offence was committed, whereas in the present case the complaint was not made until after the lapse of several months. [His Lordship referred to a passage from the summing-up and continued:] It is said that the opening portion of that passage was likely to convey to the minds of the jury that although the girl's statement to her mother was in the circumstances not admissible in evidence, nevertheless the jury could draw the inference, from what the mother did, that the girl had said that the appellant was responsible for her condition, and that that amounted to corroboration of the girl's story. That direction would be wrong. Any such inference as to what the girl had told her mother could not amount to corroboration of the girl's story, because it proceeded from the girl herself; it was merely the girl's story at second hand. In order that evidence may amount to corroboration it must be extraneous to the witness who is to be corroborated. A girl cannot corroborate herself, otherwise it is only necessary for her to repeat her story some twenty-five times in order to get twenty-five corroborations of it.'
Appeal allowed.

Leach LJ: Presumably, Mr Atkyn, the same would apply to such things as previous inconsistent statements and memory-refreshing documents, in those cases where they are admissible.

Mr Atkyn: My Lord, indeed. The same point is illustrated by the provisions of Section 6(4) of the Civil Evidence Act 1968. When certain hearsay statements were rendered admissible in civil cases by Part 1 of the Act, it was necessary to deal with the situation where such statements might be tendered in addition to the oral evidence of the witness. Clearly, this was another case where there was no independent source and where it would therefore be wrong for such hearsay statements to be capable of corroborating the evidence of the witness. The section provides that they are not.

Civil Evidence Act 1968 s.6(4)

6(4) For the purpose of any enactment or rule of law or practice requiring evidence to be corroborated or regulating the manner in which uncorroborated evidence is to be treated —
(a)   a statement which is admissible in evidence by virtue of Section 2 or 3 of this Act shall not be capable of corroborating evidence given by the maker of the statement; and
(b)   a statement which is admissible in evidence by virtue of Section 4 of this Act shall not be capable of corroborating evidence given by the person who originally supplied the information from which the record containing the statement was compiled.

East LJ: I can see the force of that argument in relation to the recent complaint, but that surely does not affect the corroborative value of the evidence of Dr Vesey and Dr Espinasse?

Mr Atkyn: My Lord, that evidence is clearly from an independent source. But in order to be corroborative in law, the evidence must show not only that an offence was committed but that it was committed by the defendant. In this connection, Your Lordships may find helpful the principle set out in the affiliation case of:

Cracknell v *Smith* [1960] 1 WLR 1239 (DC)

The complainant in affiliation proceedings gave evidence that she had had intercourse with the defendant at about the likely time of conception (March 1958). Her mother testified that the defendant had visited her home to see the complainant in January and February 1958, and had met the complainant at the corner of the street on various occasions. The justices were of opinion that the evidence of the mother was sufficient corroboration of the complainant's evidence, and accordingly adjudged the defendant the putative father of the child. The defendant appealed.

LORD PARKER CJ, giving the judgment of the court, said: 'For my part, I am perfectly satisfied that the evidence of the mother was not sufficient corroboration or, perhaps more accurately, any corroboration, because the weight to be attached to the evidence is a matter for the justices. Quite apart from the fact that she was only speaking in regard to January and February, 1958, and not in regard to March, it is quite clear that her evidence was as to mere opportunity. Mere evidence of opportunity and nothing more can be no corroboration. There are, of course, cases, of which *Moore* v *Hewitt* [1947] KB 831 is an example, and also *Harvey* v *Anning* [1902] 87 LT 687, in both of which there was something more than mere opportunity. In both cases, unlike the present case, there was evidence that the complainant was not being intimate with or associating with anybody else. Secondly, in *Harvey* v *Anning* there was, as an additional factor, the great difference in the social position of the parties, and in both cases there was real evidence of courtship and association together, and not the very vague association spoken to by the mother in the present case.'
Appeal allowed.

And, My Lords, more directly in the case of *James* v *R*, a case of alleged rape, it was held that mere medical evidence of sexual intercourse did not in itself corroborate evidence that the complainant had been raped, as opposed to merely having sexual intercourse.

James v *R* (1970) 55 Cr App R 299 (PC)

The appellant was convicted of rape. The complainant alleged that a man whom she subsequently identified as the appellant had raped her at knife point. There was medical evidence showing that the complainant had had sexual intercourse at about a time consistent with her allegation. The trial judge directed that this evidence might corroborate that of the complainant.

VISCOUNT DILHORNE, delivering the judge of the Board, said: 'In their Lordships' view, this direction was entirely wrong. Independent evidence that intercourse had taken place is not evidence confirming in some material particular either that the crime of rape had been committed or, if it had been, that it had been committed by the accused. It does not show that the intercourse took place without consent or that the accused was a party to it. There was in this case no evidence capable of amounting to corroboration of Miss Hall's evidence that she had been raped, and raped by the accused. The judge should have told the jury that. His failure to do so was a serious misdirection, so serious as to make it inevitable that the conviction should be quashed.

Not only did the judge fail so to direct the jury; he went on to tell them wrongly that the medical evidence could amount to corroboration and having said that, he said that two questions had to be considered, was it without her consent and was he the man? Despite what he had said earlier about corroboration being particularly necessary where the issue is consent or no consent, he failed to direct the jury as to the need for corroboration on both these questions. Indeed the passage cited above suggests that the jury might well have thought that, if they accepted the medical evidence, they were entitled to disregard the warning he had given against the danger of acting on uncorroborated evidence.'

Conviction quashed.

Leach LJ: I accept the principle of that case, of course, Mr Atkyn. But I don't think it helps you, because in this case there is no dispute that it was your client who had sexual intercourse with Miss Blackstone. Had there been a dispute about that, I agree that the evidence would not have implicated Mr Coke or anyone in the commission of an offence. But on the facts as they appear to us, while I would probably agree with your point in relation to the recent complaint, I do not see how you can criticise the summing up on the medical evidence when your client does not dispute having had sexual intercourse.

Mr Atkyn: My Lord, that evidence does not point to lack of consent.

Leach LJ: I agree. But the requirement as stated by Lord Reading CJ in *R* v *Baskerville* was only that it should confirm the evidence in a material particular. I think it does.

14.4 Commentary

R v *Coke and Littleton* on appeal against conviction. At the trial, Margaret Blackstone gave evidence on oath. Angela Blackstone, following questioning by Holt J, was permitted to give evidence unsworn under the provisions of s.38(1) of the Children and Young Persons Act 1933 (see also 11.9 et seq). In the course of the summing up, Holt J makes no reference to the subject of corroboration. Mr Atkyn and Mr Bacon both contend that the conviction must be quashed because of this omission.

14.5 Argument

Leach LJ: Mr Atkyn, we will deal with your appeal first. Although you are obviously concerned with the evidence of both girls to some extent, I imagine you are principally concerned with that of Margaret?

Mr Atkyn: My Lord, that is right. In my submission, it was incumbent on the learned judge to direct the jury about corroboration.

East LJ: This is not one of the cases where the jury could not have convicted on uncorroborated evidence, because she gave evidence on oath.

Mr Atkyn: My Lord, that is correct. Her evidence required to be corroborated as a matter of practice. I accept that there may well have been corroborative evidence available, and that in any event the jury would have been entitled to convict in its absence but in my submission, the absence of warning is fatal to the conviction because the jury were not made aware of the danger.

Cox LJ: On what basis do you say that practice required corroboration?

Mr Atkyn: My Lord, on two grounds. The first is that she was a child of tender years, and the second is that she was the complainant as to an act of sexual misconduct. If I may deal with her age first, it is settled law that there is always a danger in acting on the uncorroborated evidence of children, particularly where there is some realistic possibility of collusion, as there was here between these two sisters.

Leach LJ: Mr Atkyn, that may be all very well in principle, but I see from the papers that this witness was born on 3 May, 1962 and was not far off eighteen when she gave evidence. Can you realistically maintain that she falls within the definition of a child of tender years?

Mr Atkyn: My Lord, in my submission there is no defined age at which one ceases to be of tender years. The matter is one for the discretion of the judge, who must take into account the maturity of the witness and the likelihood of collusion. I must concede that if my argument is right it is an unusual case. But it is a question to which the judge should have addressed his mind, and it appears that he did not. I refer Your Lordships to:

R v *Morgan* [1978] 1 WLR 735 (CA)

The defendant was tried on a charge of indecent assault on a boy aged 11. Evidence on oath about the incident was given by the victim, his brother aged 12 and a boy aged 16 at the time of the incident, which had occurred some 12 months before the trial. Neither the brother nor the boy aged 16 was a victim. The defendant did not give evidence. In relation to the victim the jury were warned of the risks in convicting on his evidence unless it was corroborated; no such warning was given in relation to the brother or the boy aged 16. The defendant was convicted.

ROSKILL LJ, giving the judgment of the court, said: 'We think, with great respect to the judge,...that he was guilty of an omission in not extending what he said to the jury as to the need for corroboration in the case of the victim to the brother, who was only a little older than the victim. We think that he should have given a similar warning that the jury ought to have in mind that this boy was only 12 years of age at the time of the incident and 13 at the time of the trial and that, therefore, exactly·the same considerations applied to testing his evidence and to the need to support from other sources as applied in the case of the victim himself.

So far as the older boy is concerned, reliance was placed on a decision of the Court of Criminal Appeal in *R v Gammon* (1959) 43 Cr App R 155. I have already said, the elder boy was 17 years of age at the time of the trial and 16 at the time of the incidents. He was, therefore, substantially older, and it has been suggested that the omission which I have mentioned in relation to the brother is applicable also to the case of the older boy.

We do not think it possible to state as a general proposition what the age is above which it becomes unnecessary for a judge to give a warning such as I have already mentioned. This is an example of a situation where the trial judge is much better placed to consider the matter than any appellate court can be. The judge will, in those circumstances, obviously apply his mind to the problem and ask himself the question whether, having seen this boy in the witness box, he was of an age which made it desirable to give this warning. He might say to the jury: "If you think that this boy is of an age where the sort of risks exist against which the rule regarding corroboration is a safeguard, then you should look and see what corroboration exists." '

(The court applied the proviso to s.2(1) of the Criminal Appeal Act 1968.)

Appeal dismissed.

East LJ: I am not sure that I am inclined to criticise the learned judge on that score. But I think there may be more force in your second point.

Mr Atkyn: My Lord, yes. There are of course some cases under the Sexual Offences Act 1956, sections 2, 3, 4, 22 and 23 where corroboration is required as a matter of law. The offences deal with procurement. This is not such a case. But nonetheless at common law the evidence of the complainant in a sexual case should be corroborated and the jury should be directed to look for corroboration. In my submission, this rule has no exceptions. I would refer Your Lordships to the case of:

R v *Midwinter* (1971) 55 Cr App R 523 (CA)

The defendant was convicted of indecent assault on a girl. There had been no visual identification by the girl of the defendant as her assailant either at an identification parade or in court, but she had given a description of her assailant to the police. The summing up contained no reference to corroboration.

CAIRNS LJ, reading the judgment of the court, said: 'The rule has been laid down as a rule to which there are few, if any, exceptions that in a case of a sexual nature such as this it is essential that there should be a direction to the jury on corroboration. The case which may be regarded as final in deciding that proposition beyond doubt is *Trigg* (1963) 47 Cr App R 94; [1963] 1 WLR 305. It is true that it was said in the later case of *O'Reilly* (1967) 51 Cr App R 345; [1967] 2 QB 722, that the word "corroboration" need not be used so long as there is given a solemn warning to the same effect, but there may be cases where a direction on corroboration is unnecessary, as in the earlier case of *Rolfe* (1952) 36 Cr App R 4, where the accused had actually gone into the witness box and had admitted in the witness box that he committed the indecent assault. Indeed, in reading the report in the case of *Rolfe (supra)* it is impossible to say, and Mr Clapham was not able to enlighten us, what possible defence or ground of appeal there could have been in that case.

However, Mr Clapham says this was not a case for corroboration because the girl herself had not identified the man at all, it turned upon the alleged confession of the appellant. The Court does not accept that view of the matter. It is true that the girl had not identified the man either at an identification parade or in court, and it may well be that counsel for the prosecution exercised a proper discretion in not inviting the girl to identify the man in court which, as we all know, has its dangers. But when one looks at the summing up one finds this passage: "And so the sole vital issue which you must determine is: Was the youth who committed that indecent assault and whose description I have read to you as given by Christine, was it this defendant?" The position, therefore, was that the girl had given a description of her assailant and no doubt one question to which the jury would direct their minds was: Does the accused man fit that description? It is on that point that it seems to this Court that it is vital that there should have been added the warning that corroboration of the girl's evidence of the description that she had given was required.

If indeed it were the fact that nothing that the girl had said could be regarded as evidence of identification, then no doubt the warning would have to be in a different form and the word "corroboration" would not be appropriate. That would be in complete accordance with the position in *O'Reilly (supra)*, but in this case it seems to us that the word "corroboration" would have been appropriate and that, whether that actual word was used or not, it was essential that the jury should be directed that the girl's evidence must be supported or confirmed, whatever word one likes to choose, by evidence which the jury accepted. On that ground this Court is of the opinion that the direction here was not a sufficient one.' Conviction quashed.

This case shows the importance of the rule, because the conviction was quashed even though the corroboration could have related only to marginal issues. Further, My Lords, very much the same rule applies to the evidence of the complainants of sexual misconduct in matrimonial cases. The analogy may be helpful, and I refer Your Lordships to the case of:

Alli v *Alli* [1965] 3 All ER 480 (DC)

A wife brought proceedings before justices against her husband, alleging desertion and wilful neglect to provide reasonable maintenance for her and for their child. Having heard evidence from the wife and the husband only, the justices found for the wife on both allegations. Their reasons did not refer to the need for, or desirability of, corroboration. The husband appealed.

SIR JOCELYN SIMON P said: 'To sum up, then, our view of the authorities so far: (a) where a matrimonial offence is alleged, the court will look for corroboration of the complainant's evidence; (b) the court will normally, before finding a matrimonial offence proved, require such corroboration if, on the face of the complainant's own evidence, it is available; (c) these are not rules of law, but of practice only. They spring from the gravity of the consequences of proof of a matrimonial offence; and because, we would add, experience has shown the risk of a miscarriage of justice in acting on the uncorroborated testimony of a spouse in this class of case; (d) it is, nevertheless, open to a court to act on the uncorroborated evidence of a spouse if it is in no doubt where the truth lies; (e) these statements are equally applicable to proceedings in courts of summary jurisdiction as to those in the High Court.

It follows, we think, that justices should remind themselves, as they proceed to adjudication, of the desirability of corroboration, not least where, on the face of the complainant's evidence, it is available, just as they should remind themselves of the onus and standard of proof; see *Saunders* v *Saunders* [1965] 1 All ER 838, at 843, 846.

The question then arises for decision whether it is incumbent on the justices, in their reasons for their decision prepared for this court, to signify that they have had the question of corroboration in mind; and whether the court will quash the decision if there is no such reference?...[His Lordship stated that there were two relevant classes of case, and continued:] In the first — those alleging sexual misconduct and those where the evidence of adultery is that of a willing participant — experience has shown that there is such an exceptional risk of a miscarriage of justice unless the court has in mind the danger of acting on uncorroborated evidence that an appellate court will intervene unless the trial court has expressly warned itself of that danger. However, in other classes of case, the risk is less acute and the absence of an express indication that the desirability of corroboration was in mind will not of itself call for the intervention of the appellate court; though no doubt such absence may, together with other matters, convince the appellate court that the trial court must have proceeded oblivious of the rules of practice to which we have referred, and that it would not be safe to let the decision stand.'
Appeal dismissed.

Leach LJ: Yes. Before we hear from you further, Mr Atkyn, perhaps we should hear from Mr Bacon as to why the evidence of Angela Blackstone should be corroborated.

Mr Bacon: Your Lordship will appreciate that quite apart from the specific matters to which I shall come, Angela also was a complainant of sexual misconduct, and as such the arguments advanced by my learned friend on behalf of Coke apply equally. Nonetheless, there was a further consideration in her case. Because of her age and the answers she gave to the judge, it was ordered at the trial that Angela give evidence unsworn under the provisions of Section 38(1) of the Children and Young Persons Act 1933.

Leach LJ: Perhaps you would remind us of the terms of that section.

Mr Bacon: My Lords, certainly. The subsection provides:

> Where, in any proceedings against any person or for any offence, any child of tender years called as a witness does not in the opinion of the court understand the nature of an oath, his evidence may be received, though not given upon oath, if, in the opinion of the court, he is possessed of sufficient intelligence to justify the reception of the evidence, and understands the duty of speaking the truth.

My Lords, this subsection contains a proviso that:

> Where evidence admitted by virtue of this section is given on behalf of the prosecution the accused shall not be liable to be convicted of the offence unless that evidence is corroborated by some other material evidence in support thereof implicating him.

East LJ: That is a mandatory provision, so that in the absence of any corroborating evidence the judge would be obliged to withdraw the case from the jury?

Mr Bacon: My Lord, yes.

Cox LJ: And whatever view this court may take of Mr Atkyn's arguments in respect of Margaret Blackstone, it seems clear that the learned judge would have been justified in regarding Angela as a child of tender years, in which case her evidence would be required to be corroborated as a matter of practice, even if she had been sworn.

Mr Bacon: My Lord, that is right.

Leach LJ: One matter that concerns us in the case of both appeals is to what extent the evidence of these two girls could amount to mutual corroboration. In other words, on the assumption that both girls required corroboration, could they provide it for each other and thereby satisfy the requirement in both cases?

Mr Bunbury: My Lord, in my submission they could. The position relating to unsworn evidence was considered in detail by the House of Lords in *DPP* v *Hester* where facts similar to the present case arose.

DPP v *Hester* [1973] AC 296 (HL)

The respondent was charged with indecent assault on the complainant, a girl of 12. The complainant gave evidence on oath. Her nine-year-old sister gave unsworn evidence for the prosecution under section 38 of the Children and Young Persons Act 1933. The deputy chairman directed the jury that the evidence of an unsworn child could, in law, amount to corroboration of evidence given on oath by another child who had been sworn. The respondent was convicted. The Court of Appeal held that the deputy chairman's direction had been wrong and quashed the conviction. The Crown appealed to the House of Lords.

VISCOUNT DILHORNE, having read s.38(1), continued: 'While it may be that this proviso only contemplated unsworn evidence being given by a child who was the victim of an assault or other crime, I do not myself think that this is probable, for the earlier provision of the Children Act 1908, which contained a similar proviso, referred to "the child in respect of

whom the offence is charged to have been committed, or any other child of tender years"
[section 30]. In the Act of 1933, a consolidation Act, the reference to the "child in respect of
whom the offence is charged to have been committed" was left out, no doubt as its inclusion
was thought unnecessary.

The "evidence admitted by virtue of this section" must mean the unsworn evidence
admitted, whether given by one child or more than one child. The effect of the proviso is to
secure that no person is liable to be convicted solely on unsworn testimony: "that evidence,"
i.e. the unsworn evidence, must be corroborated by some other material evidence implicating
the accused.

The deputy chairman correctly told the jury that if the only evidence implicating the
accused was that of unsworn children it would have been his duty to have stopped the case.
He also told them that in law the evidence of an unsworn child could amount to
corroboration of evidence given by another child who had been sworn. This direction the
Court of Appeal held was wrong, and that court certified that the point of law was one of
public general importance, while refusing leave to appeal which was later granted by this
House.

This first question for consideration is whether the requirements of the proviso to section
38 were fulfilled in this case. Was there evidence which was not unsworn evidence
corroborating June's evidence and implicating the accused? If there was not, June's evidence
should have been ignored. While the deputy chairman did tell the jury that the unsworn
evidence needed some corroborating evidence, he did not direct them as to whether or not
there was any evidence capable of amounting to such corroboration. He really only directed
them on the question of corroboration of Valerie's evidence.

The only evidence capable of amounting to corroboration of June's was Valerie's. The jury
were rightly told that though they could convict on her evidence alone it was not safe to do so
in the absence of corroboration. So the question arises, can the evidence of a witness which,
for it to be safe to convict, itself requires corroboration amount to corroboration of unsworn
testimony of a child so as to satisfy the proviso?

To hold that it cannot do so involves reading into the proviso words which are not there
and the introduction of a qualification that the other material evidence implicating the
accused must not be sworn testimony for which corroboration is required or desirable. I see
no reason for reading in anything of this kind. In my opinion, the requirements of the proviso
could have been satisfied by Valerie's evidence.

Those requirements having been met, could June's evidence then be capable of providing
corroboration of Valerie's evidence? I see no reason why it should not. The Court of Appeal
held that it could not, and based its conclusion on two cases, *Rex* v *Davies,* 11 Cr App R 272
and *R* v *Manser,* 25 Cr App R 18. In *R* v *Davies* the judge had failed to direct the jury not to
convict on the unsworn evidence of a child in the absence of corroboration and it was on that
ground that the conviction was quashed. The question whether the evidence of the boy's
mother (which itself required corroboration for it to be safe to act on) could corroborate the
child's evidence was never considered. Counsel for the prosecution did suggest that the
evidence of another boy might amount to corroboration, but the court, while recognising that
there might be a case where the corroboration was so clear and ample that the court would
not interfere with the conviction, said that it could not come to the conclusion that with such
a caution from the judge the jury in that case would have arrived at the same verdict.

I cannot regard this decision as any authority for the proposition that the sworn evidence
of one person cannot, if a conviction would only be safe if it was corroborated, itself amount
to corroboration of unsworn testimony or for the proposition that unsworn evidence if
corroborated cannot provide corroboration of other evidence.

The report of *R* v *Manser,* 25 Cr App R 18 does not in terms state whether one of the two
girls in that case was sworn. One was not. In *R* v *Campbell* [1956] 2 QB 432 Lord Goddard
CJ treated the case as establishing that unsworn evidence could not be corroborated by other
unsworn evidence. There are, in my view, some indications in the report of *R* v *Manser* which
would lead one to the conclusion that one of the girls was sworn and the other not. If that
was the case then *R* v *Manser* is a decision on the question at issue in this case. In *R* v
Manser it was contended for the Crown that the jury were entitled to regard the evidence of
the two girls as being mutually corroborative. This contention was described by Lord Hewart
CJ as an argument in a circle and rejected. He said that the unsworn evidence was not

corroborative and was clearly not corroborated by the other girl. But apart from drawing attention to the circular nature of the argument he gave no reason for that conclusion.

I do not regard this decision as at all satisfactory. If it be the case that one of the girls was sworn, I think the case should not be followed in future. I do not consider that the mere statement that an argument is circular in nature really justifies putting a gloss and a qualification upon the words of a statute. In my opinion Lord Goddard CJ was right when he said in *R* v *Campbell* [1956] 2 QB 432, 436 that the court saw no reason why the corroboration of unsworn evidence could not be the evidence of another child who was sworn.

So, here, if Valerie's evidence was corroborative of June's, in my opinion the proviso was satisfied and, being satisfied, June's evidence became capable of being treated as corroborative of Valerie's. I therefore have reached the conclusion that the contentions advanced by the appellant on this question are right.

In *R* v *Campbell* Lord Goddard CJ made some general observations as to the need to give a careful warning in relation to the evidence of children. It is not necessary for me to repeat them but I would desire to emphasise the necessity for especially careful warning in relation to the weight to be placed on the evidence of two children, one sworn and one unsworn, when their evidence is being relied upon as mutually corroborative of each other.

Had an adequate warning been given in this case as to the care that should have been exercised before the acceptance of June's evidence then I do not myself feel any doubt but that the jury would have found the accused not guilty on the third count. They had not acted on Valerie's evidence in relation to the first two counts. I cannot believe having regard to the nature of that evidence in relation to the third count that they would have acted on her evidence alone and if they had been directed not only as to the need to examine her evidence with care, but also as to the necessity for great caution in accepting the evidence of June, I feel no doubt that the result would have been different from what it was. In these circumstances I think the Court of Appeal was right in the conclusion it reached, namely, that the conviction must be quashed, and that that decision of the Court of Appeal should not be altered.

LORD DIPLOCK said: 'My Lords, if a summing up is to perform its proper function in a criminal trial by jury it should not contain a general disquisition on the law of corroboration couched in lawyer's language but should be tailored to the particular circumstances of the case.

It would be highly dangerous to suppose that there is any such thing as a model summing up appropriate to all cases of this kind. No doubt if there is unsupported evidence on oath of a child complainant fit to be left to the jury the judge should tell them that it is open to them to convict upon her evidence alone, though he should remind them forcibly of the danger of doing so. But there is no need for him to tell them of what kind of evidence *could* amount to corroboration of her story if in fact there is none at all.

That was the position on the first two counts in the instant case, on which there was no corroboration of Valerie's evidence. On the third count too the summing up did not call for any general exposition of what in law could amount to corroboration because every relevant allegation of each witness was confirmed by the evidence of the other. Nor do I think that it was necessary to make any express reference to the provisions of the statute or to use the not very familiar word "corroboration" at all. What the jury needed to be told with respect to the third count was that the only evidence inculpating the accused was that of the two children, Valerie and June, and that in considering whether their evidence could be accepted as true they should bear in mind the danger that any child as young as these were, particularly June, might be incapable of fully understanding or remembering and describing accurately events which had happened at some time past and that young children are prone to be both imaginative and suggestible. They might then appropriately have been reminded of Valerie's account of the events which formed the subject of the first charge (which bordered upon the utterly incredible) and told that if they felt, as well they might, that all that was imagined they would no doubt feel that very little reliance could be placed on any of the rest of Valerie's evidence. If that was their general view as to the reliability of Valerie's evidence they ought next to consider whether the fact that the story which she told as to the third count was supported by the evidence of her little sister June really made such a difference as to convince them that on this part of her evidence at any rate Valerie was telling the truth. June was a very young child, too young even to understand the nature of an oath. Valerie was her elder sister, with whom she shared a bed, and likely at their ages to have great influence over June. The incident took place at night when June might be expected to be sleeping. The two sisters must have talked and talked together about what happened that night before either of them gave evidence. Bearing all that in mind the jury had to ask themselves whether the fact that June told the same story as Valerie carried any real conviction to their minds that that story must be true.

My Lords, the jury did not convict on the evidence of Valerie on the first two counts. Had they been directed on the lines which I have suggested on the third count I do not think that they could have failed to acquit the accused on that count also. That they did not was, I think, due to their being bewildered by the actual direction given to them on corroboration — accurate though it was as an exposition of the law.'
(LORDS MORRIS of BORTH-Y-GEST, PEARSON, and CROSS of CHELSEA delivered concurring judgments.)
Appeal dismissed.

Hence, My Lords, although two children giving evidence unsworn could not corroborate one another, where one of them is sworn mutual corroboration is possible.

East LJ: I think the only other case where mutual corroboration is not possible is the case of two or more accomplices who are *participes criminis.*

Mr Bunbury: My Lord, that is right.

Leach LJ: Suppose for a moment you had the situation where children were giving evidence about different offences, but offences which were admissible each as evidence to prove the other under the similar fact principle. Could those children corroborate each other, even though they dealt with different offences? Because what is happening in the present case is that Angela is giving evidence primarily of one offence and Margaret primarily of the other, although I appreciate that their evidence when regarded as a whole does relate to both.

Mr Bunbury: My Lords, in my submission it does relate to both because each girl described what happened to the other as well as to herself. But in answer to Your Lordship's question, the House of Lords in *DPP v Kilbourne* held that although the children were dealing with unrelated offences, the fact that the evidence on each was admissible under the similar fact principle allowed mutual corroboration as between the children.

DPP v *Kilbourne* [1973] AC 729 (HL)

The respondent was convicted of one offence of buggery, one of attempted buggery, and five offences of indecent assault on two groups of boys. Counts one to four related to offences in 1970 against the first group of boys, and counts five to seven related to offences against the second group of boys in 1971. The defence was one of innocent association. The judge directed the jury that they would be entitled to take the uncorroborated evidence of the second group of boys, if they were satisfied that the boys were speaking the truth as to what the respondent had done to them, as supporting evidence given by the first group of boys. The Court of Appeal having quashed the convictions, the Crown appealed to the House of Lords.

LORD HAILSHAM LC said: 'There are two manifest distinctions to be drawn between the facts in *Hester* and the present case. *Hester's* case was concerned with the alleged mutual corroboration of two witnesses, one of whom (the victim of the alleged offence) was sworn, and one of whom was an unsworn child who gave her evidence pursuant to section 38 of the

Children and Young Persons Act 1933. In the present case all the witnesses were sworn. Secondly, in *Hester's* case, both the witnesses whose evidence was in question gave evidence purporting to deal with the same incident, which each claimed to have witnessed. In the present case, of the five boys in question, only two pairs claimed actually to have seen the same incident, and in the way in which the trial judge's summing up was framed, the corroboration in fact placed before the jury related to incidents similar in character to one another, but in respect of each of which the evidence alleged to be mutually corroborative was supported by witnesses from the other group....

The difficulty which has arisen in the present case was complicated by the fact that the witnesses requiring corroboration were said to be corroborated by witnesses not of the same incident, but of incidents of a similar character themselves all of the class requiring corroboration. A considerable part of the time taken up in argument was devoted to a consideration whether such evidence of similar incidents could be used against the accused to establish his guilt at all, and we examined the authorities in some depth from *Makin* v *Attorney-General for New South Wales* [1894] AC 57, through Lord Sumner's observations in *Thompson* v *The King* [1918] AC 221, to *Harris* v *Director of Public Prosecutions* [1952] AC 694. I do not myself feel that the point really arises in the present case. Counsel for the respondent was in the end constrained to agree that all the evidence in this case was both admissible and relevant, and that the Court of Appeal was right to draw attention [1972] 1 WLR 1365, 1370 to the "striking features of the resemblance" between the acts alleged to have been committed in one count and those alleged to have been committed in the others, and to say that this made it "more likely that John was telling the truth when he said that the appellant had behaved in the same way to him." In my view, this was wholly correct. With the exception of one incident

> each accusation bears a resemblance to the other and shows not merely that [Kilbourne] was a homosexual, which would not have been enough to make the evidence admissible, but that he was one whose proclivities in that regard took a particular form [1972] 1 WLR 1365, 1369.

I also agree with the Court of Appeal in saying that the evidence of each child went to contradict any possibility of innocent association. As such it was admissible as part of the prosecution case, and since, by the time the judge came to sum up, innocent association was the foundation of the defence put forward by the accused, the admissibility, relevance, and, indeed cogency of the evidence was beyond question. The word "corroboration" by itself means no more than evidence tending to confirm other evidence. In my opinion, evidence which is (a) admissible and (b) relevant to the evidence requiring corroboration, and, if believed, confirming it in the required particulars, is capable of being corroboration of that evidence and, when believed, is in fact such corroboration.

As Professor Cross well says in his book on *Evidence,* 3rd p 316:

> The ground of the admissibility of this type of evidence was succinctly stated by Hallett J, when delivering the judgment by the Court of Criminal Appeal: "If the jury are precluded by some rule of law from taking the view that something is coincidence which is against all probabilities if the accused person is innocent, then it would seem to be a doctrine of law which prevents a jury from using what looks like common sense." *R* v *Robinson* (1953) 37 Cr App R 95, 106–107....

Corroboration is only required or afforded if the witness requiring corroboration or giving it is otherwise credible. If his evidence is not credible, a witness's testimony should be rejected and the accused acquitted, even if there could be found evidence capable of being corroboration in other testimony. Corroboration can only be afforded to or by a witness who is otherwise to be believed. If a witness's testimony falls of its own inanition the question of his needing, or being capable of giving, corroboration does not arise. It is for this reason that evidence of complaint is acceptable in rape cases to defeat any presumption of consent and to establish consistency of conduct, but not as corroboration. The jury is entitled to examine any evidence of complaint, in order to consider the question whether the witness is credible at all. It is not entitled to treat that evidence as corroboration because a witness, though otherwise

credible, "cannot corroborate himself," i.e. the evidence is not "independent testimony" to
satisfy the requirements of corroboration in *R* v *Baskerville* [1916] 2 KB 658, 667. Of course,
the moment at which the jury must make up its mind is at the end of the case. They must look
at the evidence as a whole before asking themselves whether the evidence of a given witness is
credible in itself and whether, if otherwise credible, it is corroborated. Nevertheless,
corroboration is a doctrine applying to otherwise credible testimony and not to testimony
incredible in itself. In the present case Mark's evidence (count 3) was corroborated. But it was
not credible and the conviction founded on it was rightly quashed.

It seems to me that the only way in which the doctrine upon which the decision of the
Court of Appeal was founded can be supported, would be if there were some general rule of
law to the effect that witnesses of a class requiring corroboration could not corroborate one
another. For this rule of law counsel for the respondent expressly contended. I do not believe
that such a rule of law exists. It is probably true that the testimony of one unsworn child
cannot corroborate the testimony of another unsworn child (see *Cross on Evidence* at p 164),
but, if so, this is probably because this is expressly prohibited by statute (see *R* v *Hester*
[1973] AC 296). It is not "other" testimony within the meaning of the proviso to the Children
and Young Persons Act 1933, section 38(1). This House has now decided in *R* v *Hester* that
the sworn testimony of a child can be corroborated by the unsworn testimony of another
child and vice versa. In so doing the House disapproved the "circular argument" doctrine first
enunciated by Lord Hewart CJ in *R* v *Manser* (1934) 25 Cr App R 18 which was at one time
generally accepted, and which is probably the only real support for the general proposition
contended for on behalf of the respondent. There Lord Hewart CJ said, at pp 20–21:

> The argument for the prosecution is therefore an argument in a circle. Let it be granted
> that the evidence of Barbara [the elder child witness for the prosecution who may have
> been sworn or unsworn] has to be corroborated: it is corroborated by the evidence of
> Doris [the younger child witness who was unsworn]. She, however, also needs to be
> corroborated. The answer is that she is corroborated by the evidence of Barbara, and that
> is called "mutual corroboration." In truth and in fact the evidence of the girl Doris ought
> to have been obliterated altogether from the case, inasmuch as it was not corroborated.

In *R* v *Hester* [1973] AC 296 this House has stigmatised this argument as fallacious. With
respect, I wholly agree, and I hope no more will be heard of it.

The other ground upon which the general proposition may be defended is the bald
proposition that one accomplice cannot corroborate another. In support of this proposition
were cited *R* v *Noakes* (1832) 5 C & P 326 *per* Littledale J; *R* v *Gay* (1909) 2 Cr App R 327;
R v *Prater* [1960] 2 QB 464, 465 *per* Edmund Davies J; *R* v *Baskerville* [1916] 2 KB 658, 664
citing *Noakes;* and *R* v *Cratchley* (1913) 9 Cr App R 232....

Whatever else it is, the rule about fellow accomplices is not authority for the proposition
that no witness who may himself require corroboration may afford corroboration for another
to whom the same consideration applies, and this alone is what would help the respondent.
When a small boy relates a sexual incident implicating a given man he may be indulging in
fantasy. If another small boy relates such an incident it may be a coincidence if the detail is
insufficient. If a large number of small boys relate similar incidents in enough detail about the
same person, if it is not conspiracy it may well be that the stories are true. Once there is a
sufficient nexus it must be for the jury to say what weight is given to the combined testimony
of a number of witnesses.'

LORD REID said: 'The main difficulty in the case is caused by observations in the case of
R v *Manser* (1934) 25 Cr App R 18 to the effect that the evidence of one witness which
required corroboration cannot be used as corroboration of that of another witness which also
requires corroboration. For some unexplained reason it was held that there can be no mutual
corroboration in such a case.

I do not see why that should be so. There is nothing technical in the idea of corroboration.
When in the ordinary affairs of life one is doubtful whether or not to believe a particular
statement one naturally looks to see whether it fits in with other statements or circumstances
relating to the particular matter; the better it fits in, the more one is inclined to believe it. The
doubted statement is corroborated to a greater or lesser extent by the other statements or

circumstances with which it fits in.

In ordinary life we should be, and in law we are required to be, careful in applying this idea. We must be astute to see that the apparently corroborative statement is truly independent of the doubted statement. If there is any real chance that there has been collusion between the makers of the two statements we should not accept them as corroborative. And the law says that a witness cannot corroborate himself. In ordinary affairs we are often influenced by the fact that the maker of the doubled statement has consistently said the same thing ever since the event described happened. But the justification for the legal view must, I think, be that generally it would be too dangerous to take this into account and therefore it is best to have a universal rule.

So when we are considering whether there can be mutual corroboration between witnesses each of whom requires corroboration, the question must or at least ought to be whether it would be too dangerous to allow this. It might often be dangerous if there were only two children. But here we are dealing with cases where there is a "system," and I do not think that only two instances would be enough to establish a "system." Where several children, between whom there can have been no collaboration in concocting a story, all tell similar stories it appears to me that the conclusion that each is telling the truth is likely to be inescapable and the corroboration is very strong. So I can see no ground at all for the law refusing to recognise the obvious. Once there are enough children to show a "system" I can see no ground for refusing to recognise that they can corroborate each other.

Many of the authorities cited deal with accomplices where the rule as to the need of warning that there should be corroboration is similar to the rule with regard to children. I do not think it useful to regard children as accomplices; the rule with regard to children applies whether or not they are accomplices.

In most of the authorities the accomplices were accomplices to a single crime so the danger that they collaborated in concocting their story is obvious, and it is therefore quite right that there should be a general rule that accomplices cannot corroborate each other. Whether that should be a universal rule I greatly doubt, but I need not pursue that matter in this case.'

(LORD MORRIS OF BORTH-Y-GEST agreed with LORD HAILSHAM. LORD SIMON OF GLAISDALE and LORD CROSS OF CHELSEA delivered judgments to the same effect.)

Appeal allowed.

My Lords, in my submission this case is stronger, in that each girl gave direct evidence of the offence and not merely evidence admissible under the similar fact principle. (Leach LJ indicated that the court had formed the view that the summing up was seriously defective.)

14.6 Commentary

R v *Coke and Littleton* on appeal against conviction.   At the trial, Coke elected to plead guilty and to give evidence for the prosecution against Littleton. His evidence was that Littleton had visited his flat on 8 July 1979 and had there committed an offence against Angela Blackstone. Coke also admitted in the presence of the jury that he had raped Margaret Blackstone and had pleaded guilty to that offence, and that Holt J had postponed sentence upon him until the end of the trial of Littleton. In cross-examination, it was suggested to Coke that his motive for giving evidence against Littleton was the hope of attracting a lenient sentence. Coke denied this, and affirmed the truth of this evidence. No mention was made in the summing up of the question of corroboration of Coke's evidence. Mr Bacon on behalf of Littleton appeals on the ground of this omission.

14.7 Argument

Mr Bacon: My Lords, in my submission Coke was an accomplice in the offence charged and therefore the jury should have been directed to look for corroboration as a matter of practice, and warned of the dangers of acting on his uncorroborated evidence. I would refer Your Lordships to:

Davies v DPP [1954] AC 378 (HL)

The defendant, together with other youths, attacked with their fists another group, one of whom subsequently died from stab wounds inflicted by a knife. Six youths, including the defendant and one Lawson, were charged with murder but finally the defendant alone was convicted, Lawson having been amoung four against whom no evidence was offered and who were found not guilty of murder but convicted of common assault. At the defendant's trial Lawson gave evidence for the prosecution as to an admission by the defendant of the use of a knife by him but the judge did not warn the jury of the danger of accepting his evidence without corroboration. The defendant's conviction was affirmed by the Court of Criminal Appeal, and he appealed to the House of Lords.

LORD SIMONDS LC said: 'There is in the authorities no formal definition of the term "accomplice": and your Lordships are forced to deduce a meaning for the word from the cases in which X, Y and Z have been held to be, or held liable to be treated as, accomplices. On the cases it would appear that the following persons, if called as witnesses for the prosecution, have been treated as falling within the category:—
    (1) On any view, persons who are participes criminis in respect of the actual crime charged, whether as principals or accessories before or after the fact (in felonies) or persons committing, procuring or aiding and abetting (in the case of misdemeanors). This is surely the natural and primary meaning of the term "accomplice." But in two cases, persons falling strictly outside the ambit of this category have, in particular decisions been held to be accomplices for the purpose of the rule: viz.:
    (2) Receivers have been held to be accomplices of the thieves from whom they receive goods on a trial of the latter for larceny (R v Jennings (1912) 7 Cr App R 242: R v Dixon (1925) 19 Cr App R 36):
    (3) When X has been charged with a specific offence on a particular occasion, and evidence is admissible, and has been admitted, of his having committed crimes of this identical type on other occasions, as proving system and intent and negativing accident; in such cases the court has held that in relation to such other similar offences, if evidence of them were given by parties to them, the evidence of such other parties should not be left to the jury without a warning that it is dangerous to accept it without corroboration. (R v Farid (1945) 30 Cr App R 168).
    In both of these cases (2) and (3) a person not a party or not necessarily a party to the substantive crime charged was treated as an accomplice for the purpose of the requirement of warning. (I say "not necessarily" to cover the case of receivers. A receiver may on the facts of a particular case have procured the theft, or aided and abetted it, or may have helped to shield the thief from justice. But he can be a receiver without doing any of these things.) The primary meaning of the term "accomplice," then, has been extended to embrace these two anomalous cases. In each case there are special circumstances to justify or at least excuse the extension. A receiver is not only committing a crime intimately allied in character with that of theft: he could not commit the crime of receiving at all without the crime of theft having preceded it. The two crimes are in a relationship of "one-sided dependence." In the case of "system," the requirement of warning within the special field of similar crimes committed is a logical application within that collateral field of the general principle, though it involves a warning as to the evidence of persons not accomplices to the substantive crime charged.'
(LORDS PORTER, OAKSEY, TUCKER and ASQUITH OF BISHOPSTONE concurred.)
Appeal dismissed.

East LJ: You would say that Coke was a participant in the alleged offence and therefore fell within the first category?
    Mr Bacon: My Lord, yes. I am not submitting to Your Lordships that there was no corroborative evidence, purely that the learned judge erred in omitting to give the

jury a direction.

Leach LJ: Of course, this problem arises because Coke pleaded guilty and therefore became a competent witness for the prosecution. Presumably, had he pleaded not guilty and had there been a joint trial, if Coke had given evidence in his defence implicating your client he would not have been an accomplice.

Mr Bacon: My Lord, that is correct. A defendant who gives evidence in his own defence is not an accomplice. I refer Your Lordship to the case of:

R v *Barnes; R* v *Richards* [1940] 2 All ER 229 (CCA)

The defendants were indicted, together with three other persons, a man and two women, for the murder of A, and were convicted. They had all been concerned in the preparation, the placing and the explosion of a bomb which had been left in a busy street. In consequence of the explosion five persons were killed including A. Each of the two women co-defendants made statements inculpating the two defendants. The judge pointed out differences between the evidence of the women given at the trial, and the earlier statements made by them. He made no reference to the fact that their evidence was that of accomplices and might need corroboration. The defendants were convicted and appealed.

LORD HEWART CJ, delivering the judgment of the court, said: 'The witnesses whose evidence, it is said, needed corroboration are the two women prisoners. They were not called as witnesses for the prosecution. They went into the witness box to give evidence, and they gave evidence on their own behalf. The rule with regard to corroboration of accomplices does not seem to apply to such a case. As was stated in *R* v *Baskerville* in this court, at p 665:

The rule of practice as to corroborative evidence has arisen in consequence of the danger of convicting a person upon the unconfirmed testimony of one who is admittedly a criminal. What is required is some additional evidence rendering it probable that the story of the accomplice is true and that it is reasonably safe to act upon it.

In no respect is it true to say that the evidence which is referred to in this part of the notice of appeal was evidence called by the prosecution. Nor was the jury being asked by the prosecution to act upon the evidence given by either of those two women. One looks in vain for any case in which it has been decided that, where prisoners are tried together on the charge of being jointly concerned in the commission of a crime, and they elect to give evidence, and in so doing one of them happens incidentally to give a piece of evidence which tells against another of the accused, it is requisite that the warning as to the evidence of accomplices should be given.'
Appeal dismissed.

However, Your Lordships will be aware that there is authority holding that whenever a prosecution witness has some personal motive or interest in giving evidence, it is desirable for the judge to give a warning to the jury of the danger of uncorroborated evidence, even though the case may not fall strictly within one of the generally accepted categories. I refer Your Lordships to:

R v *Prater* [1960] 2 QB 464 (CCA)

The defendant was convicted of conspiring to defraud and uttering forged documents. He appealed against his conviction on the ground, *inter alia,* that the evidence of his co-accused at the trial, Welham, who gave evidence on his own behalf, required to be corroborated, and that there should have been a warning given by the judge of the danger of convicting the defendant on the evidence of his co-accused.

EDMUND-DAVIES J, delivering the judgment of the court, said: 'For the purposes of this present appeal, this court is content to accept that whether the label to be attached to Welham in this case was strictly that of an accomplice or not, in practice it is desirable that a warning should be given that the witness, whether he comes from the dock, as in this case, or whether he be a Crown witness, may be a witness with some purpose of his own to serve. It is, however, to be observed that in *Davies* v *DPP* [1954] AC 378 Lord Simonds, in enunciating his third proposition, deals with the matter in these terms [1954] AC 378, 399: "Where the judge fails to warn the jury in accordance with this rule, the conviction will be quashed, even if in fact there be ample corroboration of the evidence of the accomplice, unless the appellate court can apply the proviso to section 4(1) of the Criminal Appeal Act, 1907. The rule, it will be observed, applies only to witnesses for the prosecution."

In the circumstances of the present appeal it is sufficient for this court to express the view that it is desirable that, in cases where a person may be regarded as having some purpose of his own to serve, the warning against uncorroborated evidence should be given. But every case must be looked at in the light of its own facts, and in *R* v *Garland* Humphreys J used words completely apposite to the present case, namely, that if there be evidence so clear and convincing that this court is satisfied that no miscarriage of justice has arisen by reason of the omission of a warning to the jury, it will not interfere. On those grounds, and bearing in mind also the proviso to section 4(1) of the Act of 1907, this court sees no reason to disturb the finding of the jury in respect of the first ground relied on by counsel for the appellant.' Appeal dismissed.

Leach LJ: The difficulty I have with this case is whether or not Coke was an accomplice, because they were charged with different offences. As I understand it, the prosecution did not suggest that Coke played any part in Littleton's alleged offence against Angela Blackstone and indeed his evidence was that he did not expect such a thing and was horrified when he discovered it.

Mr Bacon: My Lord, the question of who is an accomplice is not always an easy one. Sometimes the participants in an offence have nothing to do with each other in a direct physical sense, as with the case of:

R v *Sidhu; R* v *Singh* (1976) 63 Cr App R 24 (CA)

The defendants were each convicted of affray. The prosecution's case was that the defendants chased two men to a particular street, and then deliberately attacked them there. It was said that the resulting fight amounted to an affray in which the defendants were the principal parties. The defence was the exact opposite: that, far from having pursued the principal witnesses for the prosecution, it was the latter who had enticed them into the street.

LAWTON LJ, giving the judgment of the court, said: 'Before we leave this case we must deal with one point which was put before us by Mr Fletcher-Cooke on behalf of the appellants, as they now are. It was submitted by Mr Fletcher-Cooke that the four Sikh witnesses, on the defence account of what happened, could be considered as accomplices, and it followed, according to the usual practice of our Courts, that the learned judge should have asked the jury to consider whether those four witnesses or any of them were accomplices, and, if they thought they might be, then they should bear in mind that there was no corroboration of their evidence.

In my judgment the use of the terms "accomplice" and "corroboration" in affray cases would be a most unfortunate development in the law, the reason being that, although from a lawyer's point of view all those taking part in an affray are taking part in one offence, nevertheless the word "accomplice" as it would be understood by a jury would be foreign to that concept. Nevertheless in this class of case, all too common nowadays in our Courts, it seems to us necessary that the judge should point out to the jury, without using the words "accomplice" and "corroboration," the essence of what is required. Judges would be well advised to tell jurors that those fighting who were called on behalf of the prosecution, if they were not defending themselves, may have been doing the very thing which the accused were charged with doing. Then the judge should go on to point out that in those circumstances it

would be dangerous to convict those charged on evidence coming from such persons unless there was some independent evidence which supported the evidence of those called by the prosecution. We think that that approach is much more satisfactory than using words with a legalistic connotation such as "accomplice" and "corroboration." '
Appeal allowed.

East LJ: Yes, but that is not quite the same situation. There the defendants were charged with the same offence, even though they played different parts and may have had no physical contact.

Mr Bacon: At the same time, My Lords, Coke and Littleton were, on the prosecution case, involved in something of a joint enterprise, and the jury should have been directed that Coke had an obvious motive for giving evidence for the prosecution. This would follow the *Prater* principle even if Coke was not technically an accomplice.

Cox LJ: Well, suppose that Coke had given evidence favourable to the appellant Littleton. What would you say then?

Mr Bacon: My Lord, there is some authority that the judge may still find it necessary to give a warning to the jury, though in my submission he should not set out to impeach a prosecution witness who does not come up to proof. But even if the evidence is partly unfavourable to a defendant, the judge should at least consider giving a warning. In my submission, the correct approach was that of the court in:

R v Royce-Bentley [1974] 1 WLR 535 (CA)

The defendant was charged with theft. A prosecution witness, who on his own evidence could have been an accomplice in the theft, gave evidence which was mainly favourable to the defence but in some respects supported the prosecution's case. Before summing up to the jury, the judge consulted with both counsel as to whether the witness ought to be put before the jury as a potential accomplice. Defence counsel stated that he would prefer that no direction was given on the issue whether the witness was an accomplice. The judge agreed and gave no direction to the jury on the matter. The defendant was convicted. He appealed against conviction on the grounds that the judge failed to leave to the jury the issue whether the witness was an accomplice and that he misdirected the jury by failing to warn them, if they found that the witness was an accomplice, of the danger of convicting the defendant on his uncorroborated evidence.

LORD WIDGERY CJ, delivering the judgment of the court, said: 'We start today with that proposition, that if the so-called accomplice does not in fact give evidence adverse to the defendant, no warning is required for the reason there given. Today we have to move on to the slightly different situation in which the alleged accomplice has given some evidence which is favourable to the defence and some evidence which is potentially favourable to the prosecution as well. It seems we have to face up, perhaps for the first time, to laying down a principle as to the conduct of the trial judge in that situation.

We approach it on the footing that in this case there was in the extract from the transcript which I have read some evidence given by the boy which could be treated as adverse to the defendant, and also some evidence given by the boy which might entitle the jury to hold him to be an accomplice, but there was also, as I have said, a good deal of other evidence given by the boy which was favourable to the defence.

Cases will obviously arise in which a witness who gives evidence of these two different characters may wish to be upheld by the defence because, on the whole, he is more favourable to them, and cases will therefore arise where the defence do not want the credibility of the witness attacked by an accomplice direction because they attach too much importance to that evidence themselves.

In our judgment, where a trial judge is faced with the situation which arises here, he should of course consult counsel in the absence of the jury before taking any final decision, but having done that, he ought to consider whether on the whole, more harm to the defence would be done by giving the accomplice direction than by not giving it, and if he comes to the conclusion that on the whole more harm would be done in that way, then it is no irregularity on his part in the conduct of the trial if he decides not to give the accomplice direction.

It may still, of course, be possible to attack a conviction thus obtained on other general grounds, that it was unsafe or unsatisfactory, but we do not regard the judge as committing an irregularity for the purposes of the Criminal Appeal Act 1968, if having considered both aspects of the alleged accomplice evidence, he comes to conclusion on balance that more harm would be done by giving the direction than by refraining from giving it.

It follows if he comes to that conclusion with the active encouragement of counsel for the defence, the more clear is it that no irregularity has taken place.'
Appeal dismissed.

(The court later indicated that there was evidence on which the jury could have found a joint enterprise and that Coke had some motive for giving evidence for the prosecution. Accordingly, the court felt that some warning ought to have been given as to the desirability of corroboration and as to what corroborative evidence was available.)

14.8   Commentary

R v *Coke and Littleton* on appeal against conviction. At the trial of Coke and Littleton, Coke elected to give evidence in his defence. In the course of giving evidence, Coke admitted that he had been sexually attracted to Margaret Blackstone prior to the date of the alleged offence and did plan to invite her to his flat for the purpose of having sexual relations with her. He denied, however, any intention to do so without her consent. Mr Atkyn on behalf of Coke now complains about the following passage in the summing up of Holt J to the jury:

Members of the jury, you have heard argument from counsel and I have directed you to the effect that you should look for corroboration of Margaret's evidence, and that it would be dangerous, you may think, to convict unless that evidence was corroborated. In those circumstances, where can you find corroboration? It may occur to you to look at the evidence of the defendant Coke himself. He was not obliged to give evidence, but he elected to do so and you can consider that evidence. Bear in mind that on his own admission, he found himself sexually attracted to this girl and fully intended to have sexual relations with her. If you wish, you might regard that as some support for the account which Margaret has given you from the witness box. It may also be, though it is entirely a matter for you, that you do not accept what the defendant Coke says about his intentions, or about Margaret's consent. Well, if you disbelieve him, what better support could there be for Margaret's evidence? You would be entitled to regard that as corroborative, and you may well find that that removes some of the danger you would feel in acting on her unsupported evidence.

14.9   Argument

Mr Atkyn: My Lords, in my submission the mere fact that the jury may disbelieve the defendant, while perhaps making them more ready to convict, cannot of itself amount to corroboration of evidence given for the prosecution. I would refer Your Lordships to:

R v *Chapman; R* v *Baldwin* [1973] QB 774 (CA)

The defendant C was charged with several offences of theft and false accounting and the defendant B with offences of theft and handling stolen goods. On some of the counts, the main prosecution witness was an accomplice of the defendants. The judge warned the jury that it was dangerous to convict on the uncorroborated evidence of an accomplice but directed them that, if they did not believe the defendants' evidence, that false evidence was capable of amounting to corroboration of the accomplice's evidence. C was convicted on 3 counts of theft and B on 15 counts of handling stolen goods; the accomplice's evidence only related to two of the convictions for theft and five of the convictions for handling stolen goods.

ROSKILL LJ, reading the judgment of the court said: 'In the view of this court the judge's direction was wrong, both on principle and on authority, to none of which was his attention drawn. It was wrong in principle for this reason: if the question is whether A's evidence or B's evidence is true, the mere rejection of B's evidence does not of itself mean that A's evidence must be accepted as true. B might have a separate and independent reason for lying or otherwise giving unreliable evidence or evidence which is for some reason incapable of belief. Mere rejection of evidence is not affirmative proof of the contrary of the evidence which has been rejected.

The most recent decision on this question is *Tumahole Bereng* v *The King* [1949] AC 253, a decision of the Judicial Committee of the Privy Council which included both Lord MacDermott and Lord Reid. It is not necessary to relate the complex facts of that case. Lord MacDermott, delivering the opinion of the Board said, at p 270:

> The circumstances that the appellants (other than No. 2) elected not to give evidence is equally incapable of constituting corroboration, though on more general grounds. Silence on the part of an accused person which is tantamount to an admission by conduct may, on occasion, amount to corroboration. But an accused admits nothing by exercising at his trial the right which the law gives him of electing not to deny the charge on oath. Silence of that kind — and it is the only kind relevant to this appeal — affords no corroboration to satisfy the rule of practice under consideration. Nor does an accused corroborate an accomplice merely by giving evidence which is not accepted and must therefore be regarded as false. Corroboration may well be found in the evidence of an accused person; but that is a different matter, for there confirmation comes, if at all, from what is said, and not from the falsity of what is said. It is, of course, correct to say that these circumstances — the failure to give evidence or the giving of false evidence — may bear against an accused and assist in his conviction if there is other material sufficient to sustain a verdict against him. But if the other material is insufficient either in its quality or extent they cannot be used as a make-weight. To hold otherwise would be to undermine the presumption of innocence in a manner as repugnant to the Proclamation of 1938 as to the common law of England.

That passage is, of course, not strictly binding on this court, but is the highest persuasive authority. For some reason that decision is not cited in *Archbold Criminal Pleading Evidence & Practice*, 37th ed (1969).

Two years later in *Credland* v *Knowler* (1951) 35 Cr App R 48, 54, 55, Lord Goddard CJ, delivering the judgment of the Divisional Court, treated as axiomatic the proposition that the fact that a defendant's evidence ought to be rejected did not of itself amount to corroboration. Lord Goddard CJ went on to refer to a judgment of Lord President Dunedin in the First Division of the Inner House in *Dawson* v *M'Kenzie* (1908) 45 ScLR 473, later approved by the Divisional Court in *Jones* v *Thomas* [1934] 1 KB 323....

Those two decisions of the Inner House are in precise accord with the passages from the opinion of the Board in *Tumahole Bereng* v *The King* [1949] AC 253, though neither decision nor *Jones* v *Thomas* appears to have been cited in argument before that Judicial Committee and *Tumahole's* case does not appear to have been cited to the Divisional Court in *Credland v Knowler*, 35 Cr App R 48. Curiously enough this point seems never to have arisen for direct decision by the Court of Appeal in this country either in a civil or criminal case. But this court has no doubt both on principle and authority that the statements quoted are correct and respectfully adopts them all....

There is no doubt that a lie told out of court is capable in some circumstances of constituting corroboration, though it may not necessarily do so. There may be an explanation of the lie which will clearly prevent it being corroboration: see, for example, *R v Clynes* (1960) 44 Cr App R 158, 163–164. But, in the view of this court, there is a clear distinction in principle between a lie told out of court and evidence given in the witness box which the jury rejects as incapable of belief or as otherwise unreliable. Proof of a lie told out of court is capable of being direct evidence, admissible at the trial, amounting to affirmative proof of the untruth of the defendant's denial of guilt. This in turn may tend to confirm the evidence against him and to implicate him in the offence charged. But a denial in the witness box which is untruthful or otherwise incapable of belief is not positive proof of anything. It leads only to the rejection of the evidence given, which then has to be treated as if it had not been given. Mere rejection of evidence is not of itself affirmative or confirmatory proof of the truth of other evidence to the contrary.

For these reasons we are clearly of the view that the judge's direction on corroboration was wrong and cannot be supported. It is, of course, always open to a jury to convict on the uncorroborated evidence of an accomplice, provided they are fully warned of the dangers of so doing and are convinced, whilst always bearing that warning in mind, that the uncorroborated evidence is true. The Judicial Committee observed in the passage quoted from *Tumahole Bereng v The King* [1949] AC 253 that failure to give evidence or the giving of false evidence may bear against an accused and assist in his conviction if there is other material sufficient to sustain a verdict against him.

The relevant other material in the present case (so far as concerns the counts depending upon Thatcher's evidence) was the uncorroborated evidence of Thatcher. It was for the jury to decide whether or not, in the light of the judge's warning, that uncorroborated evidence was sufficient to justify conviction. If they took the view that, having rejected as they plainly did the evidence of the defendants on all the counts, including those counts in which Thatcher was not involved, they had disbelieved the two persons best qualified to give the lie to Thatcher's evidence on the counts to which his evidence was directed, and that this disbelief led them irresistibly to accept Thatcher's evidence directed to those counts though uncorroborated as clearly true, no one could have challenged their reasoning or their verdicts.

If the defence is an alibi and the alibi breaks down the jury must not be told that they may convict merely because the alibi has broken down, but they are entitled to ask themselves the single question: "Why has a false alibi been tendered?" If there is only one possible answer to that question they are entitled to give their answer by their verdict. Similarly in a case such as the present if the accused are found to have given evidence which is incapable of belief or otherwise unreliable, the jury are entitled to ask the single question: "Why has this evidence which we have rejected been tendered to us?" If there is only one possible answer — that the accomplice, though uncorroborated, was telling the truth — once again they are entitled to give their answer in their verdict, provided, of course, that the trial judge has properly warned them of the dangers of acting on the accomplice's uncorroborated evidence.'

Appeal dismissed. (The court applied the proviso to s. 2(1) of the Criminal Appeal Act 1968.)

If would be equally wrong to hold the defendant's failure to give evidence as being capable of amounting to corroboration. The reason in that case would be that to do so would greatly weaken the defendant's power of decision as to whether to give evidence. I refer Your Lordships to:

R v Jackson (1953) 37 Cr App R 43 (CCA)

The appellant was convicted of being accessory before the fact to the larceny of a quantity of motor tyres and of receiving the tyres knowing them to have been stolen. The evidence against the defendant on the counts on which he was convicted consisted mainly of that of the thieves. The appellant did not go into the witness box.

LORD GODDARD CJ, giving the judgment of the court, said: 'The difficulty that arises in this case is on the direction that the learned judge gave. Having pointed out and emphasised the danger of acting on the evidence of accomplices and having indicated who might be regarded as accomplices, in commenting on the fact that the appellant had not gone into the box to give evidence, he said: "You, members of the jury, will attach just what weight you think right to that and if you say: "Well, that, in our view, forms ample corroboration that those thieves were telling the truth, that he has refrained from going into the witness box because he does not dare; he thinks he will only make matters worse if he does" — if you come to that conclusion — the weight you attach to his silence is entirely a matter for you." That came just at the end of the learned judge's summing up, and could only, in our view, have been understood by the jury as meaning that the fact that the appellant had not gone into the witness box might amount to corroboration, if they thought fit to treat it as such. In the opinion of the court, that is not correct. One cannot say that the fact that a prisoner had not gone into the witness box to give evidence is of itself corroboration of accomplices' evidence. It is a matter which the jury very properly could, and very probably would, take into account but it should be clearly understood that that direction is wrong in law. Appeal dismissed.

Leach LJ: I think that point is well taken, Mr Atkyn. But surely there can be no objection to some corroboration being found in the substance of the defendant's evidence. What do you say about the various admissions he made?

Mr Atkyn: My Lord, I would concede that if the jury consider the admissions to be damaging, then they would be entitled to regard them as corroborative. The same would apply if it is satisfactorily proved that the defendant has told a lie, as distinct from the case where the jury merely disbelieve him. This appears from the decision in:

R v Lucas [1981] 3 WLR 120 (CA)

The appellant was tried on a count charging an offence in respect of which evidence implicating her was given by an accomplice. The appellant gave evidence which was challenged as being partly lies. The jury were warned of the dangers of convicting on the accomplice's uncorroborated evidence and were directed in terms which suggested that lies told by the appellant in court could be considered as corroborative of the accomplice's evidence. The appellant was convicted and appealed.

LORD LANE CJ, delivering the judgment of the court, said: 'We accept that the words used in the context in which they were, were probably taken by the jury as a direction that lies told by the defendant in the witness box could be considered as corroborative of an accomplice's evidence, and we approach the case on that footing.

The fact that the jury may feel sure that the accomplice's evidence is to be preferred to that of the defendant and that the defendant accordingly must have been lying in the witness box is not of itself somthing which can be treated by the jury as corroboration of the accomplice's evidence. It is only if the accomplice's evidence is believed that there is any necessity to look for corroboration of it. If the belief that the accomplice is truthful means that the defendant was untruthful and if that untruthfulness can be used as corroboration, the practical effect would be to dispense with the need of corroboration altogether.

The matter was put in this way by Lord MacDermott in *Tumahole Bereng* v *The King* [1949] AC 253, 270:

> Nor does an accused corroborate an accomplice merely by giving evidence which is not accepted and must therefore be regarded as false. Corroboration may well be found in the evidence of an accused person; but that is a different matter, for there confirmation comes, if at all, from what is said, and not from the falsity of what is said.

There is, without doubt, some confusion in the authorities as to the extent to which lies may in some circumstances provide corroboration and it was this confusion which probably and understandably led the judge astray in the present case. In our judgment the position is as follows. Statements made out of court, for example, statements to the police, which are proved or admitted to be false may in certain circumstances amount to corroboration. There is no shortage of authority for this proposition: see, for example, *R* v *Knight* [1966] 1 WLR 230, *Credland* v *Knowler* (1951) 35 Cr App R 48. It accords with good sense that a lie told by a defendant about a material issue may show that the liar knew if he told the truth he would be sealing his fate. In the words of Lord Dunedin in *Dawson* v *M'Kenzie*, 1908 SC 648, 649, cited with approval by Lord Goddard CJ in *Credland* v *Knowler*, 35 Cr App R 48, 55:

> ...the opportunity may have a complexion put upon it by statements made by the defender which are proved to be false. It is not that a false statement made by the defender provers that the pursuer's statements are true, but it may give to a proved opportunity a different complexion from what it would have borne had no such false statement been made.

To be capable of amounting to corroboration the lie told out of court must first of all be deliberate. Secondly it must relate to a material issue. Thirdly the motive for the lie must be a realisation of guilt and a fear of the truth. The jury should in appropriate cases be reminded that people sometimes lie, for example, in an attempt to bolster up a just cause, or out of shame or out of a wish to conceal disgraceful behaviour from their family. Fourthly the statement must be clearly shown to be a lie by evidence other than that of the accomplice who is to be corroborated that is to say by admission or by evidence from an independent witness.

As a matter of good sense it is difficult to see why, subject to the same safeguards, lies proved to have been told in court by a defendant should not equally be capable of providing corroboration. In other common law jurisdictions they are so treated; see the cases collated by Professor J D Heydon in "Can Lies Corroborate?" (1973) 89 LQR 552, 561, and cited with apparent approval in *Cross on Evidence*, 5th ed (1979), p 210 (footnote).

It has been suggested that there are dicta in *R* v *Chapman* [1973] QB 774, to the effect that lies so told in court can never be capable of providing corroboration of other evidence given against a defendant. We agree with the comment upon this case in *Cross on Evidence*, 5th ed, pp 210–211, that the court there may only have been intending to go no further than to apply the passage from the speech of Lord MacDermott in *Tumahole Bereng* v *The King* [1949] AC 253, 270 which we have already cited.

In our view the decision in *R* v *Chapman* [1973] QB 774 on the point there in issue was correct. The decision should not, however, be regarded as going any further than we have already stated. Properly understood, it is not authority for the proposition that in no circumstances can lies told by a defendant in court provide material corroboration of an accomplice. We find ourselves in agreement with the comment upon this decision made by this court in *R* v *Boardman* [1975] AC 421, 428–429. That point was not subsequently discussed when that case was before the House of Lords.

The main evidence against Chapman and Baldwin was a man called Thatcher, who was undoubtedly an accomplice in the alleged theft and dishonest handling of large quantities of clothing. The defence was that Thatcher was lying when he implicated the defendants and that he must himself have stolen the goods. The judge gave the jury the necessary warning about accomplice evidence and the requirement of corroboration, and then went on to say, at p 779:

> If you think that Chapman's story about the disappearance of the van and its contents is so obviously untrue that you do not attach any weight to it at all — in other words, you think Chapman is lying to you — then I direct you that that is capable of corroborating Thatcher, because, members of the jury, if Chapman is lying about the van, can there be any explanation except that Thatcher is telling the truth about how it came to disappear?...My direction is that it is capable in law of corroborating Thatcher. Similarly in the case of Baldwin, if you think that Baldwin's story about going up to London and buying these...is untrue — in other words he has told you lies about that — then...that I direct you, so far as he is concerned, is capable of amounting to corroboration of Thatcher.

That being the direction which this court was then considering, the decision is plainly correct, because the jury were being invited to prefer the evidence of the accomplice to that of the defendant and then without more to use their disbelief of the defendant as corroboration of the accomplice.

Providing that the lies told in court fulfil the four criteria which we have set out above, we are unable to see why they should not be available for the jury to consider in just the same way as lies told out of court. So far as the instant case is concerned, the judge, we feel, fell into the same error as the judge did in *R v Chapman* [1973] QB 774.

The lie told by the appellant was clearly not shown to be a lie by evidence other than that of the accomplice who was to be corroborated and consequently the apparent direction that a lie was capable of providing corroboration was erroneous.'

Appeal allowed.

East LJ: Is not the present case one containing an admission? The authorities do not suggest that the admissions must go all the way. How does the case differ from that of *R v Dossi* (1918) 13 Cr App Rep 158, where although the defendant said that his handling of the child was platonic, that admission was nonetheless corroborative of the child's evidence of indecent assault?

R v Dossi (1918) 13 Cr App R 158 (CCA)

The appellant was convicted of indecent assault against two young girls.

ATKIN J, delivering the judgment of the court, said: 'The substantial point made by Sir Ernest Wild was with regard to the direction by the Chairman to the jury on the question of corroboration. There can be no doubt that in cases of this kind the jury are entitled to act on the uncorroborated evidence of a child who is able to give evidence on oath, but judges must warn juries not to convict a prisoner on the uncorroborated evidence of a child except after weighing it with extreme care. (See *R v Graham*, 4 Cr App R 218, 1910; *R v Pitts*, 8 Cr App R 126, 1912; and *R v Cratchley*, 9 Cr App R 232, 1913.) Those cases sufficiently shew what kind of direction should be given to the jury in cases of this kind, and the question arises whether or not the summing up of the Deputy-Chairman offended against the rules which are there laid down. He told the jury that "The law does not require corroboration.... What the law does require is that it must be most carefully pointed out to a jury that they ought to act with great caution and with the greatest deliberation, if there is no corroboration of the story in such a case as this.... It is for you to say whether or not you are satisfied that that little girl was trying to tell you the truth. I say that you must be very careful before you act without corroboration, but that you are entitled, if you are convinced beyond all reasonable doubt that the little girl is telling the truth, to act on her story even without corroboration." If the summing up had stopped there it could not have been contended that it was open to any objection. The law is stated as the authorities which I have cited laid it down, and the caution to the jury is framed in careful words. But the Deputy-Chairman went on to say in reference to the question of corroboration: "It does seem to me that it is infinitely less dangerous to act on the uncorroborated testimony of little children who allege that they have been indecently assaulted than to act on the uncorroborated testimony of older people who allege that they have been assaulted, and I will tell you why. I should always practically tell a jury that they must not convict on the uncorroborated testimony of a woman of full years, because it is so easy to make a charge, for purposes that you can well imagine, either against the wrong man when there is a right man, or against a person who has had no dealings with her at all, or for the purpose of blackmail. But with regard to small children there is less incentive for them to make up a false story about a particular man in a matter of this sort than there often is in the case of an older woman. Children are less likely to suggest a wrong man when there is a right man, and they are less likely to be open to the purposes of blackmail than older people." We think that those were dangerous remarks to make to the jury. No doubt, the considerations which the Deputy-Chairman had in his mind were perfectly sensible. But, on the other hand, small children are possibly more under the influence of third persons — sometimes their parents — than are adults, and they are apt to allow their imaginations to run away with them and to invent untrue stories. There seems to us no reason to distinguish between the

amount of corroboration required in the one case and that required in the other. But doubtless the jury looked on this summing up as advice on a matter on which they were quite able to form an opinion. They had heard the beginning of the summing up where they were directed quite accurately, and immediately after the passage I last read the Deputy-Chairman said: "You must act with great care in the case of the little girl White. You must act with great care also in the case of Rebecca Barnett." In our view, the repetition of that caution prevented the other parts of the summing up from having the serious effect on the jury they might have had. White's story had very slight corroboration and, indeed, it might be said that, at the end of the case for the prosecution, there was none. But the question of corroboration often assumes an entirely different aspect after the accused person has gone into the witness box and has been cross examined. The appellant in this case stated in evidence that he was in the habit of fondling the little girls and described how he took them up, and the jury might well have refused to accept his story that these things were done innocently. There was evidence to support the verdict, there was no substantial misdirection on the facts or on the law, and the appeal must, therefore, be dismissed.'
Appeal dismissed.

Mr Atkyn: My Lords, on that point I think I must concede defeat.

14.10 Questions for Counsel

14.10.1 R v *Coke and Littleton:* Construct a passage to be used by Holt J in his summing up which would adequately deal with the requirements for corroboration of the evidence of Angela and Margaret Blackstone, on the assumptions (a) that Angela gives evidence unsworn, and (b) that Angela gives evidence on oath.

14.10.2 R v *Coke and Littleton:* Do you agree that Coke in giving evidence for the prosecution against Littleton should be regarded as an accomplice? If so, how should Holt J direct the jury with regard to his evidence?

15   Documentary and Real Evidence

A: DOCUMENTARY EVIDENCE

15.1 Proof of contents: introductory notes

15.1.1 This chapter deals with the proof and use in evidence of private documents, as opposed to documents admissible under the public document rule considered in Chapter 6. The word 'document' has been variously defined. At common law, the main characteristic of a document is that it should contain and convey information. Although the word primarily applies to information conveyed in writing or by other inscription, in modern times the storing of information in diagrammatic form or computer coding, or the audio or video recording of information is probably equally acceptable. The Criminal Evidence Act 1965 and the Civil Evidence Act 1968 contain wide definitions of the word 'document.'

15.1.2 The rules of evidence apply to documents as they do to any form of evidence. Where a party seeks to tender a document in evidence, it must first be established whether the contents of the document are relied upon as direct evidence or hearsay admissible under Part 1 of the Civil Evidence Act 1968. In the latter case, the Act contains statutory provision for the proof of contents under 6(1), which is dealt with in Chapter 8. Where, however, the contents of the document are relied upon as direct evidence, a rule of commmon law requires that the contents shall be proved by 'primary' as opposed to 'secondary' evidence. The usual and most satisfactory form of primary evidence is the production of the original of the document, but in suitable cases an opponent's admission of the contents of a document, and in the case of enrolled documents an official copy, are also regarded as primary.

15.1.3 Primary evidence is not required unless the contents of the documents themselves are relied upon as direct evidence. Thus, where evidence is directed only to proving the existence of or to identifying the document, secondary evidence will suffice. Where the document is used merely to prove the existence of some other state of affairs and no reliance is placed on the detail of its contents, secondary evidence is similarly admissible.

15.1.4 Secondary evidence of the contents of a document is admissible in certain cases, namely:

(a) Where the opponent fails after notice to produce an original document in his possession.

(b)   Where a stranger to proceedings lawfully refuses to produce the original in his possession.

(c)   Where the original of a document is lost and cannot be found after due search.

(d)   Where production of the original is impossible.

(e)   Where the document is or forms part of a banker's book within the meaning of the Bankers' Books Evidence Act 1879. (*A Practical Approach to Evidence*, pp 387–93.)

15.2   Commentary

Blackstone v *Coke* at trial.   Mr Noy for the plaintiff applies to Hardwicke J to admit into evidence copies of the Coke handwriting exhibits used at the criminal trial, the sheets of notepaper allegedly written by Coke (Exhibit GG1) and the known specimen of Coke's handwriting (Exhibit GG3). Mr Atkyn for Coke objects to the admissibility of these pieces of evidence on the ground that Mr Noy does not propose to produce the original documents.

15.3   Argument

Mr Atkyn: My Lord, the plaintiff seeks to rely on the content of these documents as direct evidence, and in my submission the plaintiff ought to produce the original documents and so supply the court with primary evidence of the contents.

Hardwicke J: Yes. This rule of evidence seems frequently to be overlooked, but it is one which should be followed in cases governed by common law. Before I hear Mr Noy, perhaps we might look at what the rule requires. First of all, Mr Atkyn, is there any rule as to what amounts to a document?

Mr Atkyn: My Lord, various definitions have been offered. In certain cases, Parliament has provided some statutory definition for limited purposes. These modern definitions tend to be wide in their scope. For example, Your Lordship might be assisted by looking at:

Criminal Evidence Act 1965, s.1(4)

1(4)…'document' includes any device by means of which information is recorded or stored…

The Civil Evidence Act 1968 also has its own definition provided in:

Civil Evidence Act 1968, s.10(1)

10(1)…'document' includes, in addition to a document in writing —
   (a)   any map, plan, graph or drawing;
   (b)   any photograph;
   (c)   any disc, tape, sound track or other device in which sounds or other data (not being visual images) are embodied so as to be capable (with or without the aid of some other equipment) of being reproduced therefrom; and
   (d)   any film, negative, tape or other device in which one or more visual images are embodied so as to be capable (as aforesaid) of being reproduced therefrom…

In cases at common law not covered by those definitions, my submission is that in modern times the word should be given a wide meaning as in:

R v Daye [1908] 2 KB 333 (DC)

A sealed packet supposed to contain a secret process for making diamonds had been deposited by two persons with a bank which had undertaken not to give the packet to any person without the consent of both depositors. A criminal matter was pending in a French court against one of the depositors, and in the course of proceedings under the Extradiction Act 1873 a subpoena was issued to the representative of the bank to produce the sealed packet as being a document within the meaning of that Act. The bank refused to produce the packet, as one of the depositors objected.

DARLING J said: 'On behalf of the bank it has been contended that the sealed envelope and what is inside it does not come within the term "document." I think that it is perfectly plain that the sealed envelope itself might be a document. Nothing but the sealed envelope might be required. But I should myself say that any written thing capable of being evidence is properly described as a document and that it is, immaterial on what the writing may be inscribed. It might be inscribed on paper, as is the common case now; but the common case once was that it was not on paper, but on parchment; and long before that it was on stone, marble, or clay, and it might be, and often was, on metal. So I should desire to guard myself against being supposed to assent to the argument that a thing is not a document unless it be a paper writing. I should say it is a document no matter upon what material it be, provided it is writing or printing and capable of being evidence.'

In more recent times, the courts have extended the form which a document may take to include more modern media, such as tape recordings, for example, in *Grant and another* v *Southwestern and County Properties Ltd. and another* [1975] Ch 185.

Hardwicke J: Mr Noy, I have of course only had these documents described to me and have not yet had the advantage of seeing them. Although I have formed some idea of what their contents are, I would be obliged to hear from you whether you propose to use the documents as direct or hearsay evidence.

Mr Noy: My Lord, the contents are to be used as direct evidence. In the case of Exhibit GG1, that will be tendered as evidence of the defendant Coke's state of mind at the time he wrote it, and of course Exhibit GG3 is tendered as being direct evidence of handwriting upon which it is hoped to base evidence of a scientific comparison.

Hardwicke J: Must you not then produce the original? I have in mind the case of:

MacDonnell v Evans (1852) 11 CB 930 (CP)

In an action of assumpsit upon a bill of exchange a witness for the plaintiff was asked in cross-examination whether a letter of his which was produced was written in reply to a letter charging him with forgery. The last-mentioned letter was not produced, and the question was disallowed on the ground that this was an attempt to get in evidence the contents of a document without producing the document itself.

JERVIS CJ said: 'The rule of evidence which governs this case, is applicable to all cases where witnesses are sworn to give evidence upon the trial of an issue. That rule is, that the best evidence in the possession or power of the party must be produced. What the best evidence is, must depend upon circumstances. Generally speaking, the original document is the best evidence; but circumstances may arise in which secondary evidence of the contents may be given. In the present case, those circumstances do not exist. For anything that appeared, the defendant's counsel might have had the letter in his hand when he put the question. It was sought to give secondary evidence of the contents of a letter, without in any way accounting for its absence, or shewing any attempt made to obtain it. It is enough for us to decide upon the application of the general rule.'

MAULE J said: 'Undoubtedly, if the question had been answered, it might have been letting in evidence whence the jury might have inferred that the letter spoken of contained certain things, the letter not having been produced, or its non-production accounted for. It is a general rule, — subject, it may be, to an exception in the case of an examination upon the voir dire, which is an inquiry of a special nature, in which it is the province of the judge, and not of the jury, to determine whether or not the witness is competent to give evidence, — that, if you want to get at the contents of a written document, the proper way is, to produce it, if you can. That is a rule in which the common sense of mankind concurs. If the paper is in the possession of the party who seeks to have the jury infer something from its contents, he should let them see it. That is the general and ordinary rule: the contents can only be proved by the writing itself.'
(CRESSWELL and WILLIAMS JJ concurred.)

As I understand it this is a classic decision at common law which illustrates the application of the rule.

Mr Noy: My Lord, I accept the rule to be as Your Lordship has stated it. I have two arguments to make on that subject. The first is that I am tendering the documents only as a foundation for further evidence, in this case the evidence of the scientific office of Mr Hale. Thus, the precise contents of the documents are in a sense immaterial, and it is the form and substance of the handwriting on which I seek to rely. If that is right and I can introduce the documents for a purpose other than strictly proving their contents as such, I can bring myself within the class of case such as:

R v *Elworthy* (1867) LR 1 CCR 103

KELLY CB said: 'This was a trial for perjury, the perjury being assigned on a statement made by the defendant that there was no draft of a certain statutory declaration; and the question arose whether, in order to give secondary evidence of the contents of that draft, it was necessary to give notice to produce it to the defendant, into whose possession it was alleged to have come. I am of opinion that such notice was necessary. It is very important to conform to the rules of law, which protect the accused from the admission of evidence of a doubtful and uncertain character, when certain evidence can be obtained. Here the perjury assigned was, that there was no draft of the statutory declaration. In the course of the trial the exact contents of that draft became essential, because on them depended the materiality of the perjury assigned; and the prosecution proceeded to give evidence that such a draft existed and was in the defendant's hands, and then to give secondary evidence of its contents without having given any notice to produce it, on the principle that in this case notice might be dispensed with.

Now, to take first of all the example of a civil action, it has been held that, in an action in trover for a deed or other writing, notice may be dispensed with, on the ground that the action itself is notice to the defendant of the nature and contents of the document. That doctrine is inapplicable here. Secondly, in a criminal prosecution for stealing a document, it has been held unnecessary to give notice to produce. In *Aickle's Case* 1 Leach 294, 299 it is said: "If it had been in the prisoner's possession, the next best evidence to the bill itself would have been admissible; for, as a prisoner cannot be compelled, or even legally required, to produce any evidence which may operate against himself, the next best evidence which it is in the power of the prosecutor to produce is always admitted." But there is also another reason that by the form of the indictment the prisoner has notice that he is charged with the possession of the very document, and will be required to produce it. This reason is inapplicable in this case. The defendant swore there was no draft; and there was nothing on the face of the indictment to shew that the draft necessarily came into his possession, or remained in it, so as to entitle the prosecution to say that he ought to have produced it. It was necessary to prove that the defendant swore there was no draft, that he knew that to be false, and that the perjury was material to the issue; and he might in reality have alluded to another document. This, therefore, is different'from the other cases where this principle alluded to has been applied; and under these circumstances there is nothing to call upon us to apply it here. I think for myself that the principle of admitting evidence which is not the best evidence ought not to be extended.'

BRAMWELL B said: 'If the question had been only as to the existence of the draft, it might have been different; but here the prosecution gave evidence of the alterations and contents in order to shew wilful perjury. These contents therefore became material; and the general rule then applied that you must give the best evidence.'
(BYLES, LUSH and WILLES JJ concurred.)
Conviction quashed.

Hardwicke J: I think you may have difficulty in persuading me that you fall within that rule. You have already indicated that it is your intention to place some reliance on the contents of the documents as evidence of the defendant's state of mind, assuming, that is, that you prove him to be the author. If I am against you on that point, what do you say?

Mr Noy: If Your Lordship is against me on that point, then although for reasons to which I shall come shortly, I am unable to produce the original of the documents, I would seek to rely upon an admission as to the contents made by the defendant Coke or by counsel on his behalf during the criminal trial about which Your Lordship has heard. It was not disputed at that trial what the contents of the original documents were, and indeed the original documents were produced in that case and shown to the jury. I am in a position to prove by reference to the transcript of the trial that such an admission was in fact made, and the rule of common law allows an admission to be made informally and orally as well as in writing. I refer Your Lordship to:

Slatterie v Pooley (1840) 6 M & W 664 (Exch)

The plaintiff sued on a covenant indemnifying him against certain debts. The debts covered by the indemnity were contained in the schedule to a deed, which was inadmissible for want of a proper stamp. An oral admission by the defendant that a certain debt was included in the schedule was disallowed by the trial judge.

PARKE B said: '...we who heard the argument...entertain no doubt that the defendant's own declarations were admissible in evidence to prove the identity of the debt sued for, with that mentioned in the schedule, although such admissions involved the contents of a written instrument not produced...The reason why such parol statements are admissible, without notice to produce, or accounting for the absence of the written instrument, is, that they are not open to the same objection which belongs to parol evidence from other sources, where the written evidence might have been produced; for such evidence is excluded from the presumption of its untruth, arising from the very nature of the case, where better evidence is withheld; whereas what a party himself admits to be true, may reasonably be presumed to be so.'
(LORD ABINGER CB, GURNEY and ROLFE BB concurred.)

Hardwicke J: Mr Noy, perhaps you could tell me where the originals are.
Mr Noy: My Lord, unhappily I cannot. Owing to some administrative error they appear to have been lost either by the police officers or the criminal court at some stage after the trial concluded and in those circumstances, it was my intention to continue by seeking to persuade Your Lordship that secondary evidence of the documents might be admissible.
Hardwicke J: Yes. Under what circumstances am I permitted to entertain

secondary evidence?

Mr Noy: My Lord, dealing with the cases recognised by the common law, one can eliminate impossibility of production and of course the exception relating to bankers' books. But I firstly rely on the rule that where the original document is lost and cannot be found or identified after due search, its contents may be proved by secondary evidence. I accept that I will have to produce some evidence to satisfy Your Lordship of due search, and if Your Lordship accepts the argument, I propose to do so in due course. I refer to:

Saltern v Melhuish (1754) Amb 248 (Ch)

The plaintiff, in order to prove the contents of a deed which was charged in his bill to have been destroyed and lost by the defendant, produced a deed engrossed, but not executed, which was proved to be a copy of the deed supposed to be destroyed.

LORD HARDWICKE, CHANCELLOR said: 'I am fully satisfied this deed ought to be read...There are several rules by which evidence, even parol, may be given of the contents of a deed: First, it is ground sufficient to show that the deed is in the hands of the opposite party, and that he had notice to produce it, and does not. Second, another ground is, to give reasonable account of the deed being lost or destroyed. Rule of law is, that the best evidence must be given which the nature of the case will admit, and in no case is that rule construed with greater latitude than in cases of this sort.'

Hardwicke J: In the circumstances, I should have thought you might rely also upon one of the exceptions applicable where the document is in the possession of another party or a stranger. Did you give notice to produce?

Mr Noy: My Lord, we did. We were able to discover that the documents were apparently not in the possession of the defendant, because there was no reference to them in his list of documents. Had that been the case, I could have relied upon the provisions of RSC Order 27, Rule 4(3), which states:

A party to a cause or matter by whom a list of documents is served on any other party...shall be deemed to have been served by that other party with a notice requiring him to produce at the trial of the cause or matter such of the documents specified in the list as are in his possession, custody or power.

Mr Atkyn: My Lord, the answer is that the documents are not in the defendant's possession. They were in the possession of the police and prosecuting authorities for the purpose of the criminal trial, and so far as I am aware would have been retained by the court after having been produced in evidence until the time for appeal had run, and then returned to the prosecution. In those circumstances, it is not open to my learned friend to say that we have failed to produce the documents.

Hardwicke J: Yes. Has anyone sought to obtain the documents by referring to the police?

Mr Noy: Yes, My Lord. No one seemed to be able to give us any account of where the documents were. The court apparently does not have them, and states that they have been returned to the prosecuting authorities. There was some suggestion in the letter from the prosecuting solicitors that they would not in any event be prepared to release these documents for the purpose of evidence in this case, and that they might assert some lawful reason for withholding them. In that event, I would have invited Your Lordship to test that question by issuing a subpoena and if Your Lordship found the refusal to be lawful then another exception would have entitled me to produce secondary evidence. I would refer Your Lordship to:

Mills v *Oddy* (1834) 6 C & P 728 (Nisi Prius)

Oddy had purchased at an auction an under-lessee's interest in a house, and refused to pay a cheque which he had given for the deposit, because the ground-rent payable to the superior landlord was greater than it was stated to be at the sale. The superior landlord's solicitor was not compellable to produce the counterpart of the original lease; and a person who had advanced money on that lease, and held it as equitable mortgagee, could also not be compelled to produce the lease itself.

PARKE B said: 'If you have anyone who has seen this lease, who does not claim under it as one of his title-deeds, and who is not privileged as attorney or solicitor, he may give secondary evidence of its contents. There is an impossibility of your producing it, as the person who has it cannot be compelled to produce it under his subpoena.'

Of course from the plaintiff's point of view, it would be more satisfactory that the failure to produce should be laid at the defendant's door, in that not only would I be entitled to rely on secondary evidence, but the defendant would then not be able to show by other evidence what the contents of the original were to contradict the copies. I would refer Your Lordship to:

Doe d. Thompson v *Hodgeson* (1840) 12 A & E 135 (QB)

On the trial of an ejectment by landlord against tenant, the case for the lessor of the plaintiff was that the defendant was his tenant from year to year, and had received due notice to quit. To prove the tenancy, the lessor of the plaintiff relied upon the payment of rent by the defendant. He had given notice to the defendant to produce the receipts, which, at the trial, counsel for the defendant refused to do. Other evidence was the given of the payment. The defendant's counsel afterwards, as part of his own case, put in the receipts, for the purpose of showing that the rent was paid to the lessor of the plaintiff and another jointly.

LORD DENMAN CJ delivering the judgment of the court, said: 'In this case the question was whether a party, who, at the trial, had refused to produce a writing which he possessed, and thereby had drawn the other party to give secondary evidence of its contents, could afterwards produce it. I thought at the trial that he could not; considering it to be the rule that, where he had the opportunity, and had declined to produce the writing, he could not afterwards bring forward its contents. Our opinion is, that that is the rule of practice; and that, when that refusal has taken place, the party who had refused to produce the writing could not afterwards be at liberty to give it in evidence.'

Hardwicke J   What do you say, Mr Atkyn?

Mr Atkyn: My Lord, it would seem that Your Lordship ought to investigate whether it is possible to compel production of the originals from the police and if not whether it ought to be found that the originals have been lost despite due search. In my submission, until those findings are made, my learned friend is not entitled to introduce secondary evidence. I would further say that the secondary evidence must be strictly proved, by which I mean that copies of the documents will only be admissible if it is shown to Your Lordship's satisfaction that they are in fact true copies of the missing originals. I would refer to:

R v *Collins* (1960) 44 Cr App R 170 (CCA)

The defendant was convicted of obtaining money by false pretences. The charge related to the cashing of a cheque by the defendant which was returned marked 'Account closed'. In proof of the knowledge that the account was closed, a bank manager was called. He sought to produce a document purporting to be a copy of a letter sent previously to the defendant which informed him that the account was closed. The original letter was called for and was not produced, and the manager then produced the document, which was not the carbon copy, but was said to be a copy of the carbon copy. He gave evidence that, in the absence of his co-manager who had actually written the letter, he had searched the files of the bank and extracted certain copies of letters of which the letter in question was one.

LORD PARKER CJ, giving the judgment of the court, stated the facts, dealt with another ground of appeal and continued: 'It is then said that if secondary evidence is going to be given by means of a copy, it must be the original copy and the original copy only, and not a copy made from the original copy, and Mr Du Cann has referred us to paragraph 1282 in the current edition of *Archbold* and to the two cases there referred to, *Liebman* v *Pooley* (1816) 1 Stark NP 167 and *Everingham* v *Roundell* (1838) 2 M & Rob 138. Again, this court finds it unnecessary to come to any final conclusion on the matter, although, as at present advised, they can see no objection to a copy of a copy being produced, provided that somebody is called who can verify not only that the copy produced is a true copy of the original copy, but also that it is in the same terms as the original. Where the court feels that the case for the prosecution broke down is that Mr Everitt was quite unable to say, or at any rate did not say, that he had checked the document which he had produced with the carbon copy which was on the file and that what he was producing was a true copy of the original letter. That step in the proof was completely missing and accordingly, in the judgment of this court, the letters, and in particular the letter of April 9, 1959, were wrongly admitted.
(The court nevertheless dismissed the appeal, applying the proviso to s.4(1) of the Criminal Appeal Act 1907.)

Of course, My Lord, I accept that there are no degrees of secondary evidence, so that my learned friend could introduce oral evidence or copies of copies to prove what the contents were. But he is nonetheless obliged to produce proof of the accuracy of the secondary evidence.

Hardwicke J: Yes. Mr Noy rather abandoned the impossibility approach. But I note that in *Mortimer* v *M'Callan* (1846) M&W 58 (Exch), Alderson B held that it was in effect impossible to produce the original books of the Bank of England because of the obvious resulting inconvenience [see following case].

Mr Noy: My Lord, yes. And in *Owner* v *Bee Hive Spinning Company Limited* the court recognised a principle of legal impossibility where the original of a notice was obliged by law to remain on the wall of a factory in a particular place.

Owner v Bee Hive Spinning Company Ltd. [1914] 1 KB 105 (DC)

The occupier of a factory was prosecuted for allowing a young person employed in the factory to remain in a room in which a manufacturing process was being carried on during the time allowed for meals, contrary to s.33 of the Factory and Workshop Act 1901. The justices ruled that secondary evidence could not be given to prove the contents of the notice specifying the times allowed in the factory for meals, which notice had under s.32 to be affixed in the factory.

RIDLEY J said: 'No doubt it is the ordinary and very proper rule of evidence that before secondary evidence can be given of the contents of a written document which is in the possession of the other side a notice to produce the original must be given. But in my opinion the justices were wrong in applying that rule to this particular case, for the facts bring it within the exception which permits secondary evidence to be given in cases where the production of the original document would be either physically impossible or highly inconvenient. We have been referred to the case of *Mortimer* v *M'Callan* 6 M & W 58. In the course of that case it became necessary to prove that an entry in the books of the Bank of England relating to a transfer of stock had been signed by the defendant. An examined copy of the Bank books was produced, and a witness was called who said he had seen the signature in the books at the Bank and that it was in the handwriting of the defendant. It was contended that the books themselves ought to have been produced. The Court held that the removal of the books from the Bank would be so inconvenient that copies of them might be received in evidence. Lord Abinger in the course of his judgment said 6 M & W at 68: "A case has been aptly put by my brother Alderson, that if a writing were on a wall, might you not give evidence of the character of the handwriting, as probable evidence of who wrote it, without producing the wall in Court?" The present case appears to me to be somewhat akin to that, for s.128 of the Factory and Workshop Act, 1901, enacts that this notice shall be kept constantly affixed at the factory, and a breach of that provision renders the occupier of the factory liable to a fine. In my opinion *Mortimer* v *M'Callan* is an authority for saying that secondary evidence of the contents of this notice ought to have been accepted. The appeal will, therefore, be allowed.'

(SCRUTTON and BAILHACHE JJ agreed.)

Appeal allowed.

Mr Atkyn: My Lord, while accepting the principle of those cases, all that has happened here is that the document cannot be found. Nobody suggests that there would be any impossibility about producing the documents if they were to hand or could be compelled.

Hardwicke J: Yes, I think that is right. I shall defer ruling on this matter until I have heard evidence of the whereabouts of these documents and made some investigation of the practicality of finding them.

15.4 Proof of due execution: introductory notes

15.4.1 In certain cases, due execution of the document must be proved to the court. Unlike public documents, the execution of which is generally proved by the mere production of certified copy, private documents must be proved to have been properly executed if this is disputed. This is normally of importance in relation to documents whose formal validity depends upon due execution, for example wills, but may be of importance in relationship to authorship of documents generally.

15.4.2 Due execution may be admitted for the purpose of either civil or criminal proceedings. Proof of due execution may further be dispensed with where an opponent refuses to produce a document after notice to do so. Due execution will be presumed in the case of a private document which is more than 20 years old and comes from proper custody. In all other cases, due execution is to be proved by evidence.

15.4.3 Where evidence is required, due execution may be proved either by direct evidence of a person who perceived the document being executed, by opinion evidence from any witness familiar with the handwriting of the purported executor, or by scientific comparison by means of expert evidence of the disputed writing with writing proved to the satisfaction of the judge to be the genuine writing of the purported executor. Scientific comparison of samples is a matter for expert evidence, and should not be left to the unaided observation of the tribunal of fact. Documents which require attestation may be proved by the evidence of the attesting witnesses or one of them. Formerly this manner of proof was required in the case of such documents but it is now optional, except in relation to wills when probate is not granted in common form. An attesting witness is called as the witness of the court and may be cross-examined and contradicted by any party. (*A Practical Approach to Evidence*, pp 393-5.)

15.5 Commentary

Blackstone v *Coke* at trial.   Following the argument in 15.3, Hardwicke J allows the plaintiff to tender secondary evidence to prove the contents of Exhibits GG1 and GG3, on the ground that the originals have been lost and cannot be found after due search. Mr Noy then tenders in evidence copies of these documents, having called D/1 Glanvil and Mr Hale to prove that they are in fact true copies of the originals. Mr Noy now proposes to call Mr Hale to make a scientific comparison with a view to proving that Coke wrote document GG1. Mr Atkyn indicates that Coke's authorship of this document is denied, and Hardwicke J inquires of Mr Noy what means of proof may be used to prove or disprove authorship.

15.6 Argument

Hardwicke J: I am concerned, Mr Noy, because clearly authorship is not admitted for the purpose of these proceedings, and since the documents do not purport to be more than twenty years old, there is no applicable presumption in your favour. The document GG1 does not purport to be dated, and even this cannot be presumed in your favour. Had I ruled that this was a case where the defendant had refused to produce the documents after due notice, then by analogy with the cases on formal validity, I think I could have dispensed with proof of execution. I have in mind the old decision in:

Cooke v *Tanswell* (1818) 8 Taunt 450 (CP)

The declaration in covenant on an indenture of apprenticeship averred that the deed was in the possession of the defendant, who pleaded *non est factum*. At the trial the deed was proved to be in the hands of the defendants, who had received notice to produce it, the notice stating the name of the subscribing witness. On non-production of the deed, the plaintiff gave parol evidence of its contents, without calling the subscribing witness, who was in court.

GIBBS CJ said: 'I do not think that the knowledge of the name of the subscribing witness makes any difference in the case. I take the question to be, whether when one party calls for a deed of the other, who does not produce it, and the party calling for the deed is consequently driven to give parol evidence of its contents, it is necessary for him to call the subscribing witness. In cases where *non est factum* is not pleaded, as in ejectment, when a party so situated gives evidence of the contents of a deed, I never yet heard it contended that it was necessary to call the subscribing witness. Here, the deed was in the hands of the defendant; if he wished to throw on the plaintiff the burden of calling the subscribing witness, he might have produced the deed. It was alleged on the record, that the deed was in the defendant's hands, that allegation was admitted, and the defendant being called on to produce it, and refusing to do so, it was not necessary that the plaintiff should call the subscribing witness to the deed before he gave evidence of the contents.'
(PARK and BURROUGH JJ agreed.)

Mr Noy: My Lord, in my submission the evidence of Mr Hale which is expert evidence of a scientific comparison is proper in this case. It is true that the most satisfactory evidence of execution of a document is to call the witness who perceived the document being executed. But in this case, no such witness is known to the plaintiff. Nor is the plaintiff in a position to call any witness who is generally familiar with the handwriting of the defendant Mr Coke, so as to be able to state his opinion as to the similarity. For those reasons, my Lord, I rely on the evidence of Mr Hale. The basis for such evidence is a statutory one, namely Section 8 of the Criminal Procedure Act 1865. This provides:

> Comparison of a disputed writing with any writing proved to the satisfaction of the judge to be genuine shall be permitted to be made by witnesses; and such writings, and the evidence of witnesses respecting the same, may be submitted to the court and jury as evidence of the genuineness or otherwise of the writing in dispute.

Hardwicke J: I imagine it may well be that there will be no dispute that the document GG3 is the known writing of defendant Coke, but I am somewhat puzzled as to the degree to which that must be proved to my satisfaction as required by the section.

Mr Noy: My Lord, in my submission the proper standard of proof is that on the balance of probabilities. Even in a criminal case, it has been held by the Criminal Division of the Court of Appeal that this standard is sufficient. All Your Lordship is doing at this stage is to satisfy himself that there is a *prima facie* case for the genuineness of this document, as a precondition of allowing it to be compared. I refer Your Lordship to:

R v *Angeli* [1979] 1 WLR 26 (CA)

The defendant was charged with assault with intent to rob and, at the trial, the prosecution's case was that he had pretended to deliver a parcel at the victim's house and, when she had opened the door to receive it, he and another man had attacked her. The prosecution alleged that the writing on the parcel had been written by the defendant and sought to call a handwriting expert to compare that writing with samples of the defendant's handwriting. As the defendant did not acknowledge that eight documents included in the sample had been written by him, the judge heard evidence concerning those documents and then ruled that he was satisfied on the balance of probability that the documents had been written by the defendant and, therefore, they were admissible under s.8 of the Criminal Procedure Act 1865. The handwriting expert gave evidence and the defendant was subsequently convicted.

BRIDGE LJ, giving the judgment of the court, said: 'The short point which Mr Challenger, who has presented a powerful argument to the court, takes on the defendant's behalf was that the judge·was wrong in law in directing himself under section 8 of the Criminal Procedure Act 1865 by the civil standard of proof and should, it is submitted, have directed himself to apply and have applied the criminal standard of proof. He should not have admitted the disputed writings in evidence for the purpose of comparison unless he was satisfied so as to be sure, or satisfied beyond a reasonable doubt, that they were genuine writings of this defendant.

Certainly the point as such is not one which is decided by any authority which has been put before us. A number of authorities have been drawn to our attention, but the court finds, with respect to Mr Challenger's argument, singularly little assistance from them. The first point to be observed is that they are all authorities decided in civil and and not in criminal cases, because the provision which is now section 8 of the Criminal Procedure Act 1865 follows a provision in identical terms which applied to the admissibility of evidence of this character in civil cases ever since the Common Law Procedure Act 1854 and the Criminal Procedure Act 1865, as we will see in a minute, had the effect of applying that same provision to criminal courts as to civil courts.

Apart from reliance upon authority, from which we do not, as stated, derive assistance, the other limb of Mr Challenger's argument which at first blush is more compelling, rests upon a submission that it is a general principle which applies whenever the admissibility of evidence in a criminal trial depends upon some disputed question of fact that the judge at the trial within a trial, having to decide on a question of fact, should only decide it in favour of the prosecution and against the defence if he is satisfied, on whatever the issue of fact may be, by the criminal standard so that he is sure and satisfied beyond reasonable doubt.

Of course, the familiar example of an application of that principle is in the instance which causes 99 out of 100 trials within trials which have to be held when the voluntary character of an admission or confession on which the prosecution seek to rely is challenged. The admissibility of the admission or confession has to be determined by the judge before he decides whether the jury shall be allowed to know about it. In those circumstances it is a very well-established rule that the judge must direct himself by the criminal standard of proof and be satisfied beyond a reasonable doubt that the statement was made voluntarily before he decides to admit it in evidence. Is that a rule of general application? We are prepared to assume that it is a rule of general application whenever the admissibility of evidence in a criminal trial turns upon some issue of fact and depends upon a rule of common law; but the vital distinction between the kind of decision which the judge has to make in relation to a disputed confession and the decision which the judge had to make as to the admissibility of disputed writings in this case is that whereas the confession evidence and its admissibility depend upon rules of common law, the admissibility of the disputed writings in this case depended wholly upon the application of the statute.

In our judgment all this court has to do here is to consider the statute which the judge was called on to apply, and it is clear that that is all the judge thought that he was doing. Approached in that light we think the answer to the issue which has been canvassed in this appeal is clear beyond argument.

The Criminal Procedure Act 1865, as already stated, applied for the first time to courts of criminal jurisdiction the statutory provision which had already been in operation in civil courts since 1854, under the Common Law Procedure Act of that year; and applied it without change of statutory language. Section 8 itself simply repeats what had been the rule applicable in civil cases for the previous 11 years. It was made applicable to criminal courts by the provisions of section 1 which so far as relevant enact: "the provisions of sections from 3 to 8, inclusive, of this Act shall apply to all courts of judicature..." That being the position under the statute, there is in our judgment no ground for construing this provision as having a different application in civil courts from its application in criminal. Whatever was the standard of proof implicit in the words: "proved to the satisfaction of the judge to be genuine" when those words applied in civil courts only as they did from 1854 to 1865, the same standard became applicable when the self-same provision was made operative in criminal courts by the enactment of the Act of 1865.

For those reasons we have come to the conclusion that the judge here correctly directed himself that he needed to be satisfied on the balance of probability....'
Appeal dismissed.

Hardwicke J: I am wondering to what extent I will be assisted by the evidence you propose to call. If the question is whether the handwriting on these two documents is the same, is that not something I can establish by looking at them closely myself, assisted by the arguments of counsel?

Mr Noy: With respect, My Lord, no. It is true that the dangers of such a course would be very much less in a civil case, when Your Lordship is sitting alone, than would be the course with a jury. But it has been held that comparison is a matter for scientific evidence to assist the court to come to its ultimate conclusion. I refer Your Lordship to *R* v *Tilley* [1961] 1 WLR 1309 (CCA) (see ante 9.5)

Hardwicke J: Yes, very well.

B: REAL EVIDENCE

15.7 Introductory notes

15.7.1 Real evidence is the name given to any evidence from which the tribunal of fact is invited to draw conclusions from its own observation and act on its own perception. Such evidence may consist of material objects, the appearance of persons or animals, the demeanour of witnesses, views of the *locus in quo* or of some object, person or animal which cannot conveniently be brought to court, and the use of tapes, photographs, films and the like whose appearance or tone may yield evidence beyond the actual content of what is recorded.

15.7.2 Before admitting a piece of real evidence, the judge must satisfy himself that the evidence tendered is what it purports to be. For this purpose, it is enough if the party tendering raises a *prima facie* case that the provenance and history of the evidence are such as to suggest that it is authentic and accurate.

15.8 Commentary

R v Coke and Littleton at trial.   Mr Bunbury for the prosecution proposes to have played in court for the benefit of the jury the cassette recording purporting to be the conversation between Littleton and Mrs Littleton at the Oxbridge Police Station, which was recorded by D/I Glanvil. He proposes that the jury should be supplied with a transcript of the recording for their use while it is being played.

15.9 Argument

Holt J: Mr Bunbury, my first concern is why it is necessary for this tape recording to be played, when D/I Glanvil could give evidence of what he overheard, refreshing his memory as far as necessary from the transcript of the recording.

Mr Bunbury: With respect, My Lord, the evidential value of this recording goes beyond the mere words of the transcript. The prosecution say that the jury are entitled to draw certain conclusions from the physical aspects of the recording, that is to say the tone of voice of the speakers and the way in which the words are spoken. It is of course to that extent a piece of real evidence. Of course, the prosecution also say that the words themselves are of evidential value, in that the words spoken by the defendant Littleton amount to a confession of guilt. But in the submission of the prosecution, this becomes clearer when one considers the tone of voice in which the words are spoken. Indeed, I understand that my learned friend, Mr Bacon, would actually agree with this position.

Mr Bacon: My Lord, I do agree. However it is my submission that the jury will in due course find the tone of words to bear another interpretation. Indeed, it is the case for the defendant Littleton that the words were spoken in a tone of-voice which indicates sarcasm or irony. Nonetheless, I do have an objection to the admissibility of the tape which is unrelated to its admission as real evidence. I would concede that if Your Lordship is against me on the objection to which I shall come, then my learned friend would be entitled to put the evidence in as real evidence.

Mr Bunbury: Perhaps I might refer Your Lordship to the decision in *The Statue of Liberty* in which the President of the Probate, Divorce and Admiralty Division admitted in evidence a cinematograph film of radar echoes for a comparable purpose.

The Statue of Liberty [1968] 1 WLR 739 (P)

In an action arising out of a collision between two ships, the plaintiffs sought to adduce in evidence film recorded by radar apparatus on shore. The defendants opposed the application on the ground that since the evidence was produced mechanically without human intervention it offended against the hearsay rule.

SIR JOCELYN SIMON P said: 'I am clearly of the opinion that the evidence is admissible and could, indeed, be a valuable piece of evidence in the elucidation of the facts in dispute. In a case concerned with mechanical recordings by tape recorder, *R v Maqsud Ali* [1966] 1 QB 688, Marshall J, delivering the judgment of the Court of Criminal Appeal, ruled that the tape recordings were admissible, and stated that the court could see no difference in principle between a tape recording and a photograph; see also *R v Senat* and *R v Sin* The Times, March 16, 1968. Moreover, *R v Maqsud Ali* makes it plain that we are not here concerned with evidence admissible under the Evidence Act, 1938, because that Act is not applicable to criminal proceedings. Mr Thomas seeks to distinguish *R v Maqsud Ali* from the present case on the ground that in the former case, the police officer set up a recording machine to overhear part of a recorded conversation and claimed to be able to identify the voices recorded. I should be sorry to think that that was a ground for distinction; for in *R v Maqsud Ali* the language was a dialect of Punjabi, not understandable by Urdu experts, let alone by English police officers.

In my view the evidence in question in the present case has nothing to do with the hearsay rule…It is in the nature of real evidence, which is conveniently defined in Cockle's Cases and Statutes on Evidence 10th ed, (1963) at p 348: "Real evidence is the evidence afforded by the production of physical objects for inspection or other examination by the court." If tape recordings are admissible, it seems that a photograph of radar reception is equally admissible — or indeed, any other type of photograph. It would be an absurd distinction that a photograph should be admissible if the camera were operated manually by a photographer, but not if it were operated by a trip or clock mechanism. Similarly, if evidence of weather conditions were relevant, the law would affront common sense if it were to say that those could be proved by a person who looked at a barometer from time to time, but not by producing a barograph record. So, too, with other types of dial recordings. Again, cards from clocking-in-and-out machines are frequently admitted in accident cases. The law is now bound to take cognisance of the fact that mechanical means replace human effort.'
Judgment for the plaintiff.

Holt J: Yes, very well.

Mr Bacon: My Lord, there is one further matter. It is for my learned friend to prove to Your Lordship's satisfaction that the cassette recording is the original and that it accurately reflects the whole of the conversation that it purports to record. My Lord, I would accept that this requirement is met if my learned friend elicits from D/I Glanvil evidence showing that the tape recording has been kept in proper police custody from the time of its making until the present time, that it has not been interfered with or edited in any way. He must make out a *prima facie* case that the recording is original and authentic.

(Mr Bacon then referred to *R v Maqsud Ali; R v Ashik Hussain* [1966] 1 QB 688; *R v Stevenson and others* [1971] 1 WLR 1 and *R v Robson; R v Harris* [1972] 1 WLR 651 and the matters referred to in 3.11 ante. Mr Bacon then went on to address His Lordship on the subject of privilege based on his contention that the contents of the recording were a matrimonial communication, see 10.16 ante.)

15.10 Questions for Counsel

15.10.1 Blackstone v *Coke:* Could you improve on the argument put forward by Mr Atkyn to prevent the proof of documents GG1 and GG3 by secondary evidence?

15.10.2 Blackstone v *Coke:* Conversely, could you improve on Mr Noy's argument with a view to showing that primary evidence was unnecessary in relation to these documents?

15.10.3 What evidence would you wish D/I Glanvil to give for the prosecution in order to establish the provenance and history of the cassette recording to the judge's satisfaction? Assuming that the recording is admitted and is played to the jury, what direction should Holt J give to them in summing up regarding the use they make of what they hear?

Subject Index